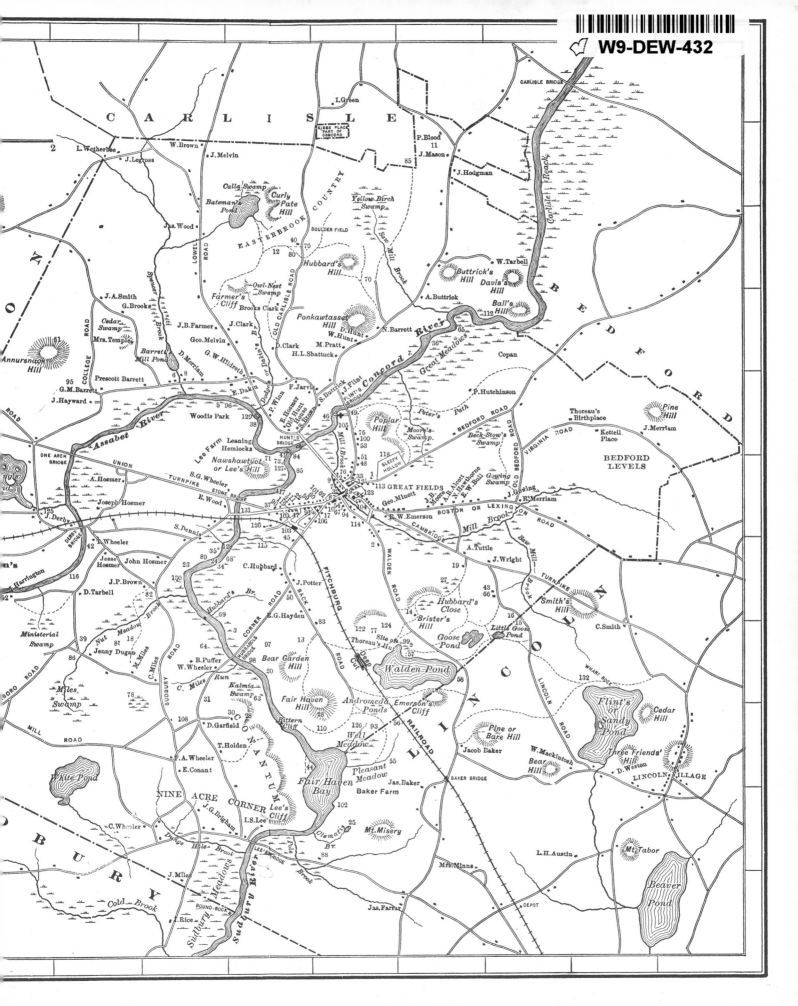

THE ANNOTATED™ WALDEN

Other Books by PHILIP VAN DOREN STERN

The Selected Writings of Thomas De Quincey
The Portable Poe
The Life and Writings of Abraham Lincoln
The Annotated *Uncle Tom's Cabin*

The dove of peace that appears on the title
page was drawn by Thoreau on the border of
two of his manuscripts. It has never been reproduced before.

THE ANNOTATED™
WALDEN

WALDEN; or, LIFE IN THE WOODS

By HENRY D. THOREAU

TOGETHER WITH "CIVIL DISOBEDIENCE," A DETAILED CHRONOLOGY
AND VARIOUS PIECES ABOUT ITS AUTHOR
THE WRITING AND PUBLISHING OF THE BOOK

Edited, with an Introduction, Notes, and Bibliography by

PHILIP VAN DOREN STERN

*Illustrated with maps, portraits, photographs,
manuscript pages, drawings, and decorations*

BRAMHALL HOUSE · NEW YORK

Designed by SALLY STEIN

Acknowledgments

The editor wants to thank the Henry E. Huntington Library of San Marino, California, for permission to use the original manuscript of *Walden* and other Thoreau manuscripts in its possession; the University of Chicago Library for the loan of the *Walden* microfilm; the Concord Free Public Library for much help and many pictures; the Concord Antiquarian Society for a photograph of Thoreau's furniture; the Berg Collection of the New York Public Library; the Boston Public Library; the Houghton Library at Harvard; the Pierpont Morgan Library; and the Yale University Library.

Also many Thoreau scholars, especially Charles R. Anderson, Kenneth Cameron, Reginald L. Cook, Walter Harding, William L. Howarth, Milton Meltzer, Sherman Paul, and James Lyndon Shanley.

And special thanks to Roland Wells Robbins for information and advice, for the use of his Herbert Gleason collection of Concord photographs, and for permission to photograph some of the objects he found when he excavated the Walden Pond cabin site.

Grateful acknowledgment is made for permission to reprint the following: the map on page 324 from *Thoreau as World Traveler*, John Aldrich Christie, Columbia University Press, N. Y., 1965; the letters from *Correspondence of Henry David Thoreau*, edited by Bode and Harding to the Huntington Library Collection, the Harvard College Library, the Henry W. and Albert A. Berg Collection of the New York Public Library, Astor Lenox and Tilden Foundations.

Photographs without credit lines were taken by the editor.

TABLE OF CONTENTS

I

THOREAU

THE NAME THOREAU

Although millions of people say Thoró, they pronounce the name incorrectly. The citizens of Concord—who should know because the Thoreau tradition has made a lasting impression on the town—say Thúrrow, as in furrow. Hawthorne's diary bears this out, for he wrote in it when he first met Henry David and did not know how to spell his name: "Mr. Thorow dined with us yesterday."

So let us settle here and now for Thúrrow, which is what the man himself almost surely said. He had a good knowledge of the French language and was fully aware of his French ancestry. His paternal grandfather had come to America from St. Helier on the Isle of Jersey about 1754. He did not come intentionally, but was brought to Boston after having been one of the crew on a Jersey privateer that had been shipwrecked and abandoned.

In his *Journal* (February 15, 1852; III, 304), Thoreau said: "Perhaps I am descended from that Northman named 'Thorer the Dog-footed.' Thorer Hund—'he was the most powerful man in the North'—to judge from his name, belonged to the same family. Thorer is one of the most, if not the most, common name in the chronicles of the Northmen."

The *Journal* for the next day continues with more about Thoreau's Northmen ancestors. One of them was supposed to have been "the grandfather of William the Bastard, from whom all the following English kings are descended." Thoreau adds: "So it seems that from one branch of the family were descended the kings of England, and from another myself."

"MR. THOROW [*sic*] dined with us yesterday. He is a singular character—a young man with much of wild original nature still remaining in him; and so far as he is sophisticated, it is in a way and method of his own. He is as ugly as sin, long-nosed, queer-mouthed, and with uncouth and somewhat rustic, although courteous manners, corresponding very well with such an exterior. But his ugliness is of an honest and agreeable fashion, and becomes him much better than beauty. On the whole, I find him a healthy and wholesome man to know."

NATHANIEL HAWTHORNE
American Notebook, September 1, 1842

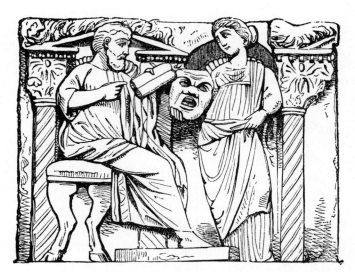

The Poet and his Muse

WALDEN: THE BOOK AND ITS MEANING

There is one book in American literature that stands out from all the others because it is so very different from them. It is an intensely individual work, the expression of a man who believed fiercely in himself even though he was constantly tortured by what he considered to be his own shortcomings, weaknesses, and failures. His doubts, however, did not prevent him from criticizing the materialism and apathy that he saw dominating his country.

What Henry David Thoreau said more than a century ago still holds true. But today more people—especially younger ones—are likely to heed his message than his contemporaries did. We have had a chance to see how empty the material rewards of an acquisitive society are.

"Things are in the saddle and will ride mankind," **1** Thoreau's friend and fellow townsman, Ralph Waldo Emerson, said. Things have been in the saddle ever since and dominate our thinking and our way of life.

Thoreau, whose life bridged the careers of Thomas Jefferson and Abraham Lincoln, saw how his country was betraying the fine promises of its founders. He denounced the Establishment of his time for its gross disregard of human rights. He deplored the poverty-stricken misery of the penniless Irish immigrants who had fled from a potato famine in their own land only to encounter ruthless exploitation and hostility in their new refuge. He was indignant about the Indians, who had been driven ever farther west into territory that nobody wanted. And he reached new heights of eloquence in denouncing slavery and all that it meant.

But *Walden* is far more than a book of social protest, although it is that too. It is an autobiography, a venture into philosophy, and a book about Nature. Most of all it is a work of literature—and a supremely good one, one of America's best.

1 *"Things are in the saddle."* From "Ode inscribed to W. H. Channing," which was written in the mid-1840's.

"Walden *is one of the very few American works to have won international acceptance as a classic, and it is also—which does not necessarily follow—one of the most widely read of nineteenth-century books."* JOSEPH WOOD KRUTCH
HENRY DAVID THOREAU, 1948

"The . . . most important cause of Thoreau's lasting success is his power over words. At his best he is a superb writer, one of those shapers of language who give age-old ideas their final form. Thanks to this, his sentences and paragraphs escape from the dead hands of time." HENRY SEIDEL CANBY
THOREAU, 1939

It is as literature that *Walden* should be judged, for Thoreau thought of himself primarily as a writer. Even his philosophy was subordinate to that. He did not pretend to be a professional naturalist, although he was a perceptive observer and a first-rate note-taker, far better than most professionals in the field, then and now. His writings on natural history belong to art rather than science, even though he did pioneering work in limnology, dendrochronology, ecology, and phenology—all terms that did not even exist in Thoreau's lifetime. And it must always be remembered that he was an active field-worker at a time when the natural sciences were still being shaped. Nor had he had any formal training in them. His education at Harvard was confined to the study of languages, ancient and modern, early English poetry, rhetoric, grammar, philosophy, theology, and history. At college his only encounters with science were optics, electricity and magnetism, and mathematics (as far as calculus). He did have a year in natural history and occasionally listened to lectures on mineralogy and anatomy, but most of his meager scientific education came from books which he read without supervision.

His *Journal*, which is our best key to his thinking and interests, has many more entries about natural history for the years after 1854, when *Walden* was published, than it does for the period before that. From late 1845 to early 1854, while Thoreau was working on the manuscript, he was far more concerned with larger human issues than with the details of natural history.

Style as well as content has made *Walden* a classic that is read throughout the world. Pithy, original, and memorable phrases make the book a delight. And beyond these are numerous poetic passages which have endeared *Walden* to generations of admirers. It is a book that people feel strongly about; even those who do not like it usually say so in forthright terms.

2 *limnology* is the scientific study of bodies of fresh water such as ponds or lakes; *dendrochronology* is the science of determining dates by counting annual tree rings; *ecology* is the study of the relationship between living things and their environment; *phenology* is the scientific study of the influence of climate on the recurrence of annual phenomena in animal life, i.e., bird migration, hibernation, change of color, and so forth.

3 *His education at Harvard.* Thoreau studied the standard curriculum and had very little choice so far as subject was concerned. According to Raymond Adams (1940), his college essays were "exercises with rigidly assigned topics and rigidly directed thinking." The truth about his four years at Harvard has been distorted by some of his classmates who found him to be "cold and unimpressible," "of an unsocial disposition," and filled with "Concord self-conceit." Later research, however, has shown that Thoreau took part in undergraduate pranks and was more normal as a student than these criticisms, written later in his classmates' lives, would indicate.

Harvard College

Walden appeals to young people, but perhaps it is best appreciated by those who have read it in their youth and then go back to it in later years. True devotees keep returning to it all their lives.

How did such a work come into being? One thing is certain; it did not just happen as a casual inspiration. Thoreau spent nearly nine years revising and restructuring his manuscript. He wrote eight versions, yet the never-satisfied author kept making further changes in the page proofs and even in the bound copies of the finished book. There is no doubt that Thoreau took his work seriously. *Walden* was to be his personal testament, the essence of all he had observed and put down in his *Journal*, the bringing together of everything he had felt and thought about.

His world consisted of only a few square miles around the little town of Concord, Massachusetts. Thoreau occasionally did go to other places in the Northeast. He also went to Canada, and he made one last long trip to Min-

Thoreau's manuscript *Journals* in the box he made for them (*Courtesy Pierpont Morgan Library*)

nesota as a dying man in search of health. He never stayed away from Concord any longer than he had to. He came back to it as Antaeus did to Mother Earth, for a renewal of strength by contact. Only at the end did that renewal fail, and it may be that by that time Thoreau wanted to die.

Much as he loved Concord, he saw its failings and was unsparing in his criticisms of its citizens' lack of interest in cultural affairs. Nevertheless, this village of 2,249 people held him entranced all his life. He had no desire to go to Europe or to see any of the far places of the earth. Yet he was enormously interested in them and read widely about them, as John Aldrich Christie's *Thoreau as World Traveler* (1965) shows.

Thoreau may have loved Concord, but he did not fully appreciate all that it had to offer. There was no small town in the Western Hemisphere in which he could have met so many distinguished people on intimate terms. Emerson was there, and for a while at least, so was Hawthorne. William Ellery Channing was Thoreau's best friend; he knew the Alcotts, and later he met Franklin Benjamin Sanborn, who was to be his biographer. Among the constant stream of visitors were Margaret Fuller, Theodore Parker, Wendell Phillips, and—fatefully—John Brown of Osawatomie fame. There were others too, for Boston is only eighteen miles away. **4**

Concord, except for its mud and dust, was then at its most beautiful, with fine big houses set back from tree-lined streets, and broad green fields and woods all around. We who live in a strife-torn, heavily polluted, and disaster-threatened age look back at Concord in Thoreau's time and are likely to think of it as an earthly paradise. It was not, of course, but to some of us it seems that way.

Thoreau saw the railroad and the telegraph come into existence and intrude on Walden Pond. He said forthrightly that the huge cloth mills of New England were **5** not operated for mankind to be "well and honestly clad, but, unquestionably, that the corporations may be enriched." He realized that an old way of life was passing and that what was replacing it was not necessarily an improvement. He lived at a time when America was beginning to be transformed from a rural economy to an industrialized urban society. It may be that his protests came from his awareness of what the future would bring.

We who live in this artificial present seldom think about Nature except to hope vaguely that some part of the natural world will be saved from the crunching jaws of our devastating machines that are equally ruthless with soil, rocks, and living things. We are so overwhelmed with the seemingly unsolvable problems of man that we tend to ignore what is going on beyond our narrow

4 *Emerson, Hawthorne, Channing,* and so on. Nearly all these people were Transcendentalists. They were all liberal and strongly opposed to slavery.

5 *cloth mills.* These were mostly in the eastern part of the state at Lowell, Manchester, Fall River, and Clinton. Thoreau describes a visit to the one in Clinton in his *Journal* for January 2, 1851; II, 134 ff.

horizon's rim. And our problems are real and horrifying, more so than any previous generation has had to face. Suddenly our world has become too crowded, and we have found out that creatures that live too closely to- **6** gether tend to become neurotic and destructive. Even worse is the shadow that looms over us for the first time in human history, the unbearable knowledge that man- kind can annihilate itself and everything that lives. **7**

Sometimes we may be impatient with Thoreau for complaining about the defects of his much simpler world. But it is the very things he complained about that have become the monstrous evils which plague us now. Henry **8** Miller, who once called America an air-conditioned nightmare, edited three of Thoreau's essays and said of their author: "He appeared at a time when we had . . . a choice as to the direction, we, the American people, would take. Like Emerson and Whitman, he pointed out the right road—the hard road. . . . As a people we chose differently. And we are now reaping the fruits of our choice. . . . It is too late now to change, we think. But it is not. As individuals, as men, it is never too late to change. That is what these sturdy forerunners of ours were emphasizing all their lives."

Many of our older people seem to believe that America's destiny has already been determined and that our leaders can pursue no other course than the one they have been following, the one that has led us into an intolerable

6 *creatures that live too closely together.* The literature on this, on animals especially, is quite large. Even man is being investigated now, and it seems that he also suffers from having too many of his fellow creatures around him all the time.

7 *can annihilate itself.* This applies not only to nuclear bombs, chemical and biological warfare, but to the pollution and poisoning of man's en- vironment as well. The population explosion goes on apace with more and more people contending for the ever-diminishing land and its products.

8 *Henry Miller.* Although often thought of only as a writer who has emphasized sex, he has always been an astute social critic who is at last beginning to be appreciated.

The Manchester Cloth Mills

state of affairs. But young people, ever rebellious, refuse to believe this and demand a radical change. Thoreau has a special appeal to them. He wanted them for his audience. In the second paragraph of *Walden* he says: "Perhaps these pages are particularly addressed to poor students." And then, a little later: "How could youths better learn to live than by at once trying the experiment of living?"

One is never too young or too old to read a book as universal as this one is. For *Walden* is not merely a printed text to be read; it is an experience to savor. Each contact with it offers us more of its riches.

The other nineteenth-century American classics, great as they are, do not convey the intensely personal message that *Walden* does. Examine them one by one, *Moby-Dick, The Scarlet Letter*, all of Poe's work, and Mark Twain's too, and you will see that they are about people, but other people, never about you. *Walden* is as personal as a letter from a close friend, a friend who wishes you well. Emerson tries to do this, but the sage of Concord sometimes addresses his audience from too lofty a perch. Whitman comes nearest, for he speaks directly to his fellow men and is deeply concerned about them. But it must be remembered that he sings primarily of himself.

Important as these authors are, none of their books has attracted the completely devoted following that *Walden* has. Even more than Emerson, Thoreau was concerned with the minds and morals of his readers. He was a mentor, a counselor, and an admonisher—a true teacher in every sense of the word. But if he had been only that he would have been forgotten along with countless other well-meaning and helpful advisers. He wrote superbly well, and they did not.

It is as a poet and a stylist that Thoreau rises to front rank in American literature. His verse, however, is much inferior to his prose. He never mastered the technical skill that formal poetry requires. And, perhaps sensing his own weakness in that medium, he lost interest in it. Most of his verse was written while he was young. Even **9** before *Walden* was published he noted that "the strains from my muse are as rare nowadays . . . as the notes of birds in the winter. . . . It never melts into song."

The critic who has best grasped the essential nature of Thoreau's great book is Charles R. Anderson, who writes about it with great perception in *The Magic Circle of Walden* (1968). The book has many facets, he says, but its style is even more important than its matter. Therefore, "why not try an entirely new approach and read *Walden* as a poem, the transformation of a vision into

9 *Most of his verse was written while he was young.* Nevertheless, Thoreau produced enough poetry to make a good-sized volume. *The Collected Poems of Henry Thoreau*, edited by Carl Bode (1965), has more than 400 pages.

"Thoreau . . . was not so optimistic as Emerson, not so wantonly inconsistent, not so preoccupied with the reconciling of opposites. Hence, starting from the same premises, he came to different and much more violent conclusions. Self-reliance was for him a doctrine to be literally observed, with no qualifications and no exceptions. When he perceived that the whole structure of society was contrary to the principles in which he believed, he did not hesitate to repudiate society. He was ready to disregard law as freely as he disregarded convention, and he had no fear of consequences. It did not occur to him to leave to the operation of divine law the elimination of evil, nor was his faith of a kind to blind him to his own duty. Even his love of the beauties of nature never befogged his vision of human injustice, and the death of John Brown killed for a time his pleasure in his native lakes and hills." GRANVILLE HICKS
THE GREAT TRADITION, 1935

words?" Many *Journal* entries show that Thoreau thought of himself primarily as a poet.

This does not mean that *Walden*'s best passages should be broken into lines of free verse, nor should one consider it a prose-poem. It can stand by itself, put together just as Thoreau wanted it to be. As Anderson says, "To read it as a poem is to assume that its meaning resides not in its logic but in its language, its structure of images, its symbolism."

What Thoreau is striving for, Anderson adds, is "rendered in an intricate series of image-clusters: animal, leaf, food and shelter, the imagery of time, the quest or journey, the cocoon, the circle, and so on."

On page 18 Professor Anderson explains *Walden*'s complex design:

"The overall structure of *Walden* may be likened to that of both a circle and a web. The spider's web is too geometric, but it will serve as a useful analogy to begin with. Walden Pond lies at the center as a symbol of the purity and harmony yearned for by man, though unattainable. Radial lines of wit run out from this, cutting across the attractions of the purely pragmatic or sensual life. And these radials are looped with circle after concentric circle of aspiration toward the ideal life of heaven —which is also mirrored in the central pond. But Thoreau was too much a poet to be content with a mechanical design. These figures—the spider's web and the formal Euclidian circle—are suggestive merely. Like the orientals he sought an asymmetrical pattern that would satisfy the esthetic sense of form and still remain true to the nature of experience, art without the appearance of artifice.

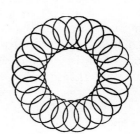

"The circle in *Walden* is less the obvious cycle of the seasons than a number of subtly suggested circular figures, overlapping as well as concentric. (This design is treated fully in a later chapter.) The web is but another name for the intricate lines of relationship that shape the total structure. But all are so woven together that the whole vibrates when any part is touched, and the ultimate motion is toward circumference. Few works of the creative imagination are more successfully unified. Few have their meaning more embedded in a complex pattern of words. *Walden* is a poem, though rendered in the guise of prose." *Walden* is a very great poem, one of America's greatest, for it expresses the noblest ideals to which this country might have aspired. That it did not attain them is a tragedy that affects the entire human race.

And *Walden* is a poem in the primeval mythic sense, as Reginald L. Cook (1965, page 98 f.) points out: "There are at least two *Walden*s. One is the homely, circumstantial, and actual record; the other is ancient, ritualistic, and hieratic. . . . The theme of the reactualization of the archetypal gestures of archaic man—the gestures of baptism and planting and harvesting, or curative ceremonials and re-birth—and their ritualistic evidences appear as naturally as the pickerel in the pond. The more searchingly *Walden* is read with Jane Harrison's statement concerning 'the darker and older shapes' in mind the more various the shapes appear. . . . Interpreted in this light these passages complement and re-enforce an extra-Christian dimension in *Walden*. It can then be read on two levels most rewardingly to the imaginative reader. There is the level of the dramatic present and the level of the prehistoric past."

Walden is a difficult book. It cannot be skimmed through or read lightly. It is all meat, compact and solid. To get from it all that it can yield requires careful reading, re-reading, and concentrated study. It is worth the effort, for it has almost anything you can want—practical advice, facts about natural phenomena, anecdotes about people, philosophical speculation, and—for those who are attuned to such things—intimations of immortality, poetic insight, and the thrill that words can give when they have been chosen and arranged by a master who endows them with more than their apparent meaning.

To have read *Walden* many years ago is not enough, no matter how well you may think you remember it. You are a different person now who will get different meanings from it if you read it again. *Walden* should never be put away; it is a book to keep close at hand so it can be referred to often.

In it are depths below depths, vistas beyond vistas, an opening and closing of doors that lead to corridors and rooms stored with treasure beyond counting. But the treasure has to be searched for. Charles Anderson has described it, but even with the clues he gives, each reader has to go on his own quest. Like all spiritual quests this one should be rewarding in itself.

This much can be promised: that hidden in *Walden*—and buried deep within it—is another book that few readers even suspect is there. Only those who bring to *Walden* the necessary sensitivity and the ability to understand implied meanings will reach the central book that is artfully concealed beneath outer wrappings of nature writing, facts and figures about house building, and other seemingly irrelevant things. (They are not irrelevant.) Like poetry, *Walden* can be appreciated to its full extent only by those who respond to symbolism, suggestion, and association. A hound, a bay horse, and a turtle-dove are there to help readers on their way, but those readers must be able to recognize their guides when they see them, for

"After the first encounter, one perceived that, if Henry Thoreau was a thorn-bush, he was the kind that bears the fragrant flowers."
    VAN WYCK BROOKS
    THE FLOWERING OF NEW ENGLAND, 1936

"[Walden] is a document of increasing pertinence; each year it seems to gain a little headway, as the world loses ground."   E. B. WHITE
    ONE MAN'S MEAT, 1944

they will not be labelled as such. (Nothing is.) The road is hard, the terrain perilous, the effort great, but the reward is beyond computing. (It would wreck anything so simple as a computer.) But seldom is so great a chance, so challenging a challenge given. Let the search begin, then stick to it manfully, always remembering that: At the heart of this inner secret book is Walden itself, but this Walden is no ordinary New England pond. It is a small bit of paradise that existed only in its creator's mind, so you will have to re-create it in yours. It belongs with literature's many lands of the heart's desire, with the **10** Forest of Brocéliande where Merlin and Vivian still live, with the fairyland where *Midsummer Night's Dream* forever casts its magic spell. These imaginary places may seem to be as insubstantial as moonbeams, yet they outlast time and transcend reality.

The reader who is going to be won over by *Walden* will hear the musical hum of the wind blowing through the telegraph wire harp as he approaches a Concord that **11** never was. In the countryside around Walden the trees are greener, the snow whiter, and the crystal-clear water of the pond bluer than anywhere else. In this enchanted forest the animals are friendly—as one would expect them to be. Here the flowers are forever in bloom, and the air is so exhilarating that just to breathe it is to make one want to renounce all previous life. Yet there is wildness **12** here too, a psychic frenzy of the kind that the worshipers of Pan experienced when they ran unrestrained through the dark woods searching for the god of passion and rebellion.

But *Walden*'s magic works only on those who are prepared to surrender themselves to it. To others it will be just another book full of words and phrases that have little significance. They literally will not be able to see the forest for the trees—and to them the trees will be just so much lumber to be calculated in board feet and sawed into planks for building fences.

After reading *Walden*, men who have been leading lives of quiet desperation may become less desperate when they find out what is troubling them. And even those who feel that the odds are against them may realize that "there is more day to dawn" and that "the sun is but a **13** morning star."

10 *the Forest of Brocéliande* is in central Brittany, between Rennes and Ploermel. It is one of the many settings for the various episodes of the Arthurian legend.

11 *the telegraph wire harp.* The bare metallic wires of the early telegraph hummed in the wind, making a musical sound that fascinated Thoreau. He often refers to it.

12 *Yet there is wildness here too.* And very important it is, as will be seen.

13 *"the sun is but a morning star." Walden* ends with these words.

Portrait bust of Thoreau

THE MAN WHO WROTE
*WALDEN**

Thoreau is many men to many people, but there is one thing about him on which everyone is likely to agree; he is very American. Perry Miller (1958, page 45) has said that "he was the most 'nationalistic' of all our writers, beyond even Melville and Whitman."

The growing nineteenth-century nation that Thoreau so often castigated was then just coming into its own as a continental power. Ahead were the dreadful Civil War years. Thoreau was to see only the first one of them, but he was so near to death then that he was probably not fully aware of what was happening.

He had tried to carry on the traditions of the founders —of Washington and Jefferson and the Adamses. But his country had failed him and had already set its feet on the way to the materialism he despised. The great war **1** that ended in freeing the slaves was not fought for that purpose but to preserve the Union.

Thoreau's life was a magnificent attempt to make his fellow men understand and appreciate the full possibilities of daily existence. He failed, but he left behind a book of rules that shows men how to live rich lives without being rich. *Walden* is the essence of that book, but what Thoreau said goes beyond *Walden*, into the *Journal*, "Civil Disobedience," "Life Without Principle," and half a **2** dozen other works.

Thoreau saw people as they actually were. His eyes penetrated their shoddy disguises and saw through their absurd pretenses. His standards were high, so high that he could not meet them himself. But he never gave up trying. In his efforts he called upon the wise men and the poets of the world. His life was an endless quest, a quest for beauty, for truth, for honesty, for understanding, for

1 *The great war.* The Civil War was fought to preserve the Union—not to free the slaves. Lincoln often said this, sometimes in no uncertain terms, particularly in his letter to Horace Greeley (August 22, 1862): "My paramount object in this struggle is to save the Union, and is not either to save or to destroy slavery."

2 *"Life Without Principle."* This was delivered as a lecture on December 6, 1854. After many changes of title it was printed in *The Atlantic Monthly*, Vol. 11, 1863, and was first published in book form in *A Yankee in Canada* in 1866. It is one of Thoreau's most important short pieces.

* The details of Thoreau's life are given in the Chronology. He is discussed here as a man and a writer.

the betterment of all mankind. He was always disappointed in his search for friendship because he eventually found out that the person he had admired so much was just another mortal and therefore imperfect, selfish, inadequate, and unworthy of the great trust he had wanted to impose upon him. He had, in fact, the very faults that Thoreau had himself.

His doubts and his questionings came from within. He may at first seem to be arrogant, too much the ever-earnest preacher, the unsparing critic, the man for whom nothing was ever good enough. But a careful reading of his work turns up phrases that deny this. "I am not worth seeing personally—the stuttering, blundering, clod-hopper that I am"; or "The writer learns to bear contempt and to despise himself." In *Walden* he said: "I never dreamed of any enormity greater than I have committed. I never knew, and never shall know, a worse man than myself."

Thoreau constantly complained that the society in which he lived did not make full use of his talents. His books did not sell, he had trouble getting lecture dates, yet he could always find employment as a carpenter, a gardener, or as a surveyor. He did not mind doing such work, but he thought that it was a waste of his valuable time. It was almost as if he knew he was fated to die while fairly young. He counted the hours and hated to see them spent on performing labor that a hundred others in Concord could do as well. He knew that he had special abilities, but he could seldom persuade others to make use of them.

Thoreau deals with the major problem faced by everyone who is not born rich. "Getting a Living" was the working title of the article that eventually became "Life Without Principle." And there is much about gaining a livelihood in *Walden*.

Few men enjoy what they do to earn a living, and those who do are fortunate no matter how little they make. Those who consider their work a distasteful job that has to be done are the mass of mankind who "lead lives of quiet desperation." Their plight has not changed from Thoreau's day to this, even though they work shorter hours and are better paid.

Thoreau understood clearly the essential nature of work. Observing, thinking, and writing were what he wanted most to do. Hoeing his bean-field, carpentry, and surveying gave him enough money for his needs. To simplify things, he reduced his wants to the fewest possible. "I learned . . . that it would cost incredibly little to obtain one's necessary food," he says in *Walden*. And he built his one-room house there at a total cost of $28.12½. He gives exact details of his income and expenses. The

"The heart of Thoreau's revolt was his continual assertion that the only true America is that country where you are able to pursue life without encumbrances. He did not want that freedom for his private self alone. His deepest reason for disliking the pinched Yankee standardization was its starvation of the minds and spirits of the citizens. One strain of his thought that has not yet been given due attention was summed up by him thus: 'To act collectively is according to the spirit of our institutions.' The context of that remark in *Walden* is where he is maintaining that the community is responsible for providing a more adequate cultural life, good libraries, distinguished lecturers at the lyceums, encouragement for the practice of all the arts. He was as opposed to private hoarding of our spiritual resources as he was to the lust for ownership in our rapacious economy. He believed that all great values should be as public as light."

F. O. MATTHIESSEN
American Renaissance, 1941

The Thoreau Lyceum's replica of the cabin at Walden Pond

prices may seem absurdly low now, but the dollar was **3** worth far more then. The principle, however, is the same.

To live as he did, of course, requires being free of **4** obligations to wives, children, or other hostages to fortune. One must be willing to forgo even small luxuries, be indifferent to public opinion, and not care about providing for old age. Thoreau's way of life was admittedly not for everyone. "I do not mean to prescribe rules to strong and valiant natures," he said. And he exempted still others, some satirically.

Thoreau had a poor opinion of most of his fellow men and avoided them as much as he could. He is best remembered for his two-year stay at Walden Pond, but his desire to be alone was a lifelong affair. Yet he was no hermit; he merely wanted to select his companions and spend time with them on his own terms. This, of course, is a sign of arrogance, but it is the arrogance that creative people sometimes have to display in order to conserve their highly useful and always limited time.

As a writer Thoreau seems to have had enormous confidence in himself, but further readings in the *Journal* show that this was not always true. Doubts and self-questioning often occur. His own physical appearance impaired his self-esteem. He was, according to his own description, "about five feet 7 inches in height—of a light complexion, rather slimly built," and, as all those who have described him agree, had a rather prominent nose. Ellery Channing (1873, page 25), who knew Thor-

3 *the dollar was worth far more then.* Much more, yet there was a curious discrepancy in prices. The very good pencils made by the Thoreaus sold for 75 cents a dozen in Elizabeth Peabody's Boston bookstore. This may seem to be unusually high, but Thoreau pencils have soared in value since then, not because of inflation but because of the demand from collectors. In 1965, when a Boston bookstore offered a dozen for sale, the price was $100.

4 *hostages to fortune.* This, of course, is Francis Bacon's famous phrase.

eau best, characterized that nose as "aquiline or very Roman, like one of the portraits of Caesar (more like a beak, as was said)." Channing then goes on to give us a word picture of Thoreau's face with "large, overhanging brows above the deepest set blue eyes that could be seen, in certain lights, in others gray,—eyes expressive of all shades of feeling, but never weak or near-sighted; the forehead not unusually broad or high, full of concentrated energy and purpose; the mouth with prominent lips, pursed up with meaning and thought when silent, and giving out when open a stream of the most varied and unusual and instructive sayings. His hair was a dark brown, exceedingly abundant, fine and soft; and for several years he wore a comely beard."

Channing also said that Thoreau "retained a peculiar pronunciation of the letter *r*, with a decided French accent. . . . His speech always had an emphasis, a *burr* in it." This was a disadvantage in public speaking. And Thoreau often became more interested in the manuscript of his lecture than in the people he was addressing and therefore tended to slur what he was saying. His platform presence was not good although Channing testifies to the forcefulness of his person: "His whole figure had an active earnestness, as if he had no moment to waste. The clenched hand betokened purpose. In walking, he made a short cut if he could, and when sitting in the shade or by the wall-side seemed merely the clearer to look forward into the next piece of activity. Even in the boat, he had a wary, transitory air, his eyes on the outlook. . . ."

There is a great deal in *Walden*—and in Thoreau's other writings—about clothes. Carlyle's *Sartor Resartus* **5** had been published in Boston in 1836, and its satirical view of mankind's apparel had a great effect on the young Thoreau. He was not only not interested in attire —and all that it meant—he was contemptuous of it. He saw garments merely as protective devices against weather, thorns, brambles, and insects. For his own use, he asked only that a fabric wear well and that it cost as little as possible. It is curious, though, that someone who had such a poor opinion of clothing should have written so much about it.

Carlyle had an important influence on Thoreau. He gave a lecture on Carlyle at the Concord Lyceum on February 4, 1846, while he was living in his Walden Pond house, and then made the lecture into an article which was published in *Graham's Magazine*, XXX, 1845.

Harvard had a greater impact on Thoreau than is generally thought. While there, he read the twenty-one volumes of Chalmers' *English Poets*, much of the work of **6** Coleridge, Wordsworth, Shakespeare, Milton, Sir Thomas

5 Sartor Resartus. Written by Thomas Carlyle, it originally appeared in 1833–1834 in England in *Fraser's Magazine;* however, it was first published in book form in Boston in 1836 and did not come out in England as a book until 1838. *Sartor Resartus* means "the tailor retailored." Only the first part of it deals with the philosophy of clothes; the second part is the story of Diogenes Teufelsdröck, an eccentric old German professor who serves as a mouthpiece for Carlyle.

6 *Chalmers'* English Poets. These small volumes edited by Alexander Chalmers (1759–1834) are still a treasure house of early English poetry.

Browne, Chaucer, Beaumont and Fletcher, as well as the seventeenth-century Cavalier poets.

In September 1836, while he was still at Harvard, Thoreau purchased a copy of Emerson's just-published book, *Nature*. Short as the book was, it was to have a tremendous effect on Thoreau's thinking. **7**

Thoreau and Emerson probably met for the first time in 1836. Emerson, who was 14 years older than the bright young man he wanted to look upon as his disciple, had been born in Boston, but his family was from Concord. When he moved there with his new wife Lidian in the autumn of 1835, Thoreau was still at Harvard, but in a small town like Concord it was inevitable that he and Emerson would soon meet. **8**

Their friendship began well, and there is no doubt that it was beneficial to Thoreau during his early years. But as he grew older—and surer of himself—he slowly came to resent the very qualities that made Emerson the sage of Concord.

John Brooks Moore (1932, page 241) has pointed out that "there are sixty important references to Thoreau in Emerson's *Journals;* while in Thoreau's *Journal* there are only between twenty and thirty really significant references to Emerson, most of them brief. Further, it ought to be noted, Thoreau's references to Emerson are often ironic and lack entirely the one of discipleship."

There are probably more references to Emerson in Thoreau's *Journal* than Moore has counted, but that is because some of them do not mention him by name. This applies particularly to those about the perfidy and untrustworthiness of alleged friends.

Again and again, Emerson says "my good Henry" or "my brave Henry," whereas Thoreau almost always calls Emerson "R.W.E." or, in a few instances, "Mr. Emerson."

By 1852, when Thoreau was thirty-five years old, he had become completely disillusioned with the kind, well-intentioned fellow townsman who undoubtedly wished him well. Thoreau's *Journal* for May 23 of that year (see Chronology) shows that he and Emerson could no longer be close friends. He found the older man too condescending for him to tolerate the relationship any longer. However, they remained on good but rather impersonal terms, and Emerson spoke well of his friend Henry for the rest of his life.

So far as most Concordians were concerned, Thoreau was just what Emerson said he was: cold, proud, anti-social, indifferent to public opinion, a man who could say no much more easily than yes, a creature who preferred the solitude of the fields to the best of whatever the town had to offer. Yet the Concordians came to respect Thoreau even though they remained a bit in awe of him. They

7 Nature. Although Emerson's first book was very short, it summarized the meaning of Transcendentalism.

8 *Lidian*. She was Emerson's second wife; the first, Ellen Louisa Tucker, had died of tuberculosis while very young. Lidian's name was really Lydia, but Emerson made her change it because he thought that Lidian Emerson sounded better.

Ralph Waldo Emerson as a young man

knew that his probity was beyond question, that his character was difficult but basically good, that his replies to any question would be completely honest, and that his attitude toward the poor and the oppressed would be democratic, while his opinion on any subject was always his own.

Walter Harding (1954b, page 22) says that Emerson's **9** eulogy of Thoreau, which was revised and printed in *The Atlantic Monthly* for August 1862, had "a most devastating effect on his fame," and that when Emerson edited Thoreau's letters in 1865 "he cut from them every line that showed his warm friendly personality and emphasized his philosophical aloofness."

It is unlikely, however, that Emerson was at any time actually hostile to Thoreau; hostility was foreign to his nature. As an older man, who had met Thoreau while he was still an undergraduate, he felt that such a bright young lad should be encouraged. Unfortunately, this paternal feeling continued. At some time in his career, Thoreau began to believe that he was not only Emerson's equal but his superior. The judgment of the years seems to have borne him out.

Emerson vitiated his own work by imbuing it with too much dicta of the kind that would be endorsed by commercial enterprises. Thoreau remained uncompromising to the end and supported John Brown openly when the **10** Government was hunting down his men and preparing to hang the Old Testament rebel.

The relationship between Emerson and Thoreau has

9 *Emerson's eulogy of Thoreau.* Nevertheless, this eulogy had much in it that praised Thoreau. Emerson was ambivalent about his friend, but he thought well of him.

10 *John Brown.* His influence on Thoreau has never been adequately appraised. It was even more important than his biographers think.

The Emerson house as it is today

never been thoroughly investigated. For one thing, some
of the key documents are lacking. And much of what the
two men felt about each other was probably never put
on paper. Thoreau was a clever jack-of-all-trades while
Emerson always cursed his useless "imbecile hands," so
the younger man was twice invited to stay at the Emerson
house with board and lodging given in exchange for a
few hours of manual work each day.

The first period began on April 26, 1841, and lasted
for nearly two years. Since Emerson was away part of the
time on lecture tours, Thoreau and Lidian Emerson were

Lidian Emerson
(Courtesy Concord Free Public Library)

often left alone. She was the very sort of woman to whom Thoreau would be attracted. She was older than he, but that would be in her favor.

Thoreau enjoyed living with the Emersons and wrote a letter of thanks on January 24, 1843, when he left. (See Chronology.) His next extended stay was between September 1847 and July 1848, after he had abandoned his Walden Pond house to take charge of the Emerson home while its master was in Europe.

Thoreau was probably as near to being in love with Lidian Emerson as he ever was with any woman. His **11** letters to her of May 22 and June 20, 1843, show that apparently she discouraged him, but she need not have worried, for the attachment was almost surely a Platonic one. The years that Thoreau spent with Lidian were probably the happiest in his life—a life that seems to have been almost devoid of any other close emotional involvement. That he thought of Lidian as a sister is meaningful, and there is good reason to believe that that was the warmest relationship he could have with a woman. An unpublished scrap of manuscript in the Huntington Library casts some light on this: "My most intimate acquaintance with woman has been a sister's relation, or at most the catholic virgin mother relations—not that it has always been free from the suspicion of a lower sympathy" (HM 13182, env. II, 1848–1850).

Only in recent years has the possibility that Thoreau might have been a homosexual been raised. In earlier times such an idea would have been thought too shocking to mention. The evidence for it is indirect and never positive. It must, however, be remembered that practically every word that Thoreau ever wrote was subject to post- **12** humous censorship by his sister Sophia and other relatives and friends.

A poem that was circulated freely in Thoreau's lifetime is perhaps the most convincing document that he was attracted to males. This is the one addressed to "the **13** gentle boy," who was 11-year-old Edmund Sewall, brother of Ellen, the 17-year-old girl who presumably rejected Thoreau's offer of marriage. (See Chronology for June 17, 1839.)

There is more evidence. In the "Lost" *Journal* for October 17, 1840, Thoreau wrote: "In the presence of my friend I am ashamed of my fingers and toes. I have no feature so fair as my love for him. There is more than a maiden modesty between us." The male friend referred to is not necessarily young Edmund Sewall. Other *Journal* entries for October and November 1840 mention such a friend again and again. The most interesting entry is

11 *His letters . . . of May 22 and June 20, 1843* (in part): I think of you as some elder sister of mine, whom I could not have avoided,—a sort of lunar influence,—only of such age as the moon, whose time is measured by her light. You must know that you represent to me woman, for I have not traveled very far or wide,—and what if I had? I like to deal with you, for I believe you do not lie or steal, and these are very rare virtues. I thank you for your influence for two years. I was fortunate to be subjected to it, and am now to remember it. It is the noblest gift we can make; what signify all others that can be bestowed? You have helped to keep my life "on loft," as Chaucer says of Griselda, and in a better sense. You always seemed to look down at me as from some elevation—some of your high humilities—and I was better for having to look up. I felt taxed not to disappoint your expectation; for could there be any accident so sad as to be respected for something better than we are? It was a pleasure even to go away from you, as it is not to meet some, as it apprised me of my high relations; and such a departure is a sort of further introduction and meeting. Nothing makes the earth seem so spacious as to have friends at a distance; they make the latitudes and longitudes.

I am almost afraid to look at your letter. I see that it will make my life very steep, but it may lead to fairer prospects than this.

You seem to me to speak out of a very clear and high heaven, where any one may be who stands so high. Your voice seems not a voice, but comes as much from the blue heavens, as from the paper.

My dear friend it was very noble in you to write me so trustful an answer. It will do as well for another world as for this. Such a voice is for no particular time nor person, and it makes him who may hear it stand for all that is lofty and true in humanity. The thought of you will constantly elevate my life; it will be something always above the horizon to behold, as when I look up at the evening star. I think I know your thoughts without seeing you, and as well here as in Concord. You are not at all strange to me.

I could hardly believe after the lapse of one night that I had such a noble letter still at hand to read—that it was not some fine dream. I looked at midnight to be sure that it was real. I feel that I am unworthy to know you, and yet they will not permit it wrongfully.

I, perhaps, am more willing to deceive by appearances than you say you are; it would not be worth the while to tell how willing—but I have the power perhaps too much to forget my meanness as soon as seen, and not be incited by permanent sorrow. My actual life is unspeakably mean, compared with what I know and see that

not prose but verse written on November 7. Note the **14** revealing last line.

Some of the early critics said that this poem was addressed to Ellen Sewall rather than to her brother. But they cannot explain away the many male references except to say that perhaps they were phrased in this way to conceal Thoreau's love for Ellen.

One thing, however, that must be kept in mind is that in Transcendentalist Concord "love" and "friendship" were practically synonymous. But this does not necessarily mean that they were always free of sex. Margaret Fuller, whose journal is more outspoken than Thoreau's, said: "It is so true that a woman may be in love with a woman, and a man with a man. . . . It is regulated by the same law as that of love between persons of different sexes; only it is partly intellectual and spiritual. . . . Why did Socrates love Alcibiades? Why did Körner love **15, 16** Schneider? How natural is the love of Wallenstein for **17** Max; that of de Staël for Récamier; mine for ———. **18** I loved ——— for a time with as much passion as I was then strong enough to feel. . . . I do not love her now with passion, but I still feel towards her as I can to no other woman."

Despite her clearly indicated Lesbian tendencies, Mar- **19** garet Fuller married Count Ossoli and bore him a child.

The interpersonal relations of the highly neurotic, intense, intellectual Concord group are so involved that they will probably never be untangled. And the individual personalities are equally complex. In Thoreau's case at least two pioneering efforts have been made to understand him in psychological terms. Both, however, **20** remain unpublished.

When a serious and detailed study is made by fully competent investigators trained in psychological techniques, more light will undoubtedly be shed on this difficult and little-explored problem. From the work that has already been done, the uncertain verdict seems to be that Thoreau had latent homoerotic tendencies. Whether they ever became overt or not may never be revealed unless some new documentation is discovered.

Closely allied to Thoreau's sexual problems are his constant dwellings upon the difficulty of finding a friend whom he can trust. His writings are filled with musings on the subject. The fairly long essay "Friendship," which he inserted into the Wednesday chapter of *A Week on the Concord and Merrimack Rivers*, was made from *Journal* entries that were written before 1849 when the book was published. This essay is a far from complete statement for it does not contain post-1849 entries, and

it might be—Yet the ground from which I see and say this is some part of it. It ranges from heaven to earth and is all things in an hour. The experience of every past moment but belies the faith of each present. We never conceive the greatness of our fates. Are not these faint flashes of light, which sometimes obscure the sun, their certain dawn?

My friend, I have read your letter as if I was not reading it. After each pause I could defer the rest forever. The thought of you will be a new motive for every right action. You are another human being whom I know, and might not our topic be as broad as the universe. What have we to do with petty rumbling news? We have our own great affairs. . . .

What wealth is it to have such friends that we cannot think of them without elevation. And we can think of them any time, and any where, and it costs nothing but the lofty disposition. I cannot tell you the joy your letter gives me—which will not quite cease till the latest time. Let me accompany your finest thought.

I send my love to my other friend and brother, whose nobleness I slowly recognize.

                                        Henry

Harding and Bode (1958, page 121) say of the second letter: " To almost anyone who will read the text with an open mind, this is a love letter."

12 *posthumous censorship*. Since Thoreau cut up his *Journals* and other manuscripts to use the clipped pages in his work, the clipping process could be continued after he was dead and not be detected.

13 *"the gentle boy."* Thoreau's title for this poem is "Sympathy."

Lately, alas, I knew a gentle boy,
  Whose features all were cast in Virtue's mould,
As one she had designed for Beauty's toy,
  But after manned him for her own stronghold.

On every side he open was as day,
  That you might see no lack of strength within,
For walls and ports do only serve alway
  For a pretense to feebleness and sin.

Say not that Caesar was victorious,
  With toil and strife who stormed the House of Fame,
In other sense this youth was glorious,
  Himself a kingdom wheresoe'er he came.

No strength went out to get him victory,
  When all was income of its own accord;

even those that were used are only a selection from a larger body of such material.

Since Thoreau was obviously obsessed with "friendship" and all its ramifications, it is an important aspect of his character and personality. Perry Miller (1958, pages 91–92) says of this that "Thoreau's frantic concern with the idea of friendship is a struggle to make it perverse, to make it a judgment on the faults of friends, to equate it with hatred. . . . One is obliged to declare that Henry clearly *wanted* the arrow of friendship to be poisoned, that he would brew the stuff and apply it himself."

Thoreau does not come out well when judged on his relations with people. Three women—his mother, his sister Sophia, and Lidian Emerson—seem to have been closest to him. He was a good family man who spent most of his life in his father's home. He was fond of his mother, even though she had the reputation of being a strongly self-willed person who was hard to get along with. He was respectful to his father but somewhat distant.

It must be remembered that Mrs. Thoreau kept a boardinghouse, with many guests living and eating there. Thoreau stayed pretty much in his attic quarters except at mealtime. Although he professed to be indifferent to food, at least one note shows that some of the dishes served at his mother's table did not meet with his approval. A fragment from his *Journal* for July 22, 1840, (now in Harvard's Houghton Library) complains about the "kitchen cabinet" which was "concocting some indigestible compound" and said that the pudding was especially terrible that day. And this from a man who, when asked which dish he preferred, indifferently said, "The nearest."

Thoreau was at his best when he was alone. He tolerated a few select individuals' company and liked to be with children, but he sought solitude and said so many times in his *Journal*, in *Walden*, and in his other writings. He justifies this desire for solitude with much weighty argument, but, like all loners, shunned people because he was ill at ease with them. He felt vastly superior to most; he found others dull; even those to whom he could talk as intellectual equals—men like Emerson, Channing, Hawthorne, and Alcott—finally turned out to have shortcomings. He got along best with hunters, fishermen, and other men who were close to Nature. They did not have to be educated, but they did have to be expert in whatever it was that they were supposed to do well.

Thoreau had the greatest admiration for Alek Therien, the French-Canadian woodchopper whom he called "a

For where he went none other was to see,
  But all were parcel of their noble lord.

He forayed like the subtile haze of summer,
  That stilly shows fresh landscapes to our eyes,
And revolutions works without a murmur,
  Or rustling of a leaf beneath the skies.

So was I taken unawares by this,
  I quite forgot my homage to confess;
Yet now am forced to know, though hard it is,
  I might have loved him had I loved him less.

Each moment as we nearer drew to each,
  A stern respect withheld us farther yet,
So that we seemed beyond each other's reach,
  And less acquainted than when first we met.

We two were one while we did sympathize,
  So could we not the simplest bargain drive;
And what avails it now that we are wise,
  If absence doth this doubleness contrive?

Eternity may not the chance repeat,
  But I must tread my single way alone,
In sad remembrance that we once did meet,
  And know that bliss irrevocably gone.

The spheres henceforth my elegy shall sing,
  For elegy has other subject none;
Each strain of music in my ears shall ring
  Knell of departure from that other one.

Make haste and celebrate my tragedy;
  With fitting strain resound ye woods and fields;
Sorrow is dearer in such case to me
  Than all the joys other occasion yields.

———

Is't then too late the damage to repair?
  Distance, forsooth, from my weak grasp hath
    reft
The empty husk, and clutched the useless tare,
  But in my hands the wheat and kernel left.

If I but love that virtue which he is,
  Though it be scented in the morning air,
Still shall we be truest acquaintances,
  Nor mortals know a sympathy more rare.

14 *verse written on November* 7 [1840].

  I'm guided in the darkest night
  By flashes of auroral light,
  Which over dart thy eastern home
  And teach me not in vain to roam.
  Thy steady light on t'other side
  Pales the sunset, makes day abide,
  And after sunrise stays the dawn,
  Forerunner of a brighter morn.

true Homeric or Paphlagonian man" in *Walden* (see pages 237 and 274). Therien doubtless deserved Thoreau's praise for his skill with an axe and his rough-and-ready good humor and honesty. But later on, when Therien took to drink, Thoreau bluntly told him to kill himself. One story says that Thoreau advised him to cut his throat; another that he recommended suicide by shooting. In either case, the meaning is the same.

Much of this, of course, is simply a reflection of Thoreau's attitude toward himself. A careful reading of the *Journal*—or even of the revealing excerpts printed in the Chronology—brings out a great deal of this. He had a high regard for his intellect and ability, but underneath he was a quagmire of uncertainty and self-abnegation. The man who could say: "The storms are happy, Concord River is happy, and I am happy too" on one day (January 6, 1857; IX, 206) and then on the very next day write: "In the street and in society I am almost invariably cheap and dissipated, my life is unspeakably mean," is obviously the victim of wide and rapid swings of mood. Since Thoreau was deeply introverted, he continually probed his mind and kept dwelling on things that a more outgoing person might be able to dismiss. Like all sensitive artists, he was a self-torturer, an expert in making himself unhappy, often for seemingly trivial—and sometimes unknown—reasons.

Yet all this was necessary for the making of a book like *Walden*. Without it, *Walden* would have been an ordinary account of a man's stay in the woods. What Thoreau added came from the depths of his inner being; it is a distillation of both his conscious and unconscious mind.

The publication of *Walden* in 1854 marked the height of Thoreau's career. It was the last time he was ever to have a book published which he had prepared for the press himself, and the sales of the first edition—the only one he was ever to see—dragged on slowly until the title was allowed to go out of print in 1859. Meanwhile, he had hundreds of copies of his only other book, *A Week on* **21** *the Concord and Merrimack Rivers*, stored in the house. He sat surrounded by reminders of failure, growing more and more bitter and retreating to his *Journal* as the only place in which he could put writings that the public apparently did not want.

John Brown's open war on slavery at Harper's Ferry **22** in October 1859 brought Thoreau fiercely—but briefly —to life. After that dramatic episode was over, he sank back into the lethargy and indifference that overtake an aging man when he feels that the world no longer needs or wants him. The *Journal* entries for these late years have few comments about people and deal almost entirely with Nature.

There is no being here to me
But staying here to be
When others laugh I am not glad,
When others cry I am not sad,
But be they grieved or be they merry
I'm supernumerary.
I am a miser without blame
Am conscience stricken without shame.
An idler am I without leisure,
A busy body without pleasure.
I did not think so bright a day
Would issue in so dark a night.
I did not think such sober play
Would leave me in so sad a plight,
And I should be most sorely spent
Where first I was most innocent.

I thought by loving all beside
To prove to you my love was wide,
And by the rites I soared above
To show you my peculiar love.

15 *Socrates . . . Alcibiades.* Socrates 470?–399 B.C.), Greek philosopher. Alcibiades (450–404 B.C.) was his pupil who later became a military leader.

16 *Körner . . . Schneider.* She is probably referring to Karl Theodor Körner (1791–1813), German poet and writer of patriotic songs, and Friedrich Schneider (1786–1853), German conductor and composer, although they cannot be positively identified by her brief last-name mention of them.

17 *Wallenstein . . . Max.* Albrecht Eusebius Wenzel von (1583–1634), Austrian general, and Maximilian I, Duke of Bavaria (1513–1651).

18 *de Staël . . . Récamier.* Madame de Staël (1766–1817), French writer, and Madame Récamier (1777–1849), French society beauty best remembered for the superb reclining portrait David made of her.

19 *Margaret Fuller* (1810–1850). This remarkable strong-willed woman was not a Concordian, but she was well known there for her unconventional views and vivid personality. Her younger sister Ellen was Ellery Channing's wife.

20 *Both . . . remain unpublished.* Literature dealing with this is exceedingly scarce. Raymond Gozzi's "Tropes and Figures: A Psychological Study of David Henry Thoreau," a doctoral thesis at New York University, and David Kalman's "A Study of Thoreau" have never been printed and are expensive and difficult to get. The first is summarized in the Thoreau Society *Bulletin*, Number 58 (Winter 1957); the second in Number 22 (January 1948). The only published work that touches on the problem and at least admits that it exists is

Thoreau continued to collect material for the book **23** on Indians which he was never to write. He did complete an article on "The Succession of Forest Trees," and he **24** did lecture on the subject in Concord in September 1860. It was his last work of any importance. His interest in tree-growth rings hastened his death. On December 3, 1860, a very cold day, he was outdoors counting the rings on tree stumps. He fell ill but insisted on keeping a lecture appointment in Waterbury, Connecticut, on December 11. The effort was too much for him, and his bad cold developed into bronchitis. He never became well again, for the terminal phase of tuberculosis had set in.

Early in 1861 he went to Minnesota, hoping that the **25** change of climate would improve his health. It did not. By July 10, he was back in Concord. For a while he was able to work with his sister Sophia, revising material which could be used as magazine articles. He kept on with this even when he was no longer able to write. Then he dictated changes and corrections to Sophia. His tubercular condition was steadily becoming worse, and he was weakening daily. He made his last entry in the *Journal* on November 3, 1861.

There is no doubt that Thoreau knew that time was running out. He had known it for a long while, perhaps longer than his family and friends suspected. It is probably no coincidence that he became ill when he did (December 3, 1860) and died when he did (May 6, 1862). He had said what he wanted to say in *Walden*, and the *Journal* contains most of what he wanted to say after that.

Carl Bode (1947, page 13) believes that "there was a tragedy in the career of Henry Thoreau. . . . The tragedy lay, I think, in the slow crumbling of Thoreau's own conception of his life's work." When he looked back at what he had tried to do, he realized that the world had not listened to him. He was to be widely read in future years, but a dying author does not know that.

The winter months passed, and spring came on. Thoreau sank down slowly into death, not resisting, but letting himself be engulfed into the great blackness from which all things come and must return.

In his funeral eulogy Emerson said that Thoreau "could **26** pace sixteen rods more accurately than another man could measure them with rod and chain. He could find his path in the woods at night, he said, better by his feet than his eyes. He could estimate the measure of a tree very well by his eye; he could estimate the weight of a calf or a pig, like a dealer. From a box containing a bushel or more of loose pencils, he could take up with his hands fast enough just a dozen pencils at every grasp. He was

Perry Miller's *Consciousness in Concord* (1958). This book, which reprints the "lost" *Journal* of 1840–1841, contains most of the material that relates to Thoreau and Ellen and Edmund Sewall—and perhaps others unnamed.

21 *hundreds of copies.* See the Chronology for October 28, 1853.

22 *Harper's Ferry.* John Brown had been in Concord in 1857, brought there by Sanborn who introduced him to Thoreau. Sanborn may have known about the plans to invade Harper's Ferry, but Thoreau probably did not.

23 *the book on Indians.* The Morgan Library has eleven manuscript notebooks with more than half a million words that Thoreau recorded for this ambitious work. Albert Keiser (1928) has examined the manuscripts and described them in a 16-page article. In the *Journal* for March 19, 1842; I, 337, Thoreau said: "When I walk in the fields of Concord and meditate on the destiny of this prosperous slip of the Saxon family, the unexhausted energies of this new country, I forget that this which is now Concord was once Musketaquid, and that the *American race* has had its destiny also. Everywhere in the fields, in the corn and grain land, the earth is strewn with the relics of a race which has vanished as completely as if trodden in with the earth. I find it good to remember the eternity behind me as well as the eternity before. Wherever I go, I tread in the tracks of the Indian. I pick up the bolt which he has but just dropped at my feet. And if I consider destiny I am on his trail. I scatter his hearthstones with my feet, and pick out of the embers of his fire the simple but enduring implements of the wigwam and the chase. In planting my corn in the same furrow which yielded its increase to his support so long, I displace some memorial of him."

24 *"The Succession of Forest Trees."* Considered by Walter Harding (1965, page 439) to be Thoreau's major contribution to scientific knowledge. It was printed in the New York *Weekly Tribune* for October 6, 1860, and first appeared in a book when *Excursions* was published in 1863.

25 *Minnesota.* Thoreau went there with young Horace Mann, son of the noted educator. Mann apparently contracted tuberculosis from Thoreau and died of it a few years later.

26 *funeral eulogy.* This was printed in *The Atlantic Monthly*, IX, 1862, and in book form as the introduction to *Excursions* in 1863.

a good swimmer, runner, skater, boatman, and would probably outwalk most countrymen in a day's journey. And the relation of body to mind was still finer than we have indicated. . . . He knew how to sit immovable, a part of the rock he rested on, until the bird, the reptile, the fish, which had retired from him, should come back and resume its habits, nay, moved by curiosity, should come to him and watch him.

"It was a pleasure and a privilege to walk with him. He knew the country like a fox or a bird, and passed through it as freely by paths of his own. He knew every track in the snow or on the ground, and what creature had taken this path before him. . . .

"Under his arm he carried an old music book to press plants; in his pocket, his diary and pencil, a spy-glass for birds, microscope, jack-knife, and twine. He wore straw hat, stout shoes, strong gray trousers to brave shrub-oaks and smilax, and to climb a tree for a hawk's or a squirrel's nest. He waded into the pool for the water-plants, and his strong legs were no insignificant part of his armor. . . . He thought, that, if waked up from a trance . . . he could tell by the plants what time of the year it was within two days.

"The country knows not yet . . . how great a son it has lost. It seems an injury that he should leave in the midst his broken task, which none else can finish,—a kind of indignity to so noble a soul, that it should depart out of Nature before yet he has been really shown to his peers for what he is. But he, at least, is content. His soul was made for the noblest society; he had in a short life exhausted the capabilities of this world; wherever there is knowledge, wherever there is virtue, wherever there is beauty, he will find a home."

"Thoreau in his life and letters shows what the pioneer movement might have come to if this great migration had sought culture rather than material conquest, and an intensity of life, rather than mere extension over the continent."

LEWIS MUMFORD
THE GOLDEN DAY, 1926

Extent, 64,230 square miles.

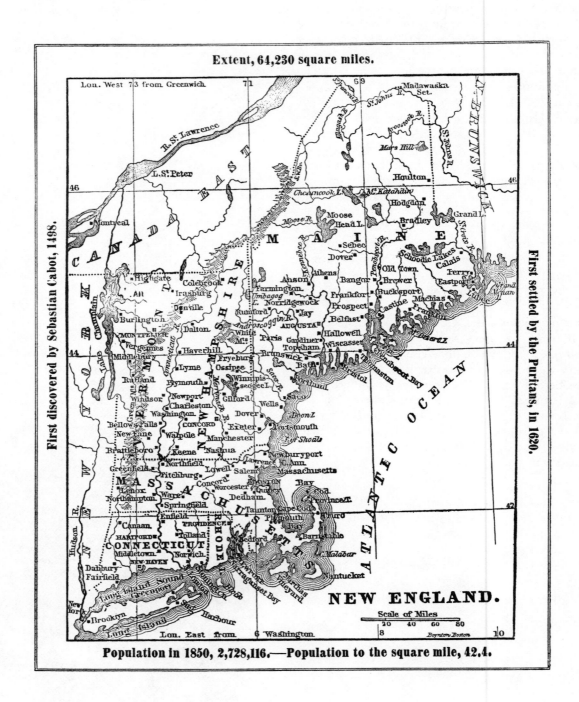

First discovered by Sebastian Cabot, 1498.

First settled by the Puritans, in 1620.

NEW ENGLAND.

Scale of Miles

Population in 1850, 2,728,116.—Population to the square mile, 42,4.

THE WRITING OF *WALDEN*

It is popularly believed that Thoreau built his little house on the shores of Walden Pond in order to write *Walden* there. That is not quite true. He wrote his first book, *A Week on the Concord and Merrimack Rivers*, while he lived in the cabin. He also did all or most of the short first draft of *Walden* at this time, but he kept working on the manuscript until it was published in 1854.

Only two of Thoreau's books were issued during his lifetime—*A Week* and *Walden*. All the others were culled from his articles and the *Journal* and were published posthumously. (See Bibliography.)

Walden was in every sense a major work that occupied the most productive years of Thoreau's life. It not only took much revising, but much thinking as well.

The manuscript from which the printer set the type for *Walden* has apparently been lost. But Thoreau's **1** working manuscript, which shows how the book was constructed, still exists. It is in the Henry E. Huntington Library in San Marino, California, where it is numbered HM924 and is kept in a steel vault along with some of the library's major literary treasures. It is, incidentally, valued at more than $100,000.

The Walden manuscript was acquired by Henry E. Huntington in August 1918 from the millionaire collector, William Keeney Bixby, chairman of the board of the American Car and Foundry Company and director of many banks and corporations. With it came dozens of now priceless manuscripts written by Shelley, Ruskin, Kipling, Burns, Dickens, and others, as well as thousands of letters from noted literary and historical figures.

The provenance of the *Walden* manuscript is clear. Thoreau's sister Sophia inherited it when he died in 1862. **2** She kept it until her death in 1876, when it went to Thoreau's friend and faithful correspondent, Harrison Gray Otis Blake of Worcester, Massachusetts. He left it to

1 *Thoreau's working manuscript.* According to James L. Shanley (1957, page 1) there are 628 leaves (1, 256 pages), but some are mere scraps of paper. The Xerox copy of the manuscript, which is used for ordinary reference, has been numbered consecutively on the back of each sheet. There are a few errors in the enumeration. Numbers 559 and 560, 1,035, and 1,036, 1,050, and 1,051, and 1,089 and 1,090 are exact duplicates, mistakenly numbered twice. The one after number 107 originally had no number on it; it is now 107A. The Xerox copy is divided into seven versions as follows:

1. "A" version	23 pp.	3 to 59 (allow 2 pp. for half titles)
"A" version	1847 240 pp. plus 2 pp.	61 to 303
2. "B" version	1848 (?) 160 pp. plus 4 pp. (1848–1849 as marked in manuscript)	305 to 468
		Note in Xerox copy: Some of the pages are in ink and hand of "C," but since the passages begin on what were "B" leaves, all the leaves are left here.
3. "C" version	probably 59 pp. 1849 plus 2 pp.	471 to 531
		Some of the pages in "B" are in the ink and hand of "C."

Elias Harlow Russell, also of Worcester; it remained in Russell's possession until he sold it to Bixby.

Bixby permitted Franklin B. Sanborn, Thoreau's biographer, to use the original manuscript for the preparation of the Bibliophile Edition of *Walden*, which was published in a limited edition of 483 copies in 1909. Sanborn added some 12,000 words from the manuscript to the text, but in doing so, rearranged the order of the book. Although Sanborn can be criticized for tampering with the text, he has never been given credit for printing long and never-before-seen passages from the manuscript. Since he knew Thoreau and the Concord of his time, he was also able to contribute many valuable footnotes.

The present edition reproduces the first printing of *Walden* intact. In the margins are corrections and changes made by Thoreau after the book was set in type, passages from the Bibliophile Edition, extracts from the *Journals* which have some bearing on the text, and hitherto unpublished material found by the editor in the Huntington Library manuscript.

Even though Sanborn used many words from the manuscript in his Bibliophile Edition, he did not make a scholarly study of the manuscript itself. This was not done until James Lyndon Shanley examined it with painstaking care and reported his findings in "A Study of the Making of *Walden*" in the *Huntington Library Quarterly* for February 1951. He then expanded this into a book, *The Making of Walden*, in 1957.

What Shanley found is of paramount interest, for it shows how Thoreau went about shaping his basic ideas into a great book. That he did not, however, intend to spend so much time on the task can be seen from the fact that *A Week on the Concord and Merrimack Rivers*, which was first issued in 1849, carries a page with the announcement: "Will soon be published, *Walden, or Life in the Woods*. By Henry D. Thoreau." But the *Week* sold only 219 copies out of a first printing of 1,000, so its publisher was naturally reluctant to bring out another book by the same author. Thoreau therefore returned to the manuscript of *Walden* and worked on it for five more years.

He wrote and rewrote the pages many times. His rapidly flowing handwriting became more and more difficult to read, and numerous passages were inserted in even harder-to-read pencil script.

The earlier drafts are written over and heavily revised, so much so that they often had to be recopied by their author. He sometimes used the margins for adding new material, and if he needed still more space to finish a passage he did not hesitate to write it vertically over the previously written horizontal lines.

3

4

Franklin B. Sanborn as a young man
(*Courtesy Concord Free Public Library*)

4. "D" version	1851–52 123 pp. plus 22 pp.	534 to 681
5. "E" version	late 1852–53 218 pp.	684 to 903
6. "F" version	1853–54 232 pp. plus 4 sm. pcs. (plus 6 pp. ?)	906 to 1,144
7. "G" version	1854 82 pp.	1,147 to 1,229

This makes a total of 1,226 pages, or 30 pages less than Shanley's figure. The difference may be explained by his remark (page 3) that "There are some torn leaves and scraps and a few leaves with irrelevant material marked 'A Week' or 'Civil Disobedience.'"

2 *Thoreau's sister Sophia inherited it.* During the fourteen years that the manuscript was in her possession, Emerson, Channing, and Harrison Blake had access to it.

3 *the Bibliophile Edition.* Copies of this have disappeared from the market and are now available only in the rare-book collections of big libraries, so it is difficult for most readers to see what passages Sanborn used. And he did not always mark unpublished material as such.

He was never satisfied. He kept canceling passages, adding new words, sentences, and paragraphs. He also changed the position of already existing material—and then often changed it again.

Thoreau's spelling was not infallible. Misspellings like "Appollo" and "beach" for beech tree occur, and, in at least one instance, an editor or typesetter betrayed him **5** by changing his correct "bell-wether" to "bell-weather." Nor was his grammar faultless. He often used "beside" when he meant "besides," and he could seldom differentiate between the time and space distinctions implicit in "farther" and "further." But these are trivial errors. Thoreau was a well-educated man, one of the best educated in Concord. And Concord was then noted for its highly cultured people.

When Shanley examined the manuscript he found that a number of the leaves were "light-blue paper . . . of the same size" (7⅞ by 9⅞ inches) and that they "bore the same embossed stationer's mark; a rose on a stem with leaves and a bud." The passages written on this easily identifiable paper "made a complete piece, save where leaves were missing. When their contents are compared with the other material in the manuscript, it is clear that they constitute the first version of *Walden* in the manuscript and, without a doubt, the first version that Thoreau wrote."

Shanley prints this rather short first version in his book. It represents the draft that was probably written in the little house near Walden Pond. This is the heart of *Walden*, and it contains some of the best writing and thinking in the entire book. But the completed work is much longer and even better. Shanley says that "The **6** final text of *Walden* has different proportions and a much larger plan than does the first version. Thoreau greatly enlarged a major aspect of the book's structure—the cycle of the seasons: he added far more material to the last third of the book than to the other parts.

"But while the manuscript reveals how much more polished, more spacious, and better designed the final text is than the first and other earlier versions, it also reveals that the essential spirit of *Walden* did not change from first to last."

A reading of the first draft shows that Thoreau—and posterity—were fortunate that the publisher of *A Week* did not print *Walden* in the condition it was in, in 1849. Good as the early versions are, they lack the stature of the final work.

In addition to isolating the pages of the first version of *Walden*, Shanley was able to determine from differences in paper, ink, handwriting, and stationers' marks that there were "seven large groups of leaves and two

4 *write it vertically*. This was not peculiar to Thoreau; anyone who has studied nineteenth-century letters and manuscripts will recall this paper-saving device which makes both the original horizontal handwriting and the vertical lines superimposed on it almost impossible to read.

5 *an editor or typesetter*. It may seem surprising that Thoreau did not change this back on the page proofs, but there comes a time in an author's life when he is so weary of being badgered by editors and printers that he lets things go which he would otherwise not tolerate.

6 *Shanley says*. The quotation is from a typewritten insert which Shanley placed on page 6 of the copy of *The Making of Walden* in the Huntington Library.

smaller ones." Only the first version was complete in itself, the others were obviously additions, rearrangements, and revisions. They show how the book took form. And then Thoreau wrote an eighth and final version for the printer. This has been lost, but the Huntington Library has the page proofs (HM925) with Thoreau's corrections on them. These give us a good idea of what the manuscript for the printer must have been like. **7 8**

They are proofs of the type locked up in three-page forms for stereotyping. Corrections were made on them by Thoreau in pencil, by the proofreader in ink. Thoreau's pencil marks appear on almost every page, although pages 229 to 246 (parts of "Higher Laws" and "Brute Neighbors") have no penciled corrections on them. His alterations are relatively few and are mostly concerned with correcting typographical errors and improving word usage and punctuation. Evidently he knew that at this advanced stage of a book's production changes are expensive and difficult to make. Toward the end of the first chapter the printer had misread Thoreau's copy "their Heaven" and set it as "these hearers," but this was caught in the page proofs. In several other places the printer wrote "Ms. not legible." **9 10**

A penciled note by Thoreau (on page 64 of the page proofs) indicates that he had given copy to the printer in installments, for he meekly says that he "will try to make the last part of the Ms. more legible."

All manuscripts were handwritten in those days, and printers developed an uncanny skill in interpreting the dreadful scrawls and hen-tracks that passed for symbols of the written word. Thoreau's hand is difficult to read until one gets used to it. Even then some words are impossible to make out. There is no doubt that certain words printed in *Walden* are not what their author intended. The printer set them in type as he thought they were supposed to be. Thoreau—even though he had a good eye for such errors—did not catch them all.

Thoreau had suffered from exceedingly bad typesetting when *A Week on the Concord and Merrimack Rivers* was published in 1849 by James Munroe & Co. And even more disturbing than the poor composition for that book was the fact that three lines of text in page 396 were left out. No one noticed the omission until the sheets were bound. (Copies exist in which Thoreau has written in the missing copy.) When Ticknor and Fields published *Walden*, the typesetting was far better than it had been for *A Week*, but again several lines were left out on page 333. This time, however, Thoreau was able to catch the error on the page proofs and correct it there.

A comparison of the existing manuscript with the page proofs shows that Thoreau's paragraphs were much **11**

A stereotype molding frame of the period

A stereotype foundry. The workman at the right is pounding papier-mâché into the type to get an impression into which hot metal from the furnace can be poured.

7 *how the book took form.* The first half of *Walden* is largely complete in the first version; it is the second half that was written in later years, mostly between 1851 and the early spring of 1854. But Thoreau kept adding material to all parts of the book, sometimes by making inserts, sometimes by rewriting and expanding previously recorded passages.

shorter when he wrote them than they are as they appear in print. It is just possible that he consolidated them on the missing final draft for the printer, but it seems much more likely that some unknown person—probably a Ticknor and Fields editor—ran them together until they became very long. Some go on for pages and make the unbroken text look unnecessarily forbidding.

This brings us to one of the greatest mysteries about *Walden*. Why did Thoreau cancel many thousands of words in the original manuscript? Much of what he eliminated was deleted in the admirable effort to condense the text into the fewest forceful phrases that would express just what he wanted to say, but there still is a large body of material of great interest; in some cases it is of more interest to a modern reader than it was to Thoreau's contemporaries. One instance is his description of cutting ice in the chapter entitled "The Pond in Winter." This begins "In the winter of '46-7 . . ." and then, significantly, the manuscript says: "as you all know." A few pages later the printed text says that the cutters divided the ice "into cakes by methods too well known to require description."

In those days, readers were familiar with ice-cutting methods, so Thoreau could shorten his account. But now that mechanical refrigerators have made the harvesting of ice obsolete, such work is as little known to us as the forging methods used in a medieval armorer's shop. Fortunately, Thoreau's account of the men at work on the ice of Walden Pond still exists in the manuscript. And F. B. Sanborn had the good sense to print it in the Bibliophile Edition of 1909. The full account has been reproduced here.

A careful examination of the manuscript and the portions of it which Sanborn printed shows that a great deal of what Thoreau took out of *Walden* is still of interest. Sometimes the canceled paragraphs seem important for themselves. Did Thoreau eliminate them, as Sanborn suggests, in order to make the text short enough for a compact and inexpensive book? Even those that may be of secondary value cast light on Thoreau's thinking and on his way of working. What the author of *Walden* considered dross may very well be of greater worth than he thought.

Beyond the 12,000 or so words that Sanborn brought to light are still others which he ignored. They are printed here for the first time. Some are of value for their own sake; others show how Thoreau changed his mind, usually but not always for the better. A few are acts of self-censorship.

8 *an eighth and final version.* This, if it were extant, would be regarded as the true manuscript of *Walden.* No one knows how it was lost. It seems unlikely that it was returned to Thoreau; if it had been, it would almost surely have been among his papers, for he seldom threw any of them away.

9 *stereotyping.* Stereotype printing plates are made by taking an impression of the type in some soft substance, usually papier-mâché, hardening it, and then pouring molten metal into the mold. The process began to be replaced in Thoreau's time by copper electrotype plates which require finely powdered graphite to serve as a conductor of electricity when depositing the copper. It was the increasing scarcity of this graphite which induced the Thoreau family to give up making pencils and specialize in supplying graphite in bulk for making electrotypes.

10 *have no penciled corrections.* The reason for this has never been found. Perhaps Thoreau worked on a duplicate set of this section. If so, it has been lost.

11 *Thoreau's paragraphs were much shorter.* The Bibliophile Edition, with its copy taken from the manuscript, preserves much of the shorter paragraphing.

On several occasions he tempers exaggerated state- **12**
ments: "A hundred times as poor" becomes "a dozen
times as poor" (page 200); "all men" is modified to "most
men" (page 222); and a "full-grown tree" is reduced to "a
well-grown" one (page 332). He also tones down his
adjectives: a long-dead woman described as "witch-like"
is merely called "inhumane" (page 382). And he changes
phrases that seem too harsh: we "who live in a climate of
so bleak a country as New England" (page 422) is remade
into "a climate of so great extremes." Sometimes the
search for a milder word goes through several phases:
"The herd of men (page 233) becomes a "mass" and then
"crowds."

The manuscript shows that some of the incidents in
Walden have fictional aspects. In the printed text of the
dialogue between the Poet (Channing) and the Hermit
(Thoreau), the Hermit eats brown bread (page 352); but
in the manuscript he says: "my boiled chestnuts will
soon be out." There are also many changes of place
names; the telegraph from Maine to Texas (page 188)
originally went to Louisiana; Lake Champlain (page 251)
was Ashuelot in the manuscript; and Siberia was Tartary
(page 301).

The heavy hand of an editor or a printer can be seen
in certain alterations of Thoreau's original copy as it was
transferred from the manuscript to the printed page. This
forgotten purist was responsible for putting words that
might be considered slang in quotation marks. Some
examples are "trainers" (page 290), "best" room (page
272), "crack" (page 392), "trotters" (page 398). This
too-zealous corrector also wrote out Thoreau's Arabic
numerals even when they were large, so that the depth
of Walden Pond which is given as 102 feet in the manuscript is stated as one hundred and two feet in the printed
text (page 409). This has been done throughout the book.

He did not, however, correct Thoreau's misuse of
"beside" where "besides" is meant. Nor did he catch some
of the typographic errors that still run through more
than two hundred editions of *Walden*. (See the notes on
pages 161, 267, and 300.)

Who decided what was to be changed or eliminated—
Thoreau, his friends in Concord, some forgotten editor at
Ticknor and Fields, or the compositor who set the type?
Thoreau probably made most of the decisions, for he was
stubborn about permitting changes, as his dealings with
other publishers reveal. But a study of his *Journal* and
correspondence shows that he was continually being advised by Horace Greeley and others to use fewer words
in his work. (Such admonitions will seem all too familiar
to present-day authors.) And Thoreau, who was completely untrammeled when he did most of his writing in

12 *he tempers exaggerated statements.* One of
Thoreau's faults was the tendency to exaggerate—
a tendency that was common in American writing
then. When he revised, he had a chance to tone
down his original statements and often did so.

Setting type by hand

his *Journals*, had to learn to discipline himself when he wrote for publication. He did so—and eventually did so very well. He could reduce pages of anecdote to a few sentences as he did with the famous passage on men who **13** lead lives of quiet desperation.

Since most of the canceled material is reproduced in the margins of the present edition, the reader can see what was eliminated. It will show him how the book was shaped and whittled down to size. Some of these long-unseen passages are very good, some give the background for what was printed in condensed form, others show Thoreau's creative mind at work.

Much of what Thoreau put into *Walden* came from his *Journal*. "The Ponds," for instance, contains a great deal of material taken from it, and some passages in that chapter are reproduced almost unchanged. Perry Miller in his *Consciousness in Concord* (1957, page 20), said that the journals which "Thoreau kept between April 3, 1842, and the spring of 1850 . . . all went into the hopper of his creative operation. They were disemboweled and **14** cannibalized. Odds and ends of work-sheets also remain— enough to show either that he did his revisions on pages of an eviscerated journal or upon pages copied from a journal manuscript. We see that this process went on ferociously, that many portions have been subjected to a dozen recastings."

Since *Walden* has no plot, no obvious structure (except for its cycle of the seasons), and has many digressions, readers have always had trouble in relocating passages that they wanted to see again. In order to overcome this difficulty the present edition has been carefully indexed by the editor, not only for words but for topics, illustrations, and notes.

13 *the famous passage on men who lead. . . .* Shanley (1957, pages 52–54) traces in detail the evolution of this passage from a long story about an organ-grinder from New York being stranded in New Hampshire to the final brief statement that appears in *Walden*.

14 *They were disemboweled and cannibalized.* Thoreau was not the only one who mutilated his manuscripts. When the twenty-volume Manuscript Edition of his works was published in 1906, an original handwritten page was bound in as a frontispiece to each first volume in the set. (Many libraries have removed these to prevent vandalism.)

Composing stick for handset type

A Boston street scene showing Ticknor's bookshop and publishing house

THE PUBLISHING OF
WALDEN

When Thoreau was trying to get a publisher in 1849 for *A Week on the Concord and Merrimack Rivers*, Ticknor and Company of Boston was among the houses that expressed interest. But he gave the book to James Munroe who did badly with it. Since then Ticknor (now Ticknor and Fields) had come up rapidly and were publishing some of the leading authors of the day. **1**

Some time in February or early in March 1854, Thoreau took the final draft of the manuscript of *Walden* to them. The *Journal* shows that he went to Boston on March 13, but this may have been to discuss contract details. The manuscript may even have gone to the printer by this time, for he received the first proofs on March 28.

Ticknor and Fields agreed to print an edition of 2,000 **2** copies and pay a 15 per cent royalty on a list price of $1 a copy. Typesetting went fast, probably because Fields was sailing to England on June 7, and he wanted to take a set of proofs with him. Thoreau had evidently promised not to make many changes, for the book went straight **3** into page proofs.

When Fields started for England he proved to be such a poor sailor that he had to leave the steamer at Halifax and return to Boston. The company wrote to Thoreau on June 10, before they learned that Fields had gotten off the ship, that "in order to secure a Cop't [copyright] in England, the book must be published there as soon as here, and at least 12 copies published and offered for sale. If Mr. F. succeeds in making a sale of the Early sheets, it will doubtless be printed in London so as to cause very little delay here, but if it be necessary to print and send out the Copies it will delay us 3 or 4 weeks. Probably not more than three weeks. You will probably prefer to delay the publication that you may be sure of your Cop't in England."

1 *leading authors.* Hawthorne, Holmes, Longfellow, Lowell, and Whittier among them.

2 *Ticknor and Fields. The Cost Books of Ticknor and Fields,* edited by Warren S. Tryon and William Charvat (1949), describes the technical details of producing *Walden:*

1854. *Walden: or Life in*		2000
the Woods		
By *Henry D. Thoreau*		
1 Vol. 16 [mo.], pp. 358.		
Thurston, Pr.		
Steo'd by Bos. Steo.		
Foundry. Cost. *$311.45*		
6 Boxes		

July 3	23 3/20 Rms. 22x37 48.			
	14	6.72	222.76	
	Engraving Map			
	Walden Pond	8.		
	Printing 2000 Do.	10.	18.	
	Baker Engraving title		10.	
12	60 Tokens	80	48.	
	Binding	10	200.	
	Copt on 1800 c @ 15%		270.	768.76
	Cost 43/ Sells $1.			
	Pub'd August 9, 1854.			
	500 Maps printed Sep.			
	1856.			

"Token" was a unit of presswork from one form.

3 *straight into page proofs.* When a book is set in type, the first proofs are ordinarily made from long galleys and are corrected before being made up into individual pages.

As a result, American publication was delayed. Printed copies were sent by steamer on July 21 and 22, but British publishers were not interested in a practically unknown American writer even though the copyright was offered to them for $100. *Walden* was not issued in Great Britain until 1884, more than 20 years after its author's death.

Thoreau got an advance copy of his book on August 2, and it was published a week later.

In Francis H. Allen's bibliography of Thoreau (1908), *Walden* is described as:

> 16mo, pp. 357. Map of Walden Pond facing p. 307. Collation: 1, title; 2, copyright and imprint (Stereotyped at the Boston Stereotype Foundry); 3, contents; 4, blank; 5–357, text. . . . The book was bound in cloth and lettered on back *Walden/ Life in the Woods/* Thoreau/Ticknor & Co.

Although 2,000 copies of the book were printed, only part of the edition was bound, and, as was customary, the rest were held as sheets. Walter Harding (1954, page x) says of the bound copies: **4**

"The binding of the first impression varies slightly. Most copies are in olive drab cloth, but occasionally some are bound in a somewhat redder brown. But again, since all the sheets were printed at once and then bound individually as they were needed, there is no great significance to the color of the binding. The endpapers of all copies of the first impression that I have seen are lemon yellow.

"The earliest advertisements [about other Ticknor and Fields books] I have discovered are April 1854 (fairly common), and the latest September, 1855. . . .

"Aside from the advertisements, the only other bibliographical point in the first impression is the engraved map of Walden Pond which in some copies faces page 306, in others page 307, and in still others is omitted entirely."

This map, which was engraved from a survey that Thoreau had made in 1846, was not put into every copy. The Ticknor and Fields cost books show that an additional 500 maps had to be printed in September 1856, probably because some of the first lot of 2,000 had been damaged or lost. Books bound up before this second lot of maps came through evidently had the map left out. There is no doubt about the position that Thoreau wanted it to have, for he wrote in the page proofs: "Let the map of the pond face page 307." **5**

Walden did not require another printing until the spring of 1862. Copies of this did not reach the book-

4 *the rest were held as sheets.* This is done to save the cost of binding books that may never be sold. It costs very little to print extra flat sheets, but binding them has always been one of the major expenses in book production.

5 *engraved from a survey.* The original drawing of this survey, now in the Concord Public Library, is quite large, but the drawing of the map from which the engraving for the book was made is small. It is in the Berg Collection of the New York Public Library.

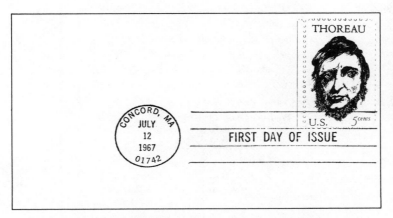

In 1967, the 150th anniversary of Thoreau's birth,
the United States Post Office issued this commem-
orative stamp designed by Leonard Baskin

Entries about *Walden* in Ticknor and Fields's cost books

stores until a short time after Thoreau's death May 6. It was a very small edition of only 280 copies, so the second impression is actually rarer than the first. This does not mean that it fetches a higher price on the rare book market; it does not. It was printed from the stereotypes made for the first impression, and they continued to be used until the 1880's, getting more and more worn and battered as time went on. Only the first impression has lemon-yellow endpapers; later editions printed from the original plates have chocolate-brown ones.

And the subtitle: "or, Life in the Woods," appears on the title page of the first impression; some later and more modern editions still carry it, but many do not.

And even in the first edition, the subtitle evidently underwent a transformation, for Thoreau penciled a note on the page proofs across the bottom of pages 352 to 354 which reads: "I should like to have the corrected title on the 5th page 'Walden, or Life,' etc., instead of 'Walden, A Life.' "

In 1862, when Thoreau requested his publisher to remove the subtitle from the forthcoming second impression, he may have felt that his account of life in the woodland cabin was far less important than the deeper philosophical implications of his book. He also may have become aware of the existence of J. T. Headley's *The* **6** *Adirondacks,* or *Life in the Woods,* which had been published in 1849. And he had certainly seen an essay entitled "Life in the Woods" by Charles Lane, which had appeared in *The Dial,* volume IV, 1844. Lane, inciden- **7** tally, was a British-born Concord man who had also gone to jail on principle rather than pay taxes which he felt were unfair.

When Walden was published in 1854, the United States had a population of 24 million or more people, of whom several million were illiterate slaves or equally illiterate recent immigrants. Yet the relatively small audience of Americans who could read purchased an amazingly large number of books, as was evidenced in 1852 when Harriet Beecher Stowe's *Uncle Tom's Cabin* came out in book form after having been serialized in a newspaper. And in the same year that *Walden* was issued, Maria Cummins' sentimental novel, *The Lamplighter,* also became a tremendous best seller. But *Walden,* which was destined to outlast everything published in America or England that year with the possible exception of Dickens' *Hard Times* or—in poetry—Tennyson's "Charge of the Light Brigade," sold very slowly. The first printing of 2,000 copies lasted until 1859, when it was allowed to go out of print. The three years between 1859 and 1862 are the only time *Walden* has not been in print. Ticknor and **8**

6 *J. T. Headley's.* Joel Tyler Headley (1813–1897), a popular Upstate New York writer and journalist. He went to the Adirondacks to regain his health. *Charles Lane* was one of the founders of the Utopian colony of Fruitlands at Harvard, just west of Concord.

7 The Dial. This short-lived periodical (1840-1844) was the mouthpiece for the Transcendentalists. It was edited by Margaret Fuller and then by Emerson. Thoreau served briefly as an editor of the April 1843 issue while Emerson was away on a lecture tour. *The Dial* was the first periodical to publish Thoreau's work, and many of his articles and poems appeared in it.

8 *Ticknor and Fields' several successors.* The most important of them is Houghton Mifflin who published the collected works, including the *Journals,* in 1906. This house had previously issued the Riverside Edition in 1893, which did not include the *Journals.*

The bookstore of Jewett and Company, publishers of *Uncle Tom's Cabin*

Fields' several successors kept bringing out new editions, and in 1910, when the copyright expired, the book became available to anyone who wanted to print it.

Copies of the first American edition were sent to England, where George Eliot reviewed it favorably in the *Westminister Review* for January 1856. The British edition of 1884 was of imported American sheets. *Walden* was finally printed in England in Walter Scott's Camelot Classics in 1886. A German edition came out in 1897, Dutch in 1902, Russian in 1910, and French in 1922, when a Japanese edition also appeared. Then came Czechoslovakian (1924), Italian (1928), Argentinian—in Spanish —(1945), Swedish (1947), Danish (1949), and finally a flood of others until *Walden* can now be read in Finnish, Greek, Hebrew, Norwegian, Portuguese, Sanskrit, Arabic, and numerous other languages including several Far Eastern, especially those of India where Gandhi did much to make Thoreau popular. It has been printed in Braille type for the blind and also in large type for those whose sight requires big letters.

Although *Walden* has long been considered an outstanding American classic, copies of the first edition did not bring high prices until recent years. In the Stephen

H. Wakeman sale (April 1924), which was particularly rich in Thoreau material, a fine copy with an autographed letter laid in went for $25, while presentation copies sold for only a little more. The one that Thoreau had given to Channing—and with Channing's comments—brought $50; one that Emerson gave to Sanborn, $90; and a copy that Thoreau had presented to H. G. O. Blake of Worcester, $50.

These prices, of course, are fractions of what these association copies would bring today. But manuscripts usually appreciate in value far more than books do. The Wakeman sale also had the manuscript of the "Lost" *Journal* of 1840–1841; it sold at what now seems the incredibly low price of $160. When it was auctioned off again in 1958 it brought $12,700. And if it were to be sold today it would surely bring still more—perhaps several times more. But it went to the Morgan Library to join the other 38 manuscript Thoreau *Journals* there. And it then took its rightful place as volume three in the wooden box which Thoreau had built to house the handwritten books which are the record of his intellectual life. The brief text of the third volume was printed in Perry Miller's *Consciousness in Concord* (1958).

When *Walden* was published on August 9, 1854, reviews began appearing almost at once. Thoreau was fortunate in that, more fortunate than authors are today, for there were more periodicals in the East then, and they gave more space to book reviews than most newspapers and magazines do now.

The first review was printed in the Providence *Journal* two days after publication. It was only a paragraph, but at least it said that the book was "worth reading." Others followed; one, in the Boston *Atlas*, was bad. But *Graham's Magazine*, which was much more important, devoted three pages to the new book and paid tribute to it and its author. Reviews in other leading publications, especially *Putnam's Monthly*, which gave it five pages, were of the kind that would attract attention.

According to Walter Harding, whose *Checklist of the Editions of Walden* (1954a) listed 132 editions that were printed during the century after the book was first published, even more have come out since then. He now estimates that there are an additional 94, making a total of 226.

Some of them are de luxe editions with fine illustrations; others are humble paperbacks selling for low prices. But all are carrying the message of *Walden* to those who want to read it.

Under way is a "new, authoritative, full edition" of Thoreau's works, which is under the sponsorship of the

"The first thing we should insist on is that Thoreau was a writer, not a man who lived in the woods or didn't pay taxes or went to jail. At his best he wrote the only really first-rate prose ever written by an American, with the possible exception of Abraham Lincoln. . . . Thoreau was not only a writer, but a writer in the great stream of the American tradition, the mythic and non-realist writers, Hawthorne and Melville, Mark Twain and Henry James, and, in our own day, as Malcolm Cowley has been most insistent in pointing out, Hemingway and Faulkner."

STANLEY EDGAR HYMAN
"Henry Thoreau in Our Time"
Atlantic Monthly, November 1946

Modern Language Association of America with the Princeton University Press acting as the publisher. *Walden*, edited by James Lyndon Shanley, who did such fine pioneering work on the first version in his book *The Making of Walden*, is to be the initial volume in the series.

THE CABIN AND WALDEN
POND

Since *Walden* has a very complete account of the way Thoreau built his dwelling, there is no point in repeating what he said. In one way or another, he makes nearly a hundred references to the famous little building. Roland Wells Robbins (1947, page 10), who excavated the site in 1945, counted the references and reported that "eighty odd of the number are 'house.' He says 'lodge' three times, 'dwelling' twice, 'apartment' twice, 'homestead' once and on only one occasion does he use the word 'hut.'" But modern biographers and critics of Thoreau seem to favor the word "cabin." **1**

There are many synonyms for such small dwelling places, and their usage is a nice exercise in semantics. "House" is a word that covers any residence, large or small. "Lodge" has upper-class overtones; "dwelling," "apartment," and "homestead" are neutral. "Hut" is a comedown, defined by Webster as "a rude small house, hovel, or cabin, esp. such as those of savage peoples." "Hovel," of course, is *déclassé*, while "cottage," "chalet," and "grange" are much too pretentious for Thoreau's 10- by 15-foot, one-room shelter near Walden Pond.

"Cabin" has become popular for the little building, perhaps because it has emotional associations, such as the log cabin in which Lincoln was born, William Butler Yeats' small cabin at Lake Innisfree, and the log-cabin presidential candidates of the nineteenth century. "Cabin" is a favored word; "hut," "hovel," and "shanty" are not, although it is interesting to note that Thoreau's New Bedford friend, Daniel Ricketson, called his retreat "The Shanty." **2**

Thoreau was not the first or the last creative person of his time to build himself a small woodland shelter where he could escape from the turmoil of the world. He had lived for some weeks with his Harvard classmate, Charles **3**

1 *"on only one occasion does he use the word 'hut.'"* Actually twice. And "cabin" twice also.

2 *Yeats' small cabin at Lake Innisfree.* This, however, was not a log cabin but one "of clay and wattles made." Yeats—in the poem at least—also cultivated beans, but only nine rows of them.

3 *Charles Stearns Wheeler.* This talented young man from nearby Lincoln had gone to Harvard with Thoreau. He went to Leipzig, Germany, for postgraduate work and died there in June 1843 when he was only 26 years old. There is a biography of him by John Olin Eidson (1951).

Stearns Wheeler, on the shores of nearby Sandy Pond; his most intimate companion, William Ellery Channing, [4] had stayed in a cabin in Illinois during the winter of 1839 and 1840; and late in 1869, a young New Yorker named Edmund Stuart Hotham built a small house near [5] the Thoreau site and lived in it for six months. Undoubtedly, there have been other instances in other places, perhaps hundreds of them.

Most of what we know about the Thoreau house comes from its builder, but there are other witnesses too. William Ellery Channing, who had a closer acquaintanceship with the building than anyone except Thoreau, hardly mentions it in his pioneering biography, *Thoreau the Poet-Naturalist* (1873), and then he calls it a shanty. But in his own copy of *Walden* he made several useful references to it; most of what he has to say, however, deals with its gradual disintegration.

Joseph Hosmer, who visited the cabin in September [6] 1845, said of the still-unfinished building: "The sides were not battened, or the walls plastered . . . the entrance to the cellar was thru' a trap door in the center of the room. The king-post was an entire tree, extending from the bottom of the cellar to the ridge-pole." This is the only mention we have of a king post, but Robbins, in his excavations of 1945, noted that "what could have been . . . a foundation [for the post] was located next to the cellar hole, on the ground level and in the very center of the house—a logical place for it to be located. Certainly Hosmer's memory would not have recalled a king-post . . . if it had not existed in some form."

Hosmer's memory, however, was far from infallible. He said that the cabin was "some thirty rods from the lake." Thoreau said "half a dozen." Since a rod is 16½ feet, Thoreau's indicated distance would be 99 feet, Hosmer's, 500. Both were very wrong. Actual measurement by Robbins shows that the cabin site is 204 feet from the shore, give or take a few feet depending on the height of water in the pond.

The nearest approach to Walden by automobile is at the eastern end of the pond where there is a parking place. Then one has to walk for nearly half a mile on the Indian path, now widened and improved, along the northern shore to reach Thoreau's cove. The railroad tracks mentioned in *Walden* are still visible at the western end of the pond. The cove runs north, and the cabin site is north and slightly west of its tip.

Thoreau said "I dug my cellar in the side of a hill." Channing, in October 1863, wrote: "There is nothing like a hill here and never was." The modern visitor will agree with Thoreau when he walks up the slope.

4 *Channing, had stayed in a cabin in Illinois.* He bought 160 acres of land there and lived in a small cabin without a floor. He was no farmer and soon returned to the East.

5 *Edmund Stuart Hotham.* A young theological student from New York who lived at Walden Pond in a cabin that Channing said "was by the pond on the bank, in front of Henry's." He stayed there from November 1869 to May 1870.·

6 *Joseph Hosmer.* He wrote this account for *The Concord Freeman*'s special edition called the "Thoreau Annex," which was published long after the cabin had been destroyed. On the first page is a poorly drawn and inaccurate sketch of what is supposed to be the little house as it looked when it was on its original site.

The stone markers that outline the site of Thoreau's cabin

Two things now mark the site: a cairn of medium-size stones which was begun by Bronson Alcott in June 1867, and beyond this, eight heavy granite posts linked together by chains. These outline the actual bit of ground where the cabin stood and also enclose the foundations of its chimney. A few feet north of this, four smaller posts show where the woodshed stood. These stone posts were put up to mark the exact locations of the cabin and the woodshed as determined by the excavations of 1945. At that time Robbins dug up numerous fragments of brick, many handmade nails, some broken bits of window panes, and a big slab of plaster. He located the cellar, which had not been in the center of the house, but just inside the door. The trap door to the attic was just above the one leading to the cellar.

Shortly after Thoreau left the cabin on September 6, 1847, it was acquired by Emerson's Irish gardener, Hugh **7** Whelan. He moved it to a new site farther away from the pond, where he intended to add a wing measuring 12 by 25 feet in order to make it large enough for his family. But too much liquor spoiled his plans. Whelan **8** abandoned his wife and Concord, and the sad little cabin began to slide down into the cellar hole he had dug for the never-to-be-built addition. Thoreau, writing to Emer-

7 *Hugh Whelan.* Thoreau's letters to Emerson of November 14 and December 15, 1847, give the details.

8 *too much liquor.* Thoreau could not resist making a pun out of Whelan's first name. In his letter to Emerson of November 14 he said: "The Ethiopian cannot change his skin nor the leopard his spots, nor indeed Hugh—his Hugh." The quotation about the Ethiopian is a paraphrase of Jeremiah XIII : 23.

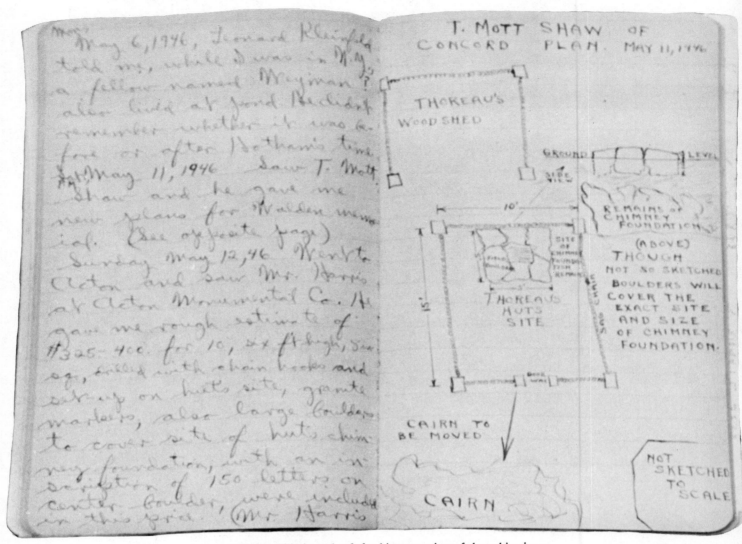

R. W. Robbins' notebook for his excavation of the cabin site

son in England on January 12, 1848, called the building a shanty for the first and only time. He thought that it could still be rented to "an honest and small-familied man, who has no affinity for moisture in him, but who has an affinity for sand."

In the summer of 1849 the cabin, somewhat the worse for neglect, was hauled away by an ox team to the Clark farm, north of the town on the old Carlisle Road, where it was used as a storage place for grain. Channing reports that it had just been pulled down when he saw its dismantled rafters on June 4, 1868, 23 years after it had been built. It would have lasted a century, Channing thought, if it had been given proper care.

The immortal little house is said to have been incorporated into a shed on the side of a barn and then used to patch the barn itself. The original material may still be there, but there is no way to identify the individual pieces. A few bits of the wood, however, were saved and are on exhibit in several places in Concord. *Sic transit. . . .*

Our best idea of what the cabin was like comes from the drawing that Thoreau's sister Sophia made of it for the title page of the first edition of *Walden*. This, however, was in 1854, when the building had long since been taken away from its idyllic site near Walden Pond. But Sophia may have made early sketches of it, and she could have visited the Clark farm where it was presumably more or less intact.

Her title-page drawing certainly portrays the building as Thoreau describes it, even to the woodshed at the rear. But Channing said that it was "a feeble caricature of the true house." Thoreau himself criticized the picture, saying that Sophia's trees were firs, not pines. And she also showed deciduous trees that did not belong in the grove of pines. The wood engraver who made the printing block may have been responsible for the kind of trees shown. We know from other existing drawings and the wood blocks made from them that the engraver often paid little attention to the authenticity of background detail.

In the corrected page proofs of *Walden*, Thoreau said: "I would suggest a little alteration, chiefly in the door, in the wide projection of the roof at the front; and that

9 *what the cabin was like*. Roland Wells Robbins, who excavated the site of the original cabin, built a full-sized replica of it near his home in Lincoln. Another has been constructed in Concord in back of the Thoreau Lyceum.

Robbins' replica of the cabin

the bank more immediately about the house be brought out more distinctly."

Since Thoreau's criticisms of the cabin picture were made on the page proofs where the finished wood engraving appears, it was too late then to make any changes unless a new block was cut. The publisher probably told the author that the picture was only a decoration and therefore did not have to be a literal representation of the actual cabin.

As a result we have no really trustworthy portrayal of what is surely the most famous small house in American literature. And perhaps the publisher was right; it does not really matter. It does not matter because the Walden cabin was not just so much wood, bricks, stone, nails, and plaster. It was a symbol of man's independence, of solitude, of a closeness to nature, of a quiet working place where dreams and ideas can be put down on paper. Thoreau's Walden cabin represents the creator who has to work out his destiny alone—and who may, in doing so, bring into being something that will outlast the most imposing buildings ever erected to celebrate politics, law, religion, and commerce.

Walden Pond, which is central to the book, is likely to **10** be a disappointment, especially when first seen from the eastern end, where there is parking space. A trailer camp is on the other side of the road, and the part of the pond that is visible from there has a beach and a large recreational building. Fortunately, Walden Pond and the acres around it have now become a state park. The often cutdown trees will at last be allowed to grow, and in a few generations should be even bigger than they were in Thoreau's time.

The old Indian path on the northern shore has been widened and buttressed, but it still follows the same course. It runs along a steep bluff and leads to a cove at the western end of the pond. This is Thoreau's Cove, which his cabin faced. Off to one side, between the shore and the house, is the little marsh mentioned in *Walden* (page 246).

The site is now surrounded by woods. Even Thoreau's **11** bean-field is covered by trees. The cove and its curving sandy beach are ordinarily quiet and undisturbed. The visitor who was disappointed when he first saw Walden Pond from the eastern end can take heart here, especially during the week, when the park is less crowded than on week ends and holidays.

Squirrels and chipmunks, descendants of the ones that Thoreau knew, still scamper through the woods. The fish, for which anglers eagerly contend, are newcomers,

The eastern end of Walden Pond

10 *likely to be a disappointment.* The degradation of Walden Pond began soon after Thoreau's death when a railroad stop was established at the western end of the lake. An article entitled "A Visit to Thoreau's Haunts in 1866," which appeared in *The Genius* for January 1880, said that "the nearer end of the lake . . . had been transformed into a picnic ground, and there were the lunch tables, the dancing platforms, the merry-go-rounds, and other abominations with which all nature's sanctuaries near our great cities are fast being polluted."

11 *now surrounded by woods.* The bean-field and the house were in clearings. The *Journal* for April 21, 1859; XII, 152, describes how Thoreau set 400 pine trees for Emerson in the former bean-field. They have all disappeared and have been replaced by later random growths.

SITE OF THOREAU'S HOUSE

From July 4, 1845 until Sept. 6, 1847
HENRY DAVID THOREAU lived here alone
transacting "some private business" in a
house which he built entirely with the
labor of his own hands. His "business" here
included the writing of his first book,
"A WEEK ON THE CONCORD AND MERRIMACK
RIVERS" and the greater part of "WALDEN"
which spread his ideas and fame eventually
throughout the world.

He was born in Concord July 12, 1817
and died there May 6, 1862

The Indian path

for the pond has been restocked. Doubtless some of the frogs carry on the ancient lineage unbroken.

12

The pond itself is unchanged. The survey which Thoreau made of it in 1846 was very accurate, and it still shows the shores and depths as they were and still are. (It should be noted that the bottom rather than the top of the map is the north side of the pond. The compass arrow indicates this, but people tend to overlook it.) The location of the house, in the lower right-hand corner, is clearly marked. (See map on page 408.)

Thoreau studied every aspect of Walden—and in all seasons. He lived on its shores for most of the two years, two months, and two days that he used the little house. But he visited Walden many times before and after this period. Allusions to it in the *Journal* are so numerous that its index does not even try to list them all. Thoreau made Walden the symbolic center of his life as well as the subject of his major book. He gave the word a certain magic which it has not lost—and never will. It means various things to various people, but they all recognize its essential quality. It gives them something which they have in common, an admiration and affection for one of the finest works of art that America has produced. And they all know that *Walden* is a guidebook, not to any place but to a way of living and of seeing truly the world around us. They know, too, that it has inner meanings for those who are responsive to them.

12 *the ancient lineage unbroken.* This should apply also to the ants which Thoreau describes in the chapter entitled "Brute Neighbors."

The cairn marking the site as it is now

A DETAILED CHRONOLOGY
OF THOREAU'S LIFE

The following chronology has been compiled from Thoreau's *Journal* (1906 and 1949), from his *Correspondence* (Harding and Bode, 1958), and from information in Walter Harding's *The Days of Henry Thoreau* (1965). Numerous minor sources were also used.

On December 27, 1855, when Thoreau was 38 years old, he made a record in his *Journal* of the houses he had lived in. The information for the first 20 years of his life is drawn largely from this.

Born, July 12, 1817, in the Minott House on the Virginia Road [Concord], where Father occupied Grandmother's thirds [a widow's share of her husband's estate], carrying on the farm. . . . Lived there about eight months. . . . I was baptized . . . by Dr. Ripley, when I was three months, and did not cry.

The Red House [Concord], where Grandmother lived. We [occupied] the west side till October, 1818. . . . According to day-book, Father hired of Proctor, October 16, 1818, and shop of Spaulding, November 10, 1818 [Chelmsford].

Chelmsford till March [21], 1821. . . . Aunt Sarah taught me to walk there when fourteen months old. Lived next the meeting-house, where they kept the powder in the garret. Father kept a grocery shop and painted signs, etc.

Pope's House, at South End in Boston, five or six(?) months, a ten-footer. Moved from Chelmsford **1** through Concord, and may have tarried in Concord a little while. Day-book says, "Moved to Pinkney Street, Sep 10th, 1821, on Monday."

Witwell's House, 4 Pinckney Street, Boston, to March, 1823 (?)

1 *Chelmsford.* In the *Journal* for January 7, 1856; VIII, 93 f., Thoreau puts down his recollections of these early years:

"They tell how I swung on a gown [?] on the stairway when I was at Chelmsford. The gown [?] gave way; I fell and fainted, and it took two pails of water to bring me to, for I was remarkable for holding my breath in those cases.

"Mother tried to milk the cow which Father took on trial, but she kicked at her and spilt the milk. (They say a dog had bitten her teats.) Proctor laughed at her as a city girl, and then he tried, but the cow kicked him over, and he finished by beating her with his cowhide shoe. . . . The cow came into the entry after pumpkins. I cut my toe, and was knocked over by a hen with chickens, etc., etc.

"Mother tells how, at the brick house, we each had a little garden a few feet square, and I came in one day, having found a potato just sprouted, which by her advice I planted in my garden. Ere long John came in with a potato which he had found and had it planted in his garden,—'Oh, mother, I have found a potato all sprouted. I mean to put it in my garden,' etc. Even Helen is said to have found one. But next I came crying that somebody had got my potato, etc., etc., but it was restored to me as the youngest and original discoverer, if not inventor, of the potato, and it grew in *my* garden, and finally its crop was dug by myself and yielded a dinner for the family.

"I was kicked down by a passing ox. Had a chicken given me by Lidy—Hannah—and peeped through the keyhole at it. Caught an eel with John. Went to bed with new boots on, and after with cap. 'Rasselas' given me, etc., etc. Asked P. Wheeler, 'Who owns all the land?' Asked Mother, having got the medal

The Virginia Road House in which Thoreau was born
(*Courtesy Concord Free Public Library*)

Brick House [Main and Walden streets], Concord, to spring of 1826.

Davis' House (next to S. Hoar's), to May 7th, 1827. **2**

Shattuck House, to spring of 1825.

Hollis Hall, Harvard, Cambridge, [September] 1833. **3**

Aunt's House, to spring of 1837. At Orestes A. Brownson's while teaching in winter of 1835 [-1836]. Went to New York with Father, peddling [pencils] in 1836. **4, 5**

(Direct quotation from the *Journal* of December 27, 1855, ends here.)

In the spring of 1837 the Thoreaus move into the Parkman House. (The Concord Library now occupies the site.) They stay there until 1845.

During the spring of 1837 Thoreau reads Emerson's first book, *Nature*, which had been published the previous year. Emerson had moved to Concord in October 1834 and was to remain there for the rest of his long life. The book had a great effect on young Thoreau. During this year his acquaintance with Emerson ripens into friendship.

for geography, 'Is Boston in Concord?' If I had gone to Miss Wheeler a little longer, should have received the chief prize book, 'Henry Lord Mayor,' etc., etc."

Thoreau's sister Helen was born in 1812, his brother John in 1815, and Sophia in 1819.

2 *(next to S. Hoar's.)* Samuel Hoar was an attorney and one of Concord's leading citizens. The houses were in Concord on Main Street. The Shattuck home was across the way.

3 *Hollis Hall, Harvard.* Room Number 20.

4 *Aunt's House.* Aunt Betsey Thoreau. The building is now the north wing of the Colonial Inn which faces the square.

5 *Orestes A. Brownson's.* Harvard then permitted impecunious students to take time off to earn money. Thoreau went to Canton, Massachusetts, to teach from December 5, 1835, to some time in March 1836. Brownson, his sponsor, was a remarkable learned man who went from one religion to another. He and Thoreau studied German together.

Aunt Betsey's house, now part of the Colonial Inn

The Parkman House. It is the one to the right of the one in front of which the single figure is standing. *(Courtesy Concord Free Public Library)*

1837

JULY 4. At the dedication ceremonies for the monument marking the site of the battle of Concord on April 19, 1775, Thoreau is a member of the choir that sings the "Concord Hymn" which Ralph Waldo Emerson had composed for the occasion.   **6**

AUGUST 30. Thoreau graduates from Harvard. The next **7** day, Emerson makes his celebrated Phi Beta Kappa speech, "The American Scholar," in Harvard Yard. **8** Thoreau begins teaching in Concord's Center School. Resigns after a few days because of disagreement about corporal punishment, which he did not want to inflict. **9**

Changes order of his name from David Henry to Henry David Thoreau.

Works in father's pencil factory where he develops a new and better method of making the graphite writ- **10** ing cores.

At some time during this summer, Thoreau stays for a while in a hut near Flint's Pond with a friend from Harvard, Charles Stearns Wheeler.

OCTOBER 22. Thoreau begins his *Journal* and says: "To be alone I find it necessary to escape the present,—I avoid myself. . . . I seek a garret."

NOVEMBER 12 (*Journal*). "I yet lack discernment to distinguish the whole lesson of to-day; but it is not lost —it will come to me at last. My desire is to know *what* I have lived, that I may know *how* to live henceforth."

DECEMBER 30. To Orestes A. Brownson: "I seek a situation in a small school, or assistant in a large one, or, what is more desirable, as private tutor in a gentleman's family. . . . I would make education a pleasant thing to both the teacher and the scholar. This discipline, which we allow to be the end of life, should not be one thing in the schoolroom, and another in the street. We should seek to be fellows with the pupil, and we should learn of, as well as with him, if we would be most helpful to him."

Financially, the year is a disastrous one for the country, and is remembered by being called "The Panic of 1837." In England, Victoria becomes Queen.

1838

MARCH 5 (*Journal*). "But what does all this scribbling amount to? What is now scribbled in the heat of the moment one can contemplate with somewhat of satisfaction, but alas! to-morrow—aye, to-night—it is stale, flat, and unprofitable,—in fine, is not, only its shell remains. . . ."

The Concord Battle Monument. Despite what the inscription says, it was actually dedicated in 1837.

MARCH 6 (*Journal*). "How can a man sit down and quietly pare his nails, while the earth goes gyrating ahead amid such a din of sphere music. . . ."

MARCH 14. Writes notes for a lecture on "Society" to be given before the Concord Lyceum on April 11. This is his first lecture. Some of the notes are: "The mass never comes up to the standard of its best member, but on the contrary degrades itself to a level with the lowest. . . . It is a levelling down, not up."

"Conversation is only a refuge from the encounter of men."

MARCH 17. Writes to his brother John, proposing that they go to the West by canalboat.

APRIL 8. Writes long poem on "Friendship."

APRIL 11. First lecture. See March 14.

APRIL 13. Hears of teaching job in Alexandria, Virginia, applies for it, but does not get it. Meanwhile, his **11** brother John is employed as a teacher in Taunton and then in Roxbury.

APRIL 26. Writes poem "The Bluebirds."

MAY 2–17. Goes to Maine, his first long trip. Visits his **12** cousins in Bangor and makes friends with an elderly Indian.

JUNE 3. Writes poem about Walden Pond.

JUNE. Thoreau opens a private school in his family's home, the Parkman House.

AUGUST 27 (*Journal**). "I have swallowed an indispensible tooth, and so am no whole man, but a lame and halting piece of manhood. . . . I have felt cheap and hardly dared hold up my head among men ever since this accident happened."

SEPTEMBER 15. He advertises for pupils in the Concord Academy, which he was able to take over, although at first it does not do well.

OCTOBER 18. Elected secretary of the Concord Lyceum; **13** then curator.

DECEMBER. Writes sections of an essay to be entitled "Sound and Silence," but it was never published. Scraps appear in the *Journal*.

1839

FEBRUARY 9. The school improves so much that John Thoreau joins his brother as a teacher in it.

* Unless otherwise noted, all quotations from now on are from Thoreau's *Journals*.

6 *the "Concord Hymn."* This was sung to the tune of "Old Hundred," and printed copies of it were distributed to the crowd so all could join in.

7 *Thoreau graduates from Harvard.* A popular myth is that Thoreau refused to accept a diploma. He got one, and it is still in existence. Harvard offered to give a master of arts degree three years after graduation for a fee of $5. It was this that he refused.

8 *"The American Scholar."* It was in this speech that Emerson advised writers to use American themes and break away from their dependence upon European culture.

9 *corporal punishment.* Channing (1873, page 24) says of this: "A knowing dean, one of the school committee, walked in and told Mr. Thoreau that he must flog and use the ferule, or the school would spoil. So he did, feruling six of his pupils after school, one of whom was the maid-servant in his own house." That evening Thoreau resigned.

10 *a new and better method.* This was already in use in Germany where fine clay was mixed with the graphite. Thoreau also designed a new graphite grinding-mill.

11 *his brother John.* John was always more fortunate in finding teaching positions than Henry was.

12 *Goes to Maine.* The trip was undertaken in order to seek work as a teacher but was unsuccessful.

13 *the Concord Lyceum.* The lyceum movement, an early effort to spread culture in America, was started by Josiah Holbrook of Derby, Connecticut, in 1826; a national group, the American Lyceum, began in 1831. It was very successful in the days before the Civil War. Noted speakers, not only American, but British, appeared on its platforms.

JUNE 17. Thoreau meets 11-year-old Edmund Sewall of Scituate, Massachusetts, and is so attracted to him that he writes in his *Journal* on

JUNE 22. "I have . . . come into contact with a pure, uncompromising spirit . . . such it is impossible not to love."

JUNE 24. He also writes a long poem entitled "Sympathy" which is addressed to "the gentle boy." **14**

JULY 20. Edmund's sister, 17-year-old Ellen, comes to Concord, where Henry and John apparently both fall in love with her.

JULY 25. On this day Thoreau writes in his *Journal* the single line: "There is no remedy for love except to love more."

AUGUST 31. The two brothers start out in a boat they had **15** built themselves on the journey that was the basis for Henry's first book, *A Week on the Concord and Merrimack Rivers*. They got to Hooksett, New Hampshire, where they leave their boat and proceed north on foot and by stagecoach to Mount Washington, which they climb. Then they return to their boat and go downstream to Concord, which they reach on September 13. They had spent a week on the rivers and a week on land. John promptly goes to Scituate to see Ellen. Henry, perhaps unhappy because of his brother's progress, writes about bravery, friendship, and love in his *Journal*.

14 *"the gentle boy."* The poem appears in the *Journal* for June 24, 1839; I, 80 ff. It is printed on page 23.

15 *a boat they had built.* At the beginning of the Saturday chapter in *A Week*, Thoreau said of it: "Our boat, which had cost us a week's labor in the spring, was in form like a fisherman's dory, fifteen feet long by three and a half in breadth at the widest part, painted green below, with a border of blue, with reference to the two elements in which it was to spend its existence. It was provided with wheels in order to be rolled around falls, as well as with two sets of oars, and several slender poles for shoving in shallow places, and also two masts, one of which served for a tent pole at night; for a buffalo skin was to be our bed, and a tent of cotton cloth our roof. It was strongly built, but heavy, and hardly of better model than usual."

Lowell, Massachusetts, where the Concord River joins the Merrimack

DECEMBER 25. Christmas. Both John and Henry visit Ellen in Scituate. Later, Henry sends her poems.

1840

MARCH. Edmund Sewall becomes a pupil at the Thoreau school and boards with the family.

JUNE. Ellen Sewall visits Concord again. The *Journal* for June 19 says: "The other day I rowed in my boat a free, even lovely young lady, and, as I plied the oars, she sat in the stern, and there was nothing but she between me and the sky." He used this passage, with some slight revision, in *A Week*. John again goes to Scituate to see Ellen, and Henry writes in his *Journal* on

JUNE 29. "Of all phenomena, my own race are the most mysterious and undiscoverable. For how many years have I striven to meet one, even on common manly ground, and have not succeeded!"

JULY. John visits Ellen, proposes to her, and is accepted. Her mother demands that she break off the engagement because the Thoreau family's well-known liberal religious views would offend her father. She does so.

JULY 1. The first issue of *The Dial* is published; Thoreau has a poem and an essay in it. In July he writes "The **16** Service," but it is rejected in December and was not published until 1902. **17**

JULY 22. "I think this the vilest world I have ever been in." (Houghton Library MS)

NOVEMBER. He writes to Ellen to propose, but her father forbids the wedding. On November 9, she writes to Henry to say that she cannot marry him. In 1844, she is married to the Reverend Joseph Osgood of Cohasset.

DECEMBER. Thoreau first meets William Ellery Channing, **18** who is to become his closest friend. The 1840 census shows a United States population of 14,189,705 whites, 2,487,355 slaves, and 386,293 free Negroes.

1841

JANUARY 4. Thoreau pays attention to an older woman, Emerson's sister-in-law, Mrs. Lucy Jackson Brown, who is staying in Concord. "I know a woman who is as true to me and as incessant with her mild rebuke as the blue sky." He writes several letters to her throughout the year. In one of them (September 8) he tells her that he has composed 300 verses. In another (July 21) he says that he grows "savager and savager every day, as if fed on raw meat." Mrs. Brown lived in Plymouth and eventually returned there.

16 *a poem and an essay.* The "gentle boy" poem first appeared in print here and then in *A Week* in 1849. The essay was on the Roman poet, Aulus Persius Flaccus.

17 *until 1902.* In a limited deluxe edition edited by F. B. Sanborn.

18 *William Ellery Channing* (1817–1901). Was named after his great-grandfather. His well-known uncle, a Unitarian minister, also had the same name.

Ellery Channing, photographed late in life
(*Courtesy Concord Public Library*)

JANUARY 26. "I had a dream last night which had reference to an act in my life in which I had been most disinterested and true to my highest instinct but completely failed in realizing my hopes; and now, after so many months, in the stillness of sleep, complete justice was rendered me. It was a divine remuneration. In my waking hours I could not have conceived of such retribution; the presumption of desert would have damned the whole. But now I was permitted to be not so much a subject as a partner to that retribution. It was the award of divine justice, which will at length be and is even now accomplished."

JANUARY 27. At the Concord Lyceum, John and Henry Thoreau debate with Bronson Alcott on the subject "Is it ever proper to offer forcible resistance?"   **19**

FEBRUARY 7. "Without great coat or drawers I have advanced thus far into the snow banks of winter, without thought and with impunity."

FEBRUARY 10 and 13. *Journal* entries indicate that Thoreau is thinking of renting or buying land and perhaps was exploring the countryside for it.   **20**

FEBRUARY 14. "Confined to the house by bronchitis."

FEBRUARY 23. "The care of the body is the highest exercise of prudence. If I have brought this weakness on my lungs I will consider calmly and disinterestedly how the thing came about, that I may find out the truth and render justice."

MARCH 27. "I must not lose any of my freedom by being a farmer and landowner. Most who enter on any profession are doomed men."

APRIL 1. Because of John Thoreau's poor health, the school, which was prospering, had to close. And on this day, on 200 acres in nearby West Roxbury, the famous Brook Farm community began its short-lived career. Although invited, neither Thoreau nor Emerson wanted any part of it.   **21**

APRIL 5. "I will build my lodge on the southern slope of some hill and take there the life the gods send me."

APRIL 7. "This staying to buy me a farm is as if the Mississippi should stop to chaffer with a clamshell. What have I to do with plows? I cut another furrow than you see."

APRIL 11. "A greater baldness my life seeks, as the crest of some bare hill, which towns and cities do not afford. I want a directer relation with the sun."

APRIL 20. "Great thoughts hallow any labor. To-day I earned seventy-five cents for heaving manure out of a pen, and made a good bargain of it."

APRIL 26. "At R.W.E.'s"—and that is the only entry in the *Journal* which records Thoreau's moving into the Emersons' home to stay for more than a year. He was to work a few hours every day on the house or garden in order to pay for his board and lodging.

MAY 30. Emerson, in writing to his friend, Thomas Carlyle, says: "One reader and friend of yours dwells now in my house—and, as I hope, for a twelve-month to come,—Henry Thoreau,—a poet whom you may one day be proud of—a noble manly youth full of melodies

19 *Bronson Alcott* (1799–1888). Teacher, writer, Transcendentalist, father of Louisa May Alcott of *Little Women* fame.

20 *thinking of renting or buying land.* This idea keeps recurring until Thoreau finally went to Walden Pond in 1845.

21 *Brook Farm.* This was one of the many American Utopian communities that were popular at this time. It lasted until 1846. Hawthorne was among the many noted people who went there. He used some of his experiences in his novel *The Blithedale Romance* (1852).

and inventions. We work together day by day in my garden, and I grow well and strong."

JUNE 26. "The best poetry has never been written, for when it might have been, the poet forgot it, and when it was too late remembered it; or when it might have been, the poet remembered it, and when it was too late forgot it."

JULY. Thoreau's poem "Sic Vita" is published in *The Dial*.

AUGUST 28. "My life hath been the poem I would have writ, but I could not both live and live to utter it."

SEPTEMBER 4. The origin of the idea for *Walden* may be in the brief *Journal* entry for this day: "I think I could write a poem to be called 'Concord.' For argument I should have the River, the Woods, the Ponds, the Hills, the Fields, the Swamps and Meadows, the Streets and Buildings, and the Villagers. Then Morning, Noon, and Evening, Spring, Summer, Autumn, and Winter, Night, Indian Summer, and the Mountains in the Horizon." **22**

SEPTEMBER 24. Isaiah T. Williams, a young law student who had lived in Concord, had moved to Buffalo. He writes the first of several letters to Thoreau and may be considered his first disciple. In his reply on September 28, Thoreau says: "I am living with Mr. Emerson in very dangerous prosperity." **23**

During the summer, a young girl, Mary Russell of Plymouth, had also been staying with the Emersons to serve as tutor to their son Waldo. Thoreau evidently had paid some brief attention to her, as is evidenced in the *Journal* entry for:

DECEMBER 12 (I, 292). "Now that lately I have heard of some traits in the character of a fair and earnest maiden whom I had known only superficially, but who has gone hence to make herself more known by distance, they sound like the strains of a wild harp music. . . . Every maiden conceals a fairer flower and more luscious fruit than any calyx in the field, and if she goes with averted face, confiding in her own purity and high resolves, she will make the heavens retrospective, and all nature will humbly confess its queen."

DECEMBER 15. "I seem to see somewhat more of my own kith and kin in the lichens on the rocks than in any books. It does seem as if mine were a peculiarly wild nature, which so yearns toward all wildness. I know of no redeeming qualities in me but a sincere love for some things, and when I am reproved I have to fall

22 *The origin of the idea for* Walden. *Walden,* however, had many sources, some of them deep in Thoreau's subconscious mind.

23 *Isaiah T. Williams.* When Williams persisted in his study of law, which Thoreau despised, he was dropped from the list of correspondents.

back on to this ground. This is my argument in reserve for all cases. My love is invulnerable. Meet me on that ground, and you will find me strong. When I am condemned, and condemn myself utterly, I think straightway, 'But I rely on my love for some things.' Therein I am whole and entire. Therein I am God-propped."

DECEMBER 24. So far Thoreau had been thinking in terms of retreating to a farm, a bare hill, or a southern slope; now his idea becomes more definite. The *Journal* entry for this day is: "I want to go soon and live away by the pond, where I shall hear only the wind whispering among the reeds. It will be success if I shall have left myself behind. But my friends ask what I will do when I get there. Will it not be employment enough to watch the progress of the seasons?"

1842

JANUARY 11. John Thoreau, while stropping his razor, cuts the tip of the ring finger of his left hand. It be-

John Thoreau, Jr., as portrayed by his sister Sophia.
From a painting owned by the Concord Antiquarian Society.
(*Courtesy Concord Free Public Library*)

comes infected and is given medical attention. But in those days germs were as yet unheard of; lockjaw develops and soon leads to death. Henry becomes terribly morose, and by January 22 displays all the symptoms of lockjaw, yet he had not cut or broken the skin. By January 24 he is on his way to recovery from the psychosomatic attack, although he had to remain in his bedroom for a month. Then, on January 27, Emerson's young son, Waldo, dies of scarlet fever. Thoreau makes no entries in his *Journal* for six weeks. On February 21, he writes: "I feel as if years had been crowded into the last month." Some time after this he leaves his father's house, where he had gone to take care of John, and rejoins the Emersons.

MARCH 14. "It is not easy to find one brave enough to play the game of love quite alone with you, but they must get some third person, or world, to countenance them. They thrust others between. Love is so delicate and fastidious that I see not how [it] can ever begin. Do you expect me to love with you, unless you make my love secondary to nothing else? Your words come tainted, if the thought of the world darted between thee and the thought of me. You are not venturous enough for love. It goes alone unscared through wildernesses.

"As soon as I see people loving what they see merely, and not their own high hopes that they form of others, I pity, and do not want their love. Such love delays me. Did I ask thee to love me who hate myself? No! Love that I love, and I will love thee that lovest it."

MARCH 20. "My friend is cold and reserved because his love for me is waxing and not waning. These are the early processes; the particles are just beginning to shoot in crystals. If the mountains came to me, I should no longer go to the mountains. So soon as that consummation takes place which I wish, it will be past. Shall I not have a friend in reserve? Heaven is to come. I hope this is not it. . . .

"Friends are those twain who feel their interests to be one. Each knows that the other might as well have said what he said. All beauty, all music, all delight springs from apparent dualism but real unity. My friend is my real brother. I see his nature groping yonder like my own. Does there go one whom I know? then I go there. . . .

"As the Indian thinks he receives into himself the courage and strength of his conquered enemy, so we add to ourselves all the character and heart of our friends. He is my creation. I can do what I will with him. There is no possibility of being thwarted; the

"There is no better prose in American literature than the clear, sinewy, fragrant writing in Walden *which discusses the homely details of house-building and kitchen economy and rejoices in the romantic loveliness of sounds at night and bird notes by day and speculates on the beauties of good living—all in plain images and simple phrases that do not change pace with the change of subject. Although his writing looks easy, only a man of keen mind and remarkable skill could have made a sentence carry so much baggage and have given living form to impulses of the imagination."*
BROOKS ATKINSON
Introduction to the Modern
Library edition of WALDEN, 1937

friend is like wax in the rays that fall from our own hearts.

"The friend does not take my word for anything, but he takes me. He trusts me as I trust myself. We only need be as true to others as we are to ourselves, that there may be ground enough for friendship. In the beginnings of friendship,—for it does not grow,—we realize such love and justice as are attributed to God."

Journal missing from April 3, 1842 to July 5, 1845.

SUMMER. The Concord Athenaeum is founded to further interest in books. It has a reading room in the First Parish Church.

JULY 8. Nathaniel Hawthorne and his wife move to Concord.

AUGUST 31. They invite Thoreau to dinner, and Hawthorne records his early impressions of him.

SEPTEMBER 1. Thoreau sells his boat to Hawthorne.

OCTOBER. *The Dial* prints eight of Thoreau's poems.

NOVEMBER 18. He is elected curator of the Concord Lyceum.

DECEMBER 21. Wendell Phillips, the noted Boston Abolitionist, speaks at the Concord Lyceum at Thoreau's invitation.

Wendell Phillips

1843

JANUARY 24. Letter to Emerson (in part):

"At the end of this strange letter I will not write—what alone I had to say—to thank you and Mrs. Emerson for your long kindness to me. It would be more ungrateful than my constant thought. I have been your pensioner for nearly two years, and still left free as under the sky. It has been as free a gift as the sun or the summer, though I have sometimes molested you with my mean acceptance of it,—I who have failed to render even those slight services of the *hand* which would have been for a sign, at least; and, by the fault of my nature, have failed of many better and higher services. But I will not trouble you with this, but for once thank you as well as Heaven.

Your friend,
H. D. T."

FEBRUARY 8. Thoreau lectures at the Lyceum on Sir **24** Walter Raleigh.

MARCH 1. He writes to Emerson in New York to help him find some kind of employment, and is engaged by

24 *Sir Walter Raleigh.* This essay was published in 1905 in a deluxe limited edition edited by F. B. Sanborn. It is not included in the collected works of 1906.

William Emerson, Ralph Waldo's brother, as a tutor **25** for his three young sons. He is to be paid $100 a year and given board and lodging in the family's Staten Island house.

MAY 6. He leaves for Staten Island. Once there, he explores the then rural island during his free time. He also visits New York but does not like the city. Yet he meets Henry James, Sr., Horace Greeley, Albert Brisbane, and several Transcendentalist writers. He also **26** visits bookstores and calls on Harper's, but that successful publishing house is not interested in young and unproved authors. During much of this time Thoreau is not well, and he is often homesick for his beloved Concord. He writes several affectionate letters to Emerson's wife, Lidian. But he is not happy with the William Emersons.

MAY. William Ellery Channing, soon to become Thoreau's best friend, moves to the Red Lodge near Emerson's house.

SUMMER. The railroad from Boston to Fitchburg, which passes Walden Pond, is being built.

JUNE 13. Charles Stearns Wheeler, Thoreau's friend and classmate at Harvard, dies in Leipzig, Germany.

AUGUST. Thoreau complains of being constantly sleepy **27** for most of this month.

25 *William Emerson.* He was a judge of the county court and a rather formal person. His oldest child was only seven.

26 *Albert Brisbane* (1809–1890). Social reformer and Fourierist, father of the journalist Arthur Brisbane.

27 *constantly sleepy.* Thoreau had been ill during the winter. This was probably an early manifestation of tuberculosis.

Staten Island with the Narrows in the distance

SEPTEMBER. In order to earn some money in his spare time, he attempts to sell subscriptions to the *American Agriculturist* in New York. He finds it difficult to place his writings with any magazines.

OCTOBER. But *The Dial* prints "A Winter Walk," and the *Democratic Review,* "The Landlord."

NOVEMBER. His review of J. A. Etzler's *The Paradise within the Reach of All* appears in the *Democratic Review.* Sometime during this month he returns to Concord and lectures there (November 29) on "The Ancient Poets."   **28**

DECEMBER 3. He goes to Staten Island to wind up his affairs so he can live in Concord permanently.

1844

JANUARY. *The Dial* publishes Thoreau's translations from Pindar. Meanwhile, he had been working in his father's pencil factory where he improved the methods for making pencils and thus produced a superior product.

APRIL 30. He goes on a boating expedition with young Edward Hoar, during which they cook some fish for lunch and accidentally set fire to the dry grass. The flames spread to the woods and burn more than 300 acres. This unfortunate episode, which was strongly criticized by the townspeople, evidently disturbed Thoreau more than he would openly admit, for he wrote about it in detail in his *Journal* some six years later (June 4, 1850; II, 21 ff.). There he told how he had not felt guilty at the time and had gone to Fair Haven Cliff to watch the fire. "It was a glorious spectacle, and I was the only one there to enjoy it." In this same *Journal* entry he also tells how to build outdoor fires safely and fight the flames if they spread.

APRIL. Young Isaac Thomas Hecker comes to Concord to study Greek and Latin. He boards with the Thoreau family and becomes acquainted with Henry. Later Hecker is converted to Catholicism and invites Thoreau to go on a pilgrimage to Rome, but Thoreau declines. Hecker eventually founds the Paulist Fathers and becomes a leading figure in the Church.   **29**

APRIL. The Channings move to a house on Lexington Road. Then, during the summer, Thoreau and Channing go for a walking trip to Mount Greylock in northern Massachusetts. From there, they go west to the Hudson and return by steamboat to New York. They arrive in Concord on August 1. They had often met, but this is the first occasion on which they spend any time together. *The Dial* ceases publication.

28 *J. A. Etzler's.* Etzler believed that man could make an earthly paradise if he would utilize all the sources of energy and employ mass-production methods. In his review Thoreau said: "The chief fault of this book is that it aims to secure the greatest degree of gross comfort and pleasure merely." We, who have accomplished what Etzler recommended, can see that his proposed solution for mankind's troubles was no solution at all.

29 *Isaac Thomas Hecker.* In later years Hecker turned against Thoreau and Trancendentalism and all that they stood for. He called Thoreau a "consecrated crank."

AUGUST 1. On this day, antislavery women are holding a fair in Concord at which Emerson was to speak. When the sexton of the First Parish Church and the town selectmen refuse to ring the bell there, Thoreau sounds the bell in the courthouse in order to attract a crowd to listen to the speech.

SEPTEMBER 10. Thoreau's father buys a lot on Texas Street where he and his son build the Texas House for the family.   **30**

30 *the Texas House.* This Thoreau-built house stood until the 1930's when it was destroyed by fire and a hurricane. The site and its stone foundations are still there. The stones were put in place by Thoreau.

31 *Ellery Channing.* Channing's advice, coming when it did, may have caused Thoreau to take action about building a woodland hut. Another precipitating factor was Emerson's recent acquisition of the pondside land which Thoreau could use free of charge.

During this year Morse's new magnetic telegraph carries word of James Polk's nomination as President. Polk is elected in November. The railroad and the telegraph, which were to change America, were both coming in at this time.

1845

During this year the Thoreau family moves into the Texas House.

MARCH 1. The annexation of Texas.

MARCH 5. Ellery Channing writes to Thoreau: "I see nothing for you . . . but that field which I once christened 'Briars'; go . . . build yourself a hut, and there begin   **31**

Site of the Texas House. The foundation stones were put into position by Thoreau.

the grand process of devouring yourself alive. I see no alternative, no other hope for you. Eat yourself up. . . ."

MARCH 12. He writes a long letter to William Lloyd Garrison, editor of the Abolitionist newspaper, *The Liberator*, which prints it on March 28. In this letter, Thoreau strikes out against the conservative people of Concord who had not wanted to allow Wendell Phillips to speak there. He praises Phillips for condemning slavery and the annexation of Texas. **32**

MARCH 25. He lectures in Concord on "Concord River."

MARCH (late). Thoreau had been thinking for years about moving to a woodlands retreat. His family's boarding-house, with its ever-present guests, did not give him the quiet he needed for writing—and he was now about to begin a full-time career as a writer. Channing's letter of March 5 may very well have induced him to make the move. And the coming of spring would add to his restlessness.

After getting permission from Emerson to use his pondside land, Thoreau borrows an axe and begins to cut down some pine trees. The beginning of the cabin is described in detail in *Walden* on page 177. In the spring he plants 2½ acres with vegetables, mostly beans.

32 *William Lloyd Garrison.* This forceful and uncompromising editor was the leader of the more radical Abolitionists.

JULY 4. He moves his few articles of furniture to the still unfinished cabin and begins to live there. During the autumn he builds a fireplace and chimney. From November 12 to December 6 he plasters the interior walls. The first writing he does in his new home is an essay on Thomas Carlyle. He also writes *A Week on the Concord and Merrimack Rivers* there and begins work on the first draft of *Walden*.

JULY 7. "I am glad to remember tonight, as I sit by my door, that I too am at least a remote descendant of that heroic race of men of whom there is tradition. I too sit here on the shore of my Ithaca, a fellow-wanderer and survivor of Ulysses. How symbolical, significant of I know not what, the pitch pine stands here before my door! Unlike any glyph I have seen sculptured or painted yet, one of Nature's later designs, yet perfect as her Grecian art. There it is, a done tree. Who can mend it? And now where is the generation of heroes whose lives are to pass amid these our northern pines, whose exploits shall appear to posterity pictured amid these strong and shaggy forms? Shall there be only arrows and bows to go with these pines on some pipestone quarry at length? There is something more respectable than railroads in these simple relics of the Indian race. What hieroglyphs shall we add to the pipestone quarry?"

SEPTEMBER (early). Channing moves into a house he has built on Punkawtasset Hill, more than a mile north of Concord.

AUTUMN. *Journal*, I, 395–396:

"The mythologies, those vestiges of ancient poems, the world's inheritance, still reflecting some of their original hues, like the fragments of clouds tinted by the departed sun, the wreck of poems, a retrospect as [of] the loftiest fames—what survives of oldest fame—some fragment will still float into the latest summer day and ally this hour to the morning of creation. These are the materials and hints for a history of the rise and progress of the race. How from the condition of ants it arrived at the condition of men, how arts were invented gradually—let a thousand surmises shed some light on this story, We will not be confined by historical, even geological, periods, which would allow us to doubt of a progress in human events. If we rise above this wisdom for the day, we shall expect that this morning of the race, in which they have been supplied with the simplest necessaries—with corn and wine and honey and oil and fire and articulate speech and agricultural and other arts—reared up by degrees from the condition of ants to men, will be succeeded by a day of

"It is the attempt to mark this sensation of maximum contact that he tried to get into his prose—'wildness,' the taste of a muskrat eaten raw, walking blind through dark woods at night, a swim in the infinite silence of Walden Pond. Fundamentally, Thoreau's best writing is an attempt to get up to the point where he can reduce human experience to communion with nature and this communion to images of total physical ecstasy. . . .

"Thoreau is a true mystic: for him there is always a lost Eden, a divine background in nature. To this he can relate what he picks up on his walks, but of this he has lost something incommunicable, 'a hound, a bay horse, and a turtle-dove.' His description of the simplest objects in nature can be unbearably moving: one feels so keenly his own trembling at the veil that keeps the world from us. Who, after all, can possess the world, can put all nature into our hands? Thoreau's imagery has all the characteristically painful longing, the Schmerz, of the romantic mystic."

ALFRED KAZIN
CONTEMPORARIES, 1962

equally progressive splendor; that, in the lapse of the divine periods, other divine agents and godlike men will assist to elevate the race as much above its present condition."

1846

FEBRUARY 4. Thoreau lectures at the Concord Lyceum on Thomas Carlyle.

MARCH 13. From here to early 1850, the *Journal* is fragmentary or missing. The manuscript of the part covering this year's trip to Maine is in the Berg Collection, New York Public Library.

MAY 8. The War with Mexico begins with a United States victory at Palo Alto. The war goes on until the autumn of 1847.

JULY 23 (or 24). Thoreau is arrested and imprisoned overnight for not having paid his poll tax. He would not support a government that was fighting the Mexican War to extend slavery. From this experience came the celebrated article on "Civil Disobedience." **33**

AUGUST 31. Thoreau sets out for Bangor and his first trip through the Maine woods with his cousin, George Thatcher. With guides, they make their way across the wilderness to Mount Katahdin, which they climb. Only Thoreau goes on to the cloud-capped summit. **34**

33 *Thoreau is arrested*. For details see the Introduction to "Civil Disobedience" and the essay itself.

34 *the Maine woods*. This was the second time that Thoreau visited Maine. That state, which then had vast areas of unsettled forests, appealed to the ever-present "wildness" in his character.

Lumbering operations in Maine

There, he sees Nature in a new and frightening way.

In his book, *The Maine Woods*, he describes what he saw: "It was, in fact, a cloud factory,—these were the cloud-works, and the wind turned them off done from the cool, bare rocks. Occasionally, when the windy columns broke in to me, I caught sight of a dark, damp crag to the right or left, the mist driving ceaselessly between it and me. . . . It was vast, Titanic, and such as man never inhabits. Some part of the beholder, even some vital part, seems to escape through the loose grating of his ribs as he ascends. . . .

"Vast, Titanic, inhuman Nature has got him at disadvantage, caught him alone, and pilfers him of some of his divine faculty. She does not smile on him as in the plains. She seems to say sternly, Why came ye here before your time. This ground is not prepared for you. Is it not enough that I smile in the valleys? I have never made this soil for thy feet, this air for thy breathing, these rocks for thy neighbors. I cannot pity nor fondle thee here, but forever relentlessly drive thee hence to where I *am* kind. Why seek me where I have not called thee, and then complain because you find me but a stepmother? Shouldst thou freeze or starve, or shudder thy life away, here is no shrine, nor altar, nor any access to my ear."

During the year 1846 Horace Greeley tries to interest magazines in publishing some of Thoreau's work. *Graham's Magazine* finally agrees to print the essay on Carlyle. On October 26, Greeley writes to Thoreau to say that the article "is in type and will be paid for liberally."

Meanwhile, Thoreau is attempting to get *A Week on the Concord and Merrimack Rivers* published as a book.

1847

FEBRUARY 10. He gives the first of the Walden lectures at the Concord Lyceum.

FEBRUARY 24. The second Walden lecture. The favorable reaction to these encourages him to continue with the book.

MARCH and APRIL. *Graham's Magazine* publishes his article on Carlyle.

MAY. Emerson writes to his brother-in-law, suggesting that Thoreau go as his assistant on a government expedition to Michigan. Thoreau wanted the job but did not get it.

MAY 28. In a letter to Wiley & Putnam about publishing **35** *A Week*, Thoreau says that he is going on a long jour-

35 *Wiley & Putnam*. Hawthorne recommended Thoreau to this house but said that "he is the most unmalleable fellow alive—the most tedious, tiresome, and intolerable—the narrowest and most notional—and yet, true as all this is, he has great qualities of intellect and character." Hawthorne also thought that there was only "one chance in a thousand" that Thoreau could write a good book.

ney (perhaps to Michigan). But this was just a hope.

SPRING and SUMMER. Thoreau supplies specimens (mostly of fish and turtles) to the Swiss naturalist, Louis Agassiz, who is in Boston at this time.   **36**

JULY 15. Emerson commissions impractical Bronson Alcott to design and build a summer house. Thoreau does most of the work.

SEPTEMBER 6. He leaves Walden, saying, "I left the woods for as good a reason as I had gone there." Actually, Emerson was going to Europe for an extended stay and wanted Thoreau to take care of his household during his absence.

SEPTEMBER 14. General Winfield Scott captures Mexico City, and the War with Mexico is virtually over.

SEPTEMBER 30. In reply to an inquiry from his class secretary at Harvard asking for personal data for the tenth anniversary of his graduation, Thoreau gives this revealing reply:

"I confess that I have very little class spirit, and have almost forgotten that I ever spent four years at Cambridge. That must have been in a former state of existence. . . . However, I will undertake at last to answer your questions as well as I can in spite of a poor memory and a defect of information. . . .

"I am not married.

"I don't know whether mine is a profession, or a trade, or what not. It is not yet learned, and in every instance has been practised before being studied. . . .

"—It is not one but legion, I will give you some of the monster's heads. I am a Schoolmaster—a private Tutor, a Surveyor—a Gardener, a Farmer—a Painter, I mean a House Painter, a Carpenter, a Mason, a Day-Laborer, a Pencil-Maker, a Glass-paper Maker, a Writer, and sometimes a Poetaster. If you will act the   **37** part of Iolas, and apply a hot iron to any of these heads, I shall be greatly obliged to you.

"My present employment is to answer such orders as may be expected from so general an advertisement as the above—that is, if I see fit, which is not always the case, for I have found out a way to live without what is commonly called employment or industry attractive or otherwise. Indeed my steadiest employment, if such it can be called, is to keep myself at the top of my condition, and ready for whatever may turn up in heaven or on earth. For the last two or three years I have lived in Concord woods alone, something more than a mile from any neighbor, in a house built entirely by myself. . . .

"P.S. I beg that the Class will not consider me an

36 *Louis Agassiz* (1807–1873). He was lecturing at Harvard at this time and was collecting specimens of American flora and fauna.

37 *the part of Iolas.* Iolas—or Iolaus—helped Hercules kill the many-headed hydra. Thoreau is complaining here of the difficulties of having too many aptitudes.

General Winfield Scott

object of charity, and if any of them are in want of pecuniary assistance, and will make known their case to me, I will engage to give them some advice of more worth than money."

OCTOBER 5. He goes to Boston to see Emerson sail to **38** Europe.

NOVEMBER 14. In a long letter to Emerson in England, Thoreau says: "Lidian [Mrs. Emerson] and I make very good housekeepers. She is a very good sister to me." He reports that Emerson's three-year-old son Eddy had said: "Mr. Thoreau, will you be my father?" He also tells Emerson that a Miss Sophia Ford, a former teacher who was 15 years older than Thoreau, had proposed to him. "I really had anticipated no such foe as this in my career." Four publishers have refused to do *A Week*. And Emerson's Irish gardener, Hugh Whelan, who had purchased the Walden cabin, is having trouble with it. (See the chapter entitled "The Cabin and Walden Pond.")

1848

JANUARY. Early this month Thoreau lectures at the Lyceum about his trip to the Maine woods. He also writes an essay on "Friendship."

JANUARY 24. John Sutter discovers gold in California, and the gold rush begins.

JANUARY 26. At the Concord Lyceum Thoreau lectures about his night in jail and the relationship of the individual to the state. Origin of "Civil Disobedience" (see May 14, 1849).

38 *to see Emerson sail to Europe.* Lidian Emerson and the Alcotts were also at the dock to wave farewell to the sailing ship *Washington Irving*.

Sutter's mill where gold was first discovered in California

FEBRUARY 2. The war with Mexico is terminated by the Treaty of Guadalupe Hidalgo.

FEBRUARY 23. Lidian Emerson is ill with jaundice—"as yellow as saffron" Thoreau writes to her husband in England. Nevertheless Emerson does not return home until late July.

MARCH 8. Thoreau says that he is revising *A Week* and that no publisher, fortunately, had taken it as it was. He has been writing lectures meanwhile and remarks that "Time and Co. are . . . the only quite honest and trustworthy publishers that we know [letter to James **39** Elliot Cabot]."

MID-MARCH. The important correspondence between Thoreau and Harrison Gray Otis Blake of Worcester, **40** Massachusetts, begins with a letter from Blake. In it he says: "When I was last in Concord, you spoke of retiring farther from our civilization. I asked you if you would feel no longings for the society of your

39 *James Elliot Cabot.* He was a naturalist who was working with Agassiz at this time.

40 *Harrison Gray Otis Blake.* He had been at Harvard with Thoreau. He then went on to the Harvard Divinity School but lost interest in theology and became a teacher. Thoreau wrote about 50 letters to him.

Harrison G. O. Blake
(*Courtesy Concord Free Public Library*)

friends. Your reply was in substance, 'No, I am nothing.' That reply was memorable to me. It indicated a depth of resources, a completeness of renunciation, a poise and repose in the universe, which to me is almost inconceivable; which in you seemed domesticated, and to which I look up with veneration. I would know of that soul which can say 'I am nothing.' "

MARCH 27. In his reply, Thoreau says:

"I have sworn no oath. I have no designs on society —or nature—or God. I am simply what I am, or I begin to be that. I *live* in the *present*. I only remember the past—and anticipate the future. I love to live, I love reform better than its modes. There is no history of how bad became better. I believe something, and there is nothing else but that. I know that I am—I know that [ano]ther is who knows more than I who takes interest in me, whose creature and yet [whose] kindred, in one sense, am I. I know that the enterprise is worthy—I know that things work well. I have heard no bad news. . . .

"Pursue, keep up with, circle round and round your life as a dog does his master's chaise. Do what you love. Know your own bone; gnaw at it, bury it, unearth it, and gnaw it [still. Do not be too] moral. You may cheat yourself out of much life so. Aim above morality. Be not *simply* good—be good for something."

MARCH 31. Thoreau writes to Greeley to say that—after a year—*Graham's Magazine* has not paid for his article on Carlyle.

APRIL 3. Greeley replies and says he will see to it that Graham's pays. He offers to take "Katahdin and the Maine Woods" and pay for it if he cannot dispose of it elsewhere more to Thoreau's advantage. He sells it as a five-part serial to Sartain's *Union Magazine*.

MAY 2. Thoreau to Blake: "I am contented with a slight and almost animal happiness. My happiness is a good deal like that of the woodchucks."

MAY 17 (?). Greeley writes to say that he has induced *Graham's* to pay for the Carlyle article. He will try to **41** sell other articles and urges Thoreau to write shorter ones.

MAY 19. When Thoreau replies he says: "For more than two years past I have lived alone in the woods, in a good plastered and shingled house entirely of my own building, earning only what I wanted, and sticking to my proper work. The fact is man need not live by the sweat of his brow—unless he sweats easier than I do— he needs so little. For two years and two months all my expenses have amounted to but 27 cents a week, and

41 *He will try to sell other articles.* Greeley was not paid for trying to get Thoreau's work published.

I have fared gloriously in all respects. If a man must have money, and he needs but the smallest amount, the true and independent way to earn it is by day-labor with his hands at a dollar a day.—I have tried many ways and can speak from experience.—Scholars are apt to think themselves privileged to complain as if their lot was a peculiarly hard one. How much have we heard about the attainment of knowledge under difficulties of poets starving in garrets—depending on the patronage of the wealthy—and finally dying mad. It is time that men sang another song. There is no reason why the scholar who professes to be a little wiser than the mass of men, should not do his work in the ditch occasionally, and by means of his superior wisdom make much less suffice for him."

(Greeley printed most of this letter in the New York *Tribune*. It was the first notice to the world of what *Walden* was about.)

Thoreau closes his letter with "Trusting that my good genius will continue to protect me on this accession of wealth. . . ." The "wealth" amounted to $75 or $100.

MAY 21. Writing to Emerson in England, Thoreau comments on a proposed new journal: "I cannot . . . join the *journalists* any more than the Fourierites—for I cannot adopt their principles—one reason is because I do not know what they are. Men talk as if you couldn't get things printed, but I *think* as if you couldn't get them written. That at least is the whole difficulty with me. I am more interested in the private journal than **42** the public one."

SUMMER. Thoreau and Ellery Channing go for a four-day trip on foot through New Hampshire. On their way they are scolded by a minister for breaking the Sabbath.

JULY. Emerson returns from Europe, and Thoreau goes to live in his father's Texas House. He obtains survey- **43** ing instruments and has a handbill printed to advertise his services.

OCTOBER 21. Hawthorne writes to offer $20 for a lecture at the Salem Lyceum.

OCTOBER 31. James Russell Lowell's *A Fable for Critics* is **44** published. The authors criticized were not identified, but readers believed that Thoreau and Ellery Channing were meant in these verses:

> There comes———, for instance; to see him's
> rare sport,
> Tread in Emerson's tracks with legs painfully short;
> How he jumps, how he strains, and gets red in the
> face,

42 *the private journal.* His own *Journal,* which continued to be the repository for his ideas and writings.

43 *He obtains surveying instruments.* His big brass sighting compass is in the Concord Public Library.

44 *James Russell Lowell's.* Thoreau distrusted Lowell after this incident. See June 22, 1858.

Salem, Massachusetts

To keep step with the mystagogue's natural pace!
He follows as close as a stick to a rocket,
His fingers exploring the prophet's each pocket.
Fie, for shame, brother bard; with good fruit of
                     your own,
Can't you let Neighbor Emerson's orchards alone?
Besides, 't is no use, you'll not find e'en a core,—
————————has picked up all the windfalls before.

Walter Harding (1965, page 299) thinks that this poem helped to bring about the break between Thoreau and Emerson.

NOVEMBER 22. Thoreau speaks in Salem on "Student Life in New England, Its Economy." Part of this lecture was used in the first chapter of *Walden.*

NOVEMBER 23. He dines at the Craigie House in Cambridge with Longfellow, Hawthorne, and Ellery Channing.

NOVEMBER. Bronson Alcott moves his family from Concord to Boston.

DECEMBER 20. Thoreau repeats his Salem lecture of October 21 at Gloucester.

1849

The California gold rush is now at its height.

JANUARY 3. Thoreau again draws on *Walden* for a lecture at the Concord Lyceum entitled "White Beans and Walden Pond."

45 *The California gold rush.* There are many references to this in Thoreau's writing, and they are always unfavorable.

45

Henry Wadsworth Longfellow
as a young man

The Craigie House

FEBRUARY 28. He lectures again at Salem.

FEBRUARY. He arranges with James Munroe and Co. to publish *A Week on the Concord and Merrimack Rivers*, but on very bad terms. **46**

MARCH 21. Thoreau lectures at Portland, Maine.

MARCH 16–APRIL 30. He is busy reading and correcting many printer's errors in the galleys for *A Week*.

MARCH 22. To George Thatcher: "I shall advertise . . . **47** 'Walden, or Life in the Woods,' in the first [book]

46 *on very bad terms*. They were to print the book while Thoreau was to let them deduct the costs from sales and guarantee that the publisher would be paid in full. It was a disastrous arrangement. See November 28, 1853.

47 *To George Thatcher*. He was Thoreau's cousin in Bangor, Maine.

Portland, Maine

which by the way I call 'A Week on the Concord and Merrimack Rivers.' "

APRIL 2. Greeley publicizes Thoreau's lectures in the New York *Tribune*.

APRIL 20. Thoreau lectures in Worcester, Massachusetts, and then gives two more lectures there a few days later.

MAY 14. Elizabeth Peabody publishes "Resistance to Civil Liberty" in the one and only issue of *Aesthetic Papers*. This now-famous piece was not called "Civil Disobedience" until 1866, when it was included in the papers in Thoreau's posthumous book, *A Yankee in Canada*.

MAY 26. Thoreau receives the first copy of his first book, *A Week on the Concord and Merrimack Rivers*.

MAY 30. It is published in an edition of 1,000 copies, fewer than half of which were bound up.

JUNE 12. Greeley's *Tribune* gives the book a long but not very favorable review. It gets a fair number of notices during the next few months, but the sales are negligible. The publisher refuses to issue *Walden* even though he had advertised it in *A Week*.

JUNE 14. Helen Thoreau, Henry's older sister, who has **48** been ill with the final stages of tuberculosis, now dies.

SUMMER. Thoreau busies himself making pencils and—probably—revising *Walden*.

SEPTEMBER 17. He persuades the president of Harvard to **49** let him borrow books from the library. "I . . . regard myself as one whom especially the library was created to serve."

SEPTEMBER 29. Thoreau's father buys the "Yellow House," **50** 73 Main Street, for his family. Nearly a year was spent on making elaborate renovations. Electrotyping, which requires large quantities of graphite for making printing plates, had come in, and the Thoreaus' business, with its special knowledge of grinding this mineral, was prospering. It may be that Henry's already delicate lungs were further affected by the ultra-fine black powder. The Yellow House was his last home.

OCTOBER 7. Edgar Allan Poe dies. **51**

OCTOBER 9. Thoreau, accompanied by Ellery Channing, goes to Cape Cod. On the way, he stops off at Cohasset **52** to see his former sweetheart, Ellen Sewall, now Mrs. Osgood. The *St. John*, a sailing ship bringing immigrants from Ireland, has been wrecked on the beach there with the loss of 145 lives. Many of the bodies lie on the rocks and sand.

48 *Helen Thoreau*. At her home funeral Thoreau played a music box while everyone sat still and listened to a melody that was "like no earthly tune."

49 *to let him borrow books*. Thoreau had had trouble about this in 1841; now, when he wanted books on Oriental literature, he wrote to President Jared Sparks and then called on him on November 9. Although the letter of permission he obtained was limited to one year, Thoreau used it for the rest of his life.

50 *the "Yellow House."* This attractive-looking and fairly large building is still standing and is now a private residence.

51 *Edgar Allan Poe dies*. Although Poe (1809–1849) and Thoreau (1817–1862) were contemporaries, they seem to have paid no attention to each other's work. The one thing they had in common was that they both were badly compensated for their writings and complained of it bitterly. Thoreau, however, must have known that Poe had violently attacked his friend Channing's book of poems in *Graham's Magazine* in August 1843.

52 *goes to Cape Cod*. Thoreau's notes on his four trips to Cape Cod resulted in the posthumous book (1865) by that title. It was edited by his sister Sophia and Ellery Channing. The first trip is the basis of the book; excerpts from the second and the third are used to fill in, and material on the fourth trip is in the *Journal* for June 12–27, 1857.

Helen Thoreau
*(Courtesy Concord
Free Public Library)*

They travel in the rain by stagecoach to Orleans and then go on foot to Truro and Provincetown where they take the steamer to Boston and the train to Concord, where Thoreau starts to read books about Cape Cod and prepare several lectures on it.

Books published in 1849: Dickens, *David Copperfield;* Macaulay, *History of England;* Melville, *Mardi,* also *Redburn.*

1850

Throughout this year Thoreau is actively busy as a land surveyor.

JANUARY 23 and 30. He lectures (in Concord) on Cape Cod.

Provincetown

FEBRUARY 18. And repeats the lecture in Danvers, Massachusetts.

MARCH 7. Compromise of 1850.   **53**

APRIL 3. To Blake: "I shall be sorry to remember that I was there but noticed nothing remarkable,—not so   **54**
much as a prince in disguise; lived in the golden age a hired man; visited Olympus even, but fell asleep after dinner, and did not hear the conversation. . . . I lived in Judea eighteen hundred years ago, but I never knew that there was such a one as Christ among my contemporaries!"

MAY. In Haverhill, Massachusetts, doing surveying work.

JUNE 25. Goes alone from Boston to Provincetown by steamer, visits only the eastern end of Cape Cod, and then returns by ship to Boston.

JULY 19. The ship carrying Margaret Fuller and her husband, Count Ossoli, and their son is wrecked on Fire   **55**
Island near New York. Emerson asks Thoreau to go there and see what can be found.

JULY 24. Thoreau leaves Concord for Fire Island. Practically nothing can be recovered by this time, but he obtains Ossoli's coat and takes a button from it.

SEPTEMBER 18. The Fugitive Slave Act becomes law.

SEPTEMBER 25. Thoreau and Ellery Channing go on a seven-dollar, ten-day excursion trip to Montreal and Quebec. From this came the posthumous book, *A Yankee in Canada*, in 1866. But the trip itself was such a disappointment that Thoreau began his text by saying: "What I got by going to Canada was a cold."

DECEMBER 6. Lectures in Newburyport, Massachusetts, and visits Thomas Wentworth Higginson.   **56**

53 *Compromise of 1850.* The bill moved slowly through Congress until September when it was adopted. Its few favorable measures—California to be admitted as a free state and the abolition of slavery in the District of Columbia—were outweighed by the Fugitive Slave Law, which outraged Northern sentiment. It permitted slave hunters to enter free states and seize and return runaway slaves. Daniel Webster's speech of March 7, in favor of the Compromise, alienated antislavery men. Whittier wrote his poem "Ichabod" about what he considered Webster's betrayal:

> ". . . from those great eyes
> The soul has fled.
> When faith is lost, when honor dies,
> The man is dead!"

54 *I was there.* The word "there" may seem puzzling, for it has no antecedent, but it is explained in what follows.

55 *Count Ossoli.* Margaret Fuller had married Giovanni Angelo, Marquis of Ossoli, who was ten years younger. They had a young son and were on their way to seek an American publisher for her manuscript on Giuseppe Mazzini, the Italian republican. It, too, was lost in the wreck.

56 *Thomas Wentworth Higginson* (1823–1911). Minister, army officer, author, and speaker, best remembered for *A Black Regiment in the Civil War*. He also wrote a number of biographies and reminiscences.

Quebec

DECEMBER 27. Elected a corresponding member of the Boston Society of Natural History, probably because he had presented a rare goshawk to it. This gave him the use of the Society's library.

United States 1850 Census: 23,911,876.

Books published in 1850; Emerson, *Representative Men;* Hawthorne, *The Scarlet Letter;* Melville, *White Jacket.*

1851

Thoreau does a great deal of surveying this year. And much lecturing too.

JANUARY 1. He lectures on Cape Cod at Clinton, Massachusetts, and visits cloth mills there.

JANUARY 22. Lectures on Walden at Medford, Massachusetts, and visits the Alcotts in Boston.

JANUARY 27. John James Audubon, the ornithologist, dies in New York.

FEBRUARY 15. "Fatal is the discovery that our friend is fallible, that he has prejudices. He is, then, only prejudiced in our favor. What is the value of his esteem who does not justly esteem another?

"Alas! Alas! when my friend begins to deal in confessions, breaks silence, makes a theme of friendship (which then is always something past), and descends to merely human relations! As long as there is a spark of love remaining, cherish that alone. Only *that* can be kindled into a flame. I thought that friendship, that love was still possible between [us]. I thought that we had not withdrawn very far asunder. But now that my

57 *visits cloth mills.* Thoreau wrote a three-page description of the Clinton mills in his *Journal* for January 2, 1851; II, 134–136. He was particularly impressed by the elaborate machinery and the operators who "succeeded only by patience, perseverance, and fidelity."

John James Audubon

friend rashly, thoughtlessly, profanely speaks, *recognizing* the distance between us, that distance seems infinitely increased.

"Of our friends we do not incline to speak, to complain, to others; we would not disturb the foundations of confidence that may still be."

APRIL 3. When Thomas Sims, a fugitive slave, is arrested in Boston, the Abolitionists try to free him but are turned back by troops.

APRIL 12. Sims, surrounded by federal marshals and militia, is taken to a ship and sent back to slavery in Georgia. Thoreau's *Journal* is filled with passages on the injustice of this.

APRIL 23. He lectures on "The Wild" in Concord and apologizes for not denouncing the Fugitive Slave Act instead.

MAY. Although he is not yet 34 years old, Thoreau has

Thomas Sims

to have all his teeth removed and replaced by dentures. The ether he was given made a great impression on him. "You exist in your roots like a tree in the winter. If you have an inclination to travel, take the ether; you go beyond the furthest star."

MAY 31. He lectures on "The Wild" in Worcester.

JUNE. Begins his night walks. One is described in detail **58** in the *Journal* for June 11. Meanwhile, he is reading Darwin's *A Naturalist's Voyage Round the World*.

JUNE 5. Harriet Beecher Stowe's *Uncle Tom's Cabin* begins as a serial in *The National Era*.

JULY 6. "There is some advantage in being the humblest, cheapest, least dignified man in the village, so that the very stable boys shall damn you. Methinks I enjoy that advantage to an unusual extent. There is many a coarsely well-meaning fellow, who knows only the skin of me, who addresses me familiarly by my Christian name. I get the whole good of him and lose nothing myself. There is 'Sam,' the jailer,—whom I never call Sam, however,—who exclaimed last evening: 'Thoreau, are you going up the street pretty soon? Well, just take a couple of these handbills along and drop one in at Hoar's piazza and one at Holbrook's, and I'll do as much for you another time.' I am not above being used, aye abused, sometimes."

JULY 9. Thoreau goes to Cambridge to see the new telescope there.

JULY 19. "Here I am thirty-four years old [on July 12], and yet my life is almost wholly unexpanded. . . . There is such an interval between my ideal and the actual in many instances that I may say I am unborn. There is the instinct for society, but no society. Life is not long enough for one success. Within another thirty-four years that miracle can hardly take place. Methinks my seasons revolve more slowly than those of nature; I am differently timed. I am contented. This rapid revolution of nature, even of nature in me, why should it hurry me? Let a man step to the music which he hears, however measured. Is it important that I should mature as soon as an apple tree? aye, as soon as an oak? May not my life in nature, in proportion as it is supernatural, be only the spring and infantile portion of my spirit's life? Shall I turn my spring to summer? May I not sacrifice a hasty and petty completeness here to entireness there? If my curve is large, why bend it to a smaller circle? My spirit's unfolding observes not the pace of nature. The society which I was made for is not here. Shall I, then, substitute for the anticipation of that this poor reality? I would

58 *night walks.* At first Thoreau was afraid that the June twilight would last too long, but once he got away from town and "deeper into the night, it was better." *Journal* for June 11, 1851; II, 234. He describes the sound made by horses and wheeled vehicles crossing wooden bridges, as well as the calls of whippoorwills and nighthawks. The moon was full on June 13, so he had the advantage of its light on these mid-month walks.

The telescope in Harvard's observatory in Cambridge, Massachusetts

[rather] have the unmixed expectation of that than this reality. If life is a waiting, so be it. I will not be shipwrecked on a vain reality. What were any reality which I can substitute? Shall I with pains erect a heaven of blue glass over myself, though when it is done I shall be sure to gaze still on the true ethereal heaven far above, as if the former were not—that still distant sky o'erarching that blue expressive eye of heaen? I am enamored of the blue-eyed arch of heaven."

JULY 21. "Men are very generally spoiled by being so civil and well-disposed. You can have no profitable conversation with them, they are so conciliatory, determined to agree with you. They exhibit such long-suffering and kindness in a short interview. I would meet with some provoking strangeness, so that we may be guest and host and refresh one another. It is possible for a man wholly to disappear and be merged in his manners."

JULY 25. He goes to Plymouth; visits Ellen Sewall Osgood on the way; then travels along the shore.

AUGUST 6. "Ah, yes, even here in Concord horizon Apollo is at work for King Admetus! Who is King Admetus? It is Business, with his four prime ministers Trade and Commerce and Manufactures and Agriculture."

AUGUST 19. "I fear that the character of my knowledge is from year to year becoming more distinct and scientific; that in exchange for views as wide as heaven's cope, I am being narrowed down to the field of the microscope. I see details, not wholes. . . ."

AUGUST 28. Thoreau watches the telegraph line from Boston to Burlington being strung through Concord.

SEPTEMBER 3. "As I went under the new telegraph-wire I heard it vibrating like a harp high overhead." But **59** there is still no telegraph office in Concord.

SEPTEMBER 14. James Fenimore Cooper dies.

SEPTEMBER 21. "Here was the cider-mill, and there the orchard, and there the hog-pasture; and so men lived, and ate, and drank, and passed away,—like vermin. Their long life was mere duration. As respectable is the life of the woodchucks, which perpetuate their race in the orchard still. That is the life of these *selectmen* (!) spun out. They will be forgotten in a few years, even by such as themselves, like vermin. . . . What, then, would redeem such a life? We only know that they ate, and drank, and built barns, and died and were buried, and still, perchance, their tombstones cumber the ground. But if I could know that there was ever entertained over their cellar-hole some divine thought, which came as a messenger of the gods, that

59 *vibrating like a harp.* This is the first of many times that Thoreau was impressed by the wind-music of the telegraph wires. On September 24, 1851; III, 13, he says, "It is as if you entered some world-famous cathedral, resounding to some vast organ. . . . I feel the very ground tremble under my feet as I stand near the post."

he who resided here acted once in his life from a noble impulse, rising superior to his grovelling and penurious life, if only a single verse of poetry or of poetic prose had ever been written or spoken or conceived here beyond a doubt, I should not think it in vain that man had lived here."

SEPTEMBER 26. "Since I perambulated the bounds of the town, I find that I have in some degree confined myself,—my vision and my walks. On whatever side I look off I am reminded of the mean and narrow-minded men whom I have lately met there. What can be uglier than a country occupied by grovelling, coarse, and low-lived men? No scenery will redeem it. What can be more beautiful than any scenery inhabited by heroes? Any landscape would be glorious to me, if I were assured that its sky was arched over a single hero. Hornets, hyenas, and baboons are not so great a curse to a country as men of a similar character. It is a charmed circle which I have drawn around my abode, having walked not with God but with the devil. I am too well aware when I have crossed this line."

SEPTEMBER 30. Henry Williams, a fugitive slave from **60** Virginia, is sheltered by the Thoreaus.

SEPTEMBER. Thoreau is accompanied by the selectmen of nearby towns while he, as a surveyor, establishes the boundaries. "Though I have been associating with the selectmen . . . I feel . . . begrimed."

The friendship between Thoreau and Emerson has been cooling for several years. Most of the entries in the *Journal* since 1849 that deal with disappointing friends probably concern Emerson even when he is not mentioned by name.

OCTOBER 10. "Ah, I yearn toward thee, my friend, but I have not confidence in thee. We do not believe in the same God. I am not thou; thou art not I. We trust each other to-day, but we distrust to-morrow. Even when I meet thee unexpectedly, I part from thee with disappointment. Though I enjoy thee more than other men, yet I am more disappointed with thee than with others. I know a noble man; what is it hinders me from knowing him better? I know not how it is that our distrust, our hate, is stronger than our love. Here I have been on what the world would call friendly terms with one fourteen years, have pleased my imagination sometimes with loving him; and yet our hate is stronger than our love. Why are we related, yet thus unsatisfactorily? We almost are a sore to one another. Ah, I am afraid because thy relations are not my relations. Because I have experienced that in some respects we are strange

60 *Henry Williams, a fugitive slave.* Thoreau went to buy a ticket for him at the Concord railroad station but saw a man there "who looked and behaved so much like a Boston policeman" that he waited until another time to put Williams on a train to Burlington, Vermont, from where he could go on to Canada and freedom.

to one another, strange as some wild creature. Ever and anon there will come the consciousness to mar our love that, change the theme but a hair's breadth, and we are tragically strange to one another. We do not know what hinders us from coming together. But when I consider what my friend's relations and acquaintances are, what his tastes and habits, then the difference between us gets named. I see that all these friends and acquaintances and tastes and habits are indeed my friend's self. In the first place, my friend is prouder than I am,—and I am very proud, perchance."

Books published in 1851: Hawthorne, *House of the Seven Gables*; Melville, *Moby-Dick*; Ruskin, *Stones of Venice*.

1852

In January, February, and March, *Putnam's Magazine* publishes an incomplete version of *A Yankee in Canada*. At this time Thoreau is subscribing to Greeley's *Weekly Tribune* (*Journal*, January 20; III, 208).

JANUARY 6. Thoreau walks through the snow to lecture at Lincoln, Massachusetts.

JANUARY 7. And then lectures in Concord.

JANUARY 21. He hears Thomas Wentworth Higginson lecture in Concord but does not like his platform manner. "He reminded me of Emerson, and I could not afford to be reminded of Christ himself."

JANUARY 22 (*Journal*; III, 314 and 316). "But why I changed? Why I left the woods? I do not think that I can tell. I have often wished myself back. I do not know any better how I ever came to go there. Perhaps it is none of my business, even if it is yours. Perhaps I wanted a change. There was a little stagnation, it may be. About 2 o'clock in the afternoon the world's axle creaked as if it needed greasing. . . . Perhaps if I lived there much longer, I might live there forever. One would think twice before he accepted Heaven on such terms. A ticket to Heaven must include tickets to Limbo, Purgatory, and Hell. . . . I must say that I do not know what made me leave the pond. I left it as unaccountably as I went to it. To speak sincerely, I went there because I had got ready to go; I left it for the same reason. . . .

"My friend invites me to read my papers to him. Gladly would I read, if he would hear. He must not hear coarsely but finely, suffering not the *least* to pass through the sieve of hearing. To associate with one for years with joy who never met you thought with thought! An overflowing sympathy while yet there is

"The single business of Henry Thoreau, during forty-odd years of eager activity, was to discover an economy calculated to provide a satisfying life. His one concern, that gave to his ramblings in Concord fields a value as of high adventure, was to explore the true meaning of wealth. . . . Walden is the handbook of an economy that endeavors to refute Adam Smith and transform the round of daily life into something nobler than a mean gospel of plus and minus. . . . Thoreau's chief business would seem to have been with life itself, and how it might best be lived by Henry Thoreau . . . so that when he came to die he might honestly say, 'I have lived.'" VERNON L. PARRINGTON
MAIN CURRENTS IN AMERICAN THOUGHT, 1927–1930

no intellectual communion. Could we not meet on higher ground with the same heartiness? It is dull work reading to one who does not apprehend you. How can it go on? I will still abide by the truth in my converse and intercourse with my friends, whether I am so brought nearer to or removed further from them. I shall not be the less your friend for answering you truly though coldly. Even the estrangement of friends is a fact to be serenely contemplated, as in the course of nature. It is of no use to lie either by word or action. Is not the everlasting truth agreeable to you?"

61 *Johnny Riordan.* The *Journal* for January 28, 1852; III, 242 f., gives more background for this.

JANUARY 28. "They showed me Johnny Riordan to-day, **61** with one thickness of ragged cloth over his little shirt for all this cold weather, with shoes with large holes in the toes, into which the snow got, as he said, without an outer garment, to walk a mile to school every day over the bleakest of causeways,—the clothes with countless patches, which hailed from, claimed descent from, were originally identical with, pantaloons of mine, which set as if his mother had fitted them to a tea-kettle first. This little mass of humanity, this tender gobbet for the fates, cast into a cold world with a torn lichen leaf wrapped about him,—Oh, I should rather hear that America's first-born were all slain than that his little fingers and toes should feel cold while I am warm. Is man so cheap that he cannot be clothed but with a mat, a rag, that we should bestow on him our *cold* victuals? Are there any fellow-creatures to whom we abandon our rags, to whom we give our old clothes and shoes when they will not fend the weather from ourselves? Let the mature rich wear the rags and insufficient clothing; let the infant poor wear the purple and fine linen. I shudder when I think of the fate of innocency. Our charitable institutions are an insult to humanity. A charity which dispenses the crumbs that fall from its overloaded tables, which are left after its feasts!"

On some loose sheets of the *Journal* is this poem, which also appears in the *Journal* for November 28, 1850.

> I am the little Irish boy
>   That lives in the shanty
> I am four years old today
>   And shall soon be one and twenty
>   I shall grow up
>   And be a great man
>   And shovel all day
>   As hard as I can.
>
> Down in the deep cut

Where the men lived
Who made the Railroad.

for supper
I have some potato
And sometimes some bread
And then if it's cold
I go right to bed.

I lie on some straw
Under my fathers coat.

My mother does not cry
And my father does not scold,
For I am a little Irish Boy
And I'm four years old.

Every day I go to school
Along the Railroad
It was so cold it made me cry
The day that it snowed.

And if my feet ache
I do not mind the cold,
For I am a little Irish boy
& I'm four years old.

JANUARY 29. "Heard C. [Channing] lecture to-night. . . . It was all genius, no talent."

JANUARY. During this month the woods at Walden were being cut. And the *Journal* entries about Emerson grow more bitter.

FEBRUARY 8. "Carried a new cloak to Johnny Riordan. . . . These Irish are not succeeding so ill after all. The little boy goes to the primary school and proves a forward boy there."

FEBRUARY 22. Goes to Plymouth to lecture.

MARCH 10. Hawthorne buys Alcott's "Hillside" house in Concord and renames it "Wayside."   **62**

MARCH 17. Thoreau lectures on Canada at the Concord Lyceum.

MARCH 20. When *Uncle Tom's Cabin* is published in Boston as a book it immediately becomes enormously successful.

MARCH 22. Thoreau lectures in Boston.

APRIL 3. Greeley wants Thoreau to write a long and important article on Emerson, but he refuses.

APRIL 6. He lectures in Boston at the Cochituate Hall in a snowstorm.   **63**

62 *"Wayside."* The house is still standing and may be visited.

63 *in a snowstorm.* As a result of the heavy snow hardly a dozen people showed up. Alcott moved the audience to the nearby mechanic's reading room, but only a few of the workmen were interested in hearing the lecture.

UNCLE TOM'S CABIN;

OR

LIFE AMONG THE LOWLY.

BY

HARRIET BEECHER STOWE.

VOL. I.

BOSTON:
JOHN P. JEWETT & COMPANY.
CLEVELAND, OHIO:
JEWETT, PROCTOR & WORTHINGTON.
1852.

The title page of the first edition of *Uncle Tom's Cabin*

APRIL 11. "For a month past life has been a thing incredible to me. None but the kind gods can make me sane."

APRIL. Takes many walks with Channing, often in the rain.

MAY 11. Louis Kossuth, the Hungarian freedom fighter, visits Concord. Thoreau is not impressed and says, "The excitement is superficial" (*Journal*, May 4).

MAY 22. Lectures at Plymouth.

JULY 5. Letter, July 13, to Sophia Thoreau: "They say that Mr. Pierce, the presidential candidate was in town **64** . . . visiting Hawthorne, whose college chum he was, and that Hawthorne is writing a life of him for electioneering purposes." This was true; Hawthorne did write a political biography of Pierce and was rewarded by being made United States consul in Liverpool after the election.

JULY 10. "I wonder if any Roman emperor ever indulged in such luxury as this—of walking up and down a river in torrid weather with only a hat to shade the head?" Thoreau was not naked; he also wore a shirt.

AUGUST 8. Alcott is in town on a genealogical tour. He tells Thoreau "to survey Concord and put down every house exactly as it stands with the name." But he did not do it.

SEPTEMBER 6–7. Thoreau goes to New Hampshire with Ellery Channing for a cross-country walk.

SEPTEMBER. The many *Journal* entries this month show that Thoreau was often visiting Walden Pond and making lengthy notes about it, most of which appear in "The Ponds."

DECEMBER. Gets a new boat and explores Walden Pond with it before the water freezes over. *Journal*, December 27; IV, 432.

   Books published in 1852: Dickens, *Bleak House;* Hawthorne, *The Blithedale Romance;* Melville, *Pierre;* Stowe, *Uncle Tom's Cabin;* Thackeray, *History of Henry Esmond.*

Franklin Pierce

1853

Thoreau continues to visit Walden Pond during the winter. But he is in a depressed state of mind all this year.

JANUARY 7. The powder mills four miles from Concord **65** blow up with great loss of life. Thoreau very sensibly says: "Put the buildings 30 rods apart, and then but one will blow up at a time."

64 *Mr. Pierce.* Franklin Pierce (1804–1869), the New Hampshire candidate on the Democratic ticket who became the fourteenth President, from 1853 to 1857.

65 *The powder mills . . . blow up.* This was a particularly gory accident. Thoreau saw human limbs and entrails and blackened naked bodies. The experience may have had some effect on what he says on January 21.

JANUARY 21. "Yesterday I was influenced with the rottenness of human relations. They appeared full of death and decay, and offended the nostrils. In the night I dreamed of delving amid the graves of the dead, and soiled my fingers with their rank mould. . . . Death is with me, and life far away."

JANUARY, FEBRUARY, and MARCH. *Putnam's Magazine* prints three out of five parts of *Excursion to Canada*. Then Thoreau cancels the deal because the publisher has been omitting "the heresies without consulting me —a privilege California is not rich enough to bid for."

MARCH 8. "Rode to Saxonville . . . to look at a small place for sale."

APRIL 11–29. "To Haverhill *via* Cambridge and Boston" on a surveying assignment.

MAY 24. "Talked, or tried to talk, with R.W.E. [Emerson]. Lost my time—nay, almost my identity. He, assuming a false opposition where there was no difference of opinion, talked to the wind—told me what I knew—and I lost my time trying to imagine myself somebody else to oppose him."

JUNE. Thoreau and Channing make several short trips on the rivers near Concord. And Thoreau often revisits Walden Pond.

JUNE 1. He is surveying the Bedford road.

JULY (late). Moncure Conway, a Virginia-born Abolitionist, visits the Thoreau family at a time when a fugitive slave had just arrived at their house. Conway said that he "watched the singularly tender and lowly devotion of the scholar to the slave. He must be fed, his swollen feet bathed, and he must think of nothing but rest. . . . This coolest and calmest of men drew near the trembling Negro and bade him feel at home, and have no fear." **66**

JULY. Hawthorne sails to England to be United States consul in Liverpool.

SEPTEMBER 13–28. Thoreau goes to the Maine woods again. **67**

OCTOBER 28. "The *Publisher*, falsely so called, has been writing . . . to ask what disposition should be made of the copies of *A Week on the Concord and Merrimack Rivers* still on hand. . . . I had them all sent to me here, and they arrived to-day by express . . . 706 copies out of an edition of 1,000 which I bought . . . four years ago and have since been paying for, and have not quite paid for yet. . . . Of the remaining 290 odd, 75 were given away, the rest sold. I have now a library of nearly 900 volumes, over 700 of which I wrote myself." **68**

66 *Moncure Conway* (1832–1907). This is from an article on Thoreau in the August 1866 issue of *Eclectic*.

67 *to the Maine woods again.* Most of what Thoreau had to say about this journey appears in his book *The Maine Woods* (1864), but some parts that were not included appear in the *Journal* for September 12–22; V, 424–432. There are interesting observations on canoe making on pages 428–431.

68 *706 copies.* These were stored in Thoreau's attic quarters in the Yellow House on Main Street. They remained there until shortly before his death in 1862.

NOVEMBER 1. A free Negro woman is at the Thoreau home while she tries to raise enough money to buy her husband from his Virginia owner. Thoreau is indignant when he hears that the slaveholder wants to make a $200 profit on the transaction.

NOVEMBER 2. Thoreau is again elected as curator of the Concord Lyceum but refuses the post because he does not believe he can find enough people to lecture.

NOVEMBER 18. Thomas Wentworth Higginson takes Channing's wife and children to Worcester because they had been badly neglected by their improvident husband and father. **69**

NOVEMBER 28 (*Journal*). Thoreau notes that he has paid $290 for having the *Week* published and has received only $15.

DECEMBER 14. Lectures in Concord on his "Journey to Moose Head Lake" in Maine.

DECEMBER 19. Declines an invitation to become a member of the Association for the Advancement of Science.

DECEMBER 22. "I would fain be employed on higher subjects. I have offered myself much more earnestly as a lecturer than a surveyor. Yet I do not get any employment as a lecturer; was not invited to lecture once last winter, and only once (without pay) this winter. But I can get surveying enough, which a hundred others in this country can do as well as I, though it is not boasting much to say that a hundred others in New England cannot lecture as well as I on my themes. But they who do not make the highest demand on you shall rue it. It is because they make a low demand on themselves. All the while that they use only your humbler faculties, your higher unemployed faculties, like an invisible cimetar [*sic*], are cutting them in twain. Woe be to the generation that lets any higher faculty in its midst go unemployed!"

DECEMBER 24. Writes at length in his *Journal*, VI, 23–24 and 35–37, about Alek Therien, the French-Canadian wood chopper.

DECEMBER 26–31. Heavy snow blankets Concord and the country around it. **70**

Books published in 1853: Hawthorne, *Tanglewood Tales;* Ruskin, *Architecture and Painting;* Thackeray, *The Newcomes.*

1854

JANUARY 1. "I would fain be a fisherman, hunter, farmer, preacher, etc., but fish, hunt, farm, preach other things than usual."

69 *Channing's wife and children.* Ellery Channing was so self-centered that he neglected his wife Ellen and was annoyed by the chatter of his four children. His family stayed in Worcester for a while and then moved to Dorchester in April 1854. The Channings were reconciled a year later, and a fifth child was born on June 15, 1856. Then the long-suffering wife died on September 22. After that the children were placed with relatives. Channing lived until 1901. The last ten years of his life were spent in Sanborn's home as a paying guest.

70 *Heavy snow.* On December 29, Thoreau tried his snowshoes. "They sink deeper than I expected, and I throw the snow upon my back. When I returned, twenty minutes after, my great tracks were not to be seen. It is the worst snow storm . . . that I remember."

A snowshoe of the period

JANUARY 21. Letter to Blake. He mentions clothes and Count d'Orsay in almost the same words that appear in *Walden*. (See page 165 of the *Walden* text.) **71**

JANUARY 23–25. In Worcester with H. G. O. Blake.

FEBRUARY and MARCH. Busy on eighth and final draft of *Walden*.

MARCH 6. Greeley wants previously published pieces to put together in a book, but Thoreau is busy with *Walden*. And he has found a publisher for it—Ticknor and Fields.

MARCH 13 (*Journal*). "To Boston." Perhaps to deliver the manuscript of *Walden* to the publisher. **72**

MARCH 28. "Got first proof of *Walden*."

MARCH 31. "When I have sent off my manuscripts to the printer, certain objectionable sentences or expressions are sure to obtrude themselves on my attention with force, though I had not consciously suspected them before. My critical instinct then at once breaks the ice and comes to the surface."

APRIL 5 "Surveying all day for Mr. Hoar in Carlisle. . . . I rode with my employer a dozen miles . . . keeping a profound silence. . . . I treated him simply as if he had bronchitis and could not speak, just as I would a sick man, a crazy man, or an idiot."

MAY. He receives a printed circular from Charles Scribner asking for biographical information for a forthcoming *Encyclopedia of American Literature* which is to have "the Lives and Writings of all American authors of importance." **73**

71 *Count d'Orsay* (1801–1852), French society leader and arbiter of fashion.

72 *Perhaps to deliver the manuscript of* Walden. It is not known just how the manuscript reached Ticknor and Fields. It may have been sent by mail or express or taken to them by someone not necessarily Thoreau. From March 13 to March 28 is a suspiciously short time for a book manuscript to be accepted and have its first printer's proofs reach Concord.

73 *a printed circular*. The original circular that was sent to Thoreau is in the Huntington Library. When the book was published in 1855 it was entitled *Cyclopaedia of American Literature*, edited by Evert and George Duyckinck. Both *A Week* and *Walden* are mentioned in it. This was Thoreau's first appearance in any work on American literature.

Worcester, Massachusetts

MAY 24. The arrest of Anthony Burns, a fugitive slave **74** who has been working in Boston, arouses New England. On May 29 Thoreau records his reactions in his *Journal*, VI, 315: "Rather than . . . be a party to this establishment; I would touch a match to blow up earth and hell together. As I love my life, I would side with the Light and let the Dark Earth roll from under me."

MAY 30. The Kansas-Nebraska Act, opening up the Nebraska country to slavery, is passed. "Popular Sovereignty" is to decide the issue locally.

JUNE. Entry after entry in the *Journal* this month shows that Thoreau is concentrating his thoughts on slavery.

JULY 4. He speaks at the Antislavery Convention at Framingham on what is later to be called "Slavery in Massachusetts." Using material from his *Journal* on both the Sims and Burns cases, he says: "We have used up all our inherited freedom. If we would save our lives we must fight for them. . . . Who can be serene in a country where both the rulers and the ruled are without principle? . . . My thoughts are murder to the State, and involuntarily go plotting against her."

AUGUST 2. Receives the *first* copy of *Walden*.
The weather is hot, and Thoreau's room under the eaves in his father's house is so unbearable that "My attic chamber has compelled me to sit below with the family for a month. I feel the necessity of deepening the stream of my life; I must cultivate privacy. It is very dissipating to be with people too much. As C. [Channing] says, it takes the edge off a man's thoughts to have been much in society. I cannot spare *my* moonlight and *my* mountains for the best of man I am likely to get in exchange."

AUGUST 8. To Blake: "Emerson says that his life is so improfitable and shabby for the most part that he is driven to all sorts of resources, and among the rest, to men. I tell him that we differ only in our resources. Mine is to get away from men."

AUGUST 9. *Walden* is published in an edition of 2,000 at one dollar a copy.

AUGUST 11. Reviews of *Walden* begin.

AUGUST 12. Thoreau receives a long letter full of praise for the book from Daniel Ricketson of New Bedford. It was the first of many that Thoreau and his new disciple were to exchange.

LATE SUMMER. Samuel Worcester Rowse boards for a **75** while with the Thoreaus. While there, he makes a crayon portrait of Henry.

74 *Anthony Burns* (1834–1862). This fugitive slave from Virginia was arrested in Boston and imprisoned there. The Abolitionists made a desperate attempt to spirit him away but were unsuccessful, and he was sent back to Virginia. Later he was purchased with Northern money, freed, and sent to Oberlin College. He then became a Baptist minister in Canada.

75 *Samuel Worcester Rowse*. Thoreau refused to pose for a portrait, but Rowse had observed him carefully. One day at breakfast he left the table and went to his room. Some hours later he emerged with the portrait that is now in the Concord Public Library. It is a romanticized picture, but it shows Thoreau as he looked during the year *Walden* was published. Rowse also made a portrait of Lidian Emerson. Photographs of Thoreau are all later than the Rowse drawing.

AUTUMN. Thomas Cholmondeley, an Oxford graduate **76** who came to Concord to see Emerson, boards with the Thoreaus and becomes quite friendly with Henry. The name is pronounced "Chumly," Thoreau explains.

SEPTEMBER (?). Written on the inside cover page of the *Journal* volume that ends here:

> My faults are:—
> Paradoxes,—saying just the opposite,—a style which may be imitated.
> Ingenious.
> Playing with words,—getting the laugh,—not always simple, strong, and broad.
> Using current phrases and maxims, when I should speak for myself.
> Not always earnest.
> "In short," "in fact," "alas!" etc.
> Want of conciseness.

OCTOBER 7–15. Goes to Plymouth to lecture on October 8 on "Night and Moonlight" and to survey Marston **77** Watson's property.

OCTOBER 19. To Wachusett Mountain with Cholmondeley and Blake.

NOVEMBER 20. To Philadelphia, 15 hours by train from Concord; lodgings, 37½ cents. Lectures on moose hunting on November 21. Goes sightseeing there and in New York, where he visits Barnum's Museum. **78**

DECEMBER 6. "To Providence to lecture. . . . After lecturing twice this winter I feel that I am in danger of cheapening myself by trying to become a successful lecturer, *i.e.*, to interest my audiences. I am disappointed to find that most that I am and value myself for is lost, or worse than lost, on my audience. I fail to get even the attention of the mass. I should suit them better if I suited myself less. I feel that the public demand an average man,—average thoughts and manners,—not originality, nor even absolute excellence. You cannot interest them except as you are like them and sympathize with them. I would rather that my audience come to me than that I should go to them, and so they be sifted; *i.e.*, I would rather write books than lectures. That is fine, this coarse. To read to a promiscuous audience who are at your mercy the fine thoughts you solaced yourself with far away is as violent as to fatten geese by cramming, and in this case they do not get fatter."

DECEMBER 8. "Winter has come unnoticed by me, I have been so busy writing. This is the life most lead in

The Rowse portrait of Thoreau
(Courtesy Concord Free Public Library)

76 *Thomas Cholmondeley.* This elegant, well-dressed, and widely traveled English gentleman, who needed much luggage and his own portable bathtub, was so taken with Thoreau that he wanted him to come to England. Thoreau, however, preferred Concord to any other place.

77 *Marston Watson's.* Mrs. Watson was the former Mary Russell to whom Thoreau had addressed his poem "To a Maiden in the East" in 1841. The survey he made was framed and hung on the walls of the family's house.

78 *Barnum's Museum.* There he saw the camelopards (giraffes) "said to be 18 and 16 feet tall." But Thoreau thought that these figures were exaggerated and estimated that the taller one was at most 15 feet high.

The giraffes—or camelopards—in Barnum's Museum

respect to Nature. How different from my habitual one! It is hasty, coarse, and trivial, as if you were a spindle in a factory. The other is leisurely, fine and glorious, like a flower. In the first case you are merely getting your living; in the second you live as you go along. You travel only on roads of the proper grade without jar or running off the track, and sweep round the hills by beautiful curves."

DECEMBER 25. To New Bedford, where he meets Daniel Ricketson for the first time. Ricketson makes a sketch **79** of him. Thoreau lectures there on December 26 and then goes to Nantucket Island on December 27 to lecture. Returns to Concord on December 29.

Published in 1854: Dickens, *Hard Times;* Tennyson, "Charge of the Light Brigade."

1855

JANUARY 4. Lectures at Worcester.

JANUARY 7. "The delicious soft, spring-suggesting air,— how it fills my veins with life! Life becomes again

79 *Ricketson makes a sketch.* See next page.

H. D. Thoreau as he presented himself, at the door of Brooklawn
Dec 25 1854 —

Age 37.

Daniel Ricketson's pencil sketch of Thoreau.
It is the only full-length figure of him.
(*Courtesy Concord Free Public Library*)

credible to me. A certain dormant life awakes in me, and I begin to love nature again. Here is my Italy, my heaven, my New England."

JANUARY 12. "Ah, bless the Lord, O my soul! bless him for wildness, for crows that will not alight within gunshot! and bless him for hens, too, that croak and cackle in the yard."

JANUARY 24. "Not strong enough for skating."

FEBRUARY 18. "Many complain of my lectures that they are transcendental—'Can't understand them. . . .' The earnest lecturer can speak only to his like, and the adapting of himself to his audience is a mere compliment which he pays them." **80**

FEBRUARY 14. Lectures at Concord.

MARCH 28. After some correspondence, Franklin B. Sanborn, who is to be Thoreau's biographer, meets him for the first time when he arrives in Concord to open a school there. **81**

APRIL 30. Thoreau unsuccessfully tries to get *A Week on the Concord and Merrimack Rivers* reissued.

SPRING. Although he does not mention it in his *Journal*, Thoreau is ill during much of this time. Evidence of this comes out in a letter to H.G.O. Blake on June 27, when he says: "I have been sick and good for nothing but to lie on my back . . . for two or three months." Tuberculosis is making itself manifest.

JUNE, JULY, and AUGUST. *Putnam's Magazine* publishes the Cape Cod articles in three installments.

JULY 4. Despite his recent illness, Thoreau starts out with Ellery Channing for a trip to Cape Cod. They stay for two weeks in a boardinghouse at Highland Light and return to Concord on July 18.

SEPTEMBER 16. "Now after four or five months of invalidity and worthlessness, I begin to feel some stirrings of life in me." But he is not yet completely well.

SEPTEMBER 26. In a letter to Blake, Thoreau says: "I do not see how strength is to be got into my legs again."

SEPTEMBER 29. Ticknor reports that 334 copies of *Walden* have been sold and that only 256 copies of the first edition are left. They pay him $51.60 as royalty. On this day Thoreau goes to visit Daniel Ricketson in New Bedford. The invitation said: "You can wear your old clothes here."

OCTOBER 3. Thoreau's British friend, Thomas Cholmondeley, sends him several large boxes containing 44 volumes of Oriental literature. **82**

80 *the adapting of himself to his audience.* Thoreau took lecturing very seriously and had a poor opinion of speakers who attempted to amuse their audiences.

81 *Franklin B. Sanborn* (1831–1917). Next to Channing, young Sanborn was to be the most important person in Thoreau's life although Thoreau was never as close to him as he was to Channing. Soon after he arrived in Concord, Sanborn rented Channing's house on Main Street and lived there with his sister.

82 *44 volumes of Oriental literature.* They were: Wilson's *Rig Veda Sanhita, Mandukya Upani-*

Thomas Cholmondeley
(Courtesy Concord Free Public Library)

OCTOBER 6. Thoreau returns to Concord.

OCTOBER 26. "I sometimes think that I must go off to some wilderness where I can have a better opportunity to play life—can find more suitable materials to build my house with, and enjoy the pleasure of collecting my fuel in the forest. I have more taste for the wild sports of hunting, fishing, wigwam-building, making garments of skins, and collecting wood wherever you find it, than for butchering, farming, carpentry, working in a factory, or going to a wood market."

NOVEMBER 30. Cholmondeley's Oriental books arrive. Thoreau makes a case for them, partly out of river driftwood.

DECEMBER 25. To Ricketson: "My legs have grown considerably stronger, and that is all that ails me."

DECEMBER 26. Emerson writes to Thoreau, asking him to correct the proofs on "Stonehenge" in his book, *English Traits*, because he will be away when the proofs are ready. Thoreau agrees to do so.

Books published in 1855: Dickens, *Little Dorrit*; Kingsley, *Westward Ho!*; Longfellow, *Hiawatha*; Melville, *Israel Potter*; Trollope, *The Warden*; Whitman, *Leaves of Grass*.

1856

JANUARY 18. Letter to Calvin Greene: "The 'Week' **83** had so poor a publisher that it is quite uncertain whether you will find it in any shop. I am not sure but authors must turn booksellers themselves." He then offers to mail a copy of the book for $1.25.

JANUARY 20. "In my experience I have found nothing so truly impoverishing as what is called wealth, i.e. the command of greater means than you had before possessed, though comparatively few and slight still, for you thus inevitably acquire a more expensive habit of living, and even the very same necessaries and comforts cost you more than they once did. Instead of gaining, you have lost some independence, and if your income should be suddenly lessened, you would find yourself poor, though possessed of the same means which once made you rich. Within the last five years I have had the command of a little more money than in the previous five years, for I have sold some books and some lectures; yet I have not been a whit better fed or clothed or warmed or sheltered, not a whit richer, except that I have been less concerned about my living, but perhaps my life has been the less serious for it, and,

shads, *Nala Damyanta*, Wilson's *Vishnu Purana*, Houghton's *Institutes of Menu*, Colebrook's *Two Treaties*, *Sankya Karika*, *Aphorisms of the Mimasma*, *Aphorisms of the Nayaya*, *Lecture on the Vedanta*, *Bhagavat Gheeta*, Wilson's *Theater of the Hindoos*, and *Sakoontala*. Some titles were in several volumes. The texts were in English, French, Latin, Greek and Sanscrit. Only Sanscrit was unfamiliar to Thoreau. The books were sent just before Cholmondeley left to go to war in the Crimea.

83 *Calvin Greene* of Rochester, Minnesota.

to balance it, I feel now that there is a possibility of failure. Who knows but I *may* come upon the town, if, as is likely, the public want no more of my books, or lectures (which last is already the case)? Before, I was much likelier to take the town upon my shoulders. That is, I have lost some of my independence on them, when they would say that I had gained an independence. If you wish to give a man a sense of poverty, give him a thousand dollars. The next hundred dollars he gets will not be worth more than ten that he used to get. Have pity on him; withhold your gifts."

FEBRUARY 10. To Calvin Greene: "You . . . have the best of me in my books. . . . I am not worth seeing personally—the stuttering, blundering, clod-hopper that I am."

MARCH 4. Greeley suggests that Thoreau come to his farm in Chappaqua, New York, to live there and be a paid tutor for his children. He accepts but later declines the offer. On this day he writes in the *Journal:*

MARCH 4. "I had two friends. The one offered me friendship on such terms that I could not accept it, without a sense of degradation. He would not meet me on equal terms, but only be to some extent my patron. He would not come to see me, but was hurt if I did not visit him. He would not readily accept a favor, but would gladly confer one. He treated me with ceremony occasionally, though he could be simple and downright sometimes; and from time to time acted a part, treating me as if I were a distinguished stranger; was on stilts, using made words. Our relation was one long tragedy, yet I did not directly speak of it. I do not believe in complaint, nor in explanation. The whole is but too plain, alas, already. We grieve that we do not love each other, that we cannot confide in each other. I could not bring myself to speak, and so recognize an obstacle to our affection.

"I had another friend, who, through a slight obtuseness, perchance, did not recognize a fact which the dignity of friendship would by no means allow me to descend so far as to speak of, and yet the inevitable effect of that ignorance was to hold us apart forever."

JUNE 13. To Worcester visiting friends. While there, he has his first photograph taken. Benjamin D. Maxham makes three daguerreotypes, all nearly identical. The **84** under-face beard, known as Galway whiskers, was recently grown, presumably to protect the throat against the cold. Thoreau says of the picture that his "friends think it is pretty good—though better looking than I."

84 *three daguerreotypes.* Calvin Greene had sent the money (50 cents each) for these so he could get a photograph of Thoreau. See next page.

One of the three Maxham daguerreotype portraits of Thoreau
(*Courtesy Concord Free Public Library*)

JUNE 19. Returns to Concord, where Daniel Ricketson is waiting for him.

JUNE 23. Thoreau goes to New Bedford with Ricketson. There he meets an Indian woman, but she has little use for the lore of her people.

JUNE 27. Goes by steamer to the offshore island of Naushon for the day.

JULY 2. Returns to Concord.

Ricketson's shanty   (*Courtesy Concord Free Public Library*)

SEPTEMBER 5. To Brattleboro and Bellows Falls, Vermont.
Then to Walpole, New Hampshire, to visit Bronson
Alcott. Much botanizing on the way.

SEPTEMBER 12. Returns to Concord.

OCTOBER 20. Letter to Thomas Cholmondeley: "There has
not been anything which you could call union between
the North and South in this country for many years,
and there cannot be so long as slavery is in the way.
I only wish that Northern—that any men—were better
material, or that I for one had more skill to deal with
them; that the north had more spirit and would settle
the question at once, and here instead of struggling
feebly and protractedly away off on the plains of Kansas. They are on the eve of a Presidential election, as
perhaps you know, and all good people are praying
that of the three candidates Fremont may be the man;

but in my opinion the issue is quite doubtful. As far as I have observed, the worst man stands the best chance in this country. But as for politics, what I most admire now-a-days, is not the regular governments but the irregular primitive ones, like the Vigilance committee in California and even the free state men in Kansas. They are the most divine. . . .

"I am sorry that I can give but a poor account of myself. I got 'run down' they say, more than a year ago, and have not yet got fairly up again. It has not touched my spirits however, for they are as indifferently tough, as sluggishly resilient, as a dried fungus. I would it were the kind called punk; that they might catch and retain some heavenly spark. I dwell as much aloof from society as ever: find it just as impossible to agree in opinion with the most intelligent of my neighbors; they not having improved one jot, nor I either. I am still immersed in nature, have much of the time a living sense of the breadth of the field on whose verge I dwell."

OCTOBER 24. To Eagleswood, a former co-operative community near Perth Amboy, New Jersey, to survey the property and lecture there. He stops off in Worcester and New York, where he revisits Barnum's Museum. **85**

NOVEMBER 1. Bronson Alcott joins him at Eagleswood; then they both go to Chappaqua to see Greeley on November 8.

NOVEMBER 4. James Buchanan is elected President.

NOVEMBER 9. Alcott and Thoreau go to Brooklyn Heights to hear Henry Ward Beecher speak at the Plymouth Church. **86**

NOVEMBER 10. They visit Walt Whitman in his Myrtle Avenue home in Brooklyn. Thoreau says of him in a letter to Blake on: **87**

NOVEMBER 19. "A. [Alcott] and I heard Beecher preach; and what was more, we visited Whitman the next morning (A. had already seen him), and were much interested and provoked. He is apparently the greatest democrat the world has seen. Kings and aristocracy go by the board at once, as they have long deserved to. A remarkably strong though coarse nature, of a sweet disposition, and much prized by his friends. Though peculiar and rough in his exterior, his skin (all over (?)) red, he is essentially a gentleman. I am still somewhat in a quandary about him,—feel that he is essentially strange to me, at any rate; but I am surprised by the sight of him. He is very broad, but, as I have said, not fine. He said that I misapprehended him. I am not quite sure that I do. He told us that he loved to ride up and down Broadway all day on an omnibus, sitting

85 *Eagleswood.* Thoreau spent a month at this communal village where a 254-foot-long stone phalanstery had been built. The community had not been doing well, and Thoreau was brought there through Bronson Alcott to survey the land so it could be made into miniature estates for New Yorkers who could commute by steamship.

86 *Henry Ward Beecher.* Beecher had made this Brooklyn church famous, and visitors to New York went out of their way to see the noted preacher in action. One of them was Abraham Lincoln, who attended services on March 11, 1860, shortly before he was nominated as the Republican candidate for the presidency.

87 *Walt Whitman.* The first edition of 800 copies of his *Leaves of Grass* had been printed in 1855. Its preface proclaimed his belief that "the United States themselves are essentially the greatest poem." Visitors found Whitman living in a miserable room with his mentally defective brother.

James Buchanan

beside the driver, listening to the roar of the carts, and sometimes gesticulating and declaiming Homer at the top of his voice. He has long been an editor and writer for the newspapers,—was editor of the 'New Orleans Crescent' once; but now has no employment but to read and write in the forenoon, and walk in the afternoon, like all the rest of the scribbling gentry."

NOVEMBER 25. After spending some more time in Eagleswood, Thoreau returns to Concord.

DECEMBER 1. "I love and could embrace the shrub oak with its scanty garment of leaves rising above the snow, lowly whispering to me, akin to winter thoughts, and sunsets, and to all virtue. Covert which the hare and the partridge seek, and I too seek. What cousin of mine is the shrub oak? How can any man suffer long? For a sense of want is a prayer, and all prayers are answered. Rigid as iron, clean as the atmosphere, hardy as virtue, innocent and sweet as a maiden is the shrub oak. In proportion as I know and love it, I am natural and sound as a partridge. I felt a positive yearning toward one bush this afternoon. There was a match found for me at last. I fell in love with a shrub oak."

DECEMBER 2. "As for the sensuality in Whitman's 'Leaves of Grass,' I do not so much wish that it was not written, as that men and women were so pure that they could read it without harm."

DECEMBER 5. "My themes shall not be far-fetched. I will tell of homely every-day phenomena. . . . Friends! Society! It seems to me that I have an abundance of it, there is so much that I rejoice and sympathize with, and men, too, that I never speak to but only know and think of. What you call bareness and poverty is to me simplicity. God could not be unkind to me if he should try. I love the winter, with its imprisonment and its cold, for it compels the prisoner to try new fields and resources. I love to have the river closed up for a season and a pause put to my boating, to be obliged to get my boat in. I shall launch it again in the spring with so much more pleasure. This is an advantage in point of abstinence and moderation compared with the seaside boating, where the boat ever lies on the shore. I love best to have each thing in its season only, and enjoy doing without it at all other times. It is the greatest of all advantages to enjoy no advantage at all. I find it invariably true, the poorer I am, the richer I am. What you consider my disadvantage, I consider my advantage. While you are pleased to get knowledge and culture in many ways, I am delighted to think that I am getting rid of them. I have never got over my surprise that I

Leaves *of* Grass.

Brooklyn, New York: 1855.

should have been born into the most estimable place in all the world, and in the very nick of time, too."

DECEMBER 7. Whitman had evidently made a great impression on Thoreau. Writing to Blake about his meeting with him, he says:

"That Walt Whitman, of whom I wrote to you, is the most interesting fact to me at present. I have just read his 2nd edition (which he gave me) and it has done me more good than any reading for a long time. Perhaps I remember best the poem of Walt Whitman an American & the Sun Down Poem. There are 2 or 3 pieces in the book which are disagreeable to say the least, simply sensual. He does not celebrate love at all. It is as if the beasts spoke. I think that men have not been ashamed of themselves without reason. No doubt, there have always been dens where such deeds were unblushingly recited, and it is no merit to compete with their inhabitants. But even on this side, he has spoken more truth than any American or modern that I know. I have found his poem exhilirating encouraging. As for its sensuality,—& it may turn out to be less sensual than it appeared—I do not so much wish that those parts were not written, as that men & women were so pure that they could read them without harm, that is, without understanding them. One woman told me that no woman could read it as if a man could read what a woman could not. Of course Walt Whitman can communicate to us no experience, and if we are shocked, whose experience is it that we are reminded of?

"On the whole it sounds to me very brave & American after whatever deductions. I do not believe that all the sermons so called that have been preached in this land put together are equal to it for preaching—

"We ought to rejoice greatly in him. He occasionally suggests something a little more than human. You cant confound him with the other inhabitants of Brooklyn or New York. How they must shudder when they read him! He is awefully good.

"To be sure I sometimes feel a little imposed on. By his heartiness & broad generalities he puts me into a liberal frame of mind prepared to see wonders—as it were sets me upon a hill or in the midst of a plain—stirs me well up, and then—throws in a thousand of brick. Though rude & sometimes ineffectual, it is a great primitive poem,—an alarum or trumpet-note ringing through the American camp. Wonderfully like the Orientals, too, considering that when I asked him if he had read them, he answered, 'No: tell me about them.'

"I did not get far in conversation with him,—two more being present,— and among the few things which I chanced to say, I remember that one was, in answer to him as representing America, that I did not think much of America or of politics, and so on, which may have been somewhat of a damper to him.

"Since I have seen him, I find that I am not disturbed by any brag or egoism in his book. He may turn out the least of a braggart of all, having a better right to be confident.

"He is a great fellow."

DECEMBER 16. In a letter from Rome, Cholmondeley says: *"Forgive my English plainness of speech.* Your love for, and intimate acquaintance with, Nature is ancillary to some affection which you have not yet discovered."

DECEMBER 18. Thoreau speaks on "Walking" in Amherst, New Hampshire. "Lectured in basement (vestry) of the orthodox church, and I trust helped to undermine it."

DECEMBER 29. "Staying in the house breeds a sort of insanity always. Every house is in this sense a hospital. A night and a forenoon is as much confinement to those wards as I can stand. I am aware that I recover some sanity which I had lost almost the instant that I come abroad."

Books published in 1856: Emerson, *English Traits;* Melville, *Piazza Tales.*

1857

JANUARY 6. "The stones are happy, Concord River is happy, and I am happy too. . . . Do you think that Concord River would have continued to flow these millions of years . . . if it had not been happy—if it had been miserable in its channel, tired of existence, and cursing its maker and the hour that it sprang?"

JANUARY 7. "In the street and in society I am almost invariably cheap and dissipated, my life is unspeakably mean. No amount of gold or respectability would in the least redeem it,—dining with the Governor or a member of Congress!! But alone in distant woods or fields, in unpretending sprout-lands or pastures tracked by rabbits, even in a bleak and, to most, cheerless day, like this, when a villager would be thinking of his inn, I come to myself, I once more feel myself grandly related, and that cold and solitude are friends of mine. I suppose that this value, in my case, is equivalent to what others get by churchgoing and prayer. I come to my solitary woodland walk as the homesick go home. I thus dispose of the superfluous and see things as they are, grand and beautiful. I have told many that I walk every day about half the daylight, but I think they do not believe it. I wish to get the Concord, the Massa-

"To those who have accepted, quite naturally, that purposeful and combative aspect of life which to our political economists is the only one in view, Thoreau seems as odd as would a Buddhist eremite to a stock-jobber. Yet a second and a steadier look at him may be disastrous to the Western concept of the strenuous life. You suspect, in sudden alarm, that there is more to life than you had been told; that it may have a nature hitherto unguessed, possibilities unknown; that, in fact, Western civilization may have taken the wrong path and may yet have to turn back—or wish desperately that it could."

H. M. TOMLINSON
"Two Americans and a Whale,"
HARPER'S MAGAZINE, April, 1926

chusetts, the America, out of my head and be sane a part of every day. If there are missionaries for the heathen, why not send them to me? I wish to know something; I wish to be made better. I wish to forget, a considerable part of every day, all mean, narrow, trivial men (and this requires usually to forego and forget all personal relations so long), and therefore I come out to these solitudes, where the problem of existence is simplified. I get away a mile or two from the town into the stillness and solitude of nature, with rocks, trees, weeds, snow about me. I enter some glade in the woods . . . and it is as if I had come to an open window. I see out and around myself. Our *skylights* are thus far away from the ordinary resorts of men. I am not satisfied with ordinary windows. I must have a true *skylight*. My true sky light is on the outside of the village. I am not thus expanded, recreated, enlightened, when I meet a company of men. It chances that the sociable, the town and county, or the farmers' club does not prove a skylight to me. I do not invariably find myself translated under those circumstances. They bore me. The man I meet with is not often so instructive as the silence he breaks. This stillness, solitude, wildness of nature is a kind of thoroughwort, or bone-set, to my intellect. This is what I go out to seek. It is as if I always met in those places some grand, serene, immortal, infinitely encouraging, though invisible, companion, and walked with him. There at last my nerves are steadied, my senses and my mind do their office. I am aware that most of my neighbors would think it a hardship to be compelled to linger here one hour, especially this bleak day, and yet I receive this sweet and ineffable compensation for it. It is the most agreeable thing I do. Truly, my coins are uncurrent with them.

"I love and celebrate nature, even in detail, merely because I love the scenery of these interviews and translations. I love to remember every creature that was at this *club*. I thus get off a certain social scurf and scaliness. I do not consider the other animals brutes in the common sense. I am attracted toward them undoubtedly because I never heard any nonsense from them. I have not convicted them of folly, or vanity, or pomposity, or stupidity, in dealing with me. Their vices, at any rate, do not interfere with me. My fairies invariably take to flight when a man appears upon the scene. In a caucus, a meeting-house, a lyceum, a club-room, there is nothing like it in my experience. But away out of the town, on Brown's scrub oak lot, which was sold the other day for six dollars an acre, I have company such as England cannot buy, nor afford. This society is what

"Reading him [Thoreau] is like eating onions—one must look out or the flavor will reach his own page."
JOHN BURROUGHS
JOURNAL, 1878

I live, what I survey, for. I subscribe generously to *this* —all that I have and am.

"*There*, in that Well Meadow Field, perhaps, I feel in my element again, as when a fish is put back into the water. I wash off all my chagrins. All things go smoothly as the axle of the universe. I can remember that when I was very young I used to have a dream night after night, over and over again, which might have been named Rough and Smooth. All existence, all satisfaction and dissatisfaction, all event was symbolized in this way. Now I seemed to be lying and tossing, perchance, on a horrible, a fatal rough surface, which must soon, indeed, put an end to my existence, though even, in the dream I knew it to be the symbol merely of my misery; and then again, suddenly, I was lying on a delicious smooth surface, as of a summer sea, as of gossamer or down or softest plush, and life was such a luxury to live. My waking experience *always* has been and is such an alternate Rough and Smooth. In other words it is Insanity and Sanity."

JANUARY 11. "For some years past I have partially offered myself as a lecturer; have been advertised as such several years. Yet I have had but two or three invitations to lecture in a year, and some years none at all. I congratulate myself on having been permitted to stay at home thus, I am so much richer for it. I do not see what I should have got of much value, but money, by going about, but I do see what I should have lost. It seems to me that I have a longer and more liberal lease of life thus. I cannot afford to be telling my experience, especially to those who perhaps will take no interest in it. I wish to be getting experience. You might as well recommend to a bear to leave his hollow tree and run about all winter scratching at all the hollow trees in the woods. He would be leaner in the spring than if he had stayed at home and sucked his claws. As for the lecture-goers, it is none of their business what I think. I perceive that most make a great account of their relations, more or less personal and direct, to many men, coming before them as lecturers, writers, or public men. But all this is impertinent and unprofitable to me. I never yet recognized, nor was recognized by, a crowd of men. I was never assured of their existence, nor they of mine."

JANUARY 18. "In Virginia a naturalist who was seen crawling through a meadow catching frogs, etc., was seized and carried before the authorities."

JANUARY 26. "At Cambridge & Boston. Saw Harbor frozen over . . . thousands on the ice. . . . Ice said to reach 14 miles."

A professional botanist of the period

FEBRUARY 3. Lectures at Fitchburg, Massachusetts.

FEBRUARY 6. "Winckelmann says: 'I am now past forty, **88** and therefore at an age when one can no longer sport freely with life. I perceive, also, that a certain delicate spirit begins to evaporate, with which I raised myself, by powerful soarings, to the contemplation of the beautiful.' "

FEBRUARY 8. "Again and again I congratulate myself on my so-called poverty. I was almost disappointed yesterday to find thirty dollars in my desk which I did not know that I possessed, though I should now be sorry to lose it. The week that I go away to lecture, however much I may get for it, is unspeakably cheapened. The preceding and succeeding days are a mere sloping down and up from it.

"In the society of many men, or in the midst of what is called success, I find my life of no account, and my spirits rapidly fall. I would rather be the barrenest pasture lying fallow than cursed with the compliments of kings, than be the sulphurous and accursed desert where Babylon once stood. But when I have only a rustling oak leaf, or the faint metallic cheep of a tree sparrow, for variety in my winter walk, my life becomes continent and sweet as the kernel of a nut. I would rather hear a single shrub oak leaf at the end of a wintry glade rustle of its own accord at my approach, than receive a shipload of stars and garters from the strange kings and peoples of the earth.

"By poverty, *i. e.* simplicity of life and fewness of incidents, I am solidified and crystallized, as a vapor or liquid by cold. It is a singular concentration of strength and energy and flavor. Chastity is perpetual acquaintance with the All. My diffuse and vaporous life becomes as the frost leaves and spiculæ radiant as gems on the weeds and stubble in a winter morning. You think that I am impoverishing myself by withdrawing from men, but in my solitude, I have woven for myself a silken web or *chrysalis*, and, nymph-like, shall ere long burst forth a more perfect creature, fitted for a higher society. By simplicity, commonly called poverty, my life is concentrated and so becomes organized, or a κόσγος, which before was inorganic and lumpish."

FEBRUARY 13. To Worcester to lecture.

MARCH 2. To Cambridge.

MARCH 4. James Buchanan is inaugurated President.

MARCH 7. The Dred Scott decision.   **89**

MARCH 20. Dines with Louis Agassiz, the Swiss naturalist, at Emerson's house.

88 *Winckelmann.* Johann Joachim Winckelmann (1717–1768), German art historian and archaeologist, early specialist in Roman antiquities.

89 *The Dred Scott decision.* This famous case, in which the United States Supreme Court held that a slave was not a citizen and therefore had no standing in court and that slaves remained slaves even when taken into free territory, helped to marshal Northern people against the South's "peculiar institution."

New Bedford

APRIL 6–16. To New Bedford to visit Daniel Ricketson. While there he meets 20-year-old Kate Brady, half-Irish and half-Yankee. He likes her because she plans to live alone in her father's abandoned house and because she loves Nature.

MAY 3. "Up and down the town, men and boys that are under subjection are polishing their shoes and brushing their go-to-meeting clothes. I, a descendant of Northmen who worshipped Thor, spend my time worshipping neither Thor nor Christ; a descendant of Northmen who sacrificed men and horses, sacrifice neither men nor horses. I care not for Thor nor for the Jews. I sympathize not to-day with those who go to church in newest clothes and sit quietly in straight-backed pews. I sympathize rather with the boy who has none to look after him, who borrows a boat and paddle and in common clothes sets out to explore these temporary vernal lakes. I meet such a boy paddling along under a sunny bank, with bare feet and his pants rolled up above his knees, ready to leap into the water at a moment's warning. Better for him to read 'Robinson Crusoe' than Baxter's 'Saints' Rest.' "

MAY 6–8. Building an arbor for Emerson.

MAY 12. "I ordinarily plod along a sort of whitewashed prison entry, subject to some indifferent or even grovelling mood. I do not distinctly realize my destiny. I have turned down my light to the merest glimmer and am doing some task which I have set myself. I take incredibly narrow views, live on the limits, and have no recollection of absolute truth. Mushroom institutions hedge me in. But suddenly, in some fortunate moment, the voice of eternal wisdom reaches me, even in the strain of the sparrow, and liberates me, whets and clarifies my senses, makes me a competent witness."

JUNE 12. Sets out for Cape Cod alone. He travels on foot and visits the new telegraph station near Highland Light. Sails from Provincetown on June 22 and arrives in Concord the same day. This was Thoreau's last trip to the Cape.

JULY 11. Finding himself "stronger than for 2 or 3 years past," he plans on making another trip to the Maine woods.

JULY 20. Starts by rail for the Maine woods in company with Edward Hoar, who had been with Thoreau in 1844 when they accidentally set the Concord woods on fire. They employ Joe Polis, an Indian, as a guide **90** and go by canoe for a 325-mile trip on the Allegash and East Branch. Thoreau's account of the journey appears in his book on the Maine woods and also in the *Journal*.

AUGUST 8. Arrives in Concord from Maine.

SEPTEMBER. Bronson Alcott returns to Concord to live. During this autumn, Thoreau grows a full beard to protect his face and throat against the winter weather.

OCTOBER 15. Because of the Panic of 1857 the Concord bank suspends payment.

OCTOBER 29. "There are some things of which I cannot at once tell whether I have dreamed them or they are real; as if they were just, perchance, establishing, or else losing, a real basis in my world. This is especially the case in the early morning hours, when there is a gradual transition from dreams to waking thoughts, from illusions to actualities, as from darkness, or perchance moon and star light, to sunlight. Dreams are real, as is the light of the stars and moon, and theirs is said to be a *dreamy* light. Such early morning thoughts as I speak of occupy a debatable ground between dreams and waking thoughts. They are a sort of permanent dream in my mind. At least, until we have for some time changed our position from prostrate to erect, and commenced or faced some of the duties of the day, we cannot tell what we have dreamed from what we have actually experienced.

"This morning, for instance, for the twentieth time at least, I thought of that mountain in the easterly part of our town (where no high hill actually is) which once or twice I had ascended, and often allowed my

90 *Joe Polis*. This 48-year-old Indian guide praised Thoreau for his ability in handling a canoe, then he showed him how to place his hands on the paddle so he would be spared unnecessary work. Polis made a lasting impression on Thoreau, so much so that acquaintance with him increased his already great respect for Indians.

thoughts alone to climb. I now contemplate it in my mind as a familiar thought which I have surely had for many years from time to time, but whether anything could have reminded me of it in the middle of yesterday, whether I ever before remembered it in broad daylight, I doubt. I can now eke out the vision I had of it this morning with my old and yesterday forgotten dreams.

"My way up used to lie through a dark and unfrequented wood at its base—I cannot now tell exactly, it was so long ago, under what circumstances I first ascended, only that I shuddered as I went along (I have an indistinct remembrance of having been out overnight alone) and then I steadily ascended along a rocky ridge half clad with stunted trees, where wild beasts haunted, till I lost myself quite in the upper air and clouds, seeming to pass an imaginary line which separates a hill, mere earth heaped up, from a mountain, into a superterranean grandeur and sublimity. What distinguishes that summit above the earthy line, is that it is unhandselled, awful, grand. It can never become familiar; you are lost the moment you set foot there. You know no path, but wander, thrilled, over the bare and pathless rock, as if it were solidified air and cloud. That rocky, misty summit, secreted in the clouds, was far more thrillingly awful and sublime than the crater of a volcano spouting fire."

NOVEMBER 14. "With this keener blast from the north, my hands suddenly fail to fulfill their office, as it were begin to die. . . . I can hardly tie and untie my shoestrings."

NOVEMBER 18. "I had yesterday a kink in my back and a general cold, and as usual it amounted to a cessation of life."

DECEMBER 31. Thoreau had done a great deal of surveying during the year. In a long *Journal* entry for this day, he satirizes some of the men he had worked for.

Books published in 1857: Borrow, *The Romany Rye;* Hughes, *Tom Brown's School Days;* Melville, *The Confidence Man;* Thackeray, *The Virginians;* Trollope, *Barchester Towers.*

1858

JANUARY 1. Thoreau's father has recovered from an attack of jaundice, but he still has a bad cough and is aging rapidly.

JANUARY 13–15. Thoreau to Lynn, Massachusetts, to lecture.

JANUARY 23. James Russell Lowell, as editor of *The Atlantic Monthly*, has asked Thoreau for an article. On this day Thoreau replies, suggesting about a hundred manuscript pages on the Maine woods.

FEBRUARY 22. In a letter to Lowell, Thoreau says that he will send the Maine woods material within a fortnight. He is to read some of it to his townsmen this week.

FEBRUARY 25. He gives the lecture in Concord.

MARCH 5. He sends some 80 pages of the Maine story to Lowell and says that there are 50 pages more. He asks for proofs. He sends in the rest of the manuscript on May 18 and again asks for proofs.

MAY 22–27. Thoreau goes on what is to be his last trip to New York. He stops off in Worcester on the way. He again visits Barnum's Museum and goes to Staten Island.

JUNE 2 to 4. To Mount Monadnock in New Hampshire with H. G. O. Blake.

JUNE 5. The first installment of the Maine experiences appears in *The Atlantic Monthly*.

JUNE 22. Letter to James Russell Lowell about cutting **91** out Thoreau's reference to a pine tree:

"When I received the proof of that portion of my story printed in the July number of your magazine, I was surprised to find that the sentence—'It is as immortal as I am, and perchance will go to as high a heaven, there to tower above me still."—(which comes directly after the words 'heals my cuts,' page 230, tenth line from the top,) have been crossed out, and it occurred to me that, after all, it was of some consequence that I should see the proofs; supposing, of course, that my 'Stet' &c in the margin would be respected, as I perceive that it was in other cases of comparatively little importance to me. However, I have just noticed that that sentence was, in a very mean and cowardly manner, omitted. I hardly need to say that this is a liberty which I will not permit to be taken with my MS. The editor has, in this case, no more right to omit a sentiment than to insert one, or put words into my mouth. I do not ask anybody to adopt my opinions, but I do expect that when they ask for them to print, they will print them, or obtain my consent to their alteration or omission. I should not read many books if I thought that they had been thus *expurgated*. I feel this treatment to be an insult, though not intended as such, for it is to presume that I can be hired to suppress my opinions.

"I do not mean to charge you with this omission, for I cannot believe that you knew anything about it, but

91   *to James Russell Lowell.* Although Thoreau was always very touchy about having his writings tampered with, he was probably expecting trouble from Lowell because of what he had said in *A Fable for Critics.* We do not know whether or not Lowell ever replied to this letter. See October 4.

there must be a responsible editor somewhere, and you, to whom I entrusted my MS. are the only party that I know in this matter. I therefore write to ask if you sanction this omission, and if there are any other sentiments to be omitted in the remainder of my article. If you do not sanction it—or whether you do or not—will you do me the justice to print that sentence, as an omitted one, indicating its place, in the August number?

"I am not willing to be associated in any way, unnecessarily, with parties who will confess themselves so bigoted & timid as this implies. I could excuse a man who was afraid of an uplifted fist, but if one habitually manifests fear at the utterance of a sincere thought, I must think that his life is a kind of nightmare continued into broad daylight. It is hard to conceive of one so completely derivative. Is this the avowed character of the Atlantic Monthly? I should like an early reply."

Apparently, there was no reply. At least, none is known.

JULY 2–19. On a trip to the White Mountains with Edward Hoar, traveling by horse and carriage. They climb Mount Washington. **92**

AUGUST 5. The first transatlantic cable is completed and messages are sent, but faulty insulation soon puts it out of commission.

AUGUST 9. "It is surprising to what extent the world is ruled by cliques. They who constitute, or at least lead, New England or New York society, in the eyes of the world, are but a clique, a few 'men of the age' and of the town, who work best in the harness provided for them. The institutions of almost all kinds are thus of a sectarian or party character. Newspapers, magazines, colleges, and all forms of government and religion express the superficial activity of a few, the mass either conforming or not attending. . . ."

"The newspapers have just told me that the transatlantic telegraph-cable is laid. That is important, but they instantly proceed to inform me how the news was received in every larger town in the United States,— how many guns they fired, or how high they jumped, —in New York, and Milwaukee, and Sheboygan; and the boys and girls, old and young, at the corners of the streets are reading it all with glistening eyes, down to the very last scrap, not omitting what they did at New Rochelle and Evansville. And all the speeches are reported, and some think of collecting them into a volume ! ! !"

AUGUST 21 to OCTOBER 15. The Lincoln-Douglas debates are held in Illinois. **93**

92 *Edward Hoar.* This was the young man who had gone to Maine with Thoreau in July 1857. When Thoreau sprained his foot on this trip he soaked it in the icy waters of a mountain stream to reduce the swelling and then put leaves from *Arnica mollis* around it. After a day in camp he was able to go on.

93 *The Lincoln-Douglas debates.* Abolitionists had little use for Lincoln. Thoreau barely mentions him in his writings.

SEPTEMBER 21–24. Thoreau goes on a walking trip with Ellery Channing to Cape Ann, Massachusetts.

OCTOBER 4. To James Russell Lowell: "I wrote to you more than a month ago respecting what was due me from the Atlantic monthly [*sic*] but I have not heard from you. . . . Your magazine is indebted to me for thirty-three pages at six dollars a page—$198." As a result of his controversy with Lowell, Thoreau refused to deal with the *Atlantic* until the middle of 1861 when James T. Fields became its new editor.

OCTOBER 12. "I think that the law is really a 'humbug', and a benefit principally to the lawyers."

NOVEMBER 1. "Give me the old familiar walk, post-office and all, with this ever new self, with this infinite expectation and faith, which does not know when it is beaten. We'll go nutting once more. We'll pluck the nut of the world, and crack it in the winter evenings. Theatres and all other sightseeing are puppet-shows in comparison. I will take another walk to the Cliff, another row on the river, another skate on the meadow, be out in the first snow, and associate with the winter birds. Here I am at home. In the bare and bleached crust of the earth I recognize my friend.

"One actual Frederick that you know is worth a million only read of. Pray, am I altogether a bachelor, or am I a widower, that I should go away and leave my bride? This Morrow that is ever knocking with irresistible force at our door, there is no such guest as that. I will stay at home and receive company.

"I want nothing new, if I can have but a tithe of the old secured to me. I will spurn all wealth beside. Think of the consummate folly of attempting to go away from *here!* When the constant endeavor should be to get nearer and nearer *here.* Here are all the friends I ever had or shall have, and as friendly as ever. Why, I never had any quarrel with a friend but it was just as sweet as unanimity could be. I do not think we budge an inch forward or backward in relation to our friends. How many things can you go away from? They see the comet from the northwest coast just as plainly as we do, and the same stars through its tail. Take the shortest way round and stay at home. A man dwells in his native valley like a corolla in its calyx, like an acorn in its cup. *Here,* of course, is all that you love, all that you expect, all that you are. Here is your bride elect, as close to you as she can be got. Here is all the best and all the worst you can imagine. What more do you want? Bear here-away then! Foolish people imagine that what they imagine is somewhere else. That stuff is not made in any factory but their own."

NOVEMBER 3. "Nothing makes me so dejected as to have met my friends, for they make me doubt if it is possible to have any friends. I feel what a fool I am. I cannot conceive of persons more strange to me than they actually are; not thinking, not believing, not doing as I do; interrupted by me. My only distinction must be that I am the greatest bore they ever had. Not in a single thought agreed; regularly balking one another. But when I get far away, my thoughts return to them. That is the way I *can* visit them. Perhaps it is unaccountable to me why I care for them. Thus I am taught that my friend is not an actual person. When I have withdrawn and am alone, I forget the actual person and remember only my ideal. Then I have a friend again."

NOVEMBER 16. "Preaching? Lecturing? Who are ye that ask for these things? What do ye want to hear, ye puling infants? A trumpet-sound that would train you up to mankind, or a nurse's lullaby? The preachers and lecturers deal with men of straw, as they are men of straw themselves. Why, a free-spoken man, of sound lungs, cannot draw a long breath without causing your rotten institutions to come toppling down by the vacuum he makes. Your church is a baby-house made of blocks, and so of the state. It would be a relief to breathe one's self occasionally among men. If there were any magnanimity in us, any grandeur of soul, anything but sects and parties undertaking to patronize God and keep the mind within bounds, how often we might encourage and provoke one another by a free expression! I will not consent to walk with my mouth muzzled, not till I am rabid, until there is danger that I shall bite the unoffending and that my bite will produce hydrophobia.

"Freedom of speech! It hath not entered into your hearts to conceive what those words mean. It is not leave given me by your sect to say this or that; it is when leave is given to your sect to withdraw. The church, the state, the school, the magazine, think they are liberal and free! It is the freedom of a prison-yard. I ask only that one fourth part of my honest thoughts be spoken aloud. What is it you tolerate, you church to-day? Not truth, but a lifelong hypocrisy. Let us have institutions framed not out of our rottenness, but out of our soundness. This factitious piety is like stale gingerbread. I would like to suggest what a pack of fools and cowards we mankind are. They want me to agree not to breathe too hard in the neighborhood of their paper castles. If I should draw a long breath in the neighborhood of these institutions, their weak and flabby sides would fall out, for my own inspiration would exhaust the air about them. The church! it is eminently the timid institution, and the heads and pillars of it are constitutionally and by principle the greatest cowards in the community. The voice that goes up from the monthly concerts is not so brave and so cheering as that which rises from the frog-ponds of the land. The best 'preachers,' so called, are an effeminate class; their bravest thoughts wear petticoats. If they have any manhood they are sure to forsake the ministry, though they were to turn their attention to baseball. Look at your editors of popular magazines. I have dealt with two or three the most liberal of them. They are afraid to print a whole sentence, a *round* sentence, a free-spoken sentence. They want to get thirty thousand subscribers, and they will do anything to get them. They consult the D.D.'s and all the letters of the alphabet before printing a sentence. I have been into many of these cowardly New England towns where they *profess* Christianity,—invited to speak, perchance,—where they were trembling in their shoes at the thought of the things you might say, as if they knew their weak side,—that they were weak on all sides. The devil they have covenanted with is a timid devil. If they would let their sores alone they might heal, and they could to the wars again like men; but instead of that they get together in meeting-house cellars, rip off the bandages and poultice them with sermons.

"One of our New England towns is sealed up hermetically like a molasses-hogshead,—such is its sweet Christianity,—only a little of the sweet trickling out at the cracks enough to daub you. The few more liberal-minded or indifferent inhabitants are the flies that buzz about it. It is Christianity bunged up. I see awful eyes looking out through a bull's-eye at the bunghole. It is doubtful if they can fellowship with me.

"The further you go up country. I think the worse it is, the more benighted they are. On the one side you will find a barroom which holds the 'Scoffers,' so called, on the other a vestry where is a monthly concert of prayer. There is just as little to cheer you in one of these companies as the other. It may be often the truth and righteousness of the barroom that saves the town. There is nothing to redeem the bigotry and moral cowardice of New-Englanders in my eyes. . . . They do not think; they adhere like oysters to what their fathers and grandfathers adhered to. How often is it that the shoemaker, by thinking over his last, can think as valuable a thought as he makes a valuable shoe?

"I have been into the town, being invited to speak to the inhabitants, not valuing, not having read even, the Assembly's Catechism, and I try to stimulate them by reporting the best of my experience. I see the craven

"Henry Thoreau . . . was conducting an experiment in economy. He had looked at the twin wonders of the age, the developing industrial system and the certainty of universal moral reform, and had seen no need to pay tribute to either. The first chapter of Walden *accurately analyzes the bank failures, bond repudiations, mortgages, farmsteads, and factories of the thirties and forties, but Thoreau's experiment dealt with a preliminary, or antecedent, problem, the survival of the mind's integrity in such a system."*

BERNARD DE VOTO, 1943
THE YEAR OF DECISION: 1846

priest looking round for a hole to escape at, alarmed because it was he that invited me thither, and an awful silence pervades the audience. They think they will never get me there again. But the seed has not all fallen in stony and shallow ground. . . ."

"It is no compliment to be invited to lecture before the rich Institutes and Lyceums. The settled lecturers are as tame as the settled ministers. The audiences do not want to hear any prophets; they do not wish to be stimulated and instructed, but entertained. They, their wives and daughters, go to the Lyceum to suck a sugar-plum. The little of medicine they get is disguised with sugar. It is never the reformer they hear there, but a faint and timid echo of him only. They seek a passtime merely. Their greatest guns and sons of thunder are only wooden guns and great-grandsons of thunder, who give them smooth words well pronounced from manuscripts well punctuated,—they who have stolen the little fire they have from prophets whom the audience would quake to hear. They ask for orators that will entertain them and leave them where they found them. The most successful lecturing on Washington, or what-not, is an awful scratching of backs to the tune, it may be, of fifty thousand dollars. Sluggards that want to have a lullaby sung to them! Such manikins as I have described are they, alas, who have made the greatest stir (and what a shallow stir) in the church and Lyceum, and in Congress. They want a medicine that will not interfere with their daily meals. . . .

"They want all of a man but his truth and independence and manhood.

"One who spoke to their condition would of course make them wince, and they would retaliate, *i.e.* kick him out, or stop their ears."

NOVEMBER 20. "Who are the religious? They who do not differ much from mankind generally, except that they are more conservative and timid and useless, but who in their conversation and correspondence talk about kindness of Heavenly Father. Instead of going bravely about their business, trusting God ever, they do like him who says 'Good sir' to the one he fears, or whistles to the dog that is rushing at him. And because they take His name in vain so often they presume that they are better than you. Oh, their religion is a rotten squash."

DECEMBER 7. Cholmondeley, Thoreau's English friend, revisits him in Concord.

DECEMBER 15. Ticknor writes that there is very little demand for *Walden*.

"*[Thoreau] was literally the most childlike, unconscious, and unblushing egotist it has ever been my fortune to encounter.*"

HENRY JAMES, SR.
Letter to the Boston HERALD,
April 24, 1881

Books published in 1858: Eliot, *Scenes of Clerical Life;* Holmes, *The Autocrat of the Breakfast Table;* Longfellow, *The Courtship of Miles Standish.*

1859

JANUARY 1. To H. G. O. Blake: "I met Mr. [Henry] James the other night at Emerson's." **94**

FEBRUARY (early). In reply to a letter from Harvard which asked for contributions to the library, Thoreau sends five dollars and writes: "I would gladly give more, but this exceeds my income from all sources together for the last four months."

FEBRUARY 3. Thoreau's father dies at the age of 71. "We **95** partially die ourselves through sympathy at the death of each of our friends or near relatives. Each experience is an assault on our vital force. It becomes a wonder that they who have lost many friends still live." As a result of his father's death, Thoreau has to take over the family's graphite business. It does fairly well.

FEBRUARY 20. "How much the writer lives and endures in coming before the public so often! A few years or books are with him equal to a long life of experience, suffering, etc. It is well if he does not become hardened. He learns how to bear contempt and to despise himself. He makes, as it were, *post-mortem* examinations of himself before he is dead."

FEBRUARY 22–23. Goes to Worcester to lecture.

MARCH 2 and 9. Lectures in Concord.

MARCH 28. "I have not decided whether I had better publish my experience in searching for arrowheads in three volumes with plates and an index, or try to compress it into one." (The book was never done.)

APRIL 3. "Men's minds run so much on work and money that the mass instantly associate all literary labor with a pecuniary reward. They are mainly curious to know how much money the lecturer or author gets for his work. . . . "What do you get for lecturing now?" I am occasionally asked. It is the more amusing since I only lecture about once a year out of my native town, often not at all; so that I might as well, if my objects were merely pecuniary, give up the business."

APRIL 8. "One of the most remarkable sources of profit opened to the Yankee within a year is the traffic in skunk-skins. I learn from the newspapers that 'the traffic in skunk-skins has suddenly become a most important branch of the fur trade, and the skins of an animal which three years ago were deemed of no value

94 *met Mr. [Henry] James.* This is the Henry James, Sr., whom Thoreau had met in New York in May 1843.

95 *Thoreau's father dies.* He coughed and spat a great deal, so it is possible that he too died of tuberculosis. Thoreau took good care of him during his last days.

Thoreau's father (*Courtesy Concord Free Public Library*)

whatever, are now in the greatest demand.' 'The principal markets are Russia and Turkey, though some are sent to Germany, where they are sold at a large profit.' Furs to Russia! 'The black skins are valued the most, and during the past winter the market price has been as high as one dollar per skin, while mottled skins brought only seventy cents.' 'Upward of 50,000 of these skins have been shipped from this city [New York] alone within the past two months.' Many of them 'are designed for the Leipsic sales, Leipsic being next to Novgorod, in Russia, the most important fur *entrepôt* in Europe. The first intimation received in this market of the value of this new description of fur came from the Hudson's Bay Company, which, having shipped a few to London at a venture, found the returns so profitable that they immediately prosecuted the business on an extensive scale.' 'The heaviest collections are made in the Middle and Eastern States, in some parts of which the mania for capturing these animals seems to have equalled the Western Pike's Peak gold excitement, men, women, and children turning out *en masse* for that purpose.' . . .

"When you get to Europe you will meet the most tender-hearted and delicately bred lady, perhaps the President of the Antislavery Society, or of that for the encouragement of humanity to animals, marching or presiding with the scales from a tortoise's back—obtained by laying live coals on it to make them curl up—stuck in her hair, rat-skin fitting as close to her fingers as erst to the rat, and, for her cloak, trimmings perchance adorned with the spoils of a hundred skunks, —rendered inodorous, we trust. Poor misguided woman! Could she not wear other armor in the war of humanity?

"When a new country like North America is discovered, a few feeble efforts are made to Christianize the natives before they are all exterminated, but they are not found to pay, in any sense. But the energetic traders of the discovering country organize themselves, or rather inevitably crystallize, into a vast rat-catching society, tempt the natives to become mere vermin-hunters and rum-drinkers, reserving half a continent for the field of their labors. Savage meets savage, and the white man's only distinction is that he is the chief.

"She says to the turtle basking on the shore of a distant isle, 'I want your scales to adorn my head' (though fire be used to raise them); she whispers to the rats in the wall, 'I want your skins to cover my delicate fingers;' and, meeting an army of a hundred skunks in her morning walk, she says, 'worthless vermin, strip off your cloaks this instant, and let me have them to adorn my robe with;' and she comes home with her hands muffled in the pelt of a gray wolf that ventured abroad to find food for its young that day.

"When the question of the protection of birds comes up, the legislatures regard only a low use and never a high use; the best-disposed legislators employ one, perchance, only to examine their crops and see how many grubs or cherries they contain, and never to study their dispositions, or the beauty of their plumage, or listen and report on the sweetness of their song. The legislature will preserve a bird professedly not because it is a beautiful creature, but because it is a good scavenger or the like. This, at least, is the defense set up. It is as if the question were whether some celebrated singer of the human race—some Jenny Lind or another —did more harm or good, should be destroyed, or not,

and therefore a committee should be appointed, not to listen to her singing at all, but to examine the contents of her stomach and see if she devoured anything which was injurious to the farmers and gardeners, or which they cannot spare."

APRIL 19 to 29. Planting trees for Emerson on his Walden Pond land.

APRIL 24. "There is a season for everything, and we do not notice a given phenomenon except at that season, if, indeed, it can be called the same phenomenon at any other season. There is a time to watch the ripples on Ripple Lake, to look for arrowheads, to study the rocks and lichens, a time to walk on sandy deserts; and the observer of nature must improve these seasons as much as the farmer his. So boys fly kites and play ball or hawkie at particular times all over the State. A wise man will know what game to play to-day, and play it. We must not be governed by rigid rules, as by the almanac, but let the season rule us. The moods and thoughts of man are revolving just as steadily and incessantly as nature's. Nothing must be postponed. Take time by the forelock. Now or never! You must live in the present, launch yourself on every wave, find your eternity in each moment. Fools stand on their island opportunities and look toward another land. There is no other land; there is no other life but this, or the like of this. Where the good husbandman is, there is the good soil. Take any other course, and life will be a succession of regrets. Let us see vessels sailing prosperously before the wind, and not simply stranded barks. There is no world for the penitent and regretful."

APRIL 26–27. Goes to Lynn, Massachusetts, to lecture.

MAY 7–8. John Brown is in Concord. Thoreau had met him in 1857 when he had been in town to visit Sanborn. At that time Sanborn had brought him to the Thoreau house for lunch, and during the afternoon Brown had told Thoreau about his battles with the proslavery forces in Kansas. Later, Brown spoke at the Concord Town Hall to raise money. Now he is to speak again in an effort to get contributions for his work. (See October 19, 1859.)

96

SUMMER. Thoreau is busy surveying the Concord River. His *Journal* is filled with notes on it.

SEPTEMBER 7–9. A militia training muster in Concord.

SEPTEMBER 16. "The hogs are in the parlor. . . . They rained down into these houses by mistake, as it is said to rain toads sometimes. They wear these advantages helter-skelter and without appreciating them, or to satisfy a vulgar taste, just as savages wear the dress of

96 *Sanborn.* Sanborn had more contact with John Brown than anyone else in Concord.

John Brown

civilized men, just as that Indian chief walked the streets of New Orleans clad in nothing but a gaudy military coat which his Great Father had given him. Some philanthropists trust that the houses will civilize the inhabitants at last. The mass of men, just like savages, strive always after the outside, the clothes and finery of civilized life, the blue beads and tinsel and centre-tables. It is a wonder that any load ever gets moved, men are so prone to put the cart before the horse.

"We do everything according to the fashion, just as the Flatheads flatten the heads of their children. We conform ourselves in a myriad ways and with infinite pains to the fashions of our time. We mourn for our lost relatives according to fashion, and as some nations hire professed mourners to howl, so we hire stone-masons to hammer and blast by the month and so express our grief. Or if a public character dies, we get up a regular wake with eating and drinking till midnight."

SEPTEMBER 22. "It would be fit that the tobacco plant should spring up on the house-site, aye on the grave, of almost every householder of Concord. These vile weeds are sown by vile men. When the house is gone they spring up in the corners of cellars where the cider-casks stood always on tap, for murder and all kindred vices will out."

SEPTEMBER 26. "The savage in man is never quite eradicated. I have just read of a family in Vermont who, several of its members having died of consumption, just *burned* the lungs, heart, and liver of the last deceased, in order to prevent any more from having it."

OCTOBER 9. Lectures in Boston at the Music Hall on what was to become "Life Without Principle." It is one of Thoreau's best explanations of his attitude toward life and is very much like *Walden*.

OCTOBER 15. "Each town should have a park, or rather a primitive forest, of five hundred or a thousand acres, where a stick should never be cut for fuel, a common possession forever, for instruction and recreation. We hear of cow-commons and ministerial lots, but we want *men*-commons and lay lots, inalienable forever. Let us keep the New World *new*, preserve all the advantages of living in the country. There is meadow and pasture and wood-lot for the town's poor. Why not a forest and huckleberry-field for the town's rich? All Walden Wood might have been preserved for our park forever, with Walden in its midst, and the Easterbrooks Country, an unoccupied area of some four square miles, might have been our huckleberry-field. If any owners of these

97

97 *"Each town should have a park."* Here, again, Thoreau is a foresighted town planner and conservationist. Communities that heeded his advice when land was cheap—or that set aside parks of their own accord—made enormous gains in capital value, convenience, and recreation facilities for their citizens.

tracts are about to leave the world without natural heirs who need or deserve to be specially remembered, they will do wisely to abandon their possession to all, and not will them to some individual who perhaps has enough already. As some give to Harvard College or another institution, why might not another give a forest or huckleberry-field to Concord? A town is an institution which deserves to be remembered."

OCTOBER 16. John Brown's raid on Harper's Ferry. Thoreau's *Journal* is filled for many weeks afterward with his reactions to it. Much of what he put down (especially on October 22) was incorporated into the speech **98** he made in Concord on October 30 in defense of Brown.

NOVEMBER 1. He speaks in Boston on John Brown.

NOVEMBER 3. And in Worcester.

NOVEMBER 17. "I have been so absorbed of late in Captain Brown's fate as to be surprised whenever I detected the old routine running still,—met persons going about their affairs indifferent. It appeared strange to

98 *speech . . . in Concord on October 30.* This first appeared in a book in *Echoes of Harpers Ferry*, edited by James Redpath, 1860; then in Thoreau's *A Yankee in Canada* in 1866.

Harper's Ferry

me that the little dipper should be still diving in the river as of yore; and this suggestion that this grebe might be diving here when Concord shall be no more. Any affecting human event may blind our eyes to natural objects."

DECEMBER 2. John Brown is hanged at Charles Town, Virginia. Thoreau wants to toll the Concord town bell at the time of his execution but is denied permission. A memorial service is held at which Thoreau reads several poems.

DECEMBER 3. Thoreau is asked to drive a seemingly de-

John Brown and one of his sons lying wounded on the floor of the engine house at Harper's Ferry

John Brown on the scaffold

mented man to the South Acton railroad station so he can take a train from there to Canada. Only later does he discover that this person was Francis Jackson Merriam, one of John Brown's men.

DECEMBER 16. To Cambridge and Boston for books from the libraries there.

DECEMBER 19. "When a man is young and his constitution and body have not acquired firmness, *i. e.*, before he has arrived at middle age, he is not an assured inhabitant of the earth, and his compensation is that he is not quite earthy, there is something peculiarly tender and divine about him. His sentiments and his weakness, nay, his very sickness and the greater uncertainty of his fate, seem to ally him to a noble race of beings, to whom he in part belongs, or with whom he is in communication. The young man is a demigod; the grown man, alas! is commonly a mere mortal. He is but half here, he knows not the men of this world, the powers that be. They know him not. Prompted by the reminiscence of that other sphere from which he so lately arrived, his actions are unintelligible to his seniors. He bathes in light. He is interesting as a stranger from another sphere. He really thinks and talks about a larger sphere of existence than this world. It takes him forty years to accommodate himself to the carapax of this world. This is the age of poetry. Afterward he may be the president of a bank, and go the way of all flesh. But a man of **99** settled views, whose thoughts are few and hardened like his bones, is truly mortal, and his only resource is to say his prayers."

Books published in 1859: Dickens, *A Tale of Two Cities;* FitzGerald, translation of *The Rubaiyat of Omar Khayyam;* Darwin, *The Origin of Species;* Eliot, *Adam Bede;* Tennyson, *Idylls of the King.*

1860

The census of 1860 shows that the population of the United States had increased to 31,443,321, of which 26,922,537 were white, while 3,953,760 were Negro slaves, and 488,070 were free Negroes. It is the decisive year in which Lincoln was elected President. Thoreau was apparently becoming more and more withdrawn from human society. His 1860 *Journal* has very few comments about people and deals almost entirely with the observed phenomena of Nature. His correspondence also is slight. The most important and revealing letter is the one to Daniel Ricketson, written on November 4. Much of Thoreau's time is spent on

99 *the way of all flesh.* John Webster (1580?–1625), *Westward Ho!* II, 3 (1603).

"*After reading Thoreau I felt how much I have lost by leaving nature out of my life.*"
F. SCOTT FITZGERALD
Letter to his daughter,
March 11, 1939

making notes for his never-to-be-published book on the Indians.

JANUARY. He is reading Darwin's recently published *Origin of Species*.   **100**

FEBRUARY 8. He lectures on "Wild Apples" at the Concord Lyceum.   **101**

FEBRUARY 14. And gives the same lecture in Lowell.

APRIL 3. Sanborn is arrested in his Concord home on an   **102** order to appear in Washington before the Senate Committe investigating the John Brown raid on Harper's Ferry. Townspeople, including Thoreau, rescue him.

APRIL 4. Sanborn goes to Boston where he is discharged from arrest by the State Supreme Court. Thoreau speaks briefly at a meeting in Concord's Town Hall during the evening. He says that the officials should have arrested the slave kidnappers instead of Sanborn.

MAY 18. Lincoln is nominated as the Republican candidate   **103** for President.

MAY 20. Letter to H. G. O. Blake (in part):

"Whether he sleeps or wakes, whether he runs or walks, whether he uses a microscope or a telescope, or his naked eye, a man never discovers anything, never overtakes anything or leaves anything behind, but himself. Whatever he says or does he merely reports himself. If he is in love, he *loves;* if he is in heaven he *enjoys,* if he is in hell he *suffers.* It is his condition that determines his locality.

"The principal, the only thing a man makes is his condition, or fate. Though commonly he does not know it, nor put up a sign to this effect, 'My own destiny made & mended here.' [not *yours*] He is a master-workman in this business. He works 24 hours a day at it and gets it done. Whatever else he neglects or botches, no man was ever known to neglect this work. . . .

"Each reaching and aspiration is an instinct with which all nature consists & cooperates, and therefore it is not in vain. But alas! each relaxing and desperation is an instinct too. To be active, well, happy, implies rare courage. To be ready to fight in a duel or a battle implies desperation, or that you hold your life cheap.

"If you take this life to be simply what old religious folks pretend, (I mean the effete, gone to seed in a drought, mere human galls stung by the Devil once), then all your joy & serenity is reduced to grinning and bearing it. The fact is, you have got to take the world on your shoulders like Atlas and put along with it. You will do this for an idea's sake, and your success will be

100 *Origin of Species.* Since this was published in England on November 24, 1859, Thoreau must have been one of the first American readers of a book that was to change man's ideas about his own past.

101 *"Wild Apples."* This became Thoreau's most successful lecture. Its sources are in the *Journals* for 1850–1852 and 1857–1860. It was published in *The Atlantic Monthly* for November 1862 and first appeared in a book in *Excursions* (1863).

102 *Sanborn is arrested.* This was the most violent episode in Concord's antislavery history. A deputy United States marshal and four aides came to the Main Street Sanborn home and entered it. Sanborn resisted fiercely while his sister ran out and summoned help. A crowd quickly gathered and blocked the officers in the house until Judge Samuel Hoar could issue a writ of habeus corpus which demanded the manacled prisoner's release. Once Sanborn was freed, the townspeople chased the arresting officers out of Concord. Thoreau is said to have been in the crowd. (He lived across the street.) The only mention of the affair in the *Journal*, which marches sedately on with observations of field and stream, is the entry on April 4, which says: "Lodged at Sanborn's last night after his *rescue,* he being away."

103 *Lincoln is nominated.* There is no mention in the *Journal* of this crucial event. And the letter to Blake which follows also ignores it.

in proportion to your devotion to ideas. It may make your back ache occasionally, but you will have the satisfaction of hanging it or twirling it to suit yourself. Cowards suffer, heroes enjoy. After a long day's walk with it, pitch it into a hollow place, sit down and eat your luncheon. Unexpectedly, by some immortal thoughts, you will be compensated. The bank whereon you sit will be a fragrant and flowery one, and your world in the hollow a sleek and light gazelle.

"Where is the 'Unexplored land' but in our own untried enterprises? To an adventurous spirit any place, —London, New York, Worcester, or his own yard, is 'unexplored land.' . . . To a sluggish & defeated spirit even the Great Basin & the Polaris are trivial places. If they ever get there (& indeed they are there now) they will want to sleep & give it up, just as they always do. These are the regions of the Known & of the Unknown. What is the use of going right over the old track again? There is an adder in the path which your own feet have worn. You must make tracks into the Unknown. That is what you have your board & clothes for. Why do you ever mend your clothes, unless that, wearing them, you may mend your ways?"

JUNE. The Hawthornes return to Concord.

JULY 7. Thoreau takes the temperature of the springs and other water sources of the Concord area.

JULY 27. Thoreau's "The Last Days of John Brown" is **104** published in *The Liberator*.

AUGUST 4. He starts out for Mount Monadnock with Ellery Channing. After much walking, climbing, and botanizing they return to Concord on August 9.

AUGUST. William Dean Howells comes to Concord where **105** he meets Thoreau and writes about him.

SEPTEMBER 8. To Lowell to lecture there on September 9. He returns to Concord on the tenth.

SEPTEMBER 11. Goes to see a lynx that was shot near Concord. **106**

SEPTEMBER 20. He reads "The Succession of Forest Trees" in the Concord Town Hall while the Middlesex Cattle Show is being held. Walter Harding calls this paper "Thoreau's major contribution to scientific knowledge."

OCTOBER 6. "The Succession of Forest Trees" is published **107** in the New York *Weekly Tribune*. Entries in the *Journal* for this autumn—particularly on October 20— show Thoreau's continuing interest in the subject—and also in determining the age of trees by counting their growth rings. During this period, when the Lincoln election is pending, Thoreau ignores politics and seems to be obsessed with trees.

104 *"The Last Days of John Brown."* This was first printed in a book in *A Yankee in Canada* (1863).

105 *William Dean Howells.* The visit to Concord was published in *Harper's Monthly* for August 1894. Howells was only 23 when he came from Lowell to Concord by stagecoach. He interviewed Hawthorne, Thoreau, and Emerson. None of the encounters was in any way noteworthy, but the one with Thoreau was the worst. The two men sat on chairs on opposite sides of a room in the Yellow House and groped for words. "I was terribly disappointed in the result," said Howells. He tried to get Thoreau to speak about Walden Pond and John Brown, but those two subjects were dearest to Thoreau's heart, and he was not going to open up on them on short acquaintance with a rash young journalist who obviously had not yet learned his business.

106 *a lynx . . . shot near Concord.* In the *Journal* for September 11–13, 1860; XIV, 78–86, Thoreau describes the dead animal in great detail. He was obviously impressed that so large and ferocious a beast could still be found in the well-settled countryside only three miles from the middle of the town. He wrote to Dr. Samuel Kneeland of the Boston Society of Natural History on October 13, 1860, about what he had seen.

107 *"The Succession of Forest Trees."* This first appeared in a book in *Excursions* (1863). It deals with the way that various kinds of trees replace forest growth that has been cut down.

NOVEMBER 4. On this day he writes a long letter to H. G. O. Blake about their mountain exploration and a short—and rather short-tempered one—to Daniel **108** Ricketson. Here are the more pertinent parts of it:

"You know that I never promised to correspond with you, & so, when I do, I do more than I promised.

"Such are my pursuits and habits that I rarely go abroad, and it is quite a habit with me to decline invitations to do so. Not that I could not enjoy such visits, if I were not otherwise occupied. I have enjoyed very much my visits to you and my rides in your neighborhood, and am sorry that I cannot enjoy such things oftener; but life is short, and there are other things also to be done. I admit that you are more social than I am, and far more attentive to 'the common courtesies of life' but this is partly for the reason that you have fewer or less exacting private pursuits.

"Not to have written a note for a year is with me a very venial offence. I think that I do not correspond with any one so often as once in six-months.

"I have a faint recollection of your invitation referred to, but I suppose that I have no new nor particular reason for declining & so made no new statements. I have felt that you would be glad to see me almost whenever I got ready to come, but I only offer myself as a rare visitor, & a still rarer correspondent.

"I am very busy, after my fashion, little as there is to show for it, and feel as if I could not spend many days nor dollars in travelling, for the shortest visit must have a fair margin to it, and the days thus affect the weeks, you know. Nevertheless, we cannot forego these luxuries altogether.

"You must not regard me as a regular diet, but at most only as acorns, which too are not to be despised, which, at least, we love to think are edible in a bracing walk. We have got along pretty well together in several directions, though we are such strangers in others."

NOVEMBER 6. Abraham Lincoln is elected a minority President of the United States—which are not to remain united for long. The stock market promptly goes down.

DECEMBER 3. While counting growth rings on tree stumps Thoreau catches a severe cold which develops into "a kind of bronchitis."

DECEMBER 11. Although he is in no condition to travel, Thoreau insists on going to Waterbury, Connecticut, to keep a lecture date. As a result he is confined to the **109** house for the winter except for occasional short trips into town.

108 *Daniel Ricketson.* In this letter Thoreau insists that he is a poor correspondent. But the volume containing his letters—and some written to him—runs to more than 600 pages. Many of his letters have been lost, and the earliest known one was written when he was 18 years old. It is difficult to understand what caused the rather unpleasant tone of this letter. Toward the end of it Thoreau relented and even wrote a pun, at the bottom of the next to the last page where he said "Turn over a new leaf." And the letter ends on a cordial note: "Please remember me to your family. I have a very pleasant recollection of your fireside, and trust that I shall revisit it—also of your shanty & the surrounding regions."

109 *to keep a lecture date.* He had made the date some time after September 22 when he wrote to the Waterbury Lyceum offering to speak there. The topic was "Autumnal Tints," which was published in *The Atlantic Monthly* for October, 1862, and in *Excursions* in 1863.

DECEMBER 20. South Carolina secedes from the Union.

Books published in 1860: Collins, *Woman in White;* Dickens, *Great Expectations;* Hawthorne, *The Marble Faun.*

1861

JANUARY 3. "How few ever get beyond feeding, clothing, **110** sheltering, and warming themselves in this world, and begin to treat themselves as human beings,—as intellectual and moral beings! Most seem not to see any further,—not to see over the ridge-pole of their barns,—or to be exhausted and accomplish nothing more than a full barn, though it may be accompanied by an empty head. They venture a little, run some risks, when it is a question of a larger crop of corn or potatoes; but they are commonly timid and count their coppers, when the question is whether their children shall be educated. He who has the reputation of being the thriftiest farmer and making the best bargains is really the most thriftless and makes the worst. It is safest to invest in knowledge, for the probability is that you can carry that with you wherever you go.

"But most men, it seems to me, do not care for Nature and would sell their share in all her beauty, as long as they may live, for a stated sum—many for a glass of rum. Thank God, men cannot as yet fly, and lay waste the sky as well as the earth! We are safe on that side for the present. It is for the very reason that some do not care for those things that we need to continue to protect all from the vandalism of a few.

"We cut down the few old oaks which witnessed the transfer of the township from the Indian to the white man, and commence our museum with a cartridge-box taken from a British soldier in 1775!

"He pauses at the end of his four or five thousand dollars, and then only fears that he has not got enough to carry him through,—that is, merely to pay for what he will eat and wear and burn and for his lodging for the rest of his life. But, pray, what does he stay here for? Suicide would be cheaper. Indeed, it would be nobler to found some good institution with the money and then cut your throat. If such is the whole upshot of their living, I think that it would be most profitable for all such to be carried or put through by being discharged from the mouth of a cannon as fast as they attained to years of such discretion.

"As boys are sometimes required to show an excuse for being absent from school, so it seems to me that men should show some excuse for being here."

110 *January 3* Journal *entry.* Here a sick and dying man makes a plea for the preservation of our natural scenery.

JANUARY–MAY. One by one the Southern states secede.

JANUARY 5. Senators from seven Southern states meet secretly in the Capitol and decide to hold a convention in Montgomery, Alabama.

FEBRUARY 4. The provisional government of the Confederate States of America is founded at the Montgomery, Alabama, convention. On February 8, Jefferson Davis is elected its president.

MARCH 4. Lincoln is inaugurated as President of the United States. On this day Thoreau says that he is "impatient with the politicians, the state of the country, the State itself, and with statesmen generally."

APRIL 10. Letter to Parker Pillsbury (in part):   **111**

"As for my prospective reader, I hope that he *ignores* Fort Sumpter [*sic*], & Old Abe, & all that, for that is just the most fatal and indeed the only fatal, weapon you can direct against evil ever; for as long as you *know* of it, you are *particeps criminis*. What business have you, if you are 'an angel of light,' to be pondering over the deeds of darkness, reading the New York Herald, & the like? I do not so much regret the present condition of things in this country (provided I regret it at all) as I do that I ever heard of it. I know one or 2 who have this year, for the first time, read a president's message; but they do not see that this implies a fall in themselves, rather than a rise in the president. Blessed were the days before you read a president's message. Blessed are the young for they do not read the president's message.

"Blessed are they who never read a newspaper, for they shall see Nature, and through her, God.

"But alas *I* have heard of Sumpter, & Pickens, & even of Buchanan, (though I did not read his message).

"I also read the New York Tribune, but then I am reading Herodotus & Strabo, & Blodget's Climatology, and Six Years in the Deserts of North America, as hard as I can, to counterbalance it."

APRIL 12. The Confederates fire on Fort Sumter in Charleston harbor, and the Civil War begins.

APRIL. The bronchitis, which Thoreau thinks is all he has, is really tuberculosis.

MAY 11. In company with the young naturalist, Horace Mann, Thoreau goes to Minnesota in search of a better   **112** climate for his rapidly failing health. They stop off at Niagara Falls, Detroit, Chicago, St. Paul, and go 300 miles up the Minnesota River to Redwood to see the Indian ceremonies being held there. Thoreau's health

111 *to Parker Pillsbury*. An antislavery speaker who had boarded at the Thoreau house in December 1857. This snarling remark about the coming war and Abraham Lincoln is one of the few that Thoreau ever made about the subject. But Channing wrote (1873, page 8) that Thoreau "used to say he 'could never recover while the war lasted.'"

112 *Thoreau goes to Minnesota. The First and Last Journeys of Thoreau,* edited by F. B. Sanborn and published in 1905 in a limited deluxe edition, gives some of the details of this trip.

Fort Sumter as it looked after the bombardment

is worse; they start home and arrive in Concord on July 10.

JUNE 25. To Sanborn: "I have seen but one eastern paper (that, by the way, *was* the Tribune) for 5 weeks. I have not taken much pains to get them; but, necessarily, I have not seen any paper at all for more than a week at a time. The people of Minnesota have *seemed* to me more cold—to feel less implicated in this war, than the people of Massachusetts. It is apparent that Massachusetts, for one state at least, is doing much more than her share, in carrying it on. However, I have dealt partly with those of southern birth, & have seen but little way beneath the surface. I was glad to be told yesterday that there was a good deal of weeping here at Redwing the other day, when the volunteers stationed at Fort Snelling followed the regulars to the seat of the war. They do not weep when their children go *up* the river to occupy the deserted forts, though they *may* have to fight the Indians there."

JULY 21. The first battle of Bull Run is a defeat for the Union troops.

AUGUST 15. To Daniel Ricketson: "My cough [is] still continuing. If I do not mend very quickly I shall be

Horace Mann, Jr.
(Courtesy Concord Free Public Library)

Minnesota Indian country

obliged to go to another climate very soon. My ordinary pursuits, both indoor and out, have been for the most part omitted, or seriously interrupted—walking, boating, scribbling, &. Indeed I have been sick so long that I have almost forgotten what it is to be well. . . ." **113**

AUGUST 19. He goes to New Bedford to visit with Ricketson for five days. Ricketson notes that "he has a bad cough and expectorates a good deal, is emaciated considerably, his spirits, however, appear as good as usual, his appetite good. . . ." E. S. Dunshee makes a photograph of him, the last ever to be taken.

SEPTEMBER (late). Thoreau makes his last visit to Walden Pond.

OCTOBER 14. Thoreau's last letter to Daniel Ricketson: "I take a ride in a wagon about every other day. My neighbor, Mr. Hoar, has two horses . . . and generously **114** offered me the use of one of them, and, as I notice, the dog throws himself in, and does scouting duty. . . . It is easy to talk, but hard to write."

113 *go to another climate.* According to Ricketson, this was to a warm climate, probably the West Indies, which an invalid could easily reach by ship from Boston. It would have been a far simpler way to travel than the overland journey to Minnesota.

114 *Mr. Hoar.* Samual Hoar, the well-to-do senator and judge, father of Edward Hoar.

The Dunshee ambrotype
portrait of Thoreau

(Courtesy Concord Free Public Library)

NOVEMBER 3. He makes the last entry in his *Journal*.   **115**

DECEMBER. During the middle of this month he has pleurisy but recovers from it.

Books published in 1861: Eliot, *Silas Marner;* Holmes, *Elsie Venner;* Palgrave, *The Golden Treasury;* Reade, *The Cloister and the Hearth;* Wood, *East Lynne.*

1862

JANUARY 7. Bronson Alcott to Daniel Ricketson: "He [Thoreau] grows feebler day by day, and is evidently failing and fading from our sight. He gets some sleep, has a pretty good appetite, reads at intervals, takes notes of his readings, and likes to see his friends, conversing, however, with difficulty, as his voice partakes of his general debility."

FEBRUARY. *The Atlantic Monthly*, under its new editor, James T. Fields, asks Thoreau for some of his work. Thoreau replies on February 11, asking what the magazine will pay for his lecture-articles. He adds: "I should expect that no sentiment or sentence be altered or   **116** omitted without my consent, and to retain the copyright of the paper after you had used it. . . ." He then goes to work with the help of his sister, Sophia, to get several articles ready for publication. She has to do most of the actual handwriting from now on.

FEBRUARY 20. He sends "Autumnal Tints" to the *Atlantic*. They pay him $100 for it.

FEBRUARY 24. He writes to Ticknor and Fields, who had published *Walden*, asking whether they would take over the 146 bound copies and 450 in sheets which he has of *A Week on the Concord and Merrimack Rivers*. He also says that they had spoken of reissuing *Walden*. He would "be happy to make an arrangement . . . to that effect."

FEBRUARY 28. He sends an article to the *Atlantic* which publishes it under the title "Life Without Principle."

MARCH 4. Letter to Ticknor and Fields: "I shall be happy to have you print 250 copies of *Walden*. . . . I wish to make one alteration in the new edition viz, to   **117** leave out from the title the words 'Or Life in the Woods.' "

MARCH 9. The battle between the *Monitor* and the *Merrimack* at Hampton Roads, Virginia.

MARCH 11. Thoreau sends his article on "Walking" to the *Atlantic*.

MARCH 21. To Myron Benton: "I *suppose* that I have not

115 *the last entry in his* Journal. After an amusing description of the way newborn kittens behave, Thoreau put down the date and then wrote briefly about the stratifications of gravel in the railroad causeway after a violent easterly storm had passed through Concord.

116 *no . . . sentence be altered or omitted without my consent.* The memory of the way the *Atlantic* had changed copy in 1858 when Lowell was its editor was still foremost in Thoreau's mind even though he knew he had only a short time left to live.

117 *to leave out from the title.* Although Thoreau's instructions to his publisher about omitting the subtitle are specific, the unwanted phrase soon crept back in, notably in Houghton Mifflin's Riverside Edition of 1893, which was used as a basic text after the copyright expired in 1910.

The battle between the *Monitor* and the *Merrimack*

many months to live; but, of course, I know nothing about it. I may add that I am enjoying existence as much as ever, and regret nothing."

MARCH 23. Sam Staples, who had been Thoreau's jailer in 1846, visits him and tells Emerson that he had "never spent an hour with more satisfaction. Never saw a man dying with so much pleasure and peace."

About this time one of his aunts asks Thoreau if he has made his peace with God. "I did not know that we had ever quarreled," he tells her.

APRIL. Sophia to Ellery Channing: "No shadow of gloom attaches to anything connected with my precious brother. His whole life impresses me as a grand miracle. I always thought him the most upright man I ever knew; and now it is a pleasure to praise him."

APRIL 2. He sends his article on "Wild Apples" to the *Atlantic*, which publishes it in November 1862.

APRIL 6. The Battle of Shiloh.

APRIL 12. James T. Fields comes to Concord to see Thoreau and takes all the unsold copies of *A Week*.

APRIL 25. Farragut's fleet captures New Orleans. The Peninsular Campaign to take Richmond gets under way.

MAY 6. Thoreau dies at 9 A. M. His last words are: "Moose". . . and "Indian."

MAY 9. The funeral ceremonies are held in Concord's **118** First Parish Church at 3 P.M. Emerson reads the eulogy.

118 *The funeral ceremonies.* Channing wrote three quotations which were placed in the coffin. They were:

"Hail to thee, O man, who art come from the transitory place to the imperishable." (Unidentified)

"Gazed on the heavens for what he missed on earth." From "The Shepherd's Pipe" by William Browne (1591–1643).

"I think for to touch also
The world which neweth everie daie,
So as I can, so as I maie." From the Prologue to *Confessio Amantis* by John Gower (1330?–1408).

Thoreau was interred in the New Burying Ground; his remains were transferred some time before 1874 to their present site on a ridge in Sleepy Hollow Cemetery where a small stone marked "Henry" is only a few feet from a larger one for the Thoreau family. The graves of Emerson, Hawthorne, Channing, and Alcott are there too.

The yellow house where Thoreau died

The Thoreau grave plot in Concord's Sleepy Hollow Cemetery

WEDNESDAY, JULY 12, 1967
11:00 A.M.
THE FIRST PARISH IN CONCORD
Concord, Massachusetts

PROGRAM

MUSIC

Presiding	G. Russell Ready, English Department
	Eastern Ontario Institute of Technology
	President, Thoreau Society
The National Anthem	
Invocation	Rev. Arthur B. Jellis, Minister
	The First Parish in Concord
Welcome	William O. Faxon, Chairman
	Concord Board of Selectmen
Introduction of Guests	
Readings from Thoreau	Sidney C. Clark, Chairman
	English Department
	Avon Old Farms School
Flute Solo	Harry C. Gatos
Address	Honorable Richard J. Murphy
	Assistant Postmaster General of
	The United States of America
Benediction	Rt. Rev. John A. York, Pastor
	St. Bernard's Church

MUSIC

Program for the celebration of the 150th anniversary of Thoreau's birth

II

WALDEN

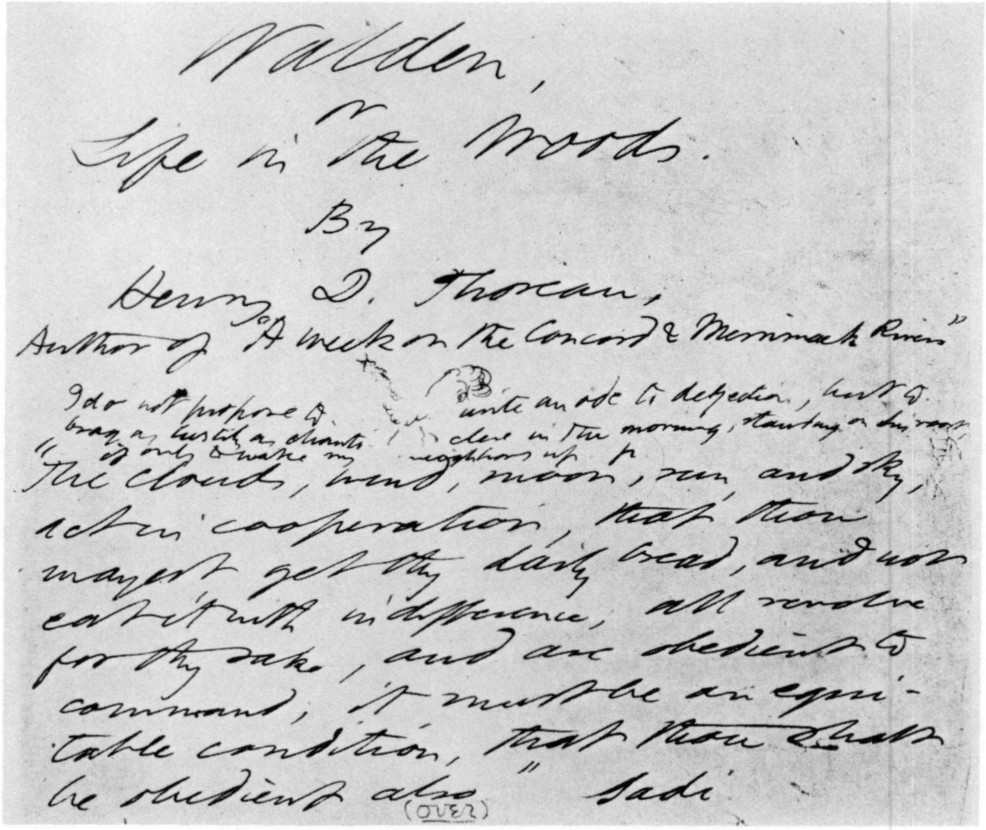

Walden,

Life in the Woods.

By

Henry D. Thoreau,

Author of "A Week on the Concord & Merrimack Rivers"

I do not propose to ... write an ode to dejection, but to
brag as lustily as chanticleer ... clear in the morning, standing on his roost,
if only to wake my neighbors up to ...

"The clouds, wind, moon, sun, and sky,
act in cooperation, that thou
mayest get thy daily bread, and not
eat it with indifference, all revolve
for thy sake, and are obedient to
command; it must be an equi-
table condition, that thou shalt
be obedient also." Sadi
(OVER)

Thoreau's draft for the title page of *Walden*

WALDEN;

OR,

LIFE IN THE WOODS.

BY HENRY D. THOREAU,

AUTHOR OF "A WEEK ON THE CONCORD AND MERRIMACK RIVERS."

I do not propose to write an ode to dejection, but to brag as lustily as chanticleer in the morning, standing on his roost, if only to wake my neighbors up. — Page 92.

BOSTON:
TICKNOR AND FIELDS.
M DCCC LIV.

The text that follows is a photographic copy of the first edition. References to manuscript pages are to those stamped on the back of the Xerox copy of HM934 in the Huntington Library.

Listings of books by authors' names and dates refer to the Bibliography which starts on page 483.

Abbreviations: NED is the 13-volume *Oxford New English Dictionary* (1933); Webster is the Merriam-Webster *New International Dictionary*, Second Edition (1934).

The evolution of the copy for the title page of *Walden* can be traced in the manuscript. At the top of ms. 61, where the first page of text begins, these pencil-written words are crammed in as if by afterthought:

> Walden or Life in
> the woods by Henry Thoreau
> Addressed to my Townsmen.
> Where I have been
> There was none seen

More complete title page copy appears on ms. 1147. Thoreau's little drawing is supposed to represent Chanticleer crowing. For comment on the woodcut of the cabin see the chapter "The Cabin and Walden Pond."

The words written in Thoreau's hand on this projected title page read:

> "I do not propose to write an ode to dejection, but to brag as lustily as Chanticleer in the morning, standing on his roost, if only to wake my neighbors up."

Then came this quotation, which was omitted from the printed book:

> "The clouds, wind, moon, sun and sky act in cooperation that thou mayest get thy daily bread, and not eat it with indifference; all revolve for thy sake, and are obedient to command; it must be an equitable condition, that thou shalt be obedient also."
>
> —SADI

CONTENTS.

---

(3)

The Table of Contents page of the first edition of *Walden*

Like the copy for the title page, both the wording and the order of the contents underwent a gradual evolution. An early draft (ms. 1148) reads:

Economy.
Where I lived and What I lived for.
Reading.
Sounds.
Solitude.
     Preface. [in another hand] Note.
Visitors.
* Beans. [rewritten as The Bean-Field]
The Village
The Ponds.
Baker Farm
* Animal Food [canceled and replaced by Higher Laws]
* Animals [canceled and replaced by Brute Neighbors]
House-warming
** Winter Animals.
** Former Inhabitants & Winter Visitors.
The Pond in Winter.
`Spring.
Conclusion.

It will be noticed that three chapters have had their titles changed (marked *) and that two have been reversed in order (**).

In the middle of this ms. page, between "Visitors" and "The Bean-Field," the following paragraph appears:

"Nearly all of this volume was written eight or nine years ago in the scenery and under the circumstances which it describes, and a considerable part was then read at the time as lectures before the Concord Lyceum. In what is now added the object has been chiefly to make it a completer and truer account of that portion of the author's life."

The Copyright page of the first edition of *Walden*

ECONOMY.

WHEN I wrote the following pages, or rather the bulk of them, I lived alone, in the woods, a mile from any neighbor, in a house which I had built myself, on the shore of Walden Pond, in Concord, Massachusetts, and earned my living by the labor of my hands only. I lived there two years and two months. At present I am a sojourner in civilized life again.

I should not obtrude my affairs so much on the notice of my readers if very particular inquiries had not been made by my townsmen concerning my mode of life, which some would call impertinent, though they do not appear to me at all impertinent, but, considering the circumstances, very natural and pertinent. Some have asked what I got to eat; if I did not feel lonesome; if I was not afraid; and the like. Others have been curious to learn what portion of my income I devoted to charitable purposes; and some, who have large families, how many poor children I maintained. I will therefore ask those of my readers who feel no particular interest in me to pardon me if I undertake to answer some of these questions in this book. In most books, the *I*, or first person, is omitted; in this it will be retained; that, in respect to egotism, is the main difference. We commonly do not remember that it is, after all, always the first person that is speaking. I should not talk so much about myself if there were any body else whom I knew as well. Unfortunately, I am confined to this theme by the narrowness of my experience. Moreover, I, on my side, require of every writer, first or last, a simple and sincere account of his own life, and not merely what he has heard of other men's lives; some such account as he would send to his kindred from a distant land; for if he has lived sincerely, it must have been in a distant land to me. Perhaps these pages are more particularly addressed to

1

2

3

4

5

6

7

1 The first paragraph is a later addition. It is not in the first draft of the manuscript. Nor is there any chapter title there—or anywhere in the first version.

2 *two years and two months*. Actually two years, two months, and two days—from July 4, 1845 to September 6, 1847.

3 *I should not obtrude my affairs*. The first version of *Walden* began here, and was worded *I should not presume to talk so much about my affairs as I shall in this lecture*.

4 *how many poor children I maintained*. In the first version this is followed by: "Some have not come to my house because I lived *there*. Others have come because I *lived* there—and others again, because *I* lived there."

"After I lectured here last winter [this probably refers to the Carlyle lecture on February 4, 1846], I heard that some had expected that I would answer some of these questions in my lecture" (ms. 62).

5 *the I . . . will be retained*. Although *Walden* is not as autobiographical as most of its readers would like it to be, Thoreau used so many capital I's that the printer sometimes ran out of them. Pages 259 to 261 of the page proofs are peppered with the black marks of type turned upside down to draw attention to the missing I's. This was then a common practice. When the hand compositor exhausted his supply of any one character, "he turns for sorts—that is, he uses a type corresponding in thickness to the proper one and turns its face to the bottom of his stick so . . . the foot will be printed in proof." *American Encyclopaedia of Printing*, edited by J. Luther Ringwalt, Philadelphia, 1871. The word index to *Walden* compiled by Sherwin and Reynolds (1960) says that there are 1,811 I's in the text.

6 *require of every writer*. This was "require of a writer or lecturer" on ms. 309 (version B).

poor students.   As for the rest of my readers, they will accept such portions as apply to them.   I trust that none will stretch the seams in putting on the coat, for it may do good service to him whom it fits.

I would fain say something, not so much concerning the Chinese and Sandwich Islanders as you who read **8** these pages, who are said to live in New England; something about your condition, especially your outward condition or circumstances in this world, in this town, what it is, whether it is necessary that it be as bad as it is, whether it cannot be improved as well as not.   I **9** have travelled a good deal in Concord; and every where, in shops, and offices, and fields, the inhabitants have appeared to me to be doing penance in a thousand remarkable ways.   What I have heard of Bramins **10** sitting exposed to four fires and looking in the face of the sun; or hanging suspended, with their heads downward, over flames; or looking at the heavens over their shoulders "until it becomes impossible for them to resume their natural position, while from the twist of the neck nothing but liquids can pass into the stomach;" or dwelling, chained for life, at the foot of a tree; or measuring with their bodies, like caterpillars, the breadth of vast empires; or standing on one leg on the tops of pillars, — even these forms of conscious penance are hardly more incredible and astonishing than the scenes which I daily witness.   The twelve labors of Hercules were trifling in comparison with those which my neighbors have undertaken; for they were only twelve, and had an end; but I could never see that these men slew

Five of the twelve labors of Hercules

7 *in a distant land to me.* A large block of copy was eliminated here. Sanborn printed it in the Bibliophile Edition (I, 3–4):

"—describing even his outward circumstances and what adventures he has had, as well as his thoughts and feelings about them. That he give me that which is most precious to him; not his life's blood, but even that for which his life's blood circulated,—what he has got by living. If anything has yielded him pleasure or instruction let him communicate it. Let the money-getter, when he takes up the pen, tell us how much he loves wealth, and what means he takes to accumulate it. He must describe those facts which he knows, better than anybody else. *He* should not write on Foreign Missions. The mechanic will naturally write about his trade, the farmer about his farm, and every man about that which he understands better than others; that is, his own affairs.

"Yet incredible mistakes are made. As if an owl were to lecture with a perverse show of learning on the solar microscope, or chanticleer on nebulous stars, when both should be sound asleep; the one in a hollow tree, the other upon his roost!"

8 *Sandwich Islanders.* Hawaiians were called that then. Captain James Cook, who discovered the islands in 1778, named them after his patron, the Earl of Sandwich. *Journal,* 1845; I, 395.

9 *I have travelled a good deal in Concord.* This famous passage—and much that follows—appears in its original state in the *Journal,* 1845–1847; I, 426 ff., where it is in this form:

"I have travelled some in New England, especially in Concord, and I found that no enterprise was on foot which it would not disgrace a man to take part in. They seemed to be employed everywhere in shops and offices and fields. They seemed, like the Brahmins of the East, to be doing penance in a thousand curious, unheard-of ways, their endurance surpassing anything I had ever seen or heard of,—Simeon Stylites, Brahmins looking in the face of the sun, standing on one leg, dwelling at the roots of trees, nothing to it; any of the twelve labors of Hercules to be matched,—the Nemean lion, Lernæan hydra, Œnœan stag, Erymanthian boar, Augean stables, Stymphalian birds, Cretan bull, Diomedes' mares, Amazonian girdle, monster Geryon, Hesperian apples, three-headed Cerberus, nothing at all in comparison, being only twelve and having an end. For I could never see that these men ever slew or captured any of their monsters, or finished any of their labors. They have no 'friend Iolaus to burn, with a hot iron, the root' of the hydra's head; for as soon as one head is crushed, two spring up.

"Men labor under a mistake; they are laying up treasures which moth and rust will corrupt and

OMVLVSETREMVLVSALVPANVTRITI~

Romulus and Remus as depicted
in a medieval manuscript

or captured any monster or finished any labor. They **11**
have no friend Iolas to burn with a hot iron the root of
the hydra's head, but as soon as one head is crushed,
two spring up.

I see young men, my townsmen, whose misfortune it **12**
is to have inherited farms, houses, barns, cattle, and
farming tools; for these are more easily acquired than
got rid of. Better if they had been born in the open
pasture and suckled by a wolf, that they might have **13**
seen with clearer eyes what field they were called to
labor in. Who made them serfs of the soil? Why
should they eat their sixty acres, when man is condemned to eat only his peck of dirt? Why should
they begin digging their graves as soon as they are
born? They have got to live a man's life, pushing all
these things before them, and get on as well as they can.
How many a poor immortal soul have I met well nigh
crushed and smothered under its load, creeping down
the road of life, pushing before it a barn seventy-five
feet by forty, its Augean stables never cleansed, and one **14**
hundred acres of land, tillage, mowing, pasture, and
wood-lot! The portionless, who struggle with no such
unnecessary inherited encumbrances, find it labor enough
to subdue and cultivate a few cubic feet of flesh.

But men labor under a mistake. The better part of **15**
the man is soon ploughed into the soil for compost. By a
seeming fate, commonly called necessity, they are employed, as it says in an old book, laying up treasures **16**
which moth and rust will corrupt and thieves break

thieves break through and steal. Northern Slavery,
or the slavery which includes the Southern, Eastern, Western, and all others."

For Thoreau's extensive reading about travel see
John A. Christie's *Thoreau as a World Traveler*
(1965).

10 *Bramins.* The Brahmins are high-caste Hindus
who subjected themselves to self-torture as a religious act. This passage was heavily revised on
ms. 62.

11 *They have no friend Iolas.* Hercules' servant,
Iolaus (as it is spelled in the *Journal* for 1845–
1847; I, 427), helped with the burning of the severed heads. The ninth one was indestructible, so
they buried it deep under a big stone.

12 *I see young men. Journal,* 1845–1847; I, 428:
"I see young men, my equals, who have inherited from their spiritual father a soul,—broad, fertile, uncultivated,—from their earthly father a
farm,—with cattle and barns and farming tools,
the implements of the picklock and the counter-
feiter. Better if they had been born in the open
pasture and suckled by a wolf, or perhaps cradled
in a manger, that they might have seen with clear
eye what was the field they were called to labor
in. The young man has got to live a man's life,
then, in this world, pushing all these things before
him, and get on as well as he can. How many a
poor immortal soul I have met, well-nigh crushed
and smothered, creeping slowly down the road of
life, pushing before it a barn seventy-five by forty
feet and one hundred acres of land,—tillage, pasture, wood-lot! This dull, opaque garment of the
flesh is load enough for the strongest spirit, but
with such an earthly garment superadded the spiritual life is soon plowed into the soil for compost.
It's a fool's life, as they will all find when they
get to the end of it. The man that goes on accumulating property when the bare necessaries of
life are cared for is a fool and knows better."

13 *suckled by a wolf.* Romulus and Remus, the
legendary founders of Rome, were supposed to
have been abandoned as infants but were mothered
by a she-wolf.

14 *its Augean stables.* The fifth labor of Hercules was to clean the huge Augean stables in one
day. He did this by diverting the courses of two
rivers and directing their water through the filth-
laden buildings.

15 *But men labor under a mistake.* This also appears in the *Journal,* 1845–1847; I, 427, where it
leads into the remarks about Negro slavery
printed a few paragraphs below.

On the back of ms. 65 Thoreau wrote:

Sir Walter Raleigh

through and steal. It is a fool's life, as they will find when they get to the end of it, if not before. It is said that Deucalion and Pyrrha created men by throwing **17** stones over their heads behind them : —

> Inde genus durum sumus, experiensque laborum,
> Et documenta damus quâ simus origine nati.

Or, as Raleigh rhymes it in his sonorous way, —

> " From thence our kind hard-hearted is, enduring pain and care,
> Approving that our bodies of a stony nature are."

So much for a blind obedience to a blundering oracle, throwing the stones over their heads behind them, and not seeing where they fell.

Most men, even in this comparatively free country, **18** through mere ignorance and mistake, are so occupied with the factitious cares and superfluously coarse labors of life that its finer fruits cannot be plucked by them. Their fingers, from excessive toil, are too clumsy and **19** tremble too much for that. Actually, the laboring man has not leisure for a true integrity day by day; he cannot afford to sustain the manliest relations to men; his labor would be depreciated in the market. He has no time to be any thing but a machine. How can he remember well his ignorance — which his growth requires — who has so often to use his knowledge? We should feed and clothe him gratuitously sometimes, and recruit him with our cordials, before we judge of him. The finest qualities of our nature, like the bloom on **20** fruits, can be preserved only by the most delicate handling. Yet we do not treat ourselves nor one another thus tenderly.

Some of you, we all know, are poor, find it hard to **21**

"To show how little men have considered what is the true end of life, or the nature of their living which they have to get, I need only remind you how many have, within the last month, started for California with the muck-rake on their shoulders. According to the precepts of the received catechism,—as if our life were a farce, and God had cast down one of his handfuls of true believing on to the mountains of California, for men to scramble for."

This was probably added later, for gold was not discovered in California until January 24, 1848, and the rush to go there did not get under way for some time.

16 *an old book.* The Bible. "Moth and rust, etc.," is a paraphrase of Matthew 6:19, as Ellery Channing points out in his copy of *Walden.* "Lay not up for yourselves treasures upon earth, where moth and rust doth corrupt, and where thieves break through and steal."

17 *Deucalion and Pyrrha.* These are the Noah and his wife in a Greek version of the biblical— and Sumerian—myth of a great deluge. They, however, survived the flood in a wooden chest instead of an ark. The two survivors had no animals but were completely alone in a desolate world. There they heard a voice say: "Cover your heads and cast the bones of your mother behind you." Deucalion realized that the earth was his mother and that her bones were rocks and stones. Those which he threw became men, while his wife's became women. Between them, they repopulated the earth. Cf. the story of Cadmus and the dragon's teeth which turned into armed warriors. The Latin quotation is from Ovid's *Metamorphoses* (Delphine Edition, I, 414–415).

The passage about Deucalion and Pyrrha, as it appeared in the manuscript, originally read:

"It is said that Deucalion and Pyrrha created men by throwing stones over their heads behind them. But that was not the best way to create men, nor the best material to create them out of. They might at least have seen where they threw the stones. But perhaps they did not rightly interpret the oracle which directed them to cast behind them the bones of their grandmother,—by which it may have meant the institutions of the dead. At any rate, men must be *re*-created after a different fashion. So much for a blind obedience to a blundering oracle."

Raleigh is Sir Walter Raleigh, about whom Thoreau had lectured in Concord on February 8, 1842. The translation is from Raleigh's *The History of the World,* 1614, page 30.

live, are sometimes, as it were, gasping for breath. I have no doubt that some of you who read this book are unable to pay for all the dinners which you have actually eaten, or for the coats and shoes which are fast wearing or are already worn out, and have come to this page to spend borrowed or stolen time, robbing your creditors of an hour. It is very evident what mean and sneaking lives many of you live, for my sight has been whetted by experience; always on the limits, trying to get **22** into business and trying to get out of debt, a very an- **23** cient slough, called by the Latins *æs alienum*, another's brass, for some of their coins were made of brass; still living, and dying, and buried by this other's brass; always promising to pay, promising to pay, to-morrow, and dying to-day, insolvent; seeking to curry favor, to get custom, by how many modes, only not state-prison offences; lying, flattering, voting, contracting yourselves **24** into a nutshell of civility, or dilating into an atmosphere of thin and vaporous generosity, that you may persuade your neighbor to let you make his shoes, or his hat, or his coat, or his carriage, or import his groceries for him; making yourselves sick, that you may lay up something against a sick day, something to be tucked away in an old chest, or in a stocking behind the plastering, or, more safely, in the brick bank; no matter where, no matter how much or how little.

I sometimes wonder that we can be so frivolous, I may almost say, as to attend to the gross but somewhat foreign form of servitude called Negro Slavery, there are so many keen and subtle masters that enslave both north and south. It is hard to have a southern over- **25** seer; it is worse to have a northern one; but worst of all when you are the slave-driver of yourself. Talk of a **26** divinity in man! Look at the teamster on the highway, wending to market by day or night; does any **27** divinity stir within him? His highest duty to fodder and water his horses! What is his destiny to him compared with the shipping interests? Does not he drive for Squire Make-a-stir? How godlike, how immortal, is he? See how he cowers and sneaks, how vaguely all the day he fears, not being immortal nor divine, but the slave and prisoner of his own opinion of himself, a fame won by his own deeds. Public opinion is a weak **28** tyrant compared with our own private opinion. What a man thinks of himself, that it is which determines, or

18 *even in this comparatively free country*. This phrase was inserted on ms. 311. So was the word "superfluously," which is two lines below.

19 *Their fingers*, etc. This sentence was inserted on the same ms. page.

20 *like the bloom on fruits*. Originally "are as difficult to preserve as the down on the peach."

21 *Some of you . . . are poor*. The origin of this passage is in the *Journal*, December 23, 1845; I, 395):

"It is generally admitted that some of you are poor, find it hard to get a living, haven't always something in your pockets, haven't paid for all the dinners you've actually eaten, or all your coats and shoes, some of which are already worn out. All this is very well known to all by hearsay and by experience. It is very evident what a mean and sneaking life you live, always in the hampers, always on the limits, trying to get into business and trying to get out of debt, a very ancient slough, called by the Latins *aes alienum*, another's brass,— some of their coins being made of brass,—and still so many living and dying and buried to-day by another's brass; always promising to pay, promising to pay, with interest, to-morrow perhaps, and die to-day, insolvent; seeking to curry favor, to get custom, lying, flattering, voting, contracting yourselves into a nutshell of civility or dilating into a world of thin and vaporous generosity, that you may persuade your neighbor to let you make his [shoes, or his hat, or his coat, or his carriage]."

22 *always on the limits*. The NED defines limit as "the amount up to which a particular customer of a bank is not permitted to overdraw," but Sanborn (Bibliophile Edition, I, 58n.) says that it is "the jail limits for imprisoned debtors."

23 *a very ancient slough*. In Bunyan's *Pilgrim's Progress* (1678), the Slough of Despond is a mire in which insolvent debtors were immersed.

24 *contracting yourselves into a nutshell*. This perhaps refers to Hamlet's "I could be bounded in a nutshell" (II, ii, 260), but may merely be concerned with the compactness with which the meat of a nut is fitted into its shell container. Thoreau was very familiar with all kinds of edible wild nuts. David M. Greene (1966, page 29) comments on this.

25 *It is hard to have a southern overseer*. From the *Journal*, 1845–1847; I, 427, which reads:

"It is hard to have a Southern overseer; it is

rather indicates, his fate. Self-emancipation even in the West Indian provinces of the fancy and imagination, — what Wilberforce is there to bring that about? **29** Think, also, of the ladies of the land weaving toilet **30** cushions against the last day, not to betray too green an interest in their fates! As if you could kill time without injuring eternity.

The mass of men lead lives of quiet desperation. **31** What is called resignation is confirmed desperation. From the desperate city you go into the desperate country, and have to console yourself with the bravery of minks and muskrats. A stereotyped but unconscious despair is concealed even under what are called the games and amusements of mankind. There is no play in them, for this comes after work. But it is a characteristic of wisdom not to do desperate things.

When we consider what, to use the words of the cate- **32** chism, is the chief end of man, and what are the true **33** necessaries and means of life, it appears as if men had deliberately chosen the common mode of living because they preferred it to any other. Yet they honestly think there is no choice left. But alert and healthy natures remember that the sun rose clear. It is never too late **34** to give up our prejudices. No way of thinking or doing, however ancient, can be trusted without proof. What every body echoes or in silence passes by as true to-day may turn out to be falsehood to-morrow, mere smoke of opinion, which some had trusted for a cloud that would sprinkle fertilizing rain on their fields. What old people say you cannot do you try and find that you can. Old deeds for old people, and new deeds for new. Old people did not know enough once, perchance, to fetch fresh fuel to keep the fire a-going; new people put a little dry **35** wood under a pot, and are whirled round the globe with the speed of birds, in a way to kill old people, as the phrase is. Age is no better, hardly so well, qualified for an instructor as youth, for it has not profited so much as it has lost. One may almost doubt if the wisest man has learned any thing of absolute value by living. Practically, the old have no very important advice to give the young, their own experience has been so partial, and their lives have been such miserable failures, for private reasons, as they must believe; and it may be that they have some faith left which belies that experience, and they are only less young than they were. I **36** have lived some thirty years on this planet, and I have

worse to have a Northern one; but worst of all when you are yourself the slave-driver. Look at the lonely teamster on the highway, wending to market by day or night; is he a son of the morning, with somewhat of divinity in him, fearless because immortal, going to receive his birthright, greeting the sun as his fellow, bounding with youthful, gigantic strength over his mother earth? See how he cowers and sneaks, how vaguely, indefinitely all the day he fears, not being immortal, not divine, the slave and prisoner of his own opinion of himself, fame which he has earned by his own deeds. Public opinion is a weak tyrant compared with private opinion. What I think of myself, that determines my fate."

Southern and Northern have been capitalized in later editions.

26 *when you are the slave-driver of yourself.* Originally "are yourself the slave driver" (ms. 314).

27 *does any divinity stir within him?* Paraphrased from Addison's *Cato*, V, i. Followed on ms. 314 by "He rolls out of the cradle into a Tom and Jerry and goes out at once to look after his team."

28 *Public opinion . . . private opinion.* Here Thoreau anticipates the modern conception of the importance of the self-image.

29 *Wilberforce.* William Wilberforce (1759–1833), who sponsored the Emancipation Act that freed all the slaves in the British Empire in 1833.

30 *weaving toilet cushions.* Here Thoreau borrows a phrase from the *Journal* (April 8, 1839; I, 76), where he says: "weavers of toilet cushions."

31 *The mass of men lead lives of quiet desperation.* This famous passage went through a long evolution and condensation. At first it concerned a "desperate" New York organ-grinder whom Thoreau encountered in New Hampshire in 1839. The Bibliophile Edition (II, 27) prints the story:

"I once met a poor wretch asking for a lodging, whom it was almost a pleasure to befriend, he was so helpless. He said that he came from New York and was seeking work. He did not know where he lodged the night before, nor where he was then, but asked, 'What place is this, Sir?' He knew only that he had travelled thirty miles that day. He could work about a stable, but he declared in a disconsolate voice that there was no work for him (as if the Fates had a spite against him). He thought that he had seriously injured himself by lying out. I asked him why he travelled so far in a day, and farther each successive day— if he was any better off at night than in the

yet to hear the first syllable of valuable or even earnest advice from my seniors. They have told me nothing, and probably cannot tell me any thing, to the purpose. Here is life, an experiment to a great extent untried by me; but it does not avail me that they have tried it. If I have any experience which I think valuable, I am sure to reflect that this my Mentors said nothing about.

One farmer says to me, "You cannot live on vegetable food solely, for it furnishes nothing to make bones with;" and so he religiously devotes a part of his day to supplying his system with the raw material of bones; walking all the while he talks behind his oxen, which, with vegetable-made bones, jerk him and his lumbering plough along in spite of every obstacle. Some things are really necessaries of life in some circles, the most helpless and diseased, which in others are luxuries merely, and in others still are entirely unknown. **38**

The whole ground of human life seems to some to have been gone over by their predecessors, both the heights and the valleys, and all things to have been cared for. According to Evelyn, "the wise Solomon **39** prescribed ordinances for the very distances of trees; and the Roman prætors have decided how often you may go into your neighbor's land to gather the acorns which fall on it without trespass, and what share belongs to that neighbor." Hippocrates has even left directions **40** how we should cut our nails; that is, even with the ends of the fingers, neither shorter nor longer. Undoubtedly the very tedium and ennui which presume to have

Hippocrates

morning—why three miles would not do as well as thirty, and better? He allowed that I had the right of it.

"I concluded that he was a desperate man who had committed some crime,—or whose whole life was a crime,—who was endeavoring to escape from himself. He travelled far, superficially, because he would not budge an inch in the direction of reform and a good conscience. He thought that nobody wished to employ him or would respect him, because he was conscious that he was unworthy to be employed, and did not respect himself. If he could have had one half-hour of sanity, he would have found a job at the next door, and all the world would have appeared his friends.

"He had travelled then 250 miles from New York in a straight line, with desperate steps, twenty-five or thirty miles a day, offering himself with a down look, anticipating failure, to do stable work at such stable yards as that radius happened to intersect; doing his part, as he would fain have believed, toward getting work; but there was none for him. He merely wished to convince the Fates that he was willing to do his part."

See *The Making of Walden* by J. Lyndon Shanley, (1957, pages 52 ff.). Originally the passage began with "It is the sum of all wisdom not to do desperate things" (ms. 536). Note the last sentence. "Mankind" rather than "men" was used and then canceled on ms. 541.

32 *Catechism* has a capital in Thoreau's manuscript.

33 *the chief end of man.* In the *New England Primer's* Shorter Catechism the chief end of man is to glorify God.

34 *It is never too late to give up our prejudices.* This starts a new paragraph on ms. 315. The passage is written on a separate scrap of paper.

35 *put a little dry wood under a pot.* This refers to the steam engine which was then beginning to serve as a source of power for ships and trains.

36 *I have lived some thirty years.* Since Thoreau was born in 1817 this would make 1847—or a few years later because of the indefinite "some"—the time when he wrote these works. But he kept revising up to the spring of 1854.

37 *on vegetable food solely.* Thoreau was not a vegetarian; he did eat meat, but not often. The text of *Walden* has many references to the various kinds of food he ate.

38 *are entirely unknown.* In ms. 71 an interesting canceled passage occurs here. "I know a ro-

exhausted the variety and the joys of life are as old as Adam. But man's capacities have never been measured; nor are we to judge of what he can do by any precedents, so little has been tried. Whatever have been thy failures hitherto, "be not afflicted, my **41** child, for who shall assign to thee what thou hast left undone?"

We might try our lives by a thousand simple tests; as, for instance, that the same sun which ripens my beans illumines at once a system of earths like ours. If I had remembered this it would have prevented some mistakes. This was not the light in which I hoed them. The stars are the apexes of what wonderful triangles! What distant and different beings in the various mansions of the universe are contemplating the same one at the same moment! Nature and human life are **42** as various as our several constitutions. Who shall say what prospect life offers to another? Could a greater miracle take place than for us to look through each other's eyes for an instant? We should live in all the ages of the world in an hour; ay, in all the worlds of the ages. History, Poetry, Mythology! — I know of no reading of another's experience so startling and informing as this would be.

The greater part of what my neighbors call good I **43** believe in my soul to be bad, and if I repent of any thing, it is very likely to be my good behavior. What demon possessed me that I behaved so well? You may say the wisest thing you can old man, — you who have **44** lived seventy years, not without honor of a kind, — I hear an irresistible voice which invites me away from all that. One generation abandons the enterprises of another like stranded vessels.

I think that we may safely trust a good deal more than we do. We may waive just so much care of ourselves as we honestly bestow elsewhere. Nature is as well adapted to our weakness as to our strength. The incessant anxiety and strain of some is a well nigh incurable form of disease. We are made to exaggerate the importance of what work we do; and yet how much is not done by us! or, what if we had been taken sick? How vigilant we are! determined not to live by faith if we can avoid it; all the day long on the alert, at night we unwillingly say our prayers and commit ourselves to uncertainties. So thoroughly and sin-

bust and hearty mother who thinks that her son who died abroad came to his end by living too low, as she has since learned that he drank only water. I heard of a very poor family in Concord this winter which would have starved if it had not been for potatoes—and tea and coffee."

39 *according to Evelyn.* John Evelyn (1620–1706). The quotation is from his book on arboriculture, *Sylva* (1664).

40 *Hippocrates.* A Greek physician who is known as "the Father of Medicine" (460?–377 B.C.). No one has traced the quotation to him.

41 *"be not afflicted, my child . . ."* A quotation from the Hindu classic, the *Vishnu Purana*.

42 *at the same moment.* Canceled copy in the manuscript that follows after this reads:
"The departing and the arriving spirit,—the joyful and the sad,—the innocent and happy child and the melancholy suicide,—the northern farmer and the southern slave."
"These are trivial instances. How many yet more distant inhabitants of our universe may be contemplating yonder fine twinkling star, which I behold at the same moment! The eye of Omniscience,—an eye in Orion, an eye in Lyra. There is the possibility of being thus related to the whole by our lives, or of remaining more and more an isolated particle in the universe."

43 *what my neighbors call good.* Here the rebel in Thoreau comes out. This passage, almost word for word the same, is in the *Journal*, January 5, 1851; I, 137.

44 *you who have lived seventy years.* According to the Psalmist (90 : 10), the allotted life-span of man is "three-score years and ten."

cerely are we compelled to live, reverencing our life, and denying the possibility of change. This is the only way, we say; but there are as many ways as there can be drawn radii from one centre. All change is a miracle to contemplate; but it is a miracle which is taking place every instant. Confucius said, "To know that we know what we know, and that we do not know what we do not know, that is true knowledge." When one man has reduced a fact of the imagination to be a fact to his understanding, I foresee that all men will at length establish their lives on that basis.

Let us consider for a moment what most of the trouble and anxiety which I have referred to is about, and how much it is necessary that we be troubled, or, at least, careful. It would be some advantage to live a primitive and frontier life, though in the midst of an outward civilization, if only to learn what are the gross necessaries of life and what methods have been taken to obtain them; or even to look over the old day-books of the merchants, to see what it was that men most commonly bought at the stores, what they stored, that is, what are the grossest groceries. For the improvements of ages have had but little influence on the essential laws of man's existence; as our skeletons, probably, are not to be distinguished from those of our ancestors.

By the words, *necessary of life*, I mean whatever, of all that man obtains by his own exertions, has been from the first, or from long use has become, so important to human life that few, if any, whether from savageness, or poverty, or philosophy, ever attempt to do without it. To many creatures there is in this sense but one necessary of life, Food. To the bison of the prairie it is a few inches of palatable grass, with water to drink; unless he seeks the Shelter of the forest or the mountain's shadow. None of the brute creation requires more than Food and Shelter. The necessaries of life for man in this climate may, accurately enough, be distributed under the several heads of Food, Shelter, Clothing, and Fuel; for not till we have secured these are we prepared to entertain the true problems of life with freedom and a prospect of success. Man has invented, not only houses, but clothes and cooked food; and pos-

45

46

47

48

49

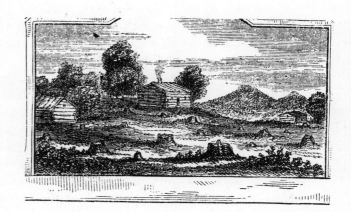

45 *as there can be drawn radii from one centre.* This is one of the many circle images in *Walden.*

46 *Confucius*, Kung Fu-tze (c. 551–479 B.C.). Lyman V. Cady, in "Thoreau's Quotations from the Confucian Books in Walden" (*American Literature*, March 1961, page 24n), identifies this as being in *The Analects*, II, Chapter XVII.

47 *on that basis.* In the manuscript, but omitted from the printed edition here, is this passage: "Men have left off rum safely, and imprisoning for debt and chattel slavery in some places; but they are not inclined to leave off hanging men, because they have not got accustomed to that way of thinking."

48 *It would be some advantage. Journal*, July 1845; I, 367.

49 *grossest groceries.* There are many puns in *Walden*, but most are more subtle than this. *Journal*, 1845–1846; I, 398.

sibly from the accidental discovery of the warmth of fire, and the consequent use of it, at first a luxury, arose the present necessity to sit by it. We observe cats and dogs acquiring the same second nature. By proper Shelter and Clothing we legitimately retain our own internal heat; but with an excess of these, or of Fuel, that is, with an external heat greater than our own internal, may not cookery properly be said to begin? Darwin, the naturalist, says of the inhabitants of Tierra del Fuego, that while his own party, who were well clothed and sitting close to a fire, were far from too warm, these naked savages, who were farther off, were observed, to his great surprise, " to be streaming with perspiration at undergoing such a roasting." So, we are told, the New Hollander goes naked with impunity, while the European shivers in his clothes. Is it impossible to combine the hardiness of these savages with the intellectualness of the civilized man? According to Liebig, man's body is a stove, and food the fuel which keeps up the internal combustion in the lungs. In cold weather we eat more, in warm less. The animal heat is the result of a slow combustion, and disease and death take place when this is too rapid; or for want of fuel, or from some defect in the draught, the fire goes out. Of course the vital heat is not to be confounded with fire; but so much for analogy. It appears, therefore, from the above list, that the expression, *animal life*, is nearly synonymous with the expression, *animal heat;* for while Food may be regarded as the Fuel which keeps up the fire within us,—and Fuel serves only to prepare that Food or to increase the warmth of our bodies by addition from without,—Shelter and Clothing also serve only to retain the *heat* thus generated and absorbed.

The grand necessity, then, for our bodies, is to keep warm, to keep the vital heat in us. What pains we accordingly take, not only with our Food, and Clothing, and Shelter, but with our beds, which are our night-clothes, robbing the nests and breasts of birds to prepare this shelter within a shelter, as the mole has its bed of grass and leaves at the end of its burrow! The poor man is wont to complain that this is a cold world; and to cold, no less physical than social, we refer directly a great part of our ails. The summer, in some climates, makes possible to man a sort of Elysian life. Fuel, except to cook his Food, is then unnecessary; the sun is his fire, and many of the fruits are sufficiently

50

51

52

53

50 *inhabitants of Tierra del Fuego.* This is from Darwin's book, *The Voyage of the "Beagle,"* an account of the trip which the young naturalist made around the world in the early 1830's.

51 *the New Hollander.* Since the early seventeenth-century discoverers of Australia were Dutch, the mainland, even as late as Thoreau's time, was called New Holland. The aborigines there have always gone naked, even in the colder parts of the south.

52 *According to Liebig.* Justus von Liebig (1803–1873), German chemist who established the fact that body heat is the result of combustion of foods in the body.

53 *a sort of Elysian life.* Elysium, or the Isles of the Blest at the ends of the earth, is the place where Greek heroes spent their happy afterlives.

cooked by its rays; while Food generally is more various, and more easily obtained, and Clothing and Shelter are wholly or half unnecessary. At the present day, and in this country, as I find by my own experience, a few implements, a knife, an axe, a spade, a wheelbarrow, &c., and for the studious, lamplight, stationery, and access to a few books, rank next to necessaries, and can all be obtained at a trifling cost. Yet some, not wise, go to the other side of the globe, to barbarous and unhealthy regions, and devote themselves to trade for ten or twenty years, in order that they may live, — that is, keep comfortably warm, — and die in New England at last. The luxuriously rich are not simply kept comfortably warm, but unnaturally hot; as I implied before, they are cooked, of course *à la mode*.   **54**

Most of the luxuries, and many of the so called comforts of life, are not only not indispensable, but positive hinderances to the elevation of mankind. With respect to luxuries and comforts, the wisest have ever lived a more simple and meagre life than the poor. The ancient philosophers, Chinese, Hindoo, Persian, and Greek, were a class than which none has been poorer in outward riches, none so rich in inward. We know not much about them. It is remarkable that *we* know so much of them as we do. The same is true of the more modern reformers and benefactors of their race. None can be an impartial or wise observer of human life but from the vantage ground of what *we* should call voluntary poverty. Of a life of luxury the fruit is luxury, whether in agriculture, or commerce, or literature, or art. There are nowadays professors of philosophy, but not philosophers. Yet it is admirable to   **55**
profess because it was once admirable to live. To be a philosopher is not merely to have subtle thoughts, nor even to found a school, but so to love wisdom as to live according to its dictates, a life of simplicity, independence, magnanimity, and trust. It is to solve some of the problems of life, not only theoretically, but practically. The success of great scholars and thinkers is commonly a courtier-like success, not kingly, not manly. They make shift to live merely by conformity, practically as their fathers did, and are in no sense the progenitors of a nobler race of men. But why do men degenerate ever? What makes families run out? What is the nature of the luxury which enervates and destroys nations? Are we sure that there is none of it

54 *unnaturally hot.* This refers to central heating which had recently been introduced into the homes of wealthy people.

55 *but not philosophers.* Thoreau had a footnote in the manuscript here: "Critics of late have been very lavish of the word 'philosopher.' According to them every century has had several. But we have forgotten what the word implies. These men were perhaps professors of philosophy,— readers of it, perhaps even utterers of it, to a slight extent."

in our own lives? The philosopher is in advance of his age even in the outward form of his life. He is not fed, sheltered, clothed, warmed, like his contemporaries. How can a man be a philosopher and not maintain his vital heat by better methods than other men?

When a man is warmed by the several modes which I have described, what does he want next? Surely not more warmth of the same kind, as more and richer food, larger and more splendid houses, finer and more abundant clothing, more numerous incessant and hotter fires, and the like. When he has obtained those things which are necessary to life, there is another alternative than to obtain the superfluities; and that is, to adventure on life now, his vacation from humbler toil having commenced. The soil, it appears, is suited to the seed, for it has sent its radicle downward, and it may now send its shoot upward also with confidence. Why has man rooted himself thus firmly in the earth, but that he may rise in the same proportion into the heavens above? — for the nobler plants are valued for the fruit they bear at last in the air and light, far from the ground, and are not treated like the humbler esculents, which, though they may be biennials, are cultivated only till they have perfected their root, and often cut down at top for this purpose, so that most would not know them in their flowering season.

I do not mean to prescribe rules to strong and valiant natures, who will mind their own affairs whether in heaven or hell, and perchance build more magnificently and spend more lavishly than the richest, without ever impoverishing themselves, not knowing how they live, — if, indeed, there are any such, as has been dreamed; nor to those who find their encouragement and inspiration in precisely the present condition of things, and cherish it with the fondness and enthusiasm of lovers, — and, to some extent, I reckon myself in this number; I do not speak to those who are well employed, in whatever circumstances, and they know whether they are well employed or not; — but mainly to the mass of men who are discontented, and idly complaining of the hardness of their lot or of the times, when they might improve them. There are some who complain most energetically and inconsolably of any, because they are, as they say, doing their duty. I also have in my mind that seemingly wealthy, but most terribly impoverished class of all, who have accumulated dross, but know not

56 *radicle.* This was "radical" in the page proofs but was changed there.

56

how to use it, or get rid of it, and thus have forged **57** their own golden or silver fetters.

If I should attempt to tell how I have desired to spend my life in years past, it would probably surprise **58** those of my readers who are somewhat acquainted with its actual history; it would certainly astonish those who know nothing about it. I will only hint at some of the enterprises which I have cherished.

In any weather, at any hour of the day or night, I have been anxious to improve the nick of time, and **59** notch it on my stick too; to stand on the meeting of two eternities, the past and future, which is precisely the present moment; to toe that line. You will pardon some obscurities, for there are more secrets in my trade than in most men's, and yet not voluntarily kept, but inseparable from its very nature. I would gladly tell all that I know about it, and never paint " No Admittance " on my gate.

I long ago lost a hound, a bay horse, and a turtle- **60** dove, and am still on their trail. Many are the travellers I have spoken concerning them, describing their tracks and what calls they answered to. I have met one or two who had heard the hound, and the tramp of the horse, and even seen the dove disappear behind a cloud, and they seemed as anxious to recover them as if they had lost them themselves.

To anticipate, not the sunrise and the dawn merely, but, if possible, Nature herself! How many mornings, summer and winter, before yet any neighbor was stirring about his business, have I been about mine! No doubt, many of my townsmen have met me returning from this enterprise, farmers starting for Boston in the twilight, or woodchoppers going to their work. It is true, I never assisted the sun materially in his rising, but, doubt not, it was of the last importance only to be present at it.

So many autumn, ay, and winter days, spent outside the town, trying to hear what was in the wind, to hear and carry it express! I well-nigh sunk all my capital in it, and lost my own breath into the bargain, running in the face of it. If it had concerned either of the political parties, depend upon it, it would have appeared in the Gazette with the earliest intelligence. At other **61**

---

57 *forged their own golden or silver fetters.* This is followed on ms. 332 by a canceled passage that reads: "This leads me to say that almost any man —if I may be pardoned the digression—knows how to earn money, but not one in a million, having amassed a fortune, knows how to spend it. If he had known as much as this, he would never have acquired it. Commonly the rich wear no better clothes, and build no better houses than their neighbors; for while they have been accumulating property, they have not been cultivating their taste or their wits. I think that, in winter (and I speak from experience), the poor man who wears cowhide is better shod than the rich, with India-rubbers over calf-skin."

58 *probably surprise.* Here Thoreau has toned down his original "startle" (ms. 337) to the milder word "surprise."

59 *improve the nick of time.* Charles R. Anderson (1968, page 272) says of this passage: "This is his [Thoreau's] witty version of the transcendental formula for escaping the wheel of time by living in the Eternal Now."

60 *I long ago lost a hound, a bay horse, and a turtledove.* This celebrated passage has produced a large body of literature of its own. Emerson said of it that Thoreau "knew well how to throw a poetic veil over his experience. All readers of *Walden* will remember his mythical record of his disappointments." (Emerson *Works*, 1904, X, 476).

Some of the interpretations are metaphysical. Francis H. Allen, in his edition of *Walden* (1910, page 371), said that the allusions may be taken "to represent the vague desires and aspirations of man's spiritual nature. . . ." John Burroughs tended to agree with him when he wrote that the fine effluence of Nature is what Thoreau meant by the hound, the horse, and the turtledove.

Others take a more practical point of view. Mark Van Doren (1916, page 16) believes that the paragraph deals with human relations. Others more specifically think the hound is the "gentle boy," Edmund Sewall; the bay horse, Thoreau's dead brother John; and the turtledove, his "lost" love, Ellen Sewell.

Thoreau, in a letter to B. B. Wiley, dated April 26, 1857, said: "How shall we account for our pursuits if they are original? We get the language with which to describe our various lives out of a common mint. If others have their losses, which they are busy repairing, so have I *mine*, & their hound & horse may *perhaps* be the symbols of some of them. But also I have lost, or am in danger of losing, a far finer & more etherial treasure, which commonly no loss of which they are conscious will symbolize—this I answer hastily &

times watching from the observatory of some cliff or tree, to telegraph any new arrival; or waiting at evening on the hill-tops for the sky to fall, that I might catch something, though I never caught much, and that, manna-wise, would dissolve again in the sun.

For a long time I was reporter to a journal, of no very wide circulation, whose editor has never yet seen fit to print the bulk of my contributions, and, as is too common with writers, I got only my labor for my pains. However, in this case my pains were their own reward. **62 63**

For many years I was self-appointed inspector of snow storms and rain storms, and did my duty faithfully; surveyor, if not of highways, then of forest paths and all across-lot routes, keeping them open, and ravines bridged and passable at all seasons, where the public heel had testified to their utility. **64**

I have looked after the wild stock of the town, which give a faithful herdsman a good deal of trouble by leaping fences; and I have had an eye to the unfrequented nooks and corners of the farm; though I did not always know whether Jonas or Solomon worked in a particular field to-day; that was none of my business. I have watered the red huckleberry, the sand cherry and the nettle tree, the red pine and the black ash, the white grape and the yellow violet, which might have withered else in dry seasons.

In short, I went on thus for a long time, I may say it without boasting, faithfully minding my business, till it became more and more evident that my townsmen would not after all admit me into the list of town officers, nor make my place a sinecure with a moderate allowance. My accounts, which I can swear to have kept faithfully, I have, indeed, never got audited, still less accepted, still less paid and settled. However, I have not set my heart on that.

Not long since, a strolling Indian went to sell baskets at the house of a well-known lawyer in my neighborhood. "Do you wish to buy any baskets?" he asked. "No, we do not want any," was the reply. "What!" exclaimed the Indian as he went out the gate, "do you mean to starve us?" Having seen his industrious white neighbors so well off, — that the lawyer had only to weave arguments, and by some magic wealth and standing followed, he had said to himself; I will go into business; I will weave baskets; it is a thing which I can do. Thinking that when he had made the baskets he **65**

---

with some hesitation, according as I now understand my own words."

In a conversation in Plymouth in 1855 or 1856, Thoreau replied to a direct request for an explanation of the passage by saying evasively that everyone meets with losses. And that was that. Since there is no clear explanation, each reader will have to supply his own. Further material on this inexhaustible subject can be found in Raymond Adams (1945d), Edith Peairs (1937), Frank Davidson (1954b), and in an unpublished 118-page master's thesis by John Girdler (1935). See the Bibliography.

Incidentally, this passage, as first written, read: "I long ago lost a hound—and a turtledove and a bay horse" (ms. 337).

61 *Gazette.* Concord then had the *Yeoman's Gazette. Journal,* 1845–1847; I, 434.

62 *a journal of no very wide circulation.* This probably means Thoreau's own *Journal.* Here his bitterness about publishers begins to show.

63 *I got only my labor for my pains.* The phrase "Literary contracts are little binding" follows this on ms. 340.

64 *I was self-appointed inspector of snow storms.* Here, in these few pages, is some of the best writing in *Walden.* The improvement over the first draft in the *Journal,* 1845–1847; I, 434–435, is evident.

"For many years I was self-appointed inspector of snow-storms and rain-storms, and did my duty faithfully, though I never received one cent for it.

"Surveyor, if not of higher ways, then of forest paths and all across-lot routes, keeping many open ravines bridged and passable at all seasons, where the public heel had testified to the importance of the same, all not only without charge, but even at considerable risk and inconvenience. Many a mower would have forborne to complain had he been aware of the invisible public good that was in jeopardy.

"So I went on, I may say without boasting, I trust, faithfully minding my business without a partner, till it became more and more evident that my townsmen would not, after all, admit me into the list of town officers, nor make the place a sinecure with moderate allowance.

"I have looked after the wild stock of the town, which pastures in common, and every one knows that these cattle give you a good deal of trouble in the way of leaping fences. I have counted and registered all the eggs I could find at least, and have had an eye to all nooks and corners of the farm, though I didn't always know whether Jonas or Solomon worked in a particular field to-day; that was none of my business. I only knew him

would have done his part, and then it would be the white man's to buy them.   He had not discovered that it was necessary for him to make it worth the other's while to buy them, or at least make him think that it was so, or to make something else which it would be worth his while to buy.   I too had woven a kind of basket of a delicate texture, but I had not made it worth any one's while to buy them.   Yet not the less, in my case, did I think it worth my while to weave them, and instead of studying how to make it worth men's while to buy my baskets, I studied rather how to avoid the necessity of selling them.   The life which men praise and regard as successful is but one kind.   Why should we exaggerate any one kind at the expense of the others?

Finding that my fellow-citizens were not likely to offer me any room in the court house, or any curacy or living any where else, but I must shift for myself, I turned my face more exclusively than ever to the woods, where I was better known.   I determined to go into business at once, and not wait to acquire the usual capital, using such slender means as I had already got.   My **66** purpose in going to Walden Pond was not to live cheaply nor to live dearly there, but to transact some private business with the fewest obstacles ; to be hindered from accomplishing which for want of a little common sense, a little enterprise and business talent, appeared not so sad as foolish.

I have always endeavored to acquire strict business **67** habits ; they are indispensable to every man.   If your trade is with the Celestial Empire, then some small counting house on the coast, in some Salem harbor, will be **68** fixture enough.   You will export such articles as the country affords, purely native products, much ice and pine timber and a little granite, always in native bottoms.   These will be good ventures.   To oversee all the details yourself in person ; to be at once pilot and captain, and owner and underwriter ; to buy and sell and keep the accounts ; to read every letter received, and write or read every letter sent ; to superintend the discharge of imports night and day ; to be upon many parts of the coast almost at the same time ; — often the richest freight will be discharged upon a Jersey shore ; **69** — to be your own telegraph, unweariedly sweeping the horizon, speaking all passing vessels bound coastwise ; to keep up a steady despatch of commodities, for the supply of such a distant and exorbitant market ; to keep

for one of the men, and trusted that he was as well employed as I was. I had to make my daily entries in the general farm book, and my duties may sometimes have made me a little stubborn and unyielding.

"Many a day spent on the hilltops waiting for the sky to fall, that I might catch something, though I never caught much, only a little, manna-wise, that would dissolve again in the sun.

"My accounts, indeed, which I can swear to have been faithfully kept, I have never got audited, still less accepted, still less paid and settled. However, I haven't set my heart upon *that*.

"I have watered the red huckleberry and the sand cherry and the hopwood tree, and the cornel and spoonhunt and yellow violet, which might have withered else in dry seasons. The white grape."

65 *a strolling Indian.* This appears in shorter form in the *Journal*, 1850; II, 84: "A squaw came to our door to-day with two pappooses, and said, 'Me want a pie.' Theirs is not common begging. You are merely the rich Indian who shares his goods with the poor. They merely offer you an opportunity to be generous and hospitable.

"Equally simple was the observation which an Indian made at Mr. Hoar's door the other day, who went there to sell his baskets. 'No, we don't want any,' said the one who went to the door. 'What! do you mean to starve us?' asked the Indian in astonishment, as he was going out the gate. The Indian seems to have said: I too will do like the white man; I will go into business. He sees his white neighbors well off around him, and he thinks that if he only enters on the profession of basket-making, riches will flow in unto him as a matter of course; just as the lawyer weaves arguments, and by some magical means wealth and standing follow. He thinks that when he has made the baskets he has done his part, now it is yours to buy them. He has not discovered that it is necessary for him to make it worth your while to buy them, or make some which it will be worth your while to buy. With great simplicity he says to himself: I too will be a man of business; I will go into trade. It isn't enough simply to make baskets. You have got to sell them."

The lawyer was Thoreau's neighbor, Samuel Hoar.

Sherman Paul (1958, page 322) thinks that the story of the Indian and his baskets represents Thoreau's unhappy experience in publishing *A Week on the Concord and Merrimack Rivers* in 1849.

66 *My purpose in going to Walden Pond.* See the Chronology for the evolution of Thoreau's wanting to go to Walden. It is well to note here Charles R. Anderson's (1968, page 11) wise re-

The semaphore telegraph station at the entrance to New York Harbor

yourself informed of the state of the markets, prospects of war and peace every where, and anticipate the tendencies of trade and civilization, — taking advantage of the results of all exploring expeditions, using new passages and all improvements in navigation; — charts to be studied, the position of reefs and new lights and buoys to be ascertained, and ever, and ever, the logarithmic tables to be corrected, for by the error of some calculator the vessel often splits upon a rock that should have reached a friendly pier, — there is the untold fate of La Perouse; — universal science to be kept pace **70** with, studying the lives of all great discoverers and navigators, great adventurers and merchants, from Han- **71** no and the Phœnicians down to our day; in fine, ac- **72** count of stock to be taken from time to time, to know how you stand. It is a labor to task the faculties of a man, — such problems of profit and loss, of interest, of tare and tret, and gauging of all kinds in it, as demand a universal knowledge.

I have thought that Walden Pond would be a good place for business, not solely on account of the railroad **73** and the ice trade; it offers advantages which it may not **74** be good policy to divulge; it is a good post and a good **75** foundation. No Neva marshes to be filled; though you must every where build on piles of your own driving. It is said that a flood-tide, with a westerly wind, and ice

mark: "Before the mythical world of *Walden* can be distinguished from the literal setting of ponds and woods and township, we must learn to separate the actual Henry Thoreau, citizen of Concord, from the fictive character who is both the persona and the voice that speaks to us in the book."

67 *strict business habits.* Thoreau's management of his father's pencil and graphite business shows that he had good common sense in commercial matters even though he despised most of the people engaged in trade and industry.

68 *some Salem harbor.* Salem was one of the chief ports for the China trade in the fast-sailing clipper ships that were then at the height of their development.

69 *upon a Jersey shore.* The references that follow came from Thoreau's stay on Staten Island in 1843.

70 *La Perouse.* Comte Jean François de Galaup de la Pérouse (1741–1788), French navigator whose ship was wrecked on Vanikoro, in the New Hebrides, where he was killed by the natives.

71 *Hanno.* A Carthaginian explorer who traveled through west Africa before 480 B.C. There is a Greek translation of his Punic report.

72 *the Phoenicians* were noted explorers, navigators, and tradesmen in early times.

in the Neva, would sweep St. Petersburg from the face **76** of the earth.

As this business was to be entered into without the usual capital, it may not be easy to conjecture where those means, that will still be indispensable to every such undertaking, were to be obtained. As for Clothing, **77** to come at once to the practical part of the question, perhaps we are led oftener by the love of novelty, and a regard for the opinions of men, in procuring it, than by a true utility. Let him who has work to do recol- **78** lect that the object of clothing is, first, to retain the vital heat, and secondly, in this state of society, to cover nakedness, and he may judge how much of any neces- sary or important work may be accomplished without adding to his wardrobe. Kings and queens who wear a suit but once, though made by some tailor or dress- maker to their majesties, cannot know the comfort of wearing a suit that fits. They are no better than wooden horses to hang the clean clothes on. Every day our garments become more assimilated to ourselves, receiv- ing the impress of the wearer's character, until we hesi- tate to lay them aside, without such delay and medical appliances and some such solemnity even as our bodies. No man ever stood the lower in my estimation for hav- ing a patch in his clothes; yet I am sure that there is greater anxiety, commonly, to have fashionable, or at least clean and unpatched clothes, than to have a sound conscience. But even if the rent is not mended, perhaps the worst vice betrayed is improvidence. I sometimes try my acquaintances by such tests as this;—who could wear a patch, or two extra seams only, over the knee? Most behave as if they believed that their prospects for life would be ruined if they should do it. It would be easier for them to hobble to town with a broken leg than with a broken pantaloon. Often if an accident happens to a **79** gentleman's legs, they can be mended; but if a similar accident happens to the legs of his pantaloons, there is no help for it; for he considers, not what is truly re- spectable, but what is respected. We know but few men, a great many coats and breeches. Dress a scare- crow in your last shift, you standing shiftless by, who would not soonest salute the scarecrow? Passing a cornfield the other day, close by a hat and coat on a

73 *not solely on account of the railroad and the ice trade.* The railroad from Boston to Fitchburg had been constructed along the western shore of Walden Pond shortly before Thoreau built his house there. See page 415 for a vivid description of ice cutting.

74 *advantages which it may not be good policy to divulge.* This paragraph has more to it than a superficial reading will reveal.

75 *it is a good post.* Here is one of the errors that have been perpetuated from edition to edition. The word is quite clearly "port" on ms. 87 and 345. Thoreau made the correction in his own copy of *Walden* which is now in the Abernethy Library of Middlebury College, Vermont. Pro- fessor Reginald L. Cook made a list of the cor- rections which was published in the Thoreau Society *Bulletin*, Number 42, Winter, 1953.

76 *St. Petersburg.* On the Neva River, it is now called Leningrad.

77 *Clothing.* What follows is obviously inspired by Carlyle's *Sartor Resartus*, which had been published in book form in Boston in 1836 although it had appeared in England in *Fraser's Magazine* in 1833 and 1834. The British book did not come out until 1838.

78 *a true utility.* This was followed on ms. 87 by two interesting paragraphs:
"It was no doubt the strongest argument against the faith of the Millerites, that most of them con- tinued to build and accumulate property so as to be prepared in case the world should not come to an end. From the stock of clothing which some are accustomed to lay in, I judge that they do not expect that the world will soon come to an end. Ay, there will be found old clothes enough in everybody's garret to last to the Millennium, if he only have faith in that.
"The bankbill that is torn in two will pass if you save the pieces, if you have got only the essential piece with the signatures. And so it is with our garments; they may be much worn and torn, even clouted, yet be passable. Lowell and Manchester think that you will let their broad- cloth currency go when it is torn; but hold on, have an eye to the signature; clout the back of it, ay, the front of it, and if it is a transmittendum, endorse the name of him from whom you re- ceived it."
The Millerites—followers of William Miller (1782–1849)—believed that the world would come to an end in 1843. When it did not, Miller told them that there had been an error and that the correct date was October 22, 1844. They gathered

in white robes on housetops and hills but were again disappointed.

79 *Often if an accident happens to a gentleman's legs.* This sentence was a last-minute thought, written up and down on the left margin of ms. 555. *Journal,* 1845–1847; I, 418.

80 *than when I saw him last.* Omitted here in the printed text but used in the Bibliophile Edition (I, 76n.) is: "The back being towards me, I missed nothing; and I thought to myself that if I were a crow, I should not fear the balance of him at all. The same coat on a stick made on me the total impression which the farmer never had made. On the other hand, I have frequently mistaken a laborer in the field for a scarecrow."

81 *Madam Pfeiffer.* This is from the *Journal* for January 17, 1852; III, 200, where Thoreau wrote practically the same words. Madam Ida Laura Pfeiffer (1797–1858) was a Viennese traveler and author of *A Lady's Voyage Round the World* (1850). It was published in America in 1852.

stake, I recognized the owner of the farm. He was only a little more weather-beaten than when I saw him **80** last. I have heard of a dog that barked at every stranger who approached his master's premises with clothes on, but was easily quieted by a naked thief. It is an interesting question how far men would retain their relative rank if they were divested of their clothes. Could you, in such a case, tell surely of any company of civilized men, which belonged to the most respected class? When Madam Pfeiffer, in her adventurous travels **81** round the world, from east to west, had got so near home as Asiatic Russia, she says that she felt the necessity of wearing other than a travelling dress, when she went to meet the authorities, for she " was now in a civilized country, where —— — people are judged of by their clothes." Even in our democratic New England towns the accidental possession of wealth, and its manifestation in dress and equipage alone, obtain for the possessor almost universal respect.   But they who yield such respect, numerous as they are, are so far heathen, and need to have a missionary sent to them.   Beside, clothes introduced sewing, a kind of work which you may call **82** endless; a woman's dress, at least, is never done.

A man who has at length found something to do will not need to get a new suit to do it in; for him the old will do, that has lain dusty in the garret for an indeterminate period.   Old shoes will serve a hero longer than **83** they have served his valet, — if a hero ever has a valet, — bare feet are older than shoes, and he can make them do.   Only they who go to soirées and legislative halls must have new coats, coats to change as often as the man changes in them.   But if my jacket and trousers, **84** my hat and shoes, are fit to worship God in, they will do; will they not?   Who ever saw his old clothes, — his old coat, actually worn out, resolved into its primitive elements, so that it was not a deed of charity to bestow it on some poor boy, by him perchance to be bestowed on some poorer still, or shall we say richer, who could do with less?   I say, beware of all enterprises that require new clothes, and not rather a new wearer of clothes.   If there is not a new man, how can the new **85** clothes be made to fit?   If you have any enterprise before you, try it in your old clothes.   All men want, not something to *do with*, but something to *do*, or rather something to *be*.   Perhaps we should never procure a new suit, however ragged or dirty the old, until we have so conducted, so enterprised or sailed in some way, that we feel like new men in the old, and that to retain it would be like keeping new wine in old bottles.   Our **86** moulting season, like that of the fowls, must be a crisis in our lives.   The loon retires to solitary ponds to spend it.   Thus also the snake casts its slough, and the caterpillar its wormy coat, by an internal industry and expansion; for clothes are but our outmost cuticle and **87** mortal coil.   Otherwise we shall be found sailing under false colors, and be inevitably cashiered at last by our own opinion, as well as that of mankind.

We don garment after garment, as if we grew like exogenous plants by addition without.   Our outside and **88** often thin and fanciful clothes are our epidermis or false skin, which partakes not of our life, and may be stripped off here and there without fatal injury; our thicker garments, constantly worn, are our cellular integument, or cortex; but our shirts are our liber or true bark, which **89**

82 *work which you may call endless. Journal,* 1845–1847; I, 419.

83 *Old shoes.* Originally "old clothes" on ms. 558. *Journal,* 1845–1846; I, 419.

84 *But if my jacket and trousers.* This is in the *Journal* for April 5, 1841; I, 224, where the question is followed by another: "Won't they, Deacon Spaulding?"

85 *how can the new clothes be made to fit?* In ms. 90 this reads: "If there is not a new man, there be a new suit, and not rather a man miss-fit and a new suit."

86 *like keeping new wine in old bottles.* A paraphrase of Matthew 9:17, which continues, "else the bottles break. . . ."

87 *our outmost cuticle and mortal coil. Journal,* 1845–1847; I, 418.

88 *exogenous plants* are those that grow by adding an annual layer just beneath the bark.

89 *liber* is the strong woody plant fiber from the outer layer of plants like flax or hemp.

cannot be removed without girdling and so destroying the man. I believe that all races at some seasons wear something equivalent to the shirt. It is desirable that a man be clad so simply that he can lay his hands on himself in the dark, and that he live in all respects so compactly and preparedly, that, if an enemy take the town, he can, like the old philosopher, walk out the gate empty-handed without anxiety. While one thick garment is, for most purposes, as good as three thin ones, and cheap clothing can be obtained at prices really to suit customers; while a thick coat can be bought for five dollars, **90** which will last as many years, thick pantaloons for two **91** dollars, cowhide boots for a dollar and a half a pair, a summer hat for a quarter of a dollar, and a winter cap for sixty-two and a half cents, or a better be made at home at a nominal cost, where is he so poor that, clad in such a suit, *of his own earning*, there will not be found wise men to do him reverence?

When I ask for a garment of a particular form, my **92** tailoress tells me gravely, "They do not make them so now," not emphasizing the "They" at all, as if she quoted

90 *a thick coat can be bought for five dollars.* The prices listed here are not such bargains as they seem to be if they are translated into terms of man-hours of labor at the wage rates that then prevailed—fifty cents to a dollar for a long day of work.

91 *thick pantaloons for two dollars.* Ms. 561 then says: "the most durable ones I ever had cost me half a dollar less." Some of the lower prices were originally stated in shillings and pence, but Thoreau translated these into dollars and cents for the printed version of *Walden*.

92 *my tailoress tells me.* Thoreau's tailoress was Miss Mary Minnott, a neighbor.

an authority as impersonal as the Fates, and I find it difficult to get made what I want, simply because she cannot believe that I mean what I say, that I am so rash. When I hear this oracular sentence, I am for a moment absorbed in thought, emphasizing to myself each word separately that I may come at the meaning of it, that I may find out by what degree of consanguinity *They* are related to *me*, and what authority they may have in an affair which affects me so nearly; and, finally, I am inclined to answer her with equal mystery, and without any more emphasis of the "they," — "It is true, they did not make them so recently, but they do **93** now." Of what use this measuring of me if she does not measure my character, but only the breadth of my shoulders, as it were a peg to hang the coat on? We worship not the Graces, nor the Parcæ, but Fashion. **94** She spins and weaves and cuts with full authority. The head monkey at Paris puts on a traveller's cap, and **95** all the monkeys in America do the same. I sometimes despair of getting any thing quite simple and honest done in this world by the help of men. They would have to be passed through a powerful press first, to squeeze their old notions out of them, so that they would not soon get upon their legs again, and then there would be some one in the company with a maggot in his head, hatched from an egg deposited there nobody knows when, for not even fire kills these things, and you would have lost your labor. Nevertheless, we will not forget that some Egyptian wheat was handed down to us by a **96** mummy.

On the whole, I think that it cannot be maintained that dressing has in this or any country risen to the dignity of an art. At present men make shift to wear what they can get. Like shipwrecked sailors, they put on what they can find on the beach, and at a little distance, whether of space or time, laugh at each other's masquerade. Every generation laughs at the old fashions, but follows religiously the new. We are amused **97** at beholding the costume of Henry VIII., or Queen Elizabeth, as much as if it was that of the King and Queen of the Cannibal Islands. All costume off a man is pitiful or grotesque. It is only the serious eye peering from and the sincere life passed within it, which restrain laughter and consecrate the costume of any people. Let Harlequin be taken with a fit of the colic and **98**

93 *but they do now*. This is followed in ms. 1149 by: "I just had a coat come home from the tailor. Ah me! who am I that should wear this coat? It was fitted upon one of the Devil's angels about my size. This is not the figure that I cut; this is the figure the tailor cut. Impertinent Fashion whispered in his ear, so that he heard no word of mine. Or as if I had said, 'Not my will, O Fashion, but thine be done.'"

The origin of this passage can be seen in the *Journal* for January 13, 1854; VII, 69 f.

94 *not the Graces, nor the Parcæ*. In classical mythology, the three Graces, "who gave life its bloom," are Aglaia (Splendor), Euphrosyne (Mirth), and Eurynome (Good Cheer). The Parcæ are the three fates, Clotho, who spins the thread of life, Lachesis, who allots each person his destiny, and Atropos, who cuts off the thread.

95 *The head monkey at Paris*, as the *Journal* for January 14, 1854, shows, was the Count D'Orsay. Thoreau did not use the fine disdain of fashion of which he had written in his *Journal*: "Oh, with what delight I could thrust a spear through her vitals or squash her under my heel! Every village might well keep constantly employed a score of knights to rid itself of this monster. It changes men into bears or monkeys with a single wave of its wand."

96 *some Egyptian wheat was handed down to us by a mummy*. Thoreau apparently had some doubts about the viability of such ancient seeds, for he changed the "was" to "is said to have been" in his printed copy of *Walden*.

The Count d'Orsay

his trappings will have to serve that mood too. When the soldier is hit by a cannon ball rags are as becoming as purple. **99**

The childish and savage taste of men and women for new patterns keeps how many shaking and squinting through kaleidoscopes that they may discover the particular figure which this generation requires to-day. The manufacturers have learned that this taste is merely whimsical. Of two patterns which differ only by a few threads more or less of a particular color, the one will be sold readily, the other lie on the shelf, though it frequently happens that after the lapse of a season the latter becomes the most fashionable. Comparatively, tattooing is not the hideous custom which it is called. **100** It is not barbarous merely because the printing is skin-deep and unalterable.

I cannot believe that our factory system is the best mode by which men may get clothing. The condition of the operatives is becoming every day more like that of the English; and it cannot be wondered at, since, as far as I have heard or observed, the principal object is, not that mankind may be well and honestly clad, but, unquestionably, that the corporations may be enriched. In the long run men hit only what they aim at. Therefore, though they should fail immediately, they had better aim at something high.

As for a Shelter, I will not deny that this is now a necessary of life, though there are instances of men having done without it for long periods in colder countries than this. Samuel Laing says that "The Laplander **101** in his skin dress, and in a skin bag which he puts over

97 *We are amused at beholding the costume.* The word "costume" was "pictures" on ms. 92.

98 *Let Harlequin.* This passage originated in the *Journal* for February 5, 1841; I, 197.

99 *When the soldier is hit. Journal,* February 5, 1841; I, 197.

100 *tattooing is not the hideous custom which it is called* was followed in the manuscript by:

"It is the same taste that prints the calico which the wearer puts off and on, and the skin itself, which is always worn; and the consistent objection is rather to the pattern of the print than to the practice itself. It is not therefore barbarous because it is skin-deep.

"When I meet a fine lady or a gentleman dressed at the top of the fashion, I wonder what they would do if there should be an earthquake, or a fire should suddenly break out; for they appear to have counted on fair weather and a smooth course only. Our dress should be such as will to a certain extent fit equally well in good and bad fortune.

"When our garments are worn out, we hang them up in the fields to scare crows with,—as if the reason why men scare crows was in their clothes. I have often experienced the difficulty of getting within gunshot of a crow. It is not because they smell powder."

101 *Samuel Laing* wrote a book about his stay in Norway (London, 1837).

Laplanders

his head and shoulders, will sleep night after night on the snow —— in a degree of cold which would extinguish the life of one exposed to it in any woollen clothing." He had seen them asleep thus. Yet he adds, "They are not hardier than other people." But, probably, man did not live long on the earth without discovering the convenience which there is in a house, the domestic comforts, which phrase may have originally signified the satisfactions of the house more than of the family; though these must be extremely partial and occasional in those climates where the house is associated in our thoughts with winter or the rainy season chiefly, and two thirds of the year, except for a parasol, is unnecessary. In our climate, in the summer, it was formerly almost solely a covering at night. In the Indian gazettes a wigwam was the symbol of a day's march, and a row of them cut or painted on the bark of a tree signified that so many times they had camped. Man was not made so large limbed and robust but that he must seek to narrow his world, and wall in a space such as fitted him. He was at first bare and out of doors; but though this was pleasant enough in serene and warm weather, by daylight, the rainy season and the winter, to say nothing of the torrid sun, would perhaps have nipped his race in the bud if he had not made haste to clothe himself with the shelter of a house. Adam and Eve, according to the fable, wore the bower before other clothes. Man wanted a home, a place of warmth, or comfort, first of physical warmth, then the warmth of the affections.

We may imagine a time when, in the infancy of the human race, some enterprising mortal crept into a hollow in a rock for shelter. Every child begins the world again, to some extent, and loves to stay out doors, even in wet and cold. It plays house, as well as horse, having an instinct for it. Who does not remember the interest with which when young he looked at shelving rocks, or any approach to a cave? It was the natural yearning of that portion of our most primitive ancestor which still survived in us. From the cave we have advanced to roofs of palm leaves, of bark and boughs, of linen woven and stretched, of grass and straw, of boards and shingles, of stones and tiles. At last, we know not what it is to live in the open air, and our lives are domestic in more senses than we think. From

102 *some enterprising mortal.* This was "a man first" on ms. 11; then "some early wight" on ms. 490.

103 *even in wet and cold.* On ms. 1153 this was: "longer than its parents think prudent."

104 *or any approach to a cave.* Sanborn printed an omitted section in the Bibliophile Edition (I, 84–85):

"We may imagine a time when, in the infancy of the human race, a man first crept into a hollow in a rock for shelter. I have tried it myself with childish delight, as one may ride on a rail. I remember well the singular interest with which, when younger, I looked at shelving rocks, or any approach to a cavern; and that sometimes I was impelled to steal away, and sit by a fire under them, in a storm. It was the natural yearning of that portion of my most primitive ancestor which still survived in me."

On another page: "After long experience of pelting storms on the bare skin, and the alternation of sunshine and shade, some inspired wit discovered how to use Nature as a shield against herself; and, doubtfully at first, yet impelled by the idea, crept into a cavity in a rock,—or perchance so far, instinct sufficed. And then some remote descendant, of more inventive genius, considering the hard fate of men who were obliged to forego the expanding plains and fertile valleys, visible afar, and restrict their wanderings to the porous hill-country,—nicely discriminating what was essential in the cave, and what adventitious,—invented the roof,—that cave above ground, the portable cave,—invented to extend palm-leaves overhead, impermeable to sun and rain, an effective protection. The record of which remains yet in all languages; in the Latin 'tectum,' in English, 'shelter' or roof,—and in the course of ages the conviction was slowly forced upon all men, that the roof was good, and deserved to prevail,—nor would the gods be displeased thereby. And lo! the plains and valleys were peopled; and the dingy, cramped and uninformed families of men were dispersed into nimble and spreading nations. And the invention has been patented in sun and rain to this day,—roofs of palm-leaves with flickering sunbeams instreaming (and dates dropping on the table); of bark and boughs, of grass and straw, of linen woven and stretched, of boards and shingles, of stones and tiles. And hence it may be, this fair-complexioned Caucasian race, so many ages in advance of its sunburned brothers. But the poet should not speak so much from under a roof; nor does the saint dwell there so long. A poet would speak always as if there were no obstruction,—not even a mote or a shadow,—between him and the celestial bodies. Generally, the

the hearth to the field is a great distance. It would be well perhaps if we were to spend more of our days and nights without any obstruction between us and the celestial bodies, if the poet did not speak so much from under a roof, or the saint dwell there so long. Birds do not sing in caves, nor do doves cherish their innocence in dovecots.

However, if one designs to construct a dwelling house, it behooves him to exercise a little Yankee shrewdness, lest after all he find himself in a workhouse, a labyrinth without a clew, a museum, an almshouse, a prison, or a splendid mausoleum instead. Consider first how slight a shelter is absolutely necessary. I have seen Penobscot Indians, in this town, living in tents of thin cotton cloth, while the snow was nearly a foot deep **106** around them, and I thought that they would be glad to have it deeper to keep out the wind. Formerly, when how to get my living honestly, with freedom left for my proper pursuits, was a question which vexed me even more than it does now, for unfortunately I am become somewhat callous, I used to see a large box by the rail- **107** road, six feet long by three wide, in which the laborers locked up their tools at night, and it suggested to me that every man who was hard pushed might get such a one for a dollar, and, having bored a few auger holes in it, to admit the air at least, get into it when it rained and at night, and hook down the lid, and so have freedom **108** in his love, and in his soul be free. This did not appear the worst, nor by any means a despicable alternative. You could sit up as late as you pleased, and, whenever you got up, go abroad without any landlord or house-lord dogging you for rent. Many a man is harassed to death to pay the rent of a larger and more luxurious box who would not have frozen to death in such a box as this. I am far from jesting. Economy **109** is a subject which admits of being treated with levity, but it cannot so be disposed of. A comfortable house for a rude and hardy race, that lived mostly out of doors, was once made here almost entirely of such materials as Nature furnished ready to their hands. Gookin, who **110** was superintendent of the Indians subject to the Massachusetts Colony, writing in 1674, says, "The best of their houses are covered very neatly, tight and warm, with barks of trees, slipped from their bodies at those seasons when the sap is up, and made into great flakes,

voices of men sound hoarse and cavernous, tinkling as from out the recesses of caves; enough to frighten bats and toads; not like bells, not like the music of birds,—not a natural melody.

"Of all the inhabitants of Concord, I know not one that dwells in Nature. If one were to inhabit her forever, he would never meet a man. This country is not settled nor discovered yet."

105 *From the hearth to the field.* This was correct in the first edition, but the word "to" was dropped in the Riverside Aldine 1889 edition of *Walden*, which was the basis for numerous later editions, many of which perpetuate the error.

106 *while the snow was nearly a foot deep.* Here Thoreau again tempered his original statement by inserting the word "nearly" on ms. 674.

107 *I used to see a large box by the railroad.* This is almost exactly the same as in the *Journal* for January 28, 1852; III, 240. Charles Anderson (1968) says that this "solution for the staggering problem of housing mankind . . . is just a ruse for playing off one extreme against another."

108 *and so have freedom in his love* is a paraphrase of "If I have freedom in my love" from Richard Lovelace's "To Althea from Prison."

109 *Economy is a subject.* Also from the *Journal* of the same day.

110 *Gookin.* Daniel Gookin (1612–1687) wrote two books on the New England Indians which were published more than a century after his death. This quotation is from *Historical Collections of the Indians in New England* (Boston, 1792). Like Thoreau, Gookin was strongly pro-Indian.

with pressure of weighty timber, when they are green.
... The meaner sort are covered with mats which they
make of a kind of bulrush, and are also indifferently
tight and warm, but not so good as the former.... Some
I have seen, sixty or a hundred feet long and thirty
feet broad.... I have often lodged in their wigwams, and
found them as warm as the best English houses." He
adds, that they were commonly carpeted and lined within with well-wrought embroidered mats, and were furnished with various utensils. The Indians had advanced
so far as to regulate the effect of the wind by a mat
suspended over the hole in the roof and moved by
a string. Such a lodge was in the first instance constructed in a day or two at most, and taken down and
put up in a few hours; and every family owned one, or
its apartment in one.

In the savage state every family owns a shelter as
good as the best, and sufficient for its coarser and simpler wants; but I think that I speak within bounds
when I say that, though the birds of the air have their **111**
nests, and the foxes their holes, and the savages their
wigwams, in modern civilized society not more than one **112**
half the families own a shelter. In the large towns and
cities, where civilization especially prevails, the number
of those who own a shelter is a very small fraction of
the whole. The rest pay an annual tax for this outside
garment of all, become indispensable summer and winter, which would buy a village of Indian wigwams, but
now helps to keep them poor as long as they live. I do
not mean to insist here on the disadvantage of hiring
compared with owning, but it is evident that the savage
owns his shelter because it costs so little, while the civilized man hires his commonly because he cannot afford
to own it; nor can he, in the long run, any better afford
to hire. But, answers one, by merely paying this tax
the poor civilized man secures an abode which is a palace compared with the savage's. An annual rent of
from twenty-five to a hundred dollars, these are the
country rates, entitles him to the benefit of the improve- **113**
ments of centuries, spacious apartments, clean paint and
paper, Rumford fireplace, back plastering, Venetian
blinds, copper pump, spring lock, a commodious cellar,
and many other things. But how happens it that he
who is said to enjoy these things is so commonly a *poor*
civilized man, while the savage, who has them not, is

111 *the birds of the air.* Matthew 8:20.

112 *not more than one half the families own a
shelter.* On ms. 96 this was "no more than one
man in a hundred"; and three lines below, "the
rest" was originally "the 99."

113 *the improvements of centuries.* The latest
and most desirable home improvements as they
were in 1854 are listed here. Central heating is not
mentioned. The Rumford fireplace had been invented a long time before by Benjamin Thomp-
son, Count Rumford (1753–1814). His principle
of having a smoke shelf that prevents downdrafts
from carrying smoke into the room is still used in
modern fireplaces. *Journal*, 1845; I, 388.

rich as a savage? If it is asserted that civilization is a real advance in the condition of man,—and I think that it is, though only the wise improve their advantages,—it must be shown that it has produced better dwellings without making them more costly; and the cost of a thing is the amount of what I will call life which is required to be exchanged for it, immediately or in the long run. An average house in this neighborhood costs perhaps eight hundred dollars, and to lay up **114** this sum will take from ten to fifteen years of the laborer's life, even if he is not encumbered with a family;— estimating the pecuniary value of every man's labor at **115** one dollar a day, for if some receive more, others receive less;—so that he must have spent more than half his life commonly before *his* wigwam will be earned. If we suppose him to pay a rent instead, this is but a doubtful choice of evils. Would the savage have been **116** wise to exchange his wigwam for a palace on these terms?

It may be guessed that I reduce almost the whole advantage of holding this superfluous property as a fund in store against the future, so far as the individual is concerned, mainly to the defraying of funeral expenses. **117** But perhaps a man is not required to bury himself. Nevertheless this points to an important distinction between the civilized man and the savage; and, no doubt, they have designs on us for our benefit, in making the life of a civilized people an *institution*, in which the life of the individual is to a great extent absorbed, in order to preserve and perfect that of the race. But I wish to show at what a sacrifice this advantage is at present obtained, and to suggest that we may possibly so live as to secure all the advantage without suffering any of the disadvantage. What mean ye by saying that the poor ye have **118** always with you, or that the fathers have eaten sour grapes, and the children's teeth are set on edge?

"As I live, saith the Lord God, ye shall not have occasion any more to use this proverb in Israel."

"Behold all souls are mine; as the soul of the father, so also the soul of the son is mine: the soul that sinneth it shall die."

When I consider my neighbors, the farmers of Concord, who are at least as well off as the other classes, I **119** find that for the most part they have been toiling twenty, **120** thirty, or forty years, that they may become the real

114 *perhaps eight hundred dollars.* Thoreau has revised his house price downward; ms. 98 said $1000.

115 *labor at one dollar a day.* This was the standard rate for many years at this time, but immigrants were often paid half of this. It is interesting to see Thoreau calculating the costs of things by the number of man-hours spent on producing them.

116 *Would the savage have been wise. Journal,* 1845; I, 389.

117 *the defraying of funeral expenses.* Ms. 566 has a novel phrase that has never been published. It follows here. "For every sickness is a beginning to die, and therefore every doctor's bill is a funeral expense."

118 *the poor ye have always with you.* Paraphrase of Matthew 26:11; *the fathers have eaten sour grapes and the children's teeth are set on edge,* Ezekiel 18:2; *As I live saith the Lord, ibid.,* 18:3.

119 *When I consider my neighbors. Journal,* 1845; I, 389.

120 *twenty, thirty, or forty years.* The word "forty" was inserted on ms. 362.

owners of their farms, which commonly they have inherited with encumbrances, or else bought with hired money, — and we may regard one third of that toil as the cost of their houses, — but commonly they have not paid for them yet. It is true, the encumbrances sometimes outweigh the value of the farm, so that the farm itself becomes one great encumbrance, and still a man is found to inherit it, being well acquainted with it, as he says. On applying to the assessors, I am surprised to learn that they cannot at once name a dozen in the town who own their farms free and clear. If you would know the history of these homesteads, inquire at the bank where they are mortgaged. The man who has actually paid for his farm with labor on it is so rare that every neighbor can point to him. I doubt if there are three such men in Concord. What has been said of the merchants, that a very large majority, even ninety-seven in a hundred, are sure to fail, is equally true of the farmers. With regard to the merchants, however, one of them says pertinently that a great part of their failures are not genuine pecuniary failures, but merely failures to fulfil their engagements, because it is inconvenient; that is, it is the moral character that breaks down. But this puts an infinitely worse face on the matter, and suggests, beside, that probably not even the other three succeed in saving their souls, but are perchance bankrupt in a worse sense than they who fail honestly. Bankruptcy and repudiation are the spring-boards from which much of our civilization vaults and turns its somersets, but the savage stands on the unelastic plank of famine. Yet the Middlesex Cattle Show goes off here with *éclat* annually, as if all the joints of the agricultural machine were suent.   **121**

The farmer is endeavoring to solve the problem of a livelihood by a formula more complicated than the problem itself. To get his shoestrings he speculates in herds of cattle. With consummate skill he has set his trap with a hair springe to catch comfort and independence, and then, as he turned away, got his own leg into it. This is the reason he is poor; and for a similar reason we are all poor in respect to a thousand savage comforts, though surrounded by luxuries. As Chapman sings, —   **122**   **123**   **124**

> " The false society of men —
>   — for earthly greatness
> All heavenly comforts rarefies to air."

121 *suent*. Thoreau defines this unusual word in his *Journal* for February 3, 1852; III, 272, where he says: " 'Suent' is an expressive word, applied to machinery whose joints are worn, which has got into working order,—apparently from sueo, to be accustomed." Today we call this "broken in."

122 *a hair springe*. Springe is an old English word for a snare or a trap. A hair springe is one that is so lightly set that the slightest touch will trip it.

123 *This is the reason he is poor. Journal*, 1845; I, 389.

124 *As Chapman sings*. The verse is from *The Tragedy of Caesar and Pompey*, V, ii, by George Chapman (1559?–1634).

Minerva

And when the farmer has got his house, he may not be the richer but the poorer for it, and it be the house that has got him.   As I understand it, that was a valid objection urged by Momus against the house which Minerva made, that she " had not made it movable, by which means a bad neighborhood might be avoided; " and it may still be urged, for our houses are such unwieldy property that we are often imprisoned rather than housed in them; and the bad neighborhood to be avoided is our own scurvy selves.   I know one or two families, at least, in this town, who, for nearly a generation, have been wishing to sell their houses in the outskirts and move into the village, but have not been able to accomplish it, and only death will set them free.

Granted that the *majority* are able at last either to own or hire the modern house with all its improvements. While civilization has been improving our houses, it has not equally improved the men who are to inhabit them. It has created palaces, but it was not so easy to create noblemen and kings.   And *if the civilized man's pursuits are no worthier than the savage's, if he is employed the greater part of his life in obtaining gross necessaries and comforts merely, why should he have a better dwelling than the former?*

But how do the poor *minority* fare?   Perhaps it will be found, that just in proportion as some have been placed in outward circumstances above the savage, others have been degraded below him.   The luxury of one class is counterbalanced by the indigence of another. On the one side is the palace, on the other are the almshouse and " silent poor."   The myriads who built the pyramids to be the tombs of the Pharaohs were fed on garlic, and it may be were not decently buried themselves.   The mason who finishes the cornice of the palace returns at night perchance to a hut not so good as a wigwam.   It is a mistake to suppose that, in a country where the usual evidences of civilization exist, the condition of a very large body of the inhabitants may not be as degraded as that of savages.   I refer to the degraded poor, not now to the degraded rich.   To know this I should not need to look farther than to the shanties which every where border our railroads, that last improvement in civilization; where I see in my daily walks human beings living in sties, and all winter with an open door, for the sake of light, without any visible,

125

126

127

128

129

130

125 *urged by Momus.* Thoreau had much more to say about Momus in the first version of *Walden:* "Momus was the god of pleasantry among the ancients. He was Jupiter's jester or fool, and many a time he set the gods in a roar. 'He was continually employed in satirizing the gods, and whatever they did was freely turned to ridicule.' Neptune, Minerva and Vulcan had a trial of skill. The first made a Bull; the second a House; the third a Man. 'Momus found fault with them all. He disliked the Bull because his horns were not placed before his eyes that he might give a surer blow.' 'He censured the House which Minerva had made because she had not made it moveable, by which means a bad neighborhood might be avoided.' 'With regard to Vulcan's Man, he said he ought to have made a window in his breast.' 'Venus herself was exposed to his satire; and when the sneering god found no fault in the body of the naked goddess, he observed, as she retired, that the noise of her feet was too loud, and greatly improper in the goddess of beauty. These reflections were the cause that Momus was driven from heaven.' What, think you, would Momus say if he were living in our day? And I am not sure but what he is."

126 *only death will set them free.* Omitted from the printed text is this passage, which Sanborn used in the Bibliophile Edition, (I, 93):
"What the rich are said to give away is not,

often imaginable, wood pile, and the forms of both old and young are permanently contracted by the long habit of shrinking from cold and misery, and the development of all their limbs and faculties is checked. It certainly is fair to look at that class by whose labor the works which distinguish this generation are accomplished. Such too, to a greater or less extent, is the condition of the operatives of every denomination in England, which is the great workhouse of the world. Or I could refer you to Ireland, which is marked as one **131** of the white or enlightened spots on the map. Contrast the physical condition of the Irish with that of the North American Indian, or the South Sea Islander, or any other savage race before it was degraded by contact with the civilized man. Yet I have no doubt that that people's rulers are as wise as the average of civilized rulers. Their condition only proves what squalidness may consist with civilization. I hardly need refer now to the laborers in our Southern States who produce the staple exports of this country, and are themselves **132** a staple production of the South. But to confine my- **133** self to those who are said to be in *moderate* circumstances.

Most men appear never to have considered what a house is, and are actually though needlessly poor all their lives because they think that they must have such a one as their neighbors have. As if one were to wear **134** any sort of coat which the tailor might cut out for him, or, gradually leaving off palmleaf hat or cap of woodchuck skin, complain of hard times because he could not afford to buy him a crown! It is possible to invent a house still more convenient and luxurious than we have, which yet all would admit that man could not afford to pay for. Shall we always study to obtain more of these things, and not sometimes to be content with less? Shall the respectable citizen thus gravely teach, by precept and example, the necessity of the young man's providing a certain number of superfluous glow- **135** shoes, and umbrellas, and empty guest chambers for empty guests, before he dies? Why should not our furniture be as simple as the Arab's or the Indian's? **136** When I think of the benefactors of the race, whom we have apotheosized as messengers from heaven, bearers of divine gifts to man, I do not see in my mind any retinue at their heels, any car-load of fashionable furniture.

commonly, a gift; but rather, so much abandoned to mankind, though it be the tenth part of their income annually. But even with money you might do something grander and more imposing. A small sum would really do much good, if the donor spent himself with it,—in other words, saw it through and did not merely relinquish it to some distant society, as the Colonization Society, or the Society for Foreign Missions, whose managers do the good or evil with it.

"How much might be done for this town with a hundred dollars! I myself have once provided a select course of twenty-five lectures for a winter, together with room, fuel and lights, with that sum; which was no inconsiderable benefit to every inhabitant. With $1000 I could purchase for Concord a more complete and select library (in my opinion) than exists in the State, outside of Cambridge and Boston,—and perhaps a more available one than any. Men sit paralyzed and helpless by the side of their buried treasures. After all, those who do the most good with money do it with the least amount; because they can do better than to acquire it."

127 *The luxury of one class.* This sentence and the next were written in between lines on heavily revised ms. *575.*

128 *"silent poor."* The silent poor are the poverty-stricken people who are too proud to ask for aid. Concord has long had a fund to take care of those who refuse to enter the poorhouse.

129 *The mason who finishes the cornice of the palace. Journal, 1845;* I, 388.

130 *the usual evidences of civilization.* This was followed on ms. 576 by "rail-roads—steamboats—printing presses—churches—and the like," but Thoreau canceled these words.

131 *Or I could refer you to Ireland.* In the 1840's, when the Irish potato crop failed, famine swept the land, and about a million people died. At this time, as the *Encyclopaedia Britannica* (Eleventh Edition, 1910, XIV, 781) says: "It was found that labour and exposure were not good for half-starved men." Hundreds of thousands of Irish left the country; large numbers came to the United States; some settled in or near Concord where Thoreau saw them daily.

132 *are themselves a staple production of the South.* This refers to slave breeding in the Southern states.

133 In his own copy of *Walden*, Thoreau placed a question mark in the margin opposite these lines.

Or what if I were to allow — would it not be a singular allowance ? — that our furniture should be more complex than the Arab's, in proportion as we are morally and intellectually his superiors! At present our houses are cluttered and defiled with it, and a good housewife would sweep out the greater part into the dust hole, and not leave her morning's work undone. Morning work! By the blushes of Aurora and the music of Memnon, what should be man's *morning work* in this world ? I had three pieces of limestone on my desk, but I was terrified to find that they required to be dusted daily, when the furniture of my mind was all undusted still, and I threw them out the window in disgust. How, then, could I have a furnished house ? I would rather sit in the open air, for no dust gathers on the grass, unless where man has broken ground.

134 *As if one were to wear. Journal,* 1845; I, 389.

135 *glowshoes.* Overshoes.

136 *furniture be as simple as the Arab's. Journal,* July 1845; I, 367.

137 *our houses are cluttered and defiled.* It must be remembered that this is the time that ornate Victorian furniture and decorative accessories were coming into fashion.

138 *By the blushes of Aurora*—goddess of the dawn.

139 *Memnon.* One of the two Egyptian colossi of Memnon near Thebes was supposed to utter a sound when the first rays of the rising sun touched it.

140 *Sardanapalus.* The Greek form of Ashurbanipal, an effeminate and cruel Assyrian ruler (c. 822 B.C.).

137

138
139

The Colossi of Memnon

It is the luxurious and dissipated who set the fashions which the herd so diligently follow. The traveller who stops at the best houses, so called, soon discovers this, for the publicans presume him to be a Sardanapalus, **140** and if he resigned himself to their tender mercies he would soon be completely emasculated. I think that in the railroad car we are inclined to spend more on luxury than on safety and convenience, and it threatens without attaining these to become no better than a modern drawing room, with its divans, and ottomans, and sunshades, and a hundred other oriental things, which we are taking west with us, invented for the ladies of the harem and the effeminate natives of the Celestial Empire, which Jonathan should be ashamed to **141** know the names of. I would rather sit on a pumpkin and have it all to myself, than be crowded on a velvet cushion. I would rather ride on earth in an ox cart with a free circulation, than go to heaven in the fancy car of an excursion train and breathe a *malaria* all the way.

The very simplicity and nakedness of man's life in the primitive ages imply this advantage at least, that they left him still but a sojourner in nature. When he **142** was refreshed with food and sleep he contemplated his journey again. He dwelt, as it were, in a tent in this world, and was either threading the valleys, or crossing the plains, or climbing the mountain tops. But lo! men have become the tools of their tools. The man who independently plucked the fruits when he was hungry is become a farmer; and he who stood under a tree for shelter, a housekeeper. We now no longer camp as for a night, but have settled down on earth and forgotten heaven. We have adopted Christianity merely as an improved method of *agri*-culture. We have built for this world a family mansion, and for the next a fami- **143** ly tomb. The best works of art are the expression of man's struggle to free himself from this condition, but the effect of our art is merely to make this low state comfortable and that higher state to be forgotten. There is actually no place in this village for a work of *fine* art, if any had come down to us, to stand, for our lives, our houses and streets, furnish no proper pedestal for it. There is not a nail to hang a picture on, nor a shelf to receive the bust of a hero or a saint. When I consider how our houses are built and paid for, or not paid for, and their internal economy managed and sustained, I wonder that the floor does not give way under the visitor while he is admiring the gewgaws upon the mantel-piece, and let him through into the cellar, to some solid and honest though earthy foundation. I cannot but perceive that this so called rich and refined life is a thing jumped at, and I do not get on in the enjoyment of the *fine* arts which adorn it, my attention being wholly occupied with the jump; for I remember that the greatest genuine leap, due to human muscles alone, on record, is that of certain

141 *which Jonathan should be ashamed to know the names of.* Just as the English were John Bull, so were Americans called Jonathan.

The following canceled and never-before-published passage occurs between the end of this sentence and the beginning of the next one (ms. 578). "And no alternative but this or the black-hole of a 2nd class car. Where is Jonathan's parlor? Jonathan's car forsooth with the seat of Jonathan omitted! To be introduced into a drawing room in which you are compelled to stand up for want of a seat, or sit on a hair cushion without the possibility of drawing a long breath owing to the encroachments of a corpulent neighbor."

This was long before the Pullman car came in during the 1860's and even before the Woodruff "Seat and Couch Railway Car" was patented in 1856. Despite the efforts to make the cars look like the Oriental harems which Thoreau has just described, the American railroads in the early 1850's were still quite primitive.

The "black-hole" refers to the black hole of Calcutta, an undersized punishment cell in India, into which 146 Europeans were crowded in 1756 so that when morning came only 23 were still alive.

142 *still but a sojourner in nature.* This, and the earlier reference to the simplicity of Arab and Indian furniture are in the *Journal* for 1845; I, 367. The "tools of their tools" reference is on page 368.

143 *for the next a family tomb.* This follows here on ms. 101: "Now the best works of art even serve comparatively but to dissipate the mind, for they themselves represent transitionary and paroxismal thought, not free and absolute thought."

wandering Arabs, who are said to have cleared twenty-five feet on level ground. Without factitious support, man is sure to come to earth again beyond that distance. The first question which I am tempted to put to the proprietor of such great impropriety is, Who bolsters you? Are you one of the ninety-seven who fail, or **144** the three who succeed? Answer me these questions, and then perhaps I may look at your bawbles and find them ornamental. The cart before the horse is neither beautiful nor useful. Before we can adorn our houses with beautiful objects the walls must be stripped, and our lives must be stripped, and beautiful housekeeping and beautiful living be laid for a foundation : now, a taste for the beautiful is most cultivated out of doors, where there is no house and no housekeeper.

Old Johnson, in his " Wonder-Working Providence," **145** speaking of the first settlers of this town, with whom he was contemporary, tells us that " they burrow themselves in the earth for their first shelter under some hillside, and, casting the soil aloft upon timber, they make a smoky fire against the earth, at the highest side." They did not " provide them houses," says he, " till the earth, by the Lord's blessing, brought forth bread to feed them," and the first year's crop was so light that " they were forced to cut their bread very thin for a long season." The secretary of the Province of New Netherland, **146** writing in Dutch, in 1650, for the information of those who wished to take up land there, states more particularly, that " those in New Netherland, and especially in New England, who have no means to build farm houses at first according to their wishes, dig a square pit in the ground, cellar fashion, six or seven feet deep, as long and as broad as they think proper, case the earth inside with wood all round the wall, and line the wood with the bark of trees or something else to prevent the caving in of the earth ; floor this cellar with plank, and wainscot it overhead for a ceiling, raise a roof of spars clear up, and cover the spars with bark or green sods, so that they can live dry and warm in these houses with their entire families for two, three, and four years, it being understood that partitions are run through those cellars which are adapted to the size of the family. The wealthy and principal men in New England, in the beginning of the colonies, commenced their first dwelling houses in this fashion for two reasons ; firstly, in order

144 *one of the ninety-seven who fail.* Again Thoreau tempers his figures. On the page proofs this was "ninety-nine" and then "one" instead of "three."

145 *Old Johnson* was Edward Johnson (1599–1672), author of *Wonder-working Providence of Zion's Saviour in New England* (1654), which covers the years 1628 to 1651, and is a primary source book for the history of the early settlement.

146 *The secretary of . . . New Netherland.* New Netherland was New York. The description of early house building that follows was taken from E. B. O'Callaghan's *The Documentary History of the State of New York*, 1851, IV, 31. At the end of it Thoreau added on ms. 1156: "Like prudent men they waited till more pressing wants were satisfied." Echoes of this can be seen in the next two sentences.

not to waste time in building, and not to want food the next season; secondly, in order not to discourage poor laboring people whom they brought over in numbers from Fatherland. In the course of three or four years, when the country became adapted to agriculture, they built themselves handsome houses, spending on them several thousands."

In this course which our ancestors took there was a show of prudence at least, as if their principle were to satisfy the more pressing wants first. But are the more pressing wants satisfied now? When I think of acquiring for myself one of our luxurious dwellings, I am deterred, for, so to speak, the country is not yet adapted to *human* culture, and we are still forced to cut our *spiritual* bread far thinner than our forefathers did their wheaten. Not that all architectural ornament is to be neglected even in the rudest periods; but let our houses first be lined with beauty, where they come in contact with our lives, like the tenement of the shell-fish, and not overlaid with it. But, alas! I have been inside one or two of them, and know what they are lined with.

Though we are not so degenerate but that we might **147** possibly live in a cave or a wigwam or wear skins to-day, it certainly is better to accept the advantages, though so dearly bought, which the invention and industry of mankind offer. In such a neighborhood as this, boards and shingles, lime and bricks, are cheaper and more easily obtained than suitable caves, or whole logs, or bark in sufficient quantities, or even well-tempered clay or flat stones. I speak understandingly on this subject, for I have made myself acquainted with it both theoretically and practically. With a little more wit we might use these materials so as to become richer than the richest now are, and make our civilization a blessing. The civilized man is a more experienced and wiser savage. But to make haste to my own experiment.

Near the end of March, 1845, I borrowed an axe **148** and went down to the woods by Walden Pond, nearest to where I intended to build my house, and began to cut **149** down some tall arrowy white pines, still in their youth, for timber. It is difficult to begin without borrowing, **150**

147 *Though we are not so degenerate.* This appears in somewhat longer form in the *Journal* for 1845; I, 387.

148 *Near the end of March, 1845.* Here the building of the Walden Pond house begins. The sentence about the axe was inserted on ms. 106. The ownership of this axe has been much disputed. Alcott said that he lent it to Thoreau; Emerson also may have had a claim to it; but Ellery Channing, in his heavily annotated copy of *Walden*, added at the end of this phrase: "(from me)." The axe itself cannot be identified. It may still be in use; perhaps it lies somewhere in the fields rusting away; or it may have been melted down for scrap iron.

149 *where I intended to build my house.* Here ms. 106 has "I told you I should put in the I." (See page 145, line 23.)

150 *It is difficult to begin without borrowing.* This is followed on ms. 368 by "Our very life is in one sense borrowed and must be returned with interest to him who lent it."

but perhaps it is the most generous course thus to permit your fellow-men to have an interest in your enterprise. The owner of the axe, as he released his hold **151** on it, said that it was the apple of his eye; but I returned it sharper than I received it. It was a pleasant hillside where I worked, covered with pine woods, through which I looked out on the pond, and a small open field

151 *The owner of the axe*. On ms. 38 this reads: "The man from whom I borrowed the axe, as he relaxed his hold on it. . . ."

152 *the lark and pewee*. The first version (ms. 106) reads: "The woodpecker & vireo."

153 *the winter of man's discontent*. Paraphrase of Shakespeare's *Richard III*, I, i.

A bit of wood and two nails from the Walden cabin (*Concord Lyceum*)

in the woods where pines and hickories were springing up. The ice in the pond was not yet dissolved, though there were some open spaces, and it was all dark colored and saturated with water. There were some slight flurries of snow during the days that I worked there; but for the most part when I came out on to the railroad, on my way home, its yellow sand heap stretched away gleaming in the hazy atmosphere, and the rails shone in the spring sun, and I heard the lark and pewee and **152** other birds already come to commence another year with us. They were pleasant spring days, in which the **153** winter of man's discontent was thawing as well as the earth, and the life that had lain torpid began to stretch itself. One day, when my axe had come off and I had cut a green hickory for a wedge, driving it with a stone, and had placed the whole to soak in a pond hole in order to swell the wood, I saw a striped snake run into the water, and he lay on the bottom, apparently without inconvenience, as long as I staid there, or more than a quarter of an hour; perhaps because he had not yet fairly come out of the torpid state. It appeared to me that for a like reason men remain in their present low and primitive condition; but if they should feel the influence of the spring of springs arousing them, they would of necessity rise to a higher and more ethereal life. I had previously seen the snakes in frosty mornings in my path with portions of their bodies still numb and inflexible, waiting for the sun to thaw them. On the 1st of April it rained and melted the ice, and in the early part of the day, which was very foggy, I heard a stray goose groping about over the pond and cackling as if lost, or **154** like the spirit of the fog.

So I went on for some days cutting and hewing timber, and also studs and rafters, all with my narrow axe, not having many communicable or scholar-like thoughts, singing to myself, —

> Men say they know many things;   **155**
> But lo! they have taken wings, —
> The arts and sciences,
> And a thousand appliances;
> The wind that blows
> Is all that any body knows.

I hewed the main timbers six inches square, most of the studs on two sides only, and the rafters and floor timbers on one side, leaving the rest of the bark on, so that they were just as straight and much stronger than sawed ones. Each stick was carefully mortised or tenoned by its stump, for I had borrowed other tools by this time. My days in the woods were not very long ones; yet I usually carried my dinner of bread and butter, and read the newspaper in which it was wrapped, at noon, sitting amid the green pine boughs which I had cut off, and to my bread was imparted some of their fragrance, for my hands were covered with a thick coat of pitch. Before I had done I was more the friend than the foe of the pine tree, though I had cut down some of them, having become better acquainted with it. Sometimes a rambler in the wood was attracted by the sound of my axe, and we chatted pleasantly over the chips which I **156** had made.

By the middle of April, for I made no haste in my work, but rather made the most of it, my house was framed and ready for the raising. I had already bought **157** the shanty of James Collins, an Irishman who worked on

154 *cackling as if lost, or.* The "or" is not on ms. 107, which reads better without it.

155 When a quotation does not have quote marks, it is Thoreau's own work.

156 *we chatted pleasantly.* Channing objected to the use of "chatted" and wrote in the margin of his copy of *Walden* "a very vile word." The NED says that chat is "an onomatopoeic abbreviation of CHATTER, which has lost . . . to some extent the depreciative force of that word." Under the definition "to converse familiarly and pleasantly," which is the way Thoreau used the word, "chat" can be found in the writings of Shakespeare, Milton, and Jane Austen.

157 *I had already bought the shanty.* The Irishmen who had built the railroad lived in crude shanties which had been built along the right of way. Now that the railroad was finished, and there was no longer any need for labor on it, the shacks were being sold for a few dollars each, while their inhabitants went elsewhere to seek work.

the Fitchburg Railroad, for boards. James Collins' shanty was considered an uncommonly fine one. When I called to see it he was not at home. I walked about the outside, at first unobserved from within, the window was so deep and high. It was of small dimensions, with a peaked cottage roof, and not much else to be seen, the dirt being raised five feet all around as if it were a compost heap. The roof was the soundest part, though a good deal warped and made brittle by the sun. Door-sill there was none, but a perennial passage for the hens under the door board. Mrs. C. came to the door and asked me to view it from the inside. The hens were driven in by my approach. It was dark, and had a dirt floor for the most part, dank, clammy, and aguish, only here a board and there a board which would not bear removal. She lighted a lamp to show me the inside of the roof and the walls, and also that the board floor extended under the bed, warning me not to step into the cellar, a sort of dust hole two feet deep. In her own words, they were "good boards overhead, good boards all around, and a good window," — of two whole squares originally, only the cat had passed out that way lately. There was a stove, a bed, and a place to sit, an infant in the house where it was born, a silk parasol, gilt-framed looking-glass, and a patent new coffee mill nailed to an oak sapling, all told. The bargain was soon concluded, for James had in the mean while returned. I to pay four dollars and twenty-five cents to-night, he to vacate at five to-morrow morning, selling to nobody else meanwhile : I to take possession at six. It were well, he said, to be there early, and anticipate certain indistinct but wholly unjust claims on the score of ground rent and fuel. This he assured me was the only encumbrance. At six I passed him and his family on the road. One large bundle held their all, — bed, coffee-mill, looking-glass, hens, — all but the cat, she took to the woods and became a wild cat, and, as I learned afterward, trod in a trap set for woodchucks, and so became a dead cat at last.

I took down this dwelling the same morning, drawing the nails, and removed it to the pond side by small cart- **158** loads, spreading the boards on the grass there to bleach and warp back again in the sun. One early thrush gave me a note or two as I drove along the woodland path. I was informed treacherously by a young Patrick

158 *by small cartloads.* The site of James Collins' shanty is not known but it was surely near the railroad and therefore not far from the place where Thoreau wanted to build his house. The cart was undoubtedly one that could be pushed by hand. He brought his furniture to the cabin on a hay-rig.

that neighbor Seeley, an Irishman, in the intervals of the carting, transferred the still tolerable, straight, and **159** drivable nails, staples, and spikes to his pocket, and then **160** stood when I came back to pass the time of day, and look freshly up, unconcerned, with spring thoughts, at the devastation; there being a dearth of work, as he said. He was there to represent spectatordom, and help make this seemingly insignificant event one with the removal of the gods of Troy.

I dug my cellar in the side of a hill sloping to the **161** south, where a woodchuck had formerly dug his burrow, down through sumach and blackberry roots, and the lowest stain of vegetation, six feet square by seven deep, to a fine sand where potatoes would not freeze in any winter. The sides were left shelving, and not stoned; but the sun having never shone on them, the sand still keeps its place. It was but two hours' work. I took particular pleasure in this breaking of ground, for in almost all latitudes men dig into the earth for an equable temperature. Under the most splendid house in the city is still to be found the cellar where they store their roots as of old, and long after the superstructure has disappeared posterity remark its dent in the earth. The house is still but a sort of porch at the entrance of a burrow.

At length, in the beginning of May, with the help of some of my acquaintances, rather to improve so good an occasion for neighborliness than from any necessity, I set up the frame of my house. No man **162** was ever more honored in the character of his raisers than I. They are destined, I trust, to assist at the raising of loftier structures one day. I began to occupy my house on the 4th of July, as soon as it was boarded and roofed, for the boards were carefully feather-edged **163** and lapped, so that it was perfectly impervious to rain; but before boarding I laid the foundation of a chimney at one end, bringing two cartloads of stones up the hill from the pond in my arms. I built the chimney after my hoeing in the fall, before a fire became necessary for warmth, doing my cooking in the mean while out of doors on the ground, early in the morning: which mode I still think is in some respects more convenient and agreeable than the usual one. When it stormed before my bread was baked, I fixed a few boards over the fire, and sat under them to watch my loaf, and passed **164**

159 *transferred the . . . nails, staples, and spikes to his pocket.* Hardware, which was then hand-made, was valuable and was carefully saved for reuse.

160 Channing, in his copy of *Walden*, took exception to the use of "drivable" and (four lines below) "spectatordom." "Bad," he noted in each instance.

161 *I dug my cellar.* See the chapter on "The Cabin and Walden Pond."

162 *No man was ever more honored in the character of his raisers.* Sanborn, in his Introduction to the Bibliophile Edition of *Walden*, quotes George Willis Cooke's list of the raisers in *Early Letters of George William Curtis to John S. Dwight* (1898): "Alcott, lately returned to Concord from the lost Paradise of Fruitlands; Emerson, Ellery Channing, the two Curtises, George and Burrill, who had migrated from Brook Farm to Ponkatassett Hill a year before; and the sturdy farmer, Edmund Hosmer, with his sons, John, Edmund, and Andrew. Alcott was then living near the Hosmers on one of the Lincoln roads, and the Curtises were in the same neighborhood."

163 *the boards were carefully feather-edged and lapped.* See illustration.

164 *and passed some pleasant hours in that way.* Sanborn (Bibliophile Edition, I, 18) placed here the Thoreau poem that is printed (in slightly different form) in "What I Lived For," note 69.

Feather-edged boards,
cut this way to keep out the rain

Stones covering the site of the fireplace
of the Walden cabin

some pleasant hours in that way. In those days, when my hands were much employed, I read but little, but the least scraps of paper which lay on the ground, my holder, or tablecloth, afforded me as much entertainment, in fact answered the same purpose as the Iliad.

It would be worth the while to build still more deliberately than I did, considering, for instance, what foundation a door, a window, a cellar, a garret, have in the nature of man, and perchance never raising any superstructure until we found a better reason for it than our temporal necessities even. There is some of the same fitness in a man's building his own house that there is in a bird's building its own nest. Who knows but if men constructed their dwellings with their own hands, and provided food for themselves and families simply and honestly enough, the poetic faculty would be universally developed, as birds universally sing when they are so engaged? But alas! we do like **165** cowbirds and cuckoos, which lay their eggs in nests which other birds have built, and cheer no traveller with their chattering and unmusical notes. Shall we forever resign the pleasure of construction to the carpenter? What does architecture amount to in the experience of the mass of men? I never in all my walks came across a man engaged in so simple and natural an occupation as building his house. We belong to the community. It is not the tailor alone who is the **166** ninth part of a man; it is as much the preacher, and the merchant, and the farmer. Where is this division of labor to end? and what object does it finally serve? No doubt another *may* also think for me; but it is not therefore desirable that he should do so to the exclusion of my thinking for myself. **167**

True, there are architects so called in this country, and I have heard of one at least possessed with the idea **168** of making architectural ornaments have a core of truth, a necessity, and hence a beauty, as if it were a revelation to him. All very well perhaps from his point of view, but only a little better than the common dilettantism. A sentimental reformer in architecture, he began at the cornice, not at the foundation. It was only how to put a core of truth within the ornaments, that every sugar plum in fact might have an almond or car-

165 *But alas!* This begins a new paragraph on the page proofs, but Thoreau wrote "no break" in the margin.

166 *It is not the tailor alone who is the ninth part of a man.* "Nine tailors make a man" is an English proverb that goes back to 1615 according to *The Oxford Dictionary of English Proverbs*, p. 314.

167 *thinking for myself.* This is followed on ms. 568 by "Folly in the gross is no more respectable than folly in detail. I do not hesitate to repeat what was revealed by another in a moment of illumination—that 'mankind is a damned fool.'" Sanborn has printed the two paragraphs after this in the Bibliophile Edition (I, 103–104):

"'Take the article ice, for instance, I say that society is foolish which so unwisely adds this to the already long list of its luxuries. My argument is this: We are exceedingly poor and bankrupt, living beyond our means—ice is a mere luxury at best and concomitant of luxuries, and it is an expensive luxury—say what you will about it.

"Have twenty mats at your door if you have leisure to shake them yourself. The fatuity with which society adopts and clutches at new luxuries! It is a roué, a débauché, and will not listen to reason—as well reason with a sick man. You must use force for his good, or let him die."

168 *and I have heard of one.* The architect is Horatio Greenough according to the *Journal* for January 11, 1852; III, 181–183. Here Thoreau says that Emerson had shown him a letter from Greenough, and it was from this that he got his conceptions—not always valid—of Greenough's theories. Those who have any interest in architecture should read carefully the ideas Thoreau expresses here. This is functionalism defined long before the word for it was invented.

away seed in it,—though I hold that almonds are most wholesome without the sugar,—and not how the inhabitant, the indweller, might build truly within and without, and let the ornaments take care of themselves. What reasonable man ever supposed that ornaments were something outward and in the skin merely,—that the tortoise got his spotted shell, or the shellfish its mother-o'-pearl tints, by such a contract as the inhabitants of Broadway their Trinity Church? But a man has no more to do with the style of architecture of his house than a tortoise with that of its shell: nor need the soldier be so idle as to try to paint the precise *color* of his virtue on his standard. The enemy will find it out. He may turn pale when the trial comes. This man seemed to me to lean over the cornice, and timidly whisper his half truth to the rude occupants who really knew it better than he. What of architectural beauty I now see, I know has gradually grown from within outward, out of the necessities and character of the indweller, who is the only builder,—out of some unconscious truthfulness, and nobleness, without ever a thought for the appearance; and whatever additional beauty of this kind is destined to be produced will be preceded by a like unconscious beauty of life. The most interesting dwellings in this country, as the painter knows, are the most unpretending, humble log huts and cottages of the poor commonly; it is the life of the in-

169

169 *Trinity Church.* The New York building mentioned here burned down and has been replaced.

Trinity Church, New York

habitants whose shells they are, and not any peculiarity in their surfaces merely, which makes them *picturesque;* and equally interesting will be the citizen's suburban box, when his life shall be as simple and as agreeable to the imagination, and there is as little straining after effect in the style of his dwelling. A great proportion of architectural ornaments are literally hollow, and a September gale would strip them off, like borrowed plumes, without injury to the substantials. They can do without *architecture* who have no olives **170** nor wines in the cellar. What if an equal ado were made about the ornaments of style in literature, and the architects of our bibles spent as much time about their cornices as the architects of our churches do? So are **171** made the *belles-lettres* and the *beaux-arts* and their professors. Much it concerns a man, forsooth, how a few sticks are slanted over him or under him, and what colors are daubed upon his box. It would signify somewhat, if, in any earnest sense, *he* slanted them and daubed it; but the spirit having departed out of the tenant, it is of a piece with constructing his own coffin, — the architecture of the grave, and " carpenter," is but another **172** name for "coffin-maker." One man says, in his despair or indifference to life, take up a handful of the earth at your feet, and paint your house that color. Is he thinking of his last and narrow house? Toss up a copper for **173** it as well. What an abundance of leisure he must have! Why do you take up a handful of dirt? Better paint your house your own complexion; let it turn pale or blush for you. An enterprise to improve the style of cottage architecture! When you have got my ornaments ready I will wear them.

Before winter I built a chimney, and shingled the sides of my house, which were already impervious to rain, with imperfect and sappy shingles made of the first slice of the log, whose edges I was obliged to straighten with a plane.

I have thus a tight shingled and plastered house, ten **174** feet wide by fifteen long, and eight-feet posts, with a garret and a closet, a large window on each side, two trap doors, one door at the end, and a brick fireplace opposite. The exact cost of my house, paying the usual price for such materials as I used, but not counting the work, all of which was done by myself, was as follows; and I give the details because very few are able to tell

170 *They can do without* architecture *who have no olives nor wines in the cellar.* This refers to the vaulted *arches* under which such things were stored.

171 *So are made the* belles-lettres. *Journal,* February 5, 1852; III, 279, where this sentence ends: "which we can do without."

172 *"carpenter."* Until recent times coffins were made by the local carpenter. The word, however, is derived from a chariot or carriage builder.

173 *Toss up a copper.* This may refer to the coin which was buried with the ancient Greeks so they could pay Charon his fare to take them across the river Styx.

174 *a tight shingled and plastered house.* Here is the most correct—and indeed the only dependable—description of the famous little house at Walden Pond.

exactly what their houses cost, and fewer still, if any, the separate cost of the various materials which compose them:— **175**

Boards, ...	$8 03½,	mostly shanty boards.
Refuse shingles for roof and sides, .	4 00	
Laths, ...	1 25	
Two second-hand windows with glass,	2 43	
One thousand old brick, . . .	4 00	
Two casks of lime, ...	2 40	That was high.
Hair, ...	0 31	More than I needed.
Mantle-tree iron, ...	0 15	
Nails, ...	3 90	
Hinges and screws, ...	0 14	
Latch, ...	0 10	
Chalk, ...	0 01	
Transportation, ...	1 40	} I carried a good part on my back.
In all, ...	$28 12½	

These are all the materials excepting the timber, stones and sand, which I claimed by squatter's right. I have also a small wood-shed adjoining, made chiefly of the stuff which was left after building the house.

I intend to build me a house which will surpass any on the main street in Concord in grandeur and luxury, as soon as it pleases me as much and will cost me no more than my present one.

I thus found that the student who wishes for a shelter can obtain one for a lifetime at an expense not greater than the rent which he now pays annually. If I seem to boast more than is becoming, my excuse is that I brag for humanity rather than for myself; and my shortcomings and inconsistencies do not affect the truth of my statement. Notwithstanding much cant and hypocrisy, — chaff which I find it difficult to separate from my wheat, but for which I am as sorry as any man, — I will breathe freely and stretch myself in this respect, it is such a relief to both the moral and physical system; and I am resolved that I will not through humility become the devil's attorney. I will endeavor to speak a good word for the truth. At Cambridge College the mere rent of a student's room, which is only a little larger than my own, is thirty dollars each year, though the corporation had the advantage of building thirty-two side by side and under one roof, and the occupant suffers the inconvenience of many and noisy **176 177**

175 *the separate cost of the various materials.* There seems to be some confusion in the itemized list that follows. Perhaps Thoreau bought more boards than those he got from James Collins for $4.25. On the page proofs it says not $8.03½, but $8.35, and the total given there is not $28.12½ but $28.44. A few things which appear on ms. 111 are not printed here. After the "two second-hand windows with glass" for $2.43, Thoreau wrote "That was high" but canceled his remark. And after "latch," he wrote: "I helped forge that."

Some of the nails from Robbins' excavation of the Walden cabin site

176 *the devil's attorney.* More properly the Advocatus Diaboli, who is the Promoter Fidei in the Sacred Congregation of Rites in the Roman Catholic Church. His duty, in a proposal for canonization, is to set forth anything that is unfavorable to the candidate's claim.

177 *Cambridge College.* Harvard College in Cambridge, Massachusetts. Thoreau's room was on the fourth floor of Hollis Hall. On the next few pages he gives his ideas on education.

neighbors, and perhaps a residence in the fourth story. I cannot but think that if we had more true wisdom in these respects, not only less education would be needed, because, forsooth, more would already have been acquired, but the pecuniary expense of getting an education would in a great measure vanish. Those conveniences which the student requires at Cambridge or elsewhere cost him or somebody else ten times as great a sacrifice of life as they would with proper management on both sides. Those things for which the most money is demanded are never the things which the student most wants. Tuition, for instance, is an important item in the term bill, while for the far more valuable education which he gets by associating with the most cultivated of his contemporaries no charge is made. The mode of founding a college is, commonly, to get up a subscription of dollars and cents, and then following blindly the principles of a division of labor to its extreme, a principle which should never be followed but with circumspection, — to call in a contractor who makes this a subject of speculation, and he employs Irishmen or other operatives actually to lay the foundations, while the students that are to be are said to be fitting themselves for it; and for these oversights successive generations have to pay. I think that it would be *better than this,* for the students, or those who desire to be benefited by it, even to lay the foundation themselves. The student who secures his coveted leisure and retirement by systematically shirking any labor necessary to man obtains but an ignoble and unprofitable leisure, defrauding himself of the experience which alone can make leisure fruitful. "But," says one, "you do not mean that the students should go to work with their hands instead of their heads?" I do not mean that exactly, but I mean something which he might think a good deal like that; I mean that they should not *play* life, or *study* it merely, while the community supports them at this expensive game, but earnestly *live* it from beginning to end. How could youths better learn to live than by at once trying the experiment of living? Methinks this would exercise their minds as much as mathematics. If I wished a boy to know something about the arts and sciences, for instance, I would not pursue the common course, which is merely to send him into the neighborhood of some professor, where any thing is professed and practised but the art of life; — to survey the world through a

178 *I cannot but think that if we.* Instead of "we," ms. 112 has "the corporation and the students."

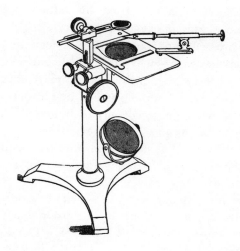

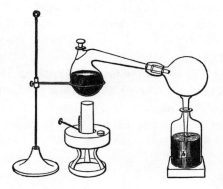

telescope or a microscope, and never with his natural eye; to study chemistry, and not learn how his bread is made, or mechanics, and not learn how it is earned; to discover new satellites to Neptune, and not detect the motes in his eyes, or to what vagabond he is a satellite himself; or to be devoured by the monsters that swarm all around him, while contemplating the monsters in a drop of vinegar. Which would have advanced the most at the end of a month,—the boy who had made his own jackknife from the ore which he had dug and smelted, reading as much as would be necessary for this, — or the boy who had attended the lectures on metallurgy at the Institute in the mean while, and had received a **179** Rogers' penknife from his father? Which would be most likely to cut his fingers? . . . To my astonishment I was informed on leaving college that I had studied navigation!—why, if I had taken one turn down the harbor I should have known more about it. Even the *poor* student studies and is taught only *political* economy, while that economy of living which is synonymous with philosophy is not even sincerely professed in our colleges. The consequence is, that while he is reading Adam Smith, Ricardo, and Say, he runs his father in **180** debt irretrievably.

As with our colleges, so with a hundred "modern improvements;" there is an illusion about them; there is not always a positive advance. The devil goes on exacting compound interest to the last for his early share and numerous succeeding investments in them. Our inventions are wont to be pretty toys, which distract our attention from serious things. They are but improved means to an unimproved end, an end which it was already but too easy to arrive at; as railroads lead to Boston or New York. We are in great haste to construct a **181** magnetic telegraph from Maine to Texas; but Maine and Texas, it may be, have nothing important to communicate. Either is in such a predicament as the man who was earnest to be introduced to a distinguished deaf woman, but when he was presented, and one end of her ear trumpet was put into his hand, had nothing to say. As if the main object were to talk fast and not to talk sensibly. We are eager to tunnel under the Atlantic and bring the old world some weeks nearer to the new; but perchance the first news that will leak through into the broad, flapping American ear will be

179 *a Rogers' penknife* should be Rodgers'. After the sentence that follows this, ms. 664 reads: "How much more aid might the agricultural chemist offer to the farmer, if he were to some extent an agriculturist himself. Of what avail if the man of science merely *shows you how* to do a thing, which he cannot do, he says, for want of leisure and you cannot understand. Forsooth, to him it is so easy—and to you it is so hard that it is not worth the while for either to try. And so the gifts of the gods are spilled."

180 *Adam Smith, Ricardo, and Say.* All economists. Smith (1723–1790) was Scottish; David Ricardo (1772–1823), English; and Jean-Baptiste Say (1767–1832), French.

181 *a magnetic telegraph from Maine to Texas.* It was at this time that telegraph lines were being extended to points far from Boston and New York. Ms. 501 has Louisiana instead of Texas.

A telegraph key of the period

that the Princess Adelaide has the whooping cough. **182**
After all, the man whose horse trots a mile in a minute
does not carry the most important messages; he is not
an evangelist, nor does he come round eating locusts
and wild honey. I doubt if Flying Childers ever car- **183**
ried a peck of corn to mill.

One says to me, "I wonder that you do not lay up
money; you love to travel; you might take the cars
and go to Fitchburg to-day and see the country." But
I am wiser than that. I have learned that the swift-
est traveller is he that goes afoot. I say to my
friend, Suppose we try who will get there first. The
distance is thirty miles; the fare ninety cents. That **184**
is almost a day's wages. I remember when wages
were sixty cents a day for laborers on this very road.
Well, I start now on foot, and get there before night;
I have travelled at that rate by the week together.
You will in the mean while have earned your fare, and
arrive there some time to-morrow, or possibly this
evening, if you are lucky enough to get a job in season.
Instead of going to Fitchburg, you will be working
here the greater part of the day. And so, if the railroad reached round the world, I think that I should
keep ahead of you; and as for seeing the country and
getting experience of that kind, I should have to cut
your acquaintance altogether.

Such is the universal law, which no man can ever
outwit, and with regard to the railroad even we may
say it is as broad as it is long. To make a railroad
round the world available to all mankind is equivalent
to grading the whole surface of the planet. Men have
an indistinct notion that if they keep up this activity of
joint stocks and spades long enough all will at length
ride somewhere, in next to no time, and for nothing;
but though a crowd rushes to the depot, and the conduct-
or shouts "All aboard!" when the smoke is blown away
and the vapor condensed, it will be perceived that a few
are riding, but the rest are run over, — and it will
be called, and will be, "A melancholy accident." No **185**
doubt they can ride at last who shall have earned
their fare, that is, if they survive so long, but they will
probably have lost their elasticity and desire to travel
by that time. This spending of the best part of one's life
earning money in order to enjoy a questionable liberty
during the least valuable part of it, reminds me of the

182 *the Princess Adelaide.* The only likely Princess Adelaide was the one who had married the Duke of Clarence in 1818. Later (1830) he became William IV. Since this Adelaide had died at the age of 57 in 1849, her whooping-cough days were a long way off.

183 *Flying Childers* was a race horse.

184 *the fare ninety cents.* The page proofs said seventy, but Thoreau changed this and explained to the printer: "They have raised the fare within a week."

185 *"A melancholy accident."* This term was then often used to describe a steamship or railroad disaster in which many lives were lost.

Englishman who went to India to make a fortune first, in order that he might return to England and live the life of a poet. He should have gone up garret at once. "What!" exclaim a million Irishmen starting up from all the shanties in the land, "is not this railroad which we have built a good thing?" Yes, I answer, *comparatively* good, that is, you might have done worse; but I wish, as you are brothers of mine, that you could have spent your time better than digging in this dirt.

Before I finished my house, wishing to earn ten or twelve dollars by some honest and agreeable method, in order to meet my unusual expenses, I planted about two **186** acres and a half of light and sandy soil near it chiefly with beans, but also a small part with potatoes, corn, peas, and turnips. The whole lot contains eleven acres, mostly growing up to pines and hickories, and was sold the preceding season for eight dollars and eight cents **187** an acre. One farmer said that it was "good for nothing but to raise cheeping squirrels on." I put no manure **188** whatever on this land, not being the owner, but merely a squatter, and not expecting to cultivate so much again, and I did not quite hoe it all once. I got out several cords of stumps in ploughing, which supplied me with fuel for a long time, and left small circles of virgin mould, easily distinguishable through the summer by the greater luxuriance of the beans there. The dead and for the most part unmerchantable wood behind my house, and the driftwood from the pond, have supplied the remainder of my fuel. I was obliged to hire a team and a man for the ploughing, though I held the plough myself. My farm outgoes for the first season were, for imple- **189** ments, seed, work, &c., $14 72½. The seed corn was given me. This never costs any thing to speak of, unless you plant more than enough. I got twelve bushels of beans, and eighteen bushels of potatoes, beside some peas and sweet corn. The yellow corn and turnips were too late to come to any thing. My whole income from the farm was

						$23 44.
Deducting the outgoes,	.	.	.	.	.	14 72½
There are left,	.	.	.	.	.	$8 71½,

beside produce consumed and on hand at the time this estimate was made of the value of $4 50,—the amount **190** on hand much more than balancing a little grass which

---

186 *my unusual expenses*. This was changed from "annual expenses" on the page proofs.

187 *eight dollars and eight cents an acre*. The land had been bought by Emerson who said in 1844 that he had paid $8.10 an acre for 11 acres. The next day he paid $125 for three or four adjoining acres. The total cost for 14 acres was therefore $214.10, or little more than $15 per acre—$15.29 to be exact.

188 *cheeping squirrels*. Thoreau had clearly written "chipping squirrels" on ms. 115 and 378 but changed the spelling on the page proofs.

189 *My farm outgoes for the first season were . . . $14 72½*. Thoreau's itemized account of this can be seen on page 293.

190 *the value of $4 50*. Following this on ms. 117: "which added to the last makes the whole profit $13 21½. By Surveying—Carpentry & day labor in the village I had earned $13 34." The second sentence, somewhat changed, appears on page 194, line 24.

MARCH.

I did not raise. All things considered, that is, considering the importance of a man's soul and of to-day, notwithstanding the short time occupied by my experiment, nay, partly even because of its transient character, I believe that that was doing better than any farmer in Concord did that year.

The next year I did better still, for I spaded up all the land which I required, about a third of an acre, and I learned from the experience of both years, not being in the least awed by many celebrated works on husbandry, Arthur Young among the rest, that if one would **191** live simply and eat only the crop which he raised, and raise no more than he ate, and not exchange it for an insufficient quantity of more luxurious and expensive things, he would need to cultivate only a few rods of ground, and that it would be cheaper to spade up that than to use oxen to plough it, and to select a fresh spot from time to time than to manure the old, and he could do all his necessary farm work as it were with his left hand at odd hours in the summer; and thus he would not be tied to an ox, or horse, or cow, or pig, as at

191 *Arthur Young* (1741–1820). English agriculturist best known for his *Travels in France* (1792), which describes the state of that country just before the Revolution.

present. I desire to speak impartially on this point, and as one not interested in the success or failure of the present economical and social arrangements. I was more independent than any farmer in Concord, for I was not anchored to a house or farm, but could follow the bent of my genius, which is a very crooked one, every moment. Beside being better off than they already, if my house had been burned or my crops had failed, I should have been nearly as well off as before.

I am wont to think that men are not so much the keepers of herds as herds are the keepers of men, the former are so much the freer. Men and oxen exchange work; but if we consider necessary work only, the oxen will be seen to have greatly the advantage, their farm is so much the larger. Man does some of his part of the exchange work in his six weeks of haying, and it is no boy's play. Certainly no nation that lived simply in all respects, that is, no nation of philosophers, would commit so great a blunder as to use the labor of animals. True, there never was and is not likely soon to be a nation of philosophers, nor am I certain it is desirable that there should be. However, *I* should never have broken a horse or bull and taken him to board for any work he might do for me, for fear I should become a horse-man or a herds-man merely; and if society seems to be the gainer by so doing, are we certain that what is one man's gain is not another's loss, and that the stable-boy has equal cause with his master to be satisfied? Granted that some public works would not have been constructed without this aid, and let man share the glory of such with the ox and horse; does it follow that he could not have accomplished works yet more worthy of himself in that case? When men begin to do, not merely unnecessary or artistic, but luxurious and idle work, with their assistance, it is inevitable that a few do all the exchange work with the oxen, or, in other words, become the slaves of the strongest. Man thus not only works for the animal within him, but, for a symbol of this, he works for the animal without him. Though we have many substantial houses of brick or stone, the prosperity of the farmer is still measured by the degree to which the barn overshadows the house. This town is said to have the largest houses for oxen, cows, and horses hereabouts, and it is not behindhand in its public buildings; but there are very few halls for free worship or free speech

192

192 *commit so great a blunder as to use the labor of animals.* This has, of course, been corrected in the twentieth century.

in this county. It should not be by their architecture, **193** but why not even by their power of abstract thought, that nations should seek to commemorate themselves? How much more admirable the Bhagvat-Geeta than all the **194** ruins of the East! Towers and temples are the luxury of princes. A simple and independent mind does not toil at the bidding of any prince. Genius is not a retainer to any emperor, nor is its material silver, or gold, or marble, except to a trifling extent. To what end, pray, is so much stone hammered? In Arcadia, when I was **195** there, I did not see any hammering stone. Nations are possessed with an insane ambition to perpetuate the memory of themselves by the amount of hammered stone they leave. What if equal pains were taken to smooth and polish their manners? One piece of good sense would be more memorable than a monument as high as the moon. I love better to see stones in place. The grandeur of Thebes was a vulgar grandeur. More sensible is a rod of stone wall that bounds an honest man's field than a hundred-gated Thebes that has wan- **196** dered farther from the true end of life. The religion and civilization which are barbaric and heathenish build splendid temples; but what you might call Christianity does not. Most of the stone a nation hammers goes toward its tomb only. It buries itself alive. As for the **197** Pyramids, there is nothing to wonder at in them so much as the fact that so many men could be found degraded enough to spend their lives constructing a tomb for some ambitious booby, whom it would have been

193 *It should not be by their architecture.* This comes from the *Journal* of June 26, 1852; IV, 152 f. There the sentence makes better sense for it reads: "but by their abstract thought." It is interesting to compare the original *Journal* entry with the final version that appears in *Walden*: "The American's taste for architecture, whether Grecian or Gothic, is like his taste for olives and wine, though the last may be made of logwood. Consider the beauty of New York architecture—and there is no very material difference between this and Baalbec—a vulgar adornment of what is vulgar. To what end pray is so much stone hammered? An insane ambition to perpetuate the memory of themselves by the amount of hammered stone they leave. Such is the glory of nations. What if equal pains were taken to smooth and polish their manners? Is not the builder of more consequence than the material? One sensible act will be more memorable than a monument as high as the moon. I love better to see stones in place. The grandeur of Thebes was a vulgar grandeur. She was not simple, and why should I be imposed on by the hundred gates of her prison? More sensible is a rod of stone wall that bounds an honest man's field than a hundred-gated Thebes that has mistaken the true end of life, that places hammered marble before honesty. The religion and civilization which are barbaric and heathenish build splendid temples, but Christianity does not."

194 *the Bhagvat-Geeta.* Also called the *Bhagavad Gita.* A Sanskrit religious classic (c. 500 B.C.) which was one of Thoreau's most revered books.

195 *In Arcadia.* Virgil called that part of ancient Greece the home of pastoral simplicity and continuing happiness.

196 *hundred-gated Thebes.* The Egyptian city where the Colossi of Memnon stood.

197 *the Pyramids.* This was written in more detail in the *Journal* for April 21, 1852; III, 453.

The ruins of Thebes

wiser and manlier to have drowned in the Nile, and then given his body to the dogs. I might possibly invent some excuse for them and him, but I have no time for it. As for the religion and love of art of the builders, it is much the same all the world over, whether the building be an Egyptian temple or the United States Bank. It costs more than it comes to. The mainspring is vanity, assisted by the love of garlic and bread and butter. Mr. Balcom, a promising young architect, designs it on the back of his Vitruvius, with hard pencil **198** and ruler, and the job is let out to Dobson & Sons, stonecutters. When the thirty centuries begin to look **199** down on it, mankind begin to look up at it. As for your high towers and monuments, there was a crazy fellow once in this town who undertook to dig through to China, and he got so far that, as he said, he heard the Chinese pots and kettles rattle; but I think that I shall not go out of my way to admire the hole which he made. Many are concerned about the monuments of the West and the East, — to know who built them. For my part, I should like to know who in those days did not build them, — who were above such trifling. But to proceed with my statistics.

By surveying, carpentry, and day-labor of various other kinds in the village in the mean while, for I have as many trades as fingers, I had earned $13 34. The expense of food for eight months, namely, from July 4th to March 1st, the time when these estimates were made, though I lived there more than two years, — not counting potatoes, a little green corn, and some peas, which I had raised, nor considering the value of what was on **200** hand at the last date, was

Rice,	$1 73½	
Molasses,	1 73	Cheapest form of the saccharine.
Rye meal,	1 04½	
Indian meal,	0 99¾	Cheaper than rye.
Pork,	0 22	
Flour,	0 88	} Costs more than Indian meal, both money and trouble.
Sugar,	0 80	
Lard,	0 65	
Apples,	0 25	
Dried apple,	0 22	
Sweet potatoes,	0 10	
One pumpkin,	0 6	
One watermelon,	0 2	
Salt,	0 3	

All experiments which failed. **201**

Yes, I did eat $8 74, all told; but I should not thus **202**

198 *Vitruvius.* Vitruvius Pollio, a well-known Roman architect of the first century B.C., author of *De Architectura*, which was used as a reliable authority for many centuries. Mr. Balcom and Dobson & Sons are unknown. Perhaps Thoreau made the names up.

199 *When the thirty centuries.* If Thoreau is citing Napoleon's speech to his soldiers at the Pyramids he should have said "forty centuries" as Napoleon did.

200 *on hand at the last date.* Following this on ms. 381 and canceled: "And now I come to something which may offend persons of a refined taste —but if I have the honor to address any who abstain from the vulgar practices of eating, drinking, and sleeping, I warn them not to look at that page in my journal which contains an accurate list —such a list makes me think as is nowhere in history—of the articles of food which I consumed during that time." After this the ms. reads: "Yes I did eat in one form or another $8 74 all told." This last sentence appears after the table here.

201 *Walter Harding* (1954a) says that in the first edition of *Walden* the bracket alongside the list of foods labeled "All experiments which failed" did not include "Salt," which obviously was essential. But the typesetter of the basic Riverside Aldine edition of 1889 "erred and extended it to include 'Salt.' This error, thus established, has persisted through most modern editions of the book."

202 *Yes, I did eat $8 74.* Charles R. Anderson (1968, page 27) draws attention to the fact that "it is probably not a coincidence that this figure tallies with one claimed as a possible food budget . . . in *The Young Housekeeper* (Boston, 1838)." Thoreau probably was familiar with this book because it had been written by one of Bronson Alcott's cousins. The proposed diet in it came to 25 cents a week, which is "exactly equivalent to the *Walden* total of $8.74 for eight months." See page 196, line 6, where Thoreau says, "about twenty-seven cents a week."

It is also possible, of course, that Thoreau, determined not to spend more than a set amount per week for food, figured out the total for the eight months involved, and then made up his table, using reasonable sums for each item, to fit the already arrived-at total. Looked at coldly, Thoreau's apparently careful accounting begins to seem less exact.

unblushingly publish my guilt, if I did not know that most of my readers were equally guilty with myself, and that their deeds would look no better in print. The next year I sometimes caught a mess of fish for my dinner, and once I went so far as to slaughter a wood-chuck which ravaged my bean-field,—effect his transmigration, as a Tartar would say,—and devour him, partly for experiment's sake; but though it afforded me a momentary enjoyment, notwithstanding a musky flavor, I saw that the longest use would not make that a good practice, however it might seem to have your wood-chucks ready dressed by the village butcher.

Clothing and some incidental expenses within the same dates, though little can be inferred from this item, amounted to

	$8 40¾
Oil and some household utensils, . . .	2 00

So that all the pecuniary outgoes, excepting for washing and mending, which for the most part were done out of the house, and their bills have not yet been received, —and these are all and more than all the ways by which money necessarily goes out in this part of the world,—were

House, ...	$28 12½
Farm one year, ...	14 72½
Food eight months, ...	8 74
Clothing, &c., eight months, ...	8 40¾
Oil, &c., eight months, ...	2 00
In all, ...	$61 99¾

I address myself now to those of my readers who have a living to get. And to meet this I have for farm produce sold

	$23 44
Earned by day-labor, ...	13 34
In all, ...	$36 78,

which subtracted from the sum of the outgoes leaves a balance of $25 21¾ on the one side,—this being very nearly the means with which I started, and the measure of expenses to be incurred,—and on the other, beside the leisure and independence and health thus secured, a comfortable house for me as long as I choose to occupy it.

203 *Tartar.* A man from Tartary in Asia; one who believed in the transmigration of souls through animals to man.

204 *dressed by the village butcher.* Thoreau had several experiences trapping woodchucks. After he had caught one of them twice, his fishing and hunting friends told him to knock the creature's brains out. But Thoreau argued that the wood-chuck had lived at Walden longer than he had and therefore had a right to be there. Instead of killing the woodchuck he took him two miles away and turned him loose.

In the Bibliophile Edition (I, 27n.), Sanborn describes another incident: "Thoreau set traps to protect his bean-field and, besides a woodchuck, once caught therein a *mephitis*, or ordinary skunk,—also an edible animal, but not to his delicate taste. Moreover, in the agonies of captivity he had malodorized the steel trap, and the naturalist tried in vain to remove the scent by washing it in the pond. Complaining to young Henry Warren, a former pupil, he was told he had not acquired all the woodman's art; for it was only needful to bury the trap in earth to disinfect it, which he then did. As for the washing and mending bills, they never came in, because that work was done by his mother's family, who also supplied Henry with occasional dainties."

205 *amounted to.* This should be on the same line as $8 40¾.

206 *washing and mending.* These, as Sanborn indicates above, were done by Thoreau's family.

207 *In all, ... $61 99¾.* This was erroneously totaled as $60.99¾ on ms. 382.

These statistics, however accidental and therefore uninstructive they may appear, as they have a certain completeness, have a certain value also. Nothing was given me of which I have not rendered some account. It appears from the above estimate, that my food alone cost me in money about twenty-seven cents a week. It was, for nearly two years after this, rye and Indian meal without yeast, potatoes, rice, a very little salt pork, molasses, and salt, and my drink water. It was fit that **208** I should live on rice, mainly, who loved so well the philosophy of India. To meet the objections of some inveterate cavillers, I may as well state, that if I dined out occasionally, as I always had done, and I trust shall have opportunities to do again, it was frequently to the detriment of my domestic arrangements. But the dining out, being, as I have stated, a constant element, does not in the least affect a comparative statement like this.

I learned from my two years' experience that it would cost incredibly little trouble to obtain one's necessary food, even in this latitude; that a man may use as simple a diet as the animals, and yet retain health and strength. I have made a satisfactory dinner, satisfactory on several accounts, simply off a dish of purslane (*Portulaca oleracea*) which I gathered in my cornfield, boiled and salted. I give the Latin on account of the savoriness of the trivial name. And pray what more can a reasonable man desire, in peaceful times, in ordinary noons, than a sufficient number of ears of green sweet-corn boiled, with the addition of salt? Even the little variety which I used was a yielding to the demands of appetite, and not of health. Yet men have come to such a pass that they frequently starve, not for want of necessaries, but for want of luxuries; and I know a good woman who thinks that her son lost his life because he took to drink- **209** ing water only.

The reader will perceive that I am treating the subject rather from an economic than a dietetic point of view, and he will not venture to put my abstemiousness to the test unless he has a well-stocked larder.

Bread I at first made of pure Indian meal and salt, genuine hoe-cakes, which I baked before my fire out of **210** doors on a shingle or the end of a stick of timber sawed off in building my house; but it was wont to get smoked and to have a piny flavor. I tried flour also; but have

208 *It was fit that I should live on rice. Journal,* January 22, 1852; III, 216.

209 *he took to drinking water only.* This probably refers to Charles Stearns Wheeler, Thoreau's friend, who had died in Leipzig, Germany.

210 *genuine hoe-cakes.* They were not genuine hoe-cakes or they would have been cooked on the iron blade of a hoe as they originally were, especially in the South.

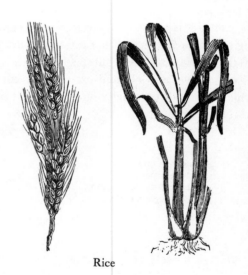

Rice

at last found a mixture of rye and Indian meal most convenient and agreeable. In cold weather it was no little amusement to bake several small loaves of this in succession, tending and turning them as carefully as an **211** Egyptian his hatching eggs. They were a real cereal fruit which I ripened, and they had to my senses a fragrance like that of other noble fruits, which I kept in as long as possible by wrapping them in cloths. I made a study of the ancient and indispensable art of bread-making, consulting such authorities as offered, going back to the primitive days and first invention of the un-leavened kind, when from the wildness of nuts and meats men first reached the mildness and refinement of this diet, and travelling gradually down in my studies through that accidental souring of the dough which, it is supposed, taught the leavening process, and through the various fermentations thereafter, till I came to "good, sweet, wholesome bread," the staff of life. Leaven, which some deem the soul of bread, the *spiritus* which fills its cellular tissue, which is religiously preserved like the vestal fire, — some precious bottle-full, I suppose, first brought over in the Mayflower, did the business for America, and its influence is still rising, swelling, spreading, in cerealian billows over the land, — **212** this seed I regularly and faithfully procured from the village, till at length one morning I forgot the rules, and scalded my yeast; by which accident I discovered that even this was not indispensable, — for my discoveries were not by the synthetic but analytic process, — and I have gladly omitted it since, though most housewives earnestly assured me that safe and wholesome bread without yeast might not be, and elderly people prophesied a speedy decay of the vital forces. Yet I find it not to be an essential ingredient, and after going without it for a year am still in the land of the living; and I am glad to escape the trivialness of carrying a bottle-full in my pocket, which would sometimes pop and discharge its contents to my discomfiture. It is simpler and more respectable to omit it. Man is an animal who more than any other can adapt himself to all climates and circumstances. Neither did I put any sal soda, or other acid or alkali, into my bread. It would seem that I made it according to the recipe which Marcus Porcius Cato gave about two centuries before **213** Christ. " Panem depsticium sic facito. Manus morta-

211 *an Egyptian . . . hatching eggs.* Both the Egyptians and the Chinese had practiced artificial incubation from earliest times.

212 *in cerealian billows.* A pun on cerulean and cereal.

213 *Marcus Porcius Cato.* The Roman statesman (239-149 B.C.), great-grandfather of the philosopher of the same name (95-46 B.C.). The quotation is from his work on agriculture, *De Re Rustica*, which is also called *De Agri Cultura*.

The *Mayflower*

riumque bene lavato. Farinam in mortarium indito, aquæ paulatim addito, subigitoque pulchre. Ubi bene subegeris, defingito, coquitoque sub testu." Which I take to mean—"Make kneaded bread thus. Wash your hands and trough well. Put the meal into the trough, add water gradually, and knead it thoroughly. When you have kneaded it well, mould it, and bake it under a cover," that is, in a baking-kettle. Not a word about leaven. But I did not always use this staff of life. At one time, owing to the emptiness of my purse, I saw none of it for more than a month.

Every New Englander might easily raise all his own breadstuffs in this land of rye and Indian corn, and not depend on distant and fluctuating markets for them. Yet so far are we from simplicity and independence that, in Concord, fresh and sweet meal is rarely sold in the shops, and hominy and corn in a still coarser form are hardly used by any. For the most part the farmer gives to his cattle and hogs the grain of his own producing, and buys flour, which is at least no more wholesome, at a greater cost, at the store. I saw that I could easily raise my bushel or two of rye and Indian corn, for the former will grow on the poorest land, and the latter does not require the best, and grind them in a hand-mill, and so do without rice and pork; and if I must have some concentrated sweet, I found by experiment that I could make a very good molasses either of pumpkins or beets, and I knew that I needed only to set out a few maples to obtain it more easily still, and while these were growing I could use various substitutes beside those which I have named. " For," as the Forefathers sang, —

214

" we can make liquor to sweeten our lips
Of pumpkins and parsnips and walnut-tree chips."

Finally, as for salt, that grossest of groceries, to obtain this might be a fit occasion for a visit to the seashore, or, if I did without it altogether, I should probably drink the less water. I do not learn that the Indians ever troubled themselves to go after it.

Thus I could avoid all trade and barter, so far as my food was concerned, and having a shelter already, it would only remain to get clothing and fuel. The pantaloons which I now wear were woven in a farmer's family,— thank Heaven there is so much virtue still in

214 *"For," as the Forefathers sang.* The verse is from J. W. Barber's (1798–1885) *Historical Collections . . . of . . . New England* (1839). Barber was an illustrator and engraver as well as an anthologist.

man ; for I think the fall from the farmer to the operative as great and memorable as that from the man to the farmer ; — and in a new country fuel is an encumbrance. As for a habitat, if I were not permitted still to squat, I might purchase one acre at the same price for which the land I cultivated was sold — namely, eight dollars and eight cents. But as it was, I considered that I enhanced the value of the land by squatting on it.

There is a certain class of unbelievers who sometimes ask me such questions as, if I think that I can live on vegetable food alone ; and to strike at the root of the matter at once, — for the root is faith, — I am accustomed to answer such, that I can live on board nails. If they cannot understand that, they cannot understand much that I have to say. For my part, I am glad to hear of experiments of this kind being tried ; as that a **215** young man tried for a fortnight to live on hard, raw corn on the ear, using his teeth for all mortar. The squirrel tribe tried the same and succeeded. The human race is interested in these experiments, though a few old women who are incapacitated for them, or who own their **216** thirds in mills, may be alarmed.

My furniture, part of which I made myself, and the **217** rest cost me nothing of which I have not rendered an account, consisted of a bed, a table, a desk, three chairs, a looking-glass three inches in diameter, a pair of tongs and andirons, a kettle, a skillet, and a frying-pan, a dipper, a wash-bowl, two knives and forks, three plates, one cup, one spoon, a jug for oil, a jug for molasses, and a japanned lamp. None is so poor that he need sit on a pumpkin. That is shiftlessness. There is a plenty of such chairs as I like best in the village garrets to be had for taking them away. Furniture ! Thank God, I can sit **218** and I can stand without the aid of a furniture warehouse. What man but a philosopher would not be ashamed to see his furniture packed in a cart and going up country exposed to the light of heaven and the eyes of men, a beggarly account of empty boxes ? That is Spaulding's **219** furniture. I could never tell from inspecting such a load whether it belonged to a so called rich man or a poor one ; the owner always seemed poverty-stricken. Indeed, the more you have of such things the poorer you are. Each load looks as if it contained the con-

215 *a young man tried . . . to live on hard, raw corn.* Channing noted in his copy of *Walden* that "this young man was Isaac Hecker, now a Catholic priest."

216 *who own their thirds.* The widow's share was one third, as is seen in the Chronology for July 12, 1817. *Journal*, May 1, 1851; II, 189.

217 *My furniture.* Most of this furniture is now on display at the Concord Antiquarian Society. On ms. 70 Thoreau did not mention the bed, the table, the desk, or the looking glass.

218 *I can sit and I can stand* then "I can go to sleep" on ms. 665.

219 *That is Spaulding's furniture.* Spaulding was a deacon. See page 202.

The furniture from the Walden cabin. It is now on display at the Concord Antiquarian Society. (*Courtesy Concord Antiquarian Society*)

tents of a dozen shanties; and if one shanty is poor, this is a dozen times as poor. Pray, for what do we *move* **220** ever but to get rid of our furniture, our *exuviæ;* at last **221** to go from this world to another newly furnished, and leave this to be burned? It is the same as if all these traps were buckled to a man's belt, and he could not move over the rough country where our lines are cast without dragging them, — dragging his trap. He was a lucky **222**

220 *a dozen times as poor.* This was "a hundred times as poor" on ms. 666.

221 exuviæ. Latin plural for discarded objects.

222 *a lucky fox.* This refers to the fox in Aesop's fable.

fox that left his tail in the trap.   The muskrat will **223**
gnaw his third leg off to be free.   No wonder man
has lost his elasticity.   How often he is at a dead set!
"Sir, if I may be so bold, what do you mean by a **224**
dead set?"   If you are a seer, whenever you meet
a man you will see all that he owns, ay, and much
that he pretends to disown, behind him, even to his
kitchen furniture and all the trumpery which he saves
and will not burn, and he will appear to be harnessed to
it and making what headway he can.   I think that the
man is at a dead set who has got through a knot hole
or gateway where his sledge load of furniture cannot
follow him.   I cannot but feel compassion when I hear
some trig, compact-looking man, seemingly free, all girded **225**
and ready, speak of his "furniture," as whether it is in-
sured or not.   "But what shall I do with my furniture?"
My gay butterfly is entangled in a spider's web then.
Even those who seem for a long while not to have any,
if you inquire more narrowly you will find have some
stored in somebody's barn.   I look upon England to-
day as an old gentleman who is travelling with a great
deal of baggage, trumpery which has accumulated from
long housekeeping, which he has not the courage to

223 *The muskrat will gnaw his third leg off.*
Thoreau had been told this by a Concord trapper,
George Melvin. *Journal,* 1837–1847; I, 481.

224 *a dead set.* Webster defines this as "a fixed
or stationary condition arising from an obstacle
or hindrance."

225 *trig.* Webster: "trim, neat, spruce, smart."

A furniture salesroom
of the period

burn; great trunk, little trunk, bandbox and bundle. Throw away the first three at least. It would surpass the powers of a well man nowadays to take up his bed **226** and walk, and I should certainly advise a sick one to lay down his bed and run. When I have met an immigrant tottering under a bundle which contained his all—looking like an enormous wen which had grown out of the nape of his neck—I have pitied him, not because that was his all, but because he had all *that* to carry. If I have got to drag my trap, I will take care that it be a light one and do not nip me in a vital part. But perchance it would be wisest never to put one's paw into it.

I would observe, by the way, that it costs me nothing for curtains, for I have no gazers to shut out but the sun and moon, and I am willing that they should look in. The moon will not sour milk nor taint meat of mine, **227** nor will the sun injure my furniture or fade my carpet, **228** and if he is sometimes too warm a friend, I find it still better economy to retreat behind some curtain which nature has provided, than to add a single item to the details of housekeeping. A lady once offered me a mat, but as I had no room to spare within the house, nor time to spare within or without to shake it, I declined it, preferring to wipe my feet on the sod before my door. It is best to avoid the beginnings of evil. **229**

Not long since I was present at the auction of a dea- **230** con's effects, for his life had not been ineffectual:—

"The evil that men do lives after them." **231**

As usual, a great proportion was trumpery which had begun to accumulate in his father's day. Among the rest was a dried tapeworm. And now, after lying half a century in his garret and other dust holes, these things were not burned; instead of a *bonfire*, or purifying destruction of them, there was an *auction*, or increasing of them. The neighbors eagerly collected to view them, bought them all, and carefully transported them to their garrets and dust holes, to lie there till their estates are settled, when they will start again. When a man dies he kicks the dust. **232**

The customs of some savage nations might, perchance, be profitably imitated by us, for they at least go through the semblance of casting their slough annually; they

226 *take up his bed and walk.* The miracle of the man sick of the palsy, Matthew 9 : 6.

227 *The moon will not sour milk nor taint meat.* These were popular beliefs in Thoreau's time.

228 *nor will the sun . . . fade my carpet.* It can, of course, but thrifty housewives prevented this by keeping their sitting rooms dark.

229 *It is best to avoid the beginnings of evil.* This is followed on ms. 1228 and 1229 by: "I saw the other day on the outskirts of the village a family which for three months had had no bed but a wisp of straw on a board and two Irish sheets—no furniture to their house but two plates, 2 bowls, 2 pewter spoons, and a knife without a handle—no house but a shanty. The husband goes three miles to his work and carries nothing but bread for his dinner. And the greater part of what he earns is sent to Ireland to forward his remaining children to this land of plenty.

"In the meanwhile, Mrs. O.D.R., president of the Charitable Society, has caught her death through a crack in the door, and Mrs. Farewell is pining away like a fly caught in a preserve pot, and calls her disease sciatica."

This may be the Irish family in which little Johnny Riordan lived. It was he who inspired Thoreau's poem "I am the Little Irish Boy." See the Chronology for January 28, 1852.

230 *the auction of a deacon's effects.* Not Deacon Spaulding but Deacon Brown. Channing wrote in his copy of *Walden:* "a penurious old curmudgeon . . . a human rat." In the *Journal* for January 27, 1854; VI, 80, Thoreau says: "Attended the auction of Deacon Brown's effects a little while to-day,—a great proportion of old traps, rubbish, or trumpery, which began to accumulate in his father's day, and now, after lying half a century in his garret and other dust-holes, is not burned, but surviving neighbors collect and view it, and buy it, and carefully transport it to their garrets and dust-holes, to lie there till their estates are settled, when it will start again. Among his effects was a dried tapeworm and various articles too numerous and worthless to mention. A pair of old snow-shoes is almost regularly sold on these occasions, though none of this generation has seen them worn here."

231 *"The evil that men do lives after them."* The next line, "The good is oft interred with their bones," was canceled on the page proofs. The verse comes from Shakespeare's *Julius Caesar* III, ii.

232 *he kicks the dust.* This may come from the Iliad where Hector is described as "kicking the

have the idea of the thing, whether they have the reality or not. Would it not be well if we were to celebrate such a "busk," or "feast of first fruits," as Bartram describes to have been the custom of the Mucclasse Indians? "When a town celebrates the busk," says he, "having previously provided themselves with new clothes, new pots, pans, and other household utensils and furniture, they collect all their worn out clothes and other despicable things, sweep and cleanse their houses, squares, and the whole town, of their filth, which with all the remaining grain and other old provisions they cast together into one common heap, and consume it with fire. After having taken medicine, and fasted for three days, all the fire in the town is extinguished. During this fast they abstain from the gratification of every appetite and passion whatever. A general amnesty is proclaimed; all malefactors may return to their town. —"

"On the fourth morning, the high priest, by rubbing dry wood together, produces new fire in the public square, from whence every habitation in the town is supplied with the new and pure flame."

They then feast on the new corn and fruits and dance and sing for three days, "and the four following days they receive visits and rejoice with their friends from neighboring towns who have in like manner purified and prepared themselves."

The Mexicans also practised a similar purification at the end of every fifty-two years, in the belief that it was time for the world to come to an end.

I have scarcely heard of a truer sacrament, that is, as the dictionary defines it, "outward and visible sign of an inward and spiritual grace," than this, and I have no doubt that they were originally inspired directly from Heaven to do thus, though they have no biblical record of the revelation.

For more than five years I maintained myself thus solely by the labor of my hands, and I found, that by working about six weeks in a year, I could meet all the expenses of living. The whole of my winters, as well as most of my summers, I had free and clear for study. I have thoroughly tried school-keeping, and found that my expenses were in proportion, or rather out of pro-

233

234

235

dust" when he was slain by Achilles, but it also may be from "another Indian kicks the dust," a popular phrase associated with Indian warfare. Sometimes it is "bites the dust."

233 *Bartram.* William Bartram (1739–1823), a naturalist who traveled through the southeastern United States looking for speciments of plants and animals.

234 *as the dictionary defines it.* Channing notes in his copy of *Walden* that the definition is from Walker's Dictionary of 1822.

235 *I have . . . tried school-keeping.* See the Chronology for August 1837 to April 1, 1841.

portion, to my income, for I was obliged to dress and train, not to say think and believe, accordingly, and I lost my time into the bargain. As I did not teach for the good of my fellow-men, but simply for a livelihood, this was a failure. I have tried trade; but I found that it would take ten years to get under way in that, and that then I should probably be on my way to the devil. I was actually afraid that I might by that time be doing what is called a good business. When formerly I was looking about to see what I could do for a living, some sad experience in conforming to the wishes of friends being fresh in my mind to tax my ingenuity, I thought often and seriously of picking huckleberries; that surely I could do, and its small profits might suffice, — for my greatest skill has been to want but little, — so little capital it required, so little distraction from my wonted moods, I foolishly thought. While my acquaintances went unhesitatingly into trade or the professions, I contemplated this occupation as most like theirs; ranging the hills all summer to pick the berries which came in my way, and thereafter carelessly dispose of them; so, to keep the flocks of Admetus. I also dreamed that I **236** might gather the wild herbs, or carry evergreens to such villagers as loved to be reminded of the woods, even to the city, by hay-cart loads. But I have since learned that trade curses every thing it handles; and though you trade in messages from heaven, the whole curse of trade attaches to the business.

As I preferred some things to others, and especially valued my freedom, as I could fare hard and yet succeed well, I did not wish to spend my time in earning rich carpets or other fine furniture, or delicate cookery, or a house in the Grecian or the Gothic style just yet. **237** If there are any to whom it is no interruption to acquire these things, and who know how to use them when acquired, I relinquish to them the pursuit. Some are "industrious," and appear to love labor for its own sake, or perhaps because it keeps them out of worse mischief; to such I have at present nothing to say. Those who would not know what to do with more leisure than they now enjoy, I might advise to work twice as hard as they do, — work till they pay for themselves, **238** and get their free papers. For myself I found that the occupation of a day-laborer was the most independent of any, especially as it required only thirty or forty

236 *to keep the flocks of Admetus.* The Apollo-Admetus concept played an important part in Thoreau's life, and references to it keep recurring. Apollo was condemned by Zeus to serve Admetus, the king of Pherae, who put him to work tending his flocks. It was an ignominious assignment for the great Apollo, but he dutifully labored in the fields, showing his power only by playing his flute, the music of which charmed wild beasts. Thoreau also played a flute, as will be seen. The *Journal* for June 22, 1853; V, 293, says: "I would watch the flocks of Admetus . . . forever, only for my board and clothes."

237 *Grecian or the Gothic style.* According to Talbot Hamlin, author of *Greek Revival Architecture in America* (1944), this period extended "roughly from 1820 to 1860." When Thoreau wrote this, the Gothic period and the Victorian furniture to accompany it were coming into fashion.

238 *till they pay for themselves, and get their free papers.* Immigrants often went into debt in advance to pay for passage from Europe to America.

Apollo

days in a year to support one. The laborer's day ends with the going down of the sun, and he is then free to devote himself to his chosen pursuit, independent of his labor; but his employer, who speculates from month to month, has no respite from one end of the year to the other.

In short, I am convinced, both by faith and experience, that to maintain one's self on this earth is not a hardship but a pastime, if we will live simply and wisely; as the pursuits of the simpler nations are still the sports of the more artificial. It is not necessary that a man should earn his living by the sweat of his brow, unless he sweats easier than I do. **239**

One young man of my acquaintance, who has inherited some acres, told me that he thought he should live as I did, *if he had the means.* I would not have any one adopt *my* mode of living on any account; for, beside that before he has fairly learned it I may have found out another for myself, I desire that there may be as many different persons in the world as possible; but I would have each one be very careful to find out and pursue *his own* way, and not his father's or his mother's or his neighbor's instead. The youth may build or plant or sail, only let him not be hindered from doing that which he tells me he would like to do. It is by a **240** mathematical point only that we are wise, as the sailor or the fugitive slave keeps the polestar in his eye; but **241** that is sufficient guidance for all our life. We may not arrive at our port within a calculable period, but we would preserve the true course.

Undoubtedly, in this case, what is true for one is truer still for a thousand, as a large house is not proportionally more expensive than a small one, since one roof may cover, one cellar underlie, and one wall separate several apartments. But for my part, I preferred the solitary dwelling. Moreover, it will commonly be cheaper to build the whole yourself than to convince another of the advantage of the common wall; and when you have done this, the common partition, to be much cheaper, must be a thin one, and that other may prove a bad neighbor, and also not keep his side in repair. The only coöperation which is commonly possible is exceedingly partial and superficial; and what little true coöperation there is, is as if it were not, being a harmony inaudible to men. If a man has faith he

239 *unless he sweats easier than I do.* In a letter to Horace Greeley, written on May 19, 1848, Thoreau had said: "The fact is man need not live by the sweat of his brow—unless he sweats easier than I do. . . ." Then, following this paragraph on ms. 273, is: "One, a handsome younger man, a sailor-like, Greek-like man—says to me to-day, 'Sir, I like your notions. I think I shall live so myself. Only I would like a wilder country where there is more game. I have been among the Indians near Appallachicola [*sic*]. I have lived with them. I like your kind of life. Good-day, I wish you success and happiness." This is also in the *Journal* for July 1845; I, 366.

Apalachicola is a seaport in Florida.

240 *he would like to do.* On ms. 124—and in the Bibliophile Edition—this is followed by: "If he is reproved for being what he is, he will find his only resource in being still more entirely what he is. Carry but yourself erect, and your garments will trail as they should. Disturb not the sailor with too many details, but let him be sure that he keep his guiding star in his eye. Everything impels us to seek our health. No doubt our instincts drive us forward in the right path, and keep us from wandering,—as faithful herdsmen do their herds. Whatever we covet is for our health. No student ever hurt his chest with writing poetry,— for that does not consist with a constrained position. No,—it was some vile copying or other drudgery that did the injury. Some say that time is money. It is more than that; it is life; and whoever exchanges much of it for money, or what money can buy, makes a wretched bargain, and will be bankrupt in the end."

241 *polestar.* This star, which indicates the north, guided fugitive slaves out of the southern states.

will coöperate with equal faith every where; if he has not faith, he will continue to live like the rest of the world, whatever company he is joined to. To coöperate, in the highest as well as the lowest sense, means *to get our living together*. I heard it proposed lately that two young men should travel together over the world, the one without money, earning his means as he went, before the mast and behind the plough, the other carrying a bill of exchange in his pocket. It was easy to see that they could not long be companions or coöperate, since one would not *operate* at all. They would part at the first interesting crisis in their adventures. Above all, as I have implied, the man who goes alone can start to-day; but he who travels with another must wait till that other is ready, and it may be a long time before they get off.

But all this is very selfish, I have heard some of my townsmen say. I confess that I have hitherto indulged very little in philanthropic enterprises. I have made some sacrifices to a sense of duty, and among others have sacrificed this pleasure also. **242** There are those who have used all their arts to persuade me to undertake the support of some poor family in the town; and if I had nothing to do, — for the devil finds employment for the idle, — I might try my hand at some such pastime as that. However, when I have thought to indulge myself in this respect, and lay their Heaven under an obligation by maintaining certain poor persons in all respects as comfortably as I maintain myself, and have even ventured so far as to make them the offer, they have one and all unhesitatingly preferred to remain poor. While my townsmen and women are devoted in so many ways to the good of their fellows, I trust that one at least may be spared to other and less humane pursuits. You must have a genius for charity as well as for any thing else. **243** As for Doing-good, that is one of the professions which are full. Moreover, I have tried it fairly, and, **244** strange as it may seem, am satisfied that it does not agree with my constitution. Probably I should not consciously and deliberately forsake my particular calling to do the good which society demands of me, to save the universe from annihilation; and I believe that a like but infinitely greater steadfastness elsewhere is all that now

242 *have sacrificed this pleasure also.* This was followed on ms. 125 by: "I may say without boasting that I have never been inside a theatre but once, and never that I remember—subscribed a cent to any charitable object."

243 *As for Doing-good.* This was written at a time when reform was in the air and philanthropy was very popular.

244 *it does not agree with my constitution.* Followed on ms. 126 by two canceled phrases: "it does not suit my genius" and "I have a natural repugnance to it."

preserves it. But I would not stand between any man and his genius; and to him who does this work, which I decline, with his whole heart and soul and life, I would say, Persevere, even if the world call it doing evil, as it is most likely they will. **245**

I am far from supposing that my case is a peculiar one; no doubt many of my readers would make a similar defence. At doing something, — I will not engage that my neighbors shall pronounce it good, — I do not hesitate to say that I should be a capital fellow to hire; but what that is, it is for my employer to find out. What *good* I do, in the common sense of that word, must **246** be aside from my main path, and for the most part wholly unintended. Men say, practically, Begin where **247** you are and such as you are, without aiming mainly to become of more worth, and with kindness aforethought go about doing good. If I were to preach at all in this strain, I should say rather, Set about being good. As if the sun should stop when he had kindled his fires up to the splendor of a moon or a star of the sixth magnitude, and go about like a Robin Goodfellow, peeping in at **248** every cottage window, inspiring lunatics, and tainting meats, and making darkness visible, instead of steadily increasing his genial heat and beneficence till he is of such brightness that no mortal can look him in the face, and then, and in the mean while too, going about the world in his own orbit, doing it good, or rather, as a truer philosophy has discovered, the world going about him getting good. When Phaeton, wishing to prove **249** his heavenly birth by his beneficence, had the sun's chariot but one day, and drove out of the beaten track, he burned several blocks of houses in the lower streets of heaven, and scorched the surface of the earth, and dried up every spring, and made the great desert of Sahara, till at length Jupiter hurled him headlong to the earth with a thunderbolt, and the sun, through grief at his death, did not shine for a year.

There is no odor so bad as that which arises from goodness tainted. It is human, it is divine, carrion. If I knew for a certainty that a man was coming to my house with the conscious design of doing me good, I should run for my life, as from that dry and parching wind of the African deserts called the simoom, which fills the mouth and nose and ears and eyes with dust till you are suffocated, for fear that I should get some of

245 *as it is most likely they will.* Sanborn's Bibliophile Edition (I, 127) printed this omitted copy:

" 'In antiquity,' said Confucius, 'those who devoted themselves to study, did it for themselves; now, those who devote themselves to study, do it for others;' as a commentator says, 'to appear learned to the eyes of others.' Now, it appears to me, those who devote themselves to charity, do it for others.

"Be assured that every man's success is in proportion to his *average* ability. The meadow flowers spring and bloom where the waters annually deposit their slime,—not where they reach in some freshet only. The truly noble and settled character of a man is not put forward,—as the king or conquerer does not march foremost in a procession. We may seem to do ourselves little credit in our own eyes; for our performance must always fall short of our aspiration and promise to ourselves,—as a stick will avail to *reach* further than it will strike effectively,—but we do not disappoint our neighbors. They indeed may affect to estimate us by our talents, but they really feel and know us by our character. A man is not his hope, nor his despair,—nor yet his past deed. The Past is in the rind, the Future in the core, and the Present between core and rind."

246 *for the most part wholly unintended.* Here ms. 391 has: "There is no doctrine preached with so much cant in these days as this of doing good, and I think that the word cant, considering its meaning, should be derived, not from the old chant, at length come to be sung more through the nose, but rather from the contraction can't, the expression of inefficiency and despair." The NED does not agree with Thoreau's theory.

247 *mainly.* This word was underlined on ms. 127 and 391.

248 *Robin Goodfellow.* Followed by "will o' the wisp" on ms. 392. This was canceled but it characterizes Robin Goodfellow, who has been called a "drudging fiend" noted for his mischievous pranks. He appears in *A Midsummer Night's Dream* as Puck.

249 *Phaeton.* The son of Apollo, god of the sun. The story is told by Ovid among others.

his good done to me, — some of its virus mingled with my blood. No, — in this case I would rather suffer evil the natural way. A man is not a good *man* to me because he will feed me if I should be starving, or warm me if I should be freezing, or pull me out of a ditch if I should ever fall·into one. I can find you a New- **250** foundland dog that will do as much. Philanthropy is not love for one's fellow-man in the broadest sense. Howard was no doubt an exceedingly kind and worthy man in his way, and has his reward; but, comparatively speaking, what are a hundred Howards to *us*, if their **251** philanthropy do not help *us* in our best estate, when we are most worthy to be helped? I never heard of a philanthropic meeting in which it was sincerely pro- posed to do any good to me, or the like of me.

The Jesuits were quite balked by those Indians who, **252** being burned at the stake, suggested new modes of tor· ture to their tormentors. Being superior to physical suffering, it sometimes chanced that they were superior to any consolation which the missionaries could offer; and the law to do as you would be done by fell with **253** less persuasiveness on the ears of those, who, for their part, did not care how they were done by, who loved their enemies after a new fashion, and came very near freely forgiving them all they did.

Be sure that you give the poor the aid they most need, though it be your example which leaves them far behind. If you give money, spend yourself with it, and do not merely abandon it to them. We make curious mistakes sometimes. Often the poor man is not so cold and hungry as he is dirty and ragged and gross. It is partly his taste, and not merely his misfortune. If you give him money, he will perhaps buy more rags with it. I was wont to pity the clumsy Irish laborers **254** who cut ice on the pond, in such mean and ragged clothes, while I shivered in my more tidy and somewhat more fashionable garments, till, one bitter cold day, one who had slipped into the water came to my house to warm him, and I saw him strip off three pairs of pants and two pairs of stockings ere he got down to the skin, though they were dirty and ragged enough, it is true, and that he could afford to refuse the *extra* garments **255** which I offered him, he had so many *intra* ones. This ducking was the very thing he needed. Then I began to pity myself, and I saw that it would be a greater charity to bestow on me a flannel shirt than a whole

250 *a Newfoundland dog.* In the Spring 1966 issue of the Thoreau Society *Bulletin*, Raymond D. Gozzi points out that in Richard B. Sheridan's play, *The Rivals*, Lydia says to her friend Julia in a similar situation: "Obligation; why a water spaniel would have done as much!"

251 *a hundred Howards.* John Howard (1726?– 1790), an English prison reformer who saw how dreadful conditions were in the jails when he became high sheriff for Bedfordshire in 1773. He also investigated hospitals and disease throughout Europe.

252 *The Jesuits.* Before this on ms. 1163 is: "Philanthropy commonly supposes a weakness greater than its own."

253 *do as you would be done by.* Here three New Testament sayings are paraphrased: Matthew 5:44, Matthew 7:12, and Luke 6:31.

254 *the clumsy Irish laborers.* See page 415 for more about them.

255 extra is outer and *intra*, inner in Latin.

slop-shop on him.   There are a thousand hacking at the branches of evil to one who is striking at the root, and it may be that he who bestows the largest amount of time and money on the needy is doing the most by his mode of life to produce that misery which he strives in vain to relieve.   It is the pious slave-breeder devoting the proceeds of every tenth slave to buy a Sunday's liberty for the rest.   Some show their kindness to the poor by employing them in their kitchens.   Would they not be kinder if they employed themselves there?   You boast of spending a tenth part of your income in charity; may be you should spend the nine tenths so, and done with it.   Society recovers only a tenth part of the property then.   Is this owing to the generosity of him in whose possession it is found, or to the remissness of the officers of justice?

Philanthropy is almost the only virtue which is sufficiently appreciated by mankind.   Nay, it is greatly overrated; and it is our selfishness which overrates it. A robust poor man, one sunny day here in Concord, praised a fellow-townsman to me, because, as he said, he was kind to the poor; meaning himself.   The kind uncles and aunts of the race are more esteemed than its true spiritual fathers and mothers.   I once heard a reverend lecturer on England, a man of learning and intelligence, after enumerating her scientific, literary, and political worthies, Shakspeare, Bacon, Cromwell, Milton, Newton, and others, speak next of her Christian heroes, whom, as if his profession required it of him, he elevated to a place far above all the rest, as the greatest of the great.   They were Penn, Howard, and Mrs. Fry.   Every one must feel the falsehood and cant of this.   The last were not England's best men and women; only, perhaps, her best philanthropists.

I would not subtract any thing from the praise that is due to philanthropy, but merely demand justice for all who by their lives and works are a blessing to mankind. I do not value chiefly a man's uprightness and benevolence, which are, as it were, his stem and leaves. Those plants of whose greenness withered we make herb tea for the sick, serve but a humble use, and are most employed by quacks.   I want the flower and fruit of a man; that some fragrance be wafted over from him to me, and some ripeness flavor our intercourse.   His goodness must not be a partial and transitory act, but a constant superfluity, which costs him

256 *every tenth slave.* This is a caustic reference to tithing, or donating one tenth of one's income to the church.

257 *and done with it.* Ms. 1162 then says: "What does all the charity of England amount to—who with her right hand withholds the soil and freedom from the masses, and with the left builds work-houses—and does not let her left hand know what her right hand does!"—a paraphrase of Matthew 6:3.

258 *Penn,* etc. William Penn (1644–1718); John Howard, see above; Elizabeth Fry (1780–1845), another British prison reformer.

259 *her best philanthropists.* Ms. 1162 then says: "Not that I love Caesar less, but Rome more"—a paraphrase of Shakespeare's *Julius Caesar,* III, ii, 23.

260 *I would not subtract any thing.* Most of this paragraph is a heavily rewritten version of ms. 130 and 131. This follows *does not spread by contagion* (below): "It has been well said that our purest and loftiest joys have no memory of, or faith in, one another, and hence we need that he of our fellows who last travelled to the sources of the sun—drank at the well of life—or tasted the fountain of God—should communicate to us some of their inspiration."

nothing and of which he is unconscious. This is a charity that hides a multitude of sins. The philanthropist too often surrounds mankind with the remembrance of his own cast-off griefs as an atmosphere, and calls it sympathy. We should impart our courage, and not our despair, our health and ease, and not our disease, and take care that this does not spread by contagion. From what southern plains comes up the voice of wailing? Under what latitudes reside the heathen to whom we would send light? Who is that intemperate and brutal man whom we would redeem? If any thing ail a man, so that he does not perform his functions, if he have a pain in his bowels even, — for that is the seat of sympathy, — he forthwith sets about reforming — the world. Being a microcosm himself, he discovers, and it is a true discovery, and he is the man to make it, — that the world has been eating green apples; to his eyes, in fact, the globe itself is a great green apple, which there is danger awful to think of that the children of men will nibble before it is ripe; and straightway his drastic philanthropy seeks out the Esquimaux and the Patagonian, and embraces the populous Indian and Chinese villages; and thus, by a few years of philanthropic activity, the powers in the mean while using him for their own ends, no doubt, he cures himself of his dyspepsia, the globe acquires a faint blush on one or both of its cheeks, as if it were beginning to be ripe, and life loses its crudity and is once more sweet and wholesome to live. I never dreamed of any enormity greater than I have committed. I never knew, and never shall know, a worse man than myself.

I believe that what so saddens the reformer is not his sympathy with his fellows in distress, but, though he be the holiest son of God, is his private ail. Let this be righted, let the spring come to him, the morning rise over his couch, and he will forsake his generous companions without apology. My excuse for not lecturing against the use of tobacco is, that I never chewed it; that is a penalty which reformed tobacco-chewers have to pay; though there are things enough I have chewed, which I could lecture against. If you should ever be betrayed into any of these philanthropies, do not let your left hand know what your right hand does, for it is not worth knowing. Rescue the drowning and tie your

261

262

263

261 *From what southern plains.* The slave states of the South.

262 *a pain in his bowels even,—for that is the seat of sympathy.* Song of Solomon, 5:4.

263 *it is not worth knowing.* Ms. 1166 then says: "Keep dark about it. That was excellent advice, for comparatively, I say, it is a deed of darkness, and will not constitute you a child of light." *Rescue the drowning*, etc., did not follow here; it was inserted.

The tobacco plant

shoe-strings. Take your time, and set about some free labor.

Our manners have been corrupted by communication with the saints. Our hymn-books resound with a melodious cursing of God and enduring him forever. One would say that even the prophets and redeemers had rather consoled the fears than confirmed the hopes of man. There is nowhere recorded a simple and irrepressible satisfaction with the gift of life, any memorable praise of God. All health and success does me good, however far off and withdrawn it may appear; all disease and failure helps to make me sad and does me evil, however much sympathy it may have with me or I with it. If, then, we would indeed restore mankind by truly Indian, botanic, magnetic, or natural means, let us first be as simple and well as Nature ourselves, dispel the clouds which hang over our own brows, and take up a little life into our pores. Do not stay to be an overseer of the poor, but endeavor to become one of the worthies of the world.

I read in the Gulistan, or Flower Garden, of Sheik **264** Sadi of Shiraz, that "They asked a wise man, saying; Of the many celebrated trees which the Most High God has created lofty and umbrageous, they call none azad, or free, excepting the cypress, which bears no fruit; what mystery is there in this? He replied; Each has its appropriate produce, and appointed season, during the continuance of which it is fresh and blooming, and during their absence dry and withered; to neither of which states is the cypress exposed, being always flourishing; and of this nature are the azads, or religious independents. — Fix not thy heart on that which is transitory; for the Dijlah, or Tigris, will continue to flow through Bagdad after the race of caliphs is extinct: if thy hand has plenty, be liberal as the date tree; but if it affords nothing to give away, be an azad, or free man, like the cypress."

264 *I read in the Gulistan.* This paragraph starts on ms. 134 with "For my own part I would fain be Azad or free like the green cypress tree." This is paraphrased below.

The Gulistan was written by the Persian poet Muslih-ud-Din Saadi—or Sadi (1184?–1291). His work was much admired by the Transcendentalists and particularly by Thoreau who mentions him several times in his *Journal*.

COMPLEMENTAL VERSES.   **265**

THE PRETENSIONS OF POVERTY.

"Thou dost presume too much, poor needy wretch,
To claim a station in the firmament,
Because thy humble cottage, or thy tub,
Nurses some lazy or pedantic virtue
In the cheap sunshine or by shady springs,
With roots and pot-herbs; where thy right hand,
Tearing those humane passions from the mind,
Upon whose stocks fair blooming virtues flourish,
Degradeth nature, and benumbeth sense,
And, Gorgon-like, turns active men to stone.
We not require the dull society
Of your necessitated temperance,
Or that unnatural stupidity
That knows nor joy nor sorrow; nor your forc'd
Falsely exalted passive fortitude
Above the active.   This low abject brood,
That fix their seats in mediocrity,
Become your servile minds; but we advance
Such virtues only as admit excess,
Brave, bounteous acts, regal magnificence,
All-seeing prudence, magnanimity
That knows no bound, and that heroic virtue
For which antiquity hath left no name,
But patterns only, such as Hercules,
Achilles, Theseus.   Back to thy loath'd cell;
And when thou seest the new enlightened sphere,
Study to know but what those worthies were."

        T. CAREW.

265 *Complemental Verses.* Thomas Carew (1595?–1645) was one of the Cavalier Poets. This is Mercury speaking to Poverty in the masque *Coelum Britannicum* (1661). Thoreau has modernized the antique spelling. On ms. 135 he wrote the phrase: "End of Economy."

WHERE I LIVED, AND WHAT I LIVED FOR.

AT a certain season of our life we are accustomed to consider every spot as the possible site of a house. I have thus surveyed the country on every side within a dozen miles of where I live. In imagination I have [1] bought all the farms in succession, for all were to be bought, and I knew their price. I walked over each farmer's premises, tasted his wild apples, discoursed on husbandry with him, took his farm at his price, at any price, mortgaging it to him in my mind; even put a higher price on it, — took every thing but a deed of it, — took his word for his deed, for I dearly love to talk, — cultivated it, and him too to some extent, I trust, and withdrew when I had enjoyed it long enough, leaving him to carry it on. This experience entitled me to be regarded as a sort of real-estate broker by my friends. Wherever I sat, there I might live, and the landscape radiated from me accordingly. What is a house but a *sedes*, a seat? — better if a country seat. I discovered many a site for a house not likely to be soon improved, which some might have thought too far from the village, but to my eyes the village was too far from it. Well, there I might live, I said; and there I did live, for an hour, a summer and a winter life; saw how I could let the years run off, buffet the winter through, and see the spring come in. The future inhabitants of this region, wherever they may place their houses, may be sure that they have been anticipated. An afternoon sufficed to lay out the land into orchard, woodlot, and pasture, and to decide what fine oaks or pines should be left to stand before the door, and whence each blasted [2]

213

1 *In imagination.* These two words were inserted on ms. 596.

2 *blasted.* "Rotten" on ms. 598.

tree could be seen to the best advantage; and then I let it lie, fallow perchance, for a man is rich in proportion to the number of things which he can afford to let alone.

My imagination carried me so far that I even had the refusal of several farms, — the refusal was all I wanted, — but I never got my fingers burned by actual possession. The nearest that I came to actual possession was when I bought the Hollowell place, and had begun to sort my seeds, and collected materials with which to make a wheelbarrow to carry it on or off with; but before the owner gave me a deed of it, his wife — every man has such a wife — changed her mind and wished to keep it, and he offered me ten dollars to release him. Now, to speak the truth, I had but ten cents in the world, and it surpassed my arithmetic to tell, if I was that man who had ten cents, or who had a farm, or ten dollars, or all together. However, I let him keep the ten dollars and the farm too, for I had carried it far enough; or rather, to be generous, I sold him the farm for just what I gave for it, and, as he was not a rich man, made him a present of ten dollars, and still had my ten cents, and seeds, and materials for a wheelbarrow left. I found thus that I had been a rich man without any damage to my poverty. But I retained the landscape, and I have since annually carried off what it yielded without a wheelbarrow. With respect to landscapes, —

> " I am monarch of all I *survey*,
>   My right there is none to dispute."

I have frequently seen a poet withdraw, having enjoyed the most valuable part of a farm, while the crusty farmer supposed that he had got a few wild apples only. Why, the owner does not know it for many years when a poet has put his farm in rhyme, the most admirable kind of invisible fence, has fairly impounded it, milked it, skimmed it, and got all the cream, and left the farmer only the skimmed milk.

The real attractions of the Hollowell farm, to me, were; its complete retirement, being about two miles from the village, half a mile from the nearest neighbor, and separated from the highway by a broad field; its bounding on the river, which the owner said protected it by its fogs from frosts in the spring, though that was nothing to me; the gray color and ruinous state of the

3 *refusal.* This has quotes on ms. 598.

4 *possession.* "Proprietorship" on ms. 598 for the second "possession."

5 *the Hollowell place.* In his copy of *Walden,* Channing said: "Henry did buy the Hollowell place, and thought to buy Weird Dell, and one side of Fairhaven Hill, that of the Orchard. He also thought of the Cliff Hill, and the Baker Farm." On this inexpensive basis Thoreau could have been considered to be the owner of all the land around Concord—and in this sense he was.

6 *"I am monarch of all I* survey." *"Survey"* is italicized. Channing helpfully says that this is "a pun on the word survey, as Henry was by trade a surveyor after he left Walden." The lines are from William Cowper's "Verses Supposed to be written by Alexander Selkirk." Daniel Defoe based *Robinson Crusoe* (1719) on the adventures of Selkirk, who was stranded for more than four years on the island of Más a Tierra, one of the Juan Fernández island group off the coast of Chile.

7 *the Hollowell farm* was on the west side of the Sudbury River near Hubbard's Bridge. This passage was taken from the *Journal* for February 3, 1854; VI, 91, many years after Thoreau had been thinking of buying the place before he went to Walden.

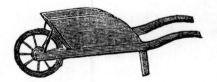

house and barn, and the dilapidated fences, which put 8
such an interval between me and the last occupant; the
hollow and lichen-covered apple trees, gnawed by rabbits, showing what kind of neighbors I should have;
but above all, the recollection I had of it from my earliest voyages up the river, when the house was concealed
behind a dense grove of red maples, through which I
heard the house-dog bark. I was in haste to buy it,
before the proprietor finished getting out some rocks,
cutting down the hollow apple trees, and grubbing up
some young birches which had sprung up in the pasture,
or, in short, had made any more of his improvements.
To enjoy these advantages I was ready to carry it on;
like Atlas, to take the world on my shoulders, — I never 9
heard what compensation he received for that, — and do
all those things which had no other motive or excuse
but that I might pay for it and be unmolested in my
possession of it; for I knew all the while that it would
yield the most abundant crop of the kind I wanted if I
could only afford to let it alone. But it turned out as I
have said.

All that I could say, then, with respect to farming on
a large scale, (I have always cultivated a garden,) was,
that I had had my seeds ready. Many think that seeds

8 *dilapidated.* This was followed by "and picturesque" on ms. 1168.

9 *Atlas.* One of the Greek Titans or elder gods
whose appointed task was to bear the world and
the vault of the sky on his shoulders.

SEPTEMBER

improve with age. I have no doubt that time discriminates between the good and the bad; and when at last I shall plant, I shall be less likely to be disappointed. But I would say to my fellows, once for all, As long as possible live free and uncommitted. It makes but little difference whether you are committed to a farm or the county jail.

Old Cato, whose " De Re Rusticâ " is my " Cultivator," says, and the only translation I have seen makes sheer nonsense of the passage, " When you think of getting a farm, turn it thus in your mind, not to buy greedily; nor spare your pains to look at it, and do not think it enough to go round it once. The oftener you go there the more it will please you, if it is good." I think I shall not buy greedily, but go round and round it as long as I live, and be buried in it first, that it may please me the more at last.

The present was my next experiment of this kind, which I purpose to describe more at length; for convenience, putting the experience of two years into one. **10** As I have said, I do not propose to write an ode to dejection, but to brag as lustily as chanticleer in the morning, standing on his roost, if only to wake my neighbors up. **11**

When first I took up my abode in the woods, that is, began to spend my nights as well as days there, which, by accident, was on Independence day, or the fourth of **12** July, 1845, my house was not finished for winter, but was merely a defence against the rain, without plastering or chimney, the walls being of rough weather-stained boards, with wide chinks, which made it cool at night. The upright white hewn studs and freshly planed door and window casings gave it a clean and airy look, especially in the morning, when its timbers were saturated with dew, so that I fancied that by noon some sweet gum would exude from them. To my imagination it retained throughout the day more or less of this auroral character, reminding me of a certain house on a **13** mountain which I had visited the year before. This was an airy and unplastered cabin, fit to entertain a travelling god, and where a goddess might trail her garments. The winds which passed over my dwelling were such as sweep over the ridges of mountains, bearing the broken strains, or celestial parts only, of ter-

10 *putting . . . two years into one.* Thoreau used his Walden Pond cabin for two years, two months, and two days, but, as he says here, he condenses this into one year—a complete cycle of the seasons. So far, however, there have been hardly any observations about Nature.

11 *I do not propose to write an ode to dejection.* This is what he said on the title page, q.v. In the *Journal* for June 2, 1853; V, 215, he wrote: "I would crow like Chanticleer in the morning, with all the lustiness that the new day imparts, without thinking of the evening, when I and all of us shall go to roost—with all the humility of the cock that takes his perch upon the highest rail and wakes the country with his clarion."

12 *the fourth of July. Journal,* January 17, 1852; III, 200, where it says that Thoreau "put a few articles of furniture into a hay-rigging" and took them to the cabin in that. He had made some of the furniture himself.

13 *a certain house on a mountain.* The *Journal* for July 5, 1845; I, 361, says: "Yesterday I came here to live. My house makes me think of some mountain houses I have seen, which seemed to have a fresher auroral atmosphere about them, as I fancy of the halls of Olympus. I lodged at the house of a saw-miller last summer, on the Catskill Mountains, high up as Pine Orchard, in the blueberry and raspberry region, where the quiet and cleanliness and coolness seemed to be all one—which had their ambrosial character. He was the miller of the Katerskill Falls. They were a clean and wholesome family, inside and out, like their house. The latter was not plastered, only lathed, and the inner doors were not hung. The house seemed high-placed, airy, and perfumed, fit to entertain a travelling god. It was so high, indeed, that all the music, the broken strains, the waifs and accompaniments of tunes, that swept over the ridge of the Catskills, passed through its aisles. Could not man be man in such an abode? And would he ever find out this grovelling life? It was the very light and atmosphere in which the works of Grecian art were composed, and in which they rest. They have appropriated to themselves a loftier hall than mortals ever occupy, at least on a level with the mountain-brows of the world. There was wanting a little of the glare of the lower vales, and in its place a pure twilight as became the precincts of heaven. Yet so equable and calm was the season there that you could not tell whether it was morning or noon or evening. Always there was the sound of the morning cricket."

restrial music.   The morning wind forever blows, the poem of creation is uninterrupted; but few are the ears that hear it.   Olympus is but the outside of the earth **14** every where.

The only house I had been the owner of before, if I except a boat, was a tent, which I used occasionally **15** when making excursions in the summer, and this is still rolled up in my garret; but the boat, after passing from hand to hand, has gone down the stream of time.   With this more substantial shelter about me, I had made some progress toward settling in the world.   This frame, so slightly clad, was a sort of crystallization around me, and reacted on the builder.   It was suggestive somewhat as a picture in outlines.   I did not need to go out doors to take the air, for the atmosphere within had lost none of its freshness.   It was not so much within doors as behind a door where I sat, even in the rainiest weather. The Harivansa says, "An abode without birds is like **16** a meat without seasoning."   Such was not my abode, for I found myself suddenly neighbor to the birds; not by having imprisoned one, but having caged myself near them.   I was not only nearer to some of those which commonly frequent the garden and the orchard, but to those wilder and more thrilling songsters of the forest which never, or rarely, serenade a villager, — the wood- **17** thrush, the veery, the scarlet tanager, the field-sparrow, the whippoorwill, and many others.

I was seated by the shore of a small pond, about a **18** mile and a half south of the village of Concord and somewhat higher than it, in the midst of an extensive wood between that town and Lincoln, and about two miles south of that our only field known to fame, Concord **19**

14 *Olympus*. The mountain where the Greek gods dwelt.

15 *a boat . . . a tent*. Thoreau had used these in 1839 when he went with his brother John on the voyage that resulted in *A Week on the Concord and Merrimack Rivers*. He had sold the boat to Hawthorne in 1842, who changed its name from *Musketaquid* to *Pond Lily*.

16 *The Harivansa*. A fifth-century A.D. epic poem about the Hindu god Krishna. Krishna was the eighth avatar of Vishnu. In the Bhagvat-Geeta he appears as a teacher. His name means black.

17 *the wood-thrush*, etc. The names of these birds were inserted later, for they are not on ms. 917.

18 *a small pond*. This was not "small" but "beautiful" on ms. 917.

19 *Concord Battle Ground*. This, of course, is the battle of April 19, 1775, that began the American Revolution. Emerson's poem:

"By the rude bridge that arched the flood,
   Their flag to April's breeze unfurled,
Here once the embattled farmers stood,
   And fired the shot heard round the world"

is inscribed on a monument near the bridge.

The Concord Battle Monument
as it was in Thoreau's time

Battle Ground; but I was so low in the woods that the opposite shore, half a mile off, like the rest, covered with wood, was my most distant horizon. For the first week, whenever I looked out on the pond it impressed me like a tarn high up on the side of a mountain, its bottom far above the surface of other lakes, and, as the sun arose, I saw it throwing off its nightly clothing of mist, and here and there, by degrees, its soft ripples or its smooth reflecting surface was revealed, while the mists, like ghosts, were stealthily withdrawing in every direction into the woods, as at the breaking up of some nocturnal conventicle. The very dew seemed to hang upon the trees later into the day than usual, as on the sides of mountains.

This small lake was of most value as a neighbor in the intervals of a gentle rain storm in August, when, both air and water being perfectly still, but the sky overcast, mid-afternoon had all the serenity of evening, and the wood-thrush sang around, and was heard from shore to shore. A lake like this is never smoother than at such a time; and the clear portion of the air above it being shallow and darkened by clouds, the water, full of light and reflections, becomes a lower heaven itself so much the more important. From a hill top near by, **20** where the wood had been recently cut off, there was a pleasing vista southward across the pond, through a wide indentation in the hills which form the shore there, where their opposite sides sloping toward each other suggested a stream flowing out in that direction through a wooded valley, but stream there was none. That way I looked between and over the near green hills to some distant and higher ones in the horizon, tinged with blue. Indeed, by standing on tiptoe I could catch a glimpse of some of the peaks of the still bluer and more distant mountain ranges in the north-west, those true-blue coins from heaven's own mint, and also of some portion of the village. But in other directions, even from this point, I could not see over or beyond the woods which surrounded me. It is well to have some water in your neighborhood, to give buoyancy to and float the earth. One value even of the smallest well is, that when you look into it you see that earth is not continent but insular. This is as important as that it keeps butter cool. When I looked across the pond from this peak toward the Sudbury meadows, which in time of flood I distin-

20 *From a hill top near by.* In his copy of *Walden* Channing says that this is Heywood's Peak. At this point *Walden,* which has thus far been about people, begins to deal with Nature.

guished elevated perhaps by a mirage in their seething valley, like a coin in a basin, all the earth beyond the pond appeared like a thin crust insulated and floated even by this small sheet of intervening water, and I was reminded that this on which I dwelt was but *dry land*.

Though the view from my door was still more contracted, I did not feel crowded or confined in the least. There was pasture enough for my imagination. The low shrub-oak plateau to which the opposite shore arose, stretched away toward the prairies of the West and the **21** steppes of Tartary, affording ample room for all the roving families of men. "There are none happy in the world but beings who enjoy freely a vast horizon," — said Damodara, when his herds required new and larger **22** pastures.

Both place and time were changed, and I dwelt nearer to those parts of the universe and to those eras in history which had most attracted me. Where I lived was as far off as many a region viewed nightly by astron- **23** omers. We are wont to imagine rare and delectable

21 *prairies of the West*. This was "pampas" on ms. 921.

22 *Damodara*. This quotation is from the poem about Krishna mentioned above. Damodara is one of the god's many names.

23 *a region viewed nightly by astronomers*. The Bibliophile Edition (I, 26) prints the following after this: "Both place and time had undergone a revolution, and I seemed to dwell nearer to those parts of the globe, and to those eras in history, which had attracted me; and as I had no clock but the sun and moon, I also lived in a more primitive time. Let us rise early, and fast or break fast gently, and without perturbation. What if the milkman does not come in season to whitewash our coffee? Let us murmur an inward prayer that we may be sustained under this trial,—and forget him."

The view from the shore
near the cabin site

places in some remote and more celestial corner of the system, behind the constellation of Cassiopeia's Chair, far from noise and disturbance. I discovered that my house actually had its site in such a withdrawn, but forever new and unprofaned, part of the universe. If it were worth the while to settle in those parts near to the **24** Pleiades or the Hyades, to Aldebaran or Altair, then I was really there, or at an equal remoteness from the life which I had left behind, dwindled and twinkling with as fine a ray to my nearest neighbor, and to be seen only in moonless nights by him. Such was that part of creation where I had squatted; —

> "There was a shepherd that did live,   **25**
>   And held his thoughts as high
> As were the mounts whereon his flocks
>   Did hourly feed him by."

What should we think of the shepherd's life if his flocks always wandered to higher pastures than his thoughts?

Every morning was a cheerful invitation to make my life of equal simplicity, and I may say innocence, with Nature herself. I have been as sincere a worshipper of Aurora as the Greeks. I got up early and bathed in **26** the pond; that was a religious exercise, and one of the best things which I did. They say that characters were engraven on the bathing tub of king Tching-thang **27** to this effect: " Renew thyself completely each day; do it again, and again, and forever again." I can understand that. Morning brings back the heroic ages. **28** I was as much affected by the faint hum of a mosquito making its invisible and unimaginable tour through my apartment at earliest dawn, when I was sitting with door and windows open, as I could be by any trumpet that **29** ever sang of fame. It was Homer's requiem; itself an Iliad and Odyssey in the air, singing its own wrath and wanderings. There was something cosmical about it; a standing advertisement, till forbidden, of the everlast- **30** ing vigor and fertility of the world. The morning, **31** which is the most memorable season of the day, is the awakening hour. Then there is least somnolence in us; and for an hour, at least, some part of us awakes which slumbers all the rest of the day and night. Little is to be expected of that day, if it can be called a day, to which we are not awakened by our Genius, but by the mechani- **32**

24 *the Pleiades*, etc. The Pleiades and Cassiopeia's Chair are prominent constellations. Aldebaran is a star in Taurus; Altair, a star in Aquila.

25 *"There was a shepherd that did live."* Channing's copy of *Walden* says that this comes from "The Shepherd's Love for Philliday," which appears in *The Muse's Garden* and that it is "Half of the first of three stanzas from [Thomas] Evans' *Old Ballads*, 1810."

26 *Aurora.* Goddess of the dawn. It is odd that a good classical scholar like Thoreau should associate this name with the Greeks, for Aurora was her Roman name. The Greeks called her Eos.

27 *king Tching-thang.* Confucius.

28 *Morning brings back the heroic ages.* Here the cycle of the day begins, and the reader is being brought close to the heart of *Walden*.

29 *any trumpet that ever sang of fame.* A paraphrase of a line in Felicia Hemans' (1793–1835) poem, "The Landing of the Pilgrims." Mrs. Hemans was held in higher regard in Thoreau's day than she is now. She is best remembered for "Casabianca" ("The boy stood on the burning deck").

30 *a standing advertisement, till forbidden.* Advertisements that ran issue after issue in a newspaper until canceled were marked "till forbidden," abbreviated TF.

31 *fertility of the world.* Again Thoreau tempered his words; "world" was "universe" on ms. 397.

32 *mechanical nudgings of some servitor.* Followed by "or by the peal of alarm bells" on ms. 925 and canceled there.

Homer

cal nudgings of some servitor, are not awakened by our own newly-acquired force and aspirations from within, accompanied by the undulations of celestial music, instead of factory bells, and a fragrance filling the air — to a higher life than we fell asleep from; and thus the darkness bear its fruit, and prove itself to be good, no less than the light. That man who does not believe that each day contains an earlier, more sacred, and auroral hour than he has yet profaned, has despaired of life, and is pursuing a descending and darkening way. After a partial cessation of his sensuous life, the soul of man, or its organs rather, are reinvigorated each day, and his Genius tries again what noble life it can make. All memorable events, I should say, transpire in morning time and in a morning atmosphere. The Vedas say, " All intelligences awake with the morning." Poetry and art, and the fairest and most memorable of the actions of men, date from such an hour. All poets and heroes, like Memnon, are the children of Aurora, and emit their music at sunrise. To him whose elastic and vigorous thought keeps pace with the sun, the day is a perpetual morning. It matters not what the clocks say or the attitudes and labors of men. Morning is when I am awake and there is a dawn in me. Moral reform is the effort to throw off sleep. Why is it that men give so poor an account of their day if they have not been slumbering? They are not such poor calculators. If they had not been overcome with drowsiness they would have performed something. The millions are awake enough for physical labor; but only one in a million is awake enough for effective intellectual exertion, only one in a hundred millions to a poetic or divine life. To be awake is to be alive. I have never yet met a man who was quite awake. How could I have looked him in the face?

We must learn to reawaken and keep ourselves awake, not by mechanical aids, but by an infinite expectation of the dawn, which does not forsake us in our soundest sleep. I know of no more encouraging fact than the unquestionable ability of man to elevate his life by a conscious endeavor. It is something to be able to paint a particular picture, or to carve a statue, and so to make a few objects beautiful; but it is far more glorious to carve and paint the very atmosphere and medium through which we look, which morally we can do. To affect the quality of the day, that is the highest of

33 *The Vedas . . . Memnon.* The Vedas are four Brahmin religious books written in prose and verse. Memnon, the son of Aurora (or Eos), was an Ethiopian and may have been black. In the Trojan War he was slain by Achilles. In Egypt the name Memnon was associated with Amenhotep III. Colossal statues of him were built near Thebes, two of which are still standing. One of them, which was damaged by an earthquake in 27 B.C., emits curious musical sounds when the rays of the rising sun warm its stones. Illustrated on page 174.

arts. Every man is tasked to make his life, even in its details, worthy of the contemplation of his most elevated and critical hour. If we refused, or rather used up, such paltry information as we get, the oracles would distinctly inform us how this might be done.

I went to the woods because I wished to live deliberately, to front only the essential facts of life, and see if I could not learn what it had to teach, and not, when I came to die, discover that I had not lived. I did not wish to live what was not life, living is so dear; nor did I wish to practise resignation, unless it was quite necessary. I wanted to live deep and suck out all the marrow of life, to live so sturdily and Spartan-like as to put to rout all that was not life, to cut a broad swath and shave close, to drive life into a corner, and reduce it to its lowest terms, and, if it proved to be mean, why then to get the whole and genuine meanness of it, and publish its meanness to the world; or if it were sublime, to know it by experience, and be able to give a true account of it in my next excursion. For most men, it appears to me, are in a strange uncertainty about it, whether it is of the devil or of God, and have *somewhat hastily* concluded that it is the chief end of man here to "glorify God and enjoy him forever."

Still we live meanly, like ants; though the fable tells us that we were long ago changed into men; like pygmies we fight with cranes; it is error upon error, and clout upon clout, and our best virtue has for its occasion a superfluous and evitable wretchedness. Our life is frittered away by detail. An honest man has hardly need to count more than his ten fingers, or in extreme cases he may add his ten toes, and lump the rest. Simplicity, simplicity, simplicity! I say, let your affairs be as two or three, and not a hundred or a thousand; instead of a million count half a dozen, and keep your accounts on your thumb nail. In the midst of this chopping sea of civilized life, such are the clouds and storms and quicksands and thousand-and-one items to be allowed for, that a man has to live, if he would not founder and go to the bottom and not make his port at all, by dead reckoning, and he must be a great calculator indeed who succeeds. Simplify, simplify. Instead of three meals a day, if it be necessary eat but one; instead of a hundred dishes, five; and reduce other things in proportion. Our life is like a German Confederacy, made up of petty states,

34 *I went to the woods.* Ms. 396 has it, "I went down to the pond." Charles Anderson (1968, page 34) says that this is "a key paragraph, buried in the center of the chapter, that will repay close reading."

35 *For most men.* Another modification; it was "all men" on ms. 45.

36 *"glorify God and enjoy him forever."* These few canceled but significant words follow on ms. 145 and 397: "when there may be no enjoyment in it. If the truth were known, they enjoy the devil a good deal more. I am not satisfied with such a lumping up and glossing over the objects of life."

37 *the fable tells us.* In order to increase a scanty population *Aeacus* beseeched Zeus to turn ants into men.

38 *like pygmies we fight with cranes.* Iliad, III, lines 2 to 6. The Trojans were the cranes.

39 *evitable wretchedness.* The Bibliophile Edition (I, 44) says here: "Our life is frittered away by detail. Its dish consists almost entirely of 'fixings,' and very little of the chicken's meat."

40 *Simplicity, simplicity, simplicity!* The *Journal* for February 8, 1857; IX, 246 (written after *Walden* was published), casts further light on Thoreau's idea of simplicity: "By poverty, i.e. simplicity of life and fewness of incidents, I am solidified and crystallized, as a vapor or liquid by cold. . . . By simplicity, commonly called poverty, my life is concentrated and so becomes organized, or a kosmos, which before was inorganic and lumpish."

41 *a German Confederacy.* This was before the unification of Germany under Bismarck, when Germany was still divided into numerous small principalities and minor kingdoms.

with its boundary forever fluctuating, so that even a German cannot tell you how it is bounded at any moment. The nation itself, with all its so called internal improvements, which, by the way, are all external and superficial, is just such an unwieldy and overgrown establishment, cluttered with furniture and tripped up by its own traps, ruined by luxury and heedless expense, by want of calculation and a worthy aim, as the million households in the land; and the only cure for it as for them is in a rigid economy, a stern and more than Spartan simplicity of life and elevation of purpose. It lives too fast. Men think that it is essential that the *Nation* have commerce, and export ice, and talk through a telegraph, and ride thirty miles an hour, without a doubt, whether *they* do or not; but whether we should live like baboons or like men, is a little uncertain. If we do not get out sleepers, and forge rails, and devote days and **42** nights to the work, but go to tinkering upon our *lives* to improve *them*, who will build railroads? And if railroads are not built, how shall we get to heaven in season? But **43** if we stay at home and mind our business, who will want railroads? We do not ride on the railroad; it rides upon us. Did you ever think what those sleepers are that underlie the railroad? Each one is a man, an Irishman, or a Yankee man. The rails are laid on them, and they are covered with sand, and the cars run smoothly over them. They are sound sleepers, I assure you. **44** And every few years a new lot is laid down and run over; so that, if some have the pleasure of riding on a rail, others have the misfortune to be ridden upon. And when they run over a man that is walking in his sleep, a supernumerary sleeper in the wrong position, and wake him up, they suddenly stop the cars, and make a hue and cry about it, as if this were an exception. I am glad to know that it takes a gang of men for every five miles to keep the sleepers down and level in their beds as it is, for this is a sign that they may sometime get up again.

Why should we live with such hurry and waste of life? We are determined to be starved before we are hungry. Men say that a stitch in time saves nine, and so they take a thousand stitches to-day to save nine to-morrow. As for *work*, we haven't any of any consequence. We have the Saint Vitus' dance, and cannot **45** possibly keep our heads still. If I should only give a **46**

42 *sleepers*. The wooden ties upon which railroad tracks are laid.

43 *how shall we get to heaven in season?* This is an allusion to Hawthorne's short story, "The Celestial Railroad."

44 *They are sound sleepers.* Here puns come thick and fast. *Riding on* a rail refers to the then popular custom of getting rid of an unwanted person by riding him out of town on a wooden rail.

45 *the Saint Vitus' dance.* In cases of rheumatic fever that involve the connective tissue of the brain, Sydenham's chorea may result. People afflicted by it make jerky, spasmodic movements.

46 *only give a few pulls at the parish bell-rope, as for a fire.* Different kinds of ringing were well-understood signals in the town.

few pulls at the parish bell-rope, as for a fire, that is, without setting the bell, there is hardly a man on his farm in the outskirts of Concord, notwithstanding that press of engagements which was his excuse so many times this morning, nor a boy, nor a woman, I might almost say, but would forsake all and follow that sound, not mainly to save property from the flames, but, if we will confess the truth, much more to see it burn, since **47** burn it must, and we, be it known, did not set it on fire, — or to see it put out, and have a hand in it, if that is done as handsomely; yes, even if it were the parish church itself. Hardly a man takes a half hour's nap after dinner, but when he wakes he holds up his head and asks, " What's the news ? " as if the rest of mankind had stood his sentinels. Some give directions to be waked every half hour, doubtless for no other purpose; and then, to pay for it, they tell what they have dreamed. After a night's sleep the news is as indispensable as the breakfast. " Pray tell me any thing new that has happened to a man any where on this globe,"— and he reads it over his coffee and rolls, that a man has had his eyes gouged out this morning on the Wachito River; **48** never dreaming the while that he lives in the dark un- **49** fathomed mammoth cave of this world, and has but the rudiment of an eye himself.

For my part, I could easily do without the post-office. **50** I think that there are very few important communications made through it. To speak critically, I never received more than one or two letters in my life—I wrote this some years ago — that were worth the postage. The penny-post is, commonly, an institution through **51**

47 *much more to see it burn.* This is a round-about reference to the time when Thoreau accidentally set the grass and wood on fire. See the *Chronology* for April 30, 1844.

48 *on the Wachito River.* Spelled Ouachito River on ms. 399. It is in southern Arkansas, where the men were tough in those days. Ouachita is the favored spelling now.

49 *the dark unfathomed mammoth cave.* Kentucky's Mammoth Cave has small blind fish in its underground waters. Gray's "Elegy":

"Full many a gem of purest ray serene
 The dark unfathom'd caves of ocean bear. . . ."

50 *I could easily do without the post-office.* Sanborn said caustically of this (Bibliophile Edition, I, 49n.) that "few residents of Concord frequented the Post Office more punctually or read the newspapers (particularly the New York *Tribune*) more eagerly than Thoreau."

51 *The penny-post.* In 1846 letters could be sent for distances under 300 miles for three cents; adhesive stamps came into use in 1847, and distances were extended for three-cent postage to 3,000 miles in 1851. This reference is really to British penny postage; such a penny was worth two American cents. American rates were reduced to two cents in 1883, but were never that low in Thoreau's lifetime.

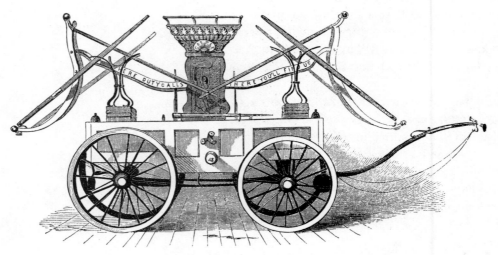

A fire engine of the time

which you seriously offer a man that penny for his thoughts which is so often safely offered in jest. And I am sure that I never read any memorable news in a newspaper. If we read of one man robbed, or murdered, or killed by accident, or one house burned, or one vessel wrecked, or one steamboat blown up, or one cow run over on the Western Railroad, or one mad dog killed, or one lot of grasshoppers in the winter, — we never need read of another. One is enough. If you are acquainted with the principle, what do you care for a myriad instances and applications? To a philosopher all *news*, as it is called, is gossip, and they who edit and read it are old women over their tea.   **52**   Yet not a few are greedy after this gossip. There was such a rush, as I hear, the other day at one of the offices to learn the foreign news by the last arrival, that several large squares of plate glass belonging to the establishment were broken by the pressure, — news which I seriously think a ready wit might write a twelvemonth or twelve years beforehand with sufficient accuracy. As for Spain, for instance, if you know how to throw in Don Carlos and the Infanta, and   **53**   Don Pedro and Seville and Granada, from time to time in the right proportions, — they may have changed the names a little since I saw the papers, — and serve up a bull-fight when other entertainments fail, it will be true to the letter, and give us as good an idea of the exact state or ruin of things in Spain as the most succinct and lucid reports under this head in the newspapers: and as for England, almost the last significant   **54**   scrap of news from that quarter was the revolution of 1649; and if you have learned the history of her crops for an average year, you never need attend to that thing again, unless your speculations are of a merely pecuniary character. If one may judge who rarely looks into the newspapers, nothing new does ever happen in foreign parts, a French revolution not excepted.   **55**

What news! how much more important to know what that is which was never old!   **56**   "Kieou-he-yu (great dignitary of the state of Wei) sent a man to Khoung-tseu to know his news. Khoung-tseu caused the messenger to be seated near him, and questioned him in these terms: What is your master doing? The messenger answered with respect: My master desires to diminish the number of his faults, but he cannot

52 *old women over their tea.* This is followed on ms. 400 by: "Uncle Sam is a man who presumes to tell you each day how many times he has stubbed his toes. No doubt such accidents do happen to a man, but let him wait at least till he stubs his nose before he bores his neighbors with the news."

53 *Don Carlos,* etc. These were Spaniards who had been prominent in politics during the 1830's and 1840's. By 1854, when *Walden* was published, they were very much out of date.

54 *the revolution of 1649.* The British monarchy was then replaced by Cromwell and the Commonwealth, which lasted until 1660.

55 *a French revolution not excepted.* News of the French revolution of 1848 had nevertheless been followed with great interest by Americans. The Bibliophile Edition (I, 50n.) prints this footnote by Thoreau: "This was written before the last (1848) Revolution broke out; but a revolution in France might be expected any day; and it would be as easy to tell where it would end, before it was born, as after it was five years old."

56 *Kieou-he-yu.* Lyman V. Cady (1961, page 25n.) points out that in the Wade system of transliteration from the Chinese this name would be rendered Chu Pai-yu and that the "h" in the *Walden* text is a printer's error for "n." The story is from the Confucian *Analects*.

The Revolution of 1848 in Paris

come to the end of them. The messenger being gone, the philosopher remarked: What a worthy messenger! What a worthy messenger!" The preacher, instead of vexing the ears of drowsy farmers on their day of rest at the end of the week, — for Sunday is the fit conclusion of an ill-spent week, and not the fresh and brave beginning of a new one, — with this one other draggletail of a sermon, should shout with thundering voice, — "Pause! Avast! Why so seeming fast, but deadly slow?"

Shams and delusions are esteemed for soundest truths, while reality is fabulous. If men would steadily observe realities only, and not allow themselves to be deluded, life, to compare it with such things as we know, would be like a fairy tale and the Arabian Nights' Entertainments. If we respected only what is inevitable and has a right to be, music and poetry would resound along the streets. When we are unhurried and wise, we perceive that only great and worthy things have any permanent and absolute existence, — that petty fears and petty pleasures are but the shadow of the reality. This is always exhilarating and sublime. By closing the eyes and slumbering, and consenting to be deceived by shows, men establish and confirm their daily life of routine and habit every where, which still is built on

57 *come to the end of them*. Thoreau changed this to "accomplish it" in his own copy of *Walden*.

58 *The preacher*. This obviously calls for a new paragraph, and on ms. 402 there is one. The passage was written in the *Journal* on July 6, 1845; I, 362, two days after Thoreau came to Walden. The ending there reads: "Stop! Avast! why so fast?" And on ms. 402 this is followed by "Why so deadly slow?"
Walter Harding (1963, page 279) thinks that this may be "an allusion to Father Taylor, the original of Father Mapple in Melville's *Moby-Dick*."

59 *Shams and delusions*. Charles Anderson (1968, page 102) calls this passage the "most abstract treatment of Idealism in *Walden*."

purely illusory foundations. Children, who play life, discern its true law and relations more clearly than men, who fail to live it worthily, but who think that they are wiser by experience, that is, by failure. I have read in a Hindoo book, that "there was a king's son, who, **60** being expelled in infancy from his native city, was brought up by a forester, and, growing up to maturity in that state, imagined himself to belong to the barbarous race with which he lived. One of his father's ministers having discovered him, revealed to him what he was, and the misconception of his character was removed, and he knew himself to be a prince. So soul," continues the Hindoo philosopher, "from the circumstances in which it is placed, mistakes its own character, until the truth is revealed to it by some holy teacher, and then it knows itself to be *Brahme*." I per-**61** ceive that we inhabitants of New England live this mean life that we do because our vision does not penetrate the surface of things. We think that that *is* which *appears* to be. If a man should walk through this town and see only the reality, where, think you, would the "Mill-dam" go to? If he should give us an ac-**62** count of the realities he beheld there, we should not recognize the place in his description. Look at a meeting-house, or a court-house, or a jail, or a shop, or

60 *a Hindoo book.* Not yet identified.

61 Brahme. Brahmā is the supreme soul, the essence of all being. Brahmā is the creative aspect of the great divinity whose other two phases are Vishnu, the preserver, and Siva, the destroyer.

62 *the "Mill-dam,"* which was just that, was one of the most frequented parts of Concord when Thoreau lived there. The various establishments mentioned three lines below were located near it. Instead of "Mill-dam," ms. 405 originally had "State Street" [Boston].

a dwelling-house, and say what that thing really is before a true gaze, and they would all go to pieces in your account of them. Men esteem truth remote, in the outskirts of the system, behind the farthest star, before Adam and after the last man. In eternity there is indeed something true and sublime. But all these times and places and occasions are now and here. God himself culminates in the present moment, and will never be more divine in the lapse of all the ages. And we are enabled to apprehend at all what is sublime and noble only by the perpetual instilling and drenching of the reality that surrounds us. The universe constantly and obediently answers to our conceptions; whether we travel fast or slow, the track is laid for us. Let us spend our lives in conceiving then. The poet or the artist never yet had so fair and noble a design but some of his posterity at least could accomplish it.

Let us spend one day as deliberately as Nature, and **63** not be thrown off the track by every nutshell and mosquito's wing that falls on the rails. Let us rise early and fast, or break fast, gently and without perturbation; let company come and let company go, let the bells ring and the children cry, — determined to make a day of it. Why should we knock under and go with the stream? Let us not be upset and overwhelmed in that **64** terrible rapid and whirlpool called a dinner, situated in the meridian shallows. Weather this danger and you are safe, for the rest of the way is down hill. With unrelaxed nerves, with morning vigor, sail by it, looking another way, tied to the mast like Ulysses. If the engine whistles, let it whistle till it is hoarse for its pains. If the bell rings, why should we run? We will consider what kind of music they are like. Let us settle ourselves, and work and wedge our feet downward through the mud and slush of opinion, and prejudice, and tradition, and delusion, and appearance, that alluvion which covers the globe, through Paris and London, through New York and Boston and Concord, through church and state, through poetry and philosophy and religion, till we come to a hard bottom and rocks in place, which we can call *reality*, and say, This is, and no mistake; and then begin, having a *point d'appui*, **65** below freshet and frost and fire, a place where you might found a wall or a state, or set a lamp-post safely, or perhaps a gauge, not a Nilometer, but a Realometer, **66**

63 *Let us spend one day as deliberately as Nature.* The *Journal* for September 7, 1851; II, 471, says: "If by watching all day and all night I may detect some trace of the Ineffable, then will it not be worth the while to watch? . . . We are surrounded by a rich and fertile mystery. May we not probe it, pry into it, employ ourselves about it, a little? To devote your life to the discovery of the divinity in nature or to the eating of oysters, would they not be attended with very different results?"

64 *that terrible rapid and whirlpool.* Here, briefly, we are on the track of Ulysses. This is the water between Scylla and Charybdis. There Ulysses had himself tied to the mast so he could hear but not succumb to the fatal song of the Sirens. Meanwhile, his crew plugged up their ears with wax in order to be deaf to the deadly music as they rowed past. After this brief return to Homer, the railroad and solid earth take over again, and "*reality* . . . is, and no mistake."

65 point d'appui. Base of operations.

66 *Nilometer.* This was a gauge placed in ancient times in the Nile at Memphis to measure the rise of the water when the river was reaching its flood stage.

that future ages might know how deep a freshet of shams and appearances had gathered from time to time. **67** If you stand right fronting and face to face to a fact, you will see the sun glimmer on both its surfaces, as if it were a cimeter, and feel its sweet edge dividing you **68** through the heart and marrow, and so you will happily conclude your mortal career. Be it life or death, we crave only reality. If we are really dying, let us hear the rattle in our throats and feel cold in the extremities; if we are alive, let us go about our business.

Time is but the stream I go a-fishing in. I drink at **69** it; but while I drink I see the sandy bottom and detect how shallow it is. Its thin current slides away, but

The cairn marking the cabin site as it was in 1906
(*Photograph by Herbert Gleason*)

67 *from time to time.* On ms. 408 this verse, written by Thoreau, follows:

He knows no change who knows the true,
    And on it keeps his eye,
Who always still the unseen doth view;
    Only the false & the apparent die.

Things change, but change not far
    From what they are not but to what they are,
Or rather 'tis our ignorance that dies;
    Forever lies the knowledge of the wise.

Carl Bode (1964, page 373) has said that "these lines, along with one other set, are as close to pure platonism as Thoreau ever comes."

68 *cimeter.* Also spelled scimitar. An oriental saber with a curved blade.

69 *Time is but the stream I go a-fishing in.* This lyrical passage was written early in the making of *Walden.* It was on ms. 145, where it was scratched out and then recopied in clear, clean form on ms. 410.

It was followed on ms. 150 to 153 by:
"When I was fairly established in my house I sang this song,

    I seek the Present Time,
    No other clime,
    Life in to-day,
    Not to sail another way,
    To Paris or to Rome,
    Or farther still from home.
    That man, whoe'er he is,
    Lives but a moral death,
    Whose life is not coeval
    With his breath.
    My feet forever stand
    On Concord fields,
    And I must live the life
    Which their soil yields.
    What are deeds done
    Away from home?
    What the best essay
    On the Ruins of Rome?
    The love of the new,
    The unfathomed blue,
    The wind in the wood,
    All fortune good,
    The sun-lit tree,
    The small chicadee,
    The dusty highways,
    What Scripture says,
    This pleasant weather
    And all signs together—
    The river's meander,
    All things, in short,
    Forbid me to wander

eternity remains. I would drink deeper; fish in the sky, whose bottom is pebbly with stars. I cannot count one. I know not the first letter of the alphabet. I have always been regretting that I was not as wise as the day I was born. The intellect is a cleaver; it discerns and rifts its way into the secret of things. I do not wish to be any more busy with my hands than is necessary. My head is hands and feet. I feel all my best faculties concentrated in it. My instinct tells me that my head is an organ for burrowing, as some creatures use their snout and fore-paws, and with it I would mine and burrow my way through these hills. I think that the richest vein is somewhere hereabouts; so by the divining rod and thin rising vapors I judge; and here I will begin to mine.

In deed or in thought,
In cold or in drouth,
Not seek the sunny South,
But make the whole tour
Of the sunny Present Hour.
For here if thou fail,
Where canst thou prevail?
If you love not
Your own land most,
You'll find nothing lovely
Upon a distant coast.
If you love not
The latest sun-set,
What is there in pictures
Or old gems set?

If no man should travel
Till he had the means,
There'd be little travelling
For Kings or for Queens.
The means! What are they?
They are the wherewithal
Great expenses to pay;–
Life got, and some to spare,
Great works on hand,
And freedom from care.
Plenty of time well spent,
To use,—
Clothes paid for, and no rent
In your shoes;—
Something to eat,
And something to burn,
And, above all, no need to return;—
For they who come back,
Say have they not failed,
Wherever they've ridden
Or steamed it, or sailed?
  All your grass hayed,—
  All your debts paid,—
  All your wills made?
Then you might as well have stayed,
For are you not dead,
Only not buried?

The way unto "Today,"
The railroad to "Here,"
They never'll grade that way,
Nor shorten it, I fear,
There are plenty of depots
All the world o'er,
But not a single station
At a man's door;
If we would get near
To the secret of things,
We shall not have to hear
When the engine bell rings."

This poem is also in the *Journal* for 1845–1847;
I, 409– 411.

READING.

With a little more deliberation in the choice of their pursuits, all men would perhaps become essentially students and observers, for certainly their nature and destiny are interesting to all alike. In accumulating **1** property for ourselves or our posterity, in founding a family or a state, or acquiring fame even, we are mortal; but in dealing with truth we are immortal, and need fear no change nor accident. The oldest Egyptian or Hindoo philosopher raised a corner of the veil from the statue of the divinity; and still the trembling robe remains raised, and I gaze upon as fresh a glory as he did, since it was I in him that was then so bold, and it is he in me that now reviews the vision. No dust has settled on that robe; no time has elapsed since that divinity was revealed. That time which we really improve, or which is improvable, is neither past, present, nor future.

My residence was more favorable, not only to thought, but to serious reading, than a university; and though I was beyond the range of the ordinary circulating library, I had more than ever come within the influence of those books which circulate round the world, whose sentences were first written on bark, and are now merely copied from time to time on to linen paper. Says the poet Mîr Camar Uddîn Mast, " Being seated **2** to run through the region of the spiritual world; I have had this advantage in books. To be intoxicated by a single glass of wine; I have experienced this pleasure when I have drunk the liquor of the esoteric doctrines." I kept Homer's Iliad on my table through the summer, **3** though I looked at his page only now and then. Inces-

In the first version of *Walden* there was no indication of a new chapter here.

1 *interesting to all alike*. On ms. 153 this was "every man." And it was followed by: "It is hard to tell of that time which we really improve to past & present & future. I might say that the student always studies antiques. In our studies we do not look forward but backward into antiquity. . . . The most adventurous student seeks the remotest antiquity, the history of a time, as it were, prior to time." The first sentence, much revised, is the last sentence of the first paragraph of the printed text.

2 *Says the poet Mîr Camar Uddîn Mast*. Thoreau found this eighteenth-century poet in a French history of Hindu literature and translated this passage. See also note 4.

3 *Homer's Iliad*. This book was the one thing that was stolen from the Walden Pond cabin during Thoreau's occupation of it.

sant labor with my hands, at first, for I had my house to finish and my beans to hoe at the same time, made more study impossible. Yet I sustained myself by the prospect of such reading in future. I read one or two **4** shallow books of travel in the intervals of my work, till that employment made me ashamed of myself, and I asked where it was then that *I* lived.

The student may read Homer or Æschylus in the **5** Greek without danger of dissipation or luxuriousness, for it implies that he in some measure emulate their heroes, and consecrate morning hours to their pages. The heroic books, even if printed in the character of our mother tongue, will always be in a language dead to degenerate times; and we must laboriously seek the meaning of each word and line, conjecturing a larger sense than common use permits out of what wisdom and valor and generosity we have. The modern cheap and fertile press, with all its translations, has done little to bring us nearer to the heroic writers of antiquity. They seem as solitary, and the letter in which they are printed as rare and curious, as ever. It is worth the expense of youthful days and costly hours, if you learn only some words of an ancient language, which are raised out of the trivialness of the street, to be perpetual suggestions and provocations. It is not in vain that the farmer remembers and repeats the few Latin words which he has heard. Men sometimes speak as if the study of the classics would at length make way for more modern and practical studies; but the adventurous student will always study classics, in whatever language they may be written and however ancient they may be. For what are the classics but the noblest recorded thoughts of man? They are the only oracles which are not decayed, and there are such answers to the most modern

4 *such reading in future.* The Bibliophile Edition (I, 134) reads: "Here, of course, I could read the Iliad, if I *would have* books, as well as in Ionia; and not wish myself in Boston or New York, in London or Rome. In such a place as this, rather, Homer lived and sang. I know that I am in good company; there is the world, its centre and metropolis; and all the palms of Asia and the laurels of Greece, and the firs of the Arctic zones incline hither.

"Where is that lost first page of History? We have never found the literature that dated from an antiquity sufficiently remote. The most adventurous student seeks the remotest antiquity, —the history of a time (as it were) prior to Time. Or, if we prefer, we may say that such is the Protean character of things; he always interprets prophecies and oracles, and is interested solely in the future."

5 *in the Greek.* This was "in the original Greek" in the *Journal* for August 6, 1845; I, 377, from which this and the next sentence were taken. Much of what follows comes from the *Journal* for July 1845; I, 370 ff.

The oracle of Apollo

inquiry in them as Delphi and Dodona never gave. **6**
We might as well omit to study Nature because she is
old.   To read well, that is, to read true books in a true
spirit, is a noble exercise, and one that will task the
reader more than any exercise which the customs of the
day esteem.   It requires a training such as the athletes
underwent, the steady intention almost of the whole
life to this object.   Books must be read as deliberately
and reservedly as they were written.   It is not enough
even to be able to speak the language of that nation by
which they are written, for there is a memorable
interval between the spoken and the written language, the language heard and the language read.
The one is commonly transitory, a sound, a tongue,
a dialect merely, almost brutish, and we learn it unconsciously, like the brutes, of our mothers.   The
other is the maturity and experience of that; if that is
our mother tongue, this is our father tongue, a reserved
and select expression, too significant to be heard by the
ear, which we must be born again in order to speak.   The   **7**
crowds of men who merely *spoke* the Greek and Latin
tongues in the middle ages were not entitled by the accident of birth to *read* the works of genius written in
those languages; for these were not written in that
Greek or Latin which they knew, but in the select language of literature.   They had not learned the nobler
dialects of Greece and Rome, but the very materials on
which they were written were waste paper to them,   **8**
and they prized instead a cheap contemporary literature.
But when the several nations of Europe had acquired
distinct though rude written languages of their own,
sufficient for the purposes of their rising literatures,
then first learning revived, and scholars were enabled to
discern from that remoteness the treasures of antiquity.
What the Roman and Grecian multitude could not *hear*,
after the lapse of ages a few scholars *read*, and a few   **9**
scholars only are still reading it.

However much we may admire the orator's occasional
bursts of eloquence, the noblest written words are commonly as far behind or above the fleeting spoken language as the firmament with its stars is behind the
clouds.   *There* are the stars, and they who can may
read them.   The astronomers forever comment on and
observe them.   They are not exhalations like our daily
colloquies and vaporous breath.   What is called elo-

6 *Delphi and Dodona.* Delphi, near Parnassus,
was Apollo's oracle; Dodona was Zeus's oracle
and was in Epirus, the land of the oak trees.

7 *The crowds.* On ms. 159 this was "herd," then
"mass," and finally "crowds."

8 *were waste paper to them.* Except for documents written on papyrus, the ancient manuscripts that survived were parchment, not paper.
All such old writings were regarded as "waste
paper" during the Middle Ages.

9 *and a few scholars only are still reading it.*
And now, fewer still!

quence in the forum is commonly found to be rhetoric in the study. The orator yields to the inspiration of a transient occasion, and speaks to the mob before him, to those who can *hear* him; but the writer, whose more equable life is his occasion, and who would be distracted by the event and the crowd which inspire the orator, speaks to the intellect and heart of mankind, to all in any age who can *understand* him.

No wonder that Alexander carried the Iliad with him on his expeditions in a precious casket. A written **10** word is the choicest of relics. It is something at once more intimate with us and more universal than any other work of art. It is the work of art nearest to life itself. It may be translated into every language, and not only be read but actually breathed from all human lips;—not be represented on canvas or in marble only, but be carved out of the breath of life itself. The symbol of an ancient man's thought becomes a modern man's speech. Two thousand summers have imparted to the monuments of Grecian literature, as to her marbles, only a maturer golden and autumnal tint, for they have carried their own serene and celestial atmosphere into all lands to protect them against the corrosion of time. Books are the treasured wealth of the world **11** and the fit inheritance of generations and nations. Books, the oldest and the best, stand naturally and rightfully on the shelves of every cottage. They have no cause of their own to plead, but while they enlighten and sustain the reader his common sense will not refuse them. Their authors are a natural and irresistible **12** aristocracy in every society, and, more than kings or emperors, exert an influence on mankind. When the illiterate and perhaps scornful trader has earned by enterprise and industry his coveted leisure and independence, and is admitted to the circles of wealth and fashion, he turns inevitably at last to those still higher but yet inaccessible circles of intellect and genius, and is sensible only of the imperfection of his culture and the vanity and insufficiency of all his riches, and further proves his good sense by the pains which he takes to secure for his children that intellectual culture whose want he so keenly feels; and thus it is that he becomes the founder of a family.

Those who have not learned to read the ancient classics in the language in which they were written

10 *A written word is the choicest of relics.* This was followed by "of thought" on ms. 160.

11 *Books are the treasured wealth of the world and the fit inheritance of generations and nations.* This sentence might suitably be inscribed on the portals of a library—and probably has been.

12 *Their authors are a natural and irresistible aristocracy in every society.* Ms. 162 has "an invisible upper class" after these words.

Alexander the Great

must have a very imperfect knowledge of the history of the human race; for it is remarkable that no transcript of them has ever been made into any modern tongue, unless our civilization itself may be regarded as such a transcript.   Homer has never yet been printed **13** in English, nor Æschylus, nor Virgil even, — works as refined, as solidly done, and as beautiful almost as the morning itself; for later writers, say what we will of their genius, have rarely, if ever, equalled the elaborate beauty and finish and the lifelong and heroic literary labors of the ancients.   They only talk of forgetting them who never knew them.   It will be soon enough to forget them when we have the learning and the genius which will enable us to attend to and appreciate them.   That age will be rich indeed when those relics which we call Classics, and the still older and more than classic but even less known Scriptures of the nations, shall have still further accumulated, when the Vaticans shall be filled with Vedas and Zendavestas and Bibles, **14** with Homers and Dantes and Shakspeares, and all the centuries to come shall have successively deposited their trophies in the forum of the world.   By such a pile we may hope to scale heaven at last.

The works of the great poets have never yet been read by mankind, for only great poets can read them. They have only been read as the multitude read the stars, at most astrologically, not astronomically.   Most men have learned to read to serve a paltry convenience, as they have learned to cipher in order to keep accounts and not be cheated in trade; but of reading as a noble intellectual exercise they know little or nothing; yet this **only is reading**, in a high sense, not that which

13 *Homer has never yet been printed in English.* All these authors long since had, of course. Thoreau means that the full rich meaning and all the overtones and subtleties do not come through in translation.

14 *Zendavestas.* The Zoroastrian scriptures.

Ancient writing materials

lulls us as a luxury and suffers the nobler faculties to sleep the while, but what we have to stand on tiptoe to read and devote our most alert and wakeful hours to.   **15**

I think that having learned our letters we should read the best that is in literature, and not be forever repeating our a b abs, and words of one syllable, in the fourth or fifth classes, sitting on the lowest and foremost form all our lives.   **16** Most men are satisfied if they read or hear read, and perchance have been convicted by the wisdom of one good book, the Bible, and for the rest of their lives vegetate and dissipate their faculties in what is called easy reading. There is a work in several volumes in our Circulating Library entitled Little Reading,   **17** which I thought referred to a town of that name which I had not been to. There are those who, like cormorants and ostriches, can digest all sorts of this, even after the fullest dinner of meats and vegetables, for they suffer nothing to be wasted. If others are the machines to provide this provender, they are the machines to read it. They read the nine thousandth tale about Zebulon and Sephronia,   **18** and how they loved as none had ever loved before, and neither did the course of their true love run smooth, — at any rate, how it did run and stumble, and get up again and go on! how some poor unfortunate got up on to a steeple, who had better never have gone up as far as the belfry; and then, having needlessly got him up there, the happy novelist rings the bell for all the world to come together and hear, O dear! how he did get down again! For my part, I think that they had better metamorphose all such aspiring heroes of universal noveldom into man weathercocks, as they used to put heroes among the constellations, and let them swing round there till they are rusty, and not come down at all to bother honest men with their pranks. The next time the novelist rings the bell I will not stir though the meeting-house burn down. "The Skip of the Tip-Toe-Hop, a Romance of the   **19** Middle Ages, by the celebrated author of 'Tittle-Tol-Tan,' to appear in monthly parts; a great rush; don't all come together." All this they read with saucer eyes, and erect and primitive curiosity, and with unwearied gizzard, whose corrugations even yet need no sharpening, just as some little four-year-old bencher his two-cent gilt-covered edition of Cinderella, — without

15 *and devote our most alert and wakeful hours to.* After this in the Bibliophile Edition (I, 140) is: "—have to gird up our robes and train ourselves for—as the wrestler trained for the combat."

16 *and not be forever repeating our a b abs.* This is a reference to the country schools of the day where all the children sat in one room and recited their lessons in turn. The youngest occupied the lowest seats in the front row.

17 *Little Reading.* There is a Reading in Pennsylvania and also in England. Both are pronounced Redding.

18 *Zebulon and Sephronia.* Perhaps there were characters with these names in the popular fiction of Thoreau's time, but they have not been identified. The name Zebulon can be found in Revelation 7:8 and in Genesis 30:20 where it is spelled Zebelun and refers to Leah's sixth son. Sephronia appears in Tasso's *Jerusalem Delivered*. Love not running smoothly is a paraphrase from *A Midsummer Night's Dream*, I, i.

19 *Tip-Toe-Hop,* etc. Various speculations have been made about the authors Thoreau may have been satirizing here. There is a good chance that he had no one in mind but was just making up odd-sounding titles.

any improvement, that I can see, in the pronunciation, or accent, or emphasis, or any more skill in extracting or inserting the moral. The result is dulness of sight, a stagnation of the vital circulations, and a general deliquium and sloughing off of all the intellectual faculties. This sort of gingerbread is baked daily and more sedulously than pure wheat or rye-and-Indian in almost every oven, and finds a surer market.

The best books are not read even by those who are called good readers. What does our Concord culture amount to? There is in this town, with a very few exceptions, no taste for the best or for very good books even in English literature, whose words all can read and spell. Even the college-bred and so called liberally educated men here and elsewhere have really little or no acquaintance with the English classics; and as for the recorded wisdom of mankind, the ancient classics and Bibles, which are accessible to all who will know of them, there are the feeblest efforts any where made to become acquainted with them. I know a woodchopper, of middle age, who takes a French paper, not for news as he says, for he is above that, but to "keep himself in practice," he being a Canadian by birth; and when I ask him what he considers the best thing he can do in this world, he says, beside this, to keep up and add to his English. This is about as much as the college bred generally do or aspire to do, and they take an English paper for the purpose. One who has just come from reading perhaps one of the best English books will find how many with whom he can converse about it? Or suppose he comes from reading a Greek or Latin classic in the original, whose praises are familiar even to the so called illiterate; he will find nobody at all to speak to, but must keep silence about it. Indeed, there is hardly the professor in our colleges, who, if he has mastered the difficulties of the language, has proportionally mastered the difficulties of the wit and poetry of a Greek poet, and has any sympathy to impart to the alert and heroic reader; and as for the sacred Scriptures, or Bibles of mankind, who in this town can tell me even their titles? Most men do not know that any nation but the Hebrews have had a scripture. A man, any man, will go considerably out of his way to pick up a silver dollar; but here are golden words, which the wisest men of antiquity have

20

21

20 *deliquium.* Webster: "Archaic. A failure of vitality; a fainting or sinking away." Thoreau is making fun of the medical language of his day.

21 *I know a woodchopper, of middle age.* This is presumably Alek Therien, although he was not middle-aged in 1854. There is much more about him in the chapter entitled "Visitors." The Bibliophile Edition (I, 143) adds to this: "My woodchopper was from Nicollet away by the Trois Rivières and spoke English as well as Canadian French."

uttered, and whose worth the wise of every succeeding age have assured us of; — and yet we learn to read only as far as **Easy Reading,** the primers and class-books, and when we leave school, the " Little Reading," and story books, which are for boys and beginners; and our reading, our conversation and thinking, are all on a very low level, worthy only of pygmies and manikins.

I aspire to be acquainted with wiser men thàn this **our Concord soil has produced,** whose names are hardly known here. Or shall I hear the name of Plato and never read his book? As if Plato were my townsman and I never saw him, — my next neighbor and I never heard him speak or attended to the wisdom of his words. But how actually is it? His Dialogues, which contain what was immortal in him, lie on the next shelf, and yet I never read them. **22** We are under-bred and low-lived and illiterate; and in this respect I confess I do not make any very broad distinction between the illiterateness of my townsman who cannot read at all, and the illiterateness of him who has learned to read only what is for children and feeble intellects. We should be as good as the worthies of antiquity, but partly by first knowing how good they were. We are a race of **23** tit-men, and soar but little higher in our intellectual flights than the columns of the daily paper.

It is not all books that are as dull as their readers. There are probably words addressed to our condition exactly, which, if we could really hear and understand, would be more salutary than the morning or the spring to our lives, and possibly put a new aspect on the face of things for us. How many a man has **24** dated a new era in his life from the reading of a book. The book exists for us perchance which will explain our miracles and reveal new ones. The at present unutterable things we may find somewhere uttered. These same questions that disturb and puzzle and confound us have in their turn occurred to all the wise men; not one has been omitted; and each has answered them, according to his ability, by his words and his life. Moreover, with wisdom we shall learn liberality. The solitary hired man on a farm in the **outskirts of Concord, who has had his second birth and 25** peculiar religious experience, and is driven as he believes into silent gravity and exclusiveness by his faith, may think it is not true; but Zoroaster, thousands of

Plato

22 *yet I never read them.* Ms. 164 adds: "I describe my own case."

23 *a race of tit-men.* Tit is a diminutive as in titlark.

24 *How many a man has dated a new era in his life from the reading of a book. Walden* would hold a high place in any list of such books.

25 *his second birth and peculiar religious experience.* Conversion.

years ago, travelled the same road and had the same experience; but he, being wise, knew it to be universal, and treated his neighbors accordingly, and is even said to have invented and established worship among men. Let him humbly commune with Zoroaster then, and, through the liberalizing influence of all the worthies, with Jesus Christ himself, and let "our church" go by the board.

We boast that we belong to the nineteenth century **26** and are making the most rapid strides of any nation. But consider how little this village does for its own culture. I do not wish to flatter my townsmen, nor to be flattered by them, for that will not advance either of us. We need to be provoked,—goaded like oxen, as we are, into a trot. We have a comparatively decent system of common schools, schools for infants only; but excepting the half-starved Lyceum in the winter, and latterly the puny beginning of a library suggested by the state, no school for ourselves. We spend more on almost any article of bodily aliment or ailment than on our

26 *We boast that we belong to the nineteenth century.* This long paragraph comes almost word for word from the *Journal* for August 29, 1852; IV, 323 ff. And this is derived from an earlier and shorter passage in the *Journal* for 1837–1847; I, 487, and another for September 26, 1851; III, 24–25.

A Concord tombstone

mental aliment. It is time that we had uncommon schools, that we did not leave off our education when we begin to be men and women. It is time that villages were universities, and their elder inhabitants the fellows of universities, with leisure — if they are indeed so well off — to pursue liberal studies the rest **27** of their lives. Shall the world be confined to one Paris **28** or one Oxford forever? Cannot students be boarded here and get a liberal education under the skies of Concord? Can we not hire some Abelard to lecture to us? Alas! what with foddering the cattle and tending the store, we are kept from school too long, and our education is sadly neglected. In this country, the village should in some respects take the place of the nobleman of Europe. It should be the patron of the fine arts. It is rich enough. It wants only the magnanimity and refinement. It can spend money enough on such things as farmers and traders value, but it is thought Utopian to propose spending money for things which more intelligent men know to be of far more worth. This town has spent seventeen thousand dollars on a town-house, thank fortune or politics, but probably it will not spend so much on living wit, the true meat to put into that shell, in a hundred years. The one hundred and twenty-five dollars annually subscribed for a Lyceum in the winter is better spent than any other equal sum raised in the town. If we live in the nineteenth century, why should we not enjoy the advantages which the nineteenth century offers? Why should our life be in any respect provincial? If we will read newspapers, why not skip the gossip of Boston and take the best newspaper in the world at once? — not be sucking the pap of "neutral family" papers, or browsing "Olive-Branches" here in New England. **29** Let the reports of all the learned societies come to us, and we will see if they know any thing. Why should we leave it to Harper & Brothers and Redding & Co. **30** to select our reading? As the nobleman of cultivated taste surrounds himself with whatever conduces to his culture, — genius — learning — wit — books — paintings — statuary — music — philosophical instruments, and the like; so let the village do, — not stop short at a **pedagogue, a parson, a sexton, a parish library, and** three selectmen, because our pilgrim forefathers got through a cold winter once on a bleak rock with these.

27 *to pursue liberal studies the rest of their lives.* Still devoutly to be wished for.

28 *one Paris or one Oxford.* Paris, the university (the Sorbonne), not the city.

29 *"Olive-Branches."* Sanborn says that this was the name of a Methodist weekly newspaper.

30 *Redding & Co.* was a book publisher; so was Harper & Brothers (now Harper & Row, Publishers).

To act collectively is according to the spirit of our institutions; and I am confident that, as our circumstances
are more flourishing, our means are greater than the
nobleman's.   New England can hire all the wise men
in the world to come and teach her. and board them
round the while, and not be provincial at all.   That is
the *uncommon* school we want.   Instead of noblemen,
let us have noble villages of men.   If it is necessary,
omit one bridge over the river, go round a little there,
and throw one arch at least over the darker gulf of
ignorance which surrounds us.

Bookbinding

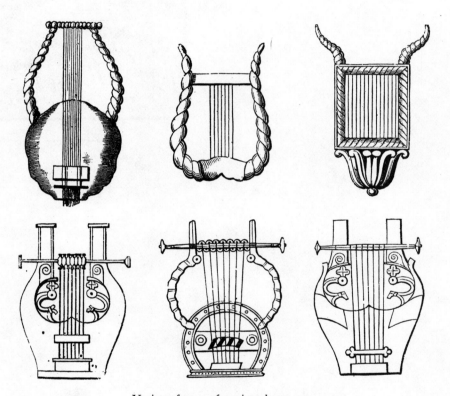

Various forms of ancient lyres

SOUNDS.

BUT while we are confined to books, though the most select and classic, and read only particular written languages, which are themselves but dialects and provincial, we are in danger of forgetting the language which all things and events speak without metaphor, which alone is copious and standard. Much is published, but little printed. The rays which stream through the shutter will be no longer remembered when the shutter is wholly removed. No method nor discipline can supersede the necessity of being forever on the alert. What is a course of history, or philosophy, or poetry, no matter how well selected, or the best society, or the most admirable routine of life, compared with the discipline of looking always at what is to be seen? Will you be a reader, a student merely, or a seer? Read your fate, see what is before you, and walk on into futurity.

I did not read books the first summer; I hoed beans. **1** Nay, I often did better than this. There were times when I could not afford to sacrifice the bloom of the present moment to any work, whether of the head or hands. I love a broad margin to my life. Sometimes, **2** in a summer morning, having taken my accustomed bath, I sat in my sunny doorway from sunrise till noon, rapt in a revery, amidst the pines and hickories and sumachs, in undisturbed solitude and stillness, while the birds sang around or flitted noiseless through the house, until by the sun falling in at my west window, or the noise of some traveller's wagon on the distant highway, I was reminded of the lapse of time. I grew

243

This chapter was heavily revised by Thoreau. Walter Harding, in his Introduction to *The Variorum Walden* (1963, page xxii), says that the second paragraph is "one of the most vivid descriptions in our literature of the mystical experience. . . . *Walden* . . . is above all a spiritual autobiography and guidebook."

Charles Anderson (1968, page 215) calls attention to the fact that this chapter has "the first elaborate use of a circle as a symbol" and "relates it significantly to the theme of wildness." The circular clearing around the cabin has "unfenced nature reaching up to your very sills."

1 *I did not read books the first summer; I hoed beans.* There is more to this passage on ms. 411 ff.: "I read very little however during the summer, for my thoughts would run upon my labor mainly, or rather where they pleased, and I had not leisure to drill myself. I only read one sentence of Homer to a week of hoeing—as for instance how Ajax struggled with the Trojans to ward off fire from the ships of the Greeks, while Patroclus was supplicating Achilles for his armor & his Myrmidons. I read no more than this—at once—still remembering & repeating it—but I imagined more things than are in Homer while I hoed."

2 *I love a broad margin to my life.* Here again the copy on ms. 412 differs widely from the printed text: "Sometimes in a spring morning, when the season of work had not yet arrived, or later in the summer, when it was already passed, having performed my accustomed ablutions, I sat in my sunny door way from the earliest dawn, wrapt in a reverie, amid the pines and hickories and sumacks, while the birds sang around and flitted noiseless over my head and out at the open window—in undisturbed solitude & stillness, ex-

NOVEMBER.

in those seasons like corn in the night, and they were far better than any work of the hands would have been. They were not time subtracted from my life, but so much over and above my usual allowance. I realized what the Orientals mean by contemplation and the forsaking of works. For the most part, I minded **3** not how the hours went. The day advanced as if to **4** light some work of mine; it was morning, and lo, now it is evening, and nothing memorable is accomplished. **5** Instead of singing like the birds, I silently smiled at my incessant good fortune. As the sparrow had its trill, sitting on the hickory before my door, so had I my chuckle or suppressed warble which he might hear out of my nest. My days were not days of the week, bearing the stamp of any heathen deity, nor were they minced into hours and fretted by the ticking of a clock; for I lived like the Puri Indians, of whom it is said **6** that "for yesterday, to-day, and to-morrow they have only one word, and they express the variety of meaning by pointing backward for yesterday, forward for to-morrow, and overhead for the passing day." This was sheer idleness to my fellow-townsmen, no doubt; but if the birds and flowers had tried me by their standard, I should not have been found wanting. A man **7**

cept when a bough fell like a fan broken by its own weight, in my sumack grove, when the atmosphere was perfume & incense, and every sound the key to unheard harmonies, until by the sun's rays falling in at my west window, or the noise of some traveller on the distant highway, I was reminded of the lapse of time. I am sensible that I waxed and grew in these intervals, as corn grows in the night, and they were far better than any work of my hands. I realized what the oriental philosophers meant by contemplation & the forsaking of works. It was quite impossible to have performed anything, and wise persons would not propose that any deed should be substituted therefor. They were little intervals during which I journeyed, and anticipated other states of existence."

3 *the forsaking of works.* Bibliophile Edition (I, 150): "It was quite impossible to have performed anything, and wise persons would not propose that any deed should be substituted therefor. They were little intervals during which I journeyed, and anticipated other states of existence."

4 *not how the hours went.* Bibliophile Edition (I, 150): "I was accustomed to say to myself,— 'Certainly I am not living that heroic life I had dreamed; and yet all my veins are full of life, and Nature whispers no reproach.' "

5 *and nothing memorable is accomplished.* Bibli-

must find his occasions in himself, it is true. The natural day is very calm, and will hardly reprove his indolence.

I had this advantage, at least, in my mode of life, over those who were obliged to look abroad for amusement, to society and the theatre, that my life itself was become my amusement and never ceased to be novel. It was a drama of many scenes and without an end. If we were always indeed getting our living, and regulating our lives according to the last and best mode we had learned, we should never be troubled with ennui. Follow your genius closely enough, and it will not fail to show you a fresh prospect every hour. Housework **8** was a pleasant pastime. When my floor was dirty, I rose early, and, setting all my furniture out of doors on the grass, bed and bedstead making but one budget, dashed water on the floor, and sprinkled white sand from the pond on it, and then with a broom scrubbed it clean and white; and by the time the villagers had broken their fast the morning sun had dried my house sufficiently to allow me to move in again, and my meditations were almost uninterrupted. It was pleasant to see my whole household effects out on the grass, making a little pile like a gypsy's pack, and my three-legged table, from which I did not remove the books and pen and ink, standing amid the pines and hickories. They seemed glad to get out themselves, and as if unwilling to be brought in. I was sometimes tempted to stretch an awning over them and take my seat there. It was worth the while to see the sun shine on these things, and hear the free wind blow on them; so much more interesting most familiar objects look out of doors than in the house. A bird sits on the next bough, life-everlasting grows under the table, and blackberry vines run round its legs; pine cones, chestnut burs, and strawberry leaves are strewn about. It looked as if this was the way these forms came to be transferred to our furniture, to tables, chairs, and bedsteads, — because they once stood in their midst.

My house was on the side of a hill, immediately on the edge of the larger wood, in the midst of a young forest of pitch pines and hickories, and half a dozen **9** rods from the pond, to which a narrow footpath led down the hill. In my front yard grew the strawberry, blackberry, and life-everlasting, johnswort and golden-

ophile Edition (I, 150–151): "and I defer to others in my thought, as if there were somewhere busier men. Yet my nature is almost content with this. What are these pines and these birds about? What is this pond a-doing? I must know a little more and be forever ready."

Sanborn then prints the passage about Homer that is in note 1, above.

6 *the Puri Indians* live in Brazil.

7 *I should not have been found wanting.* Ms. 180 and 413: "but men try one another not so. At such an hour I am not the worker but the work. The elements are working their will with me."

8 *Housework.* This clearly calls for a new paragraph and had one on ms. 181 and 414.

9 *half a dozen rods.* Here Thoreau, the surveyor, was very wrong. A rod is 16½ feet; six rods are 99 feet. By actual measurement the cabin was more than 200 feet from the shore. *Journal*, 1850; II, 12.

rod, shrub-oaks and sand-cherry, blueberry and ground-nut. Near the end of May, the sand-cherry, (*cerasus pumila*,) adorned the sides of the path with its delicate flowers arranged in umbels cylindrically about its short stems, which last, in the fall, weighed down with good sized and handsome cherries, fell over in wreaths like rays on every side. I tasted them out of compliment to Nature, though they were scarcely palatable. The sumach, (*rhus glabra*,) grew luxuriantly about the house, pushing up through the embankment which I had made, and growing five or six feet the first season. Its broad pinnate tropical leaf was pleasant though strange to look on. The large buds, suddenly pushing out late in the spring from dry sticks which had seemed to be dead, developed themselves as by magic into graceful green and tender boughs, an inch in diameter; and sometimes, as I sat at my window, so heedlessly did **10** they grow and tax their weak joints, I heard a fresh and tender bough suddenly fall like a fan to the ground, when there was not a breath of air stirring, broken off by its own weight. In August, the large masses of berries, which, when in flower, had attracted many wild bees, gradually assumed their bright velvety crimson hue, and by their weight again bent down and broke the tender limbs.

As I sit at my window this summer afternoon, hawks are circling about my clearing; the tantivy of wild **11** pigeons, flying by twos and threes athwart my view, or perching restless on the white-pine boughs behind my house, gives a voice to the air; a fishhawk dimples the glassy surface of the pond and brings up a fish; a mink **12** steals out of the marsh before my door and seizes a frog by the shore; the sedge is bending under the weight of the reed-birds flitting hither and thither; and for the last half hour I have heard the rattle of railroad cars, now dying away and then reviving like the beat of a partridge, conveying travellers from Boston to the **13** country. For I did not live so out of the world as that boy, who, as I hear, was put out to a farmer in the east part of the town, but ere long ran away and came home again, quite down at the heel and homesick. He had never seen such a dull and out-of-the-way place; the folks were all gone off; why, you couldn't even hear

10 *as I sat at my window*. The *Journal* for August 6, 1845; I, 377, then says: "like a priest of Isis, and observe the phenomena of three thousand years ago."

11 *the tantivy*. Webster: "a rushing movement." Here is one of the few places in *Walden* where Thoreau mentions wild pigeons. The passenger pigeon had once been so numerous in America that Audubon counted more than a million of them in a single flock. Constant slaughter reduced their numbers so that they were less plentiful in Thoreau's time. By 1914 the last one died in the Cincinnati Zoological Gardens.

12 *a mink steals out of the marsh*. This passage is also in the *Journal* for August 6, 1845; I, 378. But there the mink and the marsh are not mentioned. Actually, the little marsh could not be seen from the cabin because a rise in the ground cuts off the view in that direction. Ronald W. Robbins (1947, page 17) says that Thoreau drew upon his imagination for this when he rewrote the paragraph for *Walden* long after he had lived at the pond.

13 *from Boston to the country*. Ms. 173 then has: "or the first rattle and tinkle of a carriage or team along the distant highway."

the whistle! I doubt if there is such a place in Massachusetts now: —

> " In truth, our village has become a butt   **14**
>   For one of those fleet railroad shafts, and o'er
>   Our peaceful plain its soothing sound is — Concord."

The Fitchburg Railroad touches the pond about a **15** hundred rods south of where I dwell. I usually go to the village along its causeway, and am, as it were, **16** related to society by this link. The men on the freight trains, who go over the whole length of the road, bow to me as to an old acquaintance, they pass me so often, and apparently they take me for an employee; and so I am. I too would fain be a track-repairer somewhere in the orbit of the earth.

The whistle of the locomotive penetrates my woods **17** summer and winter, sounding like the scream of a hawk sailing over some farmer's yard, informing me that many restless city merchants are arriving within the circle of the town, or adventurous country traders from the other side. As they come under one horizon, they shout their warning to get off the track to the other, heard sometimes through the circles of two towns. Here come your groceries, country; your rations, countrymen! Nor is there any man so independent on his farm that he can say them nay. And here's your pay for them! screams the countryman's whistle; timber like long battering rams going twenty miles an hour against the city's walls, and chairs enough to seat all the weary and heavy laden that dwell within them. With such huge and lumbering civility the

14 *"In truth, . . ."* The three lines of verse are by Ellery Channing, as he noted in his own copy of *Walden.*

15 *The Fitchburg Railroad.* It is still there although it has now become part of the Boston and Maine.

16 *and am . . . related to society by this link.* The railroad cut is a shorter way to the western end of Concord where the Thoreau family was then living. The next sentence is in the *Journal* for January 26, 1852; III, 235.

17 *the locomotive.* This was "steam engine" on ms. 166. Here begins one of the best and earliest descriptions of a railroad in American literature. Thoreau was the first to realize the poetic possibility of trains; Thomas Wolfe, less than a century later, may be the last. They bridge the time span in which the iron horse dominated long-distance transportation.

country hands a chair to the city. All the Indian huckleberry hills are stripped, all the cranberry meadows are raked into the city. Up comes the cotton, down goes the woven cloth; up comes the silk, down goes the woollen; up come the books, but down goes the wit that writes them.

When I meet the engine with its train of cars moving off with planetary motion, — or, rather, like a comet, for the beholder knows not if with that velocity and with that direction it will ever revisit this system, since its orbit does not look like a returning curve, — with its steam cloud like a banner streaming behind in golden and silver wreaths, like many a downy cloud which I have seen, high in the heavens, unfolding its masses to the light, — as if this travelling demigod, this cloud-compeller, would ere long take the sunset sky for the livery of his train; when I hear the iron horse make the hills echo with his snort like thunder, shaking the earth with his feet, and breathing fire and smoke from his nostrils, (what kind of winged horse or fiery dragon they will put into the new Mythology I don't know,) it seems as if the earth had got a race now worthy to inhabit it. If all were as it seems, and men made the elements their servants for noble ends! If the cloud that hangs over the engine were the perspiration of heroic deeds, or as beneficent as that which floats over the farmer's fields, then the elements and Nature herself would cheerfully accompany men on their errands and be their escort.

I watch the passage of the morning cars with the same feeling that I do the rising of the sun, which is hardly more regular. Their train of clouds stretching far behind and rising higher and higher, going to heaven while the cars are going to Boston, conceals the sun for

a minute and casts my distant field into the shade, a 18 celestial train beside which the petty train of cars which hugs the earth is but the barb of the spear. The sta- 19 bler of the iron horse was up early this winter morning by the light of the stars amid the mountains, to fodder and harness his steed. Fire, too, was awakened thus early to put the vital heat in him and get him off. If the enterprise were as innocent as it is early! If the snow lies deep, they strap on his snow-shoes, and with the 20 giant plough plough a furrow from the mountains to the seaboard, in which the cars, like a following drill- 21 barrow, sprinkle all the restless men and floating merchandise in the country for seed. All day the fire-steed flies over the country, stopping only that his master may rest, and I am awakened by his tramp and defiant snort at midnight, when in some remote glen in the woods 22 he fronts the elements incased in ice and snow; and he will reach his stall only with the morning star, to start once more on his travels without rest or slumber. Or perchance, at evening, I hear him in his stable blowing off the superfluous energy of the day, that he may calm his nerves and cool his liver and brain for a few hours of iron slumber. If the enterprise were as heroic and commanding as it is protracted and unwearied!

Far through unfrequented woods on the confines of towns, where once only the hunter penetrated by day, in the darkest night dart these bright saloons without the knowledge of their inhabitants; this moment stopping at some brilliant station-house in town or city, where a social crowd is gathered, the next in the Dis- 23 mal Swamp, scaring the owl and fox. The startings and arrivals of the cars are now the epochs in the village day. They go and come with such regularity and precision, and their whistle can be heard so far, that the farmers set their clocks by them, and thus one well con- 24 ducted institution regulates a whole country. Have not men improved somewhat in punctuality since the railroad was invented? Do they not talk and think faster in the depot than they did in the stage-office?

18 *a celestial train.* Again Hawthorne's story of "The Celestial Railroad."

19 *the barb of the spear.* After this came: "Memory transports me to a different season," but the sentence was canceled on the page proofs.

20 *and with the giant plough plough a furrow.* Thoreau's original copy for this had been: "and with the giant plow, plow a furrow." Note his American spelling for "plow." And he had a comma where one belongs.

21 *drill-barrow.* An early agricultural machine that made holes in the soil, dropped the correct number of seeds into each hole, and then covered them up.

22 *in some remote glen.* Sanborn said of this: "Such a glen is in the woods southeast of Thoreau's hut, where the drifted snow sometimes stopped the heavy trains with light engines of that early period of railroading."

23 *the Dismal Swamp.* Although Thoreau is alluding to a swamp in general terms, the great Dismal Swamp is the one that lies south of Suffolk, Virginia. The next sentence regarding cars is from the *Journal*, June 8, 1850; II, 31.

24 *farmers set their clocks by them.* The coming of the railroad and the telegraph imposed an exact time schedule on rural areas where the sun had been a good enough indicator of the hours since the beginning of man's awareness of time.

There is something electrifying in the atmosphere of the former place. I have been astonished at the miracles it has wrought; that some of my neighbors, who, I should have prophesied, once for all, would never get to Boston by so prompt a conveyance, are on hand when **25** the bell rings. To do things " railroad fashion " is now the by-word; and it is worth the while to be warned so often and so sincerely by any power to get off its track. There is no stopping to read the riot act, no firing over **26** the heads of the mob, in this case. We have constructed a fate, an *Atropos*, that never turns aside. (Let that be the name of your engine.) Men are advertised that at a certain hour and minute these bolts will be shot toward particular points of the compass; yet it interferes with no man's business, and the children go to school on the other track. We live the steadier for it. We are all educated thus to be sons of Tell. The air is full of **27** invisible bolts. Every path but your own is the path of fate. Keep on your own track, then.

What recommends commerce to me is its enterprise **28** and bravery. It does not clasp its hands and pray to **29** Jupiter. I see these men every day go about their business with more or less courage and content, doing more even than they suspect, and perchance better employed than they could have consciously devised. I am less affected by their heroism who stood up for half an hour in the front line at Buena Vista, than by the steady and **30** cheerful valor of the men who inhabit the snow-plough for their winter quarters; who have not merely the three-o'-clock in the morning courage, which Bonaparte **31** thought was the rarest, but whose courage does not go to rest so early, who go to sleep only when the storm sleeps or the sinews of their iron steed are frozen. On this morning of the Great Snow, perchance, which is **32** still raging and chilling men's blood, I hear the muffled tone of their engine bell from out the fog bank of their chilled breath, which announces that the cars *are coming*, without long delay, notwithstanding the veto of a New England north-east snow storm, and I behold the ploughmen covered with snow and rime, their heads **33** peering above the mould-board which is turning down other than daisies and the nests of field-mice, like bowl- **34** ders of the Sierra Nevada, that occupy an outside place in the universe.

Commerce is unexpectedly confident and serene, alert,

25 *are on hand*. In his own copy of *Walden*, Thoreau made this "were," and, in the next line, "rings" became "rang."

26 *over the heads of the mob, in this case*. Ms. 605 then has: "Here comes somebody whom it is no use to expostulate with. Only to meet the cars on the other track is like having a tin cup shot off your head." "The other track" occurs below. And—

27 *thus to be sons of Tell*. After this on ms. 607 Thoreau put "or to stand and have tin cups shot off our heads." He was evidently looking for a place to use his "tin cup" allusion, but finally canceled it leaving only Tell to represent the fragmented thought. Tell, of course, is William Tell, the legendary Swiss hero who was forced to shoot an apple off his son's head with an arrow.

28 *What recommends commerce to me*. One does not ordinarily look to Thoreau for praise of the machine age, but this section pays tribute to the men who work on the railroad and to others as well. It is a graphic passage, an extension of what he said about the railroad on page 247. His praise of commerce, however, is not unqualified, as a careful reading will show.

29 *It does not clasp its hands*. The printer could not read these words in Thoreau's scrawled handwriting and put his complaint on the page proofs.

30 *Buena Vista*. One of the battles in the recent war with Mexico.

31 *Bonaparte*. See *Journal*, 1837–1847; I, 462, where it is spelled Buonaparte.

32 *the Great Snow*. This tremendous storm, which began on February 20, 1717, made a lasting impression on New England people. Thoreau undoubtedly knew about it at this time, but nearly two years after *Walden* was published he copied a long descriptive letter written by Cotton Mather into his *Journal* for February 3, 1856; VIII, 163 ff.

33 *snow and rime*. This was "snow and frost" on ms. 424. Thoreau changed it for the better.

34 *bowlders*. This was "boulders" on ms. 424— and in the Bibliophile Edition also. An editor or a printer has changed Thoreau's modern spelling to the less familiar form.

adventurous, and unwearied. It is very natural in its methods withal, far more so than many fantastic enterprises and sentimental experiments, and hence its singular success. I am refreshed and expanded when the freight train rattles past me, and I smell the stores which go dispensing their odors all the way from Long **35** Wharf to Lake Champlain, reminding me of foreign **36** parts, of coral reefs, and Indian oceans, and tropical climes, and the extent of the globe. I feel more like a citizen of the world at the sight of the palm-leaf which will cover so many flaxen New England heads the next summer, the Manilla hemp and cocoa-nut husks, the old junk, gunny bags, scrap iron, and rusty nails. This car-load of torn sails is more legible and interesting now than if they should be wrought into paper and printed **37** books. Who can write so graphically the history of the storms they have weathered as these rents have done? They are proof-sheets which need no correction. Here goes lumber from the Maine woods, which did not go out to sea in the last freshet, risen four dollars on the thousand because of what did go out or was split up; pine, spruce, cedar, — first, second, third and fourth qualities, so lately all of one quality, to wave over the bear, and moose, and caribou. Next rolls Thomaston lime, a **38** prime lot, which will get far among the hills before it gets slacked. These rags in bales, of all hues and qualities, the lowest condition to which cotton and linen descend, the final result of dress, — of patterns which are now no longer cried up, unless it be in Milwaukie, as those splendid articles, English, French, or American prints, ginghams, muslins, &c., gathered from all quarters both of fashion and poverty, going to become paper of one color or a few shades only, on which forsooth will be written tales of real life, high and low, and founded on fact! This closed car smells of salt fish, the strong New England and commercial scent, reminding me of the Grand Banks and the fisheries. Who has not seen a salt fish, thoroughly cured for this world, so that nothing can spoil it, and putting the perseverance of the saints to the blush? with which you may sweep or pave the streets, and split your kindlings, and the teamster shelter himself and his lading against sun wind and rain behind it, — and the trader, as a **39** Concord trader once did, hang it up by his door for a sign when he commences business, until at last his old-

35 *from Long Wharf to Lake Champlain.* Long Wharf is in Boston. Champlain was Ashuelot on ms. 424. Ashuelot Pond is in New Hampshire, while Lake Champlain is on the New York–Vermont border.

36 *foreign parts.* According to Walter Harding (1954, page xxviii), this was "foreign ports" when *Sartain's Union Magazine* serialized some of *Walden* in 1852. But it is clearly "parts" on ms. 424.

37 *wrought into paper.* Before the coming of cheap wood-fiber paper later in the nineteenth century, book paper was made from rags.

38 *Thomaston,* a town in Maine noted for its plentiful lime. Slacked is ordinarily spelled slaked. It is the process of adding water to caustic quicklime to reduce it to the more manageable slaked lime which is spread on fields to alkalinize the soil's acidity.

39 *a Concord trader.* Sanborn says that this was Deacon Parkman, in whose house the Thoreaus had lived from 1837 to 1845. (Bibliophile Edition, I, 162).

Curing and salting codfish

est customer cannot tell surely whether it be animal, vegetable, or mineral, and yet it shall be as pure as a snowflake, and if it be put into a pot and boiled, will come out an excellent dun fish for a Saturday's dinner. **40** Next Spanish hides, with the tails still preserving their twist and the angle of elevation they had when the oxen that wore them were careering over the pampas of the Spanish main, — a type of all obstinacy, and evincing how almost hopeless and incurable are all constitutional vices. I confess, that practically speaking, when I have learned a man's real disposition, I have no hopes of changing it for the better or worse in this state of existence. As the Orientals say, "A cur's tail may be warmed, and pressed, and bound round with ligatures, and after a twelve years' labor bestowed upon it, still it will retain its natural form." The only effectual cure for such inveteracies as these tails exhibit is to make glue of them, which I believe is what is usually done with them, and then they will stay put and stick. Here is a hogshead of molasses or of brandy directed to John Smith, Cuttingsville, Vermont, some trader among the Green Mountains, who imports for the farmers near his clearing, and now perchance stands over his bulk-head and thinks of the last arrivals on the coast, how they may affect the price for him, telling his customers this moment, as he has told them twenty times before this morning, that he expects some by the next train of prime quality. It is advertised in the Cuttingsville Times.

40 *dun fish*. Webster: "fish cured by dunning." And dunning is curing by salting.

While these things go up other things come down. Warned by the whizzing sound, I look up from my book and see some tall pine, hewn on far northern hills, which has winged its way over the Green Mountains and the Connecticut, shot like an arrow through the township within ten minutes, and scarce another eye beholds it; going

> " to be the mast
> Of some great ammiral."   **41**

And hark! here comes the cattle-train bearing the cattle of a thousand hills, sheepcots, stables, and cow-yards in the air, drovers with their sticks, and shepherd boys in the midst of their flocks, all but the mountain pastures, whirled along like leaves blown from the mountains by the September gales. The air is filled with the bleating of calves and sheep, and the hustling of oxen, as if a pastoral valley were going by. When the old bell-weather at the head rattles his bell, the mountains do indeed skip like rams and the little hills like lambs. A car-load of drovers, too, in the midst, on a level with their droves now, their vocation gone, but still clinging to their useless sticks as their badge of office. But their dogs, where are they? It is a stampede to them; they are quite thrown out; they have lost the scent. Methinks I hear them bark-   **42**

41 *"Of some great ammiral."* The NED says that this comes from "Fr. *le vaisseau amiral*" and that "Milton's ammiral (*Paradise Lost*, I, 294) is in imitation of it." It is "the ship that carries the admiral; the flag-ship."

42 *bell-weather*. A male sheep, leader of the flock, on whose neck a bell is hung. Thoreau had spelled this correctly as "bell-wether" on ms. 928. An overzealous editor or printer made the change and resultant error.

APRIL.

ing behind the Peterboro' Hills, or panting up the western slope of the Green Mountains. They will not be in at the death. Their vocation, too, is gone. Their fidelity and sagacity are below par now. They will slink back to their kennels in disgrace, or perchance run wild and strike a league with the wolf and the fox. So is your pastoral life whirled past and away. But the bell rings, and I must get off the track and let the cars go by; —

> What's the railroad to me ?   **43**
> I never go to see
> Where it ends.
> It fills a few hollows,
> And makes banks for the swallows,
> It sets the sand a-blowing,
> And the blackberries a-growing,

but I cross it like a cart-path in the woods. I will not have my eyes put out and my ears spoiled by its smoke and steam and hissing.

Now that the cars are gone by and all the restless world with them, and the fishes in the pond no longer feel their rumbling, I am more alone than ever. For the rest of the long afternoon, perhaps, my meditations are interrupted only by the faint rattle of a carriage or team along the distant highway.

Sometimes, on Sundays, I heard the bells, the Lincoln, Acton, Bedford, or Concord bell, when the wind was favorable, a faint, sweet, and, as it were, natural melody, worth importing into the wilderness. At a sufficient distance over the woods this sound acquires a certain vibratory hum, as if the pine needles in the horizon were the strings of a harp which it swept. All sound heard at the greatest possible distance produces one and the same effect, a vibration of the universal lyre, just as the intervening atmosphere makes a distant ridge of earth interesting to our eyes by the azure tint it imparts to it. There came to me in this case a melody which the air had strained, and which had conversed with every leaf and needle of the wood, that portion of the sound which the elements had taken up and modulated and echoed from vale to vale. The echo is, to some extent, an original sound, and therein is the magic and charm of it. It is not merely a repetition of

43 *What's the railroad to me?* This curious little poem is Thoreau's own. It is in the *Journal* for 1850; II, 58–59.

44 *the Lincoln, Acton, Bedford* was "the Lincoln bells, the Acton bell, the Bedford bell" on ms. 930. *Journal*, October 12, 1851; III, 67–68.

45 *worth importing into the wilderness.* Ms. 931 then reads: "I also heard the Sunday bells, although still with a purely secular pleasure, when crossing the fields to the village, and all nature seemed to undulate to their measure—

> Now up they go, ding,
>   Then down they go, dong,
>   And awhile they swing
>   To the same old song:
> Then changed is their measure to tone upon tone,
> And seldom it is that one sound comes alone;
> For they ring out their peals in a mingled throng,
> And the breezes waft the loud ding-dong along:
> And the metal goes round at a single bound,
> A-lulling the fields with its measured sound,
> Till the tired tongue falls with a lengthened boom,
> As solemn and loud as the crack of doom."

46 *the strings of a harp which it swept.* Ms. 930: "and is far more musical and memorable."

what was worth repeating in the bell, but partly the voice of the wood; the same trivial words and notes sung by a wood-nymph.

At evening, the distant lowing of some cow in the horizon beyond the woods sounded sweet and melodious, and at first I would mistake it for the voices of certain minstrels by whom I was sometimes serenaded, who might be straying over hill and dale; but soon I was not unpleasantly disappointed when it was prolonged into the cheap and natural music of the cow. I do not mean to be satirical, but to express my appreciation of those youths' singing, when I state that I perceived clearly that it was akin to the music of the cow, and they were at length one articulation of Nature.   **47**

Regularly at half past seven, in one part of the summer, after the evening train had gone by, the whippoor-   **48** wills chanted their vespers for half an hour, sitting on a stump by my door, or upon the ridge pole of the house. They would begin to sing almost with as much precision as a clock, within five minutes of a particular time, referred to the setting of the sun, every evening. I had a rare opportunity to become acquainted with their habits. Sometimes I heard four or five at once in different parts of the wood, by accident one a bar behind another, and so near me that I distinguished not only the cluck after each note, but often that singular buzzing sound like a fly in a spider's web, only proportionally louder. Sometimes one would circle round and round me in the woods a few feet distant as if tethered by a string, when probably I was near its eggs. They sang at intervals throughout the night, and were again as musical as ever just before and about dawn.

When other birds are still the screech owls take up the strain, like mourning women their ancient u-lu-lu. Their dismal scream is truly Ben Jonsonian. Wise midnight hags! It is no honest and blunt tu-whit   **49** tu-who of the poets, but, without jesting, a most solemn graveyard ditty, the mutual consolations of suicide lovers remembering the pangs and the delights of supernal love in the infernal groves. Yet I love to hear their wailing, their doleful responses, trilled along the woodside; reminding me sometimes of music and singing birds; as if it were the dark and tearful side of music, the regrets and sighs that would fain be sung. They are the spirits, the low spirits and melancholy fore-

47 *one articulation of Nature.* The Bibliophile Edition (I, 167) follows this with: "Sound was not made so much for convenience that we might hear when called, as to regale the sense, and fill one of the avenues of life."

48 *after the evening train had gone by.* It is interesting to compare this section with the *Journal* for August 1845; I, 378, from which it is derived:

"After the evening train has gone by and left the world to silence and to me, the whip-poor-will chants her vespers for half an hour. And when all is still at night, the owls take up the strain, like mourning women their ancient ululu. Their most dismal scream is truly Ben-Jonsonian. Wise midnight hags! It is no honest and blunt tu-whit tu-who of the poets, but, without jesting, a most solemn graveyard ditty,—but the mutual consolations of suicide lovers remembering the pangs and the delights of supernal love in the infernal groves. And yet I love to hear their wailing, their doleful responses, trilled along the woodside, reminding me sometimes of music and singing birds, as if it were the dark and tearful side of music, the regrets and sighs, that would fain be sung. The spirits, the *low* spirits and melancholy forebodings, of fallen spirits who once in human shape night-walked the earth and did the deeds of darkness, now expiating with their wailing hymns, threnodiai, their sins in the very scenery of their transgressions. They give me a new sense of the vastness and mystery of that nature which is the common dwelling of us both. 'Oh-o-o-o-o that I never had been bor-or-or-or-orn!' sighs one on this side of the pond, and circles in the restlessness of despair to some new perch in the gray oaks. Then, 'That I never had been bor-or-or-or-orn!' echoes one on the further side, with a tremulous sincerity, and 'Bor-or-or-or-orn' comes faintly from far in the Lincoln woods."

Note the paraphrases of Gray's *Elegy* ("And leaves the world to darkness and to me") and *Macbeth* IV, i ("secret, black, and midnight hags!"). See also page 263, line 15. Walter Harding (1963, page 26) questions "truly Ben-Jonsonian": "Was Thoreau thinking of 'We give thee a shout: Hoo!'?" (*Masque of Queens*, II, 317–18).

49 *tu-whit tu-who.* Harding (1963, page 286) notes that this is from what the owl says in *Love's Labour's Lost*.

bodings, of fallen souls that once in human shape night-walked the earth and did the deeds of darkness, now expiating their sins with their wailing hymns or threnodies in the scenery of their transgressions. They give me a new sense of the variety and capacity of that nature which is our common dwelling. *Oh-o-o-o-o that I never had been bor-r-r-r-n!* sighs one on this side of the pond, and circles with the restlessness of despair to some new perch on the gray oaks. Then — *that I never had been bor-r-r-r-n!* echoes another on the farther side with tremulous sincerity, and — *bor-r-r-r-n!* comes faintly from far in the Lincoln woods.

I was also serenaded by a hooting owl. Near at hand **50** you could fancy it the most melancholy sound in Nature, as if she meant by this to stereotype and make permanent in her choir the dying moans of a human being, — some poor weak relic of mortality who has left hope behind, and howls like an animal, yet with human sobs, on entering the dark valley, made more awful by a certain gurgling melodiousness, — I find myself beginning with the letters gl when I try to imitate it, — expressive of a mind which has reached the gelatinous mildewy stage in the mortification of all healthy and courageous thought. It reminded me of ghouls and idiots and insane howlings. But now one answers from far woods in a strain made really melodious by distance, — *Hoo* **51** *hoo hoo, hoorer hoo;* and indeed for the most part it suggested only pleasing associations, whether heard by day or night, summer or winter.

I rejoice that there are owls. Let them do the idiotic and maniacal hooting for men. It is a sound admirably suited to swamps and twilight woods which no day illustrates, suggesting a vast and undeveloped nature which men have not recognized. They represent the stark twilight and unsatisfied thoughts which all have. All day the sun has shone on the surface of some savage swamp, where the single spruce stands hung **52** with usnea lichens, and small hawks circulate above, and the chicadee lisps amid the evergreens, and the partridge and rabbit skulk beneath; but now a more dismal and fitting day dawns, and a different race of creatures awakes to express the meaning of Nature there.

Late in the evening I heard the distant rumbling of wagons over bridges, — a sound heard farther than almost

50 *I was also serenaded by a hooting owl.* This paragraph, in somewhat shorter form, is in the *Journal* for July 5, 1852; IV, 191.

51 Hoo hoo hoo. *Journal*, November 18, 1851; III, 122.

52 *the single spruce.* In his own copy of *Walden*, Thoreau changed "single" to "double." Double or black spruce is the only kind in the Concord area. The "single" spruce is the white variety that grows farther north.

any other at night, — the baying of dogs, and sometimes
again the lowing of some disconsolate cow in a distant
barn-yard. In the mean while all the shore rang with
the trump of bullfrogs, the sturdy spirits of ancient wine- **53**
bibbers and wassailers, still unrepentant, trying to sing
a catch in their Stygian lake, — if the Walden nymphs **54**
will pardon the comparison, for though there are almost
no weeds, there are frogs there, — who would fain keep
up the hilarious rules of their old festal tables, though
their voices have waxed hoarse and solemnly grave,
mocking at mirth, and the wine has lost its flavor, and
become only liquor to distend their paunches, and sweet
intoxication never comes to drown the memory of the
past, but mere saturation and waterloggedness and dis-
tention. The most aldermanic, with his chin upon a
heart-leaf, which serves for a napkin to his drooling
chaps, under this northern shore quaffs a deep draught
of the once scorned water, and passes round the cup
with the ejaculation *tr-r-r-oonk, tr-r-r-oonk, tr-r-r-*
oonk! and straightway comes over the water from some
distant cove the same password repeated, where the
next in seniority and girth has gulped down to his **55**
mark; and when this observance has made the circuit
of the shores, then ejaculates the master of ceremonies,
with satisfaction, *tr-r-r-oonk!* and each in his turn repeats the same down to the least distended, leakiest, and
flabbiest paunched, that there be no mistake; and then
the bowl goes round again and again, until the sun dis-

53 *sturdy spirits of ancient wine-bibbers. Journal*
for August 1845; I, 379 and 382.

54 *their Stygian lake.* In the Greek underworld
this was the subterranean body of water that separated Hades from the world of the living.

55 *down to his mark.* Early drinking cups or
horns had inside markings to indicate the amount
one drinker should take before passing the cup
on to the next man.

perses the morning mist, and only the patriarch is not under the pond, but vainly bellowing *troonk* from time to time, and pausing for a reply.

I am not sure that I ever heard the sound of cock-crowing from my clearing, and I thought that it might be worth the while to keep a cockerel for his music merely, as a singing bird. The note of this once wild **56** Indian pheasant is certainly the most remarkable of any bird's, and if they could be naturalized without being domesticated, it would soon become the most famous sound in our woods, surpassing the clangor of the goose and the hooting of the owl; and then imagine the cackling of the hens to fill the pauses when their lords' clarions rested! No wonder that man added this bird to his tame stock,—to say nothing of the eggs and drum- **57** sticks. To walk in a winter morning in a wood where these birds abounded, their native woods, and hear the wild cockerels crow on the trees, clear and shrill for miles over the resounding earth, drowning the feebler notes of other birds,— think of it! It would put na- tions on the alert. Who would not be early to rise, **58** and rise earlier and earlier every successive day of his life, till he became unspeakably healthy, wealthy, and wise? This foreign bird's note is celebrated by the **59**

56 *once wild Indian pheasant.* The common domestic fowl is descended from this ancestor.

57 *eggs and drumsticks. Journal,* July 11, 1851; II, 301.

58 *early to rise . . . till he became . . . healthy, wealthy, and wise.* Paraphrased from one of Franklin's maxims.

59 *This foreign bird's note.* Ms. 426 then goes on with "is remembered and celebrated by the English poets, along with the native skylark and the nightingale. But this faint clarion did not penetrate my woods."
This is followed by: "When I kept hens once in the village (before I went to the woods), I re- member that in one of the broods I reared, there was one white cockerel that went much by him- self, a pensive stately-paced young cockerel, that had . . . a good deal of the pheasant in him. One night he was by chance shut out of the hen-yard, and after long reconnoitering and anxious [ms. 301] going and coming—with brave thoughts exalting him, and fancies rushing thick upon him, —crowing long, memoriter-wise of his Indian origin and wild descent,—he flew, bird-like, up into the branches of a tree, and went to roost there. And I, who had witnessed this passage in his private history, forthwith wrote these verses, and inscribed them to him:"

poets of all countries along with the notes of their native songsters. All climates agree with brave Chanticleer. He is more indigenous even than the natives. His health is ever good, his lungs are sound, his spirits never flag. Even the sailor on the Atlantic and Pacific is awakened by his voice; but its shrill sound never roused me from my slumbers. I kept neither dog, cat, cow, pig, nor hens, so that you would have said there was a deficiency of domestic sounds; neither the churn, nor the spinning wheel, nor even the singing of the kettle, nor the hissing of the urn, nor children crying, to comfort one. An old-fashioned man would have lost his senses or died of ennui before this. Not even rats in the wall, for they were starved out, or rather were never baited in, — only squirrels on the roof and under the floor, a whippoorwill on the ridge pole, a blue-jay screaming beneath the window, a hare or woodchuck under the house, a screech-owl or a cat-owl behind it, a flock of wild geese or a laughing loon on the pond, and a fox to bark in the night. Not even a lark or an oriole, those mild plantation birds, ever visited my clearing. No cockerels to crow nor hens to cackle in the yard. No yard! but unfenced Nature reaching up to your very sills. A young forest growing up under

60
61

Poor bird! destined to lead thy life
  Far in the adventurous West,
And here to be debarred tonight
  From thy accustomed nest;

Must thou fall back upon old instinct now,–
Well-nigh extinct under Man's fickle care?

Did Heaven bestow its quenchless inner light
So long ago, for thy small want tonight?
Why stand'st upon thy toes to crow so late?
The Moon is deaf to thy low, feathered fate.
Or dost thou think so to possess the night,
And people the drear dark with thy brave sprite?
And now with anxious eye thou look'st about,
While the relentless shade draws on its veil,
For some sure shelter from approaching dews,
And the insidious step of nightly foes?

I fear imprisonment has dulled thy wit,
Or ingrained servitude extinguished it;
But no,—dim memory of the days of yore,
By Brahmaputra and the Jumna's shore,
Where thy proud race flew swiftly o'er the heath,
And sought its food the jungle's shade beneath,—
Has taught thy wings to seek yon friendly trees,
As erst by Indus' banks and far Ganges.

The Bibliophile Edition (II, 22) has this footnote: "This hen-keeping experience was probably while the Thoreau family lived in what has long

AUGUST.

your windows, and wild sumachs and blackberry vines breaking through into your cellar; sturdy pitch-pines rubbing and creaking against the shingles for want of room, their roots reaching quite under the house. Instead of a scuttle or a blind blown off in the gale, — a pine tree snapped off or torn up by the roots behind your house for fuel. Instead of no path to the front-yard gate in the Great Snow, — no gate — no front-yard, — and no path to the civilized world!

been the Munroe [Shattuck] house, at the corner of Main Street and Academy Lane, in the years that Henry was in college. This place, with its garden and trees, would be better adapted to poultry breeding than the Parkman house, with its narrower space and lack of trees, where the Town Library now stands. And Henry's 'Gothic window' at the Munroe house, of which he wrote in 1835, that it "overlooked the kitchen garden," would be a favorable place for watching and listening to this brave Chanticleer."

60 *his spirits never flag.* Ms. 431 then has: "I was perhaps the only inhabitant of Concord or of the state who did not hear the cock crow."

61 *Even the sailor . . . is awakened by his voice.* Ships bound on long voyages carried cooped chickens on deck to provide fresh meat at sea. The Bibliophile Edition (I, 172n.) has this note by Sanborn at the end of the chapter:

"At some point in the course of this chapter, not specially indicated in the ms., Thoreau omitted this passage:

"'I am glad to remember, as I sit by my door, that I, too, am a remote descendant of a heroic race of men, of whom there is tradition; in one sense a fellow-wanderer and survivor of Ulysses, for instance. My life passes amid the pines of New England. The pitch pine grows before my door,— unlike any symbol I have seen sculptured or painted. Where are the heroes whose exploits shall appear to posterity sculptured on monuments amid such natural forms as these? as we see heroes and demi-gods amid the lotuses and palms of the East. What new marks shall *we* add to the Red Pipe-stone Quarry?'"

This appears to have been the contents of a *Journal* page (numbered 43) written while Thoreau was at Walden, but for which he hardly found a suitable place in the volume when he edited it for printing. It stands, however, on the same four-page sheet which contains the recorded sights and sounds of a summer afternoon,—the hawks, wild pigeons, reed-birds, rattle of railroad cars, etc., near the beginning of this chapter.

SOLITUDE.

This is a delicious evening, when the whole body is one sense, and imbibes delight through every pore. I go and come with a strange liberty in Nature, a part of herself. As I walk along the stony shore of the pond in my shirt sleeves, though it is cool as well as cloudy and windy, and I see nothing special to attract me, all the elements are unusually congenial to me. The bull-frogs trump to usher in the night, and the note of the whippoorwill is borne on the rippling wind from over the water. Sympathy with the fluttering alder and poplar leaves almost takes away my breath; yet, like the lake, my serenity is rippled but not ruffled. These small waves raised by the evening wind are as remote from storm as the smooth reflecting surface. Though it is now dark, the wind still blows and roars in the wood, the waves still dash, and some creatures lull the rest with their notes. The repose is never complete. The wildest animals do not repose, but seek their prey now; the fox, and skunk, and rabbit, now roam the fields and woods without fear. They are Nature's watchmen, — links which connect the days of animated life.

When I return to my house I find that visitors have been there and left their cards, either a bunch of flow- **1** ers, or a wreath of evergreen, or a name in pencil on a yellow walnut leaf or a chip. They who come rarely to the woods take some little piece of the forest into their hands to play with by the way, which they leave, either intentionally or accidentally. One has peeled a willow wand, woven it into a ring, and dropped it on my

Charles Anderson (1968, page 62) compares this opening paragraph to Wordsworth's sonnet, "Evening on Calais Beach." He also believes that Thoreau may have been influenced by Johann Zimmerman's *Solitude* (Albany, N.Y., 1796), a copy of which he owned.

1 *a bunch of flowers*. This was "violets or houstonias" on ms. 434.

table. I could always tell if visitors had called in my absence, either by the bended twigs or grass, or the print of their shoes, and generally of what sex or age or quality they were by some slight trace left, as a flower dropped, or a bunch of grass plucked and thrown away, even as far off as the railroad, half a mile distant, or by the lingering odor of a cigar or pipe. Nay, I was frequently notified of the passage of a traveller along the highway sixty rods off by the scent of **2** his pipe.

There is commonly sufficient space about us. Our **3** horizon is never quite at our elbows. The thick wood is not just at our door, nor the pond, but somewhat is always clearing, familiar and worn by us, appropriated and fenced in some way, and reclaimed from Nature. For what reason have I this vast range and circuit, some square miles of unfrequented forest, for my privacy, abandoned to me by men? My nearest neighbor is a mile distant, and no house is visible from any place but the hill-tops within half a mile of my own. I have

2 *the scent of his pipe.* Ms. 434 then has: "Indeed my senses were as acute as an Indian's in this respect, and I saw how his habit of observation was cultivated."

3 *There is commonly sufficient space.* This was changed to "There seems always to be," but these words were then canceled, and "commonly" was restored. Ms. 266 and 435.

The railroad still runs along the western shore of Walden Pond

my horizon bounded by woods all to myself; a distant **4**
view of the railroad where it touches the pond on the one
hand, and of the fence which skirts the woodland road
on the other. But for the most part it is as solitary
where I live as on the prairies. It is as much Asia
or Africa as New England. I have, as it were, my own
sun and moon and stars, and a little world all to myself.
At night there was never a traveller passed my house,
or knocked at my door, more than if I were the first or
last man; unless it were in the spring, when at long intervals some came from the village to fish for pouts, —
they plainly fished much more in the Walden Pond of
their own natures, and baited their hooks with darkness, — but they soon retreated, usually with light baskets, and left "the world to darkness and to me," and **5**
the black kernel of the night was never profaned by
any human neighborhood. I believe that men are generally still a little afraid of the dark, though the witches
are all hung, and Christianity and candles have been
introduced.

Yet I experienced sometimes that the most sweet and
tender, the most innocent and encouraging society may
be found in any natural object, even for the poor mis-
anthrope and most melancholy man. There can be no
very black melancholy to him who lives in the midst of
Nature and has his senses still. There was never yet
such a storm but it was Æolian music to a healthy and **6**
innocent ear. Nothing can rightly compel a simple and
brave man to a vulgar sadness. While I enjoy the
friendship of the seasons I trust that nothing can make
life a burden to me. The gentle rain which waters my
beans and keeps me in the house to-day is not drear
and melancholy, but good for me too. Though it prevents my hoeing them, it is of far more worth than my
hoeing. If it should continue so long as to cause the **7**
seeds to rot in the ground and destroy the potatoes in
the low lands, it would still be good for the grass on the
uplands, and, being good for the grass, it would be good
for me. Sometimes, when I compare myself with other
men, it seems as if I were more favored by the gods than
they, beyond any deserts that I am conscious of; as
if I had a warrant and surety at their hands which my
fellows have not, and were especially guided and
guarded. I do not flatter myself, but if it be possible **8**
they flatter me. I have never felt lonesome, or in the

4 *a distant view of the railroad.* The tracks were
not so far away, but to a man who had lived for
years in the Texas House, which was literally
within a stone's throw of the railroad, the open
stretch across the pond between the Walden cabin
and the tracks must have seemed wide.

5 *and left "the world to darkness and to me."*
This is the fourth line of Thomas Gray's "Elegy
Written in a Country Churchyard." Instead of
it, ms. 435 had "and left 'the vale to solitude and
to me.'"

6 *Æolian music.* Soft sweet humming sounds
made by air currents passing over wires or other
material that will vibrate. Named after Æolus,
the Greek god of the winds. This section is from
the *Journal* for July 14, 1845; I, 364.

7 *cause the seeds to rot. Journal,* 1850; II, 12.

8 *if it be possible they flatter me.* Ms. 293 then
has: "so perhaps it appears to every one."

Hanging the witches

least oppressed by a sense of solitude, but once, and that was a few weeks after I came to the woods, when, for an hour, I doubted if the near neighborhood of man was not essential to a serene and healthy life. To be alone was something unpleasant. But I was at the same time conscious of a slight insanity in my mood, and seemed to foresee my recovery. In the midst of a gentle rain while these thoughts prevailed, I was suddenly sensible of such sweet and beneficent society in Nature, in the very pattering of the drops, and in every sound and sight around my house, an infinite and unaccountable friendliness all at once like an atmosphere sustaining me, as made the fancied advantages of human neighborhood insignificant, and I have never thought of them since. Every little pine needle expanded and swelled with sympathy and befriended me. I was so distinctly made aware of the presence of something kindred to me, even in scenes which we are accustomed to call wild and dreary, and also that the nearest of blood to me and humanest was not a person nor a villager, that I thought no place could ever be strange to me again.—

> "Mourning untimely consumes the sad;
> Few are their days in the land of the living,
> Beautiful daughter of Toscar."

Some of my pleasantest hours were during the long rain storms in the spring or fall, which confined me to the house for the afternoon as well as the forenoon, soothed by their ceaseless roar and pelting; when an early twilight ushered in a long evening in which many thoughts had time to take root and unfold themselves. In those driving north-east rains which tried the village houses so, when the maids stood ready with mop and pail in front entries to keep the deluge out, I sat behind my door in my little house, which was all entry, and thoroughly enjoyed its protection. In one heavy thunder shower the lightning struck a large pitch-pine across the pond, making a very conspicuous and perfectly regular spiral groove from top to bottom, an inch or more deep, and four or five inches wide, as you would groove a walking-stick. I passed it again the other day, and was struck with awe on looking up and beholding that mark, now more distinct than ever, where a terrific and resistless bolt came down out of the harmless sky eight years ago. Men frequently say to me, "I should think you would feel lonesome down there,

9

10
11

12

13

9 *after I came to the woods.* Ms. 293 says instead: "to the pond to live."

10 *a slight insanity in my mood.* This is one of several instances where Thoreau mentions insanity in his writings. See page 344, line 24.

11 *In the midst of a gentle rain. Journal* for July 14, 1845; I, 365.

12 *"Mourning untimely consumes the sad."* Channing noted that this was from Ossian, the legendary third-century Gaelic poet whose work was supposedly "translated" by James Macpherson (1736–1796). The genuineness of the poems was challenged by Samuel Johnson, among others. Further examination of them showed that much of the material had originated with Macpherson. Although Thoreau knew that Macpherson's *Ossian* had been denounced as a forgery, he was impressed by Patrick MacGregor's more recent *The Genuine Remains of Ossian* (1841). The quotation is from MacGregor.

13 *Men frequently say.* This obviously is the beginning of a new paragraph, and so it was on ms. 437.

and want to be nearer to folks, rainy and snowy days and nights especially." I am tempted to reply to such, — This whole earth which we inhabit is but a point in space. How far apart, think you, dwell the two most distant inhabitants of yonder star, the breadth of whose disk cannot be appreciated by our instruments? Why should I feel lonely? is not our planet in the Milky Way? This which you put seems to me not to be the most important question. What sort of space is that which separates a man from his fellows and makes him solitary? I have found that no exertion of the legs can bring two minds much nearer to one another. What do we want most to dwell near to? Not to many men surely, the depot, the post-office, the bar-room, the meeting-house, the school-house, the grocery, Beacon Hill, or the Five Points, where men **14** most congregate, but to the perennial source of our life, whence in all our experience we have found that to issue, as the willow stands near the water and sends out its roots in that direction. This will vary with different natures, but this is the place where a wise man will dig **15** his cellar. . . . I one evening overtook one of my townsmen, who has accumulated what is called "a handsome property," — though I never got a *fair* view of it, — on the Walden road, driving a pair of cattle to market, who inquired of me how I could bring my mind to give up so many of the comforts of life. I answered that I was very sure I liked it passably well; I was not joking. And so I went home to my bed, and left him to pick his way through the darkness and the mud to Brighton, **16** — or Bright-town, — which place he would reach some time in the morning.

14 *Beacon Hill, or the Five Points.* Beacon Hill was—and still is—one of the most desirable sections of downtown Boston. The Five Points, fortunately, no longer exists. It was an intersection located in New York City north of City Hall and was one of the toughest and most run-down parts of that city.

15 *where a wise man will dig his cellar.* Ms. 438: "Yet most men are not so wise as a tree, or rather are like those trees which being badly located make only wood and leaves and bear no fruit."

16 *Brighton.* Then a slaughterhouse area a few miles west of downtown Boston. Harding (1963, page 287) suggests that "Bright-town" comes from the name "Bright," which was often given to a favored ox.

Driving cattle to the Brighton market

Any prospect of awakening or coming to life to a dead man makes indifferent all times and places. The place where that may occur is always the same, and indescribably pleasant to all our senses. For the most part we allow only outlying and transient circumstances to make our occasions. They are, in fact, the cause of our distraction. Nearest to all things is that power which fashions their being. *Next* to us the grandest laws are continually being executed. *Next* to us is not the workman whom we have hired, with whom we love so well to talk, but the workman whose work we are.

"How vast and profound is the influence of the subtile powers of Heaven and of Earth!"   **17**

"We seek to perceive them, and we do not see them; we seek to hear them, and we do not hear them; identified with the substance of things, they cannot be separated from them."

"They cause that in all the universe men purify and sanctify their hearts, and clothe themselves in their holiday garments to offer sacrifices and oblations to their ancestors. It is an ocean of subtile intelligences. They are every where, above us, on our left, on our right; they environ us on all sides."

We are the subjects of an experiment which is not a little interesting to me. Can we not do without the society of our gossips a little while under these circumstances, — have our own thoughts to cheer us? Confucius says truly, "Virtue does not remain as an   **18** abandoned orphan; it must of necessity have neighbors."

With thinking we may be beside ourselves in a sane sense. By a conscious effort of the mind we can stand aloof from actions and their consequences; and all things, good and bad, go by us like a torrent. We are not wholly involved in Nature. I may be either the driftwood in the stream, or Indra in the sky looking down   **19** on it. I *may* be affected by a theatrical exhibition; on the other hand, I *may not* be affected by an actual event   **20** which appears to concern me much more. I only know myself as a human entity; the scene, so to speak, of thoughts and affections; and am sensible of a certain doubleness by which I can stand as remote from myself as from another. However intense my experience, I am conscious of the presence and criticism of a part of me, which, as it were, is not a part of me, but specta-

17 *"How vast and profound."* Lyman V. Cady (1961, page 26) identifies the passage quoted as being from the third of the Confucian Books, *The Doctrine of the Mean,* which is generally credited to Tzu Sse, Confucius' grandson, Chapter XVI, 1–3.

18 *Confucius says truly.* Just before this, on ms. 610, is: "If you want no society mind your own business." Cady (1961, page 27) says that the quotation is from *The Analects,* Book IV, Chapter XXV.

19 *Indra.* The chief of the Vedic gods, ruler of air, wind, rain, snow, and thunder.

20 *I may not be affected by an actual event.* The next few paragraphs tell a great deal about Thoreau's personality. The doubleness he speaks of will be of great interest to anyone who is familiar with Eugen Bleuler's work on psychiatry.

tor, sharing no experience, but taking note of it; and that is no more I than it is you. When the play, it may be the tragedy, of life is over, the spectator goes his way. It was a kind of fiction, a work of the imagination only, so far as he was concerned. This doubleness may easily make us poor neighbors and friends sometimes. **21**

I find it wholesome to be alone the greater part of the time. To be in company, even with the best, is soon wearisome and dissipating. I love to be alone. I never found the companion that was so companionable as solitude. We are for the most part more lonely when we go abroad among men than when we stay in our chambers. A man thinking or working is always alone, let him be where he will. Solitude is not measured by the miles of space that intervene between a man and his fellows. The really diligent student in one of the crowded hives of Cambridge College is as **22** solitary as a dervis in the desert. The farmer can **23** work alone in the field or the woods all day, hoeing or chopping, and not feel lonesome, because he is employed; but when he comes home at night he cannot sit down in a room alone, at the mercy of his thoughts, but must be where he can " see the folks," and recreate, and as he thinks remunerate, himself for his day's soli- **24** tude; and hence he wonders how the student can sit alone in the house all night and most of the day without ennui and " the blues;" but he does not realize that **25** the student, though in the house, is still at work in *his* field, and chopping in *his* woods, as the farmer in his, and in turn seeks the same recreation and society that the latter does, though it may be a more condensed form of it.

Society is commonly too cheap. We meet at very short intervals, not having had time to acquire any new value for each other. We meet at meals three times a day, and give each other a new taste of that old musty **26** cheese that we are. We have had to agree on a certain set of rules, called etiquette and politeness, to make this frequent meeting tolerable and that we need not come to open war. We meet at the post-office, and at the sociable, and about the fireside every night; we live thick and are in each other's way, and stumble over one another, and I think that we thus lose some respect for one another. Certainly less frequency would suffice

21 *poor neighbors and friends sometimes.* After this on ms. 290 are these lines from the poem eventually entitled "The Hero."

> Must we still eat
> The bread we have spurned?
> Must we re-kindle
> The faggots we've burned?

The complete poem is in Bode (1964, pages 161–163).

22 *Cambridge College.* Harvard.

23 *dervis.* The NED says that this is a variant spelling for dervish.

24 *remunerate, himself.* The comma does not appear on ms. 290 and is therefore a printer's error. Thoreau corrected it in his own copy of *Walden.* Ms. 290 has no comma after "thinks," where one should be.

25 *"the blues."* There are no quote marks on ms. 289.

26 *a new taste of that old musty cheese that we are.* Again a negative self-image.

for all important and hearty communications. Consider the girls in a factory, — never alone, hardly in their dreams. It would be better if there were but one inhabitant to a square mile, as where I live. The value of a man is not in his skin, that we should touch him.

I have heard of a man lost in the woods and dying of famine and exhaustion at the foot of a tree, whose loneliness was relieved by the grotesque visions with which, owing to bodily weakness, his diseased imagination surrounded him, and which he believed to be real. So also, owing to bodily and mental health and strength, we may be continually cheered by a like but more normal and natural society, and come to know that we are never alone.

I have a great deal of company in my house; especially in the morning, when nobody calls. Let me suggest a few comparisons, that some one may convey an idea of my situation. I am no more lonely than the loon in the pond that laughs so loud, or than Walden Pond itself. What company has that lonely lake, I pray? And yet it has not the blue devils, but the blue angels in it, in the azure tint of its waters. The sun is alone, except in thick weather, when there sometimes appear to be two, but one is a mock sun. God is alone, — but the devil, he is far from being alone; he sees a great deal of company; he is legion. I am no more lonely than a single mullein or dandelion in a pasture, or a bean leaf, or sorrel, or a horse-fly, or a humble-bee. I am no more lonely than the Mill Brook, or a weathercock, or the north star, or the south wind, or an April shower, or a January thaw, or the first spider in a new house.

I have occasional visits in the long winter evenings, when the snow falls fast and the wind howls in the wood, from an old settler and original proprietor, who is reported to have dug Walden Pond, and stoned it, and fringed it with pine woods; who tells me stories of old time and of new eternity; and between us we manage to pass a cheerful evening with social mirth and pleasant views of things, even without apples or cider, — a most wise and humorous friend, whom I love much, who keeps himself more secret than ever did Goffe or Whalley; and though he is thought to be dead, none can show where he is buried. An elderly dame, too, dwells in my neighborhood, invisible to most per-

27 *hardly in their dreams.* The Lowell factory girls slept in dormitories near the mills.

28 *he is legion.* Ms. 286 then has this: "The earth's alone—& Heaven is alone—but Hell is not at all, but when Heaven receives company or goes a-visiting *Cor ne edito*, 'eat not the heart,' saith Pythagoras. You must eat something else to be sure." Pythagoras (c.530 B.C.) was a Greek philosopher who inspired men to form a group to promulgate his teachings on political, moral, and social life.

29 *the Mill Brook* is a small stream that runs through Concord.

30 *an old settler.* This is the first appearance of this strange being; he and "the elderly dame" (described below) will be mentioned several times. Charles Anderson (1968, page 77) says of them: "The first visitor corresponds to Pan only in the sense of the Great All . . . the universal god. . . . Even the final phrase, 'he is thought to be dead,' does not necessarily refer to that story in Plutarch about the mysterious voice proclaiming 'the great god Pan is dead' at the exact moment of Christ's birth. Many voices in the nineteenth century were coming to say the same thing of Jehovah. . . ."
"The elderly dame" can be said to be the Great Mother, Mother Nature.

31 *Goffe or Whalley.* These were regicides (Edward Whalley, c.1615–c.1675, signed the death warrant of Charles I) who fled to New England at the time of the Restoration in 1660. William Goffe was Whalley's son-in-law. The two men lived for some years in Connecticut and Massachusetts and successfully avoided all attempts at arrest.

The regicides' cave in Connecticut

sons, in whose odorous herb garden I love to stroll some-
times, gathering simples and listening to her fables; for she has a genius of unequalled fertility, and her memory runs back farther than mythology, and she can tell me the original of every fable, and on what fact every one is founded, for the incidents occurred when she was young.   A ruddy and lusty old dame, who delights in all weathers and seasons, and is likely to outlive all her children yet.

The indescribable innocence and beneficence of Nature, — of sun and wind and rain, of summer and win-
ter, — such health, such cheer, they afford forever! and such sympathy have they ever with our race, that all Nature would be affected, and the sun's brightness fade, and the winds would sigh humanely, and the clouds rain tears, and the woods shed their leaves and put on mourning in midsummer, if any man should ever for a just cause grieve.   Shall I not have intelligence with **32** the earth?   Am I not partly leaves and vegetable **33** mould myself?

What is the pill which will keep us well, serene, con-
tented?   Not my or thy great-grandfather's, but our great-grandmother Nature's universal, vegetable, bo-
tanic medicines, by which she has kept herself young always, outlived so many old Parrs in her day, and fed **34** her health with their decaying fatness.   For my panacea, instead of one of those quack vials of a mixture **35** dipped from Acheron and the Dead Sea, which come **36** out of those long shallow black-schooner looking wagons

32 *intelligence.* Communication.

33 *vegetable mould myself.* Ms. 284 then has: "God is my father & my good friend—men are my brothers—but nature is my mother and my sister."

34 *old Parrs.* Thomas Parr (1483?–1635), who claimed to have lived under ten kings and queens. In September 1635 he was taken to London to be presented as a curiosity to Charles I. The experience was too much for him, and he died. William Harvey (1578–1657), discoverer of the circula-
tion of blood, performed the autopsy and found that the very old man had been in good health. Parr was buried in Westminster Abbey.

35 *those quack vials.* Here Thoreau is making fun of the nostrums that were then sold to un-
wary people. He has more to say about Nature's curative powers in the *Journal* for August 23, 1853; V, 394: "Live in each season as it passes; breathe the air, drink the drink, taste the fruit, and resign yourself to the influences of each. Let them be your only diet drink and botanical medicines. In August live on berries, not dried meats and pemmican, as if you were on shipboard mak-
ing your way through a waste ocean, or in a northern desert. Be blown on by all the winds. Open all your pores and bathe in all the tides of Nature, in all her streams and oceans, at all sea-
sons. Miasma and infection are from within, not without. The invalid, brought to the brink of the grave by an unnatural life, instead of imbibing only the great influence that Nature is, drinks only the tea made of a particular herb, while he still continues his unnatural life,—saves at the spile and wastes at the bung. He does not love Nature or his life, and so sickens and dies, and no doctor can cure him. Grow green with spring, yellow and ripe with autumn. Drink of each season's influence as a vial, a true panacea of all remedies mixed for your especial use. The vials of summer never made a man sick, but those which he stored in his cellar. Drink the wines, not of your bottling, but Nature's bottling; not kept in goat-skins or pig-skins, but the skins of a myr-
iad fair berries. Let Nature do your bottling and your pickling and preserving. For all Nature is doing her best each moment to make us well. She exists for no other end. Do not resist her. With the least inclination to be well, we should not be sick. Men have discovered—or think they have discovered—the salutariness of a few wild things only, and not of all nature. Why, "nature" is but another name for health, and the seasons are but different states of health. Some men think that they are not well in spring, or summer, or autumn or winter; it is only because they are not *well in* them."

which we sometimes see made to carry bottles, let me have a draught of undiluted morning air. Morning air! If men will not drink of this at the fountain-head of the day, why, then, we must even bottle up some and sell it in the shops, for the benefit of those who have lost their subscription ticket to morning time in this world. But remember, it will not keep quite till noonday even in the coolest cellar, but drive out the stopples long ere that and follow westward the steps of Aurora. I am no worshipper of Hygeia, who was the daughter of that old herb-doctor Æsculapius, and who is represented on monuments holding a serpent in one hand, and in the other a cup out of which the serpent sometimes drinks; but rather of Hebe, cupbearer to Jupiter, who was the daughter of Juno and wild lettuce, and who had the power of restoring gods and men to the vigor of youth. She was probably the only thoroughly sound-conditioned, healthy, and robust young lady that ever walked the globe, and wherever she came it was spring.

37

36 *Acheron.* A river of Thesprotia in southern Epirus which runs underground in some places and was therefore said to lead to Hades.

37 *Hygeia . . . Hebe.* These Greek goddesses represent health; Hygeia, the health that results from the use of good medicines; Hebe, the natural health of youth and well-being. Hebe's mother Juno ate lettuce just before she conceived her child. Æsculapius was the god of healing although he appears in mortal form in the *Iliad.* The staff and the twisted serpent—symbols that are still used—are associated with him.

Hygeia

Juno

VISITORS.

I THINK that I love society as much as most, and am ready enough to fasten myself like a bloodsucker for the time to any full-blooded man that comes in my way. I am naturally no hermit, but might possibly sit out the sturdiest frequenter of the bar-room, if my business called me thither.

I had three chairs in my house; one for solitude, two for friendship, three for society. When visitors came in larger and unexpected numbers there was but the third chair for them all, but they generally economized the room by standing up. It is surprising how many **1** great men and women a small house will contain. I have had twenty-five or thirty souls, with their bodies, at once under my roof, and yet we often parted without **2** being aware that we had come very near to one another. Many of our houses, both public and private, with their almost innumerable apartments, their huge halls and their cellars for the storage of wines and other munitions of peace, appear to me extravagantly large for their inhabitants. They are so vast and magnificent that the latter seem to be only vermin which infest them. I am surprised when the herald blows his summons before some Tremont or Astor or Middlesex House, to see **3** come creeping out over the piazza for all inhabitants a ridiculous mouse, which soon again slinks into some hole **4** in the pavement.

One inconvenience I sometimes experienced in so small a house, the difficulty of getting to a sufficient distance from my guest when we began to utter the big thoughts in big words. You want room for your thoughts to get into sailing trim and run a course or

The opening paragraph was written on ms. 440, where it was associated with the "doubleness" passage on page 266. It was placed here in a later revision.

1 *It is surprising.* Another modification; on ms. 447 this was "astonishing."

2 *under my roof.* In some texts this is "under my room," but mss. 268 and 447 clearly say "roof."

3 *Tremont or Astor or Middlesex House.* Hotels in Boston, New York, and Concord.

4 *some hole in the pavement.* Ms. 269 adds "or door step."

The Tremont House in Boston

two before they make their port. The bullet of your thought must have overcome its lateral and ricochet motion and fallen into its last and steady course before it reaches the ear of the hearer, else it may plough out again through the side of his head. Also, our sentences wanted room to unfold and form their columns in the interval. Individuals, like nations, must have suitable broad and natural boundaries, even a considerable neutral ground, between them. I have found it a singular luxury to talk across the pond to a companion on the opposite side. In my house we were so near that we could not begin to hear, — we could not speak low enough to be heard; as when you throw two stones into calm water so near that they break each other's undulations. If we are merely loquacious and loud talkers, then we can afford to stand very near together, cheek by jowl, and feel each other's breath; but if we speak reservedly and thoughtfully, we want to be farther apart, that all animal heat and moisture may have a chance to evaporate. If we would enjoy the most intimate society with that in each of us which is without, or above, being spoken to, we must not only be silent, but commonly so far apart bodily that we cannot possibly hear each other's voice in any case. Referred to this standard, speech is for the convenience of those who are hard of hearing; but there are many fine things which we cannot say if we have to shout. As the conversation began to assume a loftier and grander tone, we gradually shoved our chairs farther apart till they touched the wall in opposite corners, and then commonly there was not room enough.

My "best" room, however, my withdrawing room, always ready for company, on whose carpet the sun rarely fell, was the pine wood behind my house. Thither in summer days, when distinguished guests came, I took them, and a priceless domestic swept the floor and dusted the furniture and kept the things in order.

If one guest came he sometimes partook of my frugal meal, and it was no interruption to conversation to be stirring a hasty-pudding, or watching the rising and maturing of a loaf of bread in the ashes, in the mean while. But if twenty came and sat in my house there was nothing said about dinner, though there might be bread enough for two, more than if eating were a forsaken habit; but we naturally practised abstinence; and this

5 *neutral ground.* Ms. 269 adds "though it be disputed territory."

6 *in any case.* Ms. 449 adds "though this is what men commonly call solitude."

7 *My "best" room.* There were no quotes on ms. 450.

8 *the sun rarely fell.* Lest it fade the carpet even though this was the floor of the forest.

9 *hasty-pudding.* Corn meal stirred into boiling water or hot milk and quickly cooked.

was never felt to be an offence against hospitality, but the most proper and considerate course. The waste and decay of physical life, which so often needs repair, seemed miraculously retarded in such a case, and the vital vigor stood its ground. I could entertain thus a thousand as well as twenty; and if any ever went away disappointed or hungry from my house when they found me at home, they may depend upon it that I sympathized with them at least. So easy is it, though many housekeepers doubt it, to establish new and better customs in the place of the old. You need not rest your reputation on the dinners you give. For my own part, I was never so effectually deterred from frequenting a man's house, by any kind of Cerberus whatever, as by **10** the parade one made about dining me, which I took to be a very polite and roundabout hint never to trouble him so again. I think I shall never revisit those scenes. I should be proud to have for the motto of my cabin those lines of Spenser which one of my visitors inscribed on **11** a yellow walnut leaf for a card : —

> " Arrived there, the little house they fill,
>   Ne looke for entertainment where none was ;
> Rest is their feast, and all things at their will :
>   The noblest mind the best contentment has."

When Winslow, afterward governor of the Plymouth **12** Colony, went with a companion on a visit of ceremony to Massassoit on foot through the woods, and arrived **13** tired and hungry at his lodge, they were well received by the king, but nothing was said about eating that day. When the night arrived, to quote their own words, — " He laid us on the bed with himself and his wife, they at the one end and we at the other, it being only plank, laid a foot from the ground, and a thin mat upon them. Two more of his chief men, for want of room, pressed by and upon us ; so that we were worse weary of our lodging than of our journey." At one o'clock the next day Massassoit " brought two fishes that he had shot," about thrice as big as a bream ; " these being boiled, there were at least forty looked for a share in them. The most ate of them. This meal only we had in two nights and a day ; and had not one of us bought a partridge, we had taken our journey fasting." Fearing that they would be light-headed for want of food

10 *Cerberus.* The dog with several heads that guarded the entrance to Hades.

11 *lines of Spenser.* In his copy of *Walden,* Channing said that this verse came from *The Fairie Queen,* Book I, Canto I, Stanza 35.

12 *Winslow.* Edward Winslow (1595–1655), a passenger on the *Mayflower* and author of the journals (1622) that are the first accounts of the Plymouth Colony.

13 *Massassoit.* Indian chief (c. 1580–1661), who befriended the colonists.

Governor Winslow's signature

and also sleep, owing to "the savages' barbarous singing, (for they used to sing themselves asleep,)" and that they might get home while they had strength to travel, they departed.   As for lodging, it is true they were but poorly entertained, though what they found an inconvenience was no doubt intended for an honor; but as far as eating was concerned, I do not see how the Indians could have done better.   They had nothing to eat themselves, and they were wiser than to think that apologies could supply the place of food to their guests; so they drew their belts tighter and said nothing about it. Another time when Winslow visited them, it being a season of plenty with them, there was no deficiency in this respect.

As for men, they will hardly fail one any where.   I had more visitors while I lived in the woods than at any other period of my life; I mean that I had some. I met several there under more favorable circumstances than I could any where else.   But fewer came to see me upon trivial business.   In this respect, my company was winnowed by my mere distance from town.   I had withdrawn so far within the great ocean of solitude, into which the rivers of society empty, that for the most part, so far as my needs were concerned, only the finest sediment was deposited around me.   Beside, there were wafted to me evidences of unexplored and uncultivated continents on the other side.

Who should come to my lodge this morning but a true Homeric or Paphlagonian man, — he had so suit- **14** able and poetic a name that I am sorry I cannot print **15** it here, — a Canadian, a wood-chopper and post-maker,

14 *Paphlagonian man.* Paphlagonia was a heavily forested mountainous region in ancient Asia Minor which supplied troops to Xerxes in 480 B.C. A leader of the Paphlagonians is one of the characters in the *Iliad*.

15 *a name . . . I cannot print it here.* Ms. 282 and the *Journal* for July 14, 1845; I, 365 ff. give his name as Alek Therien. See index. He is an important figure in *Walden*, in the *Journal*, and in Thoreau's life. See also the *Journal* for December 24, 1853; V, 23–24, and for December 29, 1853; V, 35–36.

LUMBER   CUTTING

who can hole fifty posts in a day, who made his last supper on a woodchuck which his dog caught. He, too, has heard of Homer, and, "if it were not for books," would "not know what to do rainy days," though perhaps he has not read one wholly through for many rainy seasons. Some priest who could pronounce the Greek itself taught him to read his verse in the testament in his native parish far away; and now I must translate to him, while he holds the book, Achilles' reproof to Patroclus for his sad countenance. — "Why are you in tears, Patroclus, like a young girl?" — **16**

> "Or have you alone heard some news from Phthia?
> They say that Menœtius lives yet, son of Actor,
> And Peleus lives, son of Æacus, among the Myrmidons,
> Either of whom having died, we should greatly grieve."

He says, "That's good." He has a great bundle of white-oak bark under his arm for a sick man, gathered this Sunday morning. "I suppose there's no harm in going after such a thing to-day," says he. To him Homer was a great writer, though what his writing was about he did not know. A more simple and natural man it would be hard to find. Vice and disease, which cast such a sombre moral hue over the world, seemed to have hardly any existence for him. He was about twenty-eight years old, and had left Canada and his father's house a dozen years before to work in the States, and earn money to buy a farm with at last, perhaps in his native country. He was cast in the coarsest mould; a stout but sluggish body, yet gracefully carried, with a thick sunburnt neck, dark bushy hair, and dull sleepy blue eyes, which were occasionally lit up with expression. He wore a flat gray cloth cap, a dingy wool-colored greatcoat, and cowhide boots. He was a great consumer of meat, usually carrying his dinner to his work a couple of miles past my house, — for he chopped all summer, — in a tin pail; cold meats, often cold woodchucks, and coffee in a stone bottle which dangled by a string from his belt; and sometimes he offered me a drink. He came along early, crossing my bean-field, though without anxiety or haste to get to his work, such as Yankees exhibit. He wasn't a-going to hurt himself. He didn't care if he only earned his board. Frequently he would leave his dinner in the bushes, when his dog had caught a woodchuck by the **17**

16 "*Why are you in tears, Patroclus, like a young girl?*" This and the verse that follows are from the *Iliad*, Book XVI.

17 *a great bundle.* This is clearly "a neat bundle" in the *Journal*, July 1845; I, 366.

way, and go back a mile and a half to dress it and leave it in the cellar of the house where he boarded, after deliberating first for half an hour whether he could not sink it in the pond safely till nightfall, — loving to dwell long upon these themes. He would say, as he went by in the morning, "How thick the pigeons are! If working every day were not my trade, I could get all the meat I should want by hunting, — pigeons, woodchucks, rabbits, partridges, — by gosh! I could get all I should want for a week in one day." **18**

He was a skilful chopper, and indulged in some flourishes and ornaments in his art. He cut his trees level and close to the ground, that the sprouts which came up afterward might be more vigorous and a sled might slide over the stumps; and instead of leaving a whole tree to support his corded wood, he would pare it away to a slender stake or splinter which you could break off with your hand at last.

He interested me because he was so quiet and solitary and so happy withal; a well of good humor and contentment which overflowed at his eyes. His mirth was without alloy. Sometimes I saw him at his work in the woods, felling trees, and he would greet me with a laugh of inexpressible satisfaction, and a salutation in Canadian French, though he spoke English as well. **19** When I approached him he would suspend his work, and with half-suppressed mirth lie along the trunk of a pine which he had felled, and, peeling off the inner bark, roll it up into a ball and chew it while he laughed and talked. Such an exuberance of animal spirits had he that he sometimes tumbled down and rolled on the ground with laughter at any thing which made him think and tickled him. Looking round upon the trees he would exclaim, — "By George! I can enjoy myself well enough here chopping; I want no better sport." Sometimes, when at leisure, he amused himself all day in the woods with a pocket pistol, firing salutes to himself at regular intervals as he walked. **20** In the winter he had a fire by which at noon he warmed his coffee in a kettle; and as he sat on a log to eat his dinner the chicadees would sometimes come round and alight on his arm and peck at the potato in his fingers; and he said that he "liked to have the little *fellers* about **21** him."

In him the animal man chiefly was developed. In

18 *by gosh!* On ms. 278 "by George" was canceled and this was written in. But "by George" is used below. H. L. Mencken called such expressions "denaturized profanity" (*The American Language*, 1936, page 316). It is likely that Therien used much more forthright curses and that Thoreau—and his editors—toned them down for use in print.

19 *though he spoke English as well.* Ms. 277 then has: "And when I asked him in which he thought now, and if he spoke aloud to himself which language he used—you know we sometimes talk to ourselves— 'Yes, sometimes,' answered he. He said it was in English."

20 *firing salutes . . . as he walked.* Ms. 278 then has: "He loved also to frighten his dog when alone with him in the woods—by pointing his pistol at him & firing powder only." Thoreau canceled this passage, wrote it in again, and then finally suppressed it, perhaps because it was detrimental to the image of the man he admired so much.

21 *"liked to have the little* fellers *about him."* Journal, 1845–1846; I, 399.

physical endurance and contentment he was cousin to the pine and the rock. I asked him once if he was not sometimes tired at night, after working all day; and he answered, with a sincere and serious look, " Gorrappit, I never was tired in my life." But the intellectual and what is called spiritual man in him were slumbering as in an infant. He had been instructed only in that innocent and ineffectual way in which the Catholic priests teach the aborigines, by which the pupil is never educated to the degree of consciousness, but only to the degree of trust and reverence, and a child is not made a man, but kept a child. When Nature made him, she gave him a strong body and contentment for his portion, and propped him on every side with reverence and reliance, that he might live out his threescore years and ten a child. He was so genuine and unsophisticated that no introduction would serve to introduce him, more than if you introduced a woodchuck to your neighbor. He had got to find him out as you did. He would not play any part. Men paid him wages for work, and so helped to feed and clothe him; but he never exchanged opinions with them. He was so simply and naturally humble — if he can be called humble who never aspires — that humility was no distinct quality in him, nor could he conceive of it. Wiser men were demigods to him. If you told him that such a one was coming, he did as if he thought that any thing so grand would expect nothing of himself, but take all the responsibility on itself, and let him be forgotten still. He never heard the sound of praise. He particularly reverenced the writer and the preacher. Their performances were miracles. When I told him that I wrote considerably, he thought for a long time that it was merely the handwriting which I meant, for he could write a remarkably good hand himself. I sometimes found the name of his native parish handsomely written in the snow by the highway, with the proper French accent, and knew that he had passed. I asked him if he ever wished to write his thoughts. He said that he had read and written letters for those who could not, but he never tried to write thoughts, — no, he could not, he could not tell what to put first, it would kill him, and then there was spelling to be attended to at the same time !

I heard that a distinguished wise man and reformer asked him if he did not want the world to be changed;

22 *"I never was tired in my life."* Ms. 716 adds: "It sounded like the triumph of the physical man."

23 *he might live out his threescore years and ten a child.* Ms. 444: "We sometimes tell our friends of a man whom we value and whom we have met with—and he tells him also of our friend whom we wish him to know. When they meet [,] our hero knows that he has a part to perform and performs it."

24 *He would not play any part.* Ms. 443: "Like all children he lived alone, not in society, nor where rumor and fame react."

25 *he could write a remarkably good hand himself.* Ms. 274 then adds: "indeed much better than I commonly do." Thoreau's handwriting, which had been copperplate clear at Harvard, got steadily worse. By the time he wrote *Walden* it was quite bad. It varies, however, from fairly legible to difficult and then to impossible.

but he answered with a chuckle of surprise in his Canadian accent, not knowing that the question had ever been entertained before, " No, I like it well enough." It would have suggested many things to a philosopher to have dealings with him.   To a stranger he appeared to know nothing of things in general; yet I sometimes saw in him a man whom I had not seen before, and I did not know whether he was as wise as Shakspeare or as simply ignorant as a child, whether to suspect him of a fine poetic consciousness or of stupidity. A townsman told me that when he met him sauntering through the village in his small close-fitting cap, and whistling to himself, he reminded him of a prince in disguise.

His only books were an almanac and an arithmetic, in which last he was considerably expert.   The former was a sort of cyclopædia to him, which he supposed to contain an abstract of human knowledge, as indeed it does to a considerable extent.   I loved to sound him on the various reforms of the day, and he never failed to look at them in the most simple and practical light.   He had never heard of such things before.   Could he do without factories? I asked.   He had worn the home-made Vermont gray, he said, and that was good.   Could he dispense with tea and coffee?   Did this country afford any beverage beside water?   He had soaked hemlock **26** leaves in water and drank it, and thought that was better than water in warm weather.   When I asked him if he could do without money, he showed the convenience of money in such a way as to suggest and coincide with the most philosophical accounts of the origin of this institution, and the very derivation of the word *pecunia*.   If an ox were his property, and he **27** wished to get needles and thread at the store, he thought it would be inconvenient and impossible soon to go on mortgaging some portion of the creature each time to that amount.   He could defend many institutions better than any philosopher, because, in describing them as they concerned him, he gave the true reason for their prevalence, and speculation had not suggested to him any other.   At another time, hearing Plato's definition of a man, — a biped without feathers, — and that one ex- **28** hibited a cock plucked and called it Plato's man, he thought it an important difference that the *knees* bent the wrong way.   He would sometimes exclaim, " How

26 *He had soaked hemlock leaves in water and drank it.* This is the evergreen hemlock tree (*Tsuga canadensis*)—and its "leaves" are needles —not the hemlock plant (*Conium maculatum*), which is a common weed imported from Europe. It was an extract of *Conium maculatum* that was used to put Socrates to death. Just as poisonous is the American water hemlock plant (*Cicuta maculata*), which grows in wet areas.

27 pecunia. Latin for money. The word is derived from *pecus*, cattle, as the next sentence implies.

28 *that one exhibited a cock plucked.* The "one" was Diogenes.

I love to talk! By George, I could talk all day!" I asked him once, when I had not seen him for many months, if he had got a new idea this summer. "Good Lord," said he, "a man that has to work as I do, if he does not forget the ideas he has had, he will do well. May be the man you hoe with is inclined to race; then, by gorry, your mind must be there; you think of weeds." He would sometimes ask me first on such occasions, if I had made any improvement. One winter day I asked him if he was always satisfied with himself, wishing to suggest a substitute within him for the priest without, and some higher motive for living. "Satisfied!" said he; "some men are satisfied with one thing, and some with another. One man, perhaps, if he has got enough, will be satisfied to sit all day with his back to the fire and his belly to the table, by George!" Yet I never, by any manœuvring, could get him to take the spiritual view of things; the highest that he appeared to conceive of was a simple expediency, such as you might expect an animal to appreciate; and this, practically, is true of most men. If I suggested any improvement in his mode of life, he merely answered, without expressing any regret, that it was too late. Yet he thoroughly believed in honesty and the like virtues.

There was a certain positive originality, however slight, to be detected in him, and I occasionally observed that he was thinking for himself and expressing his own opinion, a phenomenon so rare that I would any day walk ten miles to observe it, and it amounted to the re-origination of many of the institutions of society. Though he hesitated, and perhaps failed to express himself distinctly, he always had a presentable thought behind. Yet his thinking was so primitive and immersed in his animal life, that, though more promising than a merely learned man's, it rarely ripened to any thing which can be reported. He suggested that there might be men of genius in the lowest grades of life, however permanently humble and illiterate, who take their own view always, or do not pretend to see at all; who are as bottomless even as Walden Pond was thought to be, though they may be dark and muddy.

Many a traveller came out of his way to see me and the inside of my house, and, as an excuse for calling,

29 *"Good Lord."* Journal, November 14, 1851; III, 117.

30 *One winter day.* The *Journal* for December 29, 1853; VI, 36, dates this incident.

asked for a glass of water. I told them that I drank at the pond, and pointed thither, offering to lend them a **31** dipper. Far off as I lived, I was not exempted from that annual visitation which occurs, methinks, about the first of April, when every body is on the move; and I had my share of good luck, though there were some curious specimens among my visitors. Half-witted men from the almshouse and elsewhere came to see me; but I endeavored to make them exercise all the wit they had, and make their confessions to me; in such cases making wit the theme of our conversation; and so was compensated. Indeed, I found some of them to be wiser than the so called *overseers* of the poor and selectmen of the town, and thought it was time that the tables were turned. With respect to wit, I learned that there was not much difference between the half and the whole. One day, in particular, an inoffensive, simple-minded pauper, whom with others I had often **32** seen used as fencing stuff, standing or sitting on a bushel

31 *offering to lend them a dipper*. In the *Journal* for January 17, 1852; III, 198, Thoreau tells a story about the dipper that reveals a great deal about certain aspects of his own personality. The *Journal* entry was obviously made many months after the incident happened, for the pond was then frozen over, but the recollection still rankled. Two young women came to the door of the hut and asked for water. Thoreau lent them his dipper, which they did not return—or even leave on the shore. "I had a right to suppose that they came to steal," he began and then denounced them fiercely: "They were a disgrace to their sex and to humanity. Pariahs of the moral world. Evil spirits that thirsted not for water but threw the dipper into the lake. Such as Dante saw. What [was] the lake to them but liquid fire and brimstone? They will never know peace till they have returned the dipper. In all the worlds this is decreed."

32 *simple-minded pauper*. Channing, in his copy of *Walden*, suggested that this might be a man named David Flint. See the *Journal* for January 16, 1852; III, 198, and January 17, 1852; III, 200.

in the fields to keep cattle and himself from straying, visited me, and expressed a wish to live as I did. He told me, with the utmost simplicity and truth, quite superior, or rather *inferior*, to any thing that is called humility, that he was "deficient in intellect." These were his words. The Lord had made him so, yet he supposed the Lord cared as much for him as for another. "I have always been so," said he, "from my childhood; I never had much mind; I was not like other children; I am weak in the head. It was the Lord's will, I suppose." And there he was to prove the truth of his words. He was a metaphysical puzzle to me. I have rarely met a fellow-man on such promising ground, — it was so simple and sincere and so true all that he said. And, true enough, in proportion as he appeared to humble himself was he exalted. I did not know at first but it was the result of a wise policy. It seemed that from such a basis of truth and frankness as the poor weak-headed pauper had laid, our intercourse might go forward to something better than the intercourse of sages.

I had some guests from those not reckoned commonly among the town's poor, but who should be; who are among the world's poor, at any rate; guests who appeal, not to your hospitality, but to your *hospitalality;* who earnestly wish to be helped, and preface their appeal with the information that they are resolved, for one thing, never to help themselves. I require of a visitor that he be not actually starving, though he may have the very best appetite in the world, however he got it. Objects of charity are not guests. Men who did not know when their visit had terminated, though I went about my business again, answering them from greater **33** and greater remoteness. Men of almost every degree of wit called on me in the migrating season. Some who had more wits than they knew what to do with; runaway slaves with plantation manners, who listened from time to time, like the fox in the fable, as if they heard the hounds a-baying on their track, and looked at me beseechingly, as much as to say, —

    "O Christian, will you send me back?"   **34**

One real runaway slave, among the rest, whom I **35** helped to forward toward the northstar. Men of one idea, like a hen with one chicken, and that a duckling;

33 *greater and greater remoteness.* Ms. 520 and 619 then have this verse of Thoreau's:

> I'm contented you should stay
> For ever and aye
> If you can take yourself away
> Any day.

34 *"O Christian, will you send me back?"* Christian is the hero in John Bunyan's *Pilgrim's Progress.*

35 *One real runaway slave.* See the Chronology for late July 1853.

men of a thousand ideas, and unkempt heads, like those hens which are made to take charge of a hundred chickens, all in pursuit of one bug, a score of them lost in every morning's dew, — and become frizzled and mangy in consequence; men of ideas instead of legs, a sort of intellectual centipede that made you crawl all over. One man proposed a book in which visitors should write their names, as at the White Moun- **36** tains; but, alas! I have too good a memory to make that necessary.

I could not but notice some of the peculiarities of my visitors. Girls and boys and young women generally seemed glad to be in the woods. They looked in the pond and at the flowers, and improved their time. Men of business, even farmers, thought only of solitude and employment, and of the great distance at which I dwelt from something or other; and though they said that they loved a ramble in the woods ococa- **37** sionally, it was obvious that they did not. Restless committed men, whose time was all taken up in getting a living or keeping it; ministers who spoke of God as if they enjoyed a monopoly of the subject, who could not bear all kinds of opinions; doctors, lawyers, uneasy housekeepers who pried into my cupboard and bed when I was out, — how came Mrs. —— to know that my sheets were not as clean as hers? — young men who had ceased to be young, and had concluded that it was safest to follow the beaten track of the professions, — all these generally said that it was not possible to do so much good in my position. Ay! there was **38** the rub. The old and infirm and the timid, of whatever age or sex, thought most of sickness, and sudden accident and death; to them life seemed full of danger, — what danger is there if you don't think of any? — and they thought that a prudent man would carefully select the safest position, where Dr. B. might be on hand at a **39** moment's warning. To them the village was literally a *com-munity*, a league for mutual defence, and you would suppose that they would not go a-huckleberrying without a medicine chest. The amount of it is, if a man is alive, there is always *danger* that he may die, though the danger must be allowed to be less in proportion as he is dead-and-alive to begin with. A man sits as many risks as he runs. Finally, there were the

36 *as at the White Mountains.* The Bibliophile Edition (I, 204) says of this: "said he would be at the expense of it! As if it were of any significance for a man who had failed to make any impression on you to leave his name!—No, I kept a book;—it needed only a small one—to put their names in,—I was at the expense of it." *Journal,* January 22, 1852; III, 215.

37 *occcasionally.* This absurd tripling of the c's occurs only in the plates of the first edition, but it was not corrected for many years and appears in the many printings that were made from them.

38 *Ay! there was the rub.* Hamlet makes this remark (in the present tense) in the "To be, or not to be" speech (III, i), when he weighs the possibility of suicide.

39 *Dr. B.* Probably Dr. Josiah Bartlett, a well-known physician in Concord, who practiced there for 57 years.

self-styled reformers, the greatest bores of all, who thought that I was forever singing, —

> This is the house that I built; 40
> This is the man that lives in the house that I built;

but they did not know that the third line was, —

> These are the folks that worry the man
> That lives in the house that I built.

I did not fear the hen-harriers, for I kept no chickens; but I feared the men-harriers rather. 41

I had more cheering visitors than the last. Children 42 come a-berrying, railroad men taking a Sunday morning walk in clean shirts, fishermen and hunters, poets and 43 philosophers, in short, all honest pilgrims, who came out to the woods for freedom's sake, and really left the village behind, I was ready to greet with, — " Welcome, Englishmen! welcome, Englishmen!" for I had had communication with that race.

ENGLISH.

40 *This is the house*. Thoreau's own parody of the Mother Goose rhyme, "This Is the House That Jack Built."

41 *the men-harriers*. These were the professional slave hunters who were looking for fugitive slaves from the Southern states.

42 *I had more cheering visitors*. Ms. 723 then has "of whom I shall speak in another place."

43 *fishermen and hunters*. Ms. 724: "—all in short who really got to the woods & left the world behind them were welcomed."

At the end of this chapter Sanborn printed several passages in the Bibliophile Edition (I, 206n.–208n.), which he thought would be of interest:

"Among the many visitors to Thoreau in his pine wood, he counted also some of the birds, and thus expressed himself about them: . . . "In due time in the spring I heard the martins twittering over my clearing, though it had not appeared that the town contained so many that it could afford any to me. I fancied they were rather of the ancient stock that dwelt in Walden trees before the white man came, than the modern village race that live in boxes. Let a man live in any part of the globe and he will hear the same simple spring sounds to cheer him along the while; and the Orinoco and the Missippi birds of the same genus migrate everywhere. The Romans greeted the swallow. Everywhere the frog and the turtle greet the season. The Temperate and Frigid salute the Torrid zone again; and birds fly, and plants and winds blow to correct this oscillation of the poles and preserve the equilibrium of Nature.

"Circumstances and employment affect but slowly the finer qualities of our nature. I observed in some of these men an inextinguishable and ineradicable refinement and delicacy of nature (older and of more worth than the sun and moon) which are commonly thought to adorn the drawing-rooms only. Sometimes I fancied a genuine magnanimity–more than Greek or Roman—equal to the least occasion of unexplored and uncontaminated descent. Greater traits methought I noticed in the shortest intercourse than are recorded of any of the worthies, Epaminondas, Socrates or Cato. They had faces homely, hard and seamed like the rocks, but human and wise, embracing Copt and Mussulman, all races and nations, A Pacha or Sultan—Selim—Mustapha or Mahmoud in disguise.

"There is no more real rudeness in laborers or washerwomen than in gentlemen and ladies. Under some of the ancient and wrinkled, almost forlorn visages, as of an Indian chieftain, slumber the world-famous humanities of man. There is the race, and you need look no further. You can tell a nobleman's head among a thousand—though he may be shovelling gravel six rods off in the midst of a gang, with a cotton handkerchief tied about it. Such a one as is to succeed the worthies of history. Their humble occupation and that they take no airs upon themselves, are no disadvantage. Civilization makes bright only the superficial film of the eye. Most men are wrecked upon their consciences."

THE BEAN-FIELD.

MEANWHILE my beans, the length of whose rows, added together, was seven miles already planted, were impatient to be hoed, for the earliest had grown considerably before the latest were in the ground; indeed they were not easily to be put off. What was the meaning of this so steady and self-respecting, this small Herculean labor, I knew not. I came to love my rows, my beans, though so many more than I wanted. They attached me to the earth, and so I got strength like Antæus. **1** But why should I raise them? Only Heaven knows. This was my curious labor all summer, — to make this portion of the earth's surface, which had yielded only cinquefoil, blackberries, johnswort, and the like, before, sweet wild fruits and pleasant flowers, produce instead this pulse. What shall I learn of beans **2** or beans of me? I cherish them, I hoe them, early and late I have an eye to them; and this is my day's work. It is a fine broad leaf to look on. My auxiliaries are the dews and rains which water this dry soil, and what fertility is in the soil itself, which for the most part is lean and effete. My enemies are worms, cool days, and most of all woodchucks. The last have nibbled for me a quarter of an acre clean. But what right had I to **3** oust johnswort and the rest, and break up their ancient herb garden? Soon, however, the remaining beans will be too tough for them, and go forward to meet new foes.

When I was four years old, as I well remember, **4** I was brought from Boston to this my native town, **5** through these very woods and this field, to the pond. It is one of the oldest scenes stamped on my memory. **6**

285

Thoreau, as will be seen, was not a good farmer. Hoeing beans in the hot sun is back-breaking, monotonous labor which soon bored him. He admits that he did not get all the weeds out and left many beans for the woodchucks. In *A Week* he explains how he felt about farming:

"My genius dates from an older era than the agricultural. . . . There is in my nature, methinks, a singular yearning toward all wildness. . . . What have I to do with plows? I cut another furrow than you see."

1 *I got strength like Antæus.* Antæus, child of Mother Earth, could renew his strength by contact with the soil. Hercules conquered him by holding him aloft and killing him before he could touch the earth again.

2 *What shall I learn of beans or beans of me?* "What's Hecuba to him, or he to Hecuba?" *Hamlet*, II, ii.

3 *a quarter of an acre.* This was "an eighth of an acre" in the *Journal* for July 7, 1845; I, 364. Since this is only two days after Thoreau came to Walden Pond, the beans had obviously been planted early in the spring.

4 *When I was four years old.* There seems to have been some doubt in Thoreau's mind about this, for the *Journal* for August 1845; I, 380, says: "Twenty-three years since, when I was five years old." But ms. 935 says four.

5 *I was brought from Boston.* Ms. 453: "to this recess among the pines, where sunshine and shadow were about the only inhabitants that varied the scene, over the tumultuous and varied city, as if here were my proper nursery."

And now to-night my flute has waked the echoes over **7** that very water.   The pines still stand here older than I ; or, if some have fallen, I have cooked my supper with their stumps, and a new growth is rising all around, preparing another aspect for new infant eyes.   Almost the same johnswort springs from the same perennial root in this pasture, and even I have at length helped to clothe that fabulous landscape of my infant dreams, and one of the results of my presence and influence is seen in these bean leaves, corn blades, and potato vines.

I planted about two acres and a half of upland ; and as it was only about fifteen years since the land was cleared, and I myself had got out two or three cords of stumps, I did not give it any manure ; but in the **8** course of the summer it appeared by the arrow-heads which I turned up in hoeing, that an extinct nation had **9** anciently dwelt here and planted corn and beans ere white men came to clear the land, and so, to some extent, had exhausted the soil for this very crop.

Before yet any woodchuck or squirrel had run across the road, or the sun had got above the shrub-oaks, while all the dew was on, though the farmers warned me against it, — I would advise you to do all your work if possible while the dew is on, — I began to level the ranks of haughty weeds in my bean-field and throw dust upon their heads.   Early in the morning I worked barefooted, dabbling like a plastic artist in the **10** dewy and crumbling sand, but later in the day the sun blistered my feet.   There the sun lighted me to hoe beans, pacing slowly backward and forward over that yellow gravelly upland, between the long green rows, fifteen rods, the one end terminating in a shrub oak copse where I could rest in the shade, the other in a blackberry field where the green berries deepened their tints by the time I had made another bout.   Removing the weeds, putting fresh soil about the bean stems, and encouraging this weed which I had sown, making the yellow soil express its summer thought in bean leaves and blossoms rather than in wormwood and piper and millet grass, making the earth say beans instead of grass, — this was my daily work.   As I had little aid from horses or cattle, or hired men or boys, or improved implements of husbandry, I was much slower, and became much more intimate with my beans than usual.   But labor of the hands, even when pursued to the verge of drudgery, is perhaps never the worst form of idleness. It has a constant and imperishable moral, and to the scholar it yields a classic result.   A very *agricola labo-* **11**

6 *one of the oldest scenes.* Ms. 453 has "one of the most ancient scenes stamped on the tablets of my memory." This is then followed by: "and that woodland vision for a long time occupied my dreams."

7 *my flute.* This rather primitive flute is now in the possession of the Concord Antiquarian Society.

8 *I did not give it any manure.* Ms. 454: "However, as it had lain fallow so long I got a good crop."

9 *an extinct nation.* Ms. 454: "an extinct tribe." Thoreau had fabulous luck in finding Indian relics. His collection of them is now in the Fruitlands Museum, Harvard, Massachusetts.

10 *I worked barefooted.* Yes, Thoreau sometimes went barefoot, as this instance shows.

11 agricola laboriosus. A hard-working farmer.

riosus was I to travellers bound westward through Lincoln and Wayland to nobody knows where; they sitting at their ease in gigs, with elbows on knees, and reins loosely hanging in festoons; I the home-staying, laborious native of the soil. But soon my homestead was out of their sight and thought. It was the only open and cultivated field for a great distance on either side of the road; so they made the most of it; and sometimes the man in the field heard more of travellers' gossip and comment than was meant for his ear: " Beans so late! peas so late! " — for I continued to plant when others had began to hoe, — the ministerial husbandman had not suspected it. " Corn, my boy, for fodder; corn **12**

12 *"Corn . . . for fodder."* On ms. 260 this has an exclamation point. And is followed by: "By the way I have heard it said that clergymen are as a class the best gardeners in N.E. [New England], better gardeners than shepherds."

The road that goes past the site of the bean-field

for fodder." "Does he *live* there?" asks the black bonnet of the gray coat; and the hard-featured farmer reins up his grateful dobbin to inquire what you are doing where he sees no manure in the furrow, and recommends a little chip dirt, or any little waste stuff, or it may be ashes or plaster. But here were two acres and a half of furrows, and only a hoe for cart and two hands to draw it, — there being an aversion to other carts and horses, — and chip dirt far away. Fellow-travellers as they rattled by compared it aloud with the fields which they had passed, so that I came to know how I stood in the agricultural world. This was one field not in Mr. Coleman's report. And, by the way, who estimates the value of the crop which Nature yields in the still wilder fields unimproved by man? The crop of *English* hay is carefully weighed, the moisture calculated, the silicates and the potash; but in all dells and pond holes in the woods and pastures and swamps grows a rich and various crop only unreaped by man. Mine was, as it were, the connecting link between wild and cultivated fields; as some states are civilized, and others half-civilized, and others savage or barbarous, so my field was, though not in a bad sense, a half-cultivated field. They were beans cheerfully returning to their wild and primitive state that I cultivated, and my hoe played the *Rans des Vaches* for them. **14**

Near at hand, upon the topmost spray of a birch, sings the brown-thrasher — or red mavis, as some love to

13

13 *Mr. Coleman's report.* Henry Colman had published four surveys on the state of agriculture in Massachusetts a few years before this.

14 Rans des Vaches. More commonly Ranz-des-Vaches, a Swiss pastoral song for calling the cows home.

JUNE.

call him — all the morning, glad of your society, that would find out another farmer's field if yours were not here. While you are planting the seed, he cries, — "Drop it, drop it, — cover it up, cover it up, — pull it up, pull it up, pull it up." But this was not corn, and so it was safe from such enemies as he. You may wonder what his rigmarole, his amateur Paganini performances **15** on one string or on twenty, have to do with your planting, and yet prefer it to leached ashes or plaster. It was a cheap sort of top dressing in which I had entire faith. **16**

As I drew a still fresher soil about the rows with my hoe, I disturbed the ashes of unchronicled nations who in primeval years lived under these heavens, and their small implements of war and hunting were brought to the light of this modern day. They lay mingled with other natural stones, some of which bore the marks of having been burned by Indian fires, and some by the sun, and also bits of pottery and glass brought hither by the recent cultivators of the soil. When my hoe tinkled against the stones, that music echoed to the woods and the sky, and was an accompaniment to my labor which yielded an instant and immeasurable crop. It was no longer beans that I hoed, nor I that hoed beans; and I remembered with as much pity as pride, if I remembered at all, my acquaintances who had gone to the city to attend the oratorios. The night-hawk circled overhead in the sunny afternoons — for I sometimes made a day of it — like a mote in the eye, or in heaven's eye, falling from time to time with a swoop and a sound as if the heavens were rent, torn at last to very rags and tatters, and yet a seamless cope remained; small imps that fill the air and lay their eggs on the ground on bare sand or rocks on the tops of hills, where few have found them; graceful and slender like ripples caught up from the pond, as leaves are raised by the wind to float in the heavens; such kindredship is in Nature. The hawk is aerial brother of the wave which he sails over and surveys, those his perfect air-inflated wings answering to the elemental unfledged pinions of the sea. Or sometimes I watched a pair of hen-hawks circling high in the sky, alternately soaring and descending, approaching and leaving one another, as if they were the imbodiment of my own thoughts. Or I was attracted by the passage of wild pigeons from this wood to that, with a slight quivering winnowing sound and

15 *Paganini.* Nicolò Paganini (1782–1840), the world-famous Italian violinist and composer, who toured Europe with great acclaim.

16 *in which I had entire faith.* Ms. 259: "and I am not sure that the beans didn't grow up the better for it."

carrier haste; or from under a rotten stump my hoe turned up a sluggish portentous and outlandish spotted salamander, a trace of Egypt and the Nile, yet our contemporary. When I paused to lean on my hoe, these sounds and sights I heard and saw any where in the row, a part of the inexhaustible entertainment which the country offers.

On gala days the town fires its great guns, which **17** echo like popguns to these woods, and some waifs of martial music occasionally penetrate thus far. To me, away there in my bean-field at the other end of the town, the big guns sounded as if a puff ball had burst; and when there was a military turnout of which I was ignorant, I have sometimes had a vague sense all the day of some sort of itching and disease in the horizon, as if some eruption would break out there soon, either scarlatina or canker-rash, until at length some more favorable puff of wind, making haste over the fields and up the Wayland road, brought me information of the "trainers." It seemed by the distant hum as if some- **18** body's bees had swarmed, and that the neighbors, according to Virgil's advice, by a faint *tintinnabulum* **19** upon the most sonorous of their domestic utensils, were endeavoring to call them down into the hive again. And when the sound died quite away, and the hum had ceased, and the most favorable breezes told no tale, I knew that they had got the last drone of them all safely into the Middlesex hive, and that now their minds were bent on the honey with which it was smeared.

I felt proud to know that the liberties of Massachusetts and of our fatherland were in such safe keeping; and as I turned to my hoeing again I was filled with an inexpressible confidence, and pursued my labor cheerfully with a calm trust in the future.

When there were several bands of musicians, it sounded as if all the village was a vast bellows, and all the buildings expanded and collapsed alternately with a din. But sometimes it was a really noble and inspiring strain that reached these woods, and the **20** trumpet that sings of fame, and I felt as if I could spit a Mexican with a good relish, — for why should we **21** always stand for trifles? — and looked round for a woodchuck or a skunk to exercise my chivalry upon. These

17 *On gala days.* Sanborn (Bibliophile Edition II, 7) has an explanatory footnote for this: "The gala days of Concord were the 19th of April (anniversary of the Concord fight of 1775) and the 4th of July (anniversary of the Declaration of Independence). During Thoreau's residence at Walden the pro-slavery war with Mexico was going on, and it is occasionally mentioned by him. . . . The fact that the country was at war brought out the martial spirit of the Concord farmers and mechanics, especially on the Democratic side,—for Concord was quite equally divided in those days between Democrats and Whigs, with a fair sprinkling of voting abolitionists. There were two volunteer militia companies in the town, and several colonels and captains."

18 *"trainers."* Uniformed men in the state militia.

19 tintinnabulum. This word, meaning "a small tinkling bell" (NED) or the ringing of it, goes back to 1398. Harding (1963, page 292) says that the word is not in the concordance to Virgil's works. Poe used the similar word "tintinabulation" in his poem, "The Bells."

20 *the trumpet that sings of fame.* Another reference to Mrs. Hemans' poem, "The Landing of the Pilgrims."

21 *spit a Mexican.* A satirical reference to the war with Mexico which was then going on.

martial strains seemed as far away as Palestine, and reminded me of a march of crusaders in the horizon, with a slight tantivy and tremulous motion of the elm-tree tops which overhang the village.   This was one of the *great* days; though the sky had from my clearing only the same everlastingly great look that it wears daily, and I saw no difference in it.

It was a singular experience that long acquaintance which I cultivated with beans, what with planting, and hoeing, and harvesting, and threshing, and picking over, and selling them, — the last was the hardest of all, — I might add eating, for I did taste. I was determined to know beans. When they were growing, I used to hoe from five o'clock in the morning till noon, and commonly spent the rest of the day about other affairs.   Consider the intimate and curious acquaintance one makes with various kinds of weeds, — it will bear some iteration in the account, for there was no little iteration in the labor, — disturbing their delicate organizations so ruthlessly, and making such invidious distinctions with his hoe, levelling whole ranks of one **22** species, and sedulously cultivating another.   That's

22 *levelling whole ranks.* This is Thoreau's war on weeds.

The bean-field as it looks now

Roman wormwood, — that's pigweed, — that's sorrel, — that's piper-grass, — have at him, chop him up, turn his roots upward to the sun, don't let him have a fibre in the shade, if you do he'll turn himself t'other side up and be as green as a leek in two days. A long war, not with cranes, but with weeds, those Trojans who had sun and rain and dews on their side. Daily the beans saw me come to their rescue armed with a hoe, and thin the ranks of their enemies, filling up the trenches with weedy dead. Many a lusty crest-waving Hector, **23** that towered a whole foot above his crowding comrades, fell before my weapon and rolled in the dust.

Those summer days which some of my contemporaries devoted to the fine arts in Boston or Rome, and others to contemplation in India, and others to trade in London or New York, I thus, with the other farmers of New England, devoted to husbandry. Not that I **24** wanted beans to eat, for I am by nature a Pythagorean, so far as beans are concerned, whether they mean porridge or voting, and exchanged them for rice; but, **25** perchance, as some must work in fields if only for the sake of tropes and expression, to serve a parable-maker **26** one day. It was on the whole a rare amusement, which, continued too long, might have become a dissipation. Though I gave them no manure, and did not hoe them all once, I hoed them unusually well as far as I went, and was paid for it in the end, "there being in truth," as Evelyn says, "no compost or lætation what-**27** soever comparable to this continual motion, repastination, and turning of the mould with the spade." "The earth," he adds elsewhere, "especially if fresh, has a certain magnetism in it, by which it attracts the salt, power, or virtue (call it either) which gives it life, and is the logic of all the labor and stir we keep about it, to sustain us; all dungings and other sordid temperings being but the vicars succedaneous to this improvement." Moreover, this being one of those "worn-out and exhausted lay fields which enjoy their sabbath," had perchance, as Sir Kenelm Digby thinks likely, attracted **28** "vital spirits" from the air. I harvested twelve bushels of beans.

But to be more particular, for it is complained that Mr. Coleman has reported chiefly the expensive experiments of gentlemen farmers, my outgoes were, —

23 *Many a lusty crest-waving Hector.* Hector was slain by Achilles on the plain below Troy in a particularly bloody hand-to-hand battle recounted in the *Iliad*.

24 *Pythagorean.* The Greek philosopher Pythagoras (ca. 530 B.C.) would not permit his followers to eat beans.

25 *or voting.* Beans were used as counting pieces in elections in ancient times.

26 *tropes.* Literary devices which permit a writer to use words in ways that go beyond their literal meanings. Thoreau was a master at this, and *Walden* has many examples of metaphor, metonymy, synecdoche, and irony.

27 *Evelyn.* John Evelyn (1620–1706), the diarist and author. He prided himself on his supposed knowledge of gardening, but if he believed such nonsense as is here quoted, he had only to look at the weeds springing up around a manure pile to see that the earth needs more than continual chopping up.

28 *Sir Kenelm Digby* (1603–1665), naval commander, diplomat, and author. Channing wrote in his copy of *Walden:* "No, it is not an easy matter (according to Sir K.D.) this getting your 'astral spirit,' and setting it in action when the thing itself is well burnt to ashes." In the Thoreau Society *Bulletin* for Fall 1967, T. L. Pebworth points out that only the term "vital spirits" is from Digby; the rest is from Evelyn.

For a hoe, ...	$0 54	
Ploughing, harrowing, and furrowing, . . .	7 50,	Too much.
Beans for seed, ...	3 12½	
Potatoes "	1 33	
Peas "	0 40	
Turnip seed, ...	0 06	
White line for crow fence, ...	0 02	
Horse cultivator and boy three hours, . . .	1 00	
Horse and cart to get crop, ...	0 75	
In all, ...	$14 72½	

My income was, (patrem familias vendacem, non **29** emacem esse oportet,) from

Nine bushels and twelve quarts of beans sold, .	.	$16 94
Five " large potatoes, ...	.	2 50
Nine " small, ...	.	2 25
Grass, ...	.	1 00
Stalks, ...	.	0 75
In all, ...		$23 44

Leaving a pecuniary profit, as I have elsewhere said, of $8 71¼.   **30**

This is the result of my experience in raising beans. Plant the common small white bush bean about the first of June, in rows three feet by eighteen inches apart, being careful to select fresh round and unmixed seed. First look out for worms, and supply vacancies by planting anew. Then look out for woodchucks, if it is an exposed place, for they will nibble off the earliest tender leaves almost clean as they go; and again, when the young tendrils make their appearance, they have notice of it, and will shear them off with both buds and young pods, sitting erect like a squirrel. But above all harvest as early as possible, if you would escape frosts and have a fair and salable crop; you may save much loss by this means.

This further experience also I gained. I said to myself, I will not plant beans and corn with so much **31** industry another summer, but such seeds, if the seed is not lost, as sincerity, truth, simplicity, faith, innocence, and the like, and see if they will not grow in this soil, even with less toil and manurance, and sustain me, for surely it has not been exhausted for these crops. Alas! I said this to myself; but now another summer is gone, and another, and another, and I am obliged to say to you, Reader, that the seeds which I planted, if indeed they *were* the seeds of those virtues, were wormeaten or had lost their vitality, and so did not come up. Commonly men will only be brave as their fathers were

29 *patrem familias vendacem, non emacem esse oportet.* "The head of the family should be the one who sells, not the one who buys," Cato, *De Agri Cultura.*

30 *as I have elsewhere said.* On page 60. On ms. 117 this is: "Net profit, not counting my labor $8.71½."

31 *I will not plant beans . . . another summer.* Taken from the *Journal* for August 15, 1845; I, 382. This early date shows that Thoreau had decided to quit bean farming even before his full crop was due.

brave, or timid. This generation is very sure to plant corn and beans each new year precisely as the Indians did centuries ago and taught the first settlers to do, as if there were a fate in it. I saw an old man the other day, to my astonishment, making the holes with a hoe for the seventieth time at least, and not for himself to lie down in! But why should not the New Englander try new adventures, and not lay so much stress on his grain, his potato and grass crop, and his orchards, — raise other crops than these? Why concern ourselves so much about our beans for seed, and not be concerned at all about a new generation of men? We should really be fed and cheered if when we met a man we were sure to see that some of the qualities which I have named, which we all prize more than those other productions, but which are for the most part broadcast and floating in the air, had taken root and grown in him. Here comes such a subtle and ineffable quality, for instance, as truth or justice, though the slightest amount or new variety of it, along the road. Our ambassadors should be instructed to send home such seeds as these, and Congress help to distribute them over all the land. **32** We should never stand upon ceremony with sincerity. We should never cheat and insult and banish one another by our meanness, if there were present the kernel of worth and friendliness. We should not meet thus in haste. Most men I do not meet at all, for they seem not to have time; they are busy about their beans. We would not deal with a man thus plodding ever, leaning on a hoe or a spade as a staff between his work, not as a mushroom, but partially risen out of the earth, something more than erect, like swallows alighted and walking on the ground: —

> "And as he spake, his wings would now and then   **33**
> Spread, as he meant to fly, then close again,"

so that we should suspect that we might be conversing with an angel. Bread may not always nourish us; but it always does us good, it even takes stiffness out of our joints, and makes us supple and buoyant, when we knew not what ailed us, to recognize any generosity in man or Nature, to share any unmixed and heroic joy.

Ancient poetry and mythology suggest, at least, that husbandry was once a sacred art; but it is pursued with irreverent haste and heedlessness by us, our object being to have large farms and large crops merely. We have **34**

32 *Congress.* Well into the twentieth century, congressmen sent free seeds to their constituents when requested.

33 *"And as he spake."* The verse is from *The Shepheard's Oracles* by Francis Quarles (1592–1644). The two lines were set as prose and run into the text, but Thoreau corrected the error on the page proofs.

34 *large crops merely.* The Bibliophile Edition (II, 14 f.) prints this long passage here:

"I would that my readers' thoughts on this subject should for once be as deliberate and slow as the pace of oxen, and as obedient to their divine instincts. The difference between the ancients, whoever they were, and ourselves may be seen in their different treatment of their fellow-laborer, the ox. We are accustomed to say that the ox is more profitable than the horse, because it not only costs less to keep it, but when it is past labor we can slaughter it, and it will furnish food for our families. We treat it as a slave rather than as a servant, and when it is worn out in our service, we slaughter the companion of our labors without a tear or any sign of gratitude.

"If other nations, as the Egyptians, have been idolaters in this respect, and made these animals objects of adoration, we have gone to the other— and an equally fatal—extreme, for every animal should be approached with a sentiment of reverence for its nature. I was pained to learn lately from a good authority that at Brighton, as it was found not to cause any serious diminution in the weight of their solid parts, cattle are starved for days before they are slaughtered, to save the expense of fodder. 'According to the early laws of Greece,' says a modern writer, 'the ploughing ox was held sacred, and was entitled when past service to range the pastures in freedom and repose. It was forbidden, by the decrees of Triptolemus, to put to death this faithful ally of the labors of the husbandman, who shared the toils of ploughing and threshing.

" 'Whenever therefore an ox was slaughtered, he must first be consecrated or devoted as a sacrifice (ἱερείου) by the sprinkling of the sacrificial barley; this was a precaution against the barbarous practice of eating raw flesh (βουφαγία). A peculiar sacrifice at Athens, at which the slayer of the ox fled, and the guilty axe was thrown into the sea, on the sentence of the Prytanes, yearly placed before the people a visible type of the first beginnings of their social institutions.'

"Ancient writers on agriculture speak of such things as the 'dignity of the herd.' Varro suggests that the object of the Argonautic expedition was a new species of sheep of finer wool than usual. The golden apples of the Hesperides

no festival, nor procession, nor ceremony, not excepting our Cattle-shows and so called Thanksgivings, by which the farmer expresses a sense of the sacredness of his calling, or is reminded of its sacred origin. It is the premium and the feast which tempt him. He sacrifices not to Ceres and the Terrestrial Jove, but to the infernal Plutus rather. By avarice and selfishness, and a grovelling habit, from which none of us is free, of regarding the soil as property, or the means of acquiring property chiefly, the landscape is deformed, husbandry is degraded with us, and the farmer leads the meanest of lives. He knows Nature but as a robber. Cato says that the profits of agriculture are particularly pious or just, (*maximeque pius quæstus,*) and according to Varro the old Romans " called the same earth Mother and Ceres, and thought that they who cultivated it led a pious and useful life, and that they alone were left of the race of King Saturn." **35, 36 37 38 39 40**

We are wont to forget that the sun looks on our cultivated fields and on the prairies and forests without distinction. They all reflect and absorb his rays alike, and the former make but a small part of the glorious picture which he beholds in his daily course. In his view the earth is all equally cultivated like a garden. Therefore we should receive the benefit of his light and heat with a corresponding trust and magnanimity. What though I value the seed of these beans, and harvest that in the fall of the year? This broad field which I have looked at so long looks not to me as the principal cultivator, but away from me to influences more genial to it, which water and make it green. These beans have results which are not harvested by me. Do they not grow for woodchucks partly? The ear of wheat, (in Latin *spica*, obsoletely *speca*, from *spe*, hope,) should not

were by the ambiguity of language goats and sheep which Hercules imported."

And then, at the end of this, mss. 249 and 250 have: "The stars and constellations bear the names of domestic animals. The Aegean Sea has its name from the goat."

35 *Ceres.* The ancient corn-goddess, also called Demeter.

36 *Jove.* Also called Jupiter (both roman names for Zeus). The greatest of the mythological gods, ruler of heaven and earth.

37 *infernal Plutus.* Pluto was the god who ruled Hades. Since he was known as The Rich One, he has some connection with Plutus, the god of wealth. Thoreau was a good classical scholar who doubtless knew all about the two mythological creatures. Here he is referring to Plutus and calls him "infernal" because he is speaking about property and the evils associated with the greed for it.

38 (maximeque pius quæstus). This is from the introduction to Cato's *De Agri Cultura.*

39 *Varro.* Marcus Terentius Varro (116-27 B.C.), Roman author, friend of Cæsar and Pompey. The quotation here is from his *Rerum Rusticarum,* III, 1, 5.

Jupiter

be the only hope of the husbandman; its kernel or grain (*granum*, from *gerendo*, bearing,) is not all that it bears. How, then, can our harvest fail? Shall I not rejoice also at the abundance of the weeds whose seeds are the granary of the birds? It matters little comparatively whether the fields fill the farmer's barns. The true husbandman will cease from anxiety, as the squirrels manifest no concern whether the woods will bear chestnuts this year or not, and finish his labor with every day, relinquishing all claim to the produce of his fields, and sacrificing in his mind not only his first but his last fruits also.   **41**

40 *Saturn* taught mankind how to grow crops.

41 *his last fruits also.* Ms. 428 adds: "The landscape is deformed when there is an attempt to approximate what cannot be approximated." *Journal*, March 26, 1846; I, 401. See also the *Journal* for January 29, 1854; VI, 82.

JULY.

THE VILLAGE.

AFTER hoeing, or perhaps reading and writing, in the forenoon, I usually bathed again in the pond, swimming across one of its coves for a stint, and washed the dust of labor from my person, or smoothed out the last wrinkle which study had made, and for the afternoon was absolutely free. Every day or two I strolled to the village to hear some of the gossip which is incessantly going on there, circulating either from mouth to mouth, or from newspaper to newspaper, and which, taken in homœopathic doses, was really as refreshing in its way as the rustle of leaves and the peeping of frogs. As I walked in the woods to see the birds and squirrels, so I walked in the village to see the men and boys; instead of the wind among the pines I heard the carts rattle. **1** In one direction from my house there was a colony of muskrats in the river meadows; under the grove of elms and buttonwoods in the other horizon was a village of busy men, as curious to me as if they had been prairie dogs, each sitting at the mouth of its burrow, or running over to a neighbor's to gossip. I went there frequently to observe their habits. The village appeared to me a great news room; and on one side, to support it, as once at Redding & Company's on State Street, they kept nuts and raisins, or salt and meal and other groceries. Some have such a vast appetite for the former commodity, that is, the news, and such sound digestive organs, that they can sit forever in public avenues without stirring, and let it simmer and whisper through them like the Etesian winds, or as if inhaling **2, 3** ether, it only producing numbness and insensibility to

Concord at this time had a population of 2,249. The general layout of the town was very much the same as it is now except that many structures of those days are gone, the Milldam, and the jail near it among them. Yet the Square was and still is the center of activity, and the streets become roads to Lexington, Lincoln, Sudbury, Maynard, the Actons, Carlisle, and Bedford. Boston dominated all these towns, as it has from the beginning of the settlements. Everyone in Concord knew everyone else, if not well, at least by name and reputation. Anyone entering the town was immediately sized up and assigned to a rank in the local hierarchy as a stranger, a person from one of the nearby farms, or as a fellow villager. Thoreau describes his home town well. The stores, the costumes, and the vehicles would seem period pieces to us now, but the houses would not. Their exteriors remain largely unchanged, and inside, much of the original furniture is still in use.

1 *I heard the carts rattle.* The Bibliophile Edition (II, 18–19) then has:

"How often in years gone by have I seen a country man come into town a-shopping, in a high-set wagon, whose clothes looked as if they were made before the last war by a maiden sister, —no reproach to her! His coat hung so high that you could see the whole of his waistcoat pockets beneath it; while the scant coat-tail hastened to a speedy conclusion, like a frog couchant on a bank; the funnel-shaped sleeves halting at a respectful distance from his victorious palms, and the collar, hard-rolled and round like a boa-constrictor, prompting you to run to his rescue,—or as if crisped by an agony of heat. His waistcoat striped like the zebra's skin,—a kind of coarse grating or gridiron over the furnace of his heart; his "pants" straight and round like

pain, — otherwise it would often be painful to hear, — without affecting the consciousness. I hardly ever failed, when I rambled through the village, to see a row of such worthies, either sitting on a ladder sunning themselves, with their bodies inclined forward and their eyes glancing along the line this way and that, from time to time, with a voluptuous expression, or else leaning against a barn with their hands in their pockets, like caryatides, as if to prop it up. They, being commonly out of doors, heard whatever was in the wind. These are the coarsest mills, in which all gossip is first rudely digested or cracked up before it is emptied into finer and more delicate hoppers within doors. I observed that the vitals of the village were the grocery, the bar-room, the post-office, and the bank; and, as a necessary part of the machinery, they kept a bell, a big gun, and a fire-engine, at convenient places; and the houses were so arranged as to make the most of mankind, in lanes and fronting one another, so that every traveller had to run the gantlet, and every man, woman, and child might get a lick at him. Of course, those who were stationed nearest to the head of the line, where they could most see and be seen, and have the first blow at him, paid the highest prices for their places: and the few straggling inhabitants in the outskirts, where long gaps in the line began to occur, and the traveller could get over walls or turn aside into cow paths, and so escape, paid a very slight ground or window tax. Signs were hung out on all sides to allure him; some to catch him by the appetite, as the tavern and victualling cellar; some by the fancy, as the dry goods store and the jeweller's; and others by the hair or the feet or the skirts, as the barber, the shoemaker, or the tailor. Besides, there was a still more terrible standing invitation to call at every one of these houses, and company expected about these times. For the most part I escaped wonderfully from these dangers, either by proceeding at once boldly and without deliberation to the goal, as is recommended to those who run the gantlet, or by keeping my thoughts on high things, like Orpheus, who, "loudly singing the praises of the gods to his lyre, drowned the voices of the Sirens, and kept out of danger." Sometimes I bolted suddenly, and nobody could tell my whereabouts, for I did not stand much about gracefulness, and never hesitated at a gap in a fence. I was even accustomed

4

5

6

a stove-pipe, into which his boots fitted smoke tight, at a height which preserved them "guiltless of his country's mud;" and his narrow-brimmed hat towering straight and round, like a column, to meet the sun in his rising,—of equal diameter throughout,—the torso of a shaft, or maybe a cenotaph to his brains,—with a nap as soft as a pussy, across which the dimpling shadows fly, as over a field of grain in autumn.

"I do not wonder that men read history; for I am as nearly related to the men of history as to any contemporary. Farthest India is nearer to me than Concord or Lexington.

"Toward most of my neighbors I am compelled to feel (like the Chinese philosopher), 'I am I and you are you; I am glad we can be so distinct.' "

Sanborn appended a footnote to this:

"Evidently Thoreau had carefully studied the appearance of his fellow-beings as they passed before his vision while he sat by his study-window or paced the streets of his village with long strides, as I have often seen him doing. This picture of the awkward country man from Carlisle or Boxborough is as exact as possible. The 'last war' was the war with England, 1812–13."

2 *Etesian winds.* Webster: "Winds in the Mediterranean region, esp. summer winds from the north in the Aegean Sea and the Levant." Not ordinarily capitalized.

3 *inhaling ether.* Ether was then being used in early experiments in anaesthesia.

4 *like caryatides.* Statues of draped female figures used in the place of columns.

5 *window tax.* In some old New England buildings, windows that were bricked up to avoid paying this tax can still be seen.

6 *"loudly singing the praises of the gods."* Walter Harding (1963) identifies this as a translation from the *Argonautica* by Apollonius Rhodius, IV, 903.

A caryatid

Orpheus

to make an irruption into some houses, where I was well
entertained, and after learning the kernels and very last
sieve-ful of news, what had subsided, the prospects of
war and peace, and whether the world was likely to hold
together much longer, I was let out through the rear
avenues, and so escaped to the woods again.

It was very pleasant, when I staid late in town, to
launch myself into the night, especially if it was dark
and tempestuous, and set sail from some bright village
parlor or lecture room, with a bag of rye or Indian meal
upon my shoulder, for my snug harbor in the woods,
having made all tight without and withdrawn under
hatches with a merry crew of thoughts, leaving only my
outer man at the helm, or even tying up the helm when
it was plain sailing. I had many a genial thought by
the cabin fire "as I sailed." I was never cast away
nor distressed in any weather, though I encountered
some severe storms. It is darker in the woods, even in

7 *irruption.* Webster: "a breaking or bursting
in."

8 *many a genial thought.* Ms. 460 has: "many a
genial fireside thought."

common nights, than most suppose. I frequently had to look up at the opening between the trees above the path in order to learn my route, and, where there was no cart-path, to feel with my feet the faint track which I had worn, or steer by the known relation of particular trees which I felt with my hands, passing between two pines for instance, not more than eighteen inches apart, in the midst of the woods, invariably in the darkest night. **9** Sometimes, after coming home thus late in a dark and muggy night, when my feet felt the path which my eyes could not see, dreaming and absent-minded all the way, until I was aroused by having to raise my hand to lift the latch, I have not been able to recall a single step of my walk, and I have thought that perhaps my body would find its way home if its master should forsake it, as the hand finds its way to the mouth without assistance. Several times, when a visitor chanced to stay into **10** evening, and it proved a dark night, I was obliged to conduct him to the cart-path in the rear of the house, and then point out to him the direction he was to pursue, and in keeping which he was to be guided rather by his feet than his eyes. One very dark night I directed thus on their way two young men who had been fishing in the pond. They lived about a mile off through the woods, and were quite used to the route. A day or two after one of them told me that they wandered about the greater part of the night, close by their own premises, and did not get home till toward morning, by which time, as there had been several heavy showers in the mean while, and the leaves were very wet, they were drenched to their skins. I have heard of many going astray even in the village streets, when the darkness was so thick that you could cut it with a knife, as the saying is. Some who live in the outskirts, having come to town a-shopping in their wagons, have been obliged to put up for the night; and gentlemen and ladies making a call have gone half a mile out of their way, feeling the sidewalk only with their feet, and not knowing when they turned. It is a surprising and memorable, as well as valuable experience, to be lost in the woods any time. Often in a snow storm, even by day, one will come out upon a well-known road and yet find it impossible to tell which way leads to the village. Though he knows that he has travelled it a thousand times, he cannot recognize a feature in it, but it is as strange to him

9 *invariably in the darkest night.* Thoreau put a comma after "invariably" in his own copy of *Walden,* although there was none on ms. 306. There the sentence went on: "where nothing could be seen—but all things must be felt."

10 *Several times.* The long passage that follows was taken from the *Journal* for March 29, 1853; V, 62 ff., but a section about a lost doctor is omitted. This is how it appears after *not knowing when they turned* on ms. 944, which, of course, is the *Journal* entry rewritten: "Even one of the doctors was lost in the centre of the village, on one of his nocturnal missions, and spent nearly the whole night fumbling about and feeling the fences & houses, being on several accounts ashamed to arouse his neighbors to learn where he was. If one with the vision of an owl, or as in broad daylight could have watched his motions they would have appeared very ludicrous indeed."

as if it were a road in Siberia.   By night, of course, the
perplexity is infinitely greater.   In our most trivial
walks, we are constantly, though unconsciously, steering
like pilots by certain well-known beacons and head-
lands, and if we go beyond our usual course we still carry in our minds the bearing of some neighboring cape;
and not till we are completely lost, or turned round, —
for a man needs only to be turned round once with his
eyes shut in this world to be lost, — do we appreciate
the vastness and strangeness of Nature.   Every man
has to learn the points of compass again as often as
he awakes, whether from sleep or any abstraction.   Not
till we are lost, in other words, not till we have lost the
world, do we begin to find ourselves, and realize where
we are and the infinite extent of our relations. **11**

One afternoon, near the end of the first summer, **12**
when I went to the village to get a shoe from the cob-
bler's, I was seized and put into jail, because, as I have
elsewhere related, I did not pay a tax to, or recognize
the authority of, the state which buys and sells men,
women, and children, like cattle at the door of its senate-
house.   I had gone down to the woods for other purposes.   But, wherever a man goes, men will pursue and
paw him with their dirty institutions, and, if they can,
constrain him to belong to their desperate odd-fellow
society.   It is true, I might have resisted forcibly with
more or less effect, might have run " amok " against
society; but I preferred that society should run " amok "
against me, it being the desperate party.   However, I was
released the next day, obtained my mended shoe, and
returned to the woods in season to get my dinner of
huckleberries on Fair-Haven Hill.   I was never mo- **13**
lested by any person but those who represented the
state.   I had no lock nor bolt but for the desk which
held my papers, not even a nail to put over my latch or
windows.   I never fastened my door night or day,
though I was to be absent several days; not even when
the next fall I spent a fortnight in the woods of Maine.
And yet my house was more respected than if it had
been surrounded by a file of soldiers.   The tired rambler could rest and warm himself by my fire, the literary amuse himself with the few books on my table, or
the curious, by opening my closet door, see what was
left of my dinner, and what prospect I had of a supper.
Yet, though many people of every class came this way

11 *Siberia.* This was Tartary on ms. 945.

12 *One afternoon.* This (ms. 528) is the experience that led to the writing of "Civil Disobedience." The day is July 23 or 24, 1846. The
circumstances are related in detail in the Introduction to that essay and also by Thoreau himself
in the text of "Civil Disobedience."

13 *Fair-Haven Hill.* Sanborn says of this in the
Bibliophile Edition (II, 29n.): "This hill is better
known as The Cliffs, and was a favorite picnic
resort of the Emersons, Alcotts, and other Concord families, as well as of Thoreau. It is but
half a mile from Thoreau's Cove at Walden."

In the Bibliophile Edition (II, 29n.), Sanborn
put the following comment in a footnote at the
end of this chapter: "Except for his few years at
Walden, Thoreau was habitually a villager, living here and there in its straggling extent, and
utilizing all the village opportunities. He was
versed, also, in the village traditions of its odd inhabitants."

to the pond, I suffered no serious inconvenience from these sources, and I never missed any thing but one small book, a volume of Homer, which perhaps was improperly gilded, and this I trust a soldier of our camp has found by this time. I am convinced, that if all men were to live as simply as I then did, thieving and robbery would be unknown. These take place only in communities where some have got more than is sufficient while others have not enough. The Pope's Homers would soon get properly distributed. —

> " Nec bella fuerunt,
> Faginus astabat dum scyphus ante dapes."
> " Nor wars did men molest,
> When only beechen bowls were in request."

14

" You who govern public affairs, what need have you to employ punishments? Love virtue, and the people will be virtuous. The virtues of a superior man are like the wind; the virtues of a common man are like the grass; the grass, when the wind passes over it, bends."

15

14   *"Nec bella fuerunt."* From *The Elegies of Tibullus*, 3, 11, 7-8.

15   *"You who govern public affairs."* Cady (1961, page 28) says that this is another passage from *The Confucian Analects*, XII, 19.

Main Street, Concord, as it was in the middle of the nineteenth century *(Courtesy Concord Free Public Library)*

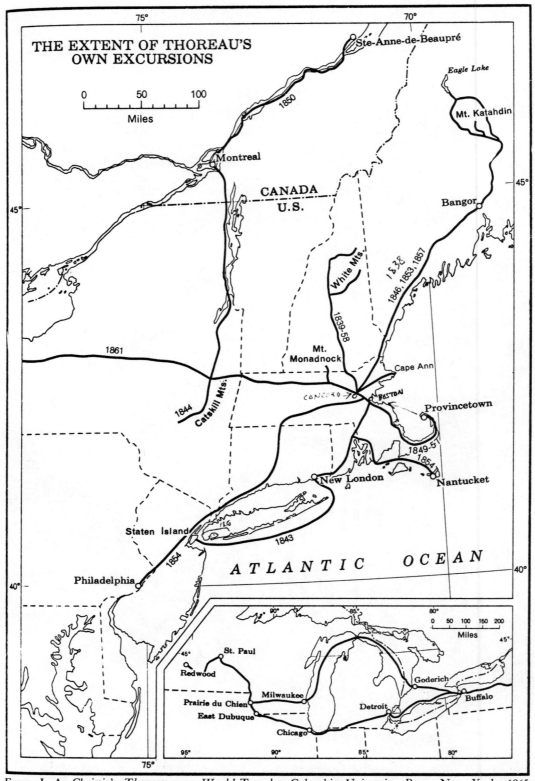

THE EXTENT OF THOREAU'S OWN EXCURSIONS

Ste-Anne-de-Beaupré

Eagle Lake

Mt. Katahdin

1850

Montreal

CANADA
U.S.

Bangor

White Mts.

1838

1846, 1853, 1857

1839-58

Mt.
Monadnock

Cape Ann

1861

CONCORD

BOSTON

Provincetown

1844

Catskill Mts.

1849-5

1854

New London

Nantucket

Staten Island

1843

1854

ATLANTIC OCEAN

Philadelphia

St. Paul

Redwood

Goderich

Milwaukee

Buffalo

Prairie du Chien

Detroit

East Dubuque

Chicago

From J. A. Christie's *Thoreau as a World Traveler*, Columbia University Press, New York, 1965. (*Reprinted with permission.*)

THE PONDS.

Sometimes, having had a surfeit of human society and gossip, and worn out all my village friends, I rambled still farther westward than I habitually dwell, into yet more unfrequented parts of the town, " to fresh **1** woods and pastures new," or, while the sun was setting, made my supper of huckleberries and blueberries on Fair Haven Hill, and laid up a store for several days. **2** The fruits do not yield their true flavor to the purchaser of them, nor to him who raises them for the market. There is but one way to obtain it, yet few take that way. If you would know the flavor of huckleberries, ask the cow-boy or the partridge. It is a vulgar error to suppose that you have tasted huckleberries who never **3, 4** plucked them. A huckleberry never reaches Boston; they have not been known there since they grew on her three hills. The ambrosial and essential part of the fruit is lost with the bloom which is rubbed off in the market cart, and they become mere provender. As long as Eternal Justice reigns, not one innocent huckleberry can be transported thither from the country's hills.

Occasionally, after my hoeing was done for the day, I joined some impatient companion who had been fishing on the pond since morning, as silent and motionless as a duck or a floating leaf, and, after practising various kinds of philosophy, had concluded commonly, by the time I arrived, that he belonged to the ancient sect of Cœnobites. There was one older man, an ex- **5** cellent fisher and skilled in all kinds of woodcraft, who was pleased to look upon my house as a building erected for the convenience of fishermen; and I was equally pleased when he sat in my doorway to arrange

Judging from the numerous extracts from the *Journal*, this chapter seems to have been written—or perhaps revised from earlier but no longer extant *Journal* entries—during the months of September, October, and November 1852. The opening section was originally part of the previous chapter, "The Village." Thoreau apparently made a number of trips to the various ponds during these months to gather more material for this chapter.

Charles Anderson (1965, page 222) says: "At the very heart of the book lies Walden Pond, the central circle image. All paths lead into this chapter, 'The Ponds,' all lines of meaning radiate from it. Here Thoreau found his ideal Self in that symbol of perfection which was the exact opposite of all those imperfections he had inveighed against in the life of society. The other ponds form a ring around Concord . . . the circle of his endless saunterings. At their center lies Walden, and at its center Thoreau glimpses the end of his quest."

1 *"to fresh woods and pastures new."* Channing identified this in his copy of *Walden* as coming from Milton's "Lycidas."

2 *Fair Haven Hill.* This is a good example of the printer's carelessness in those days. Page 186, line 17, which is only two pages back, has this as Fair-Haven Hill. It is printed both with and without the hyphen in later editions.

3 *huckleberries.* A manuscript by Thoreau on huckleberries is in the Berg Collection of the New York Public Library.

4 *who never plucked them.* Ms. 947 shows how Thoreau struggled with redundant words to get the final effect he wanted. This was followed by "from the bushes." He canceled this phrase and substituted "where they grow." Then he struck these words out and left the sentence as it is here,

his lines. Once in a while we sat together on the pond, he at one end of the boat, and I at the other; but not many words passed between us, for he had grown deaf in his later years, but he occasionally hummed a psalm, which harmonized well enough with my philosophy. Our intercourse was thus altogether one of unbroken harmony, far more pleasing to remember than if it had been carried on by speech. When, as was commonly the case, I had none to commune with, I used to raise the echoes by striking with a paddle on the side of my boat, filling the surrounding woods with circling and dilating sound, stirring them up as the keeper of a menagerie his wild beasts, until I elicited a growl from every wooded vale and hill-side.

In warm evenings I frequently sat in the boat playing the flute, and saw the perch, which I seemed to have charmed, hovering around me, and the moon travelling over the ribbed bottom, which was strewed with the wrecks of the forest. Formerly I had come to this pond adventurously, from time to time, in dark summer nights, with a companion, and making a fire close to the water's edge, which we thought attracted the fishes, we caught pouts with a bunch of worms strung on a thread; and when we had done, far in the night, threw the burning brands high into the air like skyrockets, which, coming down into the pond, were quenched with a loud

6
7
8

9

complete, and free from unnecessary qualifying clauses.

5 *Cœnobites*. Another Thoreau pun. The Cœnobites were people who lived in a religious group, but here the emphasis is not on meaning but on pronunciation: "See-no-bites."

6 *playing the flute*. As mentioned previously, this flute is now on display at the Concord Antiquarian Society. *Journal*, May 27, 1841; I, 260.

7 *seemed to have charmed*. The word is clearly written "seemed" on ms. 731, but some editions print it as "seem."

8 *with the wrecks of the forest*. The *Journal* for May 27, 1841; I, 260, then has: "and feel that nothing but the wildest imagination can conceive of the manner of life we are living. Nature is a wizard. The Concord nights are stranger than the Arabian nights."

9 *with a loud hissing*. Ms. 734 has "with a loud swizzling noise, and we would suddenly find ourselves groping in total darkness."

hissing, and we were suddenly groping in total darkness. Through this, whistling a tune, we took our way to the haunts of men again. But now I had made my home by the shore.

Sometimes, after staying in a village parlor till the family had all retired, I have returned to the woods, and, partly with a view to the next day's dinner, spent the hours of midnight fishing from a boat by moonlight, serenaded by owls and foxes, and hearing, from time to time, **10** the creaking note of some unknown bird close at hand. These experiences were very memorable and valuable to me, — anchored in forty feet of water, and twenty or thirty rods from the shore, surrounded sometimes by thousands of small perch and shiners, dimpling the surface with their tails in the moonlight, and communicating by a long flaxen line with mysterious nocturnal fishes which had their dwelling forty feet below, or sometimes dragging sixty feet of line about the pond as I drifted in the gentle night breeze, now and then feeling a slight vibration along it, indicative of some life prowling about its extremity, of dull uncertain blundering purpose there, and slow to make up its mind. At length you slowly raise, pulling hand over hand, some horned pout squeaking and squirming to the upper air. It was very queer, especially in dark nights, when your thoughts had wandered to vast and cosmogonal themes in other spheres, to feel this faint jerk, which came to interrupt your dreams and link you to Nature again. It seemed as if I might next cast my line upward into the air, as well as downward into this element which was scarcely more dense. Thus I caught two fishes as it were with one hook. **11**

The scenery of Walden is on a humble scale, and, **12** though very beautiful, does not approach to grandeur, nor can it much concern one who has not long frequented it or lived by its shore; yet this pond is so remarkable for its depth and purity as to merit a particular description. It is a clear and deep green well, half a mile long and a mile and three quarters in circumference, and contains about sixty-one and a half **13** acres; a perennial spring in the midst of pine and oak woods, without any visible inlet or outlet except by the clouds and evaporation. The surrounding hills rise abruptly from the water to the height of forty to eighty

10 *from time to time.* Ms. 732: "the note of the wood-cock or the booming of snipe a mile off, circling on the river meadows, or the croak of a bittern close at hand."

11 *with one hook.* Ms. 733: "or rather a fish and a bird."

12 *on a humble scale. Journal,* September 1, 1852; IV, 341.

13 *sixty-one and a half.* This and the numbers that follow were not written out but stated in Arabic figures on ms. 735.

The woods near Walden Pond

feet, though on the south-east and east they attain to about one hundred and one hundred and fifty feet respectively, within a quarter and a third of a mile. They are exclusively woodland. All our Concord waters have two colors at least, one when viewed at a distance, and another, more proper, close at hand. The first depends more on the light, and follows the sky. In clear weather, in summer, they appear blue at a little distance, especially if agitated, and at a great distance all appear alike. In stormy weather they are sometimes of a dark slate color. The sea, however, is said to be blue one day and green another without any perceptible change in the atmosphere. I have seen our river, when, the landscape being covered with snow, both water and ice were almost as green as grass. Some consider blue "to be the color of pure water, whether liquid or solid." But, looking directly down into our waters from a boat, they are seen to be of very different colors. Walden is blue at one time and green at another, even from the same point of view. Lying between the earth and the heavens, it partakes of the color of both. Viewed from a hill-top it reflects the **14**

14 *reflects the color of the sky.* This long section on the color of the Walden water is based on numerous observations written in the *Journal* from January 24, 1852; III, 222, to January 3, 1853; IV, 447.

color of the sky, but near at hand it is of a yellowish tint next the shore where you can see the sand, then a light green, which gradually deepens to a uniform dark green in the body of the pond. In some lights, viewed even from a hill-top, it is of a vivid green next the shore. Some have referred this to the reflection of the verdure; but it is equally green there against the railroad sand-bank, and in the spring, before the leaves are expanded, and it may be simply the result of the prevailing blue mixed with the yellow of the sand. Such is the color of its iris. This is that portion, also, where in the **15** spring, the ice being warmed by the heat of the sun reflected from the bottom, and also transmitted through the earth, melts first and forms a narrow canal about the still frozen middle. Like the rest of our waters, when much agitated, in clear weather, so that the surface of the waves may reflect the sky at the right angle, or because there is more light mixed with it, it appears at a little distance of a darker blue than the sky itself; **16** and at such a time, being on its surface, and looking with divided vision, so as to see the reflection, I have discerned a matchless and indescribable light blue, such as watered or changeable silks and sword blades suggest, more cerulean than the sky itself, alternating with the original dark green on the opposite sides of the waves, which last appeared but muddy in comparison. It is a vitreous greenish blue, as I remember it, like **17** those patches of the winter sky seen through cloud vistas in the west before sundown. Yet a single glass of its water held up to the light is as colorless as an equal quantity of air. It is well known that a large plate of glass will have a green tint, owing, as the makers say, to its "body," but a small piece of the same will be colorless. How large a body of Walden water would be required to reflect a green tint I have never proved. The water of our river is black or a very dark brown to one looking directly down on it, and, like that of most ponds, imparts to the body of one bathing in it a yellow- **18** ish tinge; but this water is of such crystalline purity that the body of the bather appears of an alabaster whiteness, still more unnatural, which, as the limbs are magnified and distorted withal, produces a monstrous effect, making fit studies for a Michael Angelo. **19**

The water is so transparent that the bottom can easily be discerned at the depth of twenty-five or thirty feet. Paddling over it, you may see many feet beneath the

15 *This is that portion.* *Journal,* October 15, 1852; IV, 387.

16 *a darker blue.* *Journal,* October 26, 1852; IV, 400.

17 *a vitreous greenish blue.* *Journal,* January 24, 1852; III, 223.

18 *a yellowish tinge.* *Journal,* June 28, 1852; IV, 160.

19 *Michael Angelo.* Thoreau is thinking here of the twisted, massive lumps of heavy muscle on Michael Angelo's statues of male figures.

From Michael Angelo's frescoes for the Sistine Chapel

surface the schools of perch and shiners, perhaps only an inch long, yet the former easily distinguished by their transverse bars, and you think that they must be ascetic fish that find a subsistence there.   Once, in the winter, many years ago, when I had been cutting holes through the ice in order to catch pickerel, as I stepped ashore I tossed my axe back on to the ice, but, as if some evil **20** genius had directed it, it slid four or five rods directly into one of the holes, where the water was twenty-five **21** feet deep.   Out of curiosity, I lay down on the ice and looked through the hole, until I saw the axe a little on one side, standing on its head, with its helve erect and gently swaying to and fro with the pulse of the pond; and there it might have stood erect and swaying till in the course of time the handle rotted off, if I had not dis- **22** turbed it.   Making another hole directly over it with an ice chisel which I had, and cutting down the longest birch which I could find in the neighborhood with my knife, I made a slip-noose, which I attached to its end, and, letting it down carefully, passed it over the knob of the handle, and drew it by a line along the birch, and so pulled the axe out again.

The shore is composed of a belt of smooth rounded white stones like paving stones, excepting one or two short sand beaches, and is so steep that in many places a single leap will carry you into water over your head; and were it not for its remarkable transparency, that would be the last to be seen of its bottom till it rose on the opposite side.   Some think it is bottomless.   It is nowhere muddy, and a casual observer would say that there were no weeds at all in it; and of noticeable plants, except in the little meadows recently overflowed, which do not properly belong to it, a closer scrutiny does not detect a flag nor a bulrush, nor even a lily, yellow or white, but only a few small heart-leaves and potamoge- **23** tons, and perhaps a water-target or two; all which how- ever a bather might not perceive; and these plants are clean and bright like the element they grow in.   The stones extend a rod or two into the water, and then the bottom is pure sand, except in the deepest parts, where there is usually a little sediment, probably from the de- cay of the leaves which have been wafted on to it so many successive falls, and a bright green weed is brought up on anchors even in midwinter.

We have one other pond just like this, White Pond

20 *tossed my axe*. Changed on the page proofs from "heaved my axe."

21 *twenty-five feet deep*. Ms. 238 says "20."

22 *if I had not disturbed it*. Ms. 238: "Is a thing lost when you know where it is?"

23 *potamogetons*. Pondweeds, or, more literally, river plants.

in Nine Acre Corner, about two and a half miles wes- **24**
terly; but, though I am acquainted with most of the
ponds within a dozen miles of this centre, I do not know
a third of this pure and well-like character. Successive
nations perchance have drank at, admired, and fathomed
it, and passed away, and still its water is green and pel-
lucid as ever. Not an intermitting spring! Perhaps
on that spring morning when Adam and Eve were
driven out of Eden Walden Pond was already in existence, and even then breaking up in a gentle spring rain
accompanied with mist and a southerly wind, and covered with myriads of ducks and geese, which had not
heard of the fall, when still such pure lakes sufficed
them. Even then it had commenced to rise and fall,
and had clarified its waters and colored them of the hue
they now wear, and obtained a patent of heaven to be
the only Walden Pond in the world and distiller of celestial dews. Who knows in how many unremembered
nations' literatures this has been the Castalian Fountain? **25**
or what nymphs presided over it in the Golden Age?
It is a gem of the first water which Concord wears in
her coronet.

Yet perchance the first who came to this well have
left some trace of their footsteps. I have been surprised
to detect encircling the pond, even where a thick wood
has just been cut down on the shore, a narrow shelf-like **26**
path in the steep hill-side, alternately rising and falling,
approaching and receding from the water's edge, as old
probably as the race of man here, worn by the feet of
aboriginal hunters, and still from time to time unwit-
tingly trodden by the present occupants of the land.
This is particularly distinct to one standing on the middle of the pond in winter, just after a light snow has
fallen, appearing as a clear undulating white line, unob-
scured by weeds and twigs, and very obvious a quarter
of a mile off in many places where in summer it is hardly distinguishable close at hand. The snow reprints it,
as it were, in clear white type alto-relievo. The orna- **27**
mented grounds of villas which will one day be built
here may still preserve some trace of this.

The pond rises and falls, but whether regularly or
not, and within what period, nobody knows, though, as
usual, many pretend to know. It is commonly higher
in the winter and lower in the summer, though not corresponding to the general wet and dryness. I can re-

24 *Nine Acre Corner.* This is west of Fair
Haven Bay. See endpaper map.

25 *the Castalian Fountain.* The spring on the
slopes of Parnassus, near Delphi, and sacred to
Apollo.

26 *a narrow shelf-like path.* This is the Indian
Path which is still in use. See *Journal* for November 9, 1852; IV, 411.

27 *white type alto-relievo. Journal,* February
16, 1854; VI, 124.

The Indian path

member when it was a foot or two lower, and also when it was at least five feet higher, than when I lived by it. There is a narrow sand-bar running into it, with very deep water on one side, on which I helped boil a kettle of chowder, some six rods from the main shore, about the year 1824, which it has not been possible to do for twenty-five years; and on the other hand, my friends used to listen with incredulity when I told them, that a few years later I was accustomed to fish from a boat in a secluded cove in the woods, fifteen rods from the only shore they knew, which place was long since converted into a meadow. But the pond has risen steadily for two years, and now, in the summer of '52, is just five feet higher than when I lived there, or as high as it was thirty years ago, and fishing goes on again in the meadow. This makes a difference of level, at the outside, of six or seven feet; and yet the water shed by the surrounding hills is insignificant in amount, and this overflow must be referred to causes which affect the deep

28

28 *the year 1824.* Thoreau was seven years old then. But below, where it says "twenty-five years" is "more than twenty" in the *Journal* for August 27, 1852; IV, 321.

springs.   This same summer the pond has begun to fall again.   It is remarkable that this fluctuation, whether **29** periodical or not, appears thus to require many years for its accomplishment.   I have observed one rise and a part of two falls, and I expect that a dozen or fifteen years hence the water will again be as low as I have ever known it.   Flints' Pond, a mile eastward, allowing for the disturbance occasioned by its inlets and outlets, and the smaller intermediate ponds also, sympathize with Walden, and recently attained their greatest height at the same time with the latter.   The same is true, as far as my observation goes, of White Pond.

This rise and fall of Walden at long intervals serves this use at least; the water standing at this great height for a year or more, though it makes it difficult to walk round it, kills the shrubs and trees which have sprung up about its edge since the last rise, pitch-pines, birches, alders, aspens, and others, and, falling again, leaves an unobstructed shore; for, unlike many ponds and all waters which are subject to a daily tide, its shore is cleanest when the water is lowest.   On the side of the pond next my house, a row of pitch pines fifteen feet high has been killed and tipped over as if by a lever, and thus a stop put to their encroachments; and their size indicates how many years have elapsed since the last rise to this height.   By this fluctuation the pond asserts its title to a shore, and thus the *shore* is *shorn*, and the trees can- **30** not hold it by right of possession.   These are the lips of the lake on which no beard grows.   It licks its chaps from time to time.   When the water is at its height, the alders, willows, and maples send forth a mass of fibrous red roots several feet long from all sides of their stems in the water, and to the height of three or four feet from the ground, in the effort to maintain themselves; and I have known the high-blueberry bushes about the shore, which commonly produce no fruit, bear an abundant crop under these circumstances.

Some have been puzzled to tell how the shore became so regularly paved.   My townsmen have all heard the tradition, the oldest people tell me that they heard it in their youth, that anciently the Indians were hold- **31** ing a pow-wow upon a hill here, which rose as high into the heavens as the pond now sinks deep into the earth, and they used much profanity, as the story goes, though this vice is one of which the Indians were never guilty,

29 *It is remarkable*. The next two sentences on ms. 956–957 are written on the back of a letter dated February 26, 1854, from Thoreau to a Mr. Wood and dealing with wages owed to a man named Flannery. This was Michael Flannery, an Irish laborer who had been deprived of a four-dollar prize by his employer after Flannery had won a spading contest in the local cattle show.

30 *the* shore *is* shorn. Thoreau cannot resist a pun. This passage, revised, is from the *Journal* for December 5, 1852; IV, 425. Also for December 13, 1852; IV, 429.

31 *the Indians were holding a pow-wow*. Writing in his own copy of *Walden*, Thoreau said: "This is told of Alexander's Lake in Killingly Ct. [Connecticut] by Barber in his Con. Hist. Coll."

Thoreau's Cove

and while they were thus engaged the hill shook and
suddenly sank, and only one old squaw, named Walden,
escaped, and from her the pond was named. It has
been conjectured that when the hill shook these stones
rolled down its side and became the present shore. It
is very certain, at any rate, that once there was no pond
here, and now there is one; and this Indian fable does
not in any respect conflict with the account of that an- **32**
cient settler whom I have mentioned, who remembers
so well when he first came here with his divining rod,
saw a thin vapor rising from the sward, and the hazel
pointed steadily downward, and he concluded to dig a
well here. As for the stones, many still think that they
are hardly to be accounted for by the action of the
waves on these hills; but I observe that the surrounding hills are remarkably full of the same kind of stones,
so that they have been obliged to pile them up in walls

32 *that ancient settler.* See Index for other references to him.

on both sides of the railroad cut nearest the pond; and, moreover, there are most stones where the shore is most abrupt; so that, unfortunately, it is no longer a mystery to me. I detect the paver. If the name was not derived from that of some English locality, — Saffron Walden, for instance, — one might suppose that it was called, originally, *Walled-in* Pond.   **33**

The pond was my well ready dug. For four months in the year its water is as cold as it is pure at all times; and I think that it is then as good as any, if not the best, in the town. In the winter, all water which is exposed to the air is colder than springs and wells which are protected from it. The temperature of the pond water which had stood in the room where I sat from five o'clock in the afternoon till noon the next day, the sixth of March, 1846, the thermometer having been up to 65° or 70° some of the time, owing partly to the sun on the roof, was 42°, or one degree colder than the water of one of the coldest wells in the village just drawn. The temperature of the Boiling Spring the same day was 45°, or the warmest of any water tried, though it is the coldest that I know of in summer, when, beside, shallow and stagnant surface water is not mingled with it. Moreover, in summer, Walden never becomes so warm as most water which is exposed to the sun, on account of its depth. In the warmest weather I usually placed a pailful in my cellar, where it became cool in the night, and remained so during the day; though I also resorted to a spring in the neighborhood. It was as good when a week old as the day it was dipped, and had no taste of the pump. Whoever camps for a week in summer by the shore of a pond, needs only bury a pail of water a few feet deep in the shade of his camp to be independent on the luxury of ice.   **34**

There have been caught in Walden, pickerel, one weighing seven pounds, to say nothing of another which carried off a reel with great velocity, which the fisherman safely set down at eight pounds because he did not see him, perch and pouts, some of each weighing over two pounds, shiners, chivins or roach, (*Leuciscus pulchellus*,) a very few breams, and a couple of eels, one weighing four pounds, — I am thus particular because the weight of a fish is commonly its only title to fame, and these are the only eels I have heard of here; — also, I have a faint recollection of a little fish some five inches   **35**   **36**

33 *Saffron Walden.* In his copy of *Walden,* Channing noted that "Walden is not an unusual name; a Walden St. in New Bedford, Saffron Walden name of an English village abbey in a town in Essex." *The Concise Oxford Dictionary of English Place Names* says that Waldene or Waledene means the "valley of the Britons," but modifies this by adding that Walh or Wealh could also mean serf. And it says: "It is stated that saffron was extensively grown at the place." Thoreau noted in his copy of *Walden* that Evelyn says in his diary that "the parish of Saffron Walden, famous for the abundance of Saffron there cultivated, and esteemed the best in any foreign country." Saffron is made from the *Crocus sativus.* Walden Pond was first given its name in the seventeenth century. Note the pun at the end of the paragraph.

34 *it is pure at all times.* Since Walden has now become a state reservation, perhaps this will be true again.

35 *There have been caught in Walden.* With the exception of the pickerel, those mentioned are all pan fish.

36 *a very few breams.* After this Thoreau wrote in his own copy of *Walden:* "*Pomotis obesus* [November 26, 1858] one trout weighing a little over 5 lbs.—[November 14, 1857]." The latter entry says that the trout had been speared.

long, with silvery sides and a greenish back, somewhat dace-like in its character, which I mention here chiefly to link my facts to fable. Nevertheless, this pond is not very fertile in fish. Its pickerel, though not abundant, are its chief boast. I have seen at one time lying **37** on the ice pickerel of at least three different kinds; a long and shallow one, steel-colored, most like those caught in the river; a bright golden kind, with greenish reflections and remarkably deep, which is the most common here; and another, golden-colored, and shaped like the last, but peppered on the sides with small dark brown or black spots, intermixed with a few faint blood-red ones, very much like a trout. The specific name *reticulatus* would not apply to this; it should be *guttatus* rather. These are all very firm fish, and weigh more than their size promises. The shiners, pouts, and perch also, and indeed all the fishes which inhabit this

37 *I have seen at one time. Journal* for January 29, 1853; IV, 484–485.

Walden Pond "is not very fertile in fish"—but fishermen still try

pond, are much cleaner, handsomer, and firmer fleshed than those in the river and most other ponds, as the water is purer, and they can easily be distinguished from them.   Probably many ichthyologists would make new varieties of some of them.   There are also a clean race of frogs and tortoises, and a few muscles in it; muskrats and minks leave their traces about it, and occasionally a travelling mud-turtle visits it.   Sometimes, when I pushed off my boat in the morning, I disturbed a great mud-turtle which had secreted himself under the boat in the night.   Ducks and geese frequent it in the spring and fall, the white-bellied swallows (*Hirundo bicolor*) skim over it, and the peetweets (*Totanus macularius*) "teter" along its stony shores all summer.   I have sometimes disturbed a fishhawk sitting on a white-pine over the water; but I doubt if it is ever profaned by the wing of a gull, like Fair Haven.   At most, it tolerates one annual loon.   These are all the animals of consequence which frequent it now.

You may see from a boat, in calm weather, near the **38** sandy eastern shore, where the water is eight or ten feet deep, and also in some other parts of the pond, some circular heaps half a dozen feet in diameter by a foot in height, consisting of small stones less than a hen's egg in size, where all around is bare sand.   At first you wonder if the Indians could have formed them on the ice for any purpose, and so, when the ice melted, they sank to the bottom; but they are too regular and some of them plainly too fresh for that.   They are similar to those found in rivers; but as there are no suckers nor lampreys here, I know not by what fish they could be made.   Perhaps they are the nests of the **39** chivin.   These lend a pleasing mystery to the bottom.

The shore is irregular enough not to be monotonous. I have in my mind's eye the western indented with deep bays, the bolder northern, and the beautifully scolloped southern shore, where successive capes overlap each other and suggest unexplored coves between. The forest has never so good a setting, nor is so dis- **40** tinctly beautiful, as when seen from the middle of a small lake amid hills which rise from the water's edge; for the water in which it is reflected not only makes the best foreground in such a case, but, with its winding shore, the most natural and agreeable boundary to it. There is no rawness nor imperfection in its edge there, **41**

38 *near the sandy eastern shore. Journal* for November 9, 1852; IV, 411.

39 *nests of the chivin.* Recent biological research has showed that Thoreau was right about this.

40 *The forest has never so good a setting. Journal*, October 22, 1852; IV, 396.

41 *nor imperfection in its edge.* Ms. 972 then has: "of the wood in this case." Also *Journal* for June 14, 1853; V, 251.

as where the axe has cleared a part, or a cultivated field abuts on it. The trees have ample room to expand on the water side, and each sends forth its most vigorous branch in that direction. There Nature has woven a natural selvage, and the eye rises by just gradations from the low shrubs of the shore to the highest trees. There are few traces of man's hand to be seen. The water laves the shore as it did a thousand years ago.

A lake is the landscape's most beautiful and expressive feature. It is earth's eye; looking into which the beholder measures the depth of his own nature. The fluviatile trees next the shore are the slender eyelashes which fringe it, and the wooded hills and cliffs around are its overhanging brows.

Standing on the smooth sandy beach at the east end of the pond, in a calm September afternoon, when a slight haze makes the opposite shore line indistinct, I have seen whence came the expression, "the glassy surface of a lake." When you invert your head, it **42** looks like a thread of finest gossamer stretched across the valley, and gleaming against the distant pine woods, separating one stratum of the atmosphere from another. You would think that you could walk dry under it to the opposite hills, and that the swallows which skim over might perch on it. Indeed, they sometimes dive below the line, as it were by mistake, and are undeceived. As you look over the pond westward you are obliged to employ both your hands to defend your eyes against the reflected as well as the true sun, for they are equally bright; and if, between the two, you survey its surface critically, it is literally as smooth as glass, except where the skater insects, at equal intervals scat- **43** tered over its whole extent, by their motions in the sun produce the finest imaginable sparkle on it, or, perchance, a duck plumes itself, or, as I have said, a swallow skims so low as to touch it. It may be that in the distance a fish describes an arc of three or four feet in the air, and there is one bright flash where it emerges, and another where it strikes the water; sometimes the whole silvery arc is revealed; or here and there, perhaps, is a thistle-down floating on its surface, which the fishes dart at and so dimple it again. It is like molten glass cooled but not congealed, and the few motes in it are pure and beautiful like the imperfections in glass.

42 *When you invert your head.* This is amplified in the *Journal* for March 4, 1852; III, 333: "I look between my legs up the river across Fair Haven. Subverting the head, we refer things to the heavens; the sky becomes the ground of the picture, and where the river breaks through low hills which slope to meet each other a quarter of a mile off, appears a mountain pass, so much nearer is it to heaven." Charles Anderson (1968, page 125) says of this: "Some of the finest images and most significant meanings in *Walden* follow immediately after this experiment. . . ." See also the *Journal* for December 11, 1853; VI, 17. And for the rest of this paragraph, the *Journal* for September 1, 1852; V, 337; and September 2, 1852; V, 340.

43 *the skater insects.* Thoreau wrote the word "Hydrometer" after this in his own copy of *Walden. Journal*, October 11, 1852; IV, 382.

You may often detect a yet smoother and darker water, separated from the rest as if by an invisible cobweb, boom of the water nymphs, resting on it.   From a hill-top you can see a fish leap in almost any part; for not a pickerel or shiner picks an insect from this smooth surface but it manifestly disturbs the equilibrium of the whole lake.   It is wonderful with what elaborateness this simple fact is advertised, — this piscine murder **44** will out, — and from my distant perch I distinguish the circling undulations when they are half a dozen rods in diameter.   You can even detect a water-bug (*Gyrinus*) ceaselessly progressing over the smooth surface a quarter of a mile off; for they furrow the water slightly, making a conspicuous ripple bounded by two diverging lines, but the skaters glide over it without rippling it perceptibly.   When the surface is considerably agitated there are no skaters nor water-bugs on it, but apparently, in calm days, they leave their havens and adventurously glide forth from the shore by short impulses till they completely cover it.   It is a soothing employment, on one of those fine days in the fall when all the warmth of the sun is fully appreciated, to sit on a stump on such a height as this, overlooking the pond, and study the dimpling circles which are incessantly inscribed on its otherwise invisible surface amid the reflected skies and trees.   Over this great expanse there is no disturbance but it is thus at once gently smoothed away and assuaged, as, when a vase of water is jarred, the trembling circles seek the shore and all is smooth again.   Not a fish can leap or an insect fall on the pond but it is thus reported in circling dimples, in lines of beauty, as it were the constant welling up of its fountain, the gentle pulsing of its life, the heaving of its breast.   The thrills of joy and thrills of pain are undistinguishable.   How peaceful the phenomena of the lake!   Again the works of man shine as in the spring.   Ay, every leaf and twig and stone and cobweb sparkles now at mid-afternoon as when covered with dew in a spring morning. Every motion of an oar or an insect produces a flash of light; and if an oar falls, how sweet the echo!   **45**

In such a day, in September or October, Walden is a perfect forest mirror, set round with stones as precious to my eye as if fewer or rarer.   Nothing so fair, so pure, and at the same time so large, as a lake, perchance, lies on the surface of the earth.   Sky water.   It needs

44 *this piscine murder will out.* Chaucer says that "mordre wol out" in *The Prioresses Tale*, 1, 124, and in *The Nonne Preests Tale*, 1, 232.

45 *how sweet the echo! Journal* for September 20, 1852; IV, 358.

no fence.   Nations come and go without defiling it.   It is a mirror which no stone can crack, whose quicksilver will never wear off, whose gilding Nature continually repairs; no storms, no dust, can dim its surface ever fresh; — a mirror in which all impurity presented to it sinks, swept and dusted by the sun's hazy brush, — this the light dust-cloth, — which retains no breath that is breathed on it, but sends its own to float as clouds high above its surface, and be reflected in its bosom still.   **46**

A field of water betrays the spirit that is in the air. It is continually receiving new life and motion from above.   It is intermediate in its nature between land and sky.   On land only the grass and trees wave, but the water itself is rippled by the wind.   I see where the breeze dashes across it by the streaks or flakes of light. It is remarkable that we can look down on its surface. We shall, perhaps, look down thus on the surface of air at length, and mark where a still subtler spirit sweeps   **47** over it.

The skaters and water-bugs finally disappear in the   **48** latter part of October, when the severe frosts have come; and then and in November, usually, in a calm day, there is absolutely nothing to ripple the surface. One November afternoon, in the calm at the end of a rain storm of several days' duration, when the sky was still completely overcast and the air was full of mist, I observed that the pond was remarkably smooth, so that it was difficult to distinguish its surface; though it no longer reflected the bright tints of October, but the sombre November colors of the surrounding hills.   Though I passed over it as gently as possible, the slight undulations produced by my boat extended almost as far as I could see, and gave a ribbed appearance to the reflections.   But, as I was looking over the surface, I saw here and there at a distance a faint glimmer, as if some skater insects which had escaped the frosts might be collected there, or, perchance, the surface, being so smooth, betrayed where a spring welled up from the bottom.   Paddling gently to one of these places, I was surprised to find myself surrounded by myriads of small perch, about five inches long, of a rich bronze color in the green water, sporting there and constantly rising to the surface and dimpling it, sometimes leaving bubbles on it.   In such transparent and seemingly bottomless water, reflecting the clouds, I seemed to be floating

46 *in its bosom still.* Ms. 751 then has: "while the sun purifies them and they are distilled again in dew and rain."

47 *a still subtler spirit sweeps over it. Journal,* 1850; II, 57.

48 *in the latter part of October.* This paragraph comes from the *Journal* for November. 2, 1852; IV, 406–407.

through the air as in a balloon, and their swimming impressed me as a kind of flight or hovering, as if they were a compact flock of birds passing just beneath my level on the right or left, their fins, like sails, set all around them. There were many such schools in the pond, apparently improving the short season before winter would draw an icy shutter over their broad skylight, sometimes giving to the surface an appearance as if a slight breeze struck it, or a few rain-drops fell there. When I approached carelessly and alarmed them, they made a sudden plash and rippling with their tails, as if one had struck the water with a brushy bough, and instantly took refuge in the depths. At length the wind rose, the mist increased, and the waves began to run, and the perch leaped much higher than before, half out of water, a hundred black points, three inches long, at once above the surface. Even as late as the fifth of December, one year, I saw some dimples on the surface, and thinking it was going to rain hard immediately, the air being full of mist, I made haste to take my place at the oars and row homeward ; already the rain seemed rapidly increasing, though I felt none on my cheek, and I anticipated a thorough soaking. But suddenly the dimples ceased, for they were produced by the perch, which the noise of my oars had scared into the depths, and I saw their schools dimly disappearing ; so I spent a dry afternoon after all.

An old man who used to frequent this pond nearly **50**

49

49 *a compact flock of birds. Journal,* November 2, 1852; IV, 408.

50 *An old man. Journal* for June 16, 1853; V, 260. Also June 17, 1853; V, 265 f. for the next two paragraphs.

sixty years ago, when it was dark with surrounding forests, tells me that in those days he sometimes saw it all alive with ducks and other water fowl, and that there were many eagles about it. He came here a-fishing, and used an old log canoe which he found on the shore. It was made of two white-pine logs dug out and pinned together, and was cut off square at the ends. It was very clumsy, but lasted a great many years before it became water-logged and perhaps sank to the bottom. He did not know whose it was; it belonged to the pond. He used to make a cable for his anchor of strips of hickory bark tied together. An old man, a potter, who lived by the pond before the Revolution, told him once that there was an iron chest at the bottom, and that he had seen it. Sometimes it would come floating up to the shore; but when you went toward it, it would go back into deep water and disappear. I was pleased to hear of the old log canoe, which took the place of an Indian one of the same material but more graceful construction, which perchance had first been a tree on the bank, and then, as it were, fell into the water, to float there for a generation, the most proper vessel for the lake. I remember that when I first looked into these depths there were many large trunks to be seen indistinctly lying on the bottom, which had either been blown over formerly, or left on the ice at the last cutting, when wood was cheaper; but now they have mostly disappeared.

When I first paddled a boat on Walden, it was completely surrounded by thick and lofty pine and oak woods, and in some of its coves grape vines had run over the trees next the water and formed bowers under which a boat could pass. The hills which form its shores are so steep, and the woods on them were then so high, that, as you looked down from the west end, it had the appearance of an amphitheatre for some kind of sylvan spectacle. I have spent many an hour, when I was younger, floating over its surface as the zephyr willed, having paddled my boat to the middle, and lying on my back across the seats, in a summer forenoon, dreaming awake, until I was aroused by the boat touching the sand, and I arose to see what shore my fates had impelled me to; days when idleness was the most attractive and productive industry. Many a forenoon have I stolen away, preferring to spend thus the most valued part of the day; for I was rich, if not in money, in sunny hours and summer days, and spent them lavishly; nor do I regret that I did not waste more of them in the workshop or the teacher's desk.　But since I left those shores the woodchoppers have still further laid them waste, and now for many a year there will be no more rambling through the aisles of the wood, with occasional vistas through which you see the water.　My Muse may be excused if she is silent henceforth.　How can you expect the birds to sing when their groves are cut down?

Now the trunks of trees on the bottom, and the old log canoe, and the dark surrounding woods, are gone, and the villagers, who scarcely know where it lies, instead of going to the pond to bathe or drink, are thinking to bring its water, which should be as sacred as the Ganges at least, to the village in a pipe, to wash their dishes with! — to earn their Walden by the turning of a cock or drawing of a plug!　That devilish Iron Horse, whose ear-rending neigh is heard throughout the town, has muddied the Boiling Spring with his foot, and he it is that has browsed off all the woods on Walden shore; that Trojan horse, with a thousand men in his belly, introduced by mercenary Greeks!　Where is the country's champion, the Moore of Moore Hall, to meet him at the Deep Cut and thrust an avenging lance between the ribs of the bloated pest?

Nevertheless, of all the characters I have known, perhaps Walden wears best, and best preserves its purity.　Many men have been likened to it, but few deserve that honor.　Though the woodchoppers have laid bare first this shore and then that, and the Irish have built their sties by it, and the railroad has infringed on its border, and the ice-men have skimmed it once, it is itself unchanged, the same water which my youthful eyes fell on; all the change is in me.　It has not acquired one permanent wrinkle after all its ripples.　It is perennially young, and I may stand and see a swallow dip apparently to pick an insect from its surface as of yore.　It struck me again to-night, as if I had not seen it almost daily for more than twenty years, — Why, here is Walden, the same woodland lake that I discovered so many years ago; where a forest was cut down last winter another is springing up by its shore as lustily as ever; the same thought is welling up to its surface that was then; it is the same liquid joy and happiness to it-

51 *in the workshop or the teacher's desk.* Ms. 975 then has: "in which last two places I have spent many of them.

"What if all ponds were shallow—would it not react on the minds of men? I thank God that he made this pond deep and pure for a symbol. While men believe in the infinite some ponds will be thought bottomless."

See also the *Journal* for January 25, 1852; III, 228–229.

52 *bring its water . . . to the village in a pipe.* Sanborn says in the Bibliophile Edition (II, 55n.): "The plan of drawing water from Walden for the service of the village was given up during Thoreau's lifetime, and it was not till some eight years after his death that Flint's Pond was drawn upon for that service, as being higher, and thus furnishing a stronger pressure. I was living in the Thoreau house at the time, and introduced the pipes there."

53 *That devilish Iron Horse.* It finally comes out that Thoreau was less enamored with the railroad than he had seemed to be. *Journal,* June 17, 1853; V, 266. Or perhaps he had changed his mind about it.

54 *Moore of Moore Hall.* The hero who slew the dragon in Thomas Percy's *Reliques of Ancient English Poetry* (1765). *Journal, ibid.*

self and its Maker, ay, and it *may* be to me. It is the work of a brave man surely, in whom there was no guile! He rounded this water with his hand, deepened and clarified it in his thought, and in his will bequeathed it to Concord. I see by its face that it is visited by the same reflection; and I can almost say, Walden, is it you?

> It is no dream of mine,
> To ornament a line;
> I cannot come nearer to God and Heaven
> Than I live to Walden even.
> I am its stony shore,
> And the breeze that passes o'er;
> In the hollow of my hand
> Are its water and its sand,
> And its deepest resort
> Lies high in my thought.

55

The cars never pause to look at it; yet I fancy that the engineers and firemen and brakemen, and those passengers who have a season ticket and see it often, are better men for the sight. The engineer does not forget at night, or his nature does not, that he has beheld this vision of serenity and purity once at least during the day. Though seen but once, it helps to wash out State-street and the engine's soot. One proposes that it be called " God's Drop."

56

I have said that Walden has no visible inlet nor outlet, but it is on the one hand distantly and indirectly related to Flints' Pond, which is more elevated, by a chain of small ponds coming from that quarter, and on the other directly and manifestly to Concord River, which is lower, by a similar chain of ponds through which in some other geological period it may have flowed, and by a little digging, which God forbid, it can be made to flow thither again. If by living thus reserved and austere, like a hermit in the woods, so long, it has acquired such wonderful purity, who would not regret that the comparatively impure waters of Flints' Pond should be mingled with it, or itself should ever go to waste its sweetness in the ocean wave?

57

Flints', or Sandy Pond, in Lincoln, our greatest lake and inland sea, lies about a mile east of Walden. It is much larger, being said to contain one hundred and ninety-seven acres, and is more fertile in fish; but it is

55 *It is no dream of mine.* This poem of Thoreau's is longer on ms. 632 and in the Bibliophile Edition (II, 57):

> It is a real place,—
> (Boston, I tell it to your face;)
> It is no dream of mine,
> To ornament a line;
> I cannot come nearer to God and Heaven
> Than I live to Walden even.
> It's a part of me which I have not profaned;
> I live by the shore of me,—detained.
> Laden with my dregs
> I stand on my legs,
> While all my pure wine
> I to Nature consign.
>
> I am its stony shore,
> And the breeze that passes o'er;
> In the hollow of my hand
> Are its water and its sand,
> And its deepest resort
> Lies high in my thought.

It also appears, in somewhat different form, in the *Journal* for 1850; II, 57–58. Sanborn added this footnote: "These verses were considerably garbled in printing; the first and second lines, and lines seven to thirteen inclusive, having been omitted entirely. Perhaps the verses could well have been spared altogether, but for a few good lines, and for the extreme pantheism which they embody,—which would have been censured or laughed at in 1854. If the bad rhyme in the last lines . . . had caught Emerson's eye or ear, he would have excluded the verses; and perhaps that was the printer's reason for leaving them out."

56 *"God's Drop."* Walter Harding (1963, page 298) says that Emerson called it that in his *Journal* for April 9, 1840; V, 381.

57 *to waste its sweetness in the ocean wave.* This paragraph comes almost word for word from the *Journal* for December 5, 1852; IV, 425. The words quoted, of course, are a paraphrase of a line from Gray's "Elegy."

comparatively shallow, and not remarkably pure. A **58** walk through the woods thither was often my recreation. It was worth the while, if only to feel the wind blow on your cheek freely, and see the waves run, and remember the life of mariners. I went a-chestnutting there in the fall, on windy days, when the nuts were dropping into the water and were washed to my feet; and one day, as I crept along its sedgy shore, the fresh spray blowing in my face, I came upon the mouldering wreck of a boat, the sides gone, and hardly more than the impression of its flat bottom left amid the rushes; yet its model was sharply defined, as if it were a large decayed pad, with its veins. It was as impressive a wreck as one could imagine on the sea-shore, and had as good a moral. It is by this time mere vegetable mould and undistinguishable pond shore, through which rushes and flags have pushed up. I used to admire the ripple **59** marks on the sandy bottom, at the north end of this pond, made firm and hard to the feet of the wader by the pressure of the water, and the rushes which grew in Indian file, in waving lines, corresponding to these marks, rank behind rank, as if the waves had planted them. There also I have found, in considerable quantities, curious balls, composed apparently of fine grass or roots, of pipewort perhaps, from half an inch to four inches in diameter, and perfectly spherical. These wash back and forth in shallow water on a sandy bottom, and are sometimes cast on the shore. They are either solid grass, or have a little sand in the middle. At first you would say that they were formed by the action of the waves, like a pebble; yet the smallest are made of equally coarse materials, half an inch long, and they are produced only at one season of the year. Moreover, the waves, I suspect, do not so much construct as wear down a material which has already acquired consistency. They preserve their form when dry for an indefinite period.

Flints' Pond! Such is the poverty of our nomencla- **60** ture. What right had the unclean and stupid farmer, whose farm abutted on this sky water, whose shores he has ruthlessly laid bare, to give his name to it? Some skin-flint, who loved better the reflecting surface of a dollar, or a bright cent, in which he could see his own brazen face; who regarded even the wild ducks which settled in it as trespassers; his fingers grown into crook-

58 *A walk through the woods thither*. Ms. 240 and 753: "on such paths as the Indians used . . ."

59 *the ripple marks*. Journal, June 20, 1850; II, 38–39.

60 *the unclean and stupid farmer*. Farmer Flint had apparently incurred Thoreau's anger because he refused to let him build a cabin on the shores of his big pond. And Thoreau remembered the place fondly because he had spent some time there with Charles Stearns Wheeler, who had a crude shanty near the pond in 1837. It is always possible, of course, that Thoreau's intense dislike of Flint had some other but now unknown basis.

"Curious balls, composed apparently of fine grass or roots" (*A Herbert Gleason photograph*)

ed and horny talons from the long habit of grasping harpy-like; — so it is not named for me. I go not there to see him nor to hear of him; who never *saw* it, who never bathed in it, who never loved it, who never protected it, who never spoke a good word for it, nor thanked God that he had made it. Rather let it be named from the fishes that swim in it, the wild fowl or quadrupeds which frequent it, the wild flowers which grow by its shores, or some wild man or child the thread of whose history is interwoven with its own; not from him who could show no title to it but the deed which a like-minded neighbor or legislature gave him, — him who thought only of its money value; whose presence perchance cursed all the shore; who exhausted the land around it, and would fain have exhausted the waters within it; who regretted only that it was not English hay or cranberry meadow, — there was nothing to redeem it, forsooth, in his eyes, — and would have drained and sold it for the mud at its bottom. It did not turn his mill, and it was no *privilege* to him to behold it. I respect **61** not his labors, his farm where every thing has its price; who would carry the landscape, who would carry his God, to market, if he could get any thing for him; who goes to market *for* his god as it is; on whose farm nothing grows free, whose fields bear no crops, whose meadows no flowers, whose trees no fruits, but dollars; who loves not the beauty of his fruits, whose fruits are not ripe for him till they are turned to dollars. Give me the poverty that enjoys true wealth. Farmers are respectable and interesting to me in proportion as they are poor, — poor farmers. A model farm! where the house stands like a fungus in a muck-heap, chambers for men, horses, oxen, and swine, cleansed and uncleansed, all contiguous to one another! Stocked with men! A great grease-spot, redolent of manures and buttermilk! Under a high state of cultivation, being manured with the hearts and brains of men! As if you were to raise your potatoes in the church-yard! Such is a model farm.

No, no; if the fairest features of the landscape are to be named after men, let them be the noblest and worthiest men alone. Let our lakes receive as true names at least as the Icarian Sea, where " still the **62** shore " a " brave attempt resounds."

61 privilege. The NED defines water-privilege as "U.S. the right to use water esp. to use running water to turn machinery."

62 *Icarian Sea, where "still the shore" a "brave attempt resounds."* Walter Harding (1963, page 298) has identified this as coming from *Icarus* by William Drummond of Hawthornden (1585–1649). The Icarian Sea is that part of the Aegean where Icarus flew too near the sun and fell into the water when the wax holding the feathers in his artificial wings melted.

Goose Pond, of small extent, is on my way to Flints';
Fair-Haven, an expansion of Concord River, said to
contain some seventy acres, is a mile south-west; and
White Pond, of about forty acres, is a mile and a half
beyond Fair-Haven. This is my lake country. These, **63**
with Concord River, are my water privileges; and night
and day, year in year out, they grind such grist as I
carry to them.

Since the woodcutters, and the railroad, and I myself
have profaned Walden, perhaps the most attractive,
if not the most beautiful, of all our lakes, the gem of
the woods, is White Pond;—a poor name from its com-
monness, whether derived from the remarkable purity
of its waters or the color of its sands. In these as in
other respects, however, it is a lesser twin of Walden.
They are so much alike that you would say they must
be connected under ground. It has the same stony
shore, and its waters are of the same hue. As at Walden, in sultry dog-day weather, looking down through **64**
the woods on some of its bays which are not so deep
but that the reflection from the bottom tinges them, its
waters are of a misty bluish-green or glaucous color. **65**

63 *This is my lake country.* The Lake Country
of northern England, which consists of Cumber-
land, Westmorland, and part of Lancashire, is
associated with Wordsworth, Coleridge, and De
Quincey, who lived there and wrote about it in
the early nineteenth century.

64 *in sultry dog-day weather.* The dog days
occur in the hottest part of the summer, approxi-
mately from July 3 to August 11 when Sirius,
the Dog Star, rises with the sun. Dogs were supposed to go mad then because of the extreme heat.

65 *glaucous color.* Light blue. *Journal* for June
23, 1853; V, 297.

A model farm

Many years since I used to go there to collect the sand by cart-loads, to make sand-paper with, and I have continued to visit it ever since. One who frequents it proposes to call it Virid Lake. Perhaps it might be called Yellow-Pine Lake, from the following circumstance. About fifteen years ago you could see the top of a pitch-pine, of the kind called yellow-pine hereabouts, though it is not a distinct species, projecting above the surface in deep water, many rods from the shore. It was even supposed by some that the pond had sunk, and this was one of the primitive forest that formerly stood there. I find that even so long ago as 1792, in a " Topographical Description of the Town of Concord," by one of its citizens, in the Collections of the Massachusetts Historical Society, the author, after speaking of Walden and White Ponds, adds: " In the middle of the latter may be seen, when the water is very low, a tree which appears as if it grew in the place where it now stands, although the roots are fifty feet below the surface of the water; the top of this tree is broken off, and at that place measures fourteen inches in diameter." In the spring of '49 I talked with the man who lives nearest the pond in Sudbury, who told me that it was he who got out this tree ten or fifteen years before. As near as he could remember, it stood twelve or fifteen rods from the shore, where the water was thirty or forty feet deep. It was in the winter, and he had been getting out ice in the forenoon, and had resolved that in the afternoon, with the aid of his neighbors, he would take out the old yellow-pine. He sawed a channel in the ice toward the shore, and hauled it over and along and out on to the ice with oxen; but, before he had gone far in his work, he was surprised to find that it was wrong end upward, with the stumps of the branches pointing down, and the small end firmly fastened in the sandy bottom. It was about a foot in diameter at the big end, and he had expected to get a good saw-log, but it was so rotten as to be fit only for fuel, if for that. He had some of it in his shed then. There were marks of an axe and of woodpeckers on the but. He thought that it might have been a dead tree on the shore, but was finally blown over into the pond, and after the top had become water-logged, while the but-end was still dry and light, had drifted out and sunk wrong end up. His father, eighty years old, could not remember when it was not there.

66　*to make sand-paper with.* The Thoreau family manufactured pencils, graphite, and sand-paper.

67　*Virid.* Green.

68　*the author.* William Jones.

69　*He had some of it in his shed then.* Ms. 757: "but unfortunately I did not think it worth the while to look at it, though I should have done ny part more faithfully if I had."

70　*but-end.* Now spelled butt-end, but in Thoreau's time it could be spelled this way. See Walker's *Dictionary,* the 1822 edition, a copy of which he owned.

Several pretty large logs may still be seen lying on the bottom, where, owing to the undulation of the surface, they look like huge water snakes in motion.

This pond has rarely been profaned by a boat, for there is little in it to tempt a fisherman. Instead of the white lily, which requires mud, or the common sweet flag, the blue flag (*Iris versicolor*) grows thinly in the pure water, rising from the stony bottom all around the shore, where it is visited by humming birds in June, and the color both of its bluish blades and its flowers, and especially their reflections, are in singular harmony **71** with the glaucous water.

White Pond and Walden are great crystals on the surface of the earth, Lakes of Light. If they were permanently congealed, and small enough to be clutched, they would, perchance, be carried off by slaves, like precious stones, to adorn the heads of emperors; but being liquid, and ample, and secured to us and our successors forever, we disregard them, and run after the diamond of Kohinoor. They are too pure to have a **72** market value; they contain no muck. How much more beautiful than our lives, how much more transparent than our characters, are they! We never learned meanness of them. How much fairer than the pool before the farmer's door, in which his ducks swim! Hither the clean wild ducks come. Nature has no human inhabitant who appreciates her. The birds with their plumage and their notes are in harmony with the flowers, but what youth or maiden conspires with the wild luxuriant beauty of Nature? She flourishes most alone, far from the towns where they reside. Talk of heaven! ye disgrace earth.

71 *in singular harmony with the glaucous water.* *Journal,* June 14, 1853; V, 252.

72 *the diamond of Kohinoor.* This has been known since 1739. It was presented by the East India Company to Queen Victoria in 1850. It then weighed $186\frac{1}{2}$ carats but was recut to $106\frac{1}{16}$ carats. It is now among the British crown jewels.

BAKER FARM.

SOMETIMES I rambled to pine groves, standing like temples, or like fleets at sea, full-rigged, with wavy boughs, and rippling with light, so soft and green and shady that the Druids would have forsaken their oaks **1** to worship in them; or to the cedar wood beyond Flints' Pond, where the trees, covered with hoary blue berries, spiring higher and higher, are fit to stand before Val- **2** halla, and the creeping juniper covers the ground with wreaths full of fruit; or to swamps where the usnea lichen **3** hangs in festoons from the white-spruce trees, and toad- **4** stools, round tables of the swamp gods, cover the ground, and more beautiful fungi adorn the stumps, like butter-flies or shells, vegetable winkles; where the swamp-pink and dogwood grow, the red alder-berry glows like eyes of imps, the waxwork grooves and crushes the hardest woods in its folds, and the wild-holly berries make the beholder forget his home with their beauty, and he is dazzled and tempted by nameless other wild forbidden fruits, too fair for mortal taste. Instead of calling on some scholar, I paid many a visit to particular trees, of kinds which are rare in this neighborhood, standing far away in the middle of some pasture, or in the depths of a wood or swamp, or on a hill-top; such as the black-birch, of which we have some handsome specimens two feet in diameter; its cousin the yellow-birch, with its loose golden vest, perfumed like the first; the beech, which has so neat a bole and beautifully lichen-painted, perfect in all its details, of which, excepting scattered specimens, I know but one small grove of sizable trees left in the township, supposed by some to have been

This was originally entitled "Baker Farm and Philanthropy." Ms. 759 shows that it began: "I also visited many a nameless little mill in the woods, as interesting to me . . . as the Amazon or the Mississippi, [its water] now running underground with subdued murmurings, now sparkling and tinkling along the surface and now spreading into a swamp."

Baker Farm is on the east side of Fair Haven Bay.

1 *Druids*. Priests of a pagan religious order in Gaul, Britain, and Ireland, active at the time of Julius Caesar. Pliny said that they held mistletoe in high regard and that groves of big oak trees were their chosen retreat.

2 *Valhalla*. In Teutonic mythology this is Odin's underground hall in which the heroes bravely killed in battle dwell forever.

3 *usnea lichen*. One of the family of fructicose lichens commonly called tree mosses.

4 *white-spruce*. Thoreau changed this to "black-spruce" in his own copy of *Walden*. See Index under Spruce.

planted by the pigeons that were once baited with beech nuts near by; it is worth the while to see the silver grain sparkle when you split this wood; the bass; the hornbeam; the *celtis occidentalis,* or false elm, of which we have but one well-grown; some taller mast of a pine, a shingle tree, or a more perfect hemlock than usual, standing like a pagoda in the midst of the woods; and many others I could mention. These were the shrines I visited both summer and winter.

Once it chanced that I stood in the very abutment of **5** a rainbow's arch, which filled the lower stratum of the atmosphere, tinging the grass and leaves around, and dazzling me as if I looked through colored crystal. It was a lake of rainbow light, in which, for a short while, I lived like a dolphin. If it had lasted longer it might have tinged my employments and life. As I walked on the railroad causeway, I used to wonder at the halo of light around my shadow, and would fain fancy myself **6** one of the elect. One who visited me declared that the shadows of some Irishmen before him had no halo about them, that it was only natives that were so distinguished. Benvenuto Cellini tells us in his memoirs, **7** that, after a certain terrible dream or vision which he had during his confinement in the castle of St. Angelo, a resplendent light appeared over the shadow of his head at morning and evening, whether he was in Italy or France, and it was particularly conspicuous when the grass was moist with dew. This was probably the same phenomenon to which I have referred, which is especially observed in the morning, but also at other times, and even by moonlight. Though a constant one, it is not commonly noticed, and, in the case of an excitable imagination like Cellini's, it would be basis enough for superstition. Beside, he tells us that he showed it to very few. But are they not indeed distinguished who are conscious that they are regarded at all?

I set out one afternoon to go a-fishing to Fair-Haven, through the woods, to eke out my scanty fare of vegetables. My way led through Pleasant Meadow, an adjunct of the Baker Farm, that retreat of which a poet **8** has since sung, beginning, —

5 *I stood in the very abutment of a rainbow's arch.* John Burroughs scoffed at this and said that it is impossible because "You can never see a rainbow at an angle. It is always facing you squarely." But Charles D. Stewart in "A Word for Thoreau" (*Atlantic,* July 1935, pages 110 ff.) comes to Thoreau's defense. See the *Journal* for August 9, 1851; II, 383, and September 12, 1851; II, 495.

6 *fancy myself one of the elect.* Ms. 762: "until I heard of another who had observed the same phenomenon, which indeed is a constant one. . . ."

7 *Benvenuto Cellini tells us . . . that, after a certain terrible dream or vision.* Cellini was an Italian artist (1500–1571) who was confined for a while in the castle of St. Angelo in Rome on an apparently false charge of having embezzled the gems of the pontifical tiara. He is as famous for his autobiography as he is for his sculpture and exquisite work in metal.

Ms. 637 goes on with: "in which certain events were communicated . . . which afterward came to pass. From the very moment that I beheld the phenomenon . . . there appeared (strange to relate!) a resplendent light over my head."

8 *a poet.* William Ellery Channing. This is from *The Woodsman and Other Poems.* The next bit of verse on page 333 is also by him.

> "Thy entry is a pleasant field,
>   Which some mossy fruit trees yield
> Partly to a ruddy brook,
>   By gliding musquash undertook,
> And mercurial trout,
>   Darting about."

I thought of living there before I went to Walden. I "hooked" the apples, leaped the brook, and scared the musquash and the trout. It was one of those afternoons which seem indefinitely long before one, in which many events may happen, a large portion of our natural life, though it was already half spent when I started. By the way there came up a shower, which compelled me to stand half an hour under a pine, piling boughs over my head, and wearing my handkerchief for a shed; and when at length I had made one cast over the pickerel-weed, standing up to my middle in water, I found myself suddenly in the shadow of a cloud, and the thunder began to rumble with such emphasis that I could do no more than listen to it. The gods must be proud, thought I, with such forked flashes to rout a poor un-armed fisherman. So I made haste for shelter to the nearest hut, which stood half a mile from any road, but so much the nearer to the pond, and had long been uninhabited: —

> "And here a poet builded,
>   In the completed years,
> For behold a trivial cabin
>   That to destruction steers."

So the Muse fables. But therein, as I found, dwelt now John Field, an Irishman, and his wife, and several **9** children, from the broad-faced boy who assisted his father at his work, and now came running by his side from the bog to escape the rain, to the wrinkled, sibyl-like, cone-headed infant that sat upon its father's knee as in the palaces of nobles, and looked out from its home in the midst of wet and hunger inquisitively upon the stranger, with the privilege of infancy, not knowing but it was the last of a noble line, and the hope and cynosure of the world, instead of John Field's poor starveling brat. There we sat together under that part of the roof which leaked the least, while it showered and thundered without. I had sat there many times of old

9 *John Field.* This long passage comes from the *Journal* for August 23, 1845; I, 383–384. It is very much the same there except for the conclusion which appears in the last paragraph of this chapter. The long section between "how poor a bargain the latter had made" and the last paragraph is not in the *Journal*.

The Muses

before the ship was built that floated this family to America. An honest, hard-working, but shiftless man plainly was John Field; and his wife, she too was brave to cook so many successive dinners in the recesses of that lofty stove; with round greasy face and bare breast, still thinking to improve her condition one day; with the never absent mop in one hand, and yet no effects of it visible any where. The chickens, which had also taken shelter here from the rain, stalked about the room like members of the family, too humanized methought to roast well. They stood and looked in my eye or pecked at my shoe significantly. Meanwhile my host told me his story, how hard he worked "bogging" for a neighboring farmer, turning up a meadow with a spade or bog hoe at the rate of ten dollars an acre and the use of the land with manure for one year, and his little broad-faced son worked cheerfully at his father's side the while, not knowing how poor a bargain the latter had made. I tried to help him with my experience, telling him that he was one of my nearest neighbors, and that I too, who came a-fishing here, and looked like a loafer, was getting my living like himself; that I lived in a tight, light, and clean house, which hardly cost more than the annual rent of such a ruin as his commonly amounts to; and how, if he chose, he might in a month or two build himself a palace of his own; that I did not use tea, nor coffee, nor butter, nor milk, nor fresh meat, and so did not have to work to get them; again, as I did not work hard, I did not have to eat hard, and it cost me but a trifle for my food; but as he began with tea, and coffee, and butter, and milk, and beef, he had to work hard to pay for them, and when he had worked hard he had to eat hard again to repair the waste of his system,—and so it was as broad as it was long, indeed it was broader than it was long, for he was discontented and wasted his life into the bargain; and yet he had rated it as a gain in coming to America, that here you could get tea, and coffee, and meat every day. But the only true America is that country where you are at liberty to pursue such a mode of life as may enable you to do without these, and where the state does not endeavor to compel you to sustain the slavery and war and other superfluous expenses which directly or indirectly result from the use of such things. For I purposely talked to him as if he were a philosopher, or desired to be one.

I should be glad if all the meadows on the earth were left in a wild state, if that were the consequence of men's beginning to redeem themselves. A man will not need to study history to find out what is best for his own culture. But alas! the culture of an Irishman is an enterprise to be undertaken with a sort of moral bog hoe. I told him, that as he worked so hard at bogging, he required thick boots and stout clothing, which yet were soon soiled and worn out, but I wore light shoes and thin clothing, which cost not half so much, though he might think that I was dressed like a gentleman, (which, however, was not the case,) and in an hour or two, without labor, but as a recreation, I could, if I wished, catch as many fish as I should want for two days, or earn enough money to support me a week. If he and his family would live simply, they might all go a-huckleberrying in the summer for their amusement. John heaved a sigh at this, and his wife stared with arms a-kimbo, and both appeared to be wondering if they had capital enough to begin such a course with, or arithmetic enough to carry it through. It was sailing by dead reckoning to them, and they saw not clearly how to make their port so; therefore I suppose they still take life bravely, after their fashion, face to face, giving it tooth and nail, not having skill to split its massive columns with any fine entering wedge, and rout it in detail;—thinking to deal with it roughly, as one should handle a thistle. But they fight at an overwhelming disadvantage,—living, John Field, alas! without arithmetic, and failing so.

"Do you ever fish?" I asked. "O yes, I catch a mess now and then when I am lying by; good perch I catch." "What's your bait?" "I catch shiners with fish-worms, and bait the perch with them." "You'd better go now, John," said his wife with glistening and hopeful face; but John demurred.

The shower was now over, and a rainbow above the eastern woods promised a fair evening; so I took my departure. When I had got without I asked for a dish, hoping to get a sight of the well bottom, to complete my survey of the premises; but there, alas! are shallows and quicksands, and rope broken withal, and bucket irrecoverable. Meanwhile the right culinary vessel was selected, water was seemingly distilled, and after consultation and long delay passed out to the thirsty one,—not yet suffered to cool, not yet to settle. Such gruel sustains life here, I thought; so, shutting my eyes, and excluding the motes by a skilfully directed under-current, I drank to genuine hospitality the heartiest draught I could. I am not squeamish in such cases when manners are concerned.

As I was leaving the Irishman's roof after the rain, bending my steps again to the pond, my haste to catch pickerel, wading in retired meadows, in sloughs and bog-holes, in forlorn and savage places, appeared for an instant trivial to me who had been sent to school and college; but as I ran down the hill toward the reddening west, with the rainbow over my shoulder, and some faint tinkling sounds borne to my ear through the cleansed air, from I know not what quarter, my Good Genius seemed to say,— Go fish and hunt far and wide day by day,— farther and wider,— and rest thee by many brooks and hearth-sides without misgiving. Remember **10** thy Creator in the days of thy youth. Rise free from care before the dawn, and seek adventures. Let the noon find thee by other lakes, and the night overtake thee every where at home. There are no larger fields than these, no worthier games than may here be played. Grow wild according to thy nature, like these sedges and brakes, which will never become English hay. Let the thunder rumble; what if it threaten ruin to farmers crops? that is not its errand to thee. Take shelter under the cloud, while they flee to carts and sheds. Let not to get a living be thy trade, but thy sport. Enjoy the land, but own it not. Through want of enterprise and faith men are where they are, buying and selling, and spending their lives like serfs.

O Baker Farm!

> " Landscape where the richest element   **11**
>   Is a little sunshine innocent." ❋ ❋

> " No one runs to revel
>   On thy rail-fenced lea." ❋ ❋

> " Debate with no man hast thou,
>   With questions art never perplexed,
>   As tame at the first sight as now,
>   In thy plain russet gabardine dressed." ❋ ❋

> " Come ye who love,
>   And ye who hate,

10 *Remember thy Creator.* Ecclesiastes, 12:1.

11 *"Landscape where the richest element."* Another of Channing's poems.

Children of the Holy Dove,
   And Guy Faux of the state,
And hang conspiracies
From the tough rafters of the trees! "

Men come tamely home at night only from the next field or street, where their household echoes haunt, and their life pines because it breathes its own breath over again; their shadows morning and evening reach farther than their daily steps. We should come home from far, from adventures, and perils, and discoveries every day, with new experience and character.

Before I had reached the pond some fresh impulse had brought out John Field, with altered mind, letting go "bogging" ere this sunset. But he, poor man, disturbed only a couple of fins while I was catching a fair string, and he said it was his luck; but when we changed seats in the boat luck changed seats too. Poor John Field!—I trust he does not read this, unless he will improve by it,—thinking to live by some derivative old country mode in this primitive new country,—to catch perch with shiners. It is good bait sometimes, I allow. With his horizon all his own, yet he a poor man, born to be poor, with his inherited Irish poverty or poor life, his Adam's grandmother and boggy ways, not to rise in this world, he nor his posterity, till their wading webbed bog-trotting feet get *talaria* to their heels.   **12**

12 talaria. These were the winged heels of some of the younger Greek male gods such as Hermes and Perseus.

Talaria

HIGHER LAWS.

As I came home through the woods with my string of fish, trailing my pole, it being now quite dark, I caught a glimpse of a woodchuck stealing across my path, and felt a strange thrill of savage delight, and was strongly tempted to seize and devour him raw; not that I was hungry then, except for that wildness which he represented. Once or twice, however, while I lived at the pond, I found myself ranging the woods, like a half-starved hound, with a strange abandonment, seeking some kind of venison which I might devour, and no morsel could have been too savage for me. The wildest scenes had become unaccountably familiar. I found in myself, and still find, an instinct toward a higher, or, as it is named, spiritual life, as do most men, and another **1** toward a primitive rank and savage one, and I rever- **2** ence them both. I love the wild not less than the good. The wildness and adventure that are in fishing still recommended it to me. I like sometimes to take rank hold on life and spend my day more as the animals do. Perhaps I have owed to this employment and to hunting, when quite young, my closest acquaintance with Nature. They early introduce us to and detain us in scenery with which otherwise, at that age, we should have little acquaintance. Fishermen, hunters, woodchoppers, and others, spending their lives in the fields and woods, in a peculiar sense a part of Nature themselves, are often in a more favorable mood for observing her, in the intervals of their pursuits, than philosophers or poets even, who approach her with expectation. She is not afraid to exhibit herself to them. The traveller on the prairie

This was entitled "Animal Food" on ms. 976. The opening bit about the woodchuck comes from the *Journal* for August 23, 1845; I, 385.

This chapter, with its moral and religious overtones, has been much commented on. See John B. Pickard's article, "The Religion of 'Higher Laws'" (1965), and C. Roland Wagner's article, "Lucky Fox at *Walden*" (1962) among others. Charles Anderson's *The Magic Circle of Walden* (1968, Chapter V) also deals with the subject in some detail. And John Burroughs in Chapter XIII of *Literary Values* (1902) talks about Thoreau's wildness.

1 *spiritual life*. Ms. 976 then has: "I used this word with hesitation, because, though we have the idea, we have not the reality."

2 *I reverence them both*. Ms. 976: "Some would say that the one impulse was directly from God and the other through Nature."

is naturally a hunter, on the head waters of the Missouri and Columbia a trapper, and at the Falls of St. **3** Mary a fisherman. He who is only a traveller learns things at second-hand and by the halves, and is poor authority. We are most interested when science reports what those men already know practically or instinctively, for that alone is a true *humanity*, or account of human experience.

They mistake who assert that the Yankee has few amusements, because he has not so many public holidays, and men and boys do not play so many games as they do in England, for here the more primitive but solitary amusements of hunting fishing and the like have not yet given place to the former. Almost every New England boy among my contemporaries shouldered a fowling piece between the ages of ten and fourteen ; and his hunting and fishing grounds were not limited like the preserves of an English nobleman, but were more boundless even than those of a savage. No wonder, then, that he did not oftener stay to play on the common. But already a change is taking place, owing, not to an increased humanity, but to an increased scarcity of game, for perhaps the hunter is the greatest friend of the animals hunted, not excepting the Humane Society.

Moreover, when at the pond, I wished sometimes to add fish to my fare for variety. I have actually fished from the same kind of necessity that the first fishers did. Whatever humanity I might conjure up against it was all factitious, and concerned my philosophy more than my feelings. I speak of fishing only now, for I had long felt differently about fowling, and sold my gun before I went to the woods. Not that I am less humane than others, but I did not perceive that my feelings were much affected. I did not pity the fishes nor the worms. This was habit. As for fowling, during the last years that I carried a gun my excuse was that I was studying ornithology, and sought only new or rare birds. But I confess that I am now inclined to think that there is a finer way of studying ornithology than this. It requires so much closer attention to the habits of the birds, that, if for that reason only, I have been **4** willing to omit the gun. Yet notwithstanding the objection on the score of humanity, I am compelled to doubt if equally valuable sports are ever substituted for these ; and when some of my friends have asked me

3 *Falls of St. Mary*. Since there are several waterfalls by this name in North America there is no telling which one of them Thoreau meant.

4 *I have been willing to omit the gun. Journal* for May 3, 1852; IV, 11.

anxiously about their boys, whether they should let them hunt, I have answered, yes,—remembering that it was **5** one of the best parts of my education,—*make* them hunters, though sportsmen only at first, if possible, mighty hunters at last, so that they shall not find game large enough for them in this or any vegetable wilderness,—hunters as well as fishers of men. Thus far I **6** am of the opinion of Chaucer's nun, who **7**

> " yave not of the text a pulled hen
> That saith that hunters ben not holy men."

There is a period in the history of the individual, as of the race, when the hunters are the " best men," as the Algonquins called them. We cannot but pity the boy who has never fired a gun; he is no more humane, while his education has been sadly neglected. This was my answer with respect to those youths who were bent on this pursuit, trusting that they would soon outgrow it. No humane being, past the thoughtless age of boyhood, will wantonly murder any creature, which holds its life by the same tenure that he does. The hare in its extremity cries like a child. I warn you, mothers, that my sympathies do not always make the usual philanthropic distinctions.

Such is oftenest the young man's introduction to the **8** forest, and the most original part of himself. He goes thither at first as a hunter and fisher, until at last, if he has the seeds of a better life in him, he distinguishes his proper objects, as a poet or naturalist it may be, and leaves the gun and fish-pole behind. The mass of men are still and always young in this respect. In some countries a hunting parson is no uncommon sight. Such a one might make a good shepherd's dog, but is far from being the Good Shepherd. I have been surprised to consider that the only obvious employment, except wood-chopping, ice-cutting, or the like business, which ever to my knowledge detained at Walden Pond for a whole half day any of my fellow-citizens, whether fathers or children of the town, with just one exception, was fishing. Commonly they did not think that they were lucky, or well paid for their time, unless they got a long string of fish, though they had the opportunity of seeing the pond all the while. They might go there a thousand times before the sediment of fishing would sink to the bottom and leave their purpose pure; but no

5 *I have answered, yes.* Thoreau's attitude toward guns may surprise many readers. But they should remember that those were different days, and even New England was wilder than it is now. See also below: "We cannot but pity the boy who has never fired a gun."

Sanborn, in a note in the Bibliophile Edition (II, 90n.) adds: "In an earlier *Journal* used in compiling *The Week,* and entered there under Wednesday, September 4, 1839, but probably written some years later, Thoreau said: 'There are few tools to be compared with a gun for efficiency and compactness. I do not know of another so complete an *arm.* It is almost a companion, like a dog. I have seen the time when I could carry a gun in my hand all day on a journey, and not feel it heavy, though I did not use it once. In the country a boy's love is apt to be divided between a gun and a watch; but the more active and manly choose the gun. Like the first settlers, who rarely went to the field—hardly even to church—without their guns, we, their descendants, have not yet quite outgrown this habit of pioneers.' "

6 *fishers of men.* Mark 1:17.

7 *Chaucer's nun.* In the Prologue to *The Canterbury Tales.* Thoreau was wrong here. Chaucer was speaking about the monk, not the nun.

8 *the young man's introduction to the forest. Journal* for June 26, 1853; V, 304.

doubt such a clarifying process would be going on all the while. The governor and his council faintly remember the pond, for they went a-fishing there when they were boys; but now they are too old and dignified to go a-fishing, and so they know it no more forever. Yet even they expect to go to heaven at last. If the legislature regards it, it is chiefly to regulate the number of hooks to be used there; but they know nothing about the hook of hooks with which to angle for the pond itself, impaling the legislature for a bait. Thus, even in civilized communities, the embryo man passes through the hunter stage of development.

I have found repeatedly, of late years, that I cannot fish without falling a little in self-respect. I have tried it again and again. I have skill at it, and, like many of my fellows, a certain instinct for it, which revives from time to time, but always when I have done I feel that it would have been better if I had not fished. I think that I do not mistake. It is a faint intimation, yet so are the first streaks of morning. There is unquestionably this instinct in me which belongs to the lower orders of creation; yet with every year I am less a fisherman, though without more humanity or even wisdom; at present I am no fisherman at all. But I see that if I were to live in a wilderness I should again be tempted to become a fisher and hunter in earnest. Beside, there is something essentially unclean about this **9** diet and all flesh, and I began to see where housework commences, and whence the endeavor, which costs so much, to wear a tidy and respectable appearance each

9 *something . . . unclean about this diet and all flesh.* Despite what he says here, Thoreau was not a complete vegetarian. Food reform was popular at this time. And Thoreau got many of his ideas from ascetic Oriental philosophers.

day, to keep the house sweet and free from all ill odors and sights.   Having been my own butcher and scullion and cook, as well as the gentleman for whom the dishes were served up, I can speak from an unusually complete experience.   The practical objection to animal food in my case was its uncleanness; and, besides, when I had caught and cleaned and cooked and eaten my fish, they seemed not to have fed me essentially.   It was insignificant and unnecessary, and cost more than it came to. A little bread or a few potatoes would have done as well, with less trouble and filth.   Like many of my **10** contemporaries, I had rarely for many years used animal food, or tea, or coffee, &c.; not so much because of any ill effects which I had traced to them, as because they were not agreeable to my imagination.   The repugnance to animal food is not the effect of experience, but is an instinct.   It appeared more beautiful to live low and fare hard in many respects; and though I never did so, I went far enough to please my imagination.   I believe that every man who has ever been earnest to preserve his higher or poetic faculties in the best condition has been particularly inclined to abstain from animal food, and from much food of any kind.   It is a significant fact, stated by entomologists, I find it in Kirby and **11** Spence, that "some insects in their perfect state, though furnished with organs of feeding, make no use of them;" and they lay it down as "a general rule, that almost all insects in this state eat much less than in that of larvæ. The voracious caterpillar when transformed into a butterfly," . . "and the gluttonous maggot when become a fly," content themselves with a drop or two of honey or some other sweet liquid.   The abdomen under the wings of the butterfly still represents the larva.   This is the tid-bit which tempts his insectivorous fate.   The gross feeder is a man in the larva state; and there are whole nations in that condition, nations without fancy or imagination, whose vast abdomens betray them.

It is hard to provide and cook so simple and clean a diet as will not offend the imagination; but this, I think, is to be fed when we feed the body; they should both sit down at the same table.   Yet perhaps this may be done.   The fruits eaten temperately need not make us ashamed of our appetites, nor interrupt the worthiest pursuits.   But put an extra condiment into your dish, and it will poison you.   It is not worth the while to live

10 *Like many of my contemporaries. Journal* for November 27, 1852; IV, 417.

11 *Kirby and Spence*. William Kirby and William Spence were the authors of *An Introduction to Entomology*, which was first published in London and then in an American edition in 1846.

by rich cookery. Most men would feel shame if caught preparing with their own hands precisely such a dinner, whether of animal or vegetable food, as is every day prepared for them by others. Yet till this is otherwise we are not civilized, and, if gentlemen and ladies, are not true men and women. This certainly suggests what change is to be made. It may be vain to ask why the imagination will not be reconciled to flesh and fat. I **12** am satisfied that it is not. Is it not a reproach that man is a carniverous animal? True, he can and does live, **13** in a great measure, by preying on other animals; but this is a miserable way, — as any one who will go to snaring rabbits, or slaughtering lambs, may learn, — and he will be regarded as a benefactor of his race who shall teach **14** man to confine himself to a more innocent and wholesome diet. Whatever my own practice may be, I have no doubt that it is a part of the destiny of the human race, in its gradual improvement, to leave off eating animals, as surely as the savage tribes have left off eating each other when they came in contact with the more civilized.

If one listens to the faintest but constant suggestions **15** of his genius, which are certainly true, he sees not to what extremes, or even insanity, it may lead him; and yet that way, as he grows more resolute and faithful, his road lies. The faintest assured objection which one healthy man feels will at length prevail over the arguments and customs of mankind. No man ever followed **16** his genius till it misled him. Though the result were bodily weakness, yet perhaps no one can say that the consequences were to be regretted, for these were a life in conformity to higher principles. If the day and the night are such that you greet them with joy, and life emits a fragrance like flowers and sweet-scented herbs, is more elastic, more starry, more immortal, — that is your success. All nature is your congratulation, and you have cause momentarily to bless yourself. The greatest gains and values are farthest from being appreciated. We easily come to doubt if they exist. We soon forget them. They are the highest reality. Perhaps the facts most astounding and most real are never communicated by man to man. The true harvest of my daily life is somewhat as intangible and indescribable as the tints of morning or evening. It is a little star-dust caught, a segment of the rainbow which I have clutched.

12 *will not be reconciled to flesh and fat.* Ms. 776: "I speak now while I am bringing home a string of fish, a partridge or a rabbit which I have snared, or if you prefer, a lamb which I have slaughtered." See the text four lines below.

13 *carniverous.* No, carnivorous was not spelled that way in the 1850's. The error was not caught in the page proofs or in the early printings but has been corrected in later editions.

14 *a benefactor of his race.* Ms. 779: "along with Prometheus and Christ." *Journal*, August 16, 1851; II, 390.

15 *If one listens.* This sentence was written in the first person singular on ms. 223.

16 *No man ever followed his genius till it misled him.* Sanborn adds this footnote (Bibliophile Edition, II 98n.): "This was a favorite thought of Thoreau. In November, 1850, he wrote: 'I find it to be the height of wisdom not to endeavor to oversee myself, and live a life of prudence and common sense; but to see over and above myself, entertain sublime conjectures, make myself the thoroughfare of thrilling thoughts, live all that can be lived.' Again, at the end of 1852 he wrote: 'Keep the time; observe the hours of the Universe, not of the cars. What are threescore years and ten, hurriedly and coarsely lived, to moments of divine leisure, in which your life is coincident with the life of the Universe?'"

Yet, for my part, I was never unusually squeamish; I could sometimes eat a fried rat with a good relish, if it were necessary. I am glad to have drunk water so long, for the same reason that I prefer the natural sky to an opium-eater's heaven. I would fain keep sober always; and there are infinite degrees of drunkenness. I believe that water is the only drink for a wise man; wine is not so noble a liquor; and think of dashing the hopes of a morning with a cup of warm coffee, or of an evening with a dish of tea! Ah, how low I fall when I am tempted by them! Even music may be intoxicating. Such apparently slight causes destroyed Greece and Rome, and will destroy England and America. Of all ebriosity, who does not prefer to be intoxicated by the air he breathes? I have found it to be the most serious objection to coarse labors long continued, that they compelled me to eat and drink coarsely also. But to tell the truth, I find myself at present somewhat less particular in these respects. I carry less religion to the table, ask no blessing; not because I am wiser than I was, but, I am obliged to confess, because, however much it is to be regretted, with years I have grown more coarse and indifferent. Perhaps these questions are entertained only in youth, as most believe of poetry. My practice is "nowhere," my opinion is here. Nevertheless I am far from regarding myself as one of those privileged ones to whom the Ved refers when it says, that "he who has true faith in the Omnipresent Supreme Being may eat all that exists," that is, is not bound to inquire what is his food, or who prepares it; and even in their case it is to be observed, as a Hindoo commentator has remarked, that the Vedant limits this privilege to "the time of distress."

Who has not sometimes derived an inexpressible satisfaction from his food in which appetite had no share? I have been thrilled to think that I owed a mental perception to the commonly gross sense of taste, that I have been inspired through the palate, that some berries which I had eaten on a hill-side had fed my genius. "The soul not being mistress of herself," says Thseng-tseu, "one looks, and one does not see; one listens, and one does not hear; one eats, and one does not know the savor of food." He who distinguishes the true savor of his food can never be a glutton; he who does not cannot be otherwise. A puritan may go to his brown-bread crust with as gross an appetite as ever an alderman to

17

18

19

20

21

17 *an opium-eater's heaven.* Probably a reference to Thomas De Quincey's *Confessions of an English Opium-eater,* which had been published in 1822.

18 *Even music may be intoxicating. Journal,* September 1850; II, 70.

19 *"he who has true faith . . ."* Walter Harding (1963, page 301) identifies this as coming from the Rajah Rammohun Roy's *Translation of Several . . . of the Vedas,* London, 1832.

20 *the commonly gross sense of taste. Journal,* July 11, 1852; IV, 219.

21 *says Thseng-tseu.* Confucius. Cady (1961) identifies this as coming from the second of the Confucian books, *The Great Learning.* Ms. 783 then has: "Confucius says: 'Of all men there is not one who does not eat and drink, but very few among them know how to distinguish savor.'"

A dram drinker of the time

his turtle. Not that food which entereth into the mouth defileth a man, but the appetite with which it is eaten. It is neither the quality nor the quantity, but the devotion to sensual savors; when that which is eaten is not a viand to sustain our animal, or inspire our spiritual life, but food for the worms that possess us. If the hunter has a taste for mud-turtles, muskrats, and other such savage tid-bits, the fine lady indulges a taste for jelly **22** made of a calf's foot, or for sardines from over the sea, and they are even. He goes to the mill-pond, she to her preserve-pot. The wonder is how they, how you and I, can live this slimy beastly life, eating and drinking. **23**

Our whole life is startlingly moral. There is never **24** an instant's truce between virtue and vice. Goodness is the only investment that never fails. In the music of the harp which trembles round the world it is the insisting on this which thrills us. The harp is the travelling patterer for the Universe's Insurance Company, recommending its laws, and our little goodness is all the assessment that we pay. Though the youth at last grows indifferent, the laws of the universe are not indifferent, but are forever on the side of the most sensitive. Listen to every zephyr for some reproof, for it **25** is surely there, and he is unfortunate who does not hear it. We cannot touch a string or move a stop but the charming moral transfixes us. Many an irksome noise, go a long way off, is heard as music, a proud sweet satire on the meanness of our lives.

We are conscious of an animal in us, which awakens **26** in proportion as our higher nature slumbers. It is reptile and sensual, and perhaps cannot be wholly expelled; like the worms which, even in life and health, occupy our bodies. Possibly we may withdraw from it, but never change its nature. I fear that it may enjoy a certain health of its own; that we may be well, yet not pure. The other day I picked up the lower jaw of a **27** hog, with white and sound teeth and tusks, which suggested that there was an animal health and vigor distinct from the spiritual. This creature succeeded by other means than temperance and purity. "That in which men differ from brute beasts," says Mencius, "is **28** a thing very inconsiderable; the common herd lose it very soon; superior men preserve it carefully." Who **29** knows what sort of life would result if we had attained to purity? If I knew so wise a man as could teach me

22 *the fine lady indulges a taste for.* Ms. 784: "some form of potted cheese, or . . ." Also *Journal,* 1850; II, 9.

23 *eating and drinking.* This is followed on ms. 784 by: "Though we are wont to attribute to woman a finer and more sibylline nature than to man, I am struck with the fact that in these respects she is rarely a reformer, and is intolerant of reform. I am not sure but he who seeks most faithfully to refine and ennoble life in these respects will after all find more sympathy in the intellect and philosophy of man than in the refinement and delicacy of woman."

24 *Our whole life. Journal* for June 22, 1853; V, 293.

25 *Listen to every zephyr for some reproof. Journal* for June 22, 1853; V, 294.

26 *We are conscious of an animal in us.* This was in the first person singular on ms. 1173.

27 *I picked up the lower jaw of a hog.* Sanborn (Bibliophile Edition, II, 103n.) says that this happened in Plymouth while Thoreau was visiting Marston Watson. But the *Journal* for June 15, 1850; II, 36, says that he found it in Concord.

purity I would go to seek him forthwith. "A command over our passions, and over the external senses of the body, and good acts, are declared by the Ved to be indispensable in the mind's approximation to God." Yet the spirit can for the time pervade and control every member and function of the body, and transmute what in form is the grossest sensuality into purity and devotion. **30** The generative energy, which, when we are loose, dissipates and makes us unclean, when we are continent invigorates and inspires us. Chastity is the flowering of man; and what are called Genius, Heroism, Holiness, and the like, are but various fruits which succeed it. Man flows at once to God when the channel of purity is open. By turns our purity inspires and our impurity casts us down. He is blessed who is assured that the animal is dying out in him day by day, and the divine being established. Perhaps there is none but has cause for shame on account of the inferior and brutish nature to which he is allied. I fear that we are such gods or demigods only as fauns and satyrs, the divine allied to beasts, the creatures of appetite, and that, to some extent, our very life is our disgrace. —

> "How happy's he who hath due place assigned   **31**
>   To his beasts and disaforested his mind!
> *   *   *   *   *
>   Can use his horse, goat, wolf, and ev'ry beast,
>   And is not ass himself to all the rest!
>   Else man not only is the herd of swine,
>   But he's those devils too which did incline
>   Them to a headlong rage, and made them worse."

All sensuality is one, though it takes many forms; all purity is one. It is the same whether a man eat, or drink, or cohabit, or sleep sensually. They are but one appetite, and we only need to see a person do any one of these things to know how great a sensualist he is. The impure can neither stand nor sit with purity. When the reptile is attacked at one mouth of his burrow, he shows himself at another. If you would be chaste, you must be temperate. What is chastity? How shall a man know if he is chaste? He shall not know it. We have heard of this virtue, but we know not what it is. We speak conformably to the rumor which we have heard. From exertion come wisdom and purity; from sloth ignorance and sensuality. **32** In the student sensuality is a sluggish habit of mind. An unclean person is

28 *Mencius.* Măng-tze (372?–289 B.C.), a Chinese philosopher, is held to be second only to Confucius. The quotation is from the Works of Mencius, Book IV, Chapter 19, page 1.

29 *"preserve it carefully."* Sanborn (Bibliophile Edition, II, 103) prints an omitted passage here: "I do not know how it is with other men, but I find it very difficult to be chaste. Methinks I can be chaste in my relations to persons, and yet I do not find myself clean. I have frequent cause to be ashamed of myself. I am well, but I am not pure."

30 *purity and devotion.* Ms. 638 then differs from the printed text: "The divine liquors, which when we are loose, dissipate and make us unclean and bestial, when we are continent invigorate and inspire us. A heroic man tastes his vigor sweet in his mouth. Chastity is the secret of genius." In notes that accompanied a letter to H. G. O. Blake in September 1852, Thoreau said: "Virginity, too, is a budding flower, and by an impure marriage the virgin is deflowered. Whoever loves flowers, loves virgins and chastity. Love and lust are as far asunder as a flower-garden is from a brothel." See Charles Anderson's comments on this in *The Magic Circle of Walden* (1968) pages 163 ff.

31 *"How happy's he."* Channing noted in his copy of *Walden* that this verse comes from John Donne's "To Sr. Edward Herbert . . . being at the siege of Iulyers." This is only part of the poem which begins "Man is a lumpe. . . ." Thoreau has modernized the spelling. Ms. 640 includes one more line: "For man can add weight to Heaven's heaviest curse."

32 *sloth ignorance and sensuality.* Ms. 793: "Go not to a warm latitude in order to live a simple and pure life. It would be harder there than it is here. If you migrate, let it be to a colder and more stubborn soil still. Be a highlander, a mountaineer in virtue. Virtue was not born under a palm tree. If you seek the warmth, even of affection, from a similar motive to that from which cats and dogs and slothful persons hug the fire you are on the downward road. Better the cold affection of the sun reflected from fields of ice and snow."

universally a slothful one, one who sits by a stove, whom the sun shines on prostrate, who reposes without being fatigued. If you would avoid uncleanness, and all the sins, work earnestly, though it be at cleaning a stable. **33** Nature is hard to be overcome, but she must be overcome. What avails it that you are Christian, if you are not purer than the heathen, if you deny yourself no more, if you are not more religious? I know of many systems of religion esteemed heathenish whose precepts fill the reader with shame, and provoke him to new endeavors, though it be to the performance of rites merely.

I hesitate to say these things, but it is not because of the subject,—I care not how obscene my *words* are,—but because I cannot speak of them without betraying my impurity. We discourse freely without shame of one form of sensuality, and are silent about another. We are so degraded that we cannot speak simply of the necessary functions of human nature. In earlier ages, in some countries, every function was reverently spoken of and regulated by law. Nothing was too trivial for the Hindoo lawgiver, however offensive it may be to modern taste. He teaches how to eat, drink, cohabit, void excrement and urine, and the like, elevating what is mean, and does not falsely excuse himself by calling these things trifles.

Every man is the builder of a temple, called his body, to the god he worships, after a style purely his own, nor can he get off by hammering marble instead. We are all sculptors and painters, and our material is our own flesh and blood and bones. Any nobleness begins at once to refine a man's features, any meanness or sensuality to imbrute them.

John Farmer sat at his door one September evening, **34** after a hard day's work, his mind still running on his labor more or less. Having bathed he sat down to rec- **35** reate his intellectual man. It was a rather cool evening, and some of his neighbors were apprehending a **36** frost. He had not attended to the train of his thoughts long when he heard some one playing on a flute, and **37, 38** that sound harmonized with his mood. Still he thought of his work; but the burden of his thought was, that though this kept running in his head, and he found himself planning and contriving it against his will, yet it concerned him very little. It was no more than the scurf of his skin, which was constantly shuffled off. **39**

33 *cleaning a stable.* Ms. 790: "And considering the state of the worker, how can his work be other than cleaning a stable? This is the first work he will find to do. Though it is made an important object with some reformers to put [791] the washing out and get it done by the community, they will find at last that they have got to take it further in—their washing and their purifying.

34 *John Farmer.* Ms. 794 says: "John Spaulding."

35 *recreate.* Because this word is improperly divided at the end of the line, Thoreau noted in his own copy of *Walden* that it should not be "rec-reate" but "re-create."

36 *apprehending a frost.* Ms. 1175: "but his Genius was apprehending something else."

37 *some one playing on a flute.* Thoreau, of course.

Hiram Powers' Greek slave

But the notes of the flute came home to his ears out of a different sphere from that he worked in, and suggested work for certain faculties which slumbered in him. They gently did away with the street, and the village, and the state in which he lived.   A voice said to him, **40** — Why do you stay here and live this mean moiling life, when a glorious existence is possible for you? Those same stars twinkle over other fields than these.— But how to come out of this condition and actually migrate thither?   All that he could think of was to practise some new austerity, to let his mind descend into his body and redeem it, and treat himself with ever increasing respect.

38 *and that sound*. Ms. 1175: "guided him back toward a path he had lost."

39 *constantly shuffled off*. Ms. 1176: "or rather by their effort he cast his slough from time to time."

40 *A voice*. Ms. 1176: "seemed to say."

BRUTE NEIGHBORS.

SOMETIMES I had a companion in my fishing, who
came through the village to my house from the other
side of the town, and the catching of the dinner was as
much a social exercise as the eating of it.

Hermit. I wonder what the world is doing now. I
have not heard so much as a locust over the sweet-fern
these three hours. The pigeons are all asleep upon
their roosts, — no flutter from them. Was that a farmer's noon horn which sounded from beyond the woods
just now? The hands are coming in to boiled salt beef
and cider and Indian bread. Why will men worry
themselves so? He that does not eat need not work.
I wonder how much they have reaped. Who would
live there where a body can never think for the barking
of Bose? And O, the housekeeping! to keep bright the
devil's door-knobs, and scour his tubs this bright day!
Better not keep a house. Say, some hollow tree; and
then for morning calls and dinner-parties! Only a woodpecker tapping. O, they swarm; the sun is too warm
there; they are born too far into life for me. I have
water from the spring, and a loaf of brown bread on the
shelf. — Hark! I hear a rustling of the leaves. Is it
some ill-fed village hound yielding to the instinct of the
chase? or the lost pig which is said to be in these
woods, whose tracks I saw after the rain? It comes on
apace; my sumachs and sweet-briers tremble. — Eh, Mr.
Poet, is it you? How do you like the world to-day?

Poet. See those clouds; how they hang! That's the
greatest thing I have seen to-day. There's nothing like
it in old paintings, nothing like it in foreign lands, — un-

This chapter was headed "Animals" on ms. 796;
this was changed to "Brute Neighbors" on ms.
1177. It began there with: "But practically I was
only half converted by my own arguments, for
I found myself fishing at rare intervals."

1 *a companion in my fishing.* Sanborn says in the
Bibliophile Edition (II, 109n.):

"This companion, also called 'The Poet,' was
Ellery Channing, who then lived on Punkawtasset
Hill, three miles at least from the Walden hut, in
the North Quarter of Concord township, in a
house now gone, in front of the estate of Mr.
Robb, and nearly opposite St. Andrew's School. In
his poem 'New England,' Channing spoke of it
as—

My small cottage on the lonely hill,
Where like a hermit I must bide my time.

But the Hermit in this colloquy was Thoreau, of
course."

Thomas Blanding, in the Spring 1969 issue of
the Thoreau Society *Bulletin*, shows how great
a stylistic resemblance there is between the dialogue that follows and the one in Izaak Walton's
Compleat Angler.

2 *Bose.* A popular dog's name like Fido.

3 *some hollow tree.* Various mythical people,
Merlin for instance, have lived in hollow trees.
See Index for other references. The *Journal* for
April 17, 1840; I, 133, says: "My neighbor in-
habits a hollow sycamore, and I a beech tree."

4 *a loaf of brown bread.* Ms. 797 has instead: "of
chestnuts a store."

less when we were off the coast of Spain. That's a true **5**
Mediterranean sky. I thought, as I have my living to
get, and have not eaten to-day, that I might go a-fishing. That's the true industry for poets. It is the only
trade I have learned. Come, let's along.

Hermit. I cannot resist. My brown bread will soon **6**
be gone. I will go with you gladly soon, but I am just
concluding a serious meditation. I think that I am
near the end of it. Leave me alone, then, for a while.
But that we may not be delayed, you shall be digging
the bait meanwhile. Angle-worms are rarely to be met
with in these parts, where the soil was never fattened
with manure; the race is nearly extinct. The sport of
digging the bait is nearly equal to that of catching the
fish, when one's appetite is not too keen; and this you
may have all to yourself to-day. I would advise you to
set in the spade down yonder among the ground-nuts,
where you see the johnswort waving. I think that I
may warrant you one worm to every three sods you
turn up, if you look well in among the roots of the
grass, as if you were weeding. Or, if you choose to go
farther, it will not be unwise, for I have found the increase of fair bait to be very nearly as the squares of
the distances.

Hermit alone. Let me see; where was I? Methinks I was nearly in this frame of mind; the world
lay about at this angle. Shall I go to heaven or a-fishing? If I should soon bring this meditation to an end,
would another so sweet occasion be likely to offer? I
was as near being resolved into the essence of things as
ever I was in my life. I fear my thoughts will not
come back to me. If it would do any good, I would
whistle for them. When they make us an offer, is it
wise to say, We will think of it? My thoughts have
left no track, and I cannot find the path again. What
was it that I was thinking of? It was a very hazy day.
I will just try these three sentences of Con-fut-see; **7**
they may fetch that state about again. I know not
whether it was the dumps or a budding ecstasy. Mem.
There never is but one opportunity of a kind.

Poet. How now, Hermit, is it too soon? I have got
just thirteen whole ones, beside several which are imperfect or undersized; but they will do for the smaller
fry; they do not cover up the hook so much. Those
village worms are quite too large; a shiner may make a
meal off one without finding the skewer.

5 *off the coast of Spain*. Sanborn's footnote in
the Bibliophile Edition (II, 110n.):

"In Channing's reply he had in mind his voyage
. . . through the straits of Gibraltar . . . on his way
to Italy in 1846."

Channing's one visit to Europe in the spring of
1846 gave him a few days in Marseilles, Genoa,
and Leghorn. He had only 16 days in Rome.

6 *My brown bread*. Ms. 2: "my boiled chestnuts
will soon be out." In the text, "gone" may be a
misprint for "done."

7 *Con-fut-see*. Confucius.

The Concord River

Hermit. Well, then, let's be off. Shall we to the Concord? There's good sport there if the water be not too high.

Why do precisely these objects which we behold make a world? Why has man just these species of animals for his neighbors; as if nothing but a mouse could have filled this crevice? I suspect that Pilpay & Co. **8** have put animals to their best use, for they are all beasts of burden, in a sense, made to carry some portion of our thoughts.

The mice which haunted my house were not the common ones, which are said to have been introduced into the country, but a wild native kind not found in the village. **9** I sent one to a distinguished naturalist, and it interested him much. When I was building, one of these **10** **11** had its nest underneath the house, and before I had laid the second floor, and swept out the shavings, would come out regularly at lunch time and pick up the crums at my feet. It probably had never seen a man before; and it soon became quite familiar, and would run over my shoes and up my clothes. It could readily ascend the sides of the room by short impulses, like a

8 *Pilpay & Co.* Sanborn's footnote in the Bibliophile Edition (II, 112n.) says that this is "an expression for the whole race of fabulists, from Bidpai, as Pilpay is now called, through Æsop, Babrius, Phædrus, and La Fontaine. . . ."

9 *a wild native kind.* In his own copy of *Walden*, Thoreau put the words *"mus leucopus"* after this.

10 *a distinguished naturalist.* Louis Agassiz (1807–1873).

11 *When I was building.* Ms. 231: "my house, a long-eared red-bellied field mouse had her. . . ." This passage about the mouse is from the *Journal* for July 1845; I, 368.

squirrel, which it resembled in its motions. At length, as I leaned with my elbow on the bench one day, it ran up my clothes, and along my sleeve, and round and round the paper which held my dinner, while I kept the latter close, and dodged and played at bo-peep with it; and when at last I held still a piece of cheese between my thumb and finger, it came and nibbled it, sitting in my hand, and afterward cleaned its face and paws, like a fly, and walked away.

A phœbe soon built in my shed, and a robin for protection in a pine which grew against the house. In June the partridge, (*Tetrao umbellus,*) which is so shy a bird, led her brood past my windows, from the woods in the rear to the front of my house, clucking and calling to them like a hen, and in all her behavior proving herself the hen of the woods. The young suddenly disperse on your approach, at a signal from the mother, as if a whirlwind had swept them away, and they so exactly resemble the dried leaves and twigs that many a traveller has placed his foot in the midst of a brood, and heard the whir of the old bird as she flew off, and her anxious calls and mewing, or seen her trail her wings to attract his attention, without suspecting their neighborhood. The parent will sometimes roll and spin round before you in such a dishabille, that you cannot, for a few moments, detect what kind of creature it is. The young squat still and flat, often running their heads under a leaf, and mind only their mother's directions given from a distance, nor will your approach make them run again and betray themselves. You may even tread on them, or have your eyes on them for a minute, without discovering them. I have held them in my open hand at such a time, and still their only care, obedient to their mother and their instinct, was to squat there without fear or trembling. So perfect is this instinct, that once, when I had laid them on the leaves again, and one accidentally fell on its side, it was found with the rest in exactly the same position ten minutes afterward. They are not callow like the young of most birds, but more perfectly developed and precocious even than chickens. The remarkably adult yet innocent expression of their open and serene eyes is very memorable. All intelligence seems reflected in them. They suggest not merely the purity of infancy, but a wisdom clarified by experience. Such an eye was not born when the bird was,

but is coeval with the sky it reflects. The woods do not yield another such a gem. The traveller does not often look into such a limpid well. The ignorant or reckless sportsman often shoots the parent at such a time, and leaves these innocents to fall a prey to some prowling beast or bird, or gradually mingle with the decaying leaves which they so much resemble. It is said that when hatched by a hen they will directly disperse on some alarm, and so are lost, for they never hear the mother's call which gathers them again. These were my hens and chickens.   **14**

It is remarkable how many creatures live wild and free though secret in the woods, and still sustain themselves in the neighborhood of towns, suspected by hunters only. How retired the otter manages to live here! He grows to be four feet long, as big as a small boy, perhaps without any human being getting a glimpse of him. I formerly saw the raccoon in the woods behind where my house is built, and probably still heard their whinnering at night. Commonly I rested an hour or   **15** two in the shade at noon, after planting, and ate my lunch, and read a little by a spring which was the source of a swamp and of a brook, oozing from under Brister's Hill, half a mile from my field. The approach to this was through a succession of descending grassy hollows, full of young pitch-pines, into a larger wood about the swamp. There, in a very secluded and shaded spot, under a spreading white-pine, there was yet a clean firm sward to sit on. I had dug out the spring and made a well of clear gray water, where I could dip up a pailful without roiling it, and thither I went for this purpose almost every day in midsummer, when the pond was warmest. Thither too the wood-cock led her brood, to probe the mud for worms, flying but a foot above them down the bank, while they ran in a troop beneath; but at last, spying me, she would leave her young and circle round and round me, nearer and nearer till within four or five feet, pretending broken wings and legs, to attract my attention, and get off her young, who would already have taken up their march, with faint wiry peep, single file through the swamp, as she directed. Or I heard the peep of the young when I could not see the parent bird. There too the turtle-doves sat over the spring, or fluttered from bough to bough of the soft white-pines over my head; or the red squirrel, coursing down the

12 *another such a gem.* Ms. 1179: "as the eye of a young partridge."

13 *Such a limpid well.* Ms. 1179: "Golconda and California are shallow and sandy [compared] to it."

14 *my hens and chickens.* Ms. 1180: "When plowing I discovered a ground bird's nest with young directly in the path of my plow, but though I carefully cut out the sod containing it, and set it in the ground a rod or two beyond the plowed land, where I had taken out another sod of the same size—the parents were less faithful than I for when I looked again the young had been deserted and were dead."

15 *whinnering.* The NED quotes this sentence from *Walden* to illustrate the use of this rare word which it defines as "a feeble whine." Both Carlyle and his wife are cited as using the word.

nearest bough, was particularly familiar and inquisitive. You only need sit still long enough in some attractive spot in the woods that all its inhabitants may exhibit themselves to you by turns.

I was witness to events of a less peaceful character. One day when I went out to my wood-pile, or rather my pile of stumps, I observed two large ants, the one **16** red, the other much larger, nearly half an inch long, and black, fiercely contending with one another. Having once got hold they never let go, but struggled and wrestled and rolled on the chips incessantly. Looking farther, I was surprised to find that the chips were covered with such combatants, that it was not a *duellum*, but a *bellum*, a war between two races of ants, the red always pitted against the black, and frequently two red ones to one black. The legions of these Myrmidons **17** covered all the hills and vales in my wood-yard, and the ground was already strewn with the dead and dying, both red and black. It was the only battle which I have ever witnessed, the only battle-field I ever trod while the battle was raging; internecine war; the red republicans on the one hand, and the black imperialists on the other. On every side they were engaged in deadly combat, yet without any noise that I could hear, and human soldiers never fought so resolutely. I watched a couple that were fast locked in each other's embraces, in a little sunny valley amid the chips, now at noon-day prepared to fight till the sun went down, or

16 *two large ants.* In a footnote in the Bibliophile Edition (II, 127n.) Sanborn gives the background for this miniature war:

"This famous battle of the ants was recorded by Thoreau nearly five years afterwards, when he had left his hut. . . . The date in the *Journal* is January 21, 1852; III, 209 ff.

"To prevent the date in the *Journal* from being mistaken for the time of the actual encounter, in printing his account in 1854, Thoreau fixes the date as in "the Presidency of Polk" (1845–1849), and "five years before the passage of Webster's Fugitive-Slave Bill." The exact date of that legislation was September 19, 1850 and therefore we may assume that the ants fought in September, 1845, before the Mexican War began."

17 *Myrmidons.* Achilles' numerous troops in the Trojan War.

Ant hills near the cabin site

life went out. The smaller red champion had fastened himself like a vice to his adversary's front, and through all the tumblings on that field never for an instant ceased to gnaw at one of his feelers near the root, having already caused the other to go by the board; while the stronger black one dashed him from side to side, and, as I saw on looking nearer, had already divested him of several of his members. They fought with more **18** pertinacity than bull-dogs. Neither manifested the least disposition to retreat. It was evident that their battle-cry was Conquer or die. In the mean while there came along a single red ant on the hill-side of this valley, evidently full of excitement, who either had despatched his foe, or had not yet taken part in the battle; probably the latter, for he had lost none of his limbs; whose mother had charged him to return with his shield or upon it. Or perchance he was some Achilles, who had nourished his wrath apart, and had now come to avenge or rescue his Patroclus. He saw this unequal combat from afar,—for the blacks were nearly twice the size of the red,—he drew near with rapid pace till he stood on his guard within half an inch of the combatants; then, watching his opportunity, he sprang upon the black warrior, and commenced his operations near the root of his right fore-leg, leaving the foe to select among his own members; and so there were three united for life, as if a new kind of attraction had been invented which put all other locks and cements to shame. I should not have wondered by this time to find that they had their respective musical bands stationed on some eminent chip, and playing their national airs the while, to excite the slow and cheer the dying combatants. I was myself excited somewhat even as if they had been men. The more you think of it, the less the difference. And certainly there is not the fight recorded in Concord history, at least, if in the history of America, that will bear a moment's comparison with this, whether for the numbers engaged in it, or for the patriotism and heroism displayed. For numbers and for carnage it was an Austerlitz or Dresden. Concord Fight! Two **19, 20** killed on the patriots' side, and Luther Blanchard wounded! Why here every ant was a Buttrick,— "Fire! for God's sake fire!"—and thousands shared the fate of Davis and Hosmer. There was not one hireling there. I have no doubt that it was a principle

18 *more pertinacity than bull-dogs.* Ms. 643 goes on with: "that would not let go though all their legs were cut off."

19 *Austerlitz or Dresden.* Battles in the Napoleonic wars.

20 *Concord Fight!* Thoreau knew the battle of April 19, 1775, in detail. The names that follow are those of men who took part in it. And the words: "Fire! for God's sake fire!" were spoken there. This passage, however, is also in the *Journal* for March 4, 1852; III, 331, where these words have no connection with the ant battle.

The Concord Battle Monument

they fought for, as much as our ancestors, and not to
avoid a three-penny tax on their tea; and the results of
this battle will be as important and memorable to those
whom it concerns as those of the battle of Bunker Hill,
at least.

I took up the chip on which the three I have particularly described were struggling, carried it into my house,
and placed it under a tumbler on my window-sill, in order to see the issue. Holding a microscope to the first-
mentioned red ant, I saw that, though he was assiduous-
ly gnawing at the near fore-leg of his enemy, having
severed his remaining feeler, his own breast was all
torn away, exposing what vitals he had there to the
jaws of the black warrior, whose breast-plate was apparently too thick for him to pierce; and the dark carbun-

The Bunker Hill Monument

cles of the sufferer's eyes shone with ferocity such as war only could excite. They struggled half an hour longer under the tumbler, and when I looked again the black soldier had severed the heads of his foes from their bodies, and the still living heads were hanging on either side of him like ghastly trophies at his saddle-bow, still apparently as firmly fastened as ever, and he was endeavoring with feeble struggles, being without feelers and with only the remnant of a leg, and I know not how many other wounds, to divest himself of them; which at length, after half an hour more, he accomplished. I raised the glass, and he went off over the window-sill in that crippled state. Whether he finally survived that combat, and spent the remainder of his days in some Hotel des Invalides, I do not know; but I **21** thought that his industry would not be worth much thereafter. I never learned which party was victorious, nor the cause of the war; but I felt for the rest of that day as if I had had my feelings excited and harrowed by witnessing the struggle, the ferocity and carnage, of a human battle before my door.

Kirby and Spence tell us that the battles of ants have **22** long been celebrated and the date of them recorded, though they say that Huber is the only modern author **23** who appears to have witnessed them. "Æneas Syl- **24** vius," say they, "after giving a very circumstantial account of one contested with great obstinacy by a great

21 *Hotel des Invalides.* The Hôtel des Invalides is the old soldiers' home in Paris built in the 1670's for Louis XIV by Libéral Bruant for war veterans. Napoleon's tomb has been there since 1840.

22 *Kirby and Spence.* See the Index for other references.

23 *Huber.* François Huber (1750–1831), the Swiss entomologist.

24 *"Æneas Sylvius."* Enea Silvio de' Piccolomini (1405–1464). He was Pope Pius II from 1458–1464.

and small species on the trunk of a pear tree," adds that " ' This action was fought in the pontificate of Eugenius the Fourth, in the presence of Nicholas Pistoriensis, an eminent lawyer, who related the whole history of the battle with the greatest fidelity.' A similar engagement between great and small ants is recorded by Olaus Magnus, in which the small ones, being victorious, are said to have buried the bodies of their own soldiers, but left those of their giant enemies a prey to the birds. This event happened previous to the expulsion of the tyrant Christiern the Second from Sweden." The battle which I witnessed took place in the Presidency of Polk, five years before the passage of Webster's Fugitive-Slave Bill.

Many a village Bose, fit only to course a mud-turtle in a victualling cellar, sported his heavy quarters in the woods, without the knowledge of his master, and ineffectually smelled at old fox burrows and woodchucks' holes; led perchance by some slight cur which nimbly threaded the wood, and might still inspire a natural terror in its denizens; — now far behind his guide, barking like a canine bull toward some small squirrel which had treed itself for scrutiny, then, cantering off, bending the bushes with his weight, imagining that he is on the track of some stray member of the jerbilla family. Once I was surprised to see a cat walking along the stony shore of the pond, for they rarely wander so far from home. The surprise was mutual. Nevertheless the most domestic cat, which has lain on a rug all her days, appears quite at home in the woods, and, by her sly and stealthy behavior, proves herself more native there than the regular inhabitants. Once, when berrying, I met with a cat with young kittens in the woods, quite wild, and they all, like their mother, had their backs up and were fiercely spitting at me. A few years before I lived in the woods there was what was called a " winged cat " in one of the farm-houses in Lincoln nearest the pond, Mr. Gilian Baker's. When I called to see her in June, 1842, she was gone a-hunting in the woods, as was her wont, (I am not sure whether it was a male or female, and so use the more common pronoun,) but her mistress told me that she came into the neighborhood a little more than a year before, in April, and was finally taken into their house; that she was of a dark brownish-gray color, with a white spot on her throat, and white feet, and had a large bushy tail like a fox; that in the winter the fur grew

25 *Eugenius the Fourth.* Gabriel Condulmaro (1383–1447). Pope from 1431–1447.

26 *Olaus Magnus* (1490–1558). Swedish Catholic ecclesiastic and historian.

27 *Christiern the Second* (1481–1559). Christian II, King of Denmark, Norway, and Sweden. Known as "The Cruel." The people of those countries revolted against him in 1532 and imprisoned him for the rest of his life.

28 *barking like a canine bull*. Ms. 983: "like a bull of Bashan." Psalms 22:12.

29 *the jerbilla family*. Not in any dictionary. Perhaps Thoreau meant gerbil, gerbille, or jerboa. All are jumping mice.

thick and flatted out along her sides, forming strips ten or twelve inches long by two and a half wide, and under her chin like a muff, the upper side loose, the under matted like felt, and in the spring these appendages dropped off. They gave me a pair of her "wings," which I keep still. There is no appearance of a membrane about them. Some thought it was part flying-squirrel or some other wild animal, which is not impossible, for, according to naturalists, prolific hybrids have been produced by the union of the marten and domestic cat. This would have been the right kind of cat for me to keep, if I had kept any; for why should not a poet's cat be winged as well as his horse?

In the fall the loon (*Columbus glacialis*) came, as **30** usual, to moult and bathe in the pond, making the woods ring with his wild laughter before I had risen. At rumor of his arrival all the Mill-dam sportsmen are **31** on the alert, in gigs and on foot, two by two and three by three, with patent rifles and conical balls and spy-glasses. They come rustling through the woods like autumn leaves, at least ten men to one loon. Some station themselves on this side of the pond, some on that, for the poor bird cannot be omnipresent; if he dive here he must come up there. But now the kind October wind rises, rustling the leaves and rippling the surface of the water, so that no loon can be heard or seen, though his foes sweep the pond with spy-glasses, and make the woods resound with their discharges. The **32** waves generously rise and dash angrily, taking sides with all waterfowl, and our sportsmen must beat a retreat to town and shop and unfinished jobs. But they were too often successful. When I went to get a pail of water early in the morning I frequently saw this stately bird sailing out of my cove within a few rods. If I endeavored to overtake him in a boat, in order to see how he would manoeuvre, he would dive and be completely lost, so that I did not discover him again, sometimes, till the latter part of the day. But I was more than a match for him on the surface. He commonly went off in a rain. **33**

As I was paddling along the north shore one very **34** calm October afternoon, for such days especially they settle on to the lakes, like the milkweed down, having looked in vain over the pond for a loon, suddenly one, sailing out from the shore toward the middle a few rods in front of me, set up his wild laugh and betrayed him-

30 *In the fall the loon. Journal,* 1845–1847; I, 421.

31 *the Mill-dam sportsmen.* Ms. 808: "the Concord sportsmen."

32 *The waves . . . rise and dash. Journal,* 1845–1847; I, 422.

33 *went off in a rain.* On ms. 810 this looks like "went off in a rage."

34 *As I was paddling.* From the *Journal,* October 8, 1852; IV, 379 ff.

self. I pursued with a paddle and he dived, but when he came up I was nearer than before. He dived again, but I miscalculated the direction he would take, and we were fifty rods apart when he came to the surface this time, for I had helped to widen the interval; and again he laughed long and loud, and with more reason than before. He manœuvred so cunningly that I could not get within half a dozen rods of him. Each time, when he came to the surface, turning his head this way and that, he coolly surveyed the water and the land, and apparently chose his course so that he might come up where there was the widest expanse of water and at the greatest distance from the boat. It was surprising how quickly he made up his mind and put his resolve into execution. He led me at once to the widest part of the pond, and could not be driven from it. While he was thinking one thing in his brain, I was endeavoring to divine his thought in mine. It was a pretty game, played on the smooth surface of the pond, a man against a loon. Suddenly your adversary's checker disappears beneath the board, and the problem is to place yours **35** nearest to where his will appear again. Sometimes he would come up unexpectedly on the opposite side of me, having apparently passed directly under the boat. So long-winded was he and so unweariable, that when he had swum farthest he would immediately plunge again, nevertheless; and then no wit could divine where in the deep pond, beneath the smooth surface, he might be speeding his way like a fish, for he had time and ability to visit the bottom of the pond in its deepest part. It **36** is said that loons have been caught in the New York lakes eighty feet beneath the surface, with hooks set for trout, — though Walden is deeper than that. How surprised must the fishes be to see this ungainly visitor from another sphere speeding his way amid their schools! Yet he appeared to know his course as surely under water as on the surface, and swam much faster there. Once or twice I saw a ripple where he approached the surface, just put his head out to reconnoitre, and instantly dived again. I found that it was as well for me to rest on my oars and wait his reappearing as to endeavor to calculate where he would rise; for again and again, when I was straining my eyes over the surface one way, I would suddenly be startled by his unearthly laugh behind me. But why, after displaying so much cunning, did he invariably betray himself the moment

35 *the problem is to.* Ms. 813: "divine his thought as to the."

36 *It is said that loons.* Ms. 813: "I have read that a fisherman caught a loon in Seneca Lake, New York. . . ." The Bibliophile Edition (II, 108n.) gives the date for Thoreau's encounter with the loon as having taken place on October 8, 1852.

he came up by that loud laugh? Did not his white breast enough betray him? He was indeed a silly loon, I thought. I could commonly hear the plash of the water when he came up, and so also detected him. But after an hour he seemed as fresh as ever, dived as willingly and swam yet farther than at first. It was surprising to see how serenely he sailed off with unruffled breast when he came to the surface, doing all the work with his webbed feet beneath. His usual note was this demoniac laughter, yet somewhat like that of a water-fowl; but occasionally, when he had balked me most successfully and come up a long way off, he uttered a long-drawn unearthly howl, probably more like that of a wolf than any bird; as when a beast puts his muzzle to the ground and deliberately howls. This was his looning, — perhaps the wildest sound that is ever heard here, making the woods ring far and wide. I concluded that he laughed in derision of my efforts, confident of his own resources. Though the sky was by this time overcast, the pond was so smooth that I could see where he broke the surface when I did not hear him. His white breast, the stillness of the air, and the smoothness of the water were all against him. At length, having come up fifty rods off, he uttered one of those prolonged howls, as if calling on the god of loons to aid **37** him, and immediately there came a wind from the east and rippled the surface, and filled the whole air with misty rain, and I was impressed as if it were the prayer of the loon answered, and his god was angry with me; and so I left him disappearing far away on the tumultuous surface.

For hours, in fall days, I watched the ducks cunning- **38** ly tack and veer and hold the middle of the pond, far from the sportsman; tricks which they will have less need to practise in Louisiana bayous. When compelled to rise they would sometimes circle round and round and over the pond at a considerable height, from which they could easily see to other ponds and the river, like black motes in the sky; and, when I thought they had gone off thither long since, they would settle down by a slanting flight of a quarter of a mile on to a distant part which was left free; but what beside safety they got by sailing in the middle of Walden I do not **39** know, unless they love its water for the same reason that I do.

37 *calling on the god of loons.* Clarence Anderson (1968, page 194) comments on this loon episode, but perhaps he does not go far enough into its inner significance. The derisive voice of the loon—and its ability to disappear—are tied up with wildness, not only in Nature but in the persona of Thoreau as well.

38 *For hours . . . I watched the ducks.* Journal, 1845–1847; I, 422.

39 *in the middle of Walden.* Somewhat rewritten from the *Journal* entry for October 12, 1852; IV, 383.

HOUSE-WARMING.

In October I went a-graping to the river meadows,
and loaded myself with clusters more precious for their
beauty and fragrance than for food. There too I admired, though I did not gather, the cranberries, small
waxen gems, pendants of the meadow grass, pearly and
red, which the farmer plucks with an ugly rake, leaving
the smooth meadow in a snarl, heedlessly measuring
them by the bushel and the dollar only, and sells the
spoils of the meads to Boston and New York; destined
to be *jammed*, to satisfy the tastes of lovers of Nature there. So butchers rake the tongues of bison out
of the prairie grass, regardless of the torn and droop-
ing plant. The barberry's brilliant fruit was likewise
food for my eyes merely; but I collected a small store
of wild apples for coddling, which the proprietor and
travellers had overlooked. When chestnuts were ripe
I laid up half a bushel for winter. It was very ex-
citing at that season to roam the then boundless chestnut woods of Lincoln, — they now sleep their long sleep
under the railroad, — with a bag on my shoulder, and a
stick to open burrs with in my hand, for I did not always
wait for the frost, amid the rustling of leaves and the
loud reproofs of the red-squirrels and the jays, whose
half-consumed nuts I sometimes stole, for the burrs which
they had selected were sure to contain sound ones. 1
Occasionally I climbed and shook the trees. They
grew also behind my house, and one large tree which
almost overshadowed it, was, when in flower, a bouquet
which scented the whole neighborhood, but the squirrels
and the jays got most of its fruit; the last coming in

On ms. 819 the title of this chapter and the opening sentences are written in pencil on the side of
the page.

1 *sure to contain sound ones.* Ms. 820 then has:
"Sometimes in unexplored and pathless depths
meeting some adventurous boy, even from other
towns—from Lincoln, Weston or Wayland, as
wild as myself, with his bag on his shoulder and
his stick to open burrs with. Perhaps two or
three had clubbed together and shaken a large
tree and shared the spoil."

flocks early in the morning and picking the nuts out of the burrs before they fell. I relinquished these trees to them and visited the more distant woods composed wholly of chestnut. These nuts, as far as they went, were a good substitute for bread. Many other substitutes might, perhaps, be found. Digging one day for fish-worms I discovered the ground-nut (*Apios tuberosa*) on its string, the potato of the aborigines, a sort **2** of fabulous fruit, which I had begun to doubt if I had ever dug and eaten in childhood, as I had told, and had not dreamed it. I had often since seen its crimpled red velvety blossom supported by the stems of other plants without knowing it to be the same. Cultivation has well nigh exterminated it. It has a sweetish taste, much like that of a frostbitten potato, and I found it better boiled than roasted. This tuber seemed like a faint promise of Nature to rear her own children and feed them simply here at some future period. In these days of fatted cattle and waving grain-fields, this humble root, which was once the *totem* of an Indian tribe, is quite forgotten, or known only by its flowering vine; but let wild Nature reign here once more, and the tender and luxurious English grains will probably disappear before a myriad of foes, and without the care of man the crow may carry back even the last seed of corn to the great corn-field of the Indian's God in the south-west, whence he is said to have brought it; but the now almost exterminated ground-nut will perhaps revive and flourish in spite of frosts and wildness, prove itself indigenous, and resume its ancient importance and dignity as the diet of the hunter tribe. Some Indian Ceres or Minerva must have been the inventor and **3** bestower of it; and when the reign of poetry commences here, its leaves and string of nuts may be represented on our works of art.

Already, by the first of September, I had seen two **4** or three small maples turned scarlet across the pond, beneath where the white stems of three aspens diverged, at the point of a promontory, next the water. Ah, many a tale their color told! And gradually from **5** week to week the character of each tree came out, and it admired itself reflected in the smooth mirror of the lake. Each morning the manager of this gallery substituted some new picture, distinguished by more brilliant or harmonious coloring, for the old upon the walls.

2. *the potato of the aborigines.* This differs on ms. 821 where it reads: "this, with corn, was the potato of the aborigines." See the *Journal* for October 12, 1852; IV, 384, and for May 9, 1852; IV, 43.

3 *Ceres or Minerva.* Roman names for Demeter, goddess of corn (agriculture) and Athena, goddess of wisdom.

4 *by the first of September.* Here autumn is beginning in the cycle of the year. *Journal* for September 1, 1852; IV, 337.

5 *many a tale.* Channing's annotated copy of *Walden* says that this is from Thomas Moore's "Those Evening Bells," "one of Henry's favorite poems."

The wasps came by thousands to my lodge in October, as to winter quarters, and settled on my windows within and on the walls over-head, sometimes deterring visitors from entering. Each morning, when they were numbed with cold, I swept some of them out, but I did not trouble myself much to get rid of them; I even felt complimented by their regarding my house as a desirable shelter. They never molested me seriously, though they bedded with me; and they gradually disappeared, into what crevices I do not know, avoiding winter and unspeakable cold.

Like the wasps, before I finally went into winter quarters in November, I used to resort to the north-east side of Walden, which the sun, reflected from the pitch-pine woods and the stony shore, made the fire-side of the pond; it is so much pleasanter and wholesomer to be warmed by the sun while you can be, than by an artificial fire. I thus warmed myself by the still glowing embers which the summer, like a departed hunter, had left.

When I came to build my chimney I studied masonry. My bricks being second-hand ones required to be cleaned with a trowel, so that I learned more than usual of the qualities of bricks and trowels. The mortar on them was fifty years old, and was said to be still growing harder; but this is one of those sayings which men love to repeat whether they are true or not. Such sayings themselves grow harder and adhere more firmly with age, and it would take many blows with a trowel to clean an old wiseacre of them. Many of the villages

6 *The wasps came by thousands . . . in October.*
Journal, November 8, 1850; II, 86, where it says
November instead of October.

7 *avoiding winter and unspeakable cold.* Iliad, III,
4.

Bricks from the chimney of the Thoreau cabin

of Mesopotamia are built of second-hand bricks of a very good quality, obtained from the ruins of Babylon, and the cement on them is older and probably harder still.   However that may be, I was struck by the peculiar toughness of the steel which bore so many violent blows without being worn out.   As my bricks had been in a chimney before, though I did not read the name of Nebuchadnezzar on them, I picked out as many fire-place bricks as I could find, to save work and waste, and I filled the spaces between the bricks about the fireplace with stones from the pond shore, and also made my mortar with the white sand from the same place.   I lingered most about the fireplace, as the most vital part of the house.   Indeed, I worked so deliberately, that though I commenced at the ground in the morning, a course of bricks raised a few inches above the floor served for my pillow at night; yet I did not get a stiff neck for it that I remember; my stiff neck is of older date.   I took a poet to board for a fortnight about those times, which caused me to be put to it for room.   He brought his own knife, though I had two, and we used to scour them by thrusting them into the earth.   He shared with me the labors of cooking.   I was pleased to see my work rising so square and solid by degrees, and reflected, that, if it proceeded slowly, it was calculated to endure a long time.   The chimney is to some extent an independent structure, standing on the ground and rising through the house to the heavens; even after the house is burned it still stands sometimes, and its importance and independence are apparent.   This was toward the end of summer.   It was now November.

The north wind had already begun to cool the pond, though it took many weeks of steady blowing to accomplish it, it is so deep.   When I began to have a fire at evening, before I plastered my house, the chimney carried smoke particularly well, because of the numerous chinks between the boards.   Yet I passed some cheerful evenings in that cool and airy apartment, surrounded by the rough brown boards full of knots, and rafters with the bark on high over-head.   My house never pleased my eye so much after it was plastered, though I was obliged to confess that it was more comfortable.   Should not every apartment in which man dwells be lofty

8 *Nebuchadnezzar.* Chaldean King of Babylon (605–562 B.C.). Daniel 5:25 describes the fateful writing on the walls of his palace.

9 *white sand from the same place.* Ms. 373: "Some whiter and cleaner sand I brought over from the opposite shore in a boat, several cartloads at once, together with my spade and barrow, and I was very glad to avail myself of this conveyance—a highway that never needs to be mended, and over which you pass with the heaviest loads without a jar or a scar." The copy printed on page 185—"I have thus a tight shingled and plastered house"—follows this in the ms.

10 *I took a poet to board.* Sanborn says that the poet was Ellery Channing.

enough to create some obscurity over-head, where flickering shadows may play at evening about the rafters? These forms are more agreeable to the fancy and imagination than fresco paintings or other the most expensive furniture. I now first began to inhabit my house, I may say, when I began to use it for warmth as well as shelter. I had got a couple of old fire-dogs to keep the wood from the hearth, and it did me good to see the soot form on the back of the chimney which I had built, and I poked the fire with more right and more satisfaction than usual. My dwelling was small, and I could hardly entertain an echo in it; but it seemed larger for being a single apartment and remote from neighbors. All the attractions of a house were concentrated in one room; it was kitchen, chamber, parlor, and keeping-room; and whatever satisfaction parent or child, master or servant, derive from living in a house, I enjoyed it all. Cato says, the master of a family (*patremfamilias*) must have in his rustic villa " cellam oleariam, vinariam, dolia multa, uti lubeat caritatem expectare, et rei, et virtuti, et gloriæ erit," that is, " an oil and wine cellar, many casks, so that it may be pleasant to expect hard times; it will be for his advantage, and virtue, and glory." I had in my cellar a firkin of potatoes, about two quarts of peas with the weevil in them, and on my shelf a little rice, a jug of molasses, and of rye and Indian meal a peck each.

I sometimes dream of a larger and more populous house, standing in a golden age, of enduring materials, and without ginger-bread work, which shall still consist of only one room, a vast, rude, substantial, primitive hall, without ceiling or plastering, with bare rafters and purlins supporting a sort of lower heaven over one's head, — useful to keep off rain and snow; where the king and queen posts stand out to receive your homage, when you have done reverence to the prostrate Saturn of an older dynasty on stepping over the sill; a cavernous house, wherein you must reach up a torch upon a pole to see the roof; where some may live in the fire-place, some in the recess of a window, and some on settles, some at one end of the hall, some at another, and some aloft on rafters with the spiders, if they choose; a house which you have got into when you have opened the outside door, and the ceremony is over; where the weary traveller may wash, and eat, and converse, and sleep, with-

11 *keeping-room.* Webster: A family sitting room.

12 *purlins.* Horizontal beams supporting the rafters for the roof. They are located between the pole plate and the ridgepole. The sentence that contains this word runs for 34 lines, but it is so well organized that it is grammatically clear. The house it describes, of course, is not a private residence but a dwelling for all mankind.

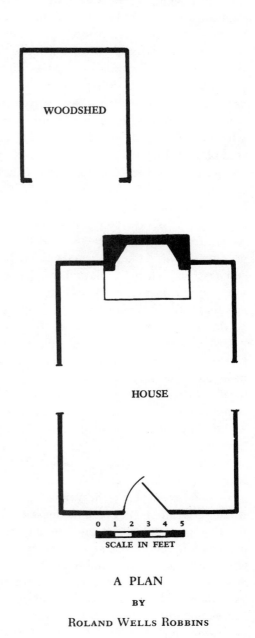

WOODSHED

HOUSE

0 1 2 3 4 5
SCALE IN FEET

A PLAN
BY
ROLAND WELLS ROBBINS

A plan made by R. W. Robbins of the Thoreau cabin

out further journey; such a shelter as you would be glad to reach in a tempestuous night, containing all the essentials of a house, and nothing for house-keeping; where you can see all the treasures of the house at one view, and every thing hangs upon its peg that a man should use; at once kitchen, pantry, parlor, chamber, store-house, and garret; where you can see so necessary a thing as a barrel or a ladder, so convenient a thing as a cupboard, and hear the pot boil, and pay your respects to the fire that cooks your dinner and the oven that bakes your bread, and the necessary furniture and utensils are the chief ornaments; where the washing is not put out, nor the fire, nor the mistress, and perhaps you are sometimes requested to move from off the trap-door, when the cook would descend into the cellar, and so learn whether the ground is solid or hollow beneath you without stamping. A house whose inside is as open and manifest as a bird's nest, and you cannot go in at the front door and out at the back without seeing some of its inhabitants; where to be a guest is to be presented with the freedom of the house, and not to be carefully excluded from seven eighths of it, shut up in a particular cell, and told to make yourself at home there, — in solitary confinement. Nowadays the host does not admit you to *his* hearth, but has got the mason to build one for yourself somewhere in his alley, and hospitality is the art of *keeping* you at the greatest distance. There is as much secrecy about the cooking as if he had a design to poison you. I am aware that I have been on many a man's premises, and might have been legally ordered off, but I am not aware that I have been in many men's houses. I might visit in my old clothes a king and queen who lived simply in such a house as I have described, if I were going their way; but backing out of a modern palace will be all that I shall desire to learn, if ever I am caught in one.

It would seem as if the very language of our parlors would lose all its nerve and degenerate into *parlaver* **13** wholly, our lives pass at such remoteness from its symbols, and its metaphors and tropes are necessarily so far fetched, through slides and dumb-waiters, as it were; in other words, the parlor is so far from the kitchen and workshop. The dinner even is only the parable of a dinner, commonly. As if only the savage dwelt near enough to Nature and Truth to borrow a trope from them.

13 parlaver. This might be a word that Thoreau made up from "parlor" plus "palaver," i.e., a room for gossiping in. It also might be an error. Dean Lyndon Shanley believes that it is, for Ms. 924 has "palaver," and Thoreau may have overlooked the misspelling in the page proof.

How can the scholar, who dwells away in the North West Territory or the Isle of Man, tell what is parliamentary in the kitchen?

However, only one or two of my guests were ever bold enough to stay and eat a hasty-pudding with me; but when they saw that crisis approaching they beat a hasty retreat rather, as if it would shake the house to its foundations. Nevertheless, it stood through a great many hasty-puddings.

I did not plaster till it was freezing weather. I brought **14** over some whiter and cleaner sand for this purpose from the opposite shore of the pond in a boat, a sort of conveyance which would have tempted me to go much farther if necessary. My house had in the mean while been shingled down to the ground on every side. In lathing I was pleased to be able to send home each nail with a single blow of the hammer, and it was my ambition to transfer the plaster from the board to the wall neatly and rapidly. I remembered the story of a conceited fellow, who, in fine clothes, was wont to lounge about the village once, giving advice to workmen. Venturing one day to substitute deeds for words, he turned up his cuffs, seized a plasterer's board, and having loaded his trowel without mishap, with a complacent look toward the lathing overhead, made a bold gesture thitherward; and straightway, to his complete discomfiture, received the whole contents in his ruffled bosom. I admired anew the economy and convenience of plastering, which so effectually shuts out the cold and takes a handsome finish, and I learned the various casualties to which the plasterer is liable. I was surprised to see how thirsty the bricks were which drank up all the moisture in my plaster before I had smoothed it, and how many pailfuls of water it takes to christen a new hearth. I had the previous winter made a small quantity of lime by burning the shells of the *Unio fluviatilis,* which our river affords, for the sake of the experiment; so that I knew where my materials came from. I might have got good limestone within a mile or two and burned it myself, if I had cared to do so.

The pond had in the mean while skimmed over in the **15** shadiest and shallowest coves, some days or even weeks before the general freezing. The first ice is especially

14 *freezing weather. Journal* for 1845; I, 387: "Left house on account of plastering, Wednesday, November 12th, at night; returned Saturday, December 6th." Thoreau probably used the house at times during this period but did not reside in it until the plastering was finished and dry. Roland W. Robbins (1947, page 52) says of this: "By leaving a newly plastered dwelling without heat during freezing weather, Thoreau displayed poor judgment."

15 *The pond had in the mean while skimmed over.* Ms. 997: "But to return to the pond. It continuously began to freeze in the shadiest and shallowest coves when it skimmed over."

Plaster from the cabin site

interesting and perfect, being hard, dark, and transparent, and affords the best opportunity that ever offers for examining the bottom where it is shallow; for you can lie at your length on ice only an inch thick, like a skater insect on the surface of the water, and study the bottom at your leisure, only two or three inches distant, like a picture behind a glass, and the water is necessarily always smooth then. There are many furrows in the [16] sand where some creature has travelled about and doubled on its tracks; and, for wrecks, it is strewn with the cases of cadis worms made of minute grains of white quartz. Perhaps these have creased it, for you find some of their cases in the furrows, though they are deep and broad for them to make. But the ice itself is the object of most interest, though you must improve the earliest opportunity to study it. If you examine it closely the morning after it freezes, you find that the greater part of the bubbles, which at first appeared to be within it, are against its under surface, and that more are continually rising from the bottom; while the ice is as yet comparatively solid and dark, that is, you see the water through it. These bubbles are from an eightieth to an eighth of an inch in diameter, very clear and beautiful, and you see your face reflected in them through the ice. There may be thirty or forty of them to a square inch. There are also already within the ice narrow oblong perpendicular bubbles about half an inch long, sharp cones with the apex upward; or oftener, if the ice is quite fresh, minute spherical bubbles one directly above another, like a string of beads. But these within the ice are not so numerous nor obvious as those beneath. I sometimes used to cast on stones to try the strength of the ice, and those which broke through carried in air with them, which formed very large and conspicuous white bubbles beneath. One day when I came to the same place forty-eight hours afterward, I found that those large bubbles were still perfect, though an inch more of ice had formed, as I could see distinctly by the seam in the edge of a cake. But as the last two days had been very warm, like an Indian summer, the ice was not now transparent, showing the dark green color of the water, and the bottom, but opaque and whitish or gray, and though twice as thick was hardly stronger than before, for the air bubbles had greatly expanded under this heat and run together, and lost their regular-

[16] *There are many furrows. Journal* for January 6, 1853; IV, 451, and January 8, 1853; IV, 458.

ity; they were no longer one directly over another, but often like silvery coins poured from a bag, one overlapping another, or in thin flakes, as if occupying slight cleavages. The beauty of the ice was gone, and it was too late to study the bottom. Being curious to know what position my great bubbles occupied with regard to the new ice, I broke out a cake containing a middling sized one, and turned it bottom upward. The new ice had formed around and under the bubble, so that it was included between the two ices. It was wholly in the lower ice, but close against the upper, and was flattish, or perhaps slightly lenticular, with a rounded edge, a quarter of an inch deep by four inches in diameter; and I was surprised to find that directly under the bubble the ice was melted with great regularity in the form of a saucer reversed, to the height of five eighths of an inch in the middle, leaving a thin partition there between the water and the bubble, hardly an eighth of an inch thick; and in many places the small bubbles in this partition had burst out downward, and probably there was no ice at all under the largest bubbles, which were a foot in diameter. I inferred that the infinite number of minute bubbles which I had first seen against the under surface of the ice were now frozen in likewise, and that each, in its degree, had operated like a burning glass on the ice beneath to melt and rot it. These are the little air-guns which contribute to make the ice crack and whoop.

At length the winter set in in good earnest, just as I had finished plastering, and the wind began to howl around the house as if it had not had permission to do so till then. Night after night the geese came lumbering in in the dark with a clangor and a whistling of wings, even after the ground was covered with snow, some to alight in Walden, and some flying low over the woods toward Fair Haven, bound for Mexico. Several times, when returning from the village at ten or eleven o'clock at night, I heard the tread of a flock of geese, or else ducks, on the dry leaves in the woods by a pond-hole behind my dwelling, where they had come up to feed, and the faint honk or quack of their leader as they hurried off. In 1845 Walden froze entirely over for **17** the first time on the night of the 22d of December, Flints' and other shallower ponds and the river having

17 *In 1845 Walden froze entirely over.* See the *Journal* for December 12, 1845; I, 394, and December 23, 1845; I, 395.

been frozen ten days or more; in '46, the 16th; in '49, about the 31st; and in '50, about the 27th of December; in '52, the 5th of January; in '53, the 31st of December. The snow had already covered the ground since the 25th of November, and surrounded me suddenly with the scenery of winter. I withdrew yet farther into my shell, and endeavored to keep a bright fire both within my house and within my breast. My employment out of doors now was to collect the dead wood in the forest, **18** bringing it in my hands or on my shoulders, or sometimes trailing a dead pine tree under each arm to my shed. An old forest fence which had seen its best days was a great haul for me. I sacrificed it to Vulcan, for **19** it was past serving the god Terminus. How much more interesting an event is that man's supper who has just been forth in the snow to hunt, nay, you might say, steal, **20** the fuel to cook it with! His bread and meat are sweet. There are enough fagots and waste wood of all kinds in the forests of most of our towns to support many fires, but which at present warm none, and, some think, hinder the growth of the young wood. There was also the drift-wood of the pond. In the course of the summer I had discovered a raft of pitch-pine logs with the bark on, pinned together by the Irish when the railroad was built. This I hauled up partly on the shore. After soaking two years and then lying high six months it was perfectly sound, though waterlogged past drying. I amused myself one winter day with sliding this piecemeal across the pond, nearly half a mile, skating behind with one end of a log fifteen feet long on my shoulder, and the other on the ice; or I tied several logs together with a birch withe, and then, with a longer birch or alder which had a hook at the end, dragged them across. Though completely waterlogged and almost as heavy as lead, they not only burned long, but made a very hot fire; nay, I thought that they burned better for the soaking, as if the pitch, being confined by the water, burned longer as in a lamp.

Gilpin, in his account of the forest borderers of England, says that "the encroachments of trespassers, and **21** the houses and fences thus raised on the borders of the forest," were "considered as great nuisances by the old forest law, and were severely punished under the name of *purprestures*, as tending *ad terrorem ferarum — ad nocumentum forestæ*, &c.," to the frightening of the game

---

18 *collect the dead wood in the forest.* Ms. 826: "*'Minuti, Blaterones, Quercum, Culi, et Curbi'* as the old forest law terms 'windfalls, dotterels, scrags, &.'" The NED defines dotteral as "a dottered tree" and dottered as "decayed, tottering or worn out with age." And scrag as the stump of a tree or a rough projection from a tree's trunk or stump.

19 *I sacrificed it to Vulcan, for it was past serving the god Terminus.* Vulcan, god of fire; Terminus, guardian of boundaries.

20 *steal, the fuel to cook it with!* See the *Journal* for February 17, 1852; III, 308, for the source of this paragraph.

21 *Gilpin.* William Gilpin (1724–1804). *Forest Scenery*, 1834. *Journal*, April 12, 1852; III, 408 f. Also for January 17, 1854; VI, 72–73.

and the detriment of the forest. But I was interested in the preservation of the venison and the vert more than the hunters or wood-choppers, and as much as though I had been the Lord Warden himself; and if any part was burned, though I burned it myself by accident, I grieved with a grief that lasted longer and was more inconsolable than that of the proprietors; nay, I grieved when it was cut down by the proprietors themselves. I would that our farmers when they cut down a forest felt some of that awe which the old Romans did when they came to thin, or let in the light to, a consecrated grove, *(lucum conlucare,)* that is, would believe that it is sacred to some god. The Roman made an expiatory offering, and prayed, Whatever god or goddess thou art to whom this grove is sacred, be propitious to me, my family, and children, &c.

It is remarkable what a value is still put upon wood even in this age and in this new country, a value more permanent and universal than that of gold. After all our discoveries and inventions no man will go by a pile of wood. It is as precious to us as it was to our Saxon and Norman ancestors. If they made their bows of it, we make our gun-stocks of it. Michaux, more than **22**

22 *Michaux.* François A. Michaux, son of the great French botanist. His book, *The North American Silva*, appeared in English in 1817–1819. See Thoreau's *Journal* for May 18, 1851; V. 201.

Bringing in wood

FEBRUARY

thirty years ago, says that the price of wood for fuel in New York and Philadelphia "nearly equals, and sometimes exceeds, that of the best wood in Paris, though this immense capital annually requires more than three hundred thousand cords, and is surrounded to the distance of three hundred miles by cultivated plains." In this town the price of wood rises almost steadily, and the only question is, how much higher it is to be this year than it was the last. Mechanics and tradesmen who come in person to the forest on no other errand, are sure to attend the wood auction, and even pay a high price for the privilege of gleaning after the wood-chopper. It is now many years that men have resorted to the forest for fuel and the materials of the arts; the New Englander and the New Hollander, the Parisian and the Celt, the farmer and Robinhood, Goody Blake and Harry Gill, in most parts of the world the prince and the peasant, the scholar and the savage, equally require still a few sticks from the forest to warm them and cook their food. Neither could I do without them.

Every man looks at his wood-pile with a kind of affection. I loved to have mine before my window, and the more chips the better to remind me of my pleasing work. I had an old axe which nobody claimed, with which by spells in winter days, on the sunny side of the house, I played about the stumps which I had got out of

23 *Goody Blake and Harry Gill.* Wordsworth's poem of this title deals with firewood. After Harry Gill prevented an old lady from gathering wood on his land, he never felt warm again.

24 *I had an old axe.* Is this the borrowed axe Thoreau built his house with—or another that he found?

my bean-field.   As my driver prophesied when I was ploughing, they warmed me twice, once while I was splitting them, and again when they were on the fire, so that no fuel could give out more heat.   As for the axe, I was advised to get the village blacksmith to "jump" it; but **25** I jumped him, and, putting a hickory helve from the woods into it, made it do.   If it was dull, it was at least hung true.

A few pieces of fat pine were a great treasure.   It is interesting to remember how much of this food for fire is still concealed in the bowels of the earth.   In previous years I had often gone "prospecting" over some **26** bare hill-side, where a pitch-pine wood had formerly **27** stood, and got out the fat pine roots.   They are almost indestructible.   Stumps thirty or forty years old, at least, will still be sound at the core, though the sapwood has all become vegetable mould, as appears by the scales of the thick bark forming a ring level with the earth four or five inches distant from the heart. With axe and shovel you explore this mine, and follow the marrowy store, yellow as beef tallow, or as if you had struck on a vein of gold, deep into the earth.   But commonly I kindled my fire with the dry leaves of the forest, which I had stored up in my shed before the snow came.   Green hickory finely split makes the woodchopper's kindlings, when he has a camp in the woods. Once in a while I got a little of this.   When the vil- **28** lagers were lighting their fires beyond the horizon, I too gave notice to the various wild inhabitants of Walden vale, by a smoky streamer from my chimney, that I was awake. —

> Light-winged Smoke, Icarian bird,   **29**
> Melting thy pinions in thy upward flight,
> Lark without song, and messenger of dawn,
> Circling above the hamlets as thy nest;
> Or else, departing dream, and shadowy form
> Of midnight vision, gathering up thy skirts;
> By night star-veiling, and by day
> Darkening the light and blotting out the sun;
> Go thou my incense upward from this hearth,
> And ask the gods to pardon this clear flame.

Hard green wood just cut, though I used but little of that, answered my purpose better than any other.   I sometimes left a good fire when I went to take a walk in a winter afternoon; and when I returned, three or four hours afterward, it would be still alive and glowing.

25 *to "jump" it.* Webster: "To thicken or enlarge by endwise blows."

26 *"prospecting."* Not in quotes but underlined on ms. 834 and 1193.

27 *had formerly stood, and.* Followed by "spent many an hour getting" on ms. 1191.

28 *Once in a while I got a little of this.* Followed on ms. 1192 by: "The old Dutch settlers on the Hudson used to say of this wood, that dried, it kept fire and sparkled like matches; and their wives preferred its coals because they lasted longer and were not burned in ashes."

29 *Light-winged Smoke, Icarian bird.* This poem has been highly praised, first by Emerson and then by F. O. Matthiessen (1941, pages 165–166).

My house was not empty though I was gone. It was as if I had left a cheerful housekeeper behind. It was I and Fire that lived there; and commonly my housekeeper proved trustworthy. One day, however, as I was splitting wood, I thought that I would just look in at the window and see if the house was not on fire; it was the only time I remember to have been particularly anxious on this score; so I looked and saw that a spark had caught my bed, and I went in and extinguished it when it had burned a place as big as my hand. But my house occupied so sunny and sheltered a position, and its roof was so low, that I could afford to let the fire go out in the middle of almost any winter day.

The moles nested in my cellar, nibbling every third potato, and making a snug bed even there of some hair left after plastering and of brown paper; for even the wildest animals love comfort and warmth as well as man, and they survive the winter only because they are so careful to secure them. Some of my friends spoke as if I was coming to the woods on purpose to freeze myself. The animal merely makes a bed, which he warms with his body in a sheltered place; but man, having discovered fire, boxes up some air in a spacious apartment, and warms that, instead of robbing himself, makes that his bed, in which he can move about divested of more cumbrous clothing, maintain a kind of summer in the midst of winter, and by means of windows even admit the light, and with a lamp lengthen out the day. Thus he goes a step or two beyond instinct, and saves a little time for the fine arts. Though, when I had been exposed to the rudest blasts a long time, my whole body began to grow torpid, when I reached the genial atmosphere of my house I soon recovered my faculties and prolonged my life. But the most luxuriously housed has little to boast of in this respect, nor need we trouble ourselves to speculate how the human race may be at last destroyed. It would be easy to cut their threads any time with a little sharper blast from the north. We go on dating from Cold Fridays and Great Snows; but a little colder Friday, or greater snow, would put a period to man's existence on the globe.

The next winter I used a small cooking-stove for economy, since I did not own the forest; but it did not keep fire so well as the open fire-place. Cooking was then, for the most part, no longer a poetic, but merely a

30 *and commonly my housekeeper proved trustworthy.* The incident about the bed being on fire was written in as an afterthought, for it was put between the lines and also on the right-hand margin of ms. 836.

31 *The moles nested in my cellar. Journal,* 1845–1847; I, 425.

32 *in a sheltered place.* Ms. 1187 then says: "He does not make a house. . . ."

33 *maintain.* Ms. 1187: "a congenial climate."

34 *my whole body began to grow torpid. Journal,* February 5, 1854; VI, 96.

35 *cut their threads.* Atropos, the third Parca, cuts the thread of life and terminates it.

36 *Cold Fridays.* The *Journal* for January 22, 1857; IX, 230, mentions this. When water, thrown into the air, struck the ground, "it was frozen and rattled like so many shot." This took place on January 19, 1810, before Thoreau was born. For the Great Snow see the Index.

37 *put a period to man's existence on the globe. Journal,* February 6, 1854; VI, 103.

chemic process.   It will soon be forgotten, in these days of stoves, that we used to roast potatoes in the ashes, after the Indian fashion.   The stove not only took up room and scented the house, but it concealed the fire, and I felt as if I had lost a companion.   You can always see a face in the fire.   The laborer, looking into it at evening, purifies his thoughts of the dross and earthiness which they have accumulated during the day.   But I could no longer sit and look into the fire, and the pertinent words of a poet recurred to me with new force. —

"Never, bright flame, may be denied to me   **38**
　　Thy dear, life imaging, close sympathy.
　　What but my hopes shot upward e'er so bright?
　　What but my fortunes sunk so low in night?

　　Why art thou banished from our hearth and hall,
　　Thou who art welcomed and beloved by all?
　　Was thy existence then too fanciful
　　For our life's common light, who are so dull?
　　Did thy bright gleam mysterious converse hold
　　With our congenial souls? secrets too bold?

　　Well, we are safe and strong, for now we sit
　　Beside a hearth where no dim shadows flit,
　　Where nothing cheers nor saddens, but a fire
　　Warms feet and hands — nor does to more aspire;
　　By whose compact utilitarian heap
　　The present may sit down and go to sleep,
　　Nor fear the ghosts who from the dim past walked,
　　And with us by the unequal light of the old wood fire
　　　　talked."

38 "*Never, bright flame.*" This is from "The Wood Fire" by Mrs. Ellen Sturgis Hooper (1812–1848), as both Thoreau and Channing note in their copies of Walden. The poem was published in the first number of *The Dial* (1840). On ms. 837 these additional beginning lines appear:

"When I am glad or gay,
　Let me walk forth into the brilliant sun,
　And with congenial rays be shone upon:
　When I am sad, or thought-bewitched would be,
　Let me glide forth in moonlight's mystery.
　But never, while I live this changeful life,
　This Past and Future with all wonders rife,
　Never, bright flame, may be denied to me, etc."

At the end of the poem, Thoreau wrote in his own copy of *Walden:* "Mrs. Hooper."

OCTOBER

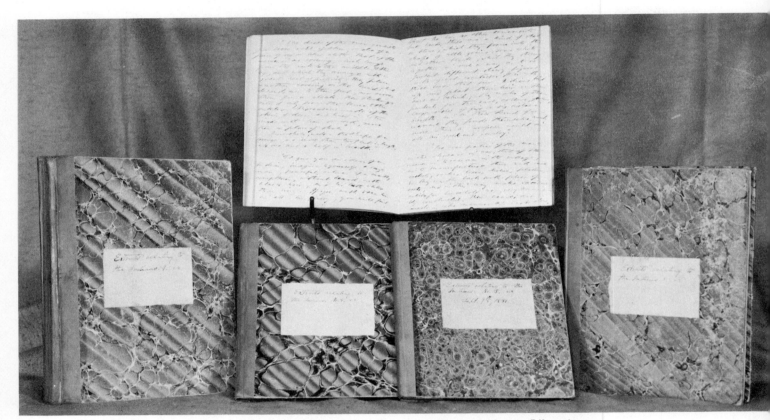

Thoreau's Indian notebooks (*Courtesy Pierpont Morgan Library*)

FORMER INHABITANTS; AND WINTER VISITORS.

I WEATHERED some merry snow storms, and spent some cheerful winter evenings by my fire-side, while the snow whirled wildly without, and even the hooting of the owl was hushed. For many weeks I met no one in my walks but those who came occasionally to cut wood and sled it to the village. The elements, however, abetted me in making a path through the deepest snow in the woods, for when I had once gone through the wind blew the oak leaves into my tracks, where they lodged, and by absorbing the rays of the sun melted the snow, and so not only made a dry bed for my feet, but in the night their dark line was my guide. For human society I was obliged to conjure up the former occupants of these woods. Within the memory of many of my townsmen the road near which my house stands resounded with the laugh and gossip of inhabitants, and the woods which border it were notched and dotted here and there with their little gardens and dwellings, though it was then much more shut in by the forest than now. In some places, within my own remembrance, the pines would scrape both sides of a chaise at once, and women and children who were compelled to go this way to Lincoln **1** alone and on foot did it with fear, and often ran a good part of the distance. Though mainly but a humble route to neighboring villages, or for the woodman's team, it once amused the traveller more than now by its variety, and lingered longer in his memory. Where now firm open fields stretch from the village to the woods, it then ran through a maple swamp on a founda-

Thoreau was always interested in Concord's historic past. Ruined mills, foundations, cellar holes, and chimney bases fascinated him. Some of his unpublished manuscripts show that he interviewed elderly people who remembered the Revolution and then put down their recollections of what happened at the Battle of Concord on April 19, 1775.

1 *this way to Lincoln.* Sanborn, who knew old Concord well, has an interesting footnote on this in the Bibliophile Edition (II, 152n.): "The shorter road from Concord village to Lincoln, the next town south-east, runs through the Walden woods and skirts the Pond, which lies partly in Lincoln. It was not the oldest road, but a makeshift of later times for access to the woods and the ponds, and naturally became the abode of denizens who rather shunned publicity, like the freed slaves of the 18th century, and white persons who had an affinity more than normal for ardent spirits."

tion of logs, the remnants of which, doubtless, still underlie the present dusty highway, from the Stratten, now the Alms House, Farm, to Brister's Hill.   **2**

East of my bean-field, across the road, lived Cato Ingraham, slave of Duncan Ingraham, Esquire, gentleman of Concord village; who built his slave a house, and gave him permission to live in Walden Woods; — Cato, not Uticensis, but Concordiensis. Some say that he was a Guinea Negro. There are a few who remember his little patch among the walnuts, which he let grow up till he should be old and need them; but a younger and whiter speculator got them at last. He too, however, occupies an equally narrow house at present. Cato's half-obliterated cellar hole still remains, though known to few, being concealed from the traveller by a fringe of pines. It is now filled with the smooth sumach, (*Rhus glabra,*) and one of the earliest species of goldenrod (*Solidago stricta*) grows there luxuriantly.   **3**   **4**

Here, by the very corner of my field, still nearer to town, Zilpha, a colored woman, had her little house, where she spun linen for the townsfolk, making the Walden Woods ring with her shrill singing, for she had a loud and notable voice. At length, in the war of 1812, her dwelling was set on fire by English soldiers, prisoners on parole, when she was away, and her cat and dog and hens were all burned up together. She led a hard life, and somewhat inhumane. One old frequenter of these woods remembers, that as he passed her house one noon he heard her muttering to herself over her gurgling pot, — "Ye are all bones, bones!" I have seen bricks amid the oak copse there.   **5**   **6**

Down the road, on the right hand, on Brister's Hill, lived Brister Freeman, "a handy Negro," slave of Squire Cummings once, — there where grow still the apple-trees which Brister planted and tended; large old trees now, but their fruit still wild and ciderish to my taste. Not long since I read his epitaph in the old Lincoln burying-ground, a little on one side, near the unmarked graves of some British grenadiers who fell in the retreat from Concord, — where he is styled " Sippio Brister," — Scipio Africanus he had some title to be called, — "a man of color," as if he were discolored. It also told me, with staring emphasis, when he died; which was but an indirect way of informing me that he ever lived. With him dwelt Fenda, his hospitable   **7**   **8**   **9**

2 *the Alms House.* This was in back of the Emerson home. The comma after it makes the sentence difficult to understand. Parentheses around "now the Alms House Farm" would have clarified the wording.

3 *East of my bean-field.* Sanborn (*ibid.*) explains the background:
"Thoreau's bean-field was the sandy pasture afterward planted by him with pines for Emerson, who owned it. . . . Duncan Ingraham, Cato's master, was a sea captain and Surinam merchant, who had made a fortune and retired to live on it in Concord village, near where the Library now stands. He was an ancestor of Captain Marryat, the novelist, and of Captain Ingraham, of the U. S. Navy, who distinguished himself by refusing to give up a Hungarian refugee on board his vessel in 1854. Cato was one of the slaves in which Ingraham occasionally dealt; when he married, his master freed him and he went to live near Walden. He died in 1805, and his master died in 1811.
"Ingraham was a Tory in the early years of our Revolution, as were the grandmother and great-uncles of Thoreau; and he may have aided in the escape of Dr. Jones, one of those uncles, from the Concord Gaol in the summer of 1775. His was also one of the houses in which Sir Archibald Campbell visited, while a prisoner on parole in Concord in 1776–77. Ingraham became reconciled to independence before the war ended, and his large property was never confiscated, as was the small estate of Daniel Bliss, a great-uncle of Emerson, living in Concord."
See also the *Journal*, 1845–1847; I, 419 ff.

4 *not Uticensis.* Cato's grandson who died at Utica and is so referred to. As to Cato's cellar hole, Channing, in his copy of *Walden*, says that it "is the one directly at the opening of the path from the Walden road to Goose pond."

5 *in the war of 1812.* Sanborn (II, 154n.): "Concord was an inland town, and therefore chosen for the residence of paroled prisoners in our two wars with England, while awaiting their exchange. Among those received in the war of 1812 were some of the officers and sailors of the *Guerrière*, captured by "Old Ironsides" not far from the Massachusetts coast; and these may have been the incendiaries of poor Zilpha's cottage."

6 *inhumane.* On ms. 1027 this was "witch-like."

wife, who told fortunes, yet pleasantly, — large, round, and black, blacker than any of the children of night, such a dusky orb as never rose on Concord before or since.

Farther down the hill, on the left, on the old road in the woods, are marks of some homestead of the Stratten family; whose orchard once covered all the slope of Brister's Hill, but was long since killed out by pitch-pines, excepting a few stumps, whose old roots furnish still the wild stocks of many a thrifty village tree. **11**

Nearer yet to town, you come to Breed's location, on **12** the other side of the way, just on the edge of the wood; ground famous for the pranks of a demon not distinctly named in old mythology, who has acted a prominent and astounding part in our New England life, and deserves, as much as any mythological character, to have his biography written one day; who first comes in the guise of a friend or hired man, and then robs and murders the whole family, — New-England Rum. But history must not yet tell the tragedies enacted here; let time intervene in some measure to assuage and lend an azure tint to them. Here the most indistinct and dubious tradition says that once a tavern stood; the well the same, which tempered the traveller's beverage and refreshed his steed. Here then men saluted one another, and heard and told the news, and went their ways again.

Breed's hut was standing only a dozen years ago, though it had long been unoccupied. It was about the size of mine. It was set on fire by mischievous boys, one Election night, if I do not mistake. I lived on the edge of the village then, and had just lost myself over Davenant's Gondibert, that winter that I labored with a **13** lethargy, — which, by the way, I never knew whether to regard as a family complaint, having an uncle who goes **14** to sleep shaving himself, and is obliged to sprout potatoes in a cellar Sundays, in order to keep awake and keep the Sabbath, or as the consequence of my attempt to read Chalmers' collection of English poetry without skipping. It fairly overcame my Nervii. I had just **15** sunk my head on this when the bells rung fire, and in hot haste the engines rolled that way, led by a straggling troop of men and boys, and I among the foremost, for I had leaped the brook. We thought it was far south over the woods, — we who had run to fires before, —

10

7 *Brister's Hill.* Channing, in his copy of *Walden*, says that "this is the place where the lilac grows. Farther down hill are several cellar-holes . . . directly as you enter the path to the pond." Sanborn has this note in the Bibliophile Edition (II, 154n.):

"Brister, who gave his name to the hill and the spring of his region, has a much longer local record than Cato, the Guinea captive. His master, "Squire Cummings," was a Scotchman by parentage, and a physician by profession, — the son of Robert Comyn, who was concerned in the Stuart rebellion of 1715, and migrated to Boston, and then to Concord, where Dr. Cummings was born and practised his profession; dying in 1788, and leaving bequests to Concord and to Harvard College, where at the age of twenty-one he graduated, — or rather got an honorary degree, in 1749.

"Brister was probably born about that time, and long survived his master. He was an active and thrifty negro, but the victim of those rude jokes that men often play on his race. The town butcher, Peter Wheeler, having a ferocious bull to slaughter, was rather afraid to bring him to the bull-ring. Seeing Brister passing his place on his way from Walden, Wheeler asked him to go into the slaughter-house and bring an axe, — with which he should have a job to do. He entered, unsuspecting, and the bull came at him, — then, finding the axe, he bravely defended himself and finally slew the bull. But when he came out, full of horror and indignation, he fled to his woods without waiting to be paid. His wife, Fenda (and perhaps himself as well), was a Guinea negro."

8 *epitaph.* The *Journal* for 1850; II, 20, gives the wording on Brister's tombstone:

"In memory of
Sippio Brister
a man of Colour
who died
Nov. 1. 1820
Æt. 64.

"But that is not telling us that he lived."

9 *Scipio Africanus.* Scipio Africanus Publius Cornelius (237–183 B.C.). The Roman general, also called Scipio the Elder. He directed the invasion of Carthage.

10 *Stratten.* In his copy of *Walden*, Thoreau corrected the spelling of this name to Stratton.

barn, shop, or dwelling-house, or all together. "It's Baker's barn," cried one. "It is the Codman Place," affirmed another. And then fresh sparks went up above the wood, as if the roof fell in, and we all shouted "Concord to the rescue!" Wagons shot past with furious speed and crushing loads, bearing, perchance, among the rest, the agent of the Insurance Company, who was bound to go however far; and ever and anon the engine bell tinkled behind, more slow and sure, and rearmost of all, as it was afterward whispered, came they who set the fire and gave the alarm. Thus we kept on like true idealists, rejecting the evidence of our senses, until at a turn in the road we heard the crackling and actually felt the heat of the fire from over the wall, and realized, alas! that we were there. The very nearness of the fire but cooled our ardor. At first we thought to throw a frog-pond on to it; but concluded to let it burn, it was so far gone and so worthless. So we stood round our engine, jostled one another, expressed our sentiments through speaking trumpets, or in lower tone referred to the great conflagrations which the world has witnessed, including Bascom's shop, and, between ourselves, we thought that, were we there in season with our "tub," and a full frog-pond by, we could turn that threatened last and universal one into another flood. We finally retreated without doing any mischief,— **16** returned to sleep and Gondibert. But as for Gondibert, I would except that passage in the preface about wit being the soul's powder,— "but most of mankind are strangers to wit, as Indians are to powder." **17**

It chanced that I walked that way across the fields the following night, about the same hour, and hearing a low moaning at this spot, I drew near in the dark, and discovered the only survivor of the family that I know, **18** the heir of both its virtues and its vices, who alone was interested in this burning, lying on his stomach and looking over the cellar wall at the still smouldering cinders beneath, muttering to himself, as is his wont. He **19** had been working far off in the river meadows all day, and had improved the first moments that he could call his own to visit the home of his fathers and his youth. He gazed into the cellar from all sides and points of view by turns, always lying down to it, as if there was some treasure, which he remembered, concealed between the stones, where there was absolutely

11 *a thrifty village tree.* He also put an X here and wrote: "Surveying for Cyrus Jarvis Dec. 23 '56—he shows me a deed of this lot containing 6A. 52 rods all on the W. of the Wayland Road— & consisting of plowland, orcharding & woodland—sold by Joseph Stratton to Samuel Swan of Concord. In holder Aug. 11th 1777."

12 *Breed's.* A note in the Bibliophile Edition (II, 156) says that "Breed was the barber . . . his vice was drink, and he had been dead for years when this fire occurred. . . . It was his son, also a toper, whom Thoreau found at the ruins the next day." See the *Journal* for 1850; II, 20. On ms. 1035 Thoreau says that Breed "kept his patrons awake by his wit. He had for a neighbor a tailor who thought himself above him, it is said, but was thus punished by Breed's muse." Thoreau adds that this is from his "collection of old Concord poetry, which contains also some scraps from the works of Jim Davis, the fiddler. . . ."
See also the *Journal*, 1845–1847; I, 424.

13 *Davenant's Gondibert.* William Davenant (1606–1668), while imprisoned in the Tower of London, wrote *Gondibert, an Heroick Poem*, which was published in 1651. It is a long dull work (with which the author himself became bored), but it has many quotable lines. See below.

14 *an uncle who goes to sleep shaving himself.* Charles Dunbar, a maternal uncle. Thoreau has much about him in the *Journal*, particularly after he died on March 27, 1856.

15 *Nervii.* Another of Thoreau's puns, this time a pretty bad one. The Nervii were a barbarian tribe defeated by Caesar. (See *The Gallic Wars*, Book II: 57 B.C.).

16 *without doing any mischief.* Ms. 1033: "and without the prospect of a civil card or of a hot chocolate."

17 *"as Indians are to powder."* Preface to *Gondibert*, 1651, p. 20.

18 *the only survivor.* Barber Breed's son as indicated above. Channing, in his copy of *Walden*, says that "this Breed . . . was a semi-idiot, like Fred Cogswell at the Poor-house."

19 *as is his wont.* Ms. 1034: "for he has a strange way of talking."

nothing but a heap of bricks and ashes. The house being gone, he looked at what there was left. He was soothed by the sympathy which my mere presence implied, and showed me, as well as the darkness permitted, where the well was covered up; which, thank Heaven, could never be burned; and he groped long about the wall to find the well-sweep which his father had cut and mounted, feeling for the iron hook or staple by which a burden had been fastened to the heavy end, — all that he could now cling to, — to convince me that it was no common "rider." I felt it, and still remark it almost daily in my walks, for by it hangs the history of a family.

Once more, on the left, where are seen the well and lilac bushes by the wall, in the now open field, lived Nutting and Le Grosse. But to return toward Lincoln.

Farther in the woods than any of these, where the road approaches nearest to the pond, Wyman the potter squatted, and furnished his townsmen with earthen ware, and left descendants to succeed him. Neither were they rich in worldly goods, holding the land by sufferance while they lived; and there often the sheriff came in vain to collect the taxes, and "attached a chip," for form's sake, as I have read in his accounts, there being nothing else that he could lay his hands on. One day in midsummer, when I was hoeing, a man who was carrying a load of pottery to market stopped his horse against my field and inquired concerning Wyman the younger. He had long ago bought a potter's wheel of him, and wished to know what had become of him. I had read of the potter's clay and wheel in Scripture, but it had never occurred to me that the pots we use were not such as had come down unbroken from those days, or grown on trees like gourds somewhere, and I was pleased to hear that so fictile an art was ever practised in my neighborhood.

The last inhabitant of these woods before me was an Irishman, Hugh Quoil, (if I have spelt his name with coil enough,) who occupied Wyman's tenement, — Col. Quoil, he was called. Rumor said that he had been a soldier at Waterloo. If he had lived I should have made him fight his battles over again. His trade here was that of a ditcher. Napoleon went to St. Helena; Quoil came to Walden Woods. All I know of him is tragic. He was a man of manners, like one who had

20 *the well-sweep.* Ms. 1035: "I have even thought to make a drawing of it for the Smithsonian Institution; for it has a peculiar curve, not to be paralleled by any that I know, whether it was so designed by the maker, or got a twist in the September Gale." The Bibliophile Edition (II, 159) then adds:

"Wells must be among the oldest monuments of man on the globe. The white man hereabouts still resorts to springs which were stoned up by the Indians. Little does the country squire think of this when he encloses one within a costly curb. One must forget himself and his age to remember how old may be the most ancient well which men use today,—coeval, almost, with the race. So, from the first, poets have derived their inspiration from a few old wells on the mountain of the Muses. Few dig anew, though some drink deeper than their brethren. But I trust that in this new country many wells are to be dug."

21 *Nutting and Le Grosse.* Harding (1963, page 308) identifies them. Also Wyman (below). They were obscure people, probably farmers.

22 *left descendants to succeed him.* Thoreau changed this on the page proofs from "his descendants dwelt there also."

23 *"attached a chip."* A legal gesture to prove that an official effort had been made to collect the debt.

24 *potter's clay and wheel in Scripture.* In his own copy of *Walden*, Thoreau placed a question mark in the margin here.

25 *fictile.* Webster: "Relating esp. to pottery or to molding in any soft material."

26 *Hugh Quoil.* There is a long account of him in the *Journal* for 1845–1847; I, 414–417. And Sanborn, in the Bibliophile Edition (II, 160n.) has this to say about him: "This Hugh Quoil was probably named Cahill in Ireland; he may have been a sergeant at Waterloo—certainly not a colonel. In his time in Concord few of the Irish peasantry had come over to the rural towns, and if an Irishman appeared he was likely to have been a discharged or deserted soldier, a printer, or some skilled but shiftless mechanic. A contemporary of Cahill, but an English tailor, had been in the British navy and seen Napoleon at St. Helena; then he came to Concord and practised his trade there. His children were perhaps pupils of Thoreau,—certainly of Ellen Fuller, the wife of Thoreau's friend Channing."

Thoreau makes a pun on his name—and an obvious one.

The battlefield of Waterloo
as it was in Thoreau's time

seen the world, and was capable of more civil speech than you could well attend to.   He wore a great coat in mid-summer, being affected with the trembling delirium, and his face was the color of carmine.   He died in the road at the foot of Brister's Hill shortly after I came to the woods, so that I have not remembered him as a neighbor.   Before his house was pulled down, when his comrades avoided it as " an unlucky castle," I visited it.   There lay his old clothes curled up by use, as if they were himself, upon his raised plank bed.   His pipe lay broken on the hearth, instead of a bowl broken at the fountain.   The last could never have been the symbol of his death, for he confessed to me that, though he had heard of Brister's Spring, he had never seen it ; and soiled cards, kings of diamonds spades and hearts, were scattered over the floor.   One black chicken which the administrator could not catch, black as night and as silent, not even croaking, awaiting Reynard, still went to roost in the next apartment.   In the rear there was the dim outline of a garden, which had been planted but had never received its first hoeing, owing to those terrible shaking fits, though it was now harvest time.   It was over-run with Roman wormwood and beggar-ticks, which last stuck to my clothes for all fruit.   The skin of a woodchuck was freshly stretched upon the back of the house, a trophy of his last Waterloo ; but no warm cap or mittens would he want more.

Now only a dent in the earth marks the site of these dwellings, with buried cellar stones, and strawberries, raspberries, thimble-berries, hazel-bushes, and sumachs

28

29

30
31

27 *All I know of him is tragic.* Ms. 1038: "I have noticed that there is something pathetic in the sedentary life of men who have travelled."

28 *after I came to the woods.* Ms. 1038: " 'There he lay' as one who found him said, 'looking better than in life.' "

29 *broken on the hearth, instead of a bowl broken at the fountain.* Paraphrased from Ecclesiastes 12:6.

30 *would he want more.* Ms. 219 adds: "whichever place he were gone to." Ms. 464 then has: "How fares it with him, what fighting or sketchwork he finds to do now—whether his thirst is quenched or still red—whether he strangles still with some liquid demon—perchance on more equal terms—till at length he shall drink him all up—I cannot by any means learn."

31 *Now only a dent in the earth. Journal,* 1845–1847; I, 420 and 424.

growing in the sunny sward there; some pitch-pine or gnarled oak occupies what was the chimney nook, and a sweet-scented black-birch, perhaps, waves where the door-stone was. Sometimes the well dent is visible, where once a spring oozed; now dry and tearless grass; or it was covered deep, — not to be discovered till some late day, — with a flat stone under the sod, when the last of the race departed. What a sorrowful act must that be, — the covering up of wells! coincident with the opening of wells of tears. These cellar dents, like deserted fox burrows, old holes, are all that is left where once were the stir and bustle of human life, and "fate, free-will, foreknowledge absolute," in some form and dialect or other were by turns discussed. But all I can learn of their conclusions amounts to just this, that " Cato and Brister pulled wool; " which is about as edifying as the history of more famous schools of philosophy.

32 , 33

Still grows the vivacious lilac a generation after the door and lintel and the sill are gone, unfolding its sweet-scented flowers each spring, to be plucked by the musing traveller; planted and tended once by children's hands, in front-yard plots, — now standing by wall-sides in retired pastures, and giving place to new-rising forests; — the last of that stirp, sole survivor of that family. Little did the dusky children think that the puny slip with its two eyes only, which they stuck in the ground in the shadow of the house and daily watered, would root itself so, and outlive them, and house itself in the rear that shaded it, and grown man's garden and orchard, and tell their story faintly to the lone wanderer a half century after they had grown up and died, — blossoming as fair, and smelling as sweet, as in that first spring. I mark its still tender, civil, cheerful, lilac colors.

34

But this small village, germ of something more, why did it fail while Concord keeps its ground? Were there no natural advantages, — no water privileges, forsooth? Ay, the deep Walden Pond and cool Brister's Spring, — privilege to drink long and healthy draughts at these, all unimproved by these men but to dilute their glass. They were universally a thirsty race. Might not the basket, stable-broom, mat-making, corn-parching, linen-spinning, and pottery business have thrived here, making the wilderness to blossom like the rose, and a

35

36

32 *the stir and bustle of human life.* Ms. 218: "and man's destiny was being consummated."

33 *"fate, free-will, foreknowledge absolute."* In his copy of *Walden*, Channing wrote: "*Paradise Lost*, II, 1.560."

34 *Still grows the vivacious lilac. Journal*, 1845–1847; I, 420.

35 *while Concord keeps its ground.* On second thought, Thoreau evidently decided that Concord was standing still, for this was originally (on ms. 217): "while Concord grows apace."

36 *making the wilderness to blossom like the rose.* This is paraphrased from Isaiah 35:1—and apparently from memory, for ms. 217 has "bloom" instead of "blossom."

Concord about 1840

numerous posterity have inherited the land of their fathers? The sterile soil would at least have been **37** proof against a low-land degeneracy. Alas! how little does the memory of these human inhabitants enhance the beauty of the landscape! Again, perhaps, Nature will try, with me for a first settler, and my house raised last spring to be the oldest in the hamlet. **38**

I am not aware that any man has ever built on the spot which I occupy. Deliver me from a city built on the site of a more ancient city, whose materials are ruins, whose gardens cemeteries. The soil is blanched and accursed there, and before that becomes necessary the earth itself will be destroyed. With such reminiscences I repeopled the woods and lulled myself asleep.

At this season I seldom had a visitor. When the **39** snow lay deepest no wanderer ventured near my house for a week or fortnight at a time, but there I lived as snug as a meadow mouse, or as cattle and poultry which are said to have survived for a long time buried in drifts, even without food; or like that early settler's family in the town of Sutton, in this state, whose cottage was completely covered by the great snow of 1717 when he was absent, and an Indian found it only by the hole which the chimney's breath made in the drift, and so relieved the family. But no friendly Indian concerned himself about me; nor needed he, for the master

37 *The sterile soil. Journal*, 1845–1847; I, 423.

38 *the oldest in the hamlet*. Ms. 216: "and with such thoughts I lulled myself to sleep." See the last sentence in the next paragraph.

39 *At this season I seldom had a visitor*. This part of Chapter XIV was apparently to be a new chapter. On the top of ms. 854 the title "Winter Visitors" is written. And the opening sentence is: "In the winter my visitors were few and far between."

of the house was at home. The Great Snow! How
cheerful it is to hear of! When the farmers could not
get to the woods and swamps with their teams, and
were obliged to cut down the shade trees before their
houses, and when the crust was harder cut off the trees
in the swamps ten feet from the ground, as it appeared
the next spring.

In the deepest snows, the path which I used from

The cairn in winter (*A Herbert Gleason photograph taken in 1906*)

the highway to my house, about half a mile long, might have been represented by a meandering dotted line, with wide intervals between the dots. For a week of even weather I took exactly the same number of steps, and of the same length, coming and going, stepping deliberately and with the precision of a pair of dividers in my own deep tracks, — to such routine the winter reduces us, — yet often they were filled with heaven's own blue. But no weather interfered fatally with my walks, or rather my going abroad, for I frequently tramped eight or ten miles through the deepest snow to keep an appointment with a beech-tree, or a yellow-birch, or an old acquaintance among the pines; when the ice and snow causing their limbs to droop, and so sharpening their tops, had changed the pines into fir-trees; wading to the tops of the highest hills when the snow was nearly two feet deep on a level, and shaking down another snow-storm on my head at every step; or sometimes creeping and floundering thither on my hands and knees, when the hunters had gone into winter quarters. One afternoon I amused myself by watching a barred owl (*Strix nebulosa*) sitting on one of the lower dead limbs of a white-pine, close to the trunk, in broad daylight, I standing within a rod of him. He could hear me when I moved and cronched the snow with my feet, but could not plainly see me. When I made most noise he would stretch out his neck, and erect his neck feathers, and open his eyes wide; but their lids soon fell again, and he began to nod. I too felt a slumberous influence after watching him half an hour, as he sat thus with his eyes half open, like a cat, winged brother of the cat. There was only a narrow slit left between their lids, by which he preserved a peninsular relation to me; thus, with half-shut eyes, looking out from the land of dreams, and endeavoring to realize me, vague object or mote that interrupted his visions. At length, on some louder noise or my nearer approach, he would grow uneasy and sluggishly turn about on his perch, as if impatient at having his dreams disturbed; and when he launched himself off and flapped through the pines, spreading his wings to unexpected breadth, I could not hear the slightest sound from them. Thus, guided amid the pine boughs rather by a delicate sense of their neighborhood than by sight, feeling his twilight way as it were with his sensitive pinions, he found a new perch,

40

40 *filled with heaven's own blue*. In his copy of *Walden*, Channing wrote: "He refers . . . to the effect of differing mediums to produce blue, also seen in the sky and the eye. He often made holes in the snow to see the blue—bluing he called it—in the air. Velvet Breughel."

where he might in peace await the dawning of his day.

As I walked over the long causeway made for the railroad through the meadows, I encountered many a blustering and nipping wind, for nowhere has it freer play ; and when the frost had smitten me on one cheek, heathen as I was, I turned to it the other also. Nor **41** was it much better by the carriage road from Brister's Hill. For I came to town still, like a friendly Indian, when the contents of the broad open fields were all piled up between the walls of the Walden road, and half an hour sufficed to obliterate the tracks of the last traveller. And when I returned new drifts would have formed, through which I floundered, where the busy north-west wind had been depositing the powdery snow round a sharp angle in the road, and not a rabbit's track, nor even the fine print, the small type, of a meadow **42** mouse was to be seen. Yet I rarely failed to find, even in mid-winter, some warm and springy swamp where the grass and the skunk-cabbage still put forth with perennial verdure, and some hardier bird occasionally **43** awaited the return of spring.

Sometimes, notwithstanding the snow, when I returned from my walk at evening I crossed the deep tracks of a woodchopper leading from my door, and found **44** his pile of whittlings on the hearth, and my house filled with the odor of his pipe. Or on a Sunday afternoon, if I chanced to be at home, I heard the cronching of

41 *I turned to it the other also.* Paraphrased from Matthew 5:39.

42 *of a meadow mouse.* Thoreau put the word "deer" in place of "meadow" in his own copy of *Walden*.

43 *perennial verdure, and.* "a robin or a large" was added after this in the page proofs.

44 *a woodchopper.* Presumably Alek Therien. See Index.

Skunk cabbage

the snow made by the step of a long-headed farmer, **45**
who from far through the woods sought my house, to
have a social "crack;" one of the few of his vocation
who are "men on their farms;" who donned a frock instead of a professor's gown, and is as ready to extract
the moral out of church or state as to haul a load of
manure from his barn-yard. We talked of rude and
simple times, when men sat about large fires in cold
bracing weather, with clear heads; and when other des-
sert failed, we tried our teeth on many a nut which wise
squirrels have long since abandoned, for those which
have the thickest shells are commonly empty.

The one who came from farthest to my lodge, through
deepest snows and most dismal tempests, was a poet. **46**
A farmer, a hunter, a soldier, a reporter, even a philosopher, may be daunted; but nothing can deter a poet, for
he is actuated by pure love. Who can predict his
comings and goings? His business calls him out at all
hours, even when doctors sleep. We made that small
house ring with boisterous mirth and resound with the
murmur of much sober talk, making amends then to
Walden vale for the long silences. Broadway was still
and deserted in comparison. At suitable intervals there
were regular salutes of laughter, which might have
been referred indifferently to the last uttered or the
forth-coming jest. We made many a "bran new" theory
of life over a thin dish of gruel, which combined the
advantages of conviviality with the clear-headedness
which philosophy requires.

I should not forget that during my last winter at the
pond there was another welcome visitor, who at one **47**
time came through the village, through snow and rain
and darkness, till he saw my lamp through the trees,
and shared with me some long winter evenings. One
of the last of the philosophers,—Connecticut gave him to
the world,—he peddled first her wares, afterwards, as he
declares, his brains. These he peddles still, prompting **48**
God and disgracing man, bearing for fruit his brain only,
like the nut its kernel. I think that he must be the
man of the most faith of any alive. His words and
attitude always suppose a better state of things than
other men are acquainted with, and he will be the last
man to be disappointed as the ages revolve. He has no **49**
venture in the present. But though comparatively disregarded now, when his day comes, laws unsuspected by

45 *a long-headed farmer*. Sanborn identifies him
in the Bibliophile Edition (II, 167n.): "The 'long-
headed farmer' was Edmund Hosmer, a native of
Concord, who had lived in Quincy and had seen
the first President Adams at church there; then
returned to his native town, and was now living
on the Cambridge Turnpike, or a little off from
that, along which his well-tilled farm extended.
This made him one of Thoreau's nearest neighbors, by a woodland path often traversed by the
"Walkers" of Concord,—Emerson, Alcott, Channing and Thoreau,—to whom I joined myself in
1855. It was in one of his houses that the Alcotts
found shelter on returning from Harvard in 1844–
45; and soon after, George Curtis and his brother
Burrill lived there for a time. Mr. Hosmer long
outlived Thoreau, and kept up his friendship with
the family to the last. By 1855 he was the owner
of an old house on what was once the farm of
John Winthrop, and there passed the last years of
his industrious life. Another and still older house
on the Winthrop, or Hunt, farm was sought by
Daniel Ricketson, but it was never occupied by
him; it was soon torn down by Mr. Hosmer."

46 *a poet*. William Ellery Channing. Sanborn
has this footnote about him in the Bibliophile Edition (II, 169n.): "During the *Walden* episode . . .
Channing was living three miles north of Walden,
—but, accustomed to long walks in all weathers,
he made nothing of the six-mile detour which
brought him to the cabin in the Emerson pine-
wood."

47 *another welcome visitor*. This was Bronson
Alcott. Sanborn's note gives an earlier version of
what Thoreau had to say about him:
"The account of Alcott was much re-written.
Earlier forms of it show these changes:—
"'Alcott is a geometer, a visionary, the Laplace
of ethics; more intellect, less of the affections,
sight beyond talents; a substratum of practical
skill and knowledge unquestionable, but overlaid and concealed by a faith in the unseen
and impracticable. Seeks to realize an entire life;
a catholic observer; habitually takes in the farthest
star and nebula into his scheme. Will be the last
man to be disappointed as the ages revolve. His
attitude is one of greater faith and expectation
than that of any man I know; with little to show;
with undue share (for a philosopher) of the
weaknesses of humanity. The most hospitable intellect, embracing high and low. For children,
how much that means! for the insane and vagabond,—for the poet and scholar.'
"These were notes made before the Walden
life, and having reference to the Fruitlands episode, of which Thoreau had much knowledge.
Again he wrote,—'When Alcott's day comes, laws

most will take effect, and masters of families and rulers will come to him for advice. —

"How blind that cannot see serenity!" **50**

A true friend of man; almost the only friend of human progress. An Old Mortality, say rather an Immortality, with unwearied patience and faith making plain the image engraven in men's bodies, the God of whom they are but defaced and leaning monuments. With his hospitable intellect he embraces children, beggars, insane, and scholars, and entertains the thought of all, adding to it commonly some breadth and elegance. I think that he should keep a caravansary on the world's highway, where philosophers of all nations might put up, and on his sign should be printed, "Entertainment for man, but not for his beast. Enter ye that have leisure and a quiet mind, who earnestly seek the right road." **52** He is perhaps the sanest man and has the fewest crotchets of any I chance to know; the same yesterday and to-morrow. Of yore we had sauntered and talked, and effectually put the world behind us; for he was pledged to no institution in it, freeborn, *ingenuus.* Whichever way we turned, it seemed that the heavens and the earth had met together, since he enhanced the **53** beauty of the landscape. A blue-robed man, whose fittest roof is the overarching sky which reflects his serenity. I do not see how he can ever die; Nature cannot spare him.

Having each some shingles of thought well dried, we **54** sat and whittled them, trying our knives, and admiring the clear yellowish grain of the pumpkin pine. We waded so gently and reverently, or we pulled together so smoothly, that the fishes of thought were not scared from the stream, nor feared any angler on the bank, but came and went grandly, like the clouds which float through the western sky, and the mother-o'-pearl flocks which sometimes form and dissolve there. There we worked, revising mythology, rounding a fable here and there, and building castles in the air for which earth offered no worthy foundation. Great Looker! **55** Great Expecter! to converse with whom was a New England Night's Entertainment. Ah! such discourse we had, hermit and philosopher, and the old settler I **56** have spoken of, — we three, — it expanded and racked **57** my little house; I should not dare to say how many

unsuspected by most will take effect; the system will crystallize according to them; all scales and falsehood will slough off; everything will be in its place.' "

48 *his brains.* Ms. 862: "with nothing to show for his pains."

49 *as the ages revolve.* Ms. 862: "for he interprets more than any. God will find it hard to astonish him."

50 *"How blind that cannot see serenity!"* Channing, in his copy of *Walden,* says that this is from Thomas Storer's *Life of Wolsey.*

51 *Old Mortality.* The leading character in a novel by Sir Walter Scott published under this title in 1816.

52 *"seek the right road."* This was "The higher road" on ms. 1044 and is followed by: "A thought floats as serenely and as much at home in his mind as a duck pluming herself on a far inland lake." This inept comparison was canceled in the manuscript.

53 *had met together.* This followed another clumsy image on ms. 1046: "and righteousness and peace had kissed each other." Also canceled.

54 *Having each some shingles of thought.* This passage has been much commented on. See James Lyndon Shanley (1957, page 62); Charles Anderson (1968, page 73). Its origin is in the *Journal* for May 9, 1853; V, 130–131. And Alcott's *Journals* commemorate this happy exchange of ideas. In them he says: "Thoreau is a walking Muse, winged at the anklets and rhyming his steps."

55 *Great Looker! Great Expecter!* Thoreau had some trouble with these. On ms. 784 he had "Great Thinker!" and on ms. 1047, "Great Seer!" with "Thinker" crossed out.

56 *the old settler.* See the Index for other references.

57 *it expanded and racked.* Again Thoreau placed a question mark opposite this line in his own copy of *Walden.*

pounds' weight there was above the atmospheric pressure on every circular inch; it opened its seams so that they had to be calked with much dulness thereafter to stop the consequent leak; — but I had enough of that kind of oakum already picked.

There was one other with whom I had "solid seasons," long to be remembered, at his house in the village, and who looked in upon me from time to time; but I had no more for society there.   **58**

There too, as every where, I sometimes expected the   **59**
Visitor who never comes. The Vishnu Purana says,   **60**
"The house-holder is to remain at eventide in his court-yard as long as it takes to milk a cow, or longer if he pleases, to await the arrival of a guest." I often performed this duty of hospitality, waited long enough to milk a whole herd of cows, but did not see the man approaching from the town.

58 *There was one other.* Emerson is quite surely meant here. Ms. 864 has: "Others there were, one or two who paid me angel visits, looking in."

59 *the Visitor who never comes.* The expected visitor who never comes is a concept among many peoples. At a Jewish Seder (Passover feast), for instance, a chair at the table is left vacant for Elijah.

60 *The Vishnu Purana.* Thoreau used H. H. Wilson's translation of this (London, 1840). He copied about 30 pages of extracts from it for future reference.

WINTER ANIMALS.

WHEN the ponds were firmly frozen, they afforded not only new and shorter routes to many points, but new views from their surfaces of the familiar landscape around them. When I crossed Flints' Pond, after it was covered with snow, though I had often paddled about and skated over it, it was so unexpectedly wide and so strange that I could think of nothing but Baffin's Bay. The Lincoln hills rose up around me at the extremity of a snowy plain, in which I did not remember to have stood before; and the fishermen, at an indeterminable distance over the ice, moving slowly about with their wolfish dogs, passed for sealers or Esquimaux, or in misty weather loomed like fabulous creatures, and I did not know whether they were giants or pygmies. I took this course when I went to lecture in Lincoln in **1** the evening, travelling in no road and passing no house between my own hut and the lecture room. In Goose **2** Pond, which lay in my way, a colony of muskrats dwelt, and raised their cabins high above the ice, though

In the original table of contents for *Walden*, "Winter Animals" preceded "Former Inhabitants; and Winter Visitors."

1 *when I went to lecture in Lincoln.* See the *Journal* for January 7, 1852; III, 177. "Last evening walked to Lincoln to lecture in a driving snow-storm." Then comes a fine three-page account of a winter landscape at night. But Thoreau was not living at Walden in 1852.

2 *between my own hut and the lecture room.* Ms. 1002: "2 or 3 miles distant."

none could be seen abroad when I crossed it. Walden, being like the rest usually bare of snow, or with only shallow and interrupted drifts on it, was my yard, where I could walk freely when the snow was nearly two feet deep on a level elsewhere and the villagers were confined to their streets. There, far from the village street, and except at very long intervals, from the jingle of sleigh-bells, I slid and skated, as in a vast moose-yard well trodden, overhung by oak woods and solemn pines bent down with snow or bristling with icicles.

For sounds in winter nights, and often in winter days, I heard the forlorn but melodious note of a hooting owl indefinitely far ; such a sound as the frozen earth would yield if struck with a suitable plectrum, the very *lingua vernacula* of Walden Wood, and quite familiar to me at last, though I never saw the bird while it was making it. I seldom opened my door in a winter evening without hearing it; *Hoo hoo hoo, hoorer hoo,* sounded sonorously, and the first three syllables accented somewhat like *how der do ;* or sometimes *hoo hoo* only. One night in the beginning of winter, before the pond froze over, about nine o'clock, I was startled by the loud honking of a goose, and, step-

ping to the door, heard the sound of their wings like a tempest in the woods as they flew low over my house. They passed over the pond toward Fair Haven, seemingly deterred from settling by my light, their commodore honking all the while with a regular beat. Suddenly an unmistakable cat-owl from very near me, with the most harsh and tremendous voice I ever heard from any inhabitant of the woods, responded at regular intervals to the goose, as if determined to expose and disgrace this intruder from Hudson's Bay by exhibiting a greater compass and volume of voice in a native, and *boo-hoo* him out of Concord horizon. What do you mean by alarming the citadel at this time of night consecrated to me? Do you think I am ever caught napping at such an hour, and that I have not got lungs and a larynx as well as yourself? *Boo-hoo, boo-hoo, boo-hoo!* It was one of the most thrilling discords I ever heard. And yet, if you had a discriminating ear, there were in it the elements of a concord such as these plains never saw nor heard.

3

4

I also heard the whooping of the ice in the pond, my great bed-fellow in that part of Concord, as if it were restless in its bed and would fain turn over, were troubled with flatulency and bad dreams; or I was waked by the cracking of the ground by the frost, as if some one had driven a team against my door, and in the morning would find a crack in the earth a quarter of a mile long and a third of an inch wide.

5

Sometimes I heard the foxes as they ranged over the snow crust, in moonlight nights, in search of a partridge or other game, barking raggedly and demoniacally like forest dogs, as if laboring with some anxiety, or seeking expression, struggling for light and to be dogs outright and run freely in the streets; for if we take the ages into our account, may there not be a civilization going on among brutes as well as men? They seemed to me to be rudimental, burrowing men, still standing on their defence, awaiting their transformation. Sometimes one came near to my window, attracted by my light, barked a vulpine curse at me, and then retreated.

6

Usually the red squirrel (*Sciurus Hudsonius*) waked me in the dawn, coursing over the roof and up and down the sides of the house, as if sent out of the woods for this purpose. In the course of the winter I threw out half a bushel of ears of sweet-corn, which had not

3 *alarming the citadel.* The sacred geese in Juno's temple roused M. Manlius from sleep when the Gauls attacked the Roman Capitol in 390 B.C. This well-known incident is told by Virgil, Lucretius, Ovid, Livy, and Martial.

4 *such as these plains never saw nor heard.* The Bibliophile Edition (II, 176) then has:

> "which
> Would ruffle up your spirits and put a tougue
> In every goose's feather, that should move
> The stones of Walden shore to rise and mutiny."

Cf. *Julius Caesar*, III, ii: ". . . that should move The stones of Rome to rise and mutiny."

5 *a third of an inch wide. Journal* for November 3, 1852; IV, 409.

6 *They seemed to me to be rudimental, burrowing men.* Thoreau expresses this idea several times in his writings. It may come from his extensive reading in Oriental literature, which takes the transmigration of souls from beasts to man for granted. *Journal*, 1845–1846; I, 396.

got ripe, on to the snow crust by my door, and was amused by watching the motions of the various animals which were baited by it.   In the twilight and the night the rabbits came regularly and made a hearty meal. All day long the red squirrels came and went, and afforded me much entertainment by their manœuvres. One would approach at first warily through the shrub-oaks, running over the snow crust by fits and starts like a leaf blown by the wind, now a few paces this way, with wonderful speed and waste of energy, making in-conceivable haste with his " trotters," as if it were for a **7** wager, and now as many paces that way, but never get-ting on more than half a rod at a time ; and then sud-denly pausing with a ludicrous expression and a gratui tous somerset, as if all the eyes in the universe were fixed on him, — for all the motions of a squirrel, even **8** in the most solitary recesses of the forest, imply specta-tors as much as those of a dancing girl, — wasting more time in delay and circumspection than would have suf-ficed to walk the whole distance, — I never saw one walk, — and then suddenly, before you could say Jack **9** Robinson, he would be in the top of a young pitch-pine, winding up his clock and chiding all imaginary specta- **10** tors, soliloquizing and talking to all the universe at the same time, — for no reason that I could ever detect, or he himself was aware of, I suspect.   At length he would reach the corn, and selecting a suitable ear, brisk **11** about in the same uncertain trigonometrical way to the top-most stick of my wood-pile, before my window, where he looked me in the face, and there sit for hours, supplying himself with a new ear from time. to time, nibbling at first voraciously and throwing the half-naked cobs about ; till at length he grew more dainty still and played with his food, tasting only the inside of the ker-nel, and the ear, which was held balanced over the stick by one paw, slipped from his careless grasp and fell to the ground, when he would look over at it with a ludi-crous expression of uncertainty, as if suspecting that it had life, with a mind not made up whether to get it again, or a new one, or be off ; now thinking of corn, then listening to hear what was in the wind.   So the little impudent fellow would waste many an ear in a forenoon ; till at last, seizing some longer and plumper one, considerably bigger than himself, and skilfully bal-ancing it, he would set out with it to the woods, like a

7 *"trotters."* Hind legs. Not in quotes on ms. 226.

8 *for all the motions of a squirrel.* Ms. 222: "The squirrels grew at last to be quite familiar and oc-casionally stepped upon my shoe when that was in the nearest way. Sometimes at the approach of spring they got under my house two at a time—directly under my feet as I sat reading and writ-ing—and kept up the queerest chuckling and chirruping—and vocal pirouetting and gurgling sounds that ever were heard—and when I stamped they only chirruped the louder as if past all fear and respect on their mad prank, defying all hu-manity to stop them. No you don't—chickaree! chickaree. They were wholly deaf to my argu-ments or failed to perceive their force—and fell into a stream of invective that was irresistible." See last sentence of the second paragraph below which has the first sentence of the passage quoted here. Much of this, paraphrased, is used on page 427.

9 *before you could say Jack Robinson.* This phrase goes back at least to the eighteenth cen-tury.

10 *winding up his clock.* Implying that the noise the squirrel makes sounds like that of a loud clock. This was originally "screwing up his clock."

11 *brisk.* Thoreau changed this to "frisk" in his own copy of *Walden.*

tiger with a buffalo, by the same zig-zag course and frequent pauses, scratching along with it as if it were too heavy for him and falling all the while, making its fall a diagonal between a perpendicular and horizontal, being determined to put it through at any rate; — a singularly frivolous and whimsical fellow; — and so he would get off with it to where he lived, perhaps carry it to the top of a pine tree forty or fifty rods distant, and I would afterwards find the cobs strewn about the woods in various directions.

At length the jays arrive, whose discordant screams were heard long before, as they were warily making their approach an eighth of a mile off, and in a stealthy **12** and sneaking manner they flit from tree to tree, nearer and nearer, and pick up the kernels which the squirrels have dropped. Then, sitting on a pitch-pine bough, they attempt to swallow in their haste a kernel which is too big for their throats and chokes them; and after great labor they disgorge it, and spend an hour in the endeavor to crack it by repeated blows with their bills. They were manifestly thieves, and I had not much respect for them; but the squirrels, though at first shy, went to work as if they were taking what was their own.

Meanwhile also came the chicadees in flocks, which, picking up the crums the squirrels had dropped, flew to the nearest twig, and, placing them under their claws, hammered away at them with their little bills, as if it were an insect in the bark, till they were sufficiently reduced for their slender throats. A little flock of these tit-mice came daily to pick a dinner out of my wood-pile, or the crums at my door, with faint flitting lisping notes, like the tinkling of icicles in the grass, or else with sprightly *day day day*, or more rarely, in spring-like days, a wiry summery *phe-be* from the wood-side. They were so familiar that at length one alighted on an armful of wood which I was carrying in, and pecked at the sticks without fear. I once had a sparrow alight upon my shoulder for a moment while I was hoeing in a village garden, and I felt that I was more distinguished by that circumstance than I should have been by any epaulet I could have worn. The squirrels also grew at last to be quite familiar, and occasionally stepped upon my shoe, when that was the nearest way.

12 *an eighth of a mile off*. Ms. 1012: "a quarter of a mile off."

When the ground was not yet quite covered, and again near the end of winter, when the snow was melted on my south hill-side and about my wood-pile, the partridges came out of the woods morning and evening to feed there. Whichever side you walk in the woods the partridge bursts away on whirring wings, jarring the snow from the dry leaves and twigs on high, which comes sifting down in the sun-beams like golden dust; for this brave bird is not to be scared by winter. It is frequently covered up by drifts, and, it is said, "sometimes plunges from on wing into the soft snow, where it remains concealed for a day or two." I used to start them in the open land also, where they had come out of the woods at sunset to "bud" the wild apple-trees. They will come regularly every evening to particular trees, where the cunning sportsman lies in wait for them, and the distant orchards next the woods suffer thus not a little. I am glad that the partridge gets fed, at any rate. It is Nature's own bird which lives on buds and diet-drink.

In dark winter mornings, or in short winter afternoons, I sometimes heard a pack of hounds threading all the woods with hounding cry and yelp, unable to resist the instinct of the chase, and the note of the hunting horn at intervals, proving that man was in the rear. The woods ring again, and yet no fox bursts forth on to the open level of the pond, nor following pack pursuing their Actæon. And perhaps at evening I see the hunters returning with a single brush trailing from their sleigh for a trophy, seeking their inn. They tell me that if the

13 *"sometimes plunges from on wing."* Ms. 1016: "One observer says 'That it is often snowed up and covered over; or sometimes plunges.'" This quotation has not been identified.

14 *the distant orchards . . . suffer thus not a little.* Ms. 1017: "If you ask the farmer why he gets no more fruit he will tell you it is because his trees are so severely budded by the partridges."

15 *In dark winter mornings.* Journal, 1845–1847; I, 422.

fox would remain in the bosom of the frozen earth he would be safe, or if he would run in a straight line away no fox-hound could overtake him; but, having left his pursuers far behind, he stops to rest and listen till they come up, and when he runs he circles round to his old haunts, where the hunters await him. Sometimes, **16** however, he will run upon a wall many rods, and then leap off far to one side, and he appears to know that water will not retain his scent. A hunter told me that he once saw a fox pursued by hounds burst out on to Walden when the ice was covered with shallow puddles, run part way across, and then return to the same shore. Ere long the hounds arrived, but here they lost the scent. Sometimes a pack hunting by themselves would pass my door, and circle round my house, and yelp and hound without regarding me, as if afflicted by a species of madness, so that nothing could divert them from the pursuit. Thus they circle until they fall upon the recent trail of a fox, for a wise hound will forsake every thing else for this. One day a man came to my hut from Lexington to inquire after his hound that made a large track, and had been hunting for a week by himself. But I fear that he was not the wiser for all I told him, for every time I attempted to answer his questions he interrupted me by asking, "What do you **17** do here?" He had lost a dog, but found a man. **18**

One old hunter who has a dry tongue, who used to come to bathe in Walden once every year when the water was warmest, and at such times looked in upon me, told me, that many years ago he took his gun one afternoon and went out for a cruise in Walden Wood; and as he walked the Wayland road he heard the cry

16 *where the hunters await him.* Ms. 1017: "Nevertheless he shows considerable cunning, for he will run upon a wall, etc."

17 *"What do you do here?"* This appears in more detail in the *Journal* for 1845–1846; I, 398–399, and also in the Bibliophile Edition (II, 187–188n.), where it is in clearer form as is shown here:

The "man from Lexington" who came to inquire after his hound amused Thoreau greatly by his curiosity, and in a fragment of the *Journal* for 1846, he thus details the conversation:

Hunter.—"Have you seen my hound, sir? (looking round him); I want to know! what? a lawyer's office? law books? want to know if you've seen anything of a hound about here? Why, what do you do here?"

Thoreau.—"I live here. No, I haven't."

H.—"Haven't you heard one in the woods anywhere?"

T.—"Oh yes,—I heard one this evening,—(*H.*— "What do you do here?") but he was some way off."

H.—"Which side did he seem to be?"

T.—"Well, I should think he was the other side of the pond."

H.—"This is a large dog,—makes a large track. He's been out hunting from Lexington for a week. How long have you lived here?"

T.—"Oh, about a year."

H.—"Somebody said there was a man up here had a camp in the woods somewhere, and he'd got him" (the hound).

T.—"Well, I don't know of anybody. There's Britton's camp over on the other road; it may be there."

H.—"Isn't there anybody in these woods?"

T.—"Yes, they are chopping right up here behind me."

H.—"How far is it?"

T.—"Only a few steps,—hark a moment; there, don't you hear the sound of their axes?"

Therien was one of these nearby choppers. Britton's camp was on the other road from Concord to Lincoln, then heavily wooded on both sides, near Flint's pond. Britton was a dealer in wood and timber, for whom Ellery Channing had cut wood a few winters earlier, as described in his poem, "The Woodman," which gave a title to the thin volume in which "Baker Farm" was first printed.

In the first passage about foxes in this chapter, the MS. reads,—"A civilization is going on among brutes as well as men. Foxes are forest dogs. I hear one barking tonight, raggedly, wildly, demoniacally in the darkness,—seeking expression, laboring with some anxiety, striving to be a dog outright, that he may carelessly run in the street.

of hounds approaching, and ere long a fox leaped the wall into the road, and as quick as thought leaped the other wall out of the road, and his swift bullet had not touched him. Some way behind came an old hound and her three pups in full pursuit, hunting on their own account, and disappeared again in the woods. Late in the afternoon, as he was resting in the thick woods south of Walden, he heard the voice of the hounds far over toward Fair Haven still pursuing the fox; and on they came, their hounding cry which made all the woods ring sounding nearer and nearer, now from Well-Meadow, now from the Baker Farm. For a long time he stood still and listened to their music, so sweet to a hunter's ear, when suddenly the fox appeared, threading the solemn aisles with an easy coursing pace, whose sound was concealed by a sympathetic rustle of the leaves, swift and still, keeping the ground, leaving his pursuers far behind; and, leaping upon a rock amid the woods, he sat erect and listening, with his back to the hunter. For a moment compassion restrained the latter's arm; but that was a short-lived mood, and as quick as thought can follow thought his piece was levelled, and *whang!* — the fox rolling over the rock lay dead on the ground. The hunter still kept his place and listened to the hounds. Still on they came, and now the near woods resounded through all their aisles with their demoniac cry. At length the old hound burst into view with muzzle to the ground, and snapping the air as if possessed, and ran directly to the rock; but spying the dead fox she suddenly ceased her hounding, as if struck dumb with amazement, and walked round and round him in silence; and one by one her pups arrived, and, like their mother, were sobered into silence by the mystery. Then the hunter came forward and stood in their midst, and the mystery was solved. They waited in silence while he skinned the fox, then followed the brush a while, and at length turned off into the woods again. That evening a Weston Squire came to the Concord hunter's cottage to inquire for his hounds, and told how for a week they had been hunting on their own account from Weston woods. The Concord hunter told him what he knew and offered him the skin; but the other declined it and departed. He did not find his hounds that night, but the next day learned that they had crossed the river and put up at a farm-house for the night, whence, having been well fed, they took their departure early in the morning.

He is but a faint man, before there were pygmies, —an imperfect, burrowing man."
Cf. page 397, line 36.

18 *He had lost a dog, but found a man.* See page 157, line 19.

The hunter who told me this could remember one Sam Nutting, who used to hunt bears on Fair Haven Ledges, and exchange their skins for rum in Concord village; who told him, even, that he had seen a moose there. Nutting had a famous fox-hound named Burgoyne, — he pronounced it Bugine, — which my informant used to borrow. In the " Wast Book " of an old trader of this town, who was also a captain, town-clerk, and representative, I find the following entry. Jan. 18th, 1742–3, " John Melven Cr. by 1 Grey Fox 0 — 2 — 3 ; " they are not now found here; and in his leger, Feb. 7th, 1743, Hezekiah Stratton has credit " by ½ a Catt skin 0 — 1 — 4½ ; " of course, a wild-cat, for Stratton was a sergeant in the old French war, and would not have got credit for hunting less noble game. Credit is given for deer skins also, and they were daily sold. One man still preserves the horns of the last deer that was killed in this vicinity, and another has told me the particulars of the hunt in which his uncle was engaged. The hunters were formerly a numerous and merry crew here. I remember well one gaunt Nimrod who would catch up a leaf by the road-side and play a strain on it wilder and more melodious, if my memory serves me, than any hunting horn.

At midnight, when there was a moon, I sometimes met with hounds in my path prowling about the woods, which would skulk out of my way, as if afraid, and stand silent amid the bushes till I had passed.

Squirrels and wild mice disputed for my store of nuts. There were scores of pitch-pines around my house, from one to four inches in diameter, which had been gnawed by mice the previous winter, — a Norwegian winter for them, for the snow lay long and deep, and they were obliged to mix a large proportion of pine bark with their other diet. These trees were alive and apparently flourishing at mid-summer, and many of them had grown a foot, though completely girdled; but after another winter such were without exception dead. It is remarkable that a single mouse should thus be allowed a whole pine tree for its dinner, gnawing round instead of up and down it; but perhaps it is necessary in order to thin these trees, which are wont to grow up densely.

The hares (*Lepus Americanus*) were very familiar. One had her form under my house all winter, separated from me only by the flooring, and she startled me each morning by her hasty departure when I began to stir, —

19 *one Sam Nutting.* The *Journal* for March 10, 1853; V, 16, has a brief description of him.

20 *Burgoyne. Journal,* May 30, 1851; II, 223.

21 *In the "Wast Book."* The *Journal* for January 27, 1854; VI, 77–80, has a long account of this. The book, which had been found in Deacon R. Brown's garret, was inscribed on the cover:

> "Mr. Ephraim Jones
> His Wast Book
> Anno Domini
> 1742"

22 *a Catt skin.* Here Thoreau underlined Catt in his own copy of *Walden* and wrote in the margin: "can it be Calf? v. Mott ledger near the beginning."

23 *Nimrod.* Genesis 10:8: "Nimrod was a mighty hunter."

24 *There were scores of pitch-pines.* From the *Journal* for 1845; V, 368. Also on ms. 1024.

25 *her hasty departure. Journal,* 1845–1847; I, 425. There the hare is a male.

thump, thump, thump, striking her head against the floor timbers in her hurry. They used to come round my door at dusk to nibble the potato parings which I had thrown out, and were so nearly the color of the ground that they could hardly be distinguished when still. Sometimes in the twilight I alternately lost and recovered sight of one sitting motionless under my window. When I opened my door in the evening, off they would go with a squeak and a bounce. Near at hand they only excited my pity. One evening one sat by my door two paces from me, at first trembling with fear, yet unwilling to move; a poor wee thing, lean and bony, with ragged ears and sharp nose, scant tail and slender paws. It looked as if Nature no longer contained the breed of **26** nobler bloods, but stood on her last toes. Its large eyes appeared young and unhealthy, almost dropsical. I took a step, and lo, away it scud with an elastic spring **27** over the snow crust, straightening its body and its limbs into graceful length, and soon put the forest between me and itself,—the wild free venison, asserting its vigor and the dignity of Nature. Not without reason was its slenderness. Such then was its nature. (*Lepus, levipes,* light-foot, some think.)

What is a country without rabbits and partridges? They are among the most simple and indigenous animal products; ancient and venerable families known to antiquity as to modern times; of the very hue and substance of Nature, nearest allied to leaves and to the ground,—and to one another; it is either winged or it is legged. It is hardly as if you had seen a wild creature when a rabbit or a partridge bursts away, only a natural one, as much to be expected as rustling leaves. The partridge and the rabbit are still sure to thrive, like true natives of the soil, whatever revolutions occur. If the forest is cut off, the sprouts and bushes which spring up afford them concealment, and they become more numerous than ever. That must be a poor country indeed that does not support a hare. Our woods teem with them both, and around every swamp may be seen the partridge or rabbit walk, beset with twiggy fences and horse-hair snares, which some cow-boy tends. **28**

26 *the breed of nobler bloods.* Cf. *Julius Caesar,* I, ii.

27 *away it scud.* Sanborn has a footnote in the Bibliophile Edition (II, 186n.) on this: "The date of the rabbit's scudding away was February 22, 1846. In the nighttime, Thoreau says elsewhere, 'The rabbits roam the fields and woods without fear. We associate wildness with the night, and silence; but the repose is never complete. Nature has her watchmen, who are links connecting the days of animated life.'"

28 *cow-boy.* Cow herder.

THE POND IN WINTER.

AFTER a still winter night I awoke with the impression that some question had been put to me, which I had been endeavoring in vain to answer in my sleep, as what — how — when — where? But there was dawning Nature, in whom all creatures live, looking in at my broad windows with serene and satisfied face, and no question on *her* lips. I awoke to an answered question, to Nature and daylight. The snow lying deep on the earth dotted with young pines, and the very slope of the hill on which my house is placed, seemed to say, Forward! Nature puts no question and answers none which we mortals ask. She has long ago taken her resolution. "O Prince, our eyes contemplate with admiration and transmit to the soul the wonderful and varied spectacle of this universe. The night veils without doubt a part of this glorious creation; but day comes to reveal to us this great work, which extends from earth even into the plains of the ether." **1**

Then to my morning work. First I take an axe and pail and go in search of water, if that be not a dream. After a cold and snowy night it needed a divining rod to find it. Every winter the liquid and trembling surface of the pond, which was so sensitive to every breath, and reflected every light and shadow, becomes solid to the depth of a foot or a foot and a half, so that it will support the heaviest teams, and perchance the snow covers it to an equal depth, and it is not to be distinguished from any level field. Like the marmots in **2** the surrounding hills, it closes its eye-lids and becomes dormant for three months or more. Standing on the

With this chapter the winter cycle in *Walden* ends, and the dark, cold months give way to the warmth and sunshine of spring.

1 *"O Prince."* Charles Anderson, in the Thoreau Society *Bulletin* for Fall 1967, page 8, says that this is from the Harivansa, an appendix to the Mahabharata, which Thoreau read in a French translation. The Mahabharata is one of India's two great epic poems. It deals with the five Pandavas and their struggles. Krishna plays an important part in it.

2 *Like the marmots. Journal* for January 12, 1854; VI, 65.

snow-covered plain, as if in a pasture amid the hills, I cut my way first through a foot of snow, and then a foot of ice, and open a window under my feet, where, kneeling to drink, I look down into the quiet parlor of the fishes, pervaded by a softened light as through a window of ground glass, with its bright sanded floor the same as in summer; there a perennial waveless serenity reigns as in the amber twilight sky, corresponding to the cool and even temperament of the inhabitants. Heaven is under our feet as well as over our heads.

Early in the morning, while all things are crisp with frost, men come with fishing reels and slender lunch, and let down their fine lines through the snowy field to take pickerel and perch; wild men, who instinctively follow other fashions and trust other authorities than their townsmen, and by their goings and comings stitch towns together in parts where else they would be ripped. They sit and eat their luncheon in stout fear-naughts on the dry oak leaves on the shore, as wise in natural lore as the citizen is in artificial. They never consulted with books, and know and can tell much less than they have done. The things which they practise are said not yet to be known. Here is one fishing for pickerel with grown perch for bait. You look into his pail with

3

4

5

6

7

3 *I cut my way.* Ms. 1051: "I" was originally "you" in this passage.

4 *Early in the morning.* Journal, 1845–1847; I, 424.

5 *to take pickerel and perch.* Ms. 216: "Who pursue their trade with as much self-respect as any mechanic or farmer does his—wisely taught by their instinct to follow other fashions and trust other authorities than their townsmen. Wild men who frequent the river meadows and solitary ponds on the horizon—connecting links between towns. . . . and with the hunter race prevent wild animals from multiplying."

6 *fear-naughts.* Warm coats made of thick winter cloth.

7 *as the citizen is in artificial.* Ms. 1052: "Their unconscious yet intimate knowledge of natural history would make a professed naturalist envious."

PIKE FISHING.

wonder as into a summer pond, as if he kept summer locked up at home, or knew where she had retreated. How, pray, did he get these in mid-winter? O, he got worms out of rotten logs since the ground froze, and so he caught them. His life itself passes deeper in Nature than the studies of the naturalist penetrate; himself a subject for the naturalist. The latter raises the moss and bark gently with his knife in search of insects; the former lays open logs to their core with his axe, and moss and bark fly far and wide. He gets his living by barking trees. Such a man has some right to fish, and I love to see Nature carried out in him. The perch swallows the grub-worm, the pickerel swallows the perch, and the fisherman swallows the pickerel; and so all the chinks in the scale of being are filled.

When I strolled around the pond in misty weather I was sometimes amused by the primitive mode which **8** some ruder fisherman had adopted. He would perhaps have placed alder branches over the narrow holes in the ice, which were four or five rods apart and an equal distance from the shore, and having fastened the end of the line to a stick to prevent its being pulled through, have passed the slack line over a twig of the alder, a foot or more above the ice, and tied a dry oak leaf to it, which, being pulled down, would show when he had a bite. These alders loomed through the mist at regular intervals as you walked half way round the pond. **9**

Ah, the pickerel of Walden! when I see them lying **10** on the ice, or in the well which the fisherman cuts in the ice, making a little hole to admit the water, I am always surprised by their rare beauty, as if they were fabulous fishes, they are so foreign to the streets, even to the woods, foreign as Arabia to our Concord life. They possess a quite dazzling and transcendent beauty which separates them by a wide interval from the cadaverous cod and haddock whose fame is trumpeted in our streets. They are not green like the pines, nor gray like the stones, nor blue like the sky; but they have, to my eyes, if possible, yet rarer colors, like flowers and precious stones, as if they were the pearls, the animalized *nuclei* or crystals of the Walden water. They, of course, are Walden all over and all through; are themselves small Waldens in the animal kingdom, Wal- **11** denses. It is surprising that they are caught here,— that in this deep and capacious spring, far beneath the

8 *by the primitive mode. Journal* for February 5, 1853; IV, 448.

9 *half way round the pond.* Ms. 1054: "Here and there, also, about the shore, on the steep wooded hillsides, you see the stone fireplaces, their charred branches, where their predecessors, the Indian fishermen, had cultivated some flame's society, and ate their lunch."

10 *Ah, the pickerel of Walden! Journal* for January 25, 1853; IV, 476. When this was transcribed to be put into the manuscript of *Walden* (ms. 1056) it was written on the back of a bill marked "Paid—Greeley and McElrath, Tribune Building, New York."

11 *Waldenses.* Sanborn has a footnote in the Bibliophile Edition (II, 194n.) on this: "Here the quaint scholarly fancy was added,—'Waldenses, Dauphins,—eldest sons of Walden; for whose behoof the whole world is but a Delphin edition to study.' The allusion is to the books prepared by the Jesuits for the use of the Dauphin of France, grandson of Louis XIV.—*Delphinus serenissimus.* These were styled 'Delphin editions.'"

Thoreau's surveying compass, now owned by the Concord Free Public Library

rattling teams and chaises and tinkling sleighs that travel the Walden road, this great gold and emerald fish swims.   I never chanced to see its kind in any market; it would be the cynosure of all eyes there.   Easily, with a few convulsive quirks, they give up their watery ghosts, like a mortal translated before his time to the thin air of heaven.

As I was desirous to recover the long lost bottom of Walden Pond, I surveyed it carefully, before the ice broke up, early in '46, with compass and chain and **12** sounding line.   There have been many stories told **13** about the bottom, or rather no bottom, of this pond, which certainly had no foundation for themselves.   It is remarkable how long men will believe in the bottomlessness of a pond without taking the trouble to sound it. **14** I have visited two such Bottomless Ponds in one walk in this neighborhood.   Many have believed that Walden reached quite through to the other side of the globe. Some who have lain flat on the ice for a long time, looking down through the illusive medium, perchance with watery eyes into the bargain, and driven to hasty con-

12 *early in '46.* Ms. 215: "last winter."

13 *sounding line.* Ms. 215: "and found it to contain a little over 61½ acres [ms. 216], and to be 102 feet deep in the middle." Edward S. Deevey, Jr., made a modern survey of Walden in 1939; in his book (1942), he showed that the pond's maximum depth was only two-tenths of a meter greater than Thoreau's figure. More recent electronic methods have also confirmed the accuracy of Thoreau's survey.

14 *taking the trouble to sound it.* Bibliophile Edition (II, 194n.) footnote: "After 'sound it,' Thoreau added in the original ms.: 'So it is with many imposing theories, in whose dark waters, concealing the muddy bottom, we see our own faces reflected; whose shallowness could easily be proved by the sounding-line of Reason. I have visited in Sudbury two such "bottomless" ponds in one week, —not to speak of the theories I have heard advanced. In fact, our imaginations require a depth in the earth, corresponding to the possible height of the Heavens above.'"

15 The printed map of Walden Pond was intended to face the next page in the first edition of *Walden.*

15

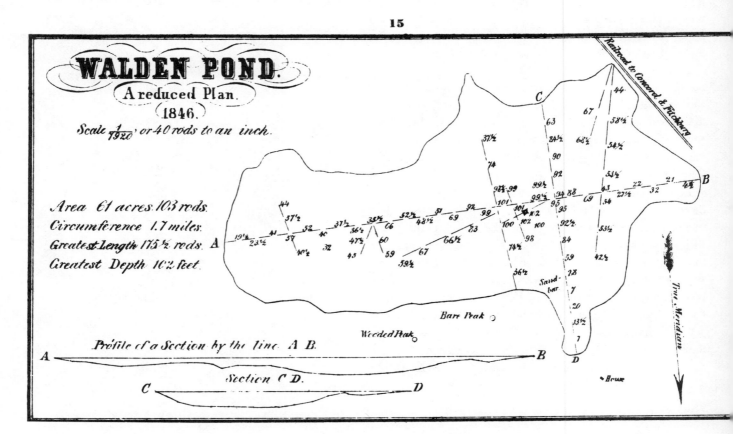

clusions by the fear of catching cold in their breasts, have seen vast holes " into which a load of hay might be driven," if there were any body to drive it, the undoubted source of the Styx and entrance to the Infernal Regions from these parts.   Others have gone down **16** from the village with a " fifty-six " and a wagon load of **17** inch rope, but yet have failed to find any bottom; for while the " fifty-six " was resting by the way, they were paying out the rope in the vain attempt to fathom their truly immeasurable capacity for marvellousness.   But I can assure my readers that Walden has a reasonably tight bottom at a not unreasonable, though at an unusual, depth.   I fathomed it easily with a cod-line and a stone weighing about a pound and a half, and could tell accurately when the stone left the bottom, by having to pull so much harder before the water got underneath to help me.   The greatest depth was exactly one hundred and two feet; to which may be added the five feet which it has risen since, making one hundred and seven.   This is a remarkable depth for so small an area; yet not an inch of it can be spared by the imagination.   What if all ponds were shallow?   Would it not react on the minds of men?   I am thankful that this pond was made deep and pure for a symbol.   While men believe in the **18** infinite some ponds will be thought to be bottomless.

A factory owner, hearing what depth I had found, thought that it could not be true, for, judging from his acquaintance with dams, sand would not lie at so steep an angle.   But the deepest ponds are not so deep in proportion to their area as most suppose, and, if drained, would not leave very remarkable valleys.   They are not like cups between the hills; for this one, which is so unusually deep for its area, appears in a vertical section through its centre not deeper than a shallow plate.   Most ponds, emptied, would leave a meadow no more hollow than we frequently see.   William Gilpin, who is **19** so admirable in all that relates to landscapes, and usually so correct, standing at the head of Loch Fyne, in Scotland, which he describes as " a bay of salt water, sixty or seventy fathoms deep, four miles in breadth," and about fifty miles long, surrounded by mountains, observes, " If we could have seen it immediately after the diluvian crash, or whatever convulsion of Nature occasioned it, before the waters gushed in, what a horrid chasm it must have appeared!

16 *from these parts.* Bibliophile Edition (II, 195n.):

"Most men do not see much more in a pond than a certain 'natural' who lived on the skirts of the village, who accosted one of my visitors with—'You have been down to the pond. It looked pooty watery, didn't it?'

"A month or two after this, as I heard, his body was found among the brush, over back of the hills,—so far decomposed that his coffin was carried to it, and it was put into it with pitchforks. But still, in spite of all, I have my suspicions that he might have died a Brahmin's death, dwelling at the roots of trees at last, and been absorbed into the spirit of Brahm. Perhaps he was one of a sect of philosophers,—the only one,—so simple, so abstracted in his thoughts and life from his contemporaries, that his wisdom was foolishness to them. His very vividness of perception, clear knowledge and insights may have made him dumb,—leaving no common consciousness and ground of parlance with mankind. I was not to be deceived, of course, by a few stupid words, or apparent stolidity."

17 *a "fifty-six."* A 56-pound weight.

18 *deep and pure for a symbol. Journal* for January 26, 1852; III, 232.

19 *William Gilpin.* See page 374. Also the *Journal* for September 1, 1852; IV, 338.

So high as heaved the tumid hills, so low
Down sunk a hollow bottom, broad, and deep,
Capacious bed of waters ——."

20

But if, using the shortest diameter of Loch Fyne, we apply these proportions to Walden, which, as we have seen, appears already in a vertical section only like a shallow plate, it will appear four times as shallow. So much for the *increased* horrors of the chasm of Loch Fyne when emptied. No doubt many a smiling valley with its stretching cornfields occupies exactly such a " horrid chasm," from which the waters have receded, though it requires the insight and the far sight of the geologist to convince the unsuspecting inhabitants of this fact. Often an inquisitive eye may detect the shores of a primitive lake in the low horizon hills, and no subsequent elevation of the plain have been necessary to conceal their history. But it is easiest, as they who **work on the highways know, to find the hollows by the puddles after a shower.** The amount of it is, the imagination, give it the least license, dives deeper and soars higher than Nature goes. So, probably, the depth of the ocean will be found to be very inconsiderable compared with its breadth.

21

22

As I sounded through the ice I could determine the shape of the bottom with greater accuracy than is possible in surveying harbors which do not freeze over, and I was surprised at its general regularity. In the deepest part there are several acres more level than almost any field which is exposed to the sun wind and plough. In one instance, on a line arbitrarily chosen, the depth did not vary more than one foot in thirty rods; and generally, near the middle, I could calculate the variation for each one hundred feet in any direction beforehand within three or four inches. Some are accustomed to speak of deep and dangerous holes even in quiet sandy ponds like this, but the effect of water under these circumstances is to level all inequalities. The regularity of the bottom and its conformity to the shores and the range of the neighboring hills were so perfect that a distant promontory betrayed itself in the soundings quite across the pond, and its direction could be determined by observing the opposite shore. Cape becomes bar, and plain shoal, and valley and gorge deep water and channel.

When I had mapped the pond by the scale of ten

20 *So high as heaved the tumid hills, so low.* Channing, in his copy of *Walden,* notes that this verse is from Milton's *Paradise Lost,* VII, 207. Thoreau ordinarily put quotation marks around material written by other authors, but he did not do so here.

21 *no subsequent elevation of the plain have been necessary.* This is another typographical error that has gone through edition after edition without being detected. Ms. 650 puts the matter right, for the verb there is not "have been necessary" but "was needed." The *Journal* for September 1, 1852; IV, 339, has "no subsequent elevation of the plain was necessary." The Bibliophile Edition (II, 197) also has it that way.

22 *So, probably, the depth of the ocean will be found to be very inconsiderable compared with its breadth.* It is indeed! The Pacific Ocean is more than 7,000 miles wide, and its greatest depth is about seven miles.

rods to an inch, and put down the soundings, more than
a hundred in all, I observed this remarkable coincidence.
Having noticed that the number indicating the greatest
depth was apparently in the centre of the map, I laid a
rule on the map lengthwise, and then breadthwise, and
found, to my surprise, that the line of greatest length
intersected the line of greatest breadth *exactly* at the
point of greatest depth, notwithstanding that the middle is so nearly level, the outline of the pond far from
regular, and the extreme length and breadth were got
by measuring into the coves ; and I said to myself, Who
knows but this hint would conduct to the deepest part of
the ocean as well as of a pond or puddle ? Is not this
the rule also for the height of mountains, regarded as the
opposite of valleys ? We know that a hill is not highest at its narrowest part.

Of five coves, three, or all which had been sounded,
were observed to have a bar quite across their mouths
and deeper water within, so that the bay tended to be
an expansion of water within the land not only horizon-
tally but vertically, and to form a basin or independent
pond, the direction of the two capes showing the course
of the bar. Every harbor on the sea-coast, also, has
its bar at its entrance. In proportion as the mouth of
the cove was wider compared with its length, the water
over the bar was deeper compared with that in the
basin. Given, then, the length and breadth of the cove,
and the character of the surrounding shore, and you
have almost elements enough to make out a formula for
all cases.

In order to see how nearly I could guess, with this
experience, at the deepest point in a pond, by observing
the outlines of its surface and the character of its shores
alone, I made a plan of White Pond, which contains
about forty-one acres. and, like this, has no island in it,
nor any visible inlet or outlet ; and as the line of greatest breadth fell very near the line of least breadth,
where two opposite capes approached each other and
two opposite bays receded, I ventured to mark a point
a short distance from the latter line, but still on the
line of greatest length, as the deepest. The deepest
part was found to be within one hundred feet of this,
still farther in the direction to which I had inclined, and
was only one foot deeper, namely, sixty feet. Of course,
a stream running through, or an island in the pond,
would make the problem much more complicated.

If we knew all the laws of Nature, we should need only one fact, or the description of one actual phenomenon, to infer all the particular results at that point. Now we know only a few laws, and our result is vitiated, not, of course, by any confusion or irregularity in Nature, but by our ignorance of essential elements in the calculation. Our notions of law and harmony are commonly confined to those instances which we detect; but the harmony which results from a far greater number of seemingly conflicting, but really concurring, laws, which we have not detected, is still more wonderful. The particular laws are as our points of view, as, to the traveller, a mountain outline varies with every step, and it has an infinite number of profiles, though absolutely but one form. Even when cleft or bored through it is not comprehended in its entirety.

What I have observed of the pond is no less true in ethics. It is the law of average. Such a rule of the two diameters not only guides us toward the sun in the system and the heart in man, but draw lines through the length and breadth of the aggregate of a man's particular daily behaviors and waves of life into his coves and inlets, and where they intersect will be the height or depth of his character. Perhaps we need only to know how his shores trend and his adjacent country or circumstances, to infer his depth and concealed bottom. If he is surrounded by mountainous circumstances, an Achillean shore, whose peaks overshadow and are reflected in his bosom, they suggest a corresponding depth in him. But a low and smooth shore proves him shallow on that side. In our bodies, a bold projecting brow falls off to and indicates a corresponding depth of thought. Also there is a bar across the entrance of our every cove, or particular inclination; each is our harbor for a season, in which we are detained and partially land-locked. These inclinations are not whimsical usually, but their form, size, and direction are determined by the promontories of the shore, the ancient axes of elevation. When this bar is gradually increased by storms, tides, or currents, or there is a subsidence of the waters, so that it reaches to the surface, that which was at first but an inclination in the shore in which a thought was harbored becomes an individual lake, cut off from the ocean, wherein the thought secures its own conditions, changes, perhaps, from salt to fresh, becomes a sweet sea, dead sea, or a

23

23 *an Achillean shore.* Thessaly, where Achilles was supposedly born, has a rocky, deeply indented, mountainous coast.

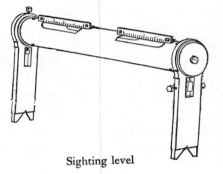

Sighting level

marsh. At the advent of each individual into this life, may we not suppose that such a bar has risen to the surface somewhere? It is true, we are such poor navigators that our thoughts, for the most part, stand off and on upon a harborless coast, are conversant only with the bights of the bays of poesy, or steer for the public ports **24** of entry, and go into the dry docks of science, where they merely refit for this world, and no natural currents concur to individualize them.

As for the inlet or outlet of Walden, I have not discovered any but rain and snow and evaporation, though perhaps, with a thermometer and a line, such places may be found, for where the water flows into the pond it will probably be coldest in summer and warmest in winter. When the ice-men were at work here in '46-7, the cakes sent to the shore were one day rejected by those who were stacking them up there, not being thick enough to lie side by side with the rest; and the cutters thus discovered that the ice over a small space was two or three inches thinner than elsewhere, which made them think that there was an inlet there. They also showed me in another place what they thought was a "leach hole," through which the pond leaked out under a hill into a neighboring meadow, pushing me out on a cake of ice to see it. It was a small cavity under ten feet of water; but I think that I can warrant the pond not to need soldering till they find a worse leak than that. One has suggested, that if such a "leach hole"

24 *bights of the bays of poesy.* Thoreau put a question mark in the margin of his own copy of *Walden* opposite this and the next line.

Cutting ice at a pond in West Cambridge where there were covered ice houses

should be found, its connection with the meadow, if any existed, might be proved by conveying some colored **25** powder or sawdust to the mouth of the hole, and then putting a strainer over the spring in the meadow, which would catch some of the particles carried through by the current.

While I was surveying, the ice, which was sixteen inches thick, undulated under a slight wind like water. It is well known that a level cannot be used on ice. At one rod from the shore its greatest fluctuation, when observed by means of a level on land directed toward a graduated staff on the ice, was three quarters of an inch, though the ice appeared firmly attached to the shore. It was probably greater in the middle. Who **26** knows but if our instruments were delicate enough we might detect an undulation in the crust of the earth? When two legs of my level were on the shore and the third on the ice, and the sights were directed over the latter, a rise or fall of the ice of an almost infinitesimal amount made a difference of several feet on a tree across the pond. When I began to cut holes for sounding, there were three or four inches of water on the ice under a deep snow which had sunk it thus far; but the water began immediately to run into these holes, and continued to run for two days in deep streams, which wore away the ice on every side, and contributed essentially, if not mainly, to dry the surface of the pond; for, as the water ran in, it raised and floated the ice. This was somewhat like cutting a hole in the bottom of a ship to let the water out. When such holes freeze, and a rain succeeds, and finally a new freezing forms a fresh smooth ice over all, it is beautifully mottled internally by dark figures, shaped somewhat like a spider's web, what you may call ice rosettes, produced by the channels worn by the water flowing from all sides to a centre. Sometimes, also, when the ice was covered with shallow puddles, I saw a double shadow of myself, one standing on the head of the other, one on the ice, the other on the trees or hill-side.

While yet it is cold January, and snow and ice are thick and solid, the prudent landlord comes from the vil- **27** lage to get ice to cool his summer drink; impressively, even pathetically wise, to foresee the heat and thirst of

25 *colored powder.* Here Thoreau foresaw the modern method of tracing the flow of underground water. Norbert Casteret (1940, pages 225–234) used 120 pounds of fluorescein to impart an intense green color to the water when he traced the true source of the Garonne River in the Pyrenees.

26 *Who knows but if our instruments were delicate enough we might detect an undulation in the crust of the earth?* And here Thoreau foresaw the modern method of detecting a coming volcanic eruption. This system is in use on the island of Hawaii, where the activity of the great shield volcanos, Mauna Loa and Mauna Kea, are forecast by tilt-meters, which show that pressure under the ground increases before eruptions take place.

27 *the prudent landlord. Journal,* 1845–1847; I, 423 and 424.

July now in January, — wearing a thick coat and mittens! when so many things are not provided for. It may be that he lays up no treasures in this world **28** which will cool his summer drink in the next. He cuts and saws the solid pond, unroofs the house of fishes, and carts off their very element and air, held fast by chains and stakes like corded wood, through the favoring winter air, to wintry cellars, to underlie the summer there. It looks like solidified azure, as, far off, it is drawn through the streets. These ice-cutters are a merry race, full of jest and sport, and when I went among them they were wont to invite me to saw pit-fashion with them, I standing underneath.

In the winter of '46-7 there came a hundred men of Hyperborean extraction swoop down on to our pond **29** one morning, with many car-loads of ungainly-looking farming tools, sleds, ploughs, drill-barrows, turf-knives, spades, saws, rakes, and each man was armed with a double-pointed pike-staff, such as is not described in the New-England Farmer or the Cultivator. I did not **30** know whether they had come to sow a crop of winter

28 *he lays up no treasures in this world*. Paraphrase of Matthew 6:20.

29 *of Hyperborean extraction*. Although this literally means a legendary race of Apollo-worshippers living in the Far North, it is evident from what is said below that Thoreau is referring to the Irish.

30 *the New-England Farmer or the Cultivator*. Sanborn says that these were weekly newspapers published in Boston.

JANUARY.

rye, or some other kind of grain recently introduced from Iceland. As I saw no manure, I judged that they meant to skim the land, as I had done, thinking the soil was deep and had lain fallow long enough. They said that a gentleman farmer, who was behind the scenes, **31** wanted to double his money, which, as I understood, amounted to half a million already; but in order to cover each one of his dollars with another, he took off the only coat, ay, the skin itself, of Walden Pond in the midst of a hard winter. They went to work at once, ploughing, harrowing, rolling, furrowing, in admirable order, as if they were bent on making this a model farm; but when I was looking sharp to see what kind of seed they dropped into the furrow, a gang of fellows by my side suddenly began to hook up the virgin mould itself, with a peculiar jerk, clean down to the sand, or rather the water,— for it was a very springy soil,—indeed all the *terra firma* there was,—and haul it away on sleds, and then I guessed that they must be cutting peat in a bog. So they came and went every day, with a peculiar shriek from the locomotive, from and to some point of the polar regions, as it seemed to me, like a flock of arctic snow-birds. But sometimes Squaw Walden had her revenge, and a hired man, walking behind his team, slipped through a crack in the ground down toward Tartarus, and he who was so brave before suddenly became but the ninth part of a man, almost gave up his animal heat, and was glad to take refuge in my house, and acknowledged that there was some virtue in a stove; or sometimes the frozen soil took a piece of steel out of a ploughshare, or a plough got set in the furrow and had to be cut out.

To speak literally, a hundred Irishmen, with Yankee overseers, came from Cambridge every day to get out **32** the ice. They divided it into cakes by methods too well known to require description, and these, being sledded to the shore, were rapidly hauled off on to an ice platform, and raised by grappling irons and block and tackle, worked by horses, on to a stack, as surely as so many barrels of flour, and there placed evenly side by side, and row upon row, as if they formed the solid base of an obelisk designed to pierce the clouds. They told me that in a good day they could get out a thousand tons, which was the yield of about one acre. Deep ruts and " cradle holes " were worn in the ice, as on *terra firma*, by the passage of the sleds over the same track, and the horses invariably ate their oats out of cakes of ice hollowed

31 *a gentleman farmer*. Sanborn calls this man "a Mr. Tudor" in the text of the Bibliophile Edition (II, 205) but in a footnote explains that "The 'gentleman-farmer' who directed this ice-cutting at Walden, which turned out badly, was no doubt the firm of Jarvis & Wyeth, large ice dealers, who had already great establishments at Fresh Pond in Cambridge, and soon after made an ice-pond at the hamlet of Assabet on the north branch of the Concord River, where now is the manufacturing town of Maynard. This also proved unlucky; for in the great gale of April, 1851, the enormous brick ice-house of the firm at Assabet blew down and was never rebuilt,—the waterfall there proving of much value for woollen mills. The Walden ice, though beautiful and pure, lacks some of the needful qualities, and the Concord families are supplied with more serviceable ice from small ponds and brooks. The lake dedicated to poetry by Thoreau and Emerson has no attribute for practical use; even its fishery is unimportant."

See the Thoreau Society *Bulletin*, Fall 1968, page 8, for more about Frederic Tudor.

32 *came from Cambridge every day*. As Thoreau says two lines below, the ice cutting was done "by methods too well known to require description," so he eliminated the long and interesting passage about the work. The Bibliophile Edition (II, 207 f.) printed the full account which follows here: "and stack it upon the shore in the open air. When Walden was covered with snow, a dozen men were incessantly engaged in scraping it off, over an area of several acres, with various kinds of scrapers drawn by horses. Two men followed with a horse and a slight cutter,—one carefully leading the horse, while the other guided the cutter within a few inches of a rope drawn straight across the ice for ten or a dozen rods. Thus a groove was made on two sides of a parallelogram. Then, with various kinds of gauge-cutters,—that is, cutters connected by a frame with parallel marks or toothless plates, at a proper distance on one or both sides, running in the last-made groove,—the whole area was finally grooved in squares of twenty-two inches, on an average.

"I was told that the best ice-cutters or plows cost over a hundred dollars, and cut four inches at a bout, but it was hard work for a horse. And then men were employed with whip-saws cutting this area into long strips the width of a cake; half a dozen poling the strips along a narrow canal to the loading place, near which one stood with a spade-like chisel to cut off the 'cake,' which consisted of two squares, and therefore measured twenty-two by forty-four inches. These cakes were to be finally divided by the shallow groove

out like buckets. They stacked up the cakes thus in the open air in a pile thirty-five feet high on one side and six or seven rods square, putting hay between the outside layers to exclude the air; for when the wind, though never so cold, finds a passage through, it will wear large cavities, leaving slight supports or studs only here and there, and finally topple it down. At first it looked like a vast blue fort or Valhalla; but when they began to tuck the coarse meadow hay into the crevices, and this became covered with rime and icicles, it looked like a venerable moss-grown and hoary ruin, built of azure-tinted marble, the abode of Winter, that old man we see in the almanac, — his shanty, as if he had a design to estivate with us. They calculated that not **33** twenty-five per cent. of this would reach its destination, and that two or three per cent. would be wasted in the cars. However, a still greater part of this heap had a different destiny from what was intended; for, either because the ice was found not to keep so well as was expected, containing more air than usual, or for some other reason, it never got to market. This heap, made in the winter of '46-7 and estimated to contain ten thousand tons, was finally covered with hay and boards; and though it was unroofed the following July, and a part of it carried off, the rest remaining exposed to the sun, it stood over that summer and the next winter, and was not quite melted till September 1848. Thus the pond recovered the greater part.

Like the water, the Walden ice, seen near at hand, **34** has a green tint, but at a distance is beautifully blue, and you can easily tell it from the white ice of the river, or the merely greenish ice of some ponds, a quarter of a mile off. Sometimes one of those great cakes slips from the ice-man's sled into the village street, and lies there for a week like a great emerald, an object of interest to all passers. I have noticed that a portion of Walden which in the state of water was green will often, when frozen, appear from the same point of view blue. So the hollows about this pond will, sometimes, in the winter, be filled with a greenish water somewhat like its own, but the next day will have frozen blue. Perhaps the blue color of water and ice is due to the light and air they contain, and the most transparent is the bluest. Ice is an interesting subject for contemplation. They told me that they had some in the ice-houses at Fresh **35** Pond five years old which was as good as ever. Why

at the loading aboard ship, so that one man might handle them.

"At the end of the canal were a dozen or fifteen men, half on each side, incessantly hauling the cakes up a narrow iron framework or railway, sunk at one end on wood and resting on a sled at the other, with pike-staffs which had a double point, one bent for hauling, the other straight for pushing. Each sled held fourteen or fifteen cakes which weighed about two tons and were drawn by one horse over the ice to the shore where they were rapidly hauled off on to an ice platform, and raised by grappling irons and block and tackle, worked by horses, on to a stack, as surely as so many barrels of flour, and there placed evenly side by side, and row upon row, as if they formed the solid base of an obelisk designed to pierce the clouds. There were sixty men employed at the stacks, about thirty above and thirty below,—about twenty in loading and sledding, and about twenty in scraping, grooving, sawing and poling."

33 *estivate.* To spend the summer.

34 *Like the water. Journal* for January 27, 1854; VI, 81; also for January 30, 1854; VI, 86, and February 14, 1854; VI, 123.

35 *Fresh Pond.* Ms. 1078: "in Cambridge."

is it that a bucket of water soon becomes putrid, but frozen remains sweet forever? It is commonly said that this is the difference between the affections and the intellect.

Thus for sixteen days I saw from my window a hundred men at work like busy husbandmen, with teams and horses and apparently all the implements of farming, such a picture as we see on the first page of the almanac; and as often as I looked out I was reminded of the fable of the lark and the reapers, or the parable of the sower, and the like; and now they are all gone, and in thirty days more, probably, I shall look from the same window on the pure sea-green Walden water there, reflecting the clouds and the trees, and sending up its evaporations in solitude, and no traces will appear that a man has ever stood there.   Perhaps I shall hear a solitary loon laugh as he dives and plumes himself, or shall see a lonely fisher in his boat, like a floating leaf, beholding his form reflected in the waves, where lately a hundred men securely labored.

Thus it appears that the sweltering inhabitants of Charleston and New Orleans, of Madras and Bombay and Calcutta, drink at my well.   In the morning I bathe my intellect in the stupendous and cosmogonal philosophy of the Bhagvat Geeta, since whose composition years of the gods have elapsed, and in comparison with which our modern world and its literature seem puny and trivial; and I doubt if that philosophy is not to be referred to a previous state of existence, so remote is its sublimity from our conceptions. I lay down the book and go to my well for water, and lo! there I meet the servant of the Bramin, priest of Brahma and Vishnu and Indra, who still sits in his temple on the Ganges reading the Vedas, or dwells at the root of a tree with his crust and water jug. I meet his servant come to draw water for his master, and our buckets as it were grate together in the same well. The pure Walden water is mingled with the sacred water of the Ganges. With favoring winds it is wafted past the site of the fabulous islands of Atlantis and the Hesperides, makes the periplus of Hanno, and, floating by Ternate and Tidore and the mouth of the Persian Gulf, melts in the tropic gales of the Indian seas, and is landed in ports of which Alexander only heard the names.

36
37

38, 39

40

41, 42
43, 44

36 *a bucket of water soon becomes putrid.* This was before the action of bacteria was discovered.

37 *the affections and the intellect.* The Bibliophile Edition (II, 210) then has this: "I was also told that southern customers objected to the blue color of the Walden ice, and preferred the Fresh Pond ice, which is white, but tastes of weeds."

38 *the fable of the lark.* Thoreau's manuscript, *Commonplace Book*, shows that he had read this fable by La Fontaine ("The Lark and Her Young Ones") in J. Payne Colliers' *Old Ballads* (1843).

39 *the parable of the sower.* Matthew 13:3–40.

40 *Bhagvat Geeta.* See Index.

41 *Atlantis.* Plato apparently was the first to record the myth of there being a large but now vanished island in the Atlantic off the Straits of Gibraltar.

42 *the Hesperides.* The mythical islands of the blessed located at the far western ends of the world.

43 *the periplus of Hanno.* A periplus is an account of a voyage around an island or a coast. The periplus of Hanno was the exploratory voyage this Carthaginian navigator made around the west coast of Africa in 480 B.C.

44 *Ternate and Tidore.* Spice islands in the Dutch East Indies which Milton mentions in *Paradise Lost*.

SPRING.

THE opening of large tracts by the ice-cutters commonly causes a pond to break up earlier; for the water, agitated by the wind, even in cold weather, wears away the surrounding ice. But such was not the effect on Walden that year, for she had soon got a thick new garment to take the place of the old. This pond never breaks up so soon as the others in this neighborhood, on account both of its greater depth and its having ro stream passing through it to melt or wear away the ice. I never knew it to open in the course of a winter, not excepting that of '52–3, which gave the ponds so severe a trial. It commonly opens about the first of April, a week or ten days later than Flints' Pond and Fair-Haven, beginning to melt on the north side and in the shallower parts where it began to freeze. It indicates better than any water hereabouts the absolute progress of the season, being least affected by transient changes of temperature. A severe cold of a few days' duration in March may very much retard the opening of the former ponds, while the temperature of Walden increases almost uninterruptedly. A thermometer thrust into the middle **1** of Walden on the 6th of March, 1847, stood at 32°, or freezing point; near the shore at 33°; in the middle of Flints' Pond, the same day, at 32½°; at a dozen rods from the shore, in shallow water, under ice a foot thick, at 36°. This difference of three and a half degrees between the temperature of the deep water and the shallow in the latter pond, and the fact that a great proportion of it is comparatively shallow, show why it should break up so much sooner than Walden. The ice in the

The word "Spring" was written on ms. 211, the last page of the previous chapter. Ms. 1080 and 1085 have the heading written in.

1 *A thermometer.* Ms. 215 has other water temperatures here, but Thoreau struck them out, probably because he felt that they would not be of interest to his readers.

shallowest part was at this time several inches thinner than in the middle.   In mid-winter the middle had been the warmest and the ice thinnest there.   So, also, every one who has waded about the shores of a pond in summer must have perceived how much warmer the water is close to the shore, where only three or four inches deep, than a little distance out, and on the surface where it is deep, than near the bottom.   In spring the sun not only exerts an influence through the increased temperature of the air and earth, but its heat passes through ice a foot or more thick, and is reflected from the bottom in shallow water, and so also warms the water and melts the under side of the ice, at the same time that it is melting it more directly above, making it uneven, and causing the air bubbles which it contains to extend themselves upward and downward until it is completely honey-combed, and at last disappears suddenly in a single spring rain.   Ice has its grain as well as wood, and when a cake begins to rot or "comb," that is, assume the appearance of honey-comb, whatever may be its position, the air cells are at right angles with what was the water surface.   Where there is a rock or a log rising near to the surface the ice over it is much thinner, and is frequently quite dissolved by this reflected heat; and I have been told that in the experiment at Cambridge to freeze water in a shallow wooden pond, though the cold air circulated underneath, and so had access to both sides, the reflection of the sun from the bottom more than counterbalanced this advantage.   When a warm **2** rain in the middle of the winter melts off the snow-ice from Walden, and leaves a hard dark or transparent ice on the middle, there will be a strip of rotten though thicker white ice, a rod or more wide, about the shores, created by this reflected heat.   Also, as I have said, the bubbles themselves within the ice operate as burning glasses to melt the ice beneath.

The phenomena of the year take place every day in a pond on a small scale.   Every morning, generally **3** speaking, the shallow water is being warmed more rapidly than the deep, though it may not be made so warm after all, and every evening it is being cooled more rapidly until the morning.   The day is an epitome of the year.   The night is the winter, the morning and evening are the spring and fall, and the noon is the summer. The cracking and booming of the ice indicate a change

2 *When a warm rain. Journal* of February 8, 1853; IV, 490.

3 *on a small scale.* On ms. 1206 this is followed by: "Other things being equal, the deeper the water the more slowly it is affected by changes of temperature, whether we consider different ponds or different parts of the same pond." This is so obvious that Thoreau canceled it.

of temperature. One pleasant morning after a cold night, February 24th, 1850, having gone to Flints' Pond to spend the day, I noticed with surprise, that when I struck the ice with the head of my axe, it resounded like a gong for many rods around, or as if I had struck on a tight drum-head. The pond began to boom about an hour after sunrise, when it felt the influence of the sun's rays slanted upon it from over the hills; it stretched itself and yawned like a waking man with a gradually increasing tumult, which was kept up three or four hours. It took a short siesta at noon, and boomed once more toward night, as the sun was withdrawing his influence. In the right stage of the weather a pond fires its evening gun with great regularity. But in the middle of the day, being full of cracks, and the air also being less elastic, it had completely lost its resonance, and probably fishes and muskrats could not then have been stunned by a blow on it. The fishermen say that the " thundering of the pond " scares the fishes and prevents their biting. The pond does not thunder every evening, and I cannot tell surely when to expect its thundering; but though I may perceive no difference in the weather, it does. Who would have suspected so large and cold and thick-skinned a thing to be so sensitive? Yet it has its law to which it thunders obedience when it should as surely as the buds expand in the spring. The earth is all alive and covered with papillæ. The largest pond is as sensitive to atmospheric changes as the globule of mercury in its tube.

One attraction in coming to the woods to live was that I should have leisure and opportunity to see the spring come in. The ice in the pond at length begins to be honey-combed, and I can set my heel in it as I walk. Fogs and rains and warmer suns are gradually melting the snow; the days have grown sensibly longer; and I see how I shall get through the winter without adding to my wood-pile, for large fires are no longer necessary. I am on the alert for the first signs of spring, to hear the chance note of some arriving bird, or the striped squirrel's chirp, for his stores must be now nearly exhausted, or see the woodchuck venture out of his winter quarters. On the 13th of March, after I had heard the bluebird, song-sparrow, and red-wing, the ice was

4 *February 24th, 1850*. The entries in the *Journal* for 1850 do not cover the period before May 31 of this year so there is no way of checking this.

still nearly a foot thick.   As the weather grew warmer, it was not sensibly worn away by the water, nor broken up and floated off as in rivers, but, though it was completely melted for half a rod in width about the shore, the middle was merely honey-combed and saturated with water, so that you could put your foot through it when six inches thick; but by the next day evening, perhaps, after a warm rain followed by fog, it would have wholly disappeared, all gone off with the fog, spirited away.   One year I went across the middle only five days before it disappeared entirely.   In 1845 Walden was first completely open on the 1st of April; in '46, the 25th of March; in '47, the 8th of April; in '51, the 28th of March; in '52, the 18th of April; in '53, the 23d of March; in '54, about the 7th of April.   **5**

Every incident connected with the breaking up of the rivers and ponds and the settling of the weather is particularly interesting to us who live in a climate of so **6** great extremes.   When the warmer days come, they who dwell near the river hear the ice crack at night with a startling whoop as loud as artillery, as if its icy fetters were rent from end to end, and within a few days see it rapidly going out.   So the alligator comes out of **7** the mud with quakings of the earth.   One old man, who has been a close observer of Nature, and seems as thoroughly wise in regard to all her operations as if she had been put upon the stocks when he was a boy, and he had helped to lay her keel,—who has come to his growth, and can hardly acquire more of natural lore if he should live to the age of Methuselah,—told me, and I was surprised to hear him express wonder at any of Nature's operations, for I thought that there were no secrets between them, that one spring day he took his gun and boat, and thought that he would have a little sport with the ducks.   There was ice still on the meadows, but it was all gone out of the river, and he dropped down without obstruction from Sudbury, where he lived, to Fair-Haven Pond, which he found, unexpectedly, covered for the most part with a firm field of ice.   It was a warm day, and he was surprised to see so great a body of ice remaining.   Not seeing any ducks, he hid his boat on the north or back side of an island in the pond, and then concealed himself in the bushes on the south side, to await them.   The ice was melted for three or four rods from the shore, and there was a smooth and

5 *in '54, about the 7th of April.* This is not on ms. 1094. The date is so late that it must have been one of the last things put into the book, for we know that Thoreau began to receive proofs on March 28. *Journal* for that day, VI, 176.

6 *a climate of so great extremes.* On ms. 890 this was "as bleak a country as New England."

7 *So the alligator comes out of the mud. Journal* for February 2, 1854; VI, 121.

warm sheet of water, with a muddy bottom, such as the ducks love, within, and he thought it likely that some would be along pretty soon.   After he had lain still there about an hour he heard a low and seemingly very distant sound, but singularly grand and impressive, unlike any thing he had ever heard, gradually swelling and increasing as if it would have a universal and memorable ending, a sullen rush and roar, which seemed to him all at once like the sound of a vast body of fowl coming in to settle there, and, seizing his gun, he started up in haste and excited; but he found, to his surprise, that the whole body of the ice had started while he lay there, and drifted in to the shore, and the sound he had heard was made by its edge grating on the shore,—at first gently nibbled and crumbled off, but at length heaving up and scattering its wrecks along the island to a considerable height before it came to a stand still.

At length the sun's rays have attained the right angle, and warm winds blow up mist and rain and melt the snow banks, and the sun dispersing the mist smiles on a checkered landscape of russet and white smoking with incense, through which the traveller picks his way from islet to islet, cheered by the music of a thousand **8** tinkling rills and rivulets whose veins are filled with the blood of winter which they are bearing off.
9
Few phenomena gave me more delight than to ob- **10** serve the forms which thawing sand and clay assume in flowing down the sides of a deep cut on the railroad through which I passed on my way to the village, a phenomenon not very common on so large a scale, though the number of freshly exposed banks of the right material must have been greatly multiplied since railroads were invented.   The material was sand of every degree of fineness and of various rich colors, commonly mixed with a little clay.   When the frost comes out in the spring, and even in a thawing day in the winter, the sand begins to flow down the slopes like lava, sometimes bursting out through the snow and overflowing it where no sand was to be seen before.   Innumerable little streams overlap and interlace one with another, exhibiting a sort of hybrid product, which obeys half way the law of currents, and half way that of vegetation.   As it flows it takes the forms of sappy leaves or vines, making heaps of pulpy sprays a foot or more in depth, and resembling, as you look down on them, the laciniated **11**

8 *thousand.* This was "myriad" on the page proofs.

9 *which they are bearing off.* This is followed on ms. 1099 by: "As I go back and forth on the rail-road through the deep cut I have seen where clayey sand like lava had flowed down when it thawed and as it streamed it assumed the form of vegetation." This is paraphrased in the next sentence.

10 *Few phenomena.* This paragraph comes from material in the *Journal* for December 30, 1851; III, 164–165, March 9, 1852; III, 344, and March 12, 1852; III, 349. Ms. 906–911 show that Thoreau had a great deal of trouble with the phrasing, for this is one of the most heavily revised sections in the entire manuscript.

A sand flow in the railroad cut
(*Photograph by Herbert Gleason*)

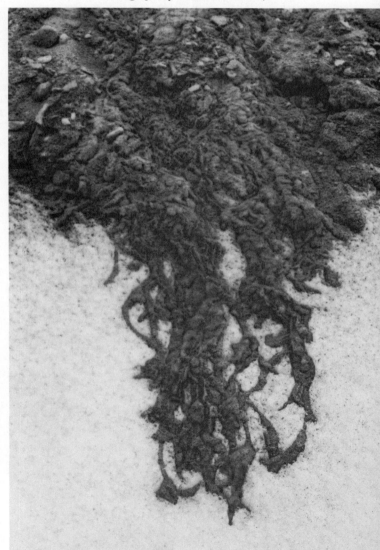

lobed and imbricated thalluses of some lichens; or you are reminded of coral, of leopards' paws or birds' feet, of brains or lungs or bowels, and excrements of all kinds. It is a truly *grotesque* vegetation, whose forms and color we see imitated in bronze, a sort of architectural foliage more ancient and typical than acanthus, chiccory, ivy, vine, or any vegetable leaves; destined perhaps, under some circumstances, to become a puzzle to future geologists. The whole cut impressed me as if it were a cave with its stalactites laid open to the light. The various shades of the sand are singularly rich and agreeable, embracing the different iron colors, brown, gray, yellowish, and reddish. When the flowing mass reaches the **12** drain at the foot of the bank it spreads out flatter into *strands*, the separate streams losing their semi-cylindrical form and gradually becoming more flat and broad, running together as they are more moist, till they form an almost flat *sand*, still variously and beautifully shaded, but in which you can trace the original forms of vegetation; till at length, in the water itself, they are converted into *banks*, like those formed off the mouths of rivers, and the forms of vegetation are lost in the ripple marks on the bottom.

The whole bank, which is from twenty to forty feet high, is sometimes overlaid with a mass of this kind of foliage, or sandy rupture, for a quarter of a mile on one or both sides, the produce of one spring day. What **13** makes this sand foliage remarkable is its springing into existence thus suddenly. When I see on the one side **14** the inert bank,—for the sun acts on one side first,— and on the other this luxuriant foliage, the creation of an hour, I am affected as if in a peculiar sense I stood in the laboratory of the Artist who made the world and me,—had come to where he was still at work, sporting on this bank, and with excess of energy strewing his fresh designs about. I feel as if I were nearer to the vitals of the globe, for this sandy overflow is something such a foliaceous mass as the vitals of the animal body. You find thus in the very sands an anticipation of the **15** vegetable leaf. No wonder that the earth expresses itself outwardly in leaves, it so labors with the idea inwardly. The atoms have already learned this law, and are pregnant by it. The overhanging leaf sees here its prototype. *Internally*, whether in the globe or animal body, it is a moist thick *lobe*, a word especially ap-

11 *laciniated . . . and imbricated thalluses.* Botanical terms: laciniated refers to edges cut into deep, irregular lobes; imbricated means overlapping like tiles on a roof; thallus is a plant so simple that it has no stem, roots, or leaves. Thoreau's reference to leopards' paws is from the *Journal*, December 31, 1851; III, 164.

12 *When the flowing mass. Journal* for January 29, 1852; III, 248.

13 *one spring day.* Ms. 1209 then has: "Sometimes it is slightly excited to productiveness by a rain in midsummer."

14 *thus suddenly.* The Bibliophile Edition (II, 221) follows this with: "as if by magic, while to the eye it has all the perfection of the most slowly formed works of Nature and Art. Just as we should think God was more alive and present if we should see the trees grow apace."

15 *an anticipation of the vegetable leaf. Journal* for March 2, 1854; VI, 148.

Fossil leaves in coal

plicable to the liver and lungs and the *leaves* of fat, (λειβω, *labor, lapsus,* to flow or slip downward, a lapsing; λοβος, *globus,* lobe, globe; also lap, flap, and many other words,) *externally* a dry thin *leaf,* even as the *f* and *v* are a pressed and dried *b.* The radicals of lobe are *lb,* the soft mass of the *b* (single lobed, or B, double lobed,) with a liquid *l* behind it pressing it forward. In globe, *glb,* the guttural *g* adds to the meaning the capacity of the throat. The feathers and wings **16** of birds are still drier and thinner leaves. Thus, also, you pass from the lumpish grub in the earth to the airy and fluttering butterfly. The very globe continually transcends and translates itself, and becomes winged in its orbit. Even ice begins with delicate crystal leaves, as if it had flowed into moulds which the fronds of water plants have impressed on the watery mirror. The whole tree itself is but one leaf, and rivers are still vaster leaves whose pulp is intervening earth, and towns and cities are the ova of insects in their axils.

When the sun withdraws the sand ceases to flow, but in the morning the streams will start once more and branch and branch again into a myriad of others. You here see perchance how blood vessels are formed. If you look closely you observe that first there pushes forward from the thawing mass a stream of softened sand with a drop-like point, like the ball of the finger, feeling its way slowly and blindly downward, until at last with more heat and moisture, as the sun gets higher, the most fluid portion, in its effort to obey the law to which the most inert also yields, separates from the latter and forms for itself a meandering channel or artery within that, in which is seen a little silvery stream glancing like lightning from one stage of pulpy leaves or branches to another, and ever and anon swallowed up in the sand. It is wonderful how rapidly yet perfectly the sand organizes itself as it flows, using the best material its mass affords to form the sharp edges of its channel. Such are the sources of rivers. In the silicious matter which the water deposits is perhaps the bony system, and in the still finer soil and organic matter the fleshy fibre or cellular tissue. What is man but a mass of thawing clay? The ball of the human finger is but a drop congealed. The fingers and toes flow to their extent from the thawing mass of the body. Who knows what the human body would expand and flow out to

16 *capacity of the throat.* Sanborn, in the Bibliophile Edition (II, 222n.), comments on this: "This singular passage is one of those in which, as Ellery Channing somewhere says, Thoreau's 'old trade of schoolmaster stuck to him.' These etymologies and analogies are rather forced, and, introduced here, they interrupt the description and the flow of thought. They were more in fashion when Thoreau was at Harvard College than they have been since, or are likely to be again."

under a more genial heaven? Is not the hand a spreading *palm* leaf with its lobes and veins? The ear may be regarded, fancifully, as a lichen, *umbilicaria*, on the side of the head, with its lobe or drop. The lip — *labium*, from *labor* (?) — laps or lapses from the sides of the cavernous mouth. The nose is a manifest congealed drop or stalactite. The chin is a still larger drop, the confluent dripping of the face. The cheeks are a slide from the brows into the valley of the face, opposed and diffused by the cheek bones. Each rounded lobe of the **17** vegetable leaf, too, is a thick and now loitering drop, larger or smaller; the lobes are the fingers of the leaf; and as many lobes as it has, in so many directions it tends to flow, and more heat or other genial influences would have caused it to flow yet farther.

Thus it seemed that this one hillside illustrated the principle of all the operations of Nature. The Maker of this earth but patented a leaf. What Champollion **18** will decipher this hieroglyphic for us, that we may turn over a new leaf at last? This phenomenon is more exhilarating to me than the luxuriance and fertility of vineyards. True, it is somewhat excrementitious in **19** its character, and there is no end to the heaps of liver lights and bowels, as if the globe were turned wrong side outward; but this suggests at least that Nature has some bowels, and there again is mother of humanity. This is the frost coming out of the ground; this is Spring. **20** It precedes the green and flowery spring, as mythology precedes regular poetry. I know of nothing more pur- **21** gative of winter fumes and indigestions. It convinces me that Earth is still in her swaddling clothes, and stretches forth baby fingers on every side. Fresh curls spring from the baldest brow. There is nothing inorganic. These foliaceous heaps lie along the bank like the slag of a furnace, showing that Nature is "in full blast" within. The earth is not a mere fragment of dead history, stratum upon stratum like the leaves of a book, to be studied by geologists and antiquaries chiefly, but living poetry like the leaves of a tree, which precede flowers and fruit, — not a fossil earth, but a living earth; compared with whose great central life all animal and vegetable life is merely parasitic. Its throes will heave our exuviæ from their graves. You may melt your metals and cast them into the most beautiful moulds you can; they will never excite me like the

17 *cheek bones.* This is followed in the Bibliophile Edition (II, 225) by: "The whole face is a continuous broad shore, and narrow below, to which the chin is a Cape of Good Hope. We might say, by the way, that the face itself is a *terra firma* broad above and narrow below, with its bald polar crown, its temperate zone of greatest breadth, and intelligence and inland seas, its equatorial but sensuous mouth, and its Dutch Cape of Good Hope or Shakespearian Patagonia."

18 *Champollion.* Jean-François Champollion (1790–1832), French Egyptologist who founded the Egyptian Museum of the Louvre. He also deciphered the Rosetta Stone, which made it possible to read hieroglyphics.

19 *somewhat excrementitious. Journal*, December 31, 1851; III, 165, where this is "foecal."

20 *This is the frost coming out of the ground. Journal*, February 8, 1854; VI, 109.

21 *I know of nothing more purgative. Journal* for January 26, 1852; III, 235. Also February 5, 1854; VI, 100.

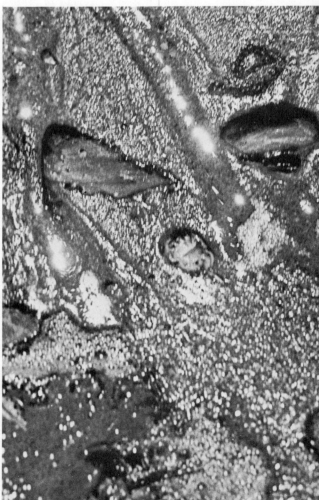

forms which this molten earth flows out into. And not only it, but the institutions upon it, are plastic like clay in the hands of the potter. **22**

Ere long, not only on these banks, but on every hill and plain and in every hollow, the frost comes out of the ground like a dormant quadruped from its burrow, and seeks the sea with music, or migrates to other climes in clouds. Thaw with his gentle persuasion is more powerful than Thor with his hammer. The one melts, **23** the other but breaks in pieces.

When the ground was partially bare of snow, and a few warm days had dried its surface somewhat, it was pleasant to compare the first tender signs of the infant year just peeping forth with the stately beauty of the withered vegetation which had withstood the winter, — life-everlasting, golden-rods, pinweeds, and graceful wild grasses, more obvious and interesting frequently than in summer even, as if their beauty was not ripe till then ; even cotton-grass, cat-tails, mulleins, johns-wort, hard-hack, meadow-sweet, and other strong **24** stemmed plants, those unexhausted granaries which entertain the earliest birds, — decent weeds, at least, which widowed Nature wears. I am particularly attracted by **25** the arching and sheaf-like top of the wool-grass ; it brings back the summer to our winter memories, and is among the forms which art loves to copy, and which, in the vegetable kingdom, have the same relation to types already in the mind of man that astronomy has. It is an antique style older than Greek or Egyptian. Many of the phenomena of Winter are suggestive of an inexpressible tenderness and fragile delicacy. We are accustomed to hear this king described as a rude and boisterous tyrant ; but with the gentleness of a lover he adorns the tresses of Summer.

At the approach of spring the red-squirrels got under my house, two at a time, directly under my feet as I sat reading or writing, and kept up the queerest chuckling and chirruping and vocal pirouetting and gurgling sounds that ever were heard ; and when I stamped they only chirruped the louder, as if past all fear and respect in their mad pranks, defying humanity to stop them. No you don't — chickaree — chickaree. They were wholly deaf to my arguments, or failed to perceive their force,

22 *like clay in the hands of the potter.* Here this fine speculative section on the shapes of Nature ends. For perceptive criticism of it see "Transcendental Pastoral " in *The Machine in the Garden: Technology and the Pastoral Ideal in America* by Leo Marx (1964, page 110).

23 *Thor.* The Scandinavian thunder-god for whom Thursday is named. *Journal* for January 26, 1852; III, 236.

24 *meadow-sweet.* Followed on ms. 1220 by "the various sedges."

25 *I am particularly attracted by.* Instead of this, ms. 203 has: "I never tire of admiring."

and fell into a strain of invective that was irresistible.

The first sparrow of spring! The year beginning with younger hope than ever! The faint silvery warblings heard over the partially bare and moist fields from the blue-bird, the song-sparrow, and the red-wing, as if the last flakes of winter tinkled as they fell! What at such a time are histories, chronologies, traditions, and all written revelations? The brooks sing carols and glees to the spring. The marsh-hawk sailing low over the meadow is already seeking the first slimy life that **26** awakes. The sinking sound of melting snow is heard in all dells, and the ice dissolves apace in the ponds. The grass flames up on the hillsides like a spring fire, — "et primitus oritur herba imbribus primoribus evocata," **27** —as if the earth sent forth an inward heat to greet the returning sun; not yellow but green is the color of its flame; — the symbol of perpetual youth, the grass-blade, like a long green ribbon, streams from the sod into the **28** summer, checked indeed by the frost, but anon pushing on again, lifting its spear of last year's hay with the fresh life below. It grows as steadily as the rill oozes out of the ground. It is almost identical with that, for in the growing days of June, when the rills are dry, the grass blades are their channels, and from year to year the herds drink at this perennial green stream, and the mower draws from it betimes their winter supply. So our human life but dies down to its root, and still puts forth its green blade to eternity.

Walden is melting apace. There is a canal two rods wide along the northerly and westerly sides, and wider still at the east end. A great field of ice has cracked off from the main body. I hear a song-sparrow singing from the bushes on the shore, — *olit, olit, olit,* — *chip,* **29** *chip, chip, che char,* — *che wiss, wiss, wiss.* He too is helping to crack it. How handsome the great sweeping curves in the edge of the ice, answering somewhat to those of the shore, but more regular! It is unusually **30** hard, owing to the recent severe but transient cold, and all watered or waved like a palace floor. But the wind slides eastward over its opaque surface in vain, till it reaches the living surface beyond. It is glorious to behold this ribbon of water sparkling in the sun, the bare face of the pond full of glee and youth, as if it spoke the **31** joy of the fishes within it, and of the sands on its shore, — a silvery sheen as from the scales of a *leuciscus,* as it

---

26 *the first slimy life that awakes.* This is followed on ms. 201 and in the Bibliophile Edition (II, 228) by Thoreau's verse:

> There is health in thy gray wing;
> Health of Nature's furnishing.

27 "*et primitus oritur herba imbribus primoribus evocata.*" "And for the first time the grass begins to grow called forth by the first rains." From Varro's *Rerum Rusticarum.*

28 *a long green ribbon.* Ms. 201: "longer than was ever woven in the factories of men."

29 *from the bushes on the shore.* The bird notes that follow come from the *Journal* for April 1, 1853; V, 79. They were a last-minute addition, for they were written in the left-hand margin of ms. 1223.

30 *but more regular!* Ms. 223 then has: "No wind blows eastward over the opaque ice." *Journal,* March 20, 1853; V, 29.

31 *full of glee and youth.* This was changed on the page from "the life and joy of youth."

were all one active fish.   Such is the contrast between winter and spring.   Walden was dead and is alive again.   **32** But this spring it broke up more steadily, as I have said.

The change from storm and winter to serene and mild weather, from dark and sluggish hours to bright and elastic ones, is a memorable crisis which all things proclaim.   It is seemingly instantaneous at last.   Suddenly an influx of light filled my house, though the evening was at hand, and the clouds of winter still overhung it, and the eaves were dripping with sleety rain.   I looked out the window, and lo! where yesterday was cold gray ice there lay the transparent pond already calm and full of **33** hope as in a summer evening, reflecting a summer evening sky in its bosom, though none was visible overhead, as if it had intelligence with some remote horizon.   I heard a robin in the distance, the first I had heard for many a thousand years, methought, whose note I shall not forget for many a thousand more, — the same sweet and powerful song as of yore.   O the evening robin, at the end of a New England summer day!   If I could ever find the twig he sits upon!   I mean *he*; I mean *the twig*.   This at least is not the *Turdus migratorius*.   **34** The pitch-pines and shrub-oaks about my house, which had so long drooped, suddenly resumed their several characters, looked brighter, greener, and more erect and alive, as if effectually cleansed and restored by the rain. I knew that it would not rain any more.   You may tell by looking at any twig of the forest, ay, at your very wood-pile, whether its winter is past or not.   As it grew darker, I was startled by the *honking* of geese flying low over the woods, like weary travellers getting in late from southern lakes, and indulging at last in unrestrained complaint and mutual consolation.   Standing at my door, I could hear the rush of their wings; when, driving toward my house, they suddenly spied my light, and with hushed clamor wheeled and settled in the pond. So I came in, and shut the door, and passed my first **35** spring night in the woods.

In the morning I watched the geese from the door **36** through the mist, sailing in the middle of the pond, fifty rods off, so large and tumultuous that Walden appeared like an artificial pond for their amusement.   But when I stood on the shore they at once rose up with a great flapping of wings at the signal of their commander, and

32 *Walden was dead and is alive again.* Channing noted in his copy of *Walden:* "Luke XV, 24."

33 *of hope as in a summer evening, reflecting a summer evening sky in its bosom, though none was visible overhead, as if it had intelligence with some remote horizon. I. . . .* These lines appear on ms. 465, but the typesetter left them out, so they were not in the page proofs. Thoreau, remembering a similar mishap in the composition of *A Week*, carefully wrote them in. Even then, the printer did not set the words correctly. Thoreau's copy called for "of hope as on" which makes better sense than "in." The error has been perpetrated ever since.

34 Turdus migratorius. This is the American thrush, commonly called a robin, although it differs from European robins. Thoreau is not very clear about it. And his previous sentence is even more incomprehensible. *Journal*, March 26, 1846; I, 400–402.

35 *and passed my first spring night in the woods.* It will be remembered that the previous spring was taken up by building the cabin. See Charles Anderson (1968, pages 250–251) for information about the cycle image here.

36 *In the morning. Journal*, 1845–1847; I, 402.

when they had got into rank circled about over my head, twenty-nine of them, and then steered straight to **Canada**, with a regular *honk* from the leader at intervals, trusting to break their fast in muddier pools. A **37** "plump" of ducks rose at the same time and took the route to the north in the wake of their noisier **38** cousins.

For a week I heard the circling groping clangor of **39** some solitary goose in the foggy mornings, seeking its companion, and still peopling the woods with the sound of a larger life than they could sustain. In April the pigeons were seen again flying express in small flocks, and in due time I heard the martins twittering over my clearing, though it had not seemed that the township contained so many that it could afford me any, and I fancied that they were peculiarly of the ancient race that dwelt in hollow trees ere white men came. In al- **40** most all climes the tortoise and the frog are among the precursors and heralds of this season, and birds fly with song and glancing plumage, and plants spring and bloom, and winds blow, to correct this slight oscillation of the poles and preserve the equilibrium of Nature.

As every season seems best to us in its turn, so the coming in of spring is like the creation of Cosmos out of Chaos and the realization of the Golden Age. —

"Eurus ad Auroram, Nabathacaque regna recessit,   **41**
    Persidaque, et radiis juga subdita matutinis."

37 *A "plump" of ducks.* A group or flock. This is one of the nouns of multitude in the ancient language of the chase in which one says: a pride of lions, a gaggle of geese, a skulk of foxes, a plague of locusts, etc. Originally it was "a compact flock" on ms. 1108.

38 *in the wake of their noisier cousins.* This is followed on ms. 1108 by:

> Behold how the wave of the sea
> Is made smooth by the calm;
> Behold how the duck dives,
> Behold how the crane travels
> And Titan shines constantly bright
> The shadows of the clouds are moving,
> The works of man shine.

39 *For a week I heard the circling.* Journal, 1845–1847; I, 422.

40 *ere white men came.* Ms. 1109 then has: "The Rhodian children greeted the swallow with a song beginning,

> 'The swallow has come,
> The swallow has come,
> Bringing beautiful hours
> Beautiful seasons, &.'

"Troops of them carrying about a swallow, sang this from door to door, and collected provisions in return. Does not the martin bring beautiful seasons to us?"

41 *"Eurus ad Auroram."* Channing, in his own copy of *Walden*, identifies this as coming from Ovid's *Metamorphoses*, I, 60.

"The East-Wind withdrew to Aurora and the Nabathæan kingdom,   **42**
    And the Persian, and the ridges placed under the morning rays.

    *   *   *   *

Man was born. Whether that Artificer of things,
The origin of a better world, made him from the divine seed;
Or the earth being recent and lately sundered from the high
Ether, retained some seeds of cognate heaven."

A single gentle rain makes the grass many shades greener. So our prospects brighten on the influx of better thoughts. We should be blessed if we lived in the present always, and took advantage of every accident that befell us, like the grass which confesses the influence of the slightest dew that falls on it; and did not spend our time in atoning for the neglect of past opportunities, which we call doing our duty. We loiter in   **43**
winter while it is already spring. In a pleasant spring morning all men's sins are forgiven. Such a day is a   **44**
truce to vice. While such a sun holds out to burn, the   **45**
vilest sinner may return. Through our own recovered innocence we discern the innocence of our neighbors. You may have known your neighbor yesterday for a thief, a drunkard, or a sensualist, and merely pitied or despised him, and despaired of the world; but the sun shines bright and warm this first spring morning, re-creating the world, and you meet him at some serene work, and see how his exhausted and debauched veins expand with still joy and bless the new day, feel the spring influence with the innocence of infancy, and all his faults are forgotten. There is not only an atmosphere of good will about him, but even a savor of holiness groping for expression, blindly and ineffectually perhaps, like a new-born instinct, and for a short hour the south hill-side echoes to no vulgar jest. You see some innocent fair shoots preparing to burst from his gnarled rind and try another year's life, tender and fresh as the youngest plant. Even he has entered into the joy of his Lord. Why the jailer does not leave open his prison doors, — why the judge does not dismiss his case, — why the preacher does not dismiss his congregation! It is because they do not obey the hint which God gives them, nor accept the pardon which he freely offers to all.

"A return to goodness produced each day in the   **46**
tranquil and beneficent breath of the morning, causes that in respect to the love of virtue and the hatred of

42 *the Nabathæan kingdom.* Usually spelled Nabatæan. The land between Syria and Arabia from the Euphrates to the Red Sea. It was an independent area between 312 B.C. and A.D. 105, when the Romans took it over.

43 *which we call doing our duty.* Ms. 1110 then has: "Though man proposeth, God disposeth all. True he is a very present help in trouble, but the chief trouble is that we live in the past and in traditions where he is not." ("He" was not capitalized in the manuscript.) "Man proposeth," etc., Thomas à Kempis, *Imitatio Christi*, I, iii. "A very present help in trouble," Psalm 46:1.

44 *all men's sins are forgiven.* Ms. 1111: Section missing, then: "and prefer the muddy and dirty ruts to the green expanding plains. We make ourselves the very cloacae [sewers] of nature." *Journal*, 1850; II, 9. Also II, 81.

45 *While such a sun holds out to burn, the vilest sinner may return.* Walter Harding (1963, page 315) identifies this as a paraphrase of a similar sentence in Isaac Watts, *Hymns and Spiritual Songs*, 1, 88.

46 *"A return to goodness."* Cady (1961) tells us that these two paragraphs come from Mencius, VI, part 1, Chapter VIII.

vice, one approaches a little the primitive nature of man, as the sprouts of the forest which has been felled. In like manner the evil which one does in the interval of a day prevents the germs of virtues which began to spring up again from developing themselves and destroys them.

"After the germs of virtue have thus been prevented many times from developing themselves, then the beneficent breath of evening does not suffice to preserve them. As soon as the breath of evening does not suffice longer to preserve them, then the nature of man does not differ much from that of the brute. Men seeing the nature of this man like that of the brute, think that he has never possessed the innate faculty of reason. Are those the true and natural sentiments of man?"

"The Golden Age was first created, which without any avenger   **47**
Spontaneously without law cherished fidelity and rectitude.
Punishment and fear were not; nor were threatening words read
On suspended brass; nor did the suppliant crowd fear
The words of their judge; but were safe without an avenger.
Not yet the pine felled on its mountains had descended
To the liquid waves that it might see a foreign world,
And mortals knew no shores but their own.
  *   *   *   *
There was eternal spring, and placid zephyrs with warm
Blasts soothed the flowers born without seed."

On the 29th of April, as I was fishing from the bank of the river near the Nine-Acre-Corner bridge, standing on the quaking grass and willow roots, where the muskrats lurk, I heard a singular rattling sound, somewhat like that of the sticks which boys play with their fingers,   **48** when, looking up, I observed a very slight and graceful hawk, like a night-hawk, alternately soaring like a ripple and tumbling a rod or two over and over, showing the underside of its wings, which gleamed like a satin ribbon in the sun, or like the pearly inside of a shell. This sight reminded me of falconry and what nobleness and poetry are associated with that sport. The Merlin it seemed to me it might be called: but I care not for its name. It was the most ethereal flight I had ever witnessed. It did not simply flutter like a butterfly, nor soar like the larger hawks, but it sported with proud reliance in the fields of air; mounting again and again with its strange chuckle, it repeated its free and beauti-

47 *"The Golden Age was first created."* Channing identifies this verse as coming from Ovid's *Metamorphoses*, I, 89.

48 *the sticks*. A game played by children using hard, elongated bits of wood or bone to make clacking sounds.

ful fall, turning over and over like a kite, and then recovering from its lofty tumbling, as if it had never set its foot on *terra firma*. It appeared to have no companion in the universe, — sporting there alone, — and to need none but the morning and the ether with which it played. It was not lonely, but made all the earth **49** lonely beneath it. Where was the parent which hatched it, its kindred, and its father in the heavens? The tenant of the air, it seemed related to the earth but by an egg hatched some time in the crevice of a crag; — or was its native nest made in the angle of a cloud, woven of the rainbow's trimmings and the sunset sky, and lined with some soft midsummer haze caught up from earth? Its eyry now some cliffy cloud.

Beside this I got a rare mess of golden and silver and bright cupreous fishes, which looked like a string of **50** jewels. Ah! I have penetrated to those meadows on the morning of many a first spring day, jumping from hummock to hummock, from willow root to willow root, when the wild river valley and the woods were bathed in so pure and bright a light as would have waked the dead, if they had been slumbering in their graves, as some suppose. There needs no stronger proof of immortality. All things must live in such a light. O **51** Death, where was thy sting? O Grave, where was thy **52** victory, then?

Our village life would stagnate if it were not for the unexplored forests and meadows which surround it. We need the tonic of wildness, — to wade sometimes in marshes where the bittern and the meadow-hen lurk, and hear the booming of the snipe; to smell the whis-

49 *but made all the earth lonely beneath it.* Ms. 195 then has: "Though it had no mate in the world."

50 *like a string of jewels.* Ms. 196: "This spring ramble was very invigorating and purgative of wintry fumes and dumps."

51 *O Death, where was thy sting?* "O death, where is thy sting? O grave, where is thy victory?" I Corinthians 15:55.

52 *thy victory, then?* This phrase is followed in the Bibliophile Edition (II, 237–238) by: "It was glorious to see the winds appeased, the sea becalmed, the soft season, the serene firmament, the still air, and the beauty of the watery scene. The silver-scaled fishes on the gravel gliding hastily, as it were, from the heat, or seen through clear streams, with fins shining brown as cinnabar, and chisel tails darted here and there. The new lustre enlightening all the land, beamed on the small pebbles, on the sides of rivers, and on the strands which looked like beryl, while the reflections of the rays played on the banks in variegated gleams. Our opaque stream did not absorb the light, but reflected it all."

A medal by Donald R. Miller issued by the Society of Medalists

pering sedge where only some wilder and more solitary fowl builds her nest, and the mink crawls with its belly close to the ground. At the same time that we are earnest to explore and learn all things, we require that all things be mysterious and unexplorable, that land and sea be infinitely wild, unsurveyed and unfathomed by us because unfathomable. We can never have enough of Nature. We must be refreshed by the sight of inexhaustible vigor, vast and Titanic features, the sea-coast with its wrecks, the wilderness with its living and its decaying trees, the thunder cloud, and the rain which lasts three weeks and produces freshets. We need to witness our own limits transgressed, and some life pasturing freely where we never wander. We are cheered when we observe the vulture feeding on the carrion which disgusts and disheartens us and deriving health and strength from the repast. There was a dead horse in the hollow by the path to my house, which compelled me sometimes to go out of my way, especially in the night when the air was heavy, but the assurance it gave me of the strong appetite and inviolable health of Nature was my compensation for this. I love to see that Nature is so rife with life that myriads can be afforded to be sacrificed and suffered to prey on one another; that tender organizations can be so serenely squashed out of existence like pulp, — tadpoles which herons gobble up, and tortoises and toads run over in the road; and that sometimes it has rained flesh and blood! With the liability to accident, we must see how little account is to be made of it. The impression made on a wise man is that of universal innocence. Poison is not poisonous after all, nor are any wounds fatal. Compassion is a very untenable ground. It must be expeditious. Its pleadings will not bear to be stereotyped.

Early in May, the oaks, hickories, maples, and other **53** trees, just putting out amidst the pine woods around the pond, imparted a brightness like sunshine to the landscape, especially in cloudy days, as if the sun were breaking through mists and shining faintly on the **54** hill-sides here and there. On the third or fourth of May I saw a loon in the pond, and during the first week of the month I heard the whippoorwill, the brown-thrasher, the veery, the wood-pewee, the chewink, and other birds. I had heard the wood-thrush long before. The phœbe had already come once more

53 *Early in May*. On the page proofs this was followed by "or by the last of April," but Thoreau struck the latter clause out.

54 *on the hill-sides here and there.* Ms. 193 then has this couplet:

> When the oaks are in the gray
> Then Farmers plant away.

and looked in at my door and window, to see if my house was cavern-like enough for her, sustaining herself on humming wings with clinched talons, as if she held by the air, while she surveyed the premises. The sulphur-like pollen of the pitch-pine soon covered the pond and the stones and rotten wood along the shore, so that you could have collected a barrel-ful. This is the "sulphur 55 showers" we hear of. Even in Calidas' drama of Sa- 56 contala, we read of "rills dyed yellow with the golden dust of the lotus." And so the seasons went rolling on into summer, as one rambles into higher and higher 57 grass.

Thus was my first year's life in the woods completed; and the second year was similar to it. I finally left 58 Walden September 6th, 1847.

55 *This is the "sulphur showers."* Ms. 896 has "These are."

56 *Calidas'.* Ordinarily spelled Kalidasa. A Hindu author, fl. 5th (?) century A.D. His best-known drama, usually spelled Sakuntala, was translated from the Sanskrit in 1789 by Sir William Jones and was extravagantly praised by Goethe. It has been produced in America and Europe in modern times.

57 *higher grass.* The Bibliophile Edition (II, 240) then has this verse by Thoreau:

He knows no change who knows the true,
   And on it keeps his eye;
Who always still the unseen doth view;
   Only the false and the apparent die.

Things change, but change not far,
   From what they are not but to what they are;
Or rather, 'tis our ignorance that dies,
   While ever lives the knowledge of the wise.

58 *and the second year was similar to it.* This, of course, was not so; it was quite different. For one thing, Thoreau went to Maine in September 1846. And the imprisonment for refusing to pay his poll tax, related in the account of the first year, actually took place during the second. But the author, for the sake of unity, wanted to make his book cover a single year. *Walden* should not be taken too literally.

The cairn as it is now with the cabin site above it

Spinning oakum

CONCLUSION.

To the sick the doctors wisely recommend a change of air and scenery. Thank Heaven, here is not all the world. The buck-eye does not grow in New England, and the mocking-bird is rarely heard here. The wild-goose is more of a cosmopolite than we; he breaks his fast in Canada, takes a luncheon in the Ohio, and plumes himself for the night in a southern bayou. Even the bison, to some extent, keeps pace with the seasons, cropping the pastures of the Colorado only till a greener and sweeter grass awaits him by the Yellow-stone. Yet we think that if rail-fences are pulled down, and stone-walls piled up on our farms, bounds are henceforth set to our lives and our fates decided. If you are chosen town-clerk, forsooth, you cannot go to Tierra del Fuego this summer: but you may go to the land of infernal fire nevertheless. The universe is wider than our views of it.

Yet we should oftener look over the tafferel of our craft, like curious passengers, and not make the voyage like stupid sailors picking oakum. The other side of the globe is but the home of our correspondent. Our voyaging is only great-circle sailing, and the doctors prescribe for diseases of the skin merely. One hastens to Southern Africa to chase the giraffe; but surely that is not the game he would be after. How long, pray, would a man hunt giraffes if he could? Snipes and woodcocks also may afford rare sport; but I trust it would be nobler game to shoot one's self. —

> " Direct your eye right inward, and you'll find
>   A thousand regions in your mind
>   Yet undiscovered. Travel them, and be
>   Expert in home-cosmography."

1 *Thank Heaven.* This is from the *Journal* for March 21, 1840; I, 130. It begins there, however, with "Thank Fortune," as it does on ms. 1130. There "takes a luncheon in the Ohio" is "Susquehanna" and "a southern bayou" is "a Louisiana bayou."

2 *If you are chosen town-clerk. Journal*, March 21, 1840; I, 131.

3 *tafferel . . . oakum.* Taffrail is the customary spelling, but Thoreau changed it from that to this on the page proofs. It is the guardrail around a ship's stern. Oakum refers to vegetable fibers treated with tar or creosote and used to calk the seams in a boat's hull. Old ropes were picked apart to obtain material.

4 *"Direct your eye right inward."* Ms. 1114 and 1131 both have this as "your eye sight," which is as it should be, for it was that way in the verse quoted from "To My Honoured Friend, Sir Ed. P. Knight" by William Habington (1605–1654). Channing gives the source in his copy of *Walden.*

What does Africa,—what does the West stand for? Is not our own interior white on the chart? black though it may prove, like the coast, when discovered. Is it the source of the Nile, or the Niger, or the Mississippi, or a North-West Passage around this continent, that we would find? Are these the problems which most concern mankind? Is Franklin the only man **5** who is lost, that his wife should be so earnest to find him? Does Mr. Grinnell know where he himself is? **6** Be rather the Mungo Park, the Lewis and Clarke and **7, 8** Frobisher, of your own streams and oceans; explore **9** your own higher latitudes,—with shiploads of preserved meats to support you, if they be necessary; and pile the **10** empty cans sky-high for a sign. Were preserved meats invented to preserve meat merely? Nay, be a Columbus to whole new continents and worlds within you, opening new channels, not of trade, but of thought. Every man is the lord of a realm beside which the earthly empire of the Czar is but a petty state, a hummock left by the ice. Yet some can be patriotic who have no *self*-respect, and sacrifice the greater to the less. They love the soil which makes their graves, but have no sympathy with the spirit which may still animate their clay. Patriotism is a maggot in their heads. What was the meaning of that South-Sea Exploring **11** Expedition, with all its parade and expense, but an indirect recognition of the fact, that there are continents and seas in the moral world, to which every man is an isthmus or an inlet, yet unexplored by him, but that it is easier to sail many thousand miles through cold and storm and cannibals, in a government ship, with five hundred men and boys to assist one, than it is to explore the private sea, the Atlantic and Pacific Ocean of one's being alone. —

> "Erret, et extremos alter scrutetur Iberos.   **12**
> Plus habet hic vitæ, plus habet ille viæ."

Let them wander and scrutinize the outlandish Australians. I have more of God, they more of the road.

It is not worth the while to go round the world to count **13** the cats in Zanzibar. Yet do this even till you can do better, and you may perhaps find some "Symmes' **14** Hole" by which to get at the inside at last. England and France, Spain and Portugal, Gold Coast and Slave

5 *Franklin.* Sir John Franklin, the Arctic explorer whose men and two ships were lost in 1847 and 1848.

6 *Grinnell.* Henry Grinnell, an American, financed an expedition to search for Franklin.

7 *Mungo Park.* A Scottish explorer whose book, *Travels in the Interior of Africa*, was published in 1799. He returned there in 1805 and was killed by the natives.

8 *Lewis and Clarke.* Headed the expedition to explore the vast territory newly acquired by the Louisiana Purchase of 1803.

9 *Frobisher.* Sir Martin Frobisher (1535?–1594), an English explorer, made several voyages to northern Canada.

10 *the empty cans.* Although few people realize it, tin cans—more properly tinned cans—were used for preserving food in those days. This is probably an allusion to the hundreds of cans of meat on Franklin's ships.

11 *South-Sea Exploring Expedition.* The one made in 1839 to 1842 under the command of Charles Wilkes of the U.S. Navy

12 *"Erret, et extremos."* We have double identification for this obscure quotation. Channing, in his copy of *Walden*, says that it is from Claudian's *Epigrammata*, II, 21. And Thoreau, in his *Journal* for May 10, 1841; I, 259, confirms this and also says that "a good warning to the restless tourists of these days is contained in the last verses of Claudian's 'Old Man of Verona.'" "Australians" is a liberty that Thoreau has taken, for "Iberos" means Spaniards.

Sir John Franklin

Coast, all front on this private sea; but no bark from them has ventured out of sight of land, though it is without doubt the direct way to India. If you would learn to speak all tongues and conform to the customs of all nations, if you would travel farther than all travellers, be naturalized in all climes, and cause the Sphinx **15** to dash her head against a stone, even obey the precept of the old philosopher, and Explore thyself. Herein are demanded the eye and the nerve. Only the defeated and deserters go to the wars, cowards that run away and enlist. Start now on that farthest western way, which does not pause at the Mississippi or the Pacific, nor conduct toward a worn-out China or Japan, but leads **16** on direct a tangent to this sphere, summer and winter, day and night, sun down, moon down, and at last earth down too.

It is said that Mirabeau took to highway robbery "to **17** ascertain what degree of resolution was necessary in order to place one's self in formal opposition to the most sacred laws of society." He declared that "a soldier who fights in the ranks does not require half so much courage as a foot-pad,"—"that honor and religion have never stood in the way of a well-considered and a firm resolve." This was manly, as the world goes; and yet it was idle, if not desperate. A saner man would have found himself often enough "in formal opposition" to what are deemed "the most sacred laws of society," through obedience to yet more sacred laws, and so have tested his resolution without going out of his way. It is not for a man to put himself in such an attitude to society, but to maintain himself in whatever attitude he find himself through obedience to the laws of his being, which will never be one of opposition to a just government, if he should chance to meet with such. **18**

I left the woods for as good a reason as I went there. **19** Perhaps it seemed to me that I had several more lives to live, and could not spare any more time for that one. It is remarkable how easily and insensibly we fall into a particular route, and make a beaten track for ourselves. I had not lived there a week before my feet wore a path from my door to the pond-side; and though it is five or six years since I trod it, it is still quite distinct. It is true, I fear that others may have fallen into it, and so helped to keep it open. The surface of the

13 *to count the cats in Zanzibar.* In his *Journal* for August 23, 1853; V, 392, Thoreau says that he had been reading Charles Pickering's *The Races of Man* (1851). This book, among many other things, tells about the cats of Zanzibar. Zanzibar is an island off the east coast of Africa, a few degrees below the equator.

14 *"Symmes' Hole."* John Symmes was the author of a pamphlet issued in 1818 and entitled: "The Symmes' Theory of Concentric Spheres, demonstrating that the earth is hollow, habitable, and widely open about the poles." This rather nonsensical idea bore fruit in literature when Poe and Jules Verne made use of it. There is also a fantasy novel that stems from it, *Symsonia: A Voyage of Discovery*, published in 1820 under the pen name, Captain Adam Seaborn.

15 *and cause the Sphinx to dash her head against a stone.* The Sphinx was a monstrous creature in ancient Greek mythology with a lion's body and the head and breast of a woman. She asked travelers a riddle saying that they could go free if they could answer it; if not, she would devour them. She terrorized the countryside until Oedipus appeared. "What goes on four feet in the morning, two at noon, and three in the evening?" she asked. When Oedipus gave "man" as the correct answer, the Sphinx obligingly killed herself by knocking her head against a rock.

16 *worn-out China or Japan.* Thoreau called these countries "worn-out" because their ancient civilizations—in his time—seemed to have become static.

17 *Mirabeau.* Honoré-Gabriel Victor Riqueti, Comte de Mirabeau (1749–1791), French revolutionist. In the *Journal* for July 21, 1851; II, 332–333, Thoreau copied parts of an article about Mirabeau which had appeared in *Harper's New Monthly*, I, 648, and which had been taken from

earth is soft and impressible by the feet of men; and so with the paths which the mind travels. How worn and dusty, then, must be the highways of the world, how deep the ruts of tradition and conformity! I did not wish to take a cabin passage, but rather to go before the mast **20** and on the deck of the world, for there I could best see the moonlight amid the mountains. I do not wish to go below now.

I learned this, at least, by my experiment; that if one advances confidently in the direction of his dreams, and endeavors to live the life which he has imagined, he will meet with a success unexpected in common hours. He will put some things behind, will pass an invisible boundary; new, universal, and more liberal laws will begin to establish themselves around and within him; or the **21** old laws be expanded, and interpreted in his favor in a more liberal sense, and he will live with the license of a higher order of beings. In proportion as he simplifies his life, the laws of the universe will appear less complex, and solitude will not be solitude, nor poverty poverty, nor weakness weakness. If you have built castles in the air, your work need not be lost; that is where they should be. Now put the foundations under them.

It is a ridiculous demand which England and America make, that you shall speak so that they can understand you. Neither men nor toad-stools grow so. As if that were important, and there were not enough to understand you without them. As if Nature could support but one order of understandings, could not sustain birds as well as quadrupeds, flying as well as creeping things, and *hush* and *who*, which Bright can under- **22** stand, were the best English. As if there were safety in stupidity alone. I fear chiefly lest my expression may not be *extra- vagant* enough, may not wander far enough **23** beyond the narrow limits of my daily experience, so as to be adequate to the truth of which I have been convinced. *Extra vagance!* it depends on how you are yarded. The migrating buffalo, which seeks new pastures in another latitude, is not extravagant like the cow which kicks over the pail, leaps the cow-yard fence, and **24** runs after her calf, in milking time. I desire to speak somewhere *without* bounds; like a man in a waking moment, to men in their waking moments; for I am convinced that I cannot exaggerate enough even to lay **25**

Chamber's Edinburgh Journal. The phrases quoted are from that. In the *Bibliophile Edition* (II, 244) is this omitted passage. "'Tell me,' said Mirabeau, 'Du Saillant,—when you lead your regiment into the heat of a battle to conquer a province to which he whom you call your master has no right whatever,—do you consider that you are performing a better action than mine, in stopping your friend on the highway and demanding his purse?' 'I obey without reasoning,' replied the Count. 'And I reason without obeying, when obedience appears to me to be contrary to reason,' rejoined Mirabeau."

18 *to meet with such.* Ms. 1119: "Let us not have a rabid virtue that will be revenged on society, and descend on it,—not like the morning dew to refresh it, but like the fervid noonday sun to wither it."

19 *I left the woods for as good a reason as I went there.* Entries in the *Journal* for January 22, 1852; III, 214 and 216, cast more light on this passage. It should be noted that it was written in the middle of winter nearly five years after Thoreau had left the cabin.

20 *a cabin passage.* There is a play on words here, deliberate or unconscious.

21 *around and within him.* This is followed on ms. 1137 by: "(heaven be about him in his manhood even.)" Cf. "Heaven lies about us in our infancy" in "Intimations of Immortality" by William Wordsworth.

22 hush *and* who, *which Bright can understand.* As has already been pointed out, Bright was a common name for an ox. Hush means "go"; who, "stop." The 1906 edition of *Walden* changed "who" to "whoa," but the editor who did it has since admitted that he was probably wrong. See Harding (1963, page 318).

the foundation of a true expression. Who that has heard a strain of music feared then lest he should speak extravagantly any more forever? In view of the future or possible, we should live quite laxly and undefined in front, our outlines dim and misty on that side; as our shadows reveal an insensible perspiration toward the sun. The volatile truth of our words should continually betray the inadequacy of the residual statement. Their truth is instantly *translated*; its literal monument alone remains. The words which express our faith and piety are not definite; yet they are significant and fragrant like frankincense to superior natures.

Why level downward to our dullest perception always, and praise that as common sense? The commonest sense is the sense of men asleep, which they express by snoring. Sometimes we are inclined to class those who are once-and-a-half witted with the half-witted, because we appreciate only a third part of their wit. Some would find fault with the morning-red, if they ever got up early enough. "They pretend," as I hear, "that the verses of Kabir have four different senses; illusion, spirit, intellect, and the exoteric doctrine of the Vedas;" but in this part of the world it is considered a ground for complaint if a man's writings admit of more than one interpretation. While England endeavors to cure the potato-rot, will not any endeavor to cure the brain-rot, which prevails so much more widely and fatally?

I do not suppose that I have attained to obscurity, but I should be proud if no more fatal fault were found with my pages on this score than was found with the Walden ice. Southern customers objected to its blue color, which is the evidence of its purity, as if it were muddy, and preferred the Cambridge ice, which is white, but tastes of weeds. The purity men love is like the mists which envelop the earth, and not like the azure ether beyond.

Some are dinning in our ears that we Americans, and moderns generally, are intellectual dwarfs compared with the ancients, or even the Elizabethan men. But what is that to the purpose? A living dog is better than a dead lion. Shall a man go and hang himself because he belongs to the race of pygmies, and not be the biggest pygmy that he can? Let every one mind his own business, and endeavor to be what he was made.

23 extra-vagant. Here Thoreau has purposely split the word in order to emphasize its original root meaning which is: *extra*=outside + *vagari*= to wander.

24 *leaps the cow-yard fence, and runs after her calf, in milking time.* These two unnecessary commas were not in the sentence on ms. 1225 and may have been added by an overprecise editor or printer.

25 *I cannot exaggerate enough. Journal* for February 5, 1854; VI, 100.

26 *like frankincense to superior natures.* This is followed in the Bibliophile Edition (II, 247n.) by: "If the reader thinks that I am vainglorious, and set myself above others, I assure him that I could tell a justified story respecting myself as well as him, if my spirits held out; could encourage him with a sufficient list of my failures, and flow as humbly as the gutters. I think worse of myself than he is likely to think of me,—and better, too, perchance,—being better acquainted with the man. Finally, I will tell him this secret, if he will not abuse my confidence,—I put the best face on the matter."
A little later he said in an omitted clause:—
"The too exquisitely cultivated I avoid, as I do the theatre. Their life lacks reality. They offer me wine instead of water. They are surrounded by things that can be bought. They have already sold themselves."

27 *"They pretend."* This is a translation from Garcin de Tassy's *Histoire de la Littérature Hindoue*. Kabar was a fifteenth-century mystic.

28 *which prevails so much more widely and fatally?* Ms. 1123 "which prevails to so damning an extent?"

29 *A living dog is better than a dead lion.* Ecclesiastes 9:4.

Why should we be in such desperate haste to succeed, and in such desperate enterprises? If a man does not keep pace with his companions, perhaps it is **30** because he hears a different drummer. Let him step to the music which he hears, however measured or far away. It is not important that he should mature as soon as an apple-tree or an oak. Shall he turn his spring into summer? If the condition of things which we were made for is not yet, what were any reality which we can substitute? We will not be shipwrecked on a vain reality. Shall we with pains erect a heaven of blue glass over ourselves, though when it is done we shall be sure to gaze still at the true ethereal heaven far above, as if the former were not?

There was an artist in the city of Kouroo who was **31** disposed to strive after perfection. One day it came into his mind to make a staff. Having considered that in an imperfect work time is an ingredient, but into a perfect work time does not enter, he said to himself, It shall be perfect in all respects, though I should do nothing else in my life. He proceeded instantly to the forest for wood, being resolved that it should not be made of unsuitable material; and as he searched for and rejected stick after stick, his friends gradually deserted him, for they grew old in their works and died, but he grew not older by a moment. His singleness of purpose and resolution, and his elevated piety, endowed him, without his knowledge, with perennial youth. As he made no compromise with Time, Time kept out of his way, and only sighed at a distance because he could not overcome him. Before he had found a stock in all **32** respects suitable the city of Kouroo was a hoary ruin, and he sat on one of its mounds to peel the stick. Before he had given it the proper shape the dynasty of the Candahars was at an end, and with the point of the stick he wrote the name of the last of that race in the sand, and then resumed his work. By the time he had smoothed and polished the staff Kalpa was no longer the pole-star; and ere he had put on the ferule and the head adorned with precious stones, Brahma had awoke and slumbered many times. But why do I stay to mention these things? When the finishing stroke was put to his work, it suddenly expanded before the eyes of the astonished artist into the fairest of all the creations of Brahma. He had made a new system in making a

30 *perhaps it is because he hears a different drummer.* It is seldom that one can trace the way a dominating idea enters a writer's mind and develops over a period of time into the form in which he wants it to appear. These few sentences in *Walden* are the final expression. Their evolution is interesting. On the night of September 2, 1839, when Thoreau and his brother John were on the voyage that resulted in *A Week on the Concord and Merrimack Rivers,* they "heard some tyro beating a drum incessantly" as they fell asleep (*A Week,* 1849, pp. 182–183).

A Week has a somewhat similar passage on page 185 of the first edition: "Marching is when the pulse of the hero beats in unison with the pulse of Nature, and he steps to the measure of the universe; then there is true courage and invincible strength."

But Thoreau was not content to leave the phrasing alone. He put down his recollections of the night on the Merrimack in the *Journal* for June 18, 1840; I, 145:

"Far into night I hear some tyro beating a drum incessantly with a view to some country muster, and am thrilled by an infinite sweetness as of a music which the breeze drew from the sinews of war. I think of the line,—

'When the drum beat at dead of night.'

"How I wish it would wake the whole world to march to its melody, but still it drums on alone in the silence and the dark. Cease not, thou drummer of the night, thou too shalt have thy reward. The stars and the firmament hear thee, and their aisles shall echo thy beat till its call is answered, and the forces are mustered. The universe is attentive as a little child to thy sound, and trembles as if each stroke bounded against an elastic vibrating firmament. I should be contented if the night never ended, for in the darkness heroism will not be deferred, and I see fields where no hero has couched his lance."

He promptly revised and improved the passage in his *Journal* for June 30, 1840; I, 156: "A man's life should be a stately march to a sweet but unheard music, and when to his fellows it shall seem irregular and inharmonious, he will only be stepping to a livelier measure or his nicer ear hurry him into a thousand symphonies and concordant variations."

Thoreau then made it part of the article "The Service," which he wrote for *The Dial.* He sent this to the editor, Margaret Fuller, some time in July 1840. After keeping the manuscript for five months she returned it. It was not published until 1902. The passage for "The Service" (p. 15) reads:

staff, a world with full and fair proportions; in which, though the old cities and dynasties had passed away, fairer and more glorious ones had taken their places. And now he saw by the heap of shavings still fresh at his feet, that, for him and his work, the former lapse of time had been an illusion, and that no more time had elapsed than is required for a single scintillation from the brain of Brahma to fall on and inflame the tinder of a mortal brain. The material was pure, and his art was pure; how could the result be other than wonderful?

No face which we can give to a matter will stead us so well at last as the truth. This alone wears well. For the most part, we are not where we are, but in a false position. Through an infirmity of our natures, we suppose a case, and put ourselves into it, and hence are in two cases at the same time, and it is doubly difficult to get out. In sane moments we regard only the facts, the case that is. Say what you have to say, not what you ought. Any truth is better than make-believe. Tom **33** Hyde, the tinker, standing on the gallows, was asked if he had any thing to say. "Tell the tailors," said he, "to remember to make a knot in their thread before they take the first stitch." His companion's prayer is forgotten.

However mean your life is, meet it and live it; do not shun it and call it hard names. It is not so bad as you are. It looks poorest when you are richest. The fault-finder will find faults even in paradise. Love your life, poor as it is. You may perhaps have some pleasant, thrilling, glorious hours, even in a poor-house. The setting sun is reflected from the windows of the alms-house as brightly as from the rich man's abode; the snow melts before its door as early in the spring. I do not see but a quiet mind may live as contentedly there, and have as cheering thoughts, as in a palace. The town's poor seem to me often to live the most independent lives of any. May be they are simply great enough to receive without misgiving. Most think that they are above being supported by the town; but it oftener happens that they are not above supporting themselves by dishonest means, which should be more disreputable. Cultivate poverty like a garden herb, like sage. Do not trouble yourself much to get new things, whether clothes or friends. Turn the old; return to them. Things do not change; we change. Sell your clothes and keep your thoughts. God will see

"A man's life should be a stately march to an unheard music; and when to his fellows it may seem irregular and inharmonious, he will be stepping to a livelier measure, which only a nicer ear can detect. There will be no halt, ever, but at most a marching on his post, or such a pause as is richer than any sound, when the deeper melody is no longer heard, but implicitly consented to with the whole life and being. He will take a false step never, even in the most arduous circumstances; for then the music will not fail to swell into greater volume, and rule the movement it inspired."

Under the uncertain dates of July and August, 1840, a poorer and subsidiary variation of the basic idea appears in the "Lost" *Journal* (Perry Miller, 1958, page 141):

"Let not the faithful sorrow that he has no ear for the more fickle and rabble harmonies of creation—if he be awake to the slower measure of virtue and truth. If his pulse does not beat in unison with the musician's quips and turns, it may accord with *their* larger periods."

This, too, with the last sentence changed to "accord with the pulse-beat of the ages," was incorporated into "The Service."

Then, eleven years later, the famous passage appears in degraded form in the *Journal* for July 14, 1851; II, 307: "For years I marched as to a music in comparison with which the military music of the streets is noise and discord."

The idea was obsessing Thoreau at this time as the *Journal* for July 19, 1851; II, 316, shows: "Let a man step to the music which he hears, however measured." Then, again on July 25, 1851; II, 346: "I am bothered to walk with those who wish to keep step with me. It is not necessary to keep step with your companion, as some endeavor to do." This prosaic rendition of the basic theme breaks it down into its simplest terms. An entry on September 7, 1851; II, 468, is merely tangential: "It is not so much the music as the marching to the music that I feel."

The idea had gone through its incubation period by this time. Thoreau now took firm hold of it and on ms. 1127 forged it into its simple, straightforward final shape. It was a last-minute revision of copy that does not appear in earlier versions of the manuscript. Only two slight changes were made in the words at this stage: "Let him step" was originally "Let a man step," and "however measured or far away" was "however measured or however far away." Once these were improved, the passage stood as it has been ever since, breathing defiance and upholding the individual against all societies of any kind. As a result it has become

that you do not want society. If I were confined to a corner of a garret all my days, like a spider, the world would be just as large to me while I had my thoughts about me. The philosopher said: " From an army of three divisions one can take away its general, and put it in disorder ; from the man the most abject and vulgar one cannot take away his thought." Do not seek so anxiously to be developed, to subject yourself to many influences to be played on; it is all dissipation. Humility like darkness reveals the heavenly lights. The shadows of poverty and meanness gather around us, " and lo ! creation widens to our view." We are often reminded that if there were bestowed on us the wealth of Crœsus, our aims must still be the same, and our means essentially the same. Moreover, if you are restricted in your range by poverty, if you cannot buy books and newspapers, for instance, you are but confined to the most significant and vital experiences; you are compelled to deal with the material which yields the most sugar and the most starch. It is life near the bone where it is sweetest. You are defended from being a trifler. No man loses ever on a lower level by magnanimity on a higher. Superfluous wealth can buy superfluities only. Money is not required to buy one necessary of the soul.

I live in the angle of a leaden wall, into whose composition was poured a little alloy of bell metal. Often, in the repose of my mid-day, there reaches my ears a confused *tintinnabulum* from without. It is the noise of my contemporaries. My neighbors tell me of their adventures with famous gentlemen and ladies, what notabilities they met at the dinner-table; but I am no more interested in such things than in the contents of the Daily Times. The interest and the conversation are about costume and manners chiefly; but a goose is a goose still, dress it as you will. They tell me of California and Texas, of England and the Indies, of the Hon. Mr. —— of Georgia or of Massachusetts, all transient and fleeting phenomena, till I am ready to leap from their court-yard like the Mameluke bey. I delight to come to my bearings, — not walk in procession with pomp and parade, in a conspicuous place, but to walk even with the Builder of the universe, if I may, — not to live in this restless, nervous, bustling, trivial Nineteenth Century, but stand or sit thoughtfully while

one of the most often quoted passages in *Walden* —and also the one which is most often parodied.

31 *There was an artist in the city of Kouroo.* This, like any good fairy story, originally began: "There was an artist who lived in the city of Kouroo" (ms. 900). Since no one has been able to find a source for the legend, it may be that Thoreau invented it. Arthur Christy (1932, page 193) thinks that it is an allegory of Thoreau's life.

32 *Before he had found a stock.* Some people think that this is a misprint for "stick," but ms. 677 and 1128 clearly say "stock." All the references to dynasties, pole-star shiftings, and the many slumbers of Brahma indicate the passing of millions of years.

33 *Tom Hyde.* Sanborn, in a footnote in the Bibliophile Edition (II, 251n.), says that this passage "is found in the *Journal* of 1849, page 383 . . . with this addition,—'Tom added, "You Boston folks and Roxbury people will want Tom Hyde to mend your kettles." ' " This *Journal* still exists in fragmentary condition and is in the Huntington Library with the entry dated: "Sun. Oct. 2, 1849."

34 *"From an army of three divisions."* Confucius.

35 *"and lo! creation widens to our view."* A line paraphrased from "To Night" by Joseph Blanco White (1775–1841), a British theological writer who is best remembered for this sonnet.

it goes by. What are men celebrating? They are all on a committee of arrangements, and hourly expect a speech from somebody. God is only the president of the day, and Webster is his orator. I love to weigh, to settle, to gravitate toward that which most strongly and rightfully attracts me; — not hang by the beam of the scale and try to weigh less, — not suppose a case, but take the case that is; to travel the only path I can, and that on which no power can resist me. It affords me no satisfaction to commence to spring an arch before I have got a solid foundation. Let us not play at kittlybenders. There is a solid bottom every where. We read that the traveller asked the boy if the swamp before him had a hard bottom. The boy replied that it had. But presently the traveller's horse sank in up to the girths, and he observed to the boy, "I thought you said that this bog had a hard bottom." "So it has," answered the latter, "but you have not got half way to it yet." So it is with the bogs and quicksands of society; but he is an old boy that knows it. Only what is thought said or done at a certain rare coincidence is good. I would not be one of those who will foolishly drive a nail into mere lath and plastering; such a deed would keep me awake nights. Give me a hammer, and let me feel for the furrowing. Do not depend on the putty. Drive a nail home and clinch it so faithfully that you can wake up in the night and think of your work with satisfaction, — a work at which you would not be ashamed to invoke the Muse. So will help you God, and so only. Every nail driven should be as another rivet in the machine of the universe, you carrying on the work.

Rather than love, than money, than fame, give me truth. I sat at a table where were rich food and wine in abundance, and obsequious attendance, but sincerity and truth were not; and I went away hungry from the inhospitable board. The hospitality was as cold as the ices. I thought that there was no need of ice to freeze them. They talked to me of the age of the wine and the fame of the vintage; but I thought of an older, a newer, and purer wine, of a more glorious vintage, which they had not got, and could not buy. The style, the house and grounds and "entertainment" pass for nothing with me. I called on the king, but he made me wait in his hall, and conducted like a man incapacitated

36 *the wealth of Crœsus. Journal* for January 29, 1852; III, 246–247. Crœsus was a sixth-century king of Lydia, who has become a legendary figure for his enormous wealth.

37 *near the bone where it is sweetest. The Oxford Dictionary of English Proverbs* says that this goes back to Percy's *Ballads*, 1559, which had: "The nearer the bone, the sweeter the flesh."

38 *You are defended from being a trifler. Journal* for January 30, 1852; III, 257–258.

39 *I live in the angle of a leaden wall. Journal,* October 1850; II, 74.

40 *the Hon. Mr. ——————— of Georgia.* Probably Robert A. Toombs, who was a congressman until 1853, when he became a United States senator. He had attracted more public attention in the North than any other Georgia congressman.

41 *the Mameluke bey.* The Mamelukes were an Egyptian military caste. When Mehemet Ali decided to massacre them in 1811, one bey is supposed to have escaped by leaping from the walls to his horse.

42 *Webster.* Daniel Webster (1782–1852), who had alienated antislavery men when he sponsored the Compromise of 1850 with its fugtive slave law. He had always been noted as an orator.

43 *to gravitate toward.* Ms. 658: "God or the devil or."

44 *kittlybenders.* Also spelled kiddly-benders and kettle-de-benders. A game in which the players run or slide over ice so thin that it bends under their weight.

45 *if the swamp . . . had a hard bottom.* This joke about the swamp had appeared in Concord's *Yeoman's Gazette* on November 22, 1828.

46 *let me feel for the furrowing.* Ms. 661 had "stud."

47 *I sat at a table.* No one has been able to find out who the people mentioned in this paragraph were. And they may, of course, not have been real.

for hospitality. There was a man in my neighborhood who lived in a hollow tree. His manners were truly regal. I should have done better had I called on him.

How long shall we sit in our porticoes practising idle and musty virtues, which any work would make impertinent? As if one were to begin the day with long-suffering, and hire a man to hoe his potatoes; and in the afternoon go forth to practise Christian meekness and charity with goodness aforethought! Consider the China pride and stagnant self-complacency of mankind. This generation reclines a little to congratulate itself on being the last of an illustrious line; and in Boston and London and Paris and Rome, thinking of its long descent, it speaks of its progress in art and science and literature with satisfaction. There are the Records of the Philosophical Societies, and the public Eulogies of *Great Men!* It is the good Adam contemplating his own virtue. "Yes, we have done great deeds, and sung **48** divine songs, which shall never die," — that is, as long as *we* can remember them. The learned societies and great men of Assyria, — where are they? What youthful philosophers and experimentalists we are! There is **49** not one of my readers who has yet lived a whole human life. These may be but the spring months in the life of the race. If we have had the seven-years' itch, **50** we have not seen the seventeen-year locust yet in Concord. We are acquainted with a mere pellicle of the globe on which we live. Most have not delved six feet beneath the surface, nor leaped as many above it. We know not where we are. Beside, we are sound asleep nearly half our time. Yet we esteem ourselves wise, and have an established order on the surface. Truly, we are deep thinkers, we are ambitious spirits! As I stand over the insect crawling amid the pine needles on the forest floor, and endeavoring to conceal itself from my sight, and ask myself why it will cherish those humble thoughts, and hide its head from me who might, perhaps, be its benefactor, and impart to its race some cheering information, I am reminded of the greater Benefactor and Intelligence that stands over me the human insect.

There is an incessant influx of novelty into the world, and yet we tolerate incredible dulness. I need only suggest what kind of sermons are still listened to in the

48 *"Yes, we have done great deeds."* Nor has the source of this quotation been traced. Thoreau may have made it up.

49 *There is not one of my readers who has yet lived a whole human life.* Read this sentence carefully; it has two meanings. After it the Bibliophile Edition (II, 256n.) has this: "The wisest reformers necessarily do not remember children, youthful men and women, not grown, but growing,— a rising generation. What are all our joy and sorrow, our repentance and reform to them? This truth bursts on us like a revelation when they are met in the street. There is an incalculable health and promise in the still growing man, which no maturity is wise enough to treat with for a moment. It can only respect it, and faintly believe in it."

50 *the seven-years' itch.* This often-used but seldom defined malady may be ordinary scabies, but the term is sometimes used facetiously to describe the boredom that seven years of marriage may bring on.

51 *we believe in the ordinary and mean.* The Bibliophile Edition (II, 257n.) places the following here: "It is a singular but consoling fact that it is as hard for a melancholy man to speak from the depth of his sadness as for the poet to give utterance to his inspiration. While he lives, and in the sunshine, he cannot be casually sad enough to convey his real meaning; and he even derives a secondary sadness from this source. The injured man resisting his age and destiny is like a tree struck by lightning,—which rustles its leaves the winter through, not having vigor enough to cast them off."

most enlightened countries. There are such words as joy and sorrow, but they are only the burden of a psalm, sung with a nasal twang, while we believe in the ordinary and mean. We think that we can change our clothes only. It is said that the British Empire is very large and respectable, and that the United States are a first-rate power. We do not believe that a tide rises and falls behind every man which can float the British Empire like a chip, if he should ever harbor it in his mind. Who knows what sort of seventeen-year locust will next come out of the ground? The government of the world I live in was not framed, like that of Britain, in after-dinner conversations over the wine. **51**

The life in us is like the water in the river. It may rise this year higher than man has ever known it, and flood the parched uplands; even this may be the eventful year, which will drown out all our muskrats. It was not always dry land where we dwell. I see far inland the banks which the stream anciently washed, before science began to record its freshets. Every one has heard the story which has gone the rounds of New England, of a strong and beautiful bug which came out of the dry leaf of an old table of apple-tree wood, which had stood in a farmer's kitchen for sixty years, first in Connecticut, and afterward in Massachusetts, — from an egg deposited in the living tree many years earlier still, as appeared by counting the annual layers beyond it; which was heard gnawing out for several weeks, hatched perchance by the heat of an urn. Who does not feel his faith in a resurrection and immortality strengthened by hearing of this? Who knows what beautiful and winged life, whose egg has been buried for ages under many concentric layers of woodenness in the dead dry life of society, deposited at first in the alburnum of the green and living tree, which has been gradually converted into the semblance of its well-seasoned tomb, — heard perchance gnawing out now for years by the astonished family of man, as they sat round the festive board, — may unexpectedly come forth from amidst society's most trivial and handselled furniture, to enjoy its perfect summer life at last! **52** **53** **54**

I do not say that John or Jonathan will realize all this; but such is the character of that morrow which mere lapse of time can never make to dawn. The light **55** **56**

52 *The life in us is like the water in the river.* *Journal*, June 1850; II, 33.

53 *a strong and beautiful bug.* This parable has attracted a sizeable body of literature, particularly since the germinal idea was also used by Herman Melville in a story which appeared two years after *Walden* had been issued. Douglas Sackman (1940, pages 448–451) in "The Original of Melville's Apple-Tree-Table," traces the tale in connection with Melville's work. Walter Harding (1956, pages 213–215) does this for Thoreau in "The Apple-Tree Table Tale." See also Charles Anderson's comment in *The Magic Circle of Walden* (1958, pages 278–279). The basic image, of course, is that of rebirth, and it is on this note that the book ends.

54 *handselled.* This word has many meanings all derived from the basic idea of giving something into the hands of another, i.e., a gift, money, etc. It can also mean cheap and shoddy, and by association with "trivial" probably does imply that here.

55 *John or Jonathan.* John Bull, an Englishman; Jonathan, an American.

56 *The light which puts out our eyes is darkness to us.* Harry Levin, in *The Power of Blackness* (1958, page 234), draws comparisons between this and passages in Hemingway's *The Old Man of the Sea* and F. Scott Fitzgerald's *The Great Gatsby*. Sanborn has a footnote on the phrase in the Bibliophile Edition (II, 259n.):
"The light that puts out our eyes is darkness to us." A curious speculation on sight also belongs here: "Our eye feels, not simply the most distant objects,—for that which we handle may be equally remote with that which we see,—but rather the subtilest emanations, which can be farthest dispersed. But the intellectual eye is a far more delicate and far-reaching sense,—having the same relation to the bodily eye that the latter has to the finger."
Sanborn then suggests that *Walden* should close with these words of Thoreau:
"We know not yet what we have done,—still less what we are doing. Wait till evening, and other parts of our day's work will shine than we had thought at noon; and we shall discover the real purport of our toil. As when the husbandman has reached the end of the furrow, and looks back, he can best tell where the pressed earth shines most."

Ms. 1224, a stray sheet at the end of the Huntington manuscript, is headed "Conclusion" and then has this copy: "René Londihouâne, [name

which puts out our eyes is darkness to us.   Only that day dawns to which we are awake.   There is more day to dawn.   The sun is but a morning star.

THE END.   57

canceled] a converted Huron, failing to comprehend the mysteries of the Godhead, said to himself, 'If a dog wished to think what are the thoughts of men, what conclusion would he naturally come to but that a man is not altogether the same as a dog.' " The words "Omit Relations" are written in at the end of this passage.

The Huron's thoughts have a curious resemblance to those recorded in 1557 by Girolamo Cardan in *De Rerum Varietate:* "A man is no more able to know about a daemon than a dog about a man. The dog knows that the man is, that he eats, drinks, walks, sleeps—no more. It also knows his form; so with a man in the case of daemons. But you say, a man has a mind, a dog has not. But the mind of a daemon differs far more in its operation from the mind of a man, than the mind of a man from the sense of a dog."

57 THE END. Walter Harding (1954, page xi) says that "In some impressions of the first edition it [The End] occurs with a period, in some without, and in some the whole phrase is omitted. . . . I have found a copy of the 1862 impression which omits the period and one of the impression of 1876 which includes it." The present editor's copy, dated 1869, has the period. The two words, incidentally, were written in at the last minute on the page proofs.

Manuscript of the last page of *Walden*
(*Courtesy the Beinecke Library, Yale University*)

III

CIVIL DISOBEDIENCE

INTRODUCTION

The exact date of Thoreau's going to jail for one night has never been determined, but written comments made by his townsmen indicate that it was late in July 1846, probably on Thursday, July 23, or Friday, July 24. As he says in *Walden*, in the chapter entitled "The Village," he was on his way to get a shoe mended when he was accosted by Sam Staples, the tax collector—and jailer—who asked him to pay his poll tax, which he had ignored for six years.

There was no conflict, no antagonism between the two men. They knew each other well, and they realized that they were playing parts assigned to them by the State of Things as They Are.

According to young Edward Emerson (1917, page 64), Staples said, "I'll pay your tax, Henry, if you're hard up." But Thoreau explained that it was a matter of principle and suggested that Staples resign. When he refused he said that if Thoreau didn't pay his tax he would have to lock him up "pretty soon." This brought the answer: "As well now as any time, Sam." And with that Thoreau went to jail.

Since he describes his experiences in the essay that follows there is no point in duplicating them here.

During the evening someone—probably from his family—came to the jail and paid the tax. In the morning Thoreau was released and went about his interrupted business. And that was all there was to it. **1**

2

The story about Emerson's visiting the jail and asking: "Henry, why are you here?" and being answered: "Waldo, why are you not here?" is apocryphal. But Emerson's *Journals* show that it was almost true, for a meeting did take place—not at the jail but later—and in slightly different words. **3**

Undoubtedly the jail experience rankled, and Thoreau

1 *probably from his family*. There has been much conjecture as to who the unknown person was, but the consensus is that it was Aunt Maria Thoreau. Emerson (*Complete Writings*, X, 458) has said that she—and perhaps some other people—paid Thoreau's taxes in advance so he would not get in trouble again.

2 *And that was all there was to it*. Except that Staples said that Thoreau was "as mad as the devil" at having to leave the jail. Staples told him that if he would not go, he would have to put him out.

3 *Emerson's* Journals. VII, 220–223.

gave a great deal of thought to its significance. Unfortunately, except for fragments, the *Journals* for this period are missing, so we do not know the evolution of his ideas on the subject.

Since people were curious about the night in jail, Thoreau spoke on January 26, 1848, at the Concord Lyceum on "The Relation of the Individual to the State," and repeated the lecture on February 23.

A year after this, Elizabeth Peabody, Hawthorne's sister-in-law who ran a bookstore in Boston, wrote to Thoreau asking him for permission to publish the lecture in the first issue of her forthcoming periodical, *Aesthetic Papers*. At this time Thoreau was correcting proofs for *A Week on the Concord and Merrimack Rivers*, but, busy as he was, he gave permission and sent her the manuscript.

The article appeared on May 14, 1849, along with contributions from Emerson and Hawthorne. It was listed in the Table of Contents as "Resistance to Civil Government; a Lecture delivered in 1847." *Aesthetic Papers* never got beyond its first issue, and for a long while it looked as though Thoreau's lecture would die with it. It came to life briefly again in 1866 when *A Yankee in Canada, with Anti-Slavery and Reform Papers* was published posthumously. In this book it first got the title by which it has been known ever since—"Civil Disobedience."

Despite its pertinence to American and world affairs during the rest of the nineteenth century, it slumbered unnoticed in *A Yankee in Canada* until Count Leo Tolstoy discovered it at the end of the century and wrote to *The North American Review*. In his letter he asked Americans why they ignored Thoreau and paid so much attention to what their moneyed people and the military said. That was 70 years ago; the question is still a good one.

Tolstoy's letter attracted little notice, and the seminal essay slumbered on. Then Mohandas K. Gandhi, who was **4** at that time an unknown law student at Oxford, learned about Thoreau from his English biographer, Henry S. Salt, and began to read whatever Thoreau books were available. Gandhi went to South Africa, where he published a newspaper for the many Indian workers living there. On October 26, 1907, he printed "Civil Disobedience" in this and then issued it as a pamphlet. Gandhi told an American journalist that he took the name of his movement from Thoreau's nearly forgotten essay.

The long-slumbering article now began to come to life. It has been a goad to men's consciences ever since.

Tolstoy and Gandhi were not the only ones to make

4 *Gandhi*, more than any one person, made "Civil Disobedience" popular throughout the world.

use of a stirring article that had been written more than half a century before to protest against taxes levied to support slavery and to finance the war with Mexico that many Northerners felt was being waged to benefit the slave states and extend their territory. It also served as an inspiration to those who were struggling against the oppression of labor in the United States in the early part of the century, and during the Second World War helped the Danish resistance movement take action against the Nazis who had invaded their country. In the 1950's, Senator Joseph McCarthy had "Civil Disobedience" removed from some local libraries and from those which the United States Information Service had established in various cities throughout the world. But American opinion turned against McCarthy and stripped him of his power.

In the 1960's, with the Negroes' struggle for civil rights **5** and with an undeclared war in Vietnam which many Americans thought unjustified, "Civil Disobedience" took on new meaning and became more widely read than ever before.

But "Civil Disobedience" is not merely a document that seems timely today; it is good for all seasons.

Those who have never read it should read it now, and those who have read it and think they know it well should read it again—carefully and with due appreciation for all that it says. For this is a message that admittedly goes beyond logic and reason; it appeals to the heart and to the emotions. The higher law cannot be justified in any courtroom, yet it resounds and reechoes down the corridors of time. It may be that the conscience of mankind is a stronger force for good than all the laws on the statute books. And it should never be forgotten that those laws were written because someone's conscience demanded them at the time.

5 *the Negroes' struggle.* The late Rev. Martin Luther King, Jr., said that when he read "Civil Disobedience" in college, he was so deeply moved that he reread it several times and that no one "has been more eloquent and passionate in getting this idea across than Henry David Thoreau."

"As a result of his [Thoreau's] writings . . . we are the heirs of a legacy of creative protest. It goes without saying that the teachings of Thoreau are alive today; indeed they are more alive today than ever before."   MARTIN LUTHER KING, JR.

A

YANKEE IN CANADA,

WITH

ANTI–SLAVERY AND REFORM PAPERS.

BY

HENRY D. THOREAU,

AUTHOR OF "A WEEK ON THE CONCORD AND MERRIMACK RIVERS,"
"WALDEN," "CAPE COD," ETC., ETC.

BOSTON:
TICKNOR AND FIELDS.
1866.

CIVIL DISOBEDIENCE.

I HEARTILY accept the motto, — " That government **1** is best which governs least"; and I should like to see it acted up to more rapidly and systematically. Carried out, it finally amounts to this, which also I believe, — "That government is best which governs not at all"; and when men are prepared for it, that will be the kind of government which they will have. Government is at best but an expedient; but most governments are usually, and all governments are sometimes, inexpedient. The objections which have been brought against a standing army, and they are many and weighty, and deserve to prevail, may also at last be brought against a standing government. The standing army is only an arm of the standing government. The government itself, which is only the mode which the people have chosen to execute their will, is equally liable to be abused and perverted before the people can act through it. Witness the pres- **2** ent Mexican war, the work of comparatively a few individuals using the standing government as their tool; for, in the outset, the people would not have consented to this measure.

This American government, — what is it but a tradition, though a recent one, endeavoring to transmit it- **3** self unimpaired to posterity, but each instant losing some of its integrity? It has not the vitality and force of a single living man; for a single man can bend it to his will. It is a sort of wooden gun to the people themselves. **4** But it is not the less necessary for this; for the people must have some complicated machinery or other, and hear its din, to satisfy that idea of government which they have. Governments show thus how successfully men can be imposed on, even impose on themselves, for their own advantage. It is excellent, we must all allow. Yet this

455

The text for "Civil Disobedience" as it appears here is the 1866 one from *A Yankee in Canada*.

1 *"That government is best which governs least."* This sounds like a famous quotation from a noted source, the kind that one expects to be in every book of quotations. But it is not. Obviously it is not original with Thoreau. He says so himself. Lee A. Pederson, in the *Thoreau Society Bulletin*, Number 67, reports that Thoreau got it from the masthead of *The Democratic Review*. That may be, but it seems likely that this journal did not originate it and that it comes from a still earlier source. Emerson in *Politics* (1841) had written: "The less government we have the better." As Thoreau says a few lines below, "That government is best which governs not at all" simply carries the basic idea one step further. "Civil Disobedience" was written at the time when the French Revolution of 1848—and its suppression—was very much in the news even though Thoreau claimed to ignore foreign affairs. And Karl Marx and Friedrich Engels had issued the *Communist Manifesto* in 1847. Thoreau may, or may not, have been familiar with what was going on in Europe, but resistance to authority was in the air. In America, objections to slavery made sensitive people disapprove of their government.

2 *the present Mexican war.* "Present" was true on January 26, 1848, when Thoreau first gave the Concord lecture on which "Civil Disobedience" was based, for the war with Mexico did not officially end until the Treaty of Guadalupe Hidalgo was signed on February 2, 1848. Apparently neither he nor the editor of *Aesthetic Papers* bothered to change the word "present" to "recent," and it has remained that way ever since.

government never of itself furthered any enterprise, but by the alacrity with which it got out of its way. *It* does not keep the country free. *It* does not settle the West. *It* does not educate. The character inherent in the American people has done all that has been accomplished; and it would have done somewhat more, if the government had not sometimes got in its way. For government is an expedient by which men would fain succeed in letting one another alone; and, as has been said, when it is most expedient, the governed are most let alone by it. Trade and commerce, if they were not made of India-rubber, would never manage to bounce over the obstacles which legislators are continually putting in their way; and, if one were to judge these men wholly by the effects of their actions and not partly by their intentions, they would deserve to be classed and punished with those mischievous persons who put obstructions on the railroads.

But, to speak practically and as a citizen, unlike those who call themselves no-government men, I ask for, not at once no government, but *at once* a better government. Let every man make known what kind of government would command his respect, and that will be one step toward obtaining it.

After all, the practical reason why, when the power is once in the hands of the people, a majority are permitted, and for a long period continue, to rule, is not because they are most likely to be in the right, nor because this seems fairest to the minority, but because they are physically the strongest. But a government in which the majority rule in all cases cannot be based on justice, even as far as men understand it. Can there not be a government in which majorities do not virtually decide right and wrong, but conscience? — in which majorities decide only those questions to which the rule of expediency is applicable? Must the citizen ever for a moment, or in the least degree, resign his conscience to the legislator? Why has every man a conscience, then? I think that we should be men first, and subjects afterward. It is not desirable to cultivate a respect for the law, so much as for the right. The only obligation which I have a right to assume, is to do at any time what I think right. It is truly enough said, that a corporation has no conscience; but a corporation of conscientious men is a corporation *with* a conscience. Law

3 *though a recent one.* The American government, if dated from the ratification of the Constitution in 1788, was only 60 years old in 1848.

4 *It is a sort of wooden gun to the people themselves.* When printed in *Aesthetic Papers* this was followed by: "and, if ever they should use it in earnest as a real one against each other, it will surely split."

5 *made of India-rubber.* India-rubber had been manufactured in America since the early 1830's, but it was poor stuff that smelled bad and did not last long. By this time, however, Charles Goodyear's new process of treating rubber had come into use.

6 *mischievous persons who put obstructions on the railroads.* Those who like to think that America in Thoreau's time was a highly civilized paradise should note this.

7 *subjects.* Although the word "subject" ordinarily means someone who is under the rule of a sovereign, it can also mean someone who owes allegiance to a government. Thoreau may have used the word purposely to indicate the individual citizen's subordination to a powerful state.

8 *a corporation has no conscience.* In 1612 Sir Edward Coke said, in connection with the case of Sutton's Hospital: "Corporations cannot commit treason, nor be outlawed, nor excommunicated, for they have no souls." Then, much later, Edward, the second Baron of Thurlow (1781–1829), is reported to have said (in Wilberforce's biography): "Did you ever expect a corporation to have a conscience, when it has no soul to be damned, and no body to be kicked?" It seems more likely that Thoreau was referring to Thurlow's statement than to Coke's.

never made men a whit more just; and, by means of their respect for it, even the well-disposed are daily made the agents of injustice. A common and natural result of an undue respect for law is, that you may see a file of soldiers, colonel, captain, corporal, privates, powder-monkeys, and all, marching in admirable order over hill and dale to the wars, against their wills, ay, against their common sense and consciences, which makes it very steep marching indeed, and produces a palpitation of the heart. They have no doubt that it is a damnable business in which they are concerned; they are all peaceably inclined. Now, what are they? **Men** at all? or small movable forts and magazines, at the service of some unscrupulous man in power? Visit the **9** Navy-Yard, and behold a marine, such a man as an American government can make, or such as it can make a man with its black arts, — a mere shadow and reminiscence of humanity, a man laid out alive and standing, and already, as one may say, buried under arms with funeral accompaniments, though it may be, —

> "Not a drum was heard, not a funeral note, **10**
>   As his corse to the rampart we hurried;
> Not a soldier discharged his farewell shot
>   O'er the grave where our hero we buried."

The mass of men serve the state thus, not as men mainly, but as machines, with their bodies. They are the standing army, and the militia, jailers, constables, posse comitatus, &c. In most cases there is no free exer- **11** cise whatever of the judgment or of the moral sense; but they put themselves on a level with wood and earth and stones; and wooden men can perhaps be manufactured that will serve the purpose as well. Such command no more respect than men of straw or a lump of dirt. They have the same sort of worth only as horses and dogs. Yet such as these even are commonly esteemed good citizens. Others, — as most legislators, politicians, lawyers, ministers, and office-holders, — serve the state chiefly with their heads; and, as they rarely make any moral distinctions, they are as likely to serve the Devil, without *intending* it, as God. A very few, as heroes, patriots, martyrs, reformers in the great sense, and *men*, serve the state with their consciences also, and so necessarily resist it for the most part; and they are commonly treated as enemies by it. A wise man will only be useful as a man, and will not submit to be " clay," and **12**

9 *Visit the Navy-Yard and behold a marine.* At this time marines were armed soldiers on warships and were completely subordinate to their naval commander.

10 *"Not a drum was heard."* From "The Burial of Sir John Moore at Corunna" by the Irish poet Charles Wolfe (1791–1823). He is remembered only for this one bit of verse which was written in 1816. Sir John Moore (1761–1809) was a British general who was killed near La Coruña, Spain, in the campaign against Napoleon there.

11 *posse comitatus.* A body of citizens called into service by an authorized official to help him preserve the peace. This is the famous "posse" of the Old West.

12 *"clay," and "stop a hole to keep the wind away."* Cf. *Hamlet*, V, i.

"stop a hole to keep the wind away," but leave that office to his dust at least : —

> "I am too high-born to be propertied,   **13**
> To be a secondary at control,
> Or useful serving-man and instrument
> To any sovereign state throughout the world."

He who gives himself entirely to his fellow-men appears to them useless and selfish ; but he who gives himself partially to them is pronounced a benefactor and philanthropist.

How does it become a man to behave toward this American government to-day ? I answer, that he cannot without disgrace be associated with it. I cannot for an instant recognize that political organization as *my* government which is the *slave's* government also.

All men recognize the right of revolution ; that is, the right to refuse allegiance to, and to resist, the government, when its tyranny or its inefficiency are great and unendurable. But almost all say that such is not the case now. But such was the case, they think, in the Revo- **14** lution of '75. If one were to tell me that this was a bad government because it taxed certain foreign commodities brought to its ports, it is most probable that I should not make an ado about it, for I can do without them. All machines have their friction ; and possibly this does enough good to counterbalance the evil. At any rate, it is a great evil to make a stir about it. But when the friction comes to have its machine, and oppression and robbery are organized, I say, let us not have such a machine any longer. In other words, when a sixth of the population of a nation which has undertaken to be the refuge of liberty are slaves, and a whole country is unjustly overrun and conquered by a foreign army, and **15** subjected to military law, I think that it is not too soon for honest men to rebel and revolutionize. What makes this duty the more urgent is the fact, that the country so overrun is not our own, but ours is the invading army.

Paley, a common authority with many on moral ques- **16** tions, in his chapter on the "Duty of Submission to Civil Government," resolves all civil obligation into expediency ; and he proceeds to say, " that so long as the interest of the whole society requires it, that is, so long as the established government cannot be resisted or changed without public inconveniency, it is the will of

13 *"I am too high-born to be propertied."* This also is from Shakespeare: *King John*, V, ii.

14 *the Revolution of '75.* Although most Americans think of the Revolution of 1776, in Concord, where the fighting began on April 19, 1775, the townspeople say that the American Revolution began there.

15 *a foreign army.* This refers to the men who were in pursuit of fugitive slaves.

16 *Paley.* William Paley (1743–1805), English divine and philosopher, author of *The Principles of Moral and Political Philosophy*, 1785, from which Chapter Six, the one Thoreau mentions, was taken.

God that the established government be obeyed, and no longer. . . . . This principle being admitted, the justice of every particular case of resistance is reduced to a computation of the quantity of the danger and grievance on the one side, and of the probability and expense of redressing it on the other." Of this, he says, every man shall judge for himself. But Paley appears never to have contemplated those cases to which the rule of expediency does not apply, in which a people, as well as an individual, must do justice, cost what it may. If I have unjustly wrested a plank from a drowning man, I must restore it to him though I drown myself. This, according to Paley, would be inconvenient. But he **17** that would save his life, in such a case, shall lose it. This people must cease to hold slaves, and to make war on Mexico, though it cost them their existence as a people.

In their practice, nations agree with Paley; but does any one think that Massachusetts does exactly what is right at the present crisis?

"A drab of state, a cloth-o'-silver slut, **18**
To have her train borne up, and her soul trail in the dirt."

Practically speaking, the opponents to a reform in Massachusetts are not a hundred thousand politicians at the South, but a hundred thousand merchants and farmers here, who are more interested in commerce and agriculture than they are in humanity, and are not prepared to do justice to the slave and to Mexico, *cost what it may.* I quarrel not with far-off foes, but with those who, near at home, co-operate with, and do the bidding **19** of, those far away, and without whom the latter would be harmless. We are accustomed to say, that the mass of men are unprepared; but improvement is slow, because the few are not materially wiser or better than the many. It is not so important that many should be as good as you, as that there be some absolute goodness somewhere; for that will leaven the whole lump. **20** There are thousands who are *in opinion* opposed to slavery and to the war, who yet in effect do nothing to put an end to them; who, esteeming themselves children of Washington and Franklin, sit down with their hands in their pockets, and say that they know not what to do, and do nothing; who even postpone the question of free-

17 *he that would save his life . . . shall lose it.* Matthew X:39.

18 *"A drab of state."* From *The Revenger's Tragedy* (1607), IV, 4, by Cyril Tourneur (1575?–1626). It should read: "A drab of State, a cloath, a silver slut."

19 *do the bidding of, those far away.* The fact that slaveowners in the South could control national policy and thus affect the North was particularly galling to antislavery men.

20 *leaven the whole lump.* Paraphrase of I Corinthians 5:6.

dom to the question of free-trade, and quietly read the prices-current along with the latest advices from Mexico, after dinner, and, it may be, fall asleep over them both. What is the price-current of an honest man and patriot to-day? They hesitate, and they regret, and sometimes they petition; but they do nothing in earnest and with effect. They will wait, well disposed, for others to remedy the evil, that they may no longer have it to regret. At most, they give only a cheap vote, and a feeble countenance and God-speed, to the right, as it goes by them. There are nine hundred and ninety-nine patrons of virtue to one virtuous man. But it is easier to deal with the real possessor of a thing than with the temporary guardian of it.

All voting is a sort of gaming, like checkers or back-gammon, with a slight moral tinge to it, a playing with right and wrong, with moral questions; and betting naturally accompanies it. The character of the voters is not staked. I cast my vote, perchance, as I think right; but I am not vitally concerned that that right should prevail. I am willing to leave it to the majority. Its obligation, therefore, never exceeds that of expediency. Even voting *for the right* is *doing* nothing for it. It is only expressing to men feebly your desire that it should prevail. A wise man will not leave the right to the mercy of chance, nor wish it to prevail through the power of the majority. There is but little virtue in the action of masses of men. When the majority shall at length vote for the abolition of slavery, it will be because they are indifferent to slavery, or because there is but little slavery left to be abolished by their vote. *They* will then be the only slaves. Only *his* vote can hasten the abolition of slavery who asserts his own freedom by his vote.

21

I hear of a convention to be held at Baltimore, or elsewhere, for the selection of a candidate for the Presidency, made up chiefly of editors, and men who are politicians by profession; but I think, what is it to any independent, intelligent, and respectable man what decision they may come to? Shall we not have the advantage of his wisdom and honesty, nevertheless? Can we not count upon some independent votes? Are there not many individuals in the country who do not attend conventions? But no: I find that the respectable man, so called, has immediately drifted from his position, and

22

21 *because there is but little slavery left to be abolished by their vote*. This turned out to be true when slavery was finally abolished on December 18, 1865, by the ratification of the Thirteenth Amendment to the Constitution.

22 *a convention to be held at Baltimore*. This was the 1848 Democratic convention which nominated Lewis Cass as its Presidential candidate. He was defeated by the Whig candidate, Zachary Taylor.

Zachary Taylor, the Whig presidential nominee in 1848

despairs of his country, when his country has more reason to despair of him. He forthwith adopts one of the candidates thus selected as the only *available* one, thus proving that he is himself *available* for any purposes of the demagogue. His vote is of no more worth than that of any unprincipled foreigner or hireling native, who may have been bought. O for a man who is a *man*, and, as my neighbor says, has a bone in his back which you cannot pass your hand through! Our statistics are at fault: the population has been returned too large. How many *men* are there to a square thousand miles in this country? Hardly one. Does not America offer any inducement for men to settle here? The American has dwindled into an Odd Fellow, — one who may be **23** known by the development of his organ of gregariousness, and a manifest lack of intellect and cheerful self-reliance; whose first and chief concern, on coming into the world, is to see that the Almshouses are in good repair; and, before yet he has lawfully donned the virile garb, to collect a fund for the support of the widows and orphans that may be; who, in short, ventures to live only by the aid of the Mutual Insurance company, which has promised to bury him decently.

It is not a man's duty, as a matter of course, to devote himself to the eradication of any, even the most enormous wrong; he may still properly have other concerns to engage him; but it is his duty, at least, to wash his hands of it, and, if he gives it no thought longer, not to give it practically his support. If I devote myself to other pursuits and contemplations, I must first see, at least, that I do not pursue them sitting upon another man's shoulders. I must get off him first, that he may pursue his contemplations too. See what gross inconsistency is tolerated. I have heard some of my townsmen say, "I should like to have them order me out to help put down an insurrection of the slaves, or to march to Mexico; — see if I would go"; and yet these very men have each, directly by their allegiance, and so indirectly, at least, by their money, furnished a substitute. The soldier is applauded who refuses to serve in an unjust war by those who do not refuse to sustain the unjust government which makes the war; is applauded by those whose own act and authority he disregards and sets at naught; as if the State were penitent to that degree that it hired one to scourge it while it sinned, but

23 *an Odd Fellow.* Although the secret, benevolent, and social Order of Odd Fellows dates back to the first half of the eighteenth century, the Independent Order of Odd Fellows was formed in Manchester, England, in 1813. It was introduced into America in 1819.

not to that degree that it left off sinning for a moment. Thus, under the name of Order and Civil Government, we are all made at last to pay homage to and support our own meanness. After the first blush of sin comes its indifference; and from immoral it becomes, as it were, *un*moral, and not quite unnecessary to that life which we have made.

The broadest and most prevalent error requires the most disinterested virtue to sustain it. The slight reproach to which the virtue of patriotism is commonly liable, the noble are most likely to incur. Those who, while they disapprove of the character and measures of a government, yield to it their allegiance and support, are undoubtedly its most conscientious supporters, and so frequently the most serious obstacles to reform. Some are petitioning the State to dissolve the Union, to disregard the requisitions of the President. Why do they not dissolve it themselves,—the union between themselves and the State,—and refuse to pay their quota into its treasury? Do not they stand in the same relation to the State, that the State does to the Union? And have not the same reasons prevented the State from resisting the Union, which have prevented them from resisting the State?

How can a man be satisfied to entertain an opinion merely, and enjoy *it*? Is there any enjoyment in it, if his opinion is that he is aggrieved? If you are cheated out of a single dollar by your neighbor, you do not rest satisfied with knowing that you are cheated, or with saying that you are cheated, or even with petitioning him to pay you your due; but you take effectual steps at once to obtain the full amount, and see that you are never cheated again. Action from principle, the perception and the performance of right, changes things and relations; it is essentially revolutionary, and does not consist wholly with anything which was. It not only divides states and churches, it divides families; ay, it divides the *individual*, separating the diabolical in him from the divine.

Unjust laws exist: shall we be content to obey them, or shall we endeavor to amend them, and obey them until we have succeeded, or shall we transgress them at once? Men generally, under such a government as this, think that they ought to wait until they have persuaded

24

24 *Some are petitioning the State to dissolve the Union.* These were the followers of William Lloyd Garrison who was soon to denounce the Constitution as "a covenant with death and an agreement with hell" and adopt the motto "No union with slaveholders."

the majority to alter them. They think that, if they should resist, the remedy would be worse than the evil. But it is the fault of the government itself that the remedy *is* worse than the evil. *It* makes it worse. Why is it not more apt to anticipate and provide for reform? Why does it not cherish its wise minority? Why does it cry and resist before it is hurt? Why does it not encourage its citizens to be on the alert to point out its faults, and *do* better than it would have them? Why does it always crucify Christ, and excommunicate Copernicus and Luther, and pronounce Washington **25** and Franklin rebels?

One would think, that a deliberate and practical denial of its authority was the only offence never contemplated by government; else, why has it not assigned its definite, its suitable and proportionate penalty? If a man who has no property refuses but once to earn nine shillings **26** for the State, he is put in prison for a period unlimited by any law that I know, and determined only by the discretion of those who placed him there; but if he should steal ninety times nine shillings from the State, he is soon permitted to go at large again.

If the injustice is part of the necessary friction of the machine of government, let it go, let it go: perchance it will wear smooth, — certainly the machine will wear out. If the injustice has a spring, or a pulley, or a rope, or a crank, exclusively for itself, then perhaps you may consider whether the remedy will not be worse than the evil; but if it is of such a nature that it requires you to be the agent of injustice to another, then, I say, break the law. Let your life be a counter friction to stop the **27** machine. What I have to do is to see, at any rate, that I do not lend myself to the wrong which I condemn.

As for adopting the ways which the State has provided for remedying the evil, I know not of such ways. They take too much time, and a man's life will be gone. I have other affairs to attend to. I came into this world, not chiefly to make this a good place to live in, but to live in it, be it good or bad. A man has not everything to do, but something; and because he cannot do *everything*, it is not necessary that he should do *something* wrong. It is not my business to be petitioning the Governor or the Legislature any more than it is theirs to petition me; and, if they should not hear my petition, what should I do

25 *Copernicus and Luther.* Nicolaus Copernicus (1473–1543), Polish astronomer whose work, *De Revolutionibus Orbium Coelestium* (1543) introduced a new system of astronomy to replace the ancient Ptolemaic idea of the universe. He was not excommunicated but only because he died just as his book was published. Martin Luther (1483–1546), German theologian and leader of the Protestant Reformation.

26 *nine shillings.* The amount of the poll tax.

27 *a counter friction.* A mechanical device that stops motion by applying friction to a moving part. Thoreau was probably thinking of the simple wagon brake, but all our modern automobile brakes work on the same principle.

then? But in this case the State has provided no way:
its very Constitution is the evil. This may seem to be **28**
harsh and stubborn and unconciliatory; but it is to treat
with the utmost kindness and consideration the only
spirit that can appreciate or deserves it. So is all change
for the better, like birth and death, which convulse the
body.

I do not hesitate to say, that those who call themselves
Abolitionists should at once effectually withdraw their
support, both in person and property, from the government of Massachusetts, and not wait till they constitute
a majority of one, before they suffer the right to prevail
through them. I think that it is enough if they have God
on their side, without waiting for that other one. Moreover, any man more right than his neighbors constitutes
a majority of one already.   **29**

I meet this American government, or its representative, the State government, directly, and face to face, once
a year — no more — in the person of its tax-gatherer; this
is the only mode in which a man situated as I am necessarily meets it; and it then says distinctly, Recognize
me; and the simplest, the most effectual, and, in the
present posture of affairs, the indispensablest mode of
treating with it on this head, of expressing your little satisfaction with and love for it, is to deny it then. My   **30**

28 *its very Constitution is the evil.* Thoreau was
not a Garrisonian, but he is in agreement with
him here.

29 *a majority of one.* This saying—and variations
of it—were particularly popular in New England
at this time, especially among Abolitionists. Wendell Phillips was to use it on November 1, 1859,
in defense of John Brown, when he said: "One on
God's side, is a majority." But the idea probably
goes back to John Knox (1505–1572), who declared that "a man with God is always in the
majority."

30 *My civil neighbor, the tax-gatherer.* This was
Sam Staples, with whom Thoreau had always
been—and would continue to be—on the best of
terms. He sometimes employed Staples as an
assistant in his surveying work.

An Abolitionist meeting on Boston Common

civil neighbor, the tax-gatherer, is the very man I have to deal with, — for it is, after all, with men and not with parchment that I quarrel, — and he has voluntarily chosen to be an agent of the government. How shall he ever know well what he is and does as an officer of the government, or as a man, until he is obliged to consider whether he shall treat me, his neighbor, for whom he has respect, as a neighbor and well-disposed man, or as a maniac and disturber of the peace, and see if he can get over this obstruction to his neighborliness without a ruder and more impetuous thought or speech corresponding with his action. I know this well, that if one thousand, if one hundred, if ten men whom I could name, — if ten *honest* men only, — ay, if *one* HONEST man, in this State of Massachusetts, *ceasing to hold slaves*, were actually to withdraw from this copartnership, and be locked up in the county jail therefor, it would be the abolition of slavery in America. For it matters not how small the beginning may seem to be: what is once well done is done forever. But we love better to talk about it: that we say is our mission. Reform keeps many scores of newspapers in its service, but not one man. If my es- **31** teemed neighbor, the State's ambassador, who will devote his days to the settlement of the question of human rights in the Council Chamber, instead of being threatened with the prisons of Carolina, were to sit down the prisoner of Massachusetts, that State which is so anxious to foist the sin of slavery upon her sister, — though at present she can discover only an act of inhospitality to be the ground of a quarrel with her, — the Legislature would not wholly waive the subject the following winter.

Under a government which imprisons any unjustly, the true place for a just man is also a prison. The proper place to-day, the only place which Massachusetts has provided for her freer and less desponding spirits, is in her prisons, to be put out and locked out of the State by her own act, as they have already put themselves out by their principles. It is there that the **32** fugitive slave, and the Mexican prisoner on parole, and the Indian come to plead the wrongs of his race, should find them; on that separate, but more free and honorable ground, where the State places those who are not *with* her, but *against* her, — the only house in a slave State in which a free man can abide with honor. If any think that their influence would be lost there, and their

31 *my esteemed neighbor, the State's ambassador.* Senator Samuel Hoar (1778–1856), of Concord, who had gone to Charleston, South Carolina, in 1844 (at the request of the State's governor) to test in the courts the constitutionality of a South Carolina law which provided that free Negroes who arrived in the state as a member of a ship's crew should be kept in jail until the ship sailed. The Senator was threatened with injury and was forced to leave.

32 *the fugitive slave . . . the Mexican prisoner . . . and the Indian.* The ethnic backgrounds of oppressed minorities have not changed in more than a century.

voices no longer afflict the ear of the State, that they would not be as an enemy within its walls, they do not know by how much truth is stronger than error, nor how much more eloquently and effectively he can combat injustice who has experienced a little in his own person. Cast your whole vote, not a strip of paper merely, but your whole influence. A minority is powerless while it conforms to the majority; it is not even a minority then; but it is irresistible when it clogs by its whole weight. If the alternative is to keep all just men in prison, or give up war and slavery, the State will not hesitate which to choose. If a thousand men were not to pay their tax-bills this year, that would not be a violent and bloody measure, as it would be to pay them, and enable the State to commit violence and shed innocent blood. This is, in fact, the definition of a peaceable revolution, if any such is possible. If the tax-gatherer, or any other public officer, asks me, as one has done, " But what shall I do?" my answer is, "If you really wish to do anything, resign your office." When the subject has refused allegiance, and the officer has resigned his office, then the revolution is accomplished. But even suppose blood should flow. Is there not a sort of blood shed when the conscience is wounded? Through this wound a man's real manhood and immortality flow out, and he bleeds to an everlasting death. I see this blood flowing now.

I have contemplated the imprisonment of the offender, rather than the seizure of his goods, — though both will serve the same purpose, — because they who assert the purest right, and consequently are most dangerous to a corrupt State, commonly have not spent much time in accumulating property. To such the State renders comparatively small service, and a slight tax is wont to appear exorbitant, particularly if they are obliged to earn it by special labor with their hands. If there were one who lived wholly without the use of money, the State itself would hesitate to demand it of him. But the rich man, — not to make any invidious comparison, — is always sold to the institution which makes him rich. Absolutely speaking, the more money, the less virtue; for money comes between a man and his objects, and obtains them for him; and it was certainly no great virtue to obtain it. It puts to rest many questions which he would otherwise be taxed to answer; while the only new question which it puts is the hard but superfluous one, how to spend it. Thus his moral ground is taken from under his feet. The opportunities of living are diminished in proportion as what are called the "means" are increased. The best thing a man can do for his culture when he is rich is to endeavor to carry out those schemes which he entertained when he was poor. Christ answered the Herodians according to their condition. "Show me the tribute-money," said he;—and one took a penny out of his pocket;—if you use money which has the image of Cæsar on it, and which he has made current and valuable, that is, *if you are men of the State*, and gladly enjoy the advantages of Cæsar's government, then pay him back some of his own when he demands it; " Render **33** therefore to Cæsar that which is Cæsar's, and to God those things which are God's," — leaving them no wiser than before as to which was which; for they did not wish to know.

When I converse with the freest of my neighbors, I perceive that, whatever they may say about the magnitude and seriousness of the question, and their regard for the public tranquillity, the long and the short of the matter is, that they cannot spare the protection of the existing government, and they dread the consequences to their property and families of disobedience to it. For my own part, I should not like to think that I ever rely on the protection of the State. But, if I deny the authority of the State when it presents its tax-bill, it will soon take and waste all my property, and so harass me and my children without end. This is hard. This makes it impossible for a man to live honestly, and at the same time comfortably, in outward respects. It will not be worth the while to accumulate property; that would be sure to go again. You must hire or squat somewhere, and raise but a small crop, and eat that soon. You must live within yourself, and depend upon yourself always tucked up and ready for a start, and not have many affairs. A man may grow rich in Turkey even, if he will be in all respects a good subject of the Turkish government. Confucius said: " If a state is gov- **34** erned by the principles of reason, poverty and misery are subjects of shame; if a state is not governed by the principles of reason, riches and honors are the subjects of shame." No: until I want the protection of Massachusetts to be extended to me in some distant Southern port, where my liberty is endangered, or until

33 *"Render therefore to Cæsar."* Matthew 22:21.

34 *Confucius said. Analects* VIII, xiii.

I am bent solely on building up an estate at home by peaceful enterprise, I can afford to refuse allegiance to Massachusetts, and her right to my property and life. It costs me less in every sense to incur the penalty of disobedience to the State, than it would to obey. I should feel as if I were worth less in that case.

Some years ago, the State met me in behalf of the Church, and commanded me to pay a certain sum toward the support of a clergyman whose preaching my father attended, but never I myself. "Pay," it said, "or be locked up in the jail." I declined to pay. But, unfortunately, another man saw fit to pay it. I did not see why the schoolmaster should be taxed to support the priest, and not the priest the schoolmaster; for I was not the State's schoolmaster, but I supported myself by voluntary subscription. I did not see why the lyceum should not present its tax-bill, and have the State to back its demand, as well as the Church. However, at the request of the selectmen, I condescended to make some such statement as this in writing: — "Know all men by these presents, that I, Henry Thoreau, do not wish to be regarded as a member of any incorporated society which I have not joined." This I gave to the town clerk; and he has it. The State, having thus learned that I did not wish to be regarded as a member of that church, has never made a like demand on me since; though it said that it must adhere to its original presumption that time. If I had known how to name them, I should then have signed off in detail from all the societies which I never signed on to; but I did not know where to find a complete list.

I have paid no poll-tax for six years. I was put into a jail once on this account, for one night; and, as I stood considering the walls of solid stone, two or three feet thick, the door of wood and iron, a foot thick, and the iron grating which strained the light, I could not help being struck with the foolishness of that institution which treated me as if I were mere flesh and blood and bones, to be locked up. I wondered that it should have concluded at length that this was the best use it could put me to, and had never thought to avail itself of my services in some way. I saw that, if there was a wall of stone between me and my townsmen, there was a still more difficult one to climb or break through, before they could get to be as free as I was. I did not for a moment feel

35 *commanded me to pay a certain sum.* Thoreau's family belonged to the First Parish Church in the center of Concord, but Thoreau never became a member of the congregation and seldom entered the building during his lifetime. His funeral, however, was held there largely because Emerson insisted on it. The church tax bill he speaks of here was sent to him in 1840. He did not pay it.

36 *I was put into a jail.* Here begins the only trustworthy account of Thoreau's night in jail. He barely mentioned it in *Walden* near the end of Chapter VIII, "The Village."

37 *walls of solid stone.* The Concord jail was a large and substantial granite building which stood near the Milldam. It was officially called the Middlesex County Jail and was a three-story structure, 65 feet long by 32 feet wide, with a yard enclosed in a brick wall ten feet high. But the prisoners were treated well, and as will be seen, were even allowed to go out to work.

HENRY DAVID THOREAU
was imprisoned for one night in a jail on
this site, July, 1846 for refusing to recognize
the right of the state to collect taxes from
him in support of slavery-an episode made
famous in his essay
"Civil Disobedience."

confined, and the walls seemed a great waste of stone and
mortar. I felt as if I alone of all my townsmen had
paid my tax. They plainly did not know how to treat
me, but behaved like persons who are underbred. In
every threat and in every compliment there was a blunder; for they thought that my chief desire was to stand
the other side of that stone wall. I could not but smile
to see how industriously they locked the door on my
meditations, which followed them out again without let
or hindrance, and *they* were really all that was dangerous. As they could not reach me, they had resolved to
punish my body; just as boys, if they cannot come at
some person against whom they have a spite, will abuse
his dog. I saw that the State was half-witted, that it
was timid as a lone woman with her silver spoons, and
that it did not know its friends from its foes, and I lost
all my remaining respect for it, and pitied it.

Thus the State never intentionally confronts a man's
sense, intellectual or moral, but only his body, his senses.
It is not armed with superior wit or honesty, but with
superior physical strength. I was not born to be forced.
I will breathe after my own fashion. Let us see who is
the strongest. What force has a multitude? They only
can force me who obey a higher law than I. They **38**
force me to become like themselves. I do not hear of
men being *forced* to live this way or that by masses of
men. What sort of life were that to live? When I

38 *a higher law.* This is the title of one of the
Walden chapters and was also a widespread concept among the more radical Abolitionists.

meet a government which says to me, "Your money or your life," why should I be in haste to give it my money? It may be in a great strait, and not know what to do: I cannot help that. It must help itself; do as I do. It is not worth the while to snivel about it. I am not responsible for the successful working of the machinery of society. I am not the son of the engineer. I perceive that, when an acorn and a chestnut fall side by side, the one does not remain inert to make way for the other, but both obey their own laws, and spring and grow and flourish as best they can, till one, perchance, overshadows and destroys the other. If a plant cannot live according to its nature, it dies; and so a man.

The night in prison was novel and interesting enough. The prisoners in their shirt-sleeves were enjoying a chat and the evening air in the doorway, when I entered. But the jailer said, "Come, boys, it is time to lock up"; and so they dispersed, and I heard the sound of their steps returning into the hollow apartments. My room-mate was introduced to me by the jailer, as "a first-rate fellow and a clever man." When the door was locked, he showed me where to hang my hat, and how he managed matters there. The rooms were whitewashed once a month; and this one, at least, was the whitest, most simply furnished, and probably the neatest apartment in the town. He naturally wanted to know where I came from, and what brought me there; and, when I had told him, I asked him in my turn how he came there, presuming him to be an honest man, of course; and, as the world goes, I believe he was. "Why," said he, "they accuse me of burning a barn; but I never did it." As near as I could discover, he had probably gone to bed in a barn when drunk, and smoked his pipe there; and so a barn was burnt. He had the reputation of being a clever man, had been there some three months waiting for his trial to come on, and would have to wait as much longer; but he was quite domesticated and contented, since he got his board for nothing, and thought that he was well treated.

He occupied one window, and I the other; and I saw, that, if one stayed there long, his principal business would be to look out the window. I had soon read all the tracts that were left there, and examined where former prisoners had broken out, and where a grate had been sawed off, and heard the history of the various occupants of that room; for I found that even here there was a history and a gossip which never circulated beyond the walls of the jail. Probably this is the only house in the town where verses are composed, which are afterward printed in a circular form, but not published. I was shown quite a long list of verses which were composed

39

40

41

42

39 *"Your money or your life."* This was, of course, the phrase made famous by highwaymen when they held up their victims.

40 *The night in prison* to *This is the whole history of "My Prisons,"* eight paragraphs away, is Thoreau's own account of his imprisonment. It was probably clipped out of his *Journals*. In the first edition in book form (1866) it is set in smaller type than the main text.

41 *the hollow apartments.* There were 18, long and narrow cells.

42 *burning a barn.* In American politics at this time, "Barnburners" were the more radical wing of the Democratic Party, whereas the conservatives were called "Hunkers." There may be some subtle allusion to this here. At any rate, the man so accused was eventually acquitted. Webster says of "Barnburner": "An allusion to the fable of the man who burned his barn to get rid of the rats."

Sam Staples, the jailer (*Courtesy Concord Free Public Library*)

by some young men who had been detected in an attempt to escape, who avenged themselves by singing them.

I pumped my fellow-prisoner as dry as I could, for fear I should never see him again; but at length he showed me which was my bed, and left me to blow out the lamp.

It was like travelling into a far country, such as I had never expected to behold, to lie there for one night. It seemed to me that I never had heard the town-clock strike before, nor the evening sounds of the village; for we slept with the windows open, which were inside the grating. It was to see my native village in the light of the Middle Ages, and our Concord was turned into a Rhine stream, and visions of knights and castles passed before me. They were the voices of old burghers that I heard in the streets. I was an involuntary spectator and auditor of whatever was done and said in the kitchen of the adjacent village-inn, — a wholly new **43** and rare experience to me. It was a closer view of my native town. I was fairly inside of it. I never had seen its institutions before. This is one of its peculiar institutions; for it is a shire town. I began to comprehend what its inhabitants were about.

43 *the adjacent village-inn.* The Middlesex Hotel, a large wooden building which was torn down about the turn of the century.

The Middlesex Hotel which stood next to the jail *(Courtesy Concord Free Public Library)*

In the morning, our breakfasts were put through the hole in the door, in small oblong-square tin pans, made to fit, and holding a pint of chocolate, with brown bread, and an iron spoon. When they called for the vessels again, I was green enough to return what bread I had left; but my comrade seized it, and said that I should lay that up for lunch or dinner. Soon after he was let out to work at haying in a neighboring field, whither he went every day, and would not be back till noon; so he bade me good-day, saying that he doubted if he should see me again.

When I came out of prison, — for some one interfered, and paid that tax, — I did not perceive that great changes had

taken place on the common, such as he observed who went in a youth, and emerged a tottering and gray-headed man; and yet a change had to my eyes come over the scene,— the town, and State, and country,—greater than any that mere time could effect. I saw yet more distinctly the State in which I lived. I saw to what extent the people among whom I lived could be trusted as good neighbors and friends; that their friendship was for summer weather only; that they did not greatly propose to do right; that they were a distinct race from me by their prejudices and superstitions, as the Chinamen and Malays are; that, in their sacrifices to humanity, they ran no risks, not even to their property; that, after all, they were not so noble but they treated the thief as he had treated them, and hoped, by a certain outward observance and a few prayers, and by walking in a particular straight though useless path from time to time, to save their souls. This may be to judge my neighbors harshly; for I believe that many of them are not aware that they have such an institution as the jail in their village.

It was formerly the custom in our village, when a poor debtor came out of jail, for his acquaintances to salute him, looking through their fingers, which were crossed to represent the grating of a jail window, "How do ye do?" My neighbors did not thus salute me, but first looked at me, and then at one another, as if I had returned from a long journey. I was put into jail as I was going to the shoemaker's to get a shoe which was mended. When I was let out the next morning, I proceeded to finish my errand, and having put on my **44** mended shoe, joined a huckleberry party, who were impatient to put themselves under my conduct; and in half an hour,— for the horse was soon tackled,— was in the midst of a huckleberry field, on one of our highest hills, two miles off, and then the State was nowhere to be seen.

This is the whole history of " My Prisons." **45**

I have never declined paying the highway tax, because I am as desirous of being a good neighbor as I am of being a bad subject; and, as for supporting schools, I am doing my part to educate my fellow-countrymen now. It is for no particular item in the tax-bill that I refuse to pay it. I simply wish to refuse allegiance to the State, to withdraw and stand aloof from it effectually. I do not care to trace the course of my dollar, if I could, till it buys a man or a musket to shoot one with,— the dollar is innocent,— but I am concerned to trace the effects of my allegiance. In fact, I quietly declare war with the State, after my fashion, though I will still make what use and get what advantage of her I can, as is usual in such cases.

44 *having put on my mended shoe*. This would imply that Thoreau had spent the night in jail with only one shoe on. Had he walked to town barefoot while he carried one shoe? Or had he carried one shoe and worn others that were ready to be repaired—or perhaps discarded? He doesn't say.

45 *This is the whole story of "My Prisons."* One thing that Thoreau omits about his night in jail was the behavior of a man in another cell. Emerson's son Edward wrote about the incident in *Henry Thoreau: As Remembered by a Young Friend*, 1917, page 65. He says that a friend told him the story, so Thoreau must have told it to this unknown friend. According to Edward Emerson, Thoreau was kept awake "by a man in the cell below ejaculating, 'What is life?' and 'So this is life!'" with a painful monotony." Thoreau asked him: "Well, what is life then?" but got no answer.

If others pay the tax which is demanded of me, from a sympathy with the State, they do but what they have already done in their own case, or rather they abet injustice to a greater extent than the State requires. If they pay the tax from a mistaken interest in the individual taxed, to save his property, or prevent his going to jail, it is because they have not considered wisely how far they let their private feelings interfere with the public good.

This, then, is my position at present. But one cannot be too much on his guard in such a case, lest his action be biassed by obstinacy, or an undue regard for the opinions of men. Let him see that he does only what belongs to himself and to the hour.

I think sometimes, Why, this people mean well; they are only ignorant; they would do better if they knew how: why give your neighbors this pain to treat you as they are not inclined to? But I think again, this is no reason why I should do as they do, or permit others to suffer much greater pain of a different kind. Again, I sometimes say to myself, When many millions of men, without heat, without ill will, without personal feeling of any kind, demand of you a few shillings only, without the possibility, such is their constitution, of retracting or altering their present demand, and without the possibility, on your side, of appeal to any other millions, why expose yourself to this overwhelming brute force? You do not resist cold and hunger, the winds and the waves, thus obstinately; you quietly submit to a thousand similar necessities. You do not put your head into the fire. But just in proportion as I regard this as not wholly a brute force, but partly a human force, and consider that I have relations to those millions as to so many millions of men, and not of mere brute or inanimate things, I see that appeal is possible, first and instantaneously, from them to the Maker of them, and, secondly, from them to themselves. But, if I put my head deliberately into the fire, there is no appeal to fire or to the Maker of fire, and I have only myself to blame. If I could convince myself that I have any right to be satisfied with men as they are, and to treat them accordingly, and not according, in some respects, to my requisitions and expectations of what they and I ought to be, then, like a good Mussulman and fatalist, I **46**

46 *a good Mussulman.* A Moslem, follower of Allah.

should endeavor to be satisfied with things as they are, and say it is the will of God. And, above all, there is this difference between resisting this and a purely brute or natural force, that I can resist this with some effect; but I cannot expect, like Orpheus, to change the nature of the rocks and trees and beasts.   **47**

I do not wish to quarrel with any man or nation. I do not wish to split hairs, to make fine distinctions, or set myself up as better than my neighbors. I seek rather, I may say, even an excuse for conforming to the laws of the land. I am but too ready to conform to them. Indeed, I have reason to suspect myself on this head and each year, as the tax-gatherer comes round, I find myself disposed to review the acts and position of the general and State governments, and the spirit of the people, to discover a pretext for conformity.

> " We must affect our country as our parents;   **48**
>   And if at any time we alienate
>   Our love or industry from doing it honor,
>   We must respect effects and teach the soul
>   Matter of conscience and religion,
>   And not desire of rule or benefit."

I believe that the State will soon be able to take all my work of this sort out of my hands, and then I shall be no better a patriot than my fellow-countrymen. Seen from a lower point of view, the Constitution, with all its faults, is very good; the law and the courts are very respectable; even this State and this American government are, in many respects, very admirable and rare things, to be thankful for, such as a great many have described them; but seen from a point of view a little higher, they are what I have described them; seen from a higher still, and the highest, who shall say what they are, or that they are worth looking at or thinking of at all?

However, the government does not concern me much, and I shall bestow the fewest possible thoughts on it. It is not many moments that I live under a government, even in this world. If a man is thought-free, fancy-free, imagination-free, that which *is not* never for a long time appearing *to be* to him, unwise rulers or reformers cannot fatally interrupt him.

I know that most men think differently from myself; but those whose lives are by profession devoted to the study of these or kindred subjects, content me as little as any. Statesmen and legislators, standing so completely within the institution, never distinctly and nakedly be-

47 *Orpheus.* His mother was the Muse Calliope who gave him the gift of music. This endowed him with a magic power to entrance wild beasts and even influence inanimate objects like rocks, mountains, and trees.

48 *"We must affect our country."* The verse is from *The Battle of Alcazar* by George Peele (1558?–1597), which was acted in 1588 and 1589 and printed in 1594. It was added to the text of the original *Aesthetic Papers* version.

hold it. They speak of moving society, but have no resting-place without it. They may be men of a certain experience and discrimination, and have no doubt invented ingenious and even useful systems, for which we sincerely thank them; but all their wit and usefulness lie within certain not very wide limits. They are wont to forget that the world is not governed by policy and expediency. Webster never goes behind government, **49** and so cannot speak with authority about it. His words are wisdom to those legislators who contemplate no essential reform in the existing government; but for thinkers, and those who legislate for all time, he never once glances at the subject. I know of those whose serene and wise speculations on this theme would soon reveal the limits of his mind's range and hospitality. Yet, compared with the cheap professions of most reformers, and the still cheaper wisdom and eloquence of politicians in general, his are almost the only sensible and valuable words, and we thank Heaven for him. Comparatively, he is always strong, original, and, above all, practical. Still his quality is not wisdom, but prudence. The lawyer's truth is not Truth, but consistency, or a consistent expediency. Truth is always in harmony with herself, and is not concerned chiefly to reveal the justice that may consist with wrong-doing. He well deserves to be called, as he has been called, the Defender of the Constitution. There are really no blows to be given by him but defensive ones. He is not a leader, but a follower. His leaders are the men of '87. **50** "I have never made an effort," he says, "and never propose to make an effort; I have never countenanced an effort, and never mean to countenance an effort, to disturb the arrangement as originally made, by which the various States came into the Union." Still thinking of the sanction which the Constitution gives to slavery, he says, "Because it was a part of the original compact, — let it stand." Notwithstanding his special acuteness and ability, he is unable to take a fact out of its merely political relations, and behold it as it lies absolutely to be disposed of by the intellect, — what, for instance, it behooves a man to do here in America today with regard to slavery, but ventures, or is driven, to make some such desperate answer as the following, while professing to speak absolutely, and as a private man, — from which what new and singular code of

49 *Webster.* This was before Daniel Webster had alienated antislavery people by voting for the Compromise of 1850 with its fugitive slave law.

50 *the men of '87.* The men who wrote the draft of the Constitution in 1787.

Daniel Webster

social duties might be inferred? "The manner," says he, "in which the governments of those States where slavery exists are to regulate it, is for their own consideration, under their responsibility to their constituents, to the general laws of propriety, humanity, and justice, and to God. Associations formed elsewhere, springing from a feeling of humanity, or any other cause, have nothing whatever to do with it. They have never received any encouragement from me, and they never will." **51**

They who know of no purer sources of truth, who have traced up its stream no higher, stand, and wisely stand, by the Bible and the Constitution, and drink at it there with reverence and humility; but they who behold where it comes trickling into this lake or that pool, gird up their loins once more, and continue their pilgrimage toward its fountain-head.

No man with a genius for legislation has appeared in **52** America. They are rare in the history of the world. There are orators, politicians, and eloquent men, by the thousand; but the speaker has not yet opened his mouth to speak, who is capable of settling the much-vexed questions of the day. We love eloquence for its own sake, and not for any truth which it may utter, or any heroism it may inspire. Our legislators have not yet learned the comparative value of free-trade and of freedom, of union, and of rectitude, to a nation. They have no genius or talent for comparatively humble questions of taxation and finance, commerce and manufactures and agriculture. If we were left solely to the wordy wit of legislators in Congress for our guidance, uncorrected by the seasonable experience and the effectual complaints of the people, America would not long retain her rank among the nations. For eighteen hundred years, though perchance I have no right to say it, the New Testament has been written; yet where is the legislator who has wisdom and practical talent enough to avail himself of the light which it sheds on the science of legislation?

The authority of government, even such as I am willing to submit to, — for I will cheerfully obey those who know and can do better than I, and in many things even those who neither know nor can do so well, — is still an impure one: to be strictly just, it must have the sanction and consent of the governed. It can have no pure right over my person and property but what I concede to it.

51 *"and they never will."* A footnote in the first edition says that these excerpts from Webster's speech on August 12, 1848 (to exclude slavery from the Territories) were "inserted since the Lecture was read."

52 *No man with a genius for legislation has appeared in America.* This seems unfair to the men who drafted the Constitution and particularly unfair to Thomas Jefferson. Thoreau probably refused to consider them because they had permitted slavery to continue.

The progress from an absolute to a limited monarchy, from a limited monarchy to a democracy, is a progress toward a true respect for the individual.   Even the Chinese philosopher was wise enough to regard the individual as the basis of the empire.   Is a democracy, such as we know it, the last improvement possible in government?   Is it not possible to take a step further towards recognizing and organizing the rights of man?   There will never be a really free and enlightened State, until the State comes to recognize the individual as a higher and independent power, from which all its own power and authority are derived, and treats him accordingly. I please myself with imagining a State at last which can afford to be just to all men, and to treat the individual with respect as a neighbor ; which even would not think it inconsistent with its own repose, if a few were to live aloof from it, not meddling with it, nor embraced by it, who fulfilled all the duties of neighbors and fellow-men. A State which bore this kind of fruit, and suffered it to drop off as fast as it ripened, would prepare the way for a still more perfect and glorious State, which also I have imagined, but not yet anywhere seen.

53 *the Chinese philosopher*. Confucius. This was added to the *Aesthetic Papers* text.

BIBLIOGRAPHY–INDEX

BIBLIOGRAPHY

THOREAU'S OWN WORKS

1849 *A Week on the Concord and Merrimack Rivers*
1854 *Walden, or Life in the Woods*

Posthumous Works

1863 *Excursions*
1864 *The Maine Woods*
1864 *Cape Cod*
1865 *Letters to Various Persons*
1866 *A Yankee in Canada, with Anti-Slavery and Reform Papers*

Edited from the Journals

1881 *Early Spring in Massachusetts*
1884 *Summer*
1888 *Winter*
1892 *Autumn*

Other Works

1894 *Miscellanies*
1894 *Familiar Letters*
1895 *Poems of Nature*
1902 *The Service* (edited by F. B. Sanborn)
1905 *Sir Walter Raleigh* (edited by F. B. Sanborn)
1905 *The First and Last Journeys of Thoreau* (edited by F. B. Sanborn)
   (*All the works listed above were published in Boston*)

1943 and 1964 *Collected Poems of Henry David Thoreau* (edited by Carl Bode), Baltimore
1958 *The Correspondence of Henry David Thoreau* (edited by Walter Harding and Carl Bode), New York
1962 *Thoreau's Minnesota Journey: Two Documents* (edited by Walter Harding), Geneseo, New York

COLLECTED WORKS

1893 Riverside Edition, Boston (11 volumes)
1906 Manuscript Edition, also the Walden Edition from the same plates (20 volumes including the 14-volume *Journal*), edited by Bradford Torrey and Francis H. Allen

1949 *The Journal of Henry D. Thoreau*, a separate issue of 14 volumes from the plates of the 1906 edition. Reprinted in cheaper form in two large volumes in 1962. Note that Perry Miller's *Consciousness in Concord*, Boston (1958), supplies the text of the "Lost Journal" of 1840–1841.

BIBLIOGRAPHIES

1908 and 1967 *A Bibliography of Henry David Thoreau* by Francis H. Allen, Boston

1939 "A Contribution to a Bibliography from 1909 to 1936 of Henry David Thoreau," by J. S. Wade (*Journal of the New York Entomological Society*, XLVII, 163–203)

1939 *A Henry David Thoreau Bibliography, 1908–1937*, by William White, Boston

1946–1947 "Contribution to a Bibliography of Thoreau, 1938–1945," by Philip E. Burnham and Carvel Collins (*Bulletin of Bibliography*, XIX, 16–18, 37–40)

1967 *A Bibliography of Scholarship about Henry David Thoreau: 1940–1967*, by Christopher A. Hildenbrand (Fort Hays Kansas State College, Bibliography Series No. 3)

1941 to date *The Thoreau Society Bulletin*, Geneseo, New York, prints a current bibliography in each issue.

BIOGRAPHY, CRITICISM, AND REFERENCE

ADAMS, RAYMOND

1930. "A Bibliographical Note on Walden," *American Literature* (May), 166–169

1932. "Thoreau's Literary Apprenticeship," *Studies in Philology*, XXIX (October), 617–629

1940. "Thoreau at Harvard: Some Unpublished Records," *New England Quarterly* (March), 24–33

1940. "Thoreau's Burials," *American Literature* (March), 105–107

1945a. "Thoreau's Diploma," *American Literature*, XII (May), 174–175

1945b. "Thoreau's Science," *Scientific Monthly*, LX (May), 379–382

1945c. "Thoreau's Sources for 'Resistance to Civil Government,'" *Studies in Philology* (July), 640–653

1945d. "Thoreau's Growth at Walden," *Christian Register*, CXXIV (July), 268–270

ALCOTT, BRONSON

1862. "The Forester," *Atlantic Monthly* (April), 443–445

1878. *Concord Days*. Boston

1938. *The Journals of Bronson Alcott* (edited by Odell Shepard), Boston

ALLEN, FRANCIS H.
1908. *Bibliography of Henry David Thoreau*, Boston
1910. *Notes on New England Birds*, Boston
1925. (Reissue) *Thoreau's Bird Lore*, Boston
1936. *Men of Concord*, Boston
1950. *Thoreau's Editors: History and Reminiscence*, Monroe, North Carolina

ANDERSON, CHARLES R.
1968. *The Magic Circle of Walden*, New York

ATKINSON, BROOKS
1927. *Henry Thoreau: the Cosmic Yankee*, New York

BAZALGETTE, LÉON
1914. *Henry Thoreau, Sauvage*, Paris
1924. English translation: *Henry Thoreau, Bachelor of Nature*, New York

BODE, CARL (editor)
1943 and 1964. *Collected Poems of Henry David Thoreau*, Chicago and Baltimore
1947 and 1964. *The Portable Thoreau*
1958. (with Walter Harding) *The Correspondence of Henry David Thoreau*, New York
1967. *American Life in the 1840s*, New York

BONNER, WILLARD H.
1963. "Mariners and Terreners: Some Aspects of Nautical Imagery in Thoreau," *American Literature*, XXXIV (January), 507–519

BRADFORD, ROBERT W.
1963. "Thoreau and Therien," *American Literature*, XXXIV (January), 499–506

BRODERICK, JOHN C.
1956. "Thoreau, Alcott, and the Poll Tax," *Studies in Philology*, LIII, 612–626

BROWN, MARY HOSMER
1926. *Memories of Concord*, Boston

BURROUGHS, JOHN
1882. "Henry D. Thoreau," *Century* (July), 368–379

CADY, LYMAN V.
1961. "Thoreau's Quotations from the Confucian Books in Walden," *American Literature*, XXXIII (March), 20–32

CAMERON, KENNETH W.
1953. "Thoreau Discovers Emerson: A College Reading Record," *Bulletin of the New York Public Library*, LVII (July), 319–334
1956a. "Thoreau and the Folklore of Walden Pond," *Emerson Society Quarterly*, No. 3, 10–12
1956b. "Thoreau's Three Months out of Harvard and His First Publication," *ESQ*, No. 5, 2–12
1959. "Thoreau's Diploma Again," *ESQ*, No. 16, 48–49
1960a. "Emerson, Thoreau, and Concord in Early Newspapers," *ESQ*, No. 21, 1–57

1960b. "Historical Notes on the Concord Academy," *ESQ*, No. 19, 46–51

1961a. "Chronology of Thoreau's Harvard Years," *ESQ*, No. 15, 2–108

1961b. "Thoreau's Walden Pond," *ESQ*, No. 22, 77–80

1962. "Thoreau's Harvard Textbooks," *ESQ*, No. 23, 19–111

1964. *Companion to Thoreau's Correspondence*, Hartford

1969. "Damning National Publicity for Thoreau in 1849," *American Transcendental Quarterly*, No. 2, 18–27

CANBY, HENRY SEIDEL

1936. "The Man Who Did What He Wanted," *Saturday Review of Literature*, December 26

1939. *Thoreau*, Boston

CASTERET, NORBERT

1940. *Ten Years Under the Earth*, London

CHANNING, WILLIAM ELLERY

1849. *The Woodsman, and Other Poems*, Boston

1873. *Thoreau: the Poet-Naturalist*, Boston

CHRISTIE, JOHN ALDRICH

1965. *Thoreau as World Traveler*, New York

CHRISTY, ARTHUR

1932 and 1963. *The Orient in American Transcendentalism: A Study of Emerson, Thoreau, and Alcott*, New York

CONDRY, WILLIAM

1954. *Thoreau*, London and New York

CONWAY, MONCURE D.

1882. *Emerson at Home and Abroad*, Boston

1904. *Autobiography*, London

COOK, REGINALD L.

1940. *The Concord Saunterer*, Middlebury, Vermont

1949 and 1966. *Passage to Walden*, Boston and New York

COOK, RICHARD C.

1959. *Henry Thoreau's Poetic Imagination: An Analysis of the Imagery of Walden*, unpublished Master's thesis, University of Maine

COOKE, G. W.

1902. *An Historical and Biographical Introduction to Accompany* The Dial, Cleveland

COSMAN, MAX

1943. "Thoreau and Staten Island," *Staten Island Historian*, VI (January–March), 1–2, 7–8

CRUICKSHANK, HELEN

1964. *Thoreau on Birds*, New York

DAVIDSON, FRANK

1954a. "Melville, Thoreau, and the Apple-Tree Table," *American Literature*, XXV, 479–488

1954b. "Thoreau's Hound, Bay Horse, and Turtle-Dove," *New England Quarterly*, XXVII (December), 521–524

DEEVEY, EDWARD S., JR.
1942. "A Re-examination of Thoreau's 'Walden,'" *The Quarterly Review of Biology*, XVII, No. 1 (March), 1–11

DE VOTO, BERNARD
1943. *The Year of Decision: 1846*, Boston

DIAS, EARL J.
1953. "Daniel Ricketson and Henry Thoreau," *New England Quarterly*, XXVI, 388–396

ECKSTORM, FANNY HARDY
1908. "Thoreau's 'Maine Woods,'" *Atlantic Monthly* (August), 242–250

EIDSON, JOHN OLIN
1951. *Charles Stearns Wheeler*, Athens, Georgia

EMERSON, EDWARD WALDO
1917 and 1968. *Henry Thoreau as Remembered by a Young Friend*, Boston and Concord

EMERSON, RALPH WALDO
1836. *Nature*, Boston
1909–1914. *Journals* (edited by Edward Waldo Emerson and Waldo Emerson Forbes), Boston (10 volumes)
1939. *Letters* (edited by Ralph L. Rusk), New York (6 volumes)

FOERSTER, NORMAN
1917. "The Intellectual Heritage of Thoreau," *Texas Review*, II, 192–212

FRENCH, ALLEN
1915. *Old Concord*, Boston

GIRDLER, JOHN
1935. *A Study of the Hound, Bay Horse, and Turtle-Dove Allusion in Thoreau's Walden*, unpublished master's thesis, University of Southern California

GLICK, WENDELL
1969. *The Recognition of Henry David Thoreau*, Ann Arbor, Michigan

GOHDES, CLARENCE L. F.
1931. *The Periodicals of American Transcendentalism*, Durham, North Carolina

GOZZI, RAYMOND
1957. *Tropes and Figures: A Psychological Study of Henry David Thoreau*, unpublished doctoral dissertation, New York University

GREENE, DAVID MASON
1966. *The Frail Duration, A Key to Symbolic Structure in Walden*, San Diego, California

GRUBER, CHRISTIAN P.
1953. *The Education of Henry Thoreau*, Harvard,

1833–1837, unpublished doctoral dissertation, Princeton University

HAMLIN, TALBOT

1944. *Greek Revival Architecture in America*, New York

HARDING, WALTER

1954a. *A Centennial Check-List of the Editions of Henry David Thoreau's* Walden, Charlottesville, Virginia

1954b. *Thoreau: A Century of Criticism*, Dallas, Texas

1956. "The Apple-Tree Table," *Boston Public Library Quarterly*, VIII, 213–215

1957. *Thoreau's Library*, Charlottesville, Virginia

1958. (With Carl Bode), *The Correspondence of Henry David Thoreau*, New York

1959. *A Thoreau Handbook*, New York

1960. *Thoreau, Man of Concord*, New York

1962. (*See* Milton Meltzer)

1964. *The Thoreau Centennial*, Albany, New York

1965. *The Days of Henry Thoreau*, New York

1968. *The Variorum Walden* and *The Variorum Civil Disobedience*, New York

HAWTHORNE, NATHANIEL

1932. *The American Notebooks* (edited by Randall Stewart), New Haven, Connecticut

HENDRICK, GEORGE

1956. "The Influence of Thoreau's 'Civil Disobedience' on Gandhi's *Satyagraha*," *New England Quarterly*, XXIX, 462–471

HICKS, GRANVILLE

1933. *The Great Tradition*, New York

HICKS, JOHN H. (editor)

1962 and 1966. *Thoreau in Our Season*, Boston

HOAGLAND, CLAYTON

1955. "The Diary of Thoreau's 'Gentle Boy,'" *New England Quarterly*, XXVIII (December), 473–489

HOELTJE, HUBERT H.

1939. "Thoreau in Concord Town and Church Records," *New England Quarterly*

1946. "Thoreau as Lecturer" (December), 485–494

1948. "Thoreau and the Concord Academy," *New England Quarterly*, XXI, 103–109

HOUGH, HENRY BEETLE

1956. *Thoreau of Walden: The Man and His Eventful Life*, New York

HOWELLS, WILLIAM DEAN

1894. "My First Visit to New England," *Harper's New Monthly Magazine* (August), 441–451

HYMAN, STANLEY EDGAR

1946. "Henry Thoreau in Our Time," *Atlantic Monthly*, CLXXVIII (November), 137–146

JAPP, ALEXANDER HAY (H. A. Page)
1877. *Thoreau: His Life and Aims,* Boston

JONES, JOSEPH
1955. *Index to Walden,* Austin, Texas

JONES, S. A.
1891. "Thoreau and His Biographers," *Lippincott's Monthly Magazine,* XLVIII, 224–228
1898. "Thoreau's Incarceration," *Inlander,* IX, 96–103; also in the Thoreau Society *Bulletin,* IV

KEISER, ALBERT
1928. "Thoreau's Manuscripts on the Indians," *Journal of English and German Philosophy,* XXVII, 183–199
1933. *The Indian in American Literature,* New York

KLEINFELD, LEONARD F.
1950. *Henry David Thoreau: Chronology,* Forest Hills, New York

KRUTCH, JOSEPH WOOD
1948. *Henry David Thoreau,* New York

LEARY, LEWIS
1956. "Thoreau" in *Eight American Authors* (edited by Floyd Stovall), New York

LOWELL, JAMES RUSSELL
1848. *A Fable for Critics,* New York

McGILL, FREDERICK T., JR.
1942. "Thoreau and College Discipline," *New England Quarterly,* XV (June), 349–353
1967. *Channing of Concord: A Life of William Ellery Channing* II, New Brunswick, New Jersey

MANNING, CLARENCE
1943. "Thoreau and Tolstoi," *New England Quarterly,* XVI (July), 234–243

MARBLE, ANNIE RUSSELL
1902. *Thoreau: His Home, Friends and Books,* New York

MARX, LEO
1964. *The Machine in the Garden, and the Pastoral Ideal in America,* New York

MATTHIESSEN, F. O.
1941. *American Renaissance: Art and Expression in the Age of Emerson and Whitman,* New York

MELTZER, MILTON, and HARDING, WALTER
1962. *A Thoreau Profile,* New York

MENCKEN, H. L.
1936. *The American Language,* New York

METZGER, C. R.
1961. *Thoreau and Whitman: A Study of Their Aesthetics,* Seattle

MILLER, HENRY (editor)
1946. *Preface to Three Essays by Henry David Thoreau,* Stanford, California

MILLER, PERRY

1958. *Consciousness in Concord: the Text of Thoreau's Hitherto "Lost Journal" (1840–1841)*, Boston

MINNEGERODE, MEADE
1924. *The Fabulous Forties: 1840–1850.* New York

MOLDENHAUER, JOSEPH J.
1959. "Images of Circularity in Thoreau's Prose," TSLL I (summer), 245–263
1964. "Paradox in *Walden*," *Graduate Journal* (University of Texas), VI, 132–146

MOORE, JOHN BROOKS
1832. "Thoreau Rejects Emerson," *American Literature*, IV (November), 241–256

PAGE, H. A. (*see* Japp, Alexander Hay)

PARRINGTON, VERNON LOUIS
1927. *Main Currents in American Thought*, New York

PAUL, SHERMAN
1949. "The Wise Silence: Sound as the Agency of Correspondence in Thoreau," *New England Quarterly*, XXII, 511–527
1958. *The Shores of America: Thoreau's Inward Exploration*, Urbana, Illinois
1962. *Thoreau: A Collection of Critical Essays*, Englewood Cliffs, New Jersey

PEAIRS, EDITH
1937. "The Hound, the Bay Horse, and the Turtle-Dove: A Study of Thoreau and Voltaire," *Publications of the Modern Language Association*, LII (September), 863–869

PICKARD, JOHN B.
1965. "The Religion of 'Higher Laws,'" *Emerson Society Quarterly*, XXXIX, 68–72

PORTE, JOEL
1966. *Emerson and Thoreau: Transcendentalists in Conflict*, Middletown, Connecticut

POWYS, LLEWELLYN
1929. "Thoreau: A Disparagement," *Bookman* (London), LXIX (April), 163–165

RAYSOR, T. M.
1926. "The Love Story of Thoreau," *Studies in Philology*, XXIII (October), 457–463

RICKETSON, ANNA AND WALTON (editors)
1902. *Daniel Ricketson and His Friends*, Boston

ROBBINS, ROLAND WELLS
1947. *Discovery at Walden*, Stoneham, Massachusetts

RULAND, RICHARD (editor)
1968. *Twentieth-Century Interpretations of Walden*, Englewood Cliffs, New Jersey

RUSK, RALPH
1949. *The Life of Ralph Waldo Emerson*, New York

SACKMAN, DOUGLAS
1940. "The Original of Melville's Apple-Tree Table,"

American Literature, XI, 448–451

SALT, HENRY S.

1890, 1896, and 1968. *Life of Henry David Thoreau*, London and Hamden, Connecticut

SANBORN, FRANKLIN BENJAMIN

1882. *Henry D. Thoreau*, Boston

1893. "Thoreau and His English Friend, Thomas Cholmondeley," *Atlantic Monthly* (December), 741–756

1901. *The Personality of Thoreau*, Boston

1909a. *Walden*, The Bibliophile Edition (editor), Boston

1909b. *Recollections of Seventy Years*, Boston

1917 and 1968. *The Life of Henry David Thoreau*, Boston and Detroit. (*See also* Thoreau's Own Works)

SCHILLER, ANDREW

1955. "Thoreau and Whitman: The Record of a Pilgrimage," *New England Quarterly* (June), 186–197

SCUDDER, TOWNSEND

1947. *Concord: American Town*, Boston

SEYBOLD, ETHEL

1951. *Thoreau: the Quest and the Classics*, New Haven, Connecticut

SHANLEY, JAMES LYNDON

1951. "A Study of the Making of *Walden*," *The Huntington Library Quarterly*, San Marino, California, XIV (February)

1957. *The Making of Walden: With the Text of the First Version*, Chicago

SHATTUCK, LEMUEL

1835. *A History of Concord*, Boston and Concord

SHEPARD, ODELL

1937. *Pedlar's Progress: The Life of Bronson Alcott*, Boston

SHERWIN, J. S., and REYNOLDS, R. C.

1960. *A Word Index to Walden: With Textual Notes.* Charlottesville, Virginia

SKWIRE, DAVID

1959. "A Check List of Word Plays in *Walden*," *American Literature* (November), 282–289

STEEL, KURT

1945. "Prophet of the Independent Man," *Progressive*, September 24

STEVENSON, ROBERT LOUIS

1882. *Familiar Studies of Men and Books*, London

STEWART, CHARLES D.

1935. "A Word for Thoreau," *Atlantic Monthly* (July), 110–116

STEWART, RANDALL

1948. *Nathaniel Hawthorne: A Biography*, New Haven

STOLLER, LEO

1956. "A Note on Thoreau's Place in the History of

Phenology," *Isis*, XLVII (June), 172–181

1957. *After Walden: Thoreau's Changing Views on Economic Man*, Stanford, California

STOWELL, ROBERT

1948. *Thoreau Gazetteer*, Calais, Vermont

STRAKER, R. L.

1941. "Thoreau's Journey to Minnesota," *New England Quarterly*, XIV, 549–555

THOREAU SOCIETY BULLETINS

1941 to date. Geneseo, New York

Ticknor and Fields, The Cost Books of

1949. Edited by Warren S. Tryon and William Charvat, New York

TORREY, BRADFORD

1896. "Thoreau," *Atlantic Monthly* (December), 822–833

VAN DOREN, MARK

1916 and 1961. *Henry David Thoreau*, Boston and New York

WAGNER, C. ROLAND

1962. "Lucky Fox at Walden," *Massachusetts Review*, IV (Autumn), 117–133

WHICHER, GEORGE

1945. *Walden Revisited: A Centennial Tribute to Henry David Thoreau*, Chicago

WHITE, E. B.

1954. "Walden," *Yale Review* (Autumn), 13–22

WHITE, VIOLA

1935. "Thoreau's Opinion of Whitman," *New England Quarterly*, VIII, 262–264

WHITFORD, KATHRYN

1950. "Thoreau and the Woodlots of Concord," *New England Quarterly* (September), 291–306

WILLSON, LAWRENCE

1959. "Thoreau's Canadian Notebook," *Huntington Library Quarterly*, XXII (May), 179–200

1960. "Thoreau's Medical Vagaries," *Journal of the History of Medicine and Allied Sciences*, XV, No. 1, 64–70

WINTERICH, JOHN T.

1929. "Walden," *Publishers' Weekly*, September 21, 163–167

WOOD, JAMES PLAYSTED

1933. "English and American Criticism of Thoreau," *New England Quarterly*, VI, 733–746

WOODSON, THOMAS MILLER

1963. *Thoreau's Prose Style*, unpublished doctoral dissertation, Yale University

INDEX

Italic figures refer to illustrations

MAP OF
CONCORD, MASS.
Showing Localities mentioned by
Thoreau in his Journals

Compiled by Herbert W. Gleason
1906

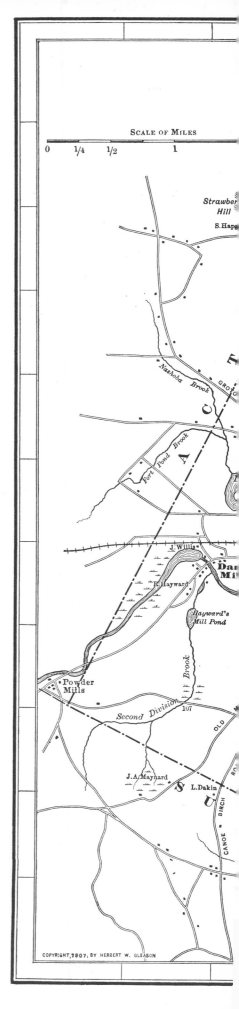

SCALE OF MILES

0   1/4   1/2   1